2004 Supplement
Constitutional Law

EDITORIAL ADVISORS

Erwin Chemerinsky
Alston & Bird Professor of Law
Duke University School of Law

Richard A. Epstein
James Parker Hall Distinguished Service Professor of Law
University of Chicago
Peter and Kirsten Bedford Senior Fellow
The Hoover Institution
Stanford University

Ronald J. Gilson
Charles J. Meyers Professor of Law and Business
Stanford University
Marc and Eva Stern Professor of Law and Business
Columbia University

James E. Krier
Earl Warren DeLano Professor of Law
University of Michigan

Richard K. Neumann, Jr.
Professor of Law
Hofstra University School of Law

Kent D. Syverud
Dean and Garner Anthony Professor
Vanderbilt University Law School

Elizabeth Warren
Leo Gottlieb Professor of Law
Harvard University

EMERITUS EDITORIAL ADVISORS

E. Allan Farnsworth
Alfred McCormack Professor of Law
Columbia University

Geoffrey C. Hazard, Jr.
Trustee Professor of Law
University of Pennsylvania

Bernard Wolfman
Fessenden Professor of Law
Harvard University

2004 Supplement

Constitutional Law

Fourth Edition

Geoffrey R. Stone
Harry Kalven, Jr., Distinguished Service Professor of Law
University of Chicago Law School

Louis M. Seidman
Professor of Law
Georgetown University Law Center

Cass R. Sunstein
Karl N. Llewellyn Professor of Jurisprudence
University of Chicago Law School and
Department of Political Science

Mark V. Tushnet
Carmack Waterhouse Professor of Constitutional Law
Georgetown University Law Center

Pamela S. Karlan
Kenneth & Harle Montgomery Professor of Public Interest Law
Stanford Law School

1185 Avenue of the Americas, New York, NY 10036
www.aspenpublishers.com

© 2004 Geoffrey R. Stone; Robert H. Seidman, Trustee; Cass R. Sunstein; Mark Tushnet; Pamela Karlan; and Rebecca and Laura Tushnet

All rights reserved. No part of this publication may be reproduced or transmitted in any form or by any means, electronic or mechanical, including photocopy, recording, or any information storage and retrieval system, without permission in writing from the publisher. Requests for permission to make copies of any part of this publication should be mailed to:

Permissions
Aspen Publishers
1185 Avenue of the Americas
New York, NY 10036

Printed in the United States of America

Library of Congress Cataloging-in-Publication Data

Constitutional law / Geoffrey R. Stone . . . [et al.]. — 4th ed.
    p.   cm.
Includes bibliographical references and index.
ISBN 0-7355-2016-X (casebound)
0-7355-4085-3 (supplement)
    1. Constitutional law — United States. I. Stone, Geoffrey R.

KF4549.C647   2001
342.73 — dc21   00-065069

ISBN 0-7355-4085-3

1 2 3 4 5 6 7 8 9 0

About Aspen Publishers

Aspen Publishers, headquartered in New York City, is a leading information provider for attorneys, business professionals, and law students. Written by preeminent authorities, our products consist of analytical and practical information covering both U.S. and international topics. We publish in the full range of formats, including updated manuals, books, periodicals, CDs, and online products.

Our proprietary content is complemented by 2,500 legal databases, containing over 11 million documents, available through our Loislaw division. Aspen Publishers also offers a wide range of topical legal and business databases linked to Loislaw's primary material. Our mission is to provide accurate, timely, and authoritative content in easily accessible formats, supported by unmatched customer care.

To order any Aspen Publishers title, go to *www.aspenpublishers.com* or call 1-800-638-8437.

To reinstate your manual update service, call 1-800-638-8437.

For more information on Loislaw products, go to *www.loislaw.com* or call 1-800-364-2512.

For Customer Care issues, email *CustomerCare@aspenpublishers.com*; call 1-800-234-1660; or fax 1-800-901-9075.

Aspen Publishers
A Wolters Kluwer Company

Contents

Table of Cases	*xi*
Table of Authorities	*xv*
Acknowledgments	*xxv*

CHAPTER 1. THE ROLE OF THE SUPREME COURT IN THE CONSTITUTIONAL ORDER   1

A.	Introduction: Some Notes on the History and Theory of the Constitution	1
B.	The Basic Framework	1
E.	"Case or Controversy" Requirements and the Passive Virtues	3
	Elk Grove Unified School District v. Newdow	3
	Vieth v. Jubelirer	9
	Bush v. Gore	17
	Note: *Bush v. Gore*	30

CHAPTER 2. THE POWERS OF CONGRESS   45

A.	Introduction	45
B.	The Basic Issues: Federalism and Judicial Review	45
C.	The Evolution of Commerce Clause Doctrine: The Lessons (?) of History	46
D.	Other Powers of Congress: Are They More (or Less) Plenary than the Commerce Power?	50

CHAPTER 3. JUDICIAL EFFORTS TO PROTECT THE EXPANSION OF THE MARKET AGAINST ASSERTIONS OF LOCAL POWER   55

A.	The Fundamental Framework	55
C.	Facially Neutral Statutes with Effects on Commerce	56

CHAPTER 4. THE DISTRIBUTION OF NATIONAL POWERS   57

A.	Introduction	57
C.	Domestic Affairs	59
D.	Foreign Affairs	63
	Hamdi v. Rumsfeld	*65*

CHAPTER 5. EQUALITY AND THE CONSTITUTION   97

B.	Equal Protection Methodology: Rational Basis Review	97
C.	Equal Protection Methodology: Heightened Scrutiny and the Problem of Race	99
	Grutter v. Bollinger	*109*
	Gratz v. Bollinger	*130*
D.	Equal Protection Methodology: Heightened Scrutiny and the Problem of Gender	134
	Nguyen v. Immigration and Naturalization Service	*136*
E.	Equal Protection Methodology: The Problem of Sexual Orientation	142
F.	Equal Protection Methodology: Other Candidates for Heightened Scrutiny	143

CHAPTER 6. IMPLIED FUNDAMENTAL RIGHTS   147

E.	Fundamental Interests and the Equal Protection Clause	147
	Vieth v. Jubelirer	*150*
F.	Modern Substantive Due Process	156
	Lawrence v. Texas	*156*
G.	Procedural Due Process	172
H.	The Contracts and Takings Clauses	173
	Palazzolo v. Rhode Island	*173*

CHAPTER 7. FREEDOM OF EXPRESSION   183

A.	Introduction	183
B.	Content-Based Restrictions: Dangerous Ideas and Information	187
C.	Overbreadth, Vagueness, and Prior Restraint	198

Contents

D.	Content-Based Restrictions: "Low" Value Speech	199
	Thompson v. Western States Medical Center	202
	Lorillard Tobacco Co. v. Reilly	205
	Ashcroft v. The Free Speech Coalition	214
	Ashcroft v. American Civil Liberties Union	219
	City of Los Angeles v. Alameda Books	223
	Virginia v. Black	*226*
E.	Content-Neutral Restrictions: Limitations on the Means of Communication and the Problem of Content-Neutrality	241
	Bartnicki v. Vopper	241
	Legal Services Corp. v. Velazquez	249
	United States v. American Library Association	253
	McConnell v. Federal Election Comm'n	268
F.	Freedom of the Press	282

CHAPTER 8. THE CONSTITUTION AND RELIGION   289

A.	Introduction	289
B.	The Establishment Clause	290
	Zelman v. Simmons-Harris	291
D.	Permissible Accommodation	298

CHAPTER 9. THE CONSTITUTION, BASELINES, AND THE PROBLEM OF PRIVATE POWER   301

C.	Constitutionally Impermissible Departures from Neutrality: State Subsidization, Approval, and Encouragement	301
	Brentwood Academy v. Tennessee Secondary School Athletic Association	*301*

Table of Cases

Italics indicate principal and intermediate cases.
All references are to page numbers in the main text.

American Amusement Machine Ass'n v. Kendrick, 1181
American Ins. Ass'n v. Garamendi, 327, 418
American Library Association v. United States, 1181, 1291, *1301*
American Mfrs. Mut. Ins. Co. v. Sullivan, 1544
Anderson v. Celebrezze, 135
Arkansas Educational Television Comm'n v. Forbes, 1298
Ashcroft v. American Civil Liberties Union (I), 1180, 1204, 1408
Ashcroft v. American Civil Liberties Union (II), 1204
Ashcroft v. Free Speech Coalition, 1184
Bartnicki v. Vopper, 1086, 1139, 1183, *1240*
B.M.W. of North America v. Gore, 920
Board of Trustees of the University of Alabama v. Garrett, 230
Boardman v. Esteva, 135
Bouie v. City of Columbia, 135
Boy Scouts of America v. Dale, 1311
Brandenburg v. Ohio, 1055
Brentwood Academy v. Tennessee Secondary School Athletic Association, 1544
Brown v. Board of Education, 135
Browning-Ferris Industries v. Kelco Disposal, Inc., 920
Bush v. Gore, 135, 744, 763
Butler, United States v., 135
Central Hudson Gas v. Public Service Comm'n of New York, 1158
City of Cuyohoga Falls v. Buckeye Community Hope Foundation, 522
Clark v. Arizona Interscholastic Assn., 1544
Cooper v. Aaron, 135

xi

Table of Cases

Cox v. Larios, 755
Detroit Free Press v. Ashcroft, 1384
Easley v. Cromartie, 552
Edmonson v. Leesville Concrete Co., 1544
Eldred v. Ashcroft, 1373
Elk Grove Unified School District v. Newdow, 112, 1419
Endo, Ex parte, 505
Erie R. Co. v. Tompkins, 135
Evans v. Newton, 1544
Fairfax's Devisee v. Hunter's Lessee, 135
FCC v. League of Women Voters, 1298
Federal Election Commission v. Beaumont, 1343
Federal Election Commission v. Colorado Republican Federal Campaign Committee, 1344
Fitzgerald v. Racing Ass'n of Central Iowa, 483, 497
Glickman v. Wileman Brothers & Elliott, Inc., 1160
Good News Club v. Milford Central School, 1285, 1497
Gratz v. Bollinger, 108, 590
Gray v. Sanders, 135
Gregory v. Ashcroft, 135
Grutter v. Bollinger, 590
Hamdi v. Rumsfeld, 410, 939
Harper v. Virginia Bd. of Elections, 135
Highland Farms Dairy v. Agnew, 135
INS v. Chadha, 397
Illinois ex rel. Madigan v. Telemarketing Associates, Inc., 1324
Kansas v. Crane, 534 U.S. 407 (2002), 920
Keystone Bituminous Coal Assn. v. DeBenedictis, 992
Korematsu v. United States, 410
Krivanek v. Take Back Tampa Political Committee, 135
Laird v. Tatum, 1090
Lamb's Chapel v. Center Moriches Union Free School Dist., 1497
Lawrence v. Texas, 494, 652, *901*
Lebron v. National Railroad Passenger Corporation, 1544
Legal Services Corporation v. Velazquez, 1298
Littleton v. Z. J. Gifts D-4, L.L.C., 1106
Locke v. Davey, 1466
Lorillard Tobacco Co. v. Reilly, 1158
Los Angeles v. Alameda Books, 1209, 1244

Table of Cases

Louisiana High School Athletic Assn. v. St. Augustine High School, 1544
Lucas v. South Carolina Coastal Council, 992
Martin v. Hunter's Lessee, 135
McConnell v. Federal Election Commission, 1346
McPherson v. Blacker, 135
Milligan, Ex parte, 410
Moore v. Ogilvie, 135
NAACP v. Alabama ex rel. Patterson, 135
NAACP v. Clairborne Hardware, 1055
Nevada Dept. of Human Resources v. Hibbs, 231, 626
New Jersey Media Group v. Ashcroft, 1384
Nguyen v. Immigration and Naturalization Service, 624
O'Brien, United States v., 1158
Pacific Mutual Ins. Co. v. Haslip, 920
Palazzolo v. Rhode Island, 992
Palm Beach County Canvassing Bd. v. Harris (*Harris I*), 135
Palm Beach County Canvassing Bd. v. Harris (*Harris III*), 135
Penn Central Transp. Co. v. New York City, 992
Pennsylvania v. Board of Directors of City Trusts of Philadelphia, 1544
Phillips v. Washington Legal Foundation, 992
Piece County v. Guillen, 203
Planned Parenthood v. American Coalition of Life Activists, 1055
Quirin, Ex parte, 410
Rasul v. Bush, 410
Rendell-Baker v. Kohn, 1544
Republican Party of Minnesota v. White, 1345
Reynolds v. Sims, 135
Rosenberger v. Rectors and Visitors of the Univ. of Virginia, 1285, 1298
Rumsfeld v. Padilla, 410
Rust v. Sullivan, 1298
Sabri v. United States, 218
Smith v. Daily Mail Publishing Co., 1240
Sinkfield v. Kelley, 551
State Farm Mut. Automobile Ins. Co. v. Campbell, 920
Tahoe-Sierra Preservation Council, Inc. v. Tahoe Regional Planning Agency, 992
Tennessee v. Lane, 230, 681
Thomas v. Chicago Park District, 1104, 1106, 1255

Thompson v. Western States Medical Center, 1157
Touchston v. McDermott, 135
TXO Prod. Corp. v. Alliance Resources Corp., 920
United Foods, United States v., 1160, 1364
Universal City Studios, Inc. v. Corley, 1323
Vieth v. Jubelirer, *120*, 755, *768*
Virginia v. Black, 1064, *1228*, 1255
Watchtower Bible & Tract Society v. Village of Stratton, 1255
Watts v. United States, 1055
West v. Atkins, 1544
Whitman v. American Trucking Ass'n, 369
Yamashita, In re, 410
Zelman v. Simmons-Harris, *1418*, *1421*, *1466*

Table of Authorities

Ackerman & Ayres, Voting with Dollars: A New Paradigm in Campaign Finance (2002), 1346
Adler, Inverting the First Amendment, 149 U. Pa. L. Rev. 921 (2001), 1183
Adler, The Perverse Law of Child Pornography, 101 Colum. L. Rev. 209 (2001), 1184
Alexander, Incitement and Freedom of Speech, in D. Kretzmer & F. Hazan, Freedom of Speech and Incitement Against Democracy 101 (2000), 1013
Amar, Intertextualism, 112 Harv. L. Rev. 748 (1999), 608
Baker & Young, Federalism and the Double Standard of Review, 51 Duke L.J. 75 (2001), 157
Barak, Foreword: A Judge on Judging: The Role of a Supreme Court in a Democracy, 116 Harv. L. Rev. 16 (2002), 45
Barber, Prelude to the Separation of Powers, 60 Cambridge L.J. 59 (2001), 334
Barron, A Localist Critique of the New Federalism, 51 Duke L.J. 377 (2001), 157
Berg, Vouchers and Religious Schools: The New Constitutional Questions, 72 U. Cin. L. Rev. 151 (2003), 1466
BeVier, The Invisible Hand of the Marketplace of Ideas, in Lee Bollinger & Geoffrey Stone, Eternally Vigilant: Free Speech in the Modern Era 233 (2002), 1120
Bezanson & Buss, The Many Faces of Government Speech, 86 Iowa L. Rev. 1377 (2001), 1301
Blasi, Free Speech and Good Character: From Milton to Brandeis to the Present, in Lee Bollinger & Geoffrey Stone, Eternal Vigilance: Free Speech in the Modern Era 61 (2002), 1003, 1028

Table of Authorities

Bollinger, Epilogue, in Lee Bollinger & Geoffrey Stone, Eternal Vigilance: Free Speech in the Modern Era 312 (2002), 1044

Bradley & Goldsmith, The Constitutional Validity of Military Commissions, 5 Green Bag 2d 249 (2002), 410

Brady, The Push to Private Religious Expression: Are We Missing Something?, 70 Fordham L. Rev. 1147 (2002), 1437

Breyer, Our Democratic Constitution, 77 N.Y.U.L. Rev. 245 (2002), 1004

Brown-Nagin, Toward a Pragmatic Understanding of Status-Consciousness: The Case of Deregulated Education, 50 Duke L.J. 753 (2000), 610

Brownstein, Protecting Religious Liberty: The False Messiahs of Free Speech Doctrine and Formal Neutrality, 18 J.L. & Pol. 119 (2002), 1484, 1485

Chemerinsky, *Bush v. Gore* Was Not Justiciable, 76 Notre Dame L. Rev. 1093 (2001), 135

_____, The Constitution and Punishment, 56 Stan. L. Rev. 1049 (2004), 920

_____, Content Neutrality as a Central Problem of Freedom of Speech, 74 S. Cal. L. Rev. 49 (2000), 1301

Choper, Taming Congress's Power Under the Commerce Clause: What Does the Near Future Portend?, 55 Ark. L. Rev. 731 (2003), 201

Clark, Separation of Powers as a Safeguard of Federalism, 79 Tex. L. Rev. 1321 (2001), 365

Cole, Enemy Aliens, 54 Sta. L. Rev. 953 (2002), 668

Currie, Rumors of Wars: Presidential and Congressional War Powers, 1809-1829, 67 U. Chi. L. Rev. 1 (2000), 413

Curtis, Free Speech, "The People's Darling Privilege" (2000), 998

Cushman, Formalism and Realism in Commerce Clause Jurisprudence, 67 U. Chi. L. Rev. 1089 (2000), 164

Delahunty & Yoo, The President's Constitutional Authority to Conduct Military Operations against Terrorist Organizations and the Nations that Harbor or Support Them, 25 Harv. JL. & Pol. 488 (2002), 410

Donner, The Age of Surveillance (1980), 1090

Dorf, Equal Protection Incorporation, 88 Va. L. Rev. 951 (2002)

Duncan, Free Exercise Is Dead, Long Live Free Exercise: *Smith, Lukumi*, and the General Applicability Requirement, 3 U. Pa. J. Const. L. 850 (2001), 1484

Table of Authorities

Eid, Federalism and Formalism, 11 Wm. & Mary Bill of Rights J. 1191 (2003), 254

Elliott's Debates on the Federal Constitution (2d ed. 1876), 135

Ely, Standing to Challenge Pro-Minority Gerrymanders, 111 Harv. L. Rev. 576 (1997), 551

Epstein, In Such Manner as the Legislature Thereof May Direct: The Outcome in *Bush v. Gore* Defended, in The Vote: Bush, Gore and the Supreme Court (Cass R. Sunstein and Richard A. Epstein eds. 2001), 135

____, Takings: Descent and Resurrection, 1987 Sup. Ct. Rev. 1, 992

____, The Constitutional Perils of Moderation: The Case of the Boy Scouts, 74 S. Cal. L. Rev. 119 (2000), 1358

Eskridge, Destabilizing Due Process and Evolutive Equal Protection, 47 UCLA L. Rev. 1183 (2000), 683

Fee, Unearthing the Denominator in Regulatory Takings Claims, 61 U. Chi. L. Rev. 1535 (1994), 992

Feldman, From Liberty to Equality: The Transformation of the Establishment Clause, 90 Cal. L. Rev. 673 (2002), 1446

____, The Intellectual Origins of the Establishment Clause, 77 N.Y.U. L. Rev. 346 (2002), 1437

Fiss, The Censorship of Television, in Lee Bollinger & Geoffrey Stone, Eternally Vigilant: Free Speech in the Modern Era 257 (2001), 1288

Fletcher, On Justice and War: Contradictions in the Proposed Military Tribunals, 25 Harv. J.L. & Pub. Pol. 635 (2002), 410

Flynn, *Trans*forming the Debate: Why We Need To Include Transgender Rights in the Struggles for Sex and Sexual Orientation Equality, 101 Colum. L. Rev. 392 (2001), 625, 657

Garrett, Institutional Lessons from the 2000 Presidential Election, 29 Fla. St. U.L. Rev. 975 (2001), 135

Gerken, Understanding the Right to an Undiluted Vote, 114 Harv. L. Rev. 1663 (2001), 230

Gewirtz, Privacy and Speech, 2001 Sup. Ct. Rev. 139, 1139, 1240

Goldsmith & Sykes, The Internet and the Dormant Commerce Clause, 110 Yale L.J. 785 (2001), 321

Gould, Mixing Bodies and Beliefs: The Predicament of Tribes, 101 Colum. L. Rev. 702 (2001), 592

Greenawalt, "Clear and Present Danger" and Criminal Speech, in Lee Bollinger & Geoffrey Stone, Eternal Vigilance: Free Speech in the Modern Era 97 (2002), 1044

Griffin, Judicial Supremacy and Equal Protection in a Democracy of Rights, 4 U. Pa. J. of Con. L. 281 (2002), 512

Gross, Chaos and Rules: Should Responses to Violent Crises Always Be Constitutional?, 112 Yale L.J. 1011 (2003), 45, 410

Gudridge, Remember Endo?, 116 Harv. L. Rev. 1933 (2003), 505

Harris, Equality Trouble: Sameness and Difference in Twentieth-Century Law, 88 Cal. L. Rev. 1923 (2000), 510

Hasday, The Principle and Practice of "Women's Full Citizenship": A Case Study of Sex-Segregated Public Education, 101 Mich. L. Rev. 755 (2002), 619

Hoffman, Book Review, 95 Nw. U.L. Rev. 1533 (2001), 135

Ides, Economic Activity as a Proxy for Federalism: Intuition and Reason in *United States v. Morrison*, 18 Const. Comment. 563 (2002), 201

Issacharoff & Karlan, Standing and Misunderstanding in Voting Rights Law, 111 Harv. L. Rev. 2276 (1998), 551

Jackson, Holistic Interpretation: Fitzpatrick v. Bitzer and Our Bifurcated Constitution, 53 Stan. L. Rev. 1259, 203

Johnson, Expressive Association and Organizational Autonomy, 85 Minn. L. Rev. 1639 (2001), 1358

Kagan, Presidential Administration, 114 Harv. L. Rev. 2245 (2001), 378

Karlan, Easing the Spring: Strict Scrutiny and Affirmative Action After the Redistricting Cases, 43 Wm. & Mary L. Rev. 1569 (2002), 230, 512, 552

_____, Elections and Change Under "Voting with Dollars," 91 Cal. L. Rev. 705 (2003), 1346

_____, Equal Protection: *Bush v. Gore* and the Making of a Precedent, in The Unfinished Election of 2000, at 159 (Jack N. Rakove ed., 2001), 763

_____, Nothing Personal: The Evolution of the Newest Equal Protection from *Shaw v. Reno* to *Bush v. Gore*, 79 N.C.L. Rev. 1345 (2001), 135

_____, "Pricking the Lines": The Due Process Clause, Punitive Damages, and Criminal Punishment, 88 Minn. L. Rev. 880 (2004), 920

_____, Two Section Twos and Two Section Fives: Voting Rights and Remedies After *Boerne*, 39 Wm. & Mary L. Rev. 725 (1998), 230

_____, Unduly Partial: The Supreme Court and the Fourteenth Amendment in *Bush v. Gore*, 29 Fla. St. U.L. Rev. 587 (2001), 135

Table of Authorities

Katyal & Tribe, Waging War, Deciding Guilt: Trying the Military Tribunals, 111 Yale L.J. 1259 (2002), 410, 668

Katz, Race and the Right to Vote after *Rice v. Cayetano*, 99 Mich. L. Rev. 491 (2000), 592

Kennedy, Nigger (2002), 1218

Klarman, *Bush v. Gore* Through the Lens of Constitutional History, 89 Calif. L. Rev. 1721 (2001), 135

Kramer, Foreword: We the Court, 115 Harv. L. Rev. 4 (2001), 35

_____, The Supreme Court in Politics in The Unfinished Election of 2000, at 105 (Jack N. Rakove ed., 2001), 135

Kreimer, Technologies of Protest: Insurgent Social Movements and the First Amendment in the Era of the Internet, 150 U. Penn. L. Rev. 119 (2001), 1407

Krent, Judging Judging: The Problem of Second-Guessing State Judges' Interpretation of State Law in *Bush v. Gore*, 29 Fla. St. U.L. Rev. 493 (2001), 135

Lawrence, Two Views of the River: A Critique of the Liberal Defense of Affirmative Action, 101 Colum. L. Rev. 928 (2001), 590

Lawson, Delegation and Original Meaning, 88 Va. L. Rev. 327 (2002), 367

Leahy, The First Amendment Gone Awry, 150 U. Pa. L. Rev. 1021 (2002), 1322

Levinson and Young, Who's Afraid of the Twelfth Amendment?, 29 Fla. St. U.L. Rev. 925 (2001), 135

Lund, The Unbearable Rightness of *Bush v. Gore*, 23 Cardozo L. Rev. 1219 (2002), 135

Lupu, Government Messages and Government Money: *Santa Fe, Mitchell v. Helms*, and the Arc of the Establishment Clause, 42 Wm. & Mary L. Rev. 771 (2001), 1469

_____ & Tuttle, Sites of Redemption: A Wide Angle Look at Government Vouchers and Sectarian Service Providers, 18 J.L. & Pol. 537 (2002), 1468

Magill, Beyond Powers and Branches in Separation of Powers Law, 150 U. Pa. L. Rev. 603 (2001), 334

_____, The Real Separation in Separation of Powers Law, 86 Va. L. Rev. 1127 (2000), 334

Mazzone, The Social Capital Argument for Federalism, 11 S. Cal. Interdis. L.J. 27 (2001), 142

Meyerson, The Neglected History of the Prior Restraint Doctrine, 34 Ind. L. Rev. 295 (2001), 997, 1112

Nadel, The First Amendment's Limitations on the Use of Internet Filtering in Public and School Libraries, 78 Tex. L. Rev. 1117 (2000), 1291

Nelson & Pushaw, Rethinking the Commerce Clause: Applying First Principles to Uphold Federal Commercial Regulations but Preserve State Control Over Social Issues, 85 Iowa L. Rev. 1 (1999), 201

Netanel, Locating Copyright Within the First Amendment, 54 Stan. L. Rev. 1 (2001), 1373

Note, Freedom of Expressive Association—Antidiscrimination Laws, 114 Harv. L. Rev. 259 (2000), 1358

Nourse, Toward a New Constitutional Anatomy, 56 Stan. L. Rev. 835 (2004), 378

Pildes, Democracy and Disorder, 68 U. Chi. L. Rev. 695 (2001), 135

Posner, R., Breaking the Deadlock: The 2000 Election, the Constitution, and the Courts (2001), 135

_____, Pragmatism versus Purposivism in First Amendment Analysis, 54 Stan. L. Rev. 737 (2002), 1036, 1044

_____, The Speech Market and the Legacy of *Schenck*, in Lee Bollinger & Geoffrey Stone, Eternal Vigilance: Free Speech in the Modern Era 121 (2002), 1036, 1056, 1232

Post, The Constitutional Status of Commercial Speech, 48 U.C.L.A. L. Rev. 1 (2000), 1158

_____, Reconciling Theory and Doctrine in First Amendment Jurisprudence, in Lee Bollinger & Geoffrey Stone, Eternal Vigilance: Free Speech in the Modern Era 153 (2002), 1002, 1004

_____ & Siegel, Equal Protection by Law: Federal Antidiscrimination Legislation After *Morrison* and *Kimel*, 110 Yale L.J. 441 (2000), 230

Prakash & Ramsey, The Executive Power over Foreign Affairs, 111 Yale L.J. 231 (2001), 403

Priest, Reanalyzing *Bush v. Gore*: Democratic Accountability and Judicial Overreaching, 72 U. Colo. L. Rev. 953 (2001), 135

Primus, Equal Protection and Disparate Impact: Round Three, 117 Harv. L. Rev. 493 (2003), 590

Rabban, Free Speech in Its Forgotten Years: 1870-1920 (1997), 998

Ramsey, Textualism and War Powers, 69 U. Chi. L. Rev. 1543 (2002), 410

Redish, Money Talks (2001), 1158

Table of Authorities

_____ & Finnery, What Did You Learn in School Today? Free Speech, Values Inculcation, and the Democratic-Educational Paradoz, 88 Cornell L. Rev. 62 (2002), 1291

Regan, Judicial Review of Member-State Regulation of Trade Within a Federal or Quasi-Federal System: Protectionism and Balancing, *Da Capo*, 99 Mich. L. Rev. 1853 (2001), 261

Rothman, Freedom of Speech and True Threats, 25 Harv. J. L. & Pub. Pol. 283 (2001), 1055

Rubenfeld, The First Amendment's Purpose, 53 Stan. L. Rev. 767 (2001), 1242, 1243, 1310, 1358

_____, The Freedom of Imagination: Copyright's Constitutionality, 112 Yale L.J. 1 (2002), 1165

Rubin, Reconnecting Doctrine and Purpose: A Comprehensive Approach to Strict Scrutiny after *Adarand* and *Shaw*, 149 U. Penn. L. Rev. 1 (2000), 512

Ryan & Heise, The Political Economy of School Choice, 111 Yale L.J. 2043 (2002), 1466

Saunders, Regulating Youth Access to Violent Video Games: Three Responses to First Amendment Concerns, 2003 L. Rev. M.S.U.-D.C.L. 51, 1181

Schapiro, Conceptions and Misconceptions of State Constitutional Law in *Bush v. Gore*, 29 Fla. St. U.L. Rev. 661 (2001), 135

Schauer, First Amendment Opportunism, in Lee Bollinger & Geoffrey Stone, Eternal Vigilance: Free Speech in the Modern Era 175 (2002), 1004

Seidman, What's So Bad About *Bush v. Gore*? An Essay on Our Unsettled Election, 47 Wayne L. Rev. 953 (2001), 135, 763

_____, The Secret Life of the Political Question Doctrine, 37 John Marshall L. Rev. 441 (2004), 410

Shane, Disappearing Democracy: How *Bush v. Gore* Undermined the Federal Right to Vote for Presidential Electors, 29 Fla. St. U. L. Rev. 535 (2001), 135

_____, Federalism's "Old Deal": What's Right and Wrong with Conservative Judicial Activism, 45 Villanova L. Rev. 201 (2000), 200

Siegel, Siegal, Equality Talk: Antisubordination and Anticlassification Values in Constitutional Struggles over Brown, 117 Harv. L. Rev. 1470 (2004), 510

_____, She the People: The Nineteenth Amendment, Sex Equality, Federalism, and the Family, 115 Harv. L. Rev. 949 (2002), 608

_____, The Use of Legislative History in a System of Separated Powers, 53 Vand. L. Rev. 1457 (2000), 397

Spiro, Treaties, Executive Agreements, and Constitutional Method, 79 Tex. L. Rev. 960 (2001), 419

St. George & Dennis, The Great Sedition Trial of 1944 (1946), 1030, 1035

Stearns, A Beautiful Mend: A Game Theoretical Analysis of the Dormant Commerce Clause Doctrine, 45 Wm. & Mary L. Rev. 1 (2003), 320

Steele, Free Speech in the Good War (1999), 1030

Stein, Evaluating the Sex Discrimination Argument for Lesbian and Gay Rights, 49 UCLA L. Rev. 471 (2001), 657

Stone, Abraham Lincoln's First Amendment, 78 N.Y.U.L. Rev. 1 (2003), 998

_____, Dialogue, in L. Bollinger & G. Stone, Eternal Vigilance: Free Speech in the Modern Era 1 (2002), 1044, 1128

_____, Judge Learned Hand and the Espionage Act of 1917: A Mystery Unraveled, 70 U. Chi. L. Rev. 335 (2003), 1011

_____, The Origins of the "Bad Tendency" Test: Free Speech in Wartime, 2002 Sup. Ct. Rev. 411, 1011

Strauss, Freedom of Speech and the Common-Law Constitution, in L. Bollinger & G. Stone, Eternal Vigilance: Free Speech in the Modern Era 1 (2002), 1004

Sullivan, The New Religion and the Constitution, 116 Harv. L. Rev. 1397 (2003), 1500

Sunder, Cultural Dissent, 54 Stan. L. Rev. 495 (2001), 1358

Sunstein, Order Without Law, in The Vote: Bush, Gore and the Supreme Court (C. Sunstein & R. Epstein eds. 2001), 135

_____ & Vermeule, Interpretation and Institutions, 101 Mich. L. Rev. 885 (2003), 45

_____, republic.com (2001), 1248, 1407

Symposium, National Securities and Civil Liberties, 69 Cornell L. Rev. 685 (1984), 1090

Telman, A Truism that Isn't True? The Tenth Amendment and Executive War Power, 51 Cath. U. L. Rev. 135 (2001), 410

Thornburgh, & Lin Youth, Pornography and the Internet (2002), 1291

Tribe, eroG v. HsuB and Its Disguises: Freeing Bush v. Gore from Its Hall of Mirrors, 115 Harv. L. Rev. 170 (2001), 135, 763

Table of Authorities

Tsesis, Destructive Messages (2002), 1218, 1226

Tubbs, Conflicting Images of Children in First Amendment Jurisprudence, 30 Pepperdine L. Rev. 1 (2002), 1204

Turner, The War on Terrorism and the Modern Relevance of the Congressional Power to "Declare War," 25 Harv. J. of Law & Pol. 519 (2002), 410

Tushnet, R., Copyright as a Model for Free Speech Law, 42 B.C. L. Rev. 1 (2000), 1333

Tushnet, M., The New Constitutional Order (2003), 22

_____, Renormalizing *Bush v. Gore*: An Anticipatory Intellectual History, 90 Geo. L.J. 113 (2001), 135

_____, Vouchers After *Zelman*, 2002 Supreme Court Rev. 1, 1466

Vermeule, Does Commerce Clause Review Have Perverse Effects?, 46 Villanova L. Rev. 1325 (2001), 201

Wiecek, The Legal Foundations of Domestic Anticommunism: The Background of *Dennis v. United States*, 2001 Sup. Ct. Rev. 375, 1037

Yoo, In Defense of the Court's Legitimacy, 68 U. Chi. L. Rev. 775 (2001), 135

_____, War and the Constitutional Text, 69 U. Chi. L. Rev. 1639 (2002), 410

Acknowledgments

Bollinger, Lee C. & Geoffrey R. Stone, eds. Eternally Vigilant: Free Speech in the Modern Era. Copyright © 2002 by the University of Chicago. All rights reserved.

Post, The Constitutional Status of Commercial Speech, 48 UCLA L. Rev. 1, 2-4, 14, 49, 53-54 (2000). Copyright © 2000, The Regents of the University of California. All rights reserved.

Rubenfeld, Jed. The First Amendment's Purpose, 53 Stan. L. Rev. 767, 768-769 (2001). Copyright © 2001 by Stanford Law Review. Reproduced with permission of Stanford Law Review in the format textbook via Copyright Clearance Center.

Sunstein, Cass. R. republic.com. Copyright © 2001 by Princeton University Press. Reprinted by permission of Princeton University Press.

2003 Supplement
Constitutional Law

1
THE ROLE OF THE SUPREME COURT IN THE CONSTITUTIONAL ORDER

A. Introduction: Some Notes on the History and Theory of the Constitution

Page 22. **At the end of section 7 of the Note, add the following:**

See also M. Tushnet, The New Constitutional Order (2003), for an argument that the constitutional arrangements that prevailed in the United States from the 1930s to the 1990s have ended. Tushnet suggests that the nation's new constitutional order is characterized by divided government, ideologically organized parties, and subdued constitutional ambition.

B. The Basic Framework

Page 35. **Before *Note: Constitutions, Democracy, and Judicial Review*, add the following:**

For a detailed treatment of the historical issues, see Larry D. Kramer, Foreword: We the Court, 115 Harv. L. Rev. 4 (2001). Kramer urges that for the framers, the "Constitution was *not* ordinary law, *not* peculiarly the stuff of courts and judges." Instead it was "a special form of popular law, law made by the people to bind their governors." Id. at 10. For many members of the revolutionary generation, constitutional principles were subject to "popular enforcement," id. at 40, that is, public insistence on compliance with the Constitution, rather than judicial activity. "It was the legislature's delegated responsibility to decide whether a proposed law was constitutionally authorized, subject to oversight by the people. Courts simply had nothing to do with it, and they were acting as interlopers if they tried to second-guess the legislature's decision." Id. at 49. Kramer traces the controversial early growth of the practice of judicial review, with many seeing it as an "act of resistance." Id. at 54. At the founding, a "handful of participants saw a role for judicial review, though few of these imagined it as a powerful or important device, and none seemed anxious to emphasize it. Others were opposed . . . . The vast majority of participants were still thinking in terms of popular constitutionalism and so focused on traditional political means of enforcing the new charter; the notion of judicial review simply never crossed their minds." Id. at 66.

In Kramer's account, constitutional limits would be enforced not through courts, but as a result of republican institutions and the citizenry's own commitment to its founding document. Kramer raises serious doubts about the account in *Marbury v. Madison* and in particular about judicial supremacy in the interpretation of the Constitution. He suggests that for some of the framers, judicial review was "a substitute for popular resistance" and to be used "only when the unconstitutionality of a law was clear beyond dispute."

Page 45. In the second paragraph, before the last sentence, add the following:

For an illuminating comparative discussion, based on the experience in Israel, see Barak, Foreword: A Judge on Judging: The Role of a Supreme Court in a Democracy, 116 Harv. L. Rev. 16 (2002). Barak emphasizes the important role of the Supreme Court of Israel (of which he is the President) in protecting civil liberties and in maintaining a balance between security and liberty; his treatment of terrorism is worth special attention. Barak stresses the general importance of a judicial check on the elected branches. For a quite different view, see Sunstein and Vermeule, Interpretation and Institutions, 101 Mich. L. Rev. 885 (2003), arguing that it is important to consider the institutional capacities (or lack thereof) of various actors, including courts, and that much is missed by approaches that emphasize what ideal courts should do. For a provocative treatment of the role of the judiciary under emergency conditions, see Gross, Chaos and Rules: Should Responses to Violent Crises Always Be Constitutional?, 112 Yale L.J. 1011 (2003).

Page 108. After the third paragraph, add the following:

A divided Court built on Northeastern Fla. Chapter in Gratz v. Bollinger, 539 U.S. 244 (2003). Patrick Hamacher, a plaintiff in the case, objected to an affirmative action program used by the University of Michigan in undergraduate admissions. The problem was that while Hamacher said that he intended to apply for admission as a transfer student, he had not actually made any such application. Dissenting, Justice Stevens urged that because Hamacher had not yet applied, his claim of injury was conjectural and hypothetical. The Court disagreed. It said that for standing, it was enough that Hamacher claimed that "he was 'able and ready' to apply as a transfer student" if the university stopped using race in undergraduate admissions. This claim of intent supported standing "to seek prospective relief with respect to the University's continued use of race in undergraduate admissions."

E. *"Case or Controversy" Requirements and the Passive Virtues*

Page 112. At the end of Note 5, add the following:

6. *Prudential Standing*

ELK GROVE UNIFIED SCHOOL DISTRICT v. NEWDOW
542 U.S. ___ (2004)

JUSTICE STEVENS delivered the opinion of the Court.

Each day elementary school teachers in the Elk Grove Unified School District (School District) lead their classes in a group recitation of the Pledge of Allegiance. Respondent, Michael A. Newdow, is an atheist whose daughter participates in that daily exercise. Because the Pledge contains the words "under God," he views the School District's policy as a religious indoctrination of his child that violates the First Amendment. [We] conclude that Newdow lacks standing and therefore reverse the Court of Appeals' decision. . . .

III

In every federal case, the party bringing the suit must establish standing to prosecute the action. [The] command to guard jealously and exercise rarely our power to make constitutional pronouncements requires strictest adherence when matters of great national significance are at stake. Even in cases concededly within our jurisdiction under Article III, we abide by "a series of rules under which [we have] avoided passing upon a large part of all the constitutional questions pressed upon [us] for decision."

[Consistent] with these principles, our standing jurisprudence contains two strands: Article III standing, which enforces the Constitution's case or controversy requirement; and prudential standing, which embodies "judicially self-imposed limits on the exercise of federal jurisdiction." Although we have not exhaustively defined the prudential dimensions of the standing doctrine, we have explained that prudential standing encompasses "the general prohibition on a litigant's raising another person's legal rights, the rule barring adjudication of generalized grievances more appropriately addressed in the representative branches, and the requirement that a plaintiff's complaint fall within the zone of interests protected by the law invoked."

[One] of the principal areas in which this Court has customarily declined to intervene is the realm of domestic relations. Long ago we observed that "the whole subject of the domestic relations of husband and wife, parent and child, belongs to the laws of the States and not to the laws of the United States." *In re Burrus,* 136 U.S. 586 (1890). [So] strong is our deference to state law in this area that we have recognized a "domestic relations exception" that "divests the federal courts of power to issue divorce, alimony, and child custody decrees." *Ankenbrandt v. Richards,* 504 U.S. 6 (1992). We have also acknowledged that it might be appropriate for the federal courts to decline to hear a case involving "elements of the domestic relationship." [Thus,] while rare instances arise in which it is necessary to answer a substantial federal question that transcends or exists apart from the family law issue, in general it is appropriate for the federal courts to leave delicate issues of domestic relations to the state courts.

[The] extent of the standing problem raised by the domestic relations issues in this case was not apparent until August 5, 2002, when Banning [the mother of the child in question] filed her motion for leave to intervene or dismiss the complaint following the Court of Appeals' initial decision. At that time, the child's custody was governed by a February 6, 2002, order of the California Superior Court. That order provided that Banning had "*sole* legal custody as to the rights and responsibilities to make decisions relating to the health, education and welfare of" her daughter. The order stated that the two parents should "consult with one another on substantial decisions relating to" the child's "'psychological and educational needs," but it authorized Banning to "exercise legal control" if the parents could not reach "'mutual agreement."

That family court order was the controlling document at the time of the Court of Appeals' standing decision. After the Court of Appeals ruled, however, the Superior Court held another conference regarding the child's custody. At a hearing on September 11, 2003, the Superior Court announced that the parents have "joint legal custody," but that Banning "makes the final decisions if the two . . . disagree."

Newdow contends that despite Banning's final authority, he retains "an unrestricted right to inculcate in his daughter—free from governmental interference—the atheistic beliefs he finds persuasive." The difficulty with that argument is that Newdow's rights, as in many cases touching upon family relations, cannot be viewed in isolation. This case concerns not merely Newdow's interest in inculcating his child with his views on religion, but also the rights of the child's mother as a parent generally and under the Superior Court orders specifically. And most important, it implicates the interests of a young child who finds herself at the center of a highly public debate over her custody, the propriety of a widespread national ritual, and the meaning of our Constitution.

The interests of the affected persons in this case are in many respects antagonistic. Of course, legal disharmony in family relations is not uncommon, and in many instances that disharmony poses no bar to federal-court adjudication of proper federal questions. What makes this case different is that Newdow's standing derives entirely from his relationship with his daughter, but he lacks the right to litigate as her next friend. [The] interests of this parent and this child are not parallel and, indeed, are potentially in conflict.

Newdow's parental status is defined by California's domestic relations law. Our custom on questions of state law ordinarily is to defer to the interpretation of the Court of Appeals for the Circuit in which the State is located. In this case, the Court of Appeals, which possesses greater familiarity with California law, concluded that state law vests in Newdow a cognizable right to influence his daughter's religious upbringing.... Nothing that either Banning or the School Board has done, however, impairs Newdow's right to instruct his daughter in his religious views. Instead, Newdow [wishes] to forestall his daughter's exposure to religious ideas that her mother, who wields a form of veto power, endorses, and to use his parental status to challenge the influences to which his daughter may be exposed in school when he and Banning disagree. The California cases simply do not stand for the proposition that Newdow has a right to dictate to others what they may and may not say to his child respecting religion.... The cases speak not at all to the problem of a parent seeking to reach outside the private parent-child sphere to restrain the acts of a third party. A next friend surely could exercise such a right, but the Superior Court's order has deprived Newdow of that status.

In our view, it is improper for the federal courts to entertain a claim by a plaintiff whose standing to sue is founded on family law rights that are in dispute when prosecution of the lawsuit may have an adverse effect on the person who is the source of the plaintiff's claimed standing. When hard questions of domestic relations are sure to affect the outcome, the prudent course is for the federal court to stay its hand rather than reach out to resolve a weighty question of federal constitutional law. There is a vast difference between Newdow's right to communicate with his child—which both California law and the First Amendment recognize—and his claimed right to shield his daughter from influences to which she is exposed in school despite the terms of the custody order. We conclude that, having been deprived under California law of the right to sue as next friend, Newdow lacks prudential standing to bring this suit in federal court.[8]

---

8. Newdow's complaint and brief cite several additional bases for standing: that Newdow "at times has himself attended—and will in the future attend—class with his daughter"; that

The judgment of the Court of Appeals is reversed.

JUSTICE SCALIA took no part in the consideration or decision of this case.

CHIEF JUSTICE REHNQUIST, with whom JUSTICE O'CONNOR joins, and with whom JUSTICE THOMAS joins as to Part I, concurring in the judgment.

The Court today erects a novel prudential standing principle in order to avoid reaching the merits of the constitutional claim. I dissent from that ruling. [On the merits, Chief Justice Rehnquist stated that he would uphold the pledge of allegiance against Establishment Clause attack.]

I

. . .

[Here] is the Court's new prudential standing principle: "It is improper for the federal courts to entertain a claim by a plaintiff whose standing to sue is founded on family law rights that are in dispute when prosecution of the lawsuit may have an adverse effect on the person who is the source of the plaintiff's claimed standing." . . .

[The] domestic relations exception is not a prudential limitation on our federal jurisdiction. It is a limiting construction of the statute defining federal diversity jurisdiction, which "divests the federal courts of power to issue divorce, alimony, and child custody decrees." This case does not involve diversity jurisdiction, and respondent does not ask this Court to issue a divorce, alimony, or child custody decree. Instead it involves a substantial federal question about the constitutionality of the School District's conducting the pledge ceremony, which is the source of our jurisdiction. Therefore, the domestic relations exception to diversity jurisdiction forms no basis for denying standing to respondent. . . .

[Sandra] Banning and respondent now share joint custody of their daughter, respondent retains the right to expose his daughter to his religious views, and the state

---

he "has considered teaching elementary school students in [the School District]"; that he "has attended and will continue to attend" school board meetings at which the Pledge is "routinely recited"; and that the School District uses his tax dollars to implement its Pledge policy. Even if these arguments suffice to establish Article III standing, they do not respond to our prudential concerns. As for taxpayer standing, Newdow does not reside in or pay taxes to the School District; he alleges that he pays taxes to the District only "indirectly" through his child support payments to Banning. That allegation does not amount to the "direct dollars-and-cents injury" that our strict taxpayer-standing doctrine requires. *Doremus v. Board of Ed. of Hawthorne*, 342 U.S. 429 (1952).

of their domestic affairs has nothing to do with the underlying constitutional claim. Abstention forms no basis for denying respondent standing. . . .

[It] seems the Court bases its new prudential standing principle, in part, on criticisms of the Court of Appeals' construction of state law, coupled with the prudential principle prohibiting third-party standing. In the Court of Appeals' original opinion, it held unanimously that respondent satisfied the Article III standing requirements, stating respondent "has standing as a parent to challenge a practice that interferes with his right to direct the education of his daughter." *Newdow v. United States Congress*, 292 F.3d 597, 602 (CA9 2002). After Banning moved for leave to intervene, the Court of Appeals reexamined respondent's standing to determine whether the parents' court-ordered custodial arrangement altered respondent's standing. *Newdow v. United States Congress*, 313 F.3d 500 (CA9 2002). The court examined whether respondent could assert an injury in fact by asking whether, under California law, "noncustodial parents maintain the right to expose and educate their children to their individual religious views, even if those religious views contradict those of the custodial parent." The Court of Appeals again unanimously concluded that the respondent satisfied Article III standing, despite the custody order, because he retained sufficient parental rights under California law. . . .

The Court does not take issue with the fact that, under California law, respondent retains a right to influence his daughter's religious upbringing and to expose her to his views. But it relies on Banning's view of the merits of this case to diminish respondent's interest, stating that the respondent "wishes to forestall his daughter's exposure to religious ideas that her mother, who wields a form of veto power, endorses, and to use his parental status to challenge the influences to which his daughter may be exposed in school when he and Banning disagree." As alleged by respondent and as recognized by the Court of Appeals, respondent wishes to enjoin the School District from endorsing a form of religion inconsistent with his own views because he has a right to expose his daughter to those views without the State's placing its *imprimatur* on a particular religion. Under the Court of Appeals' construction of California law, Banning's "veto power" does not override respondent's right to challenge the pledge ceremony. . . .

Respondent asserts that the School District's pledge ceremony infringes his right under California law to expose his daughter to his religious views. While she is intimately associated with the source of respondent's standing (the father-daughter relationship and respondent's rights thereunder), the daughter *is not the source* of respondent's standing; instead it is their relationship that provides respondent his standing, which is clear once respondent's interest is properly described. . . .

Although the Court may have succeeded in confining this novel principle almost narrowly enough to be, like the proverbial excursion ticket—good for this day only—our doctrine of prudential standing should be governed by general principles, rather than ad hoc improvisations.

Note: Standing and the Pledge

1. *In general.* Describe the Court's holding. Does the Court's prudential standing principle have any basis in previous decisions?

Why doesn't Newdow, as biological father, have a legally protected interest, under the Establishment Clause, sufficient to permit him to challenge the pledge? Would the standing issue be different if the relevant public school were attempting to indoctrinate his child in a particular religion?

2. *The passive virtues?* Consider the following view: The Court worked very hard to avoid deciding this case. It did so because the underlying issue seemed genuinely difficult to some of the justices, and because a ruling in favor of Newdow, while not implausible on the merits, would have been a political catastrophe for the Court. This was a case in which the Court attempted to display the passive virtues to avoid a contestable constitutional ruling that would undoubtedly have divided the nation, especially but not only if the Court had accepted Newdow's argument.

Page 118. Replace the discussion of Davis v. Bandemer with the following:

In Davis v. Bandemer, 478 U.S. 109 (1986), the Supreme Court held that claims of partisan gerrymandering were also justiciable. Justice White delivered the Court's opinion with respect to the political question issue: "Disposition of this question does not involve us in a matter more properly decided by a coequal branch of our Government. There is no risk of foreign or domestic disturbance, and in light of our cases since *Baker* we are not persuaded that there are no judicially discernible and manageable standards by which political gerrymander cases are to be decided." Justice White acknowledged that "the type of claim that was presented in Baker v. Carr was subsequently resolved in this Court by the formulation of the 'one person, one vote' rule. See, e.g., Reynolds v. Sims, 377 U.S., at 557-561. The mere fact, however, that we may not now similarly perceive a likely arithmetic presumption in the instant context does not compel a conclusion that the claims presented here are nonjusticiable." Justice O'Connor, writing in dissent for herself, Chief Justice Burger, and then-Justice Rehnquist, would have held claims of unconstitutional political gerrymandering nonjusticiable.

The six justices in *Bandemer* who agreed that political gerrymandering claims were justiciable split into two camps with respect to the substantive standard to be applied to such claims, with Justice White (now writing for himself and three other justices) adopting a relatively stringent standard that required plaintiffs to show that "the electoral system is arranged in a manner that will consistently degrade ... a group of voters' influence on the political process as a whole," while Justice Powell, writing for himself and Justice Stevens, proposed a more plaintiff-friendly standard that looked at factors such as the nature of the procedures by which the challenged redistricting was accomplished and the intent behind the redistricting; the shapes of the districts and their conformity with political subdivision boundaries and other "neutral" geographic criteria; and the lack of any nonpartisan explanation for the district boundaries. (The substantive standard for proving claims of unconstitutional political gerrymandering is covered in more detail in Chapter 7 infra.)

Following *Bandemer*, although a significant number of political gerrymandering cases were brought, they were uniformly unsuccessful, essentially because it was impossible to meet *Bandemer*'s "consistent degradation" test. The Court revisited the justiciability of political gerrymandering claims in the following case.

VIETH v. JUBELIRER
541 U.S. ___ (2004)

JUSTICE SCALIA announced the judgment of the Court and delivered an opinion, in which THE CHIEF JUSTICE, JUSTICE O'CONNOR, and JUSTICE THOMAS, join.

Plaintiffs-appellants Richard Vieth, Norma Jean Vieth, and Susan Furey challenge a map drawn by the Pennsylvania General Assembly establishing districts for the election of congressional Representatives, on the ground that the districting constitutes an unconstitutional political gerrymander. In Davis v. Bandemer, 478 U.S. 109 (1986), this Court held that political gerrymandering claims are justiciable, but could not agree upon a standard to adjudicate them. The present appeal presents the questions whether our decision in *Bandemer* was in error, and, if not, what the standard should be. . . .

II

Political gerrymanders are not new to the American scene. . . .

It is significant that the Framers provided a remedy for such practices in the Constitution. Article 1, § 4, while leaving in state legislatures the initial power to draw districts for federal elections, permitted Congress to "make or alter" those districts if it wished. . . .

The power bestowed on Congress to regulate elections, and in particular to restrain the practice of political gerrymandering, has not lain dormant. In the Apportionment Act of 1842, Congress provided that Representatives must be elected from single-member districts "composed of contiguous territory." [In later acts, Congress also imposed contiguity, compactness and equal population requirements.] . . . . Today, only the single-member-district-requirement remains. See 2 U.S.C. § 2c. Recent history, however, attests to Congress's awareness of the sort of districting practices appellants protest, and of its power under Article I, § 4 to control them. Since 1980, no fewer than five bills have been introduced to regulate gerrymandering in congressional districting. . . .

III

As Chief Justice Marshall proclaimed two centuries ago, "it is emphatically the province and duty of the judicial department to say what the law is." Marbury v. Madison, 5 U.S. 137 (1803). Sometimes, however, the law is that the judicial department has no business entertaining the claim of unlawfulness—because the question is entrusted to one of the political branches or involves no judicially enforceable rights. . . .

In Baker v. Carr, 369 U.S. 186 (1962), we set forth six independent tests for the existence of a political question

> [1] a textually demonstrable constitutional commitment of the issue to a coordinate political department; or [2] a lack of judicially discoverable and manageable standards for resolving it; or [3] the impossibility of deciding without an initial policy determination of a kind clearly for nonjudicial discretion; or [4] the impossibility of a court's undertaking independent resolution without expressing lack of the respect due coordinate branches of the government; or [5] an unusual need for unquestioning adherence to a political decision already made; or [6] the potentiality of embarrassment from multifarious pronouncements by various departments on one question.

These tests are probably listed in descending order of both importance and certainty. The second is at issue here . . . . One of the most obvious limitations imposed by that requirement is that judicial action must be governed by standard, by rule. Laws promulgated by the Legislative Branch can be inconsistent, illogical, and ad hoc; law pronounced by the courts must be principled, rational, and based upon reasoned distinctions.

Over the dissent of three Justices, the Court held in Davis v. Bandemer that, since it was "not persuaded that there are no judicially discernible and manageable standards by which political gerrymander cases are to be decided," such cases were justiciable. The clumsy shifting of the burden of proof for the premise (the Court was "not persuaded" that standards do not exist, rather than "persuaded" that they do) was necessitated by the uncomfortable fact that the six-Justice majority could not discern what the judicially discernible standards might be. There was no majority on that point. Four of the Justices finding justiciability believed that the standard was one thing; two believed it was something else. The lower courts have lived with that assurance of a standard (or more precisely, lack of assurance that there is no standard), coupled with that inability to specify a standard, for the past 18 years. In that time, they have considered numerous political gerrymandering claims; this Court has never revisited the unanswered question of what standard governs.

Nor can it be said that the lower courts have, over 18 years, succeeded in shaping the standard that this Court was initially unable to enunciate. . . . [I]ts application has almost invariably produced the same result (except for the incurring of attorney's fees) as would have obtained if the question were nonjusticiable: judicial intervention has been refused. . . .

Eighteen years of judicial effort with virtually nothing to show for it justify us in revisiting the question whether the standard promised *Bandemer* exists. As the following discussion reveals, no judicially discernible and manageable standards for adjudicating political gerrymandering claims have emerged. Lacking them, we must conclude that political gerrymandering claims are nonjusticiable and that *Bandemer* was wrongly decided. . . .

A

We begin our review of possible standards with that proposed by Justice White's plurality opinion in *Bandemer* because, as the narrowest ground for our decision in that case, it has been the standard employed by the lower courts. . . .

In the lower courts, the legacy of the plurality's test is one long record of puzzlement and consternation. . . . The test has been criticized for its indeterminacy by a host of academic commentators. . . .

C

[The standard proposed by Justice Powell in *Bandemer* is] essentially a totality-of-the-circumstances analysis, where all conceivable factors, none of which is dispositive, are weighed with an eye to ascertaining whether the particular gerrymander has gone too far—or, in Justice Powell's terminology, whether it is not "fair." "Fairness" does not seem to us a judicially manageable standard. . . . Some criterion more solid and more demonstrably met than that seems to us necessary to enable the state legislatures to discern the limits of their districting discretion, to meaningfully constrain the discretion of the courts, and to win public acceptance for the courts' intrusion into a process that is the very foundation of democratic decisionmaking. . . .

IV

We turn next to consideration of the standards proposed by today's dissenters. We preface it with the observation that the mere fact that these four dissenters come up with three different standards—all of them different from the two proposed in *Bandemer* and the one proposed here by appellants—goes a long way to establishing that there is no constitutionally discernible standard.

A

. . . .

Much of [Justice Stevens'] dissent is addressed to the incompatibility of severe partisan gerrymanders with democratic principles. We do not disagree with that judgment, any more than we disagree with the judgment that it would be unconstitutional for the Senate to employ, in impeachment proceedings, procedures that are incompatible with its obligation to "try" impeachments. The issue we have discussed is not whether severe partisan gerrymanders violate the Constitution, but whether it is for the courts to say when a violation has occurred, and to design a remedy. . . .

[The fact that this Court has adjudicated claims of unconstitutional racial gerrymandering is not sufficient to make claims of political gerrymandering justiciable. Thus,] the mere fact that there exist standards [from the racial gerrymandering cases] which this Court could apply — the proposition which much of Justice Stevens's opinion is devoted to establishing — does not mean that those standards are discernible in the Constitution. This Court may not willy-nilly apply standards — even manageable standards — having no relation to constitutional harms. . . .

B

. . . . Justice Souter recognizes that there is no existing workable standard for adjudicating such claims. He proposes a "fresh start" . . . complete with a five-step prima facie test sewn together from parts of, among other things, our Voting Rights Act jurisprudence, law review articles, and apportionment cases. Even if these self-styled "clues" to unconstitutionality could be manageably applied, which we doubt, there is no reason to think they would detect the constitutional crime which Justice Souter is investigating — an "extremity of unfairness" in partisan competition. . . .

While this five-part test seems eminently scientific, upon analysis one finds that [the steps require] . . . a quantifying judgment that is unguided and ill suited to the development of judicial standards . . . .

Justice Souter's proposal is doomed to failure for a more basic reason: No test — yea, not even a five-part test — can possibly be successful unless one knows what he is testing *for*. . . .

Like us, Justice Souter acknowledges and accepts that "some intent to gain political advantage is inescapable whenever political bodies devise a district plan, and some effect results from the intent." Thus, again like us, he recognizes that "the issue is one of how much is too much." And once those premises are conceded, the only line that can be drawn must be based, as Justice Souter again candidly admits, upon a substantive "notio[n] of fairness." This is the same flabby goal that deprived Justice Powell's test of all determinacy. To be sure, Justice Souter frames it somewhat differently: courts must intervene, he says, when "partisan competition has reached an *extremity* of unfairness." We do not think the problem is solved by adding the modifier.

C

. . . .

The criterion Justice Breyer proposes is nothing more precise than "the *unjustified* use of political factors to entrench a minority in power." While he invokes in passing the Equal Protection Clause, it should be clear to any reader that what constitutes *unjustified* entrenchment depends on his own theory of "effective government." While one must agree with Justice Breyer's incredibly abstract starting point that our Constitution sought to create a "basically democratic" form of government, that is a long and impassable distance away from the conclusion that the judiciary may assess whether a group (somehow defined) has achieved a level of political power (somehow defined) commensurate with that to which they would be entitled absent *unjustified* political machinations (whatever that means). . . .

[P]erhaps the most surprising omission from Justice Breyer's dissent, given his views on other matters, is the absence of any cost-benefit analysis. Justice Breyer acknowledges that "a majority normally can work its political will," and well describes the number of actors, from statewide executive officers, to redistricting commissions, to Congress, to the People in ballot initiatives and referenda, that stand ready to make that happen. He gives no instance (and we know none) of permanent frustration of majority will. But where the majority has failed to assert itself for some indeterminate period . . . , Justice Breyer simply assumes that "court action may prove necessary." Why so? In the real world, of course, court action that is available tends to be sought, not just where it is necessary, but where it is in the interest of the seeking party. And the vaguer the test for availability, the more frequently interest rather than necessity will produce litigation. Is the regular insertion of the judiciary into districting, with the delay and uncertainty that brings to the political process and the partisan *do not even enmity it brings upon the courts, worth the benefit to be achieved—an accelerated (by some unknown degree) effectuation of the majority will? We think not.*

V

Justice Kennedy recognizes that we have "demonstrated the shortcomings of the . . . standards that have been considered to date." He acknowledges, moreover, that we "lack . . . comprehensive and neutral principles for drawing electoral boundaries" and that there is an "absence of rules to limit and confine judicial intervention." From these premises, one might think that Justice Kennedy would reach the conclusion that political gerrymandering claims are nonjusticiable. Instead, however, he concludes that courts should continue to adjudicate such claims because a standard may one day be discovered.

The first thing to be said about Justice Kennedy's disposition is that it is not legally available. The District Court in this case considered the plaintiffs' claims *justiciable* but dismissed them because the standard for unconstitutionality had not been met. It is logically impossible to affirm that dismissal without either (1) finding that the unconstitutional-districting standard applied by the District Court, or some other standard that it *should* have applied, has not been met, or (2) finding (as we have) that the claim is nonjusticiable. Justice Kennedy seeks to affirm "[b]ecause, in the case before us, we have no standard." But it is *our* job, not the plaintiffs', to explicate the standard that makes the facts alleged by the plaintiffs adequate or inadequate to state a claim. We cannot nonsuit *them* for our failure to do so. . . .

Justice Kennedy worries that "[a] determination by the Court to deny all hopes of intervention could erode confidence in the courts as much as would a premature decision to intervene." But it is the function of the courts to provide relief, not hope. What we think would erode confidence is the Court's refusal to do its job—announcing that there may well be a valid claim here, but we are not yet prepared to figure it out. . . .

Reduced to its essence, Justice Kennedy's opinion boils down to this: "As presently advised, I know of no discernible and manageable standard that can render this claim justiciable. I am unhappy about that, and hope that I will be able to change my opinion in the future." What are the lower courts to make of this pronouncement? We suggest that they must treat it as a reluctant fifth vote against justiciability . . . —a vote that may change in some future case but that holds, for the time being, that this matter is nonjusticiable.

VI

We conclude that [no provision in the Constitution] . . . provides a judicially enforceable limit on the political considerations that the States and Congress may take into account when districting. . . .

While we do not lightly overturn one of our own holdings, "when governing decisions are unworkable or are badly reasoned, 'this Court has never felt constrained to follow precedent.'" Eighteen years of essentially pointless litigation have persuaded us that Bandemer is incapable of principled application. We would therefore overrule that case, and decline to adjudicate these political gerrymandering claims. . . .

JUSTICE KENNEDY, concurring in the judgment.

A decision ordering the correction of all election district lines drawn for partisan reasons would commit federal and state courts to unprecedented intervention in the American political process. The Court is correct to refrain from directing this substantial intrusion into the Nation's political life. While agreeing with the plurality that the complaint the appellants filed in the District Court must be dismissed, and while understanding that great caution is necessary when approaching this subject, I would not foreclose all possibility of judicial relief if some limited and precise rationale were found to correct an established violation of the Constitution in some redistricting cases. . . .

It is not in our tradition to foreclose the judicial process from the attempt to define standards and remedies where it is alleged that a constitutional right is burdened or denied....

[Given that the Court *has* entertained a variety of constitutional challenges to districting plans, a decision that political gerrymandering claims are nonjusticiable] hinges entirely on proof that no standard could exist. This is a difficult proposition to establish, for proving a negative is a challenge in any context.

That no such standard has emerged in this case should not be taken to prove that none will emerge in the future. Where important rights are involved, the impossibility of full analytical satisfaction is reason to err on the side of caution. Allegations of unconstitutional bias in apportionment are most serious claims, for we have long believed that "the right to vote" is one of "those political processes ordinarily to be relied upon to protect minorities." United States v. Carolene Products Co., 304 U.S. 144, 153, n. 4 (1938)....

The plurality says that 18 years, in effect, prove the negative.... [B]y the timeline of the law 18 years is rather a short period. In addition, the rapid evolution of technologies in the apportionment field suggests yet unexplored possibilities.... [T]hese new technologies may produce new methods of analysis that make more evident the precise nature of the burdens gerrymanders impose on the representational rights of voters and parties. That would facilitate court efforts to identify and remedy the burdens, with judicial intervention limited by the derived standards.

If suitable standards with which to measure the burden a gerrymander imposes on representational rights did emerge, hindsight would show that the Court prematurely abandoned the field. That is a risk the Court should not take....

JUSTICE STEVENS, dissenting.

The central question presented by this case is whether political gerrymandering claims are justiciable. Although our reasons for coming to this conclusion differ, five Members of the Court are convinced that the plurality's answer to that question is erroneous. Moreover, as is apparent from our separate writings today, we share the view that, even if these appellants are not entitled to prevail, it would be contrary to precedent and profoundly unwise to foreclose all judicial review of similar claims that might be advanced in the future. That we presently have somewhat differing views—concerning both the precedential value of some of our recent cases and the standard that should be applied in future cases—should not obscure the fact that the areas of agreement set forth in the separate opinions are of far greater significance....

[Justice Stevens's discussion of the substantive standard he would apply is set out in Chapter 7.]

The plurality candidly acknowledges that legislatures can fashion standards to remedy political gerrymandering that are perfectly manageable and, indeed, that the legislatures in Iowa and elsewhere have done so. If a violation of the Constitution is found, a court could impose a remedy patterned after such a statute. Thus, the problem, in the plurality's view, is not that there is no judicially manageable standard to fix an unconstitutional partisan gerrymander, but rather that the Judiciary lacks the ability to determine when a state legislature has violated its duty to govern impartially.

Quite obviously, however, several standards for identifying impermissible partisan influence are available to judges who have the will to enforce them. We could hold that every district boundary must have a neutral justification; we could apply Justice Powell's three-factor approach in *Bandemer*, we could apply the predominant motivation standard fashioned by the Court in its racial gerrymandering cases; or we could endorse either of the approaches advocated today by Justice Souter and Justice Breyer. What is clear is that it is not the unavailability of judicially manageable standards that drives today's decision. It is, instead, a failure of judicial will to condemn even the most blatant violations of a state legislature's fundamental duty to govern impartially. . . .

JUSTICE SOUTER, with whom JUSTICE GINSBURG joins, dissenting.
. . . .

It is undeniable that political sophisticates understand [the idea of political and representational] fairness and how to go about destroying it, although it cannot possibly be described with the hard edge of one person, one vote. The difficulty has been to translate these notions of fairness into workable criteria, as distinct from mere opportunities for reviewing courts to make episodic judgments that things have gone too far, the sources of difficulty being in the facts that some intent to gain political advantage is inescapable whenever political bodies devise a district plan, and some effect results from the intent. . . .

The plurality says, in effect, that courts have been trying to devise practical criteria for political gerrymandering for nearly 20 years, without being any closer to something workable than we were when *Davis* was decided. While this is true enough, I do not accept it as sound counsel of despair. For I take it that the principal reason we have not gone from theoretical justiciability to practical administrability in political gerrymandering cases is the [fact that the *Davis* test, which does not work, has been binding on the lower courts.] . . . .

Since this Court has created the problem no one else has been able to solve, it is up to us to make a fresh start. . . . [Justice Souter's proposed test is discussed in more detail in Chapter 7.]

The plurality says that my proposed standard would not solve the essential problem of unworkability. It says that "it does not solve the problem [of determining when gerrymandering has gone too far] to break down the original unanswerable question . . . into four more discrete but unanswerable questions." It is common sense, however, to break down a large and intractable issue into discrete fragments as a way to get a handle on the larger one, and the elements I propose are not only tractable in theory, but the very subjects that judges already deal with in practice. The plurality asks, for example, "what . . . a lower court [is] to do when, as will often be the case, the district adheres to some traditional criteria but not others?" This question already arises in cases under § 2 of the Voting Rights Act of 1965, and the district courts have not had the same sort of difficulty answering it as they have in applying the Davis v. Bandemer plurality. . . . The enquiries I am proposing are not, to be sure, as hard-edged as I wish they could be, but neither do they have a degree of subjectivity inconsistent with the judicial function. . . .

[Justice Breyer's dissent, which is devoted entirely to setting out "a set of circumstances in which the use of purely political districting criteria could conflict with constitutionally mandated democratic requirements," and for which courts could devise a workable test, is discussed in more detail in Chapter 7.]

Page 135. Before Section F, add the following:

BUSH v. GORE
531 U.S. 98 (2000)

PER CURIAM: . . .

[Following an agonizingly close presidential election in Florida, the Florida Supreme Court ordered a manual recount of undervotes—ballots on which no vote had been registered during the machine count—in all counties that had not yet completed a recount. In addition, it ordered that additional votes recovered during prior but untimely manual recounts in several other counties be included in the vote total.]

II

B

The individual citizen has no federal constitutional right to vote for electors for the President of the United States unless and until the state legislature chooses a statewide election as the means to implement its power to appoint members of the Electoral College. U.S. Const., Art. II, § 1. This is the source for the statement in McPherson v. Blacker, 146 U.S. 1, 35 (1892), that the State legislature's power to select the manner for appointing electors is plenary; it may, if it so chooses, select the electors itself, which indeed was the manner used by State legislatures in several States for many years after the Framing of our Constitution. Id., at 28-33. History has now favored the voter, and in each of the several States the citizens themselves vote for Presidential electors. When the state legislature vests the right to vote for President in its people, the right to vote as the legislature has prescribed is fundamental; and one source of its fundamental nature lies in the equal weight accorded to each vote and the equal dignity owed to each voter. The State, of course, after granting the franchise in the special context of Article II, can take back the power to appoint electors. See id., at 35 ("[T]here is no doubt of the right of the legislature to resume the power at any time, for it can neither be taken away nor abdicated") (quoting S. Rep. No. 395, 43d Cong., 1st Sess.).

The right to vote is protected in more than the initial allocation of the franchise. Equal protection applies as well to the manner of its exercise. Having once granted the right to vote on equal terms, the State may not, by later arbitrary and disparate treatment, value one person's vote over that of another. See, e.g., Harper v. Virginia Bd. of Elections, 383 U.S. 663, 665 (1966) ("[O]nce the franchise is granted to the electorate, lines may not be drawn which are inconsistent with the Equal Protection Clause of the Fourteenth Amendment"). It must be remembered that "the right of suffrage can be denied by a debasement or dilution of the weight of a citizen's vote just as effectively as by wholly prohibiting the free exercise of the franchise." Reynolds v. Sims, 377 U.S. 533, 555 (1964)....

Much of the controversy seems to revolve around ballot cards designed to be perforated by a stylus but which, either through error or deliberate omission, have not been perforated with sufficient precision for a machine to count them. In some cases a piece of the card—a chad—is hanging, say by two corners. In other cases there is no separation at all, just an indentation.

The Florida Supreme Court has ordered that the intent of the voter be discerned from such ballots. For purposes of resolving the equal protection challenge, it is not necessary to decide whether the Florida Supreme Court had the authority under the legislative scheme for resolving election disputes to define what a legal vote is and to mandate a manual recount implementing that definition. The recount mechanisms implemented in response to the decisions of the Florida Supreme Court do not satisfy the minimum requirement for non-arbitrary treatment of voters necessary to secure the fundamental right. Florida's basic command for the count of legally cast votes is to consider the "intent of the voter." This is unobjectionable as an abstract proposition and a starting principle. The problem inheres in the absence of specific standards to ensure its equal application. The formulation of uniform rules to determine intent based on these recurring circumstances is practicable and, we conclude, necessary....

An early case in our one person, one vote jurisprudence arose when a State accorded arbitrary and disparate treatment to voters in its different counties. Gray v. Sanders, 372 U.S. 368 (1963). The Court found a constitutional violation. We relied on these principles in the context of the Presidential selection process in Moore v. Ogilvie, 394 U.S. 814 (1969), where we invalidated a county-based procedure that diluted the influence of citizens in larger counties in the nominating process. There we observed that "[t]he idea that one group can be granted greater voting strength than another is hostile to the one man, one vote basis of our representative government." Id., at 819.

The State Supreme Court ratified this uneven treatment. It mandated that the recount totals from [several] counties [be] included in the certified total [even though] each of the counties used varying standards to determine what was a legal vote. Broward County used a more forgiving standard than Palm Beach County, and uncovered almost three times as many new votes, a result markedly disproportionate to the difference in population between the counties. . . .

In addition to these difficulties the actual process by which the votes were to be counted under the Florida Supreme Court's decision raises further concerns. That order did not specify who would recount the ballots. The county canvassing boards were forced to pull together ad hoc teams comprised of judges from various Circuits who had no previous training in handling and interpreting ballots. Furthermore, while others were permitted to observe, they were prohibited from objecting during the recount.

The recount process, in its features here described, is inconsistent with the minimum procedures necessary to protect the fundamental right of each voter in the special instance of a statewide recount under the authority of a single state judicial officer. Our consideration is limited to the present circumstances, for the problem of equal protection in election processes generally presents many complexities.

The question before the Court is not whether local entities, in the exercise of their expertise, may develop different systems for implementing elections. Instead, we are presented with a situation where a state court with the power to assure uniformity has ordered a statewide recount with minimal procedural safeguards. When a court orders a statewide remedy, there must be at least some assurance that the rudimentary requirements of equal treatment and fundamental fairness are satisfied. . . .

Upon due consideration of the difficulties identified to this point, it is obvious that the recount cannot be conducted in compliance with the requirements of equal protection and due process without substantial additional work. It would require not only the adoption (after opportunity for argument) of adequate statewide standards for determining what is a legal vote, and practicable procedures to implement them, but also orderly judicial review of any disputed matters that might arise. In addition, the Secretary of State has advised that the recount of only a portion of the ballots requires that the vote tabulation equipment be used to screen out undervotes, a function for which the machines were not designed. If a recount of overvotes were also required, perhaps even a second screening would be necessary. . . .

The Supreme Court of Florida has said that the legislature intended the State's electors to "participat[e] fully in the federal electoral process," as provided in 3 U.S.C. § 5. [This provision is part of a complex scheme dealing with Congressional procedures for the counting of electoral votes, enacted in the wake of the disputed presidential election of 1876. The statute provides that

> [if] any State shall have provided, by laws enacted prior to the day fixed for the appointment of the electors, for its final determination of any controversy or con-

test concerning the appointment of [electors] by judicial or other [methods], and such determination shall have been made at least six days before the time fixed for the meeting of the electors, such determination made pursuant to such law so existing on said day, and made at least six days prior to said time of meeting of the electors, shall be [conclusive]].

That statute, in turn, requires that any controversy or contest that is designed to lead to a conclusive selection of electors be completed by December 12. That date is upon us, and there is no recount procedure in place under the State Supreme Court's order that comports with minimal constitutional standards. Because it is evident that any recount seeking to meet the December 12 date will be unconstitutional for the reasons we have discussed, we reverse the judgment of the Supreme Court of Florida ordering a recount to proceed. . . .

None are more conscious of the vital limits on judicial authority than are the members of this Court, and none stand more in admiration of the Constitution's design to leave the selection of the President to the people, through their legislatures, and to the political sphere. When contending parties invoke the process of the courts, however, it becomes our unsought responsibility to resolve the federal and constitutional issues the judicial system has been forced to confront.

The judgment of the Supreme Court of Florida is reversed, and the case is remanded for further proceedings not inconsistent with this opinion.

CHIEF JUSTICE REHNQUIST, with whom JUSTICE SCALIA and JUSTICE THOMAS join, concurring.

We join the per curiam opinion. We write separately because we believe there are additional grounds that require us to reverse the Florida Supreme Court's decision.

I

We deal here not with an ordinary election, but with an election for the President of the United States. . . .

[In] Anderson v. Celebrezze, 460 U.S. 780, 794-795 (1983), we said: "In the context of a Presidential election, state-imposed restrictions implicate a uniquely important national interest. For the President and the Vice President of the United States are the only elected officials who represent all the voters in the Nation."

In most cases, comity and respect for federalism compel us to defer to the decisions of state courts on issues of state law. That practice reflects our understanding that the decisions of state courts are definitive pronouncements of the will of the States as sovereigns. Cf. Erie R. Co. v. Tompkins, 304 U.S. 64 (1938). Of course, in ordinary cases, the distribution of powers among the branches of a State's government raises no questions of federal constitutional law, subject to the requirement that the government be republican in character. See U.S. Const., Art. IV, § 4. But there are a few exceptional cases in which the Constitution imposes a duty or confers a power on a particular branch of a State's government. This is one of them. Article II, § 1, cl. 2, provides that "each State shall appoint, in such Manner as the *Legislature* thereof may direct," electors for President and Vice President. (Emphasis added.) Thus, the text of the election law itself, and not just its interpretation by the courts of the States, takes on independent significance.

In McPherson v. Blacker, 146 U.S. 1 (1892), we explained that Art. II, § 1, cl. 2, "conveys the broadest power of determination" and "leaves it to the legislature exclusively to define the method" of appointment. Id., at 27. A significant departure from the legislative scheme for appointing Presidential electors presents a federal constitutional question.

3 U.S.C. § 5 informs our application of Art. II, § 1, cl. 2, to the Florida statutory scheme, which, as the Florida Supreme Court acknowledged, took that statute into account. [If] we are to respect the legislature's Article II powers, therefore, we must ensure that postelection state-court actions do not frustrate the legislative desire to attain the "safe harbor" provided by § 5.

In Florida, the legislature has chosen to hold statewide elections to appoint the State's 25 electors. Importantly, the legislature has delegated the authority to run the elections and to oversee election disputes to the Secretary of State (Secretary), Fla. Stat. § 97.012(1) (2000), and to state circuit courts, §§ 102.168(1), 102.168(8). Isolated sections of the code may well admit of more than one interpretation, but the general coherence of the legislative scheme may not be altered by judicial interpretation so as to wholly change the statutorily provided apportionment of responsibility among these various bodies. In any election but a Presidential election, the Florida Supreme Court can give as little or as much deference to Florida's executives as it chooses, so far as Article II is concerned, and this Court will have no cause to question the court's actions. But, with respect to a Presidential election, the court must be both mindful of the legislature's role under Article II in choosing the manner of appointing electors and deferential to those bodies expressly empowered by the legislature to carry out its constitutional mandate.

In order to determine whether a state court has infringed upon the legislature's authority, we necessarily must examine the law of the State as it existed prior to the action of the court. Though we generally defer to state courts on the interpretation of state law [there] are of course areas in which the Constitution requires this Court to undertake an independent, if still deferential, analysis of state law.

For example, in NAACP v. Alabama ex rel. Patterson, 357 U.S. 449 (1958), it was argued that we were without jurisdiction because the petitioner had not pursued the correct appellate remedy in Alabama's state courts. Petitioners had sought a state-law writ of certiorari in the Alabama Supreme Court when a writ of mandamus, according to that court, was proper. We found this state-law ground inadequate to defeat our jurisdiction because we were "unable to reconcile the procedural holding of the Alabama Supreme Court" with prior Alabama precedent. 357 U.S. at 456. The purported state-law ground was so novel, in our independent estimation, that "petitioner could not fairly be deemed to have been apprised of its existence." 357 U.S. at 457.

Six years later we decided Bouie v. City of Columbia, 378 U.S. 347 (1964), in which the state court had held, contrary to precedent, that the state trespass law applied to black sit-in demonstrators who had consent to enter private property but were then asked to leave. Relying upon *NAACP*, we concluded that the South Carolina Supreme Court's interpretation of a state penal statute had impermissibly broadened the scope of that statute beyond what a fair reading provided, in violation of due process. See 378 U.S. at 361-362. What we would do in the present case is precisely parallel: Hold that the Florida Supreme Court's interpretation of the Florida election laws impermissibly distorted them beyond what a fair reading required, in violation of Article II. . . .

II

Acting pursuant to its constitutional grant of authority, the Florida Legislature has created a detailed, if not perfectly crafted, statutory scheme that provides for appointment of Presidential electors by direct election. [The] legislature has designated the Secretary of State as the "chief election officer," with the responsibility to "obtain and maintain uniformity in the application, operation, and interpretation of the election laws." § 97.012. The state legislature has delegated to county canvassing boards the duties of administering elections. § 102.141. Those boards are responsible for providing results to the state Elections Canvassing [Commission]. Cf. Boardman v. Esteva, 323 So. 2d 259, 268, n. 5 (1975) ("The election process . . . is committed to the executive branch of government through duly designated officials all charged with specific duties. . . . [The] judgments [of these officials] are entitled to be regarded by the courts as presumptively correct. . . .").

After the election has taken place, [the] county canvassing boards must file certified election returns with the Department of State by 5 p.m. on the seventh day following the election. § 102.112(1). . . .

The state legislature has also provided mechanisms both for protesting election returns and for contesting certified election results. Section 102.166 governs protests. Any protest must be filed prior to the certification of election results by the county canvassing board. § 102.166(4)(b). Once a protest has been filed, "the county canvassing board may authorize a manual recount." § 102.166(4)(c). If a sample recount conducted pursuant to § 102.166(5) "indicates an error in the vote tabulation which could affect the outcome of the election," the county canvassing board is instructed to: "(a) Correct the error and recount the remaining precincts with the vote tabulation system; (b) Request the Department of State to verify the tabulation software; or (c)

The Role of the Supreme Court in the Constitutional Order

Manually recount all ballots," § 102.166(5). In the event a canvassing board chooses to conduct a manual recount of all ballots, § 102.166(7) prescribes procedures for such a recount.

Contests to the certification of an election, on the other hand, are controlled by § 102.168. The grounds for contesting an election include "receipt of a number of illegal votes or rejection of a number of legal votes sufficient to change or place in doubt the result of the election." § 102.168(3)(c). [Section] 102.168(8) provides that "the circuit judge to whom the contest is presented may fashion such orders as he or she deems necessary to ensure that each allegation in the complaint is investigated, examined, or checked, to prevent or correct any alleged wrong, and to provide any relief appropriate under such circumstances." In Presidential elections, the contest period necessarily terminates on the date set by 3 U.S.C. § 5 for concluding the State's "final determination" of election controversies.

In its first decision, Palm Beach Canvassing Bd. v. Harris, 772 So. 2d 1220 (2000) (*Harris I*), the Florida Supreme Court extended the 7-day statutory certification deadline established by the legislature. This modification of the code, by lengthening the protest period, necessarily shortened the contest period for Presidential elections. Underlying the extension of the certification deadline and the shortchanging of the contest period was, presumably, the clear implication that certification was a matter of significance: The certified winner would enjoy presumptive validity, making a contest proceeding by the losing candidate an uphill battle. In its latest opinion, however, the court empties certification of virtually all legal consequence during the contest, and in doing so departs from the provisions enacted by the Florida Legislature.

The court determined that canvassing boards' decisions regarding whether to recount ballots past the certification deadline (even the certification deadline established by *Harris I*) are to be reviewed de novo, although the election code clearly vests discretion whether to recount in the boards, and sets strict deadlines subject to the Secretary's rejection of late tallies and monetary fines for tardiness. Moreover, the Florida court held that all late vote tallies arriving during the contest period should be automatically included in the certification regardless of the certification deadline (even the certification deadline established by *Harris I*), thus virtually eliminating both the deadline and the Secretary's discretion to disregard recounts that violate it.

Moreover, the court's interpretation of "legal vote," and hence its decision to order a contest-period recount, plainly departed from the legislative scheme. Florida statutory law cannot reasonably be thought to require the counting of improperly marked ballots. Each Florida precinct before election day provides instructions on how properly to cast a vote, § 101.46; each polling place on election day contains a working model of the voting machine it uses, § 101.5611; and each voting booth contains a sample ballot, § 101.46. In precincts using punch-card ballots, voters are instructed to punch out the ballot cleanly:

AFTER VOTING, CHECK YOUR BALLOT CARD TO BE SURE YOUR VOTING SELECTIONS ARE CLEARLY AND CLEANLY PUNCHED AND THERE ARE NO CHIPS LEFT HANGING ON THE BACK OF THE CARD.

Instructions to Voters, quoted in Touchston v. McDermott, 2000 WL 1781942, *6 & n. 19 (CA11) (Tjoflat, J., dissenting). No reasonable person would call it "an error in the vote tabulation," Fla. Stat. § 102.166(5), or a "rejection of legal votes," Fla. Stat. § 102.168(3)(c), when electronic or electromechanical equipment performs precisely in the manner designed, and fails to count those ballots that are not marked in the manner that these voting instructions explicitly and prominently specify. The scheme that the Florida Supreme Court's opinion attributes to the legislature is one in which machines are required to be "capable of correctly counting votes," § 101.5606(4), but which nonetheless regularly produces elections in which legal votes are predictably not tabulated, so that in close elections manual recounts are regularly required. This is of course absurd. The Secretary of State, who is authorized by law to issue binding interpretations of the election code, §§ 97.012, 106.23, rejected this peculiar reading of the statutes. See DE 00-13 (opinion of the Division of Elections). The Florida Supreme Court, although it must defer to the Secretary's interpretations, see Krivanek v. Take Back Tampa Political Committee, 625 So. 2d 840, 844 (Fla. 1993), rejected her reasonable interpretation and embraced the peculiar one. See Palm Beach County Canvassing Board v. Harris, No. SC00-2346 (Dec. 11, 2000) (*Harris III*).

But [in] a Presidential election the clearly expressed intent of the legislature must prevail. And there is no basis for reading the Florida statutes as requiring the counting of improperly marked ballots. . . .

III

The scope and nature of the remedy ordered by the Florida Supreme Court jeopardizes the "legislative wish" to take advantage of the safe harbor provided by 3 U.S.C. § 5. December 12, 2000, is the last date for a final determination of the Florida electors that will satisfy § 5. Yet in the late afternoon of December 8th—four days before this deadline—the Supreme Court of Florida ordered recounts of tens of thousands of so-called "undervotes" spread through 64 of the State's 67 counties. This was done in a search for elusive—perhaps delusive—certainty as to the exact count of 6 million votes. But no one claims that these ballots have not previously been tabulated; they were initially read by voting machines at the time of the election, and thereafter reread by virtue of Florida's automatic recount provision. No one claims there was any fraud in the election. The Supreme Court of Florida ordered this additional recount under the provision of the election code giving the circuit judge the authority to provide relief that is "appropriate under such circumstances." Fla. Stat. § 102.168(8) (2000).

Surely when the Florida Legislature empowered the courts of the State to grant "appropriate" relief, it must have meant relief that would have become final by the cut-off date of 3 U.S.C. § 5. In light of the inevitable legal challenges and ensuing appeals to the Supreme Court of Florida and petitions for certiorari to this Court, the entire recounting process could not possibly be completed by that date. . . .

Given all these factors, and in light of the legislative intent identified by the Florida Supreme Court to bring Florida within the "safe harbor" provision of 3 U.S.C. § 5, the remedy prescribed by the Supreme Court of Florida cannot be deemed an "appropriate" one as of December 8. It significantly departed from the statutory framework in place on November 7, and authorized open-ended further proceedings which could not be completed by December 12, thereby preventing a final determination by that date.

For these reasons, in addition to those given in the per curiam, we would reverse.

JUSTICE STEVENS, with whom JUSTICE GINSBURG and JUSTICE BREYER join, dissenting.

The Constitution assigns to the States the primary responsibility for determining the manner of selecting the Presidential electors. See Art. II, § 1, cl. 2. When questions arise about the meaning of state laws, including election laws, it is our settled practice to accept the opinions of the highest courts of the States as providing the final answers. On rare occasions, however, either federal statutes or the Federal Constitution may require federal judicial intervention in state elections. This is not such an occasion.

The federal questions that ultimately emerged in this case are not substantial. Article II provides that "[e]ach State shall appoint, in such Manner as the Legislature thereof may direct, a Number of Electors." It does not create state legislatures out of whole cloth, but rather takes them as they come—as creatures born of, and constrained by, their state constitutions. [The] legislative power in Florida is subject to judicial review pursuant to Article V of the Florida Constitution, and nothing in Article II of the Federal Constitution frees the state legislature from the constraints in the state constitution that created it. [The] Florida Supreme Court's exercise of appellate jurisdiction therefore was wholly consistent with, and indeed contemplated by, the grant of authority in Article II. . . .

Nor are petitioners correct in asserting that the failure of the Florida Supreme Court to specify in detail the precise manner in which the "intent of the voter," Fla. Stat. § 101.5614(5) (Supp. 2001), is to be determined rises to the level of a constitutional violation. We found such a violation when individual votes within the same State were weighted unequally, see, e.g., Reynolds v. Sims, but we have never before called into question the substantive standard by which a State determines that a vote has been legally cast. And there is no reason to think that the guidance provided to the factfinders, specifically the various canvassing boards, by the "intent of the voter" standard is any less sufficient—or will lead to results any less uniform—

than, for example, the "beyond a reasonable doubt" standard employed everyday by ordinary citizens in courtrooms across this country.

Admittedly, the use of differing substandards for determining voter intent in different counties employing similar voting systems may raise serious concerns. Those concerns are alleviated—if not eliminated—by the fact that a single impartial magistrate will ultimately adjudicate all objections arising from the recount process. . . .

What must underlie petitioners' entire federal assault on the Florida election procedures is an unstated lack of confidence in the impartiality and capacity of the state judges who would make the critical decisions if the vote count were to proceed. Otherwise, their position is wholly without merit. The endorsement of that position by the majority of this Court can only lend credence to the most cynical appraisal of the work of judges throughout the land. It is confidence in the men and women who administer the judicial system that is the true backbone of the rule of law. Time will one day heal the wound to that confidence that will be inflicted by today's decision. One thing, however, is certain. Although we may never know with complete certainty the identity of the winner of this year's Presidential election, the identity of the loser is perfectly clear. It is the Nation's confidence in the judge as an impartial guardian of the rule of law.

I respectfully dissent.

JUSTICE SOUTER, with whom JUSTICE BREYER joins, [dissenting]. . . .

Petitioners have raised an equal protection claim (or, alternatively, a due process claim), in the charge that unjustifiably disparate standards are applied in different electoral jurisdictions to otherwise identical facts. It is true that the Equal Protection Clause does not forbid the use of a variety of voting mechanisms within a jurisdiction, even though different mechanisms will have different levels of effectiveness in recording voters' intentions; local variety can be justified by concerns about cost, the potential value of innovation, and so on. But evidence in the record here suggests that a different order of disparity obtains under rules for determining a voter's intent that have been applied (and could continue to be applied) to identical types of ballots used in identical brands of machines and exhibiting identical physical characteristics (such as "hanging" or "dimpled" chads). I can conceive of no legitimate state interest served by these differing treatments of the expressions of voters' fundamental rights. The differences appear wholly arbitrary.

In deciding what to do about this, we should take account of the fact that electoral votes are due to be cast in six days. I would therefore remand the case to the courts of Florida with instructions to establish uniform standards for evaluating the several types of ballots that have prompted differing treatments, to be applied within and among counties when passing on such identical ballots in any further recounting (or successive recounting) that the courts might order.

The Role of the Supreme Court in the Constitutional Order Page 135

Unlike the majority, I see no warrant for this Court to assume that Florida could not possibly comply with this requirement before the date set for the meeting of electors, December 18. . . .

I respectfully dissent.

JUSTICE GINSBURG, with whom JUSTICE STEVENS joins, and with whom JUSTICE SOUTER and JUSTICE BREYER join as to Part I, dissenting.

I...

Rarely has this Court rejected outright an interpretation of state law by a state high court. Fairfax's Devisee v. Hunter's Lessee, 7 Cranch 603 (1813), NAACP v. Alabama ex rel. Patterson, 357 U.S. 449 (1958), and Bouie v. City of Columbia, 378 U.S. 347 (1964), cited by The Chief Justice, are three such rare instances. But those cases are embedded in historical contexts hardly comparable to the situation here. Fairfax's Devisee, which held that the Virginia Court of Appeals had misconstrued its own forfeiture laws to deprive a British subject of lands secured to him by federal treaties, occurred amidst vociferous States' rights attacks on the Marshall Court. The Virginia court refused to obey this Court's *Fairfax's Devisee* mandate to enter judgment for the British subject's successor in interest. That refusal led to the Court's pathmarking decision in Martin v. Hunter's Lessee, 1 Wheat. 304 (1816). *Patterson*, a case decided three months after Cooper v. Aaron, 358 U.S. 1 (1958), in the face of Southern resistance to the civil rights movement, held that the Alabama Supreme Court had irregularly applied its own procedural rules to deny review of a contempt order against the NAACP arising from its refusal to disclose membership lists. [*Bouie*], stemming from a lunch counter "sit-in" at the height of the civil rights movement, held that the South Carolina Supreme Court's construction of its trespass laws—criminalizing conduct not covered by the text of an otherwise clear statute— was "unforeseeable" and thus violated due process when applied retroactively to the petitioners.

The Chief Justice's casual citation of these cases might lead one to believe they are part of a larger collection of cases in which we said that the Constitution impelled us to train a skeptical eye on a state court's portrayal of state law. But one would be hard pressed, I think, to find additional cases that fit the mold. As Justice Breyer convincingly explains, this case involves nothing close to the kind of recalcitrance by a state high court that warrants extraordinary action by this Court. The Florida Supreme Court concluded that counting every legal vote was the overriding concern of the Florida Legislature when it enacted the State's Election Code. The court surely should not be bracketed with state high courts of the Jim Crow South.

The Chief Justice says that Article II, by providing that state legislatures shall direct the manner of appointing electors, authorizes federal superintendence over the

27

relationship between state courts and state legislatures, and licenses a departure from the usual deference we give to state court interpretations of state law. The Framers of our Constitution, however, understood that in a republican government, the judiciary would construe the legislature's enactments. See U.S. Const., Art. III; The Federalist No. 78 (A. Hamilton). In light of the constitutional guarantee to States of a "Republican Form of Government," U.S. Const., Art. IV, § 4, Article II can hardly be read to invite this Court to disrupt a State's republican regime. Yet The Chief Justice today would reach out to do just that. By holding that Article II requires our revision of a state court's construction of state laws in order to protect one organ of the State from another, The Chief Justice contradicts the basic principle that a State may organize itself as it sees fit. See, e.g., Gregory v. Ashcroft, 501 U.S. 452, 460 (1991) ("Through the structure of its government, and the character of those who exercise government authority, a State defines itself as a sovereign."); Highland Farms Dairy v. Agnew, 300 U.S. 608, 612 (1937) ("How power shall be distributed by a state among its governmental organs is commonly, if not always, a question for the state itself."). Article II does not call for the scrutiny undertaken by this Court. . . .

II . . .

I cannot agree that the recount adopted by the Florida court, flawed as it may be, would yield a result any less fair or precise than the certification that preceded that recount. . . .

I dissent.

JUSTICE BREYER . . . dissenting. . . .

II

[This portion of Justice Breyer's opinion was joined by Justices Stevens, Ginsburg, and Souter.]

Despite the reminder that this case involves "an election for the President of the United States," (Rehnquist, C.J., concurring), no preeminent legal concern, or practical concern related to legal questions, required this Court to hear this case, let alone to issue a stay that stopped Florida's recount process in its tracks. With one exception, petitioners' claims do not ask us to vindicate a constitutional provision designed to protect a basic human right. See, e.g., Brown v. Board of Education, 347 U.S. 483 (1954). Petitioners invoke fundamental fairness, namely, the need for procedural fairness, including finality. But with the one "equal protection" exception, they rely upon law that focuses, not upon that basic need, but upon the constitutional allocation of power. . . .

Of course, the selection of the President is of fundamental national importance. But that importance is political, not legal. And this Court should resist the temptation

The Role of the Supreme Court in the Constitutional Order   Page 135

unnecessarily to resolve tangential legal disputes, where doing so threatens to determine the outcome of the election.

The Constitution and federal statutes themselves make clear that restraint is appropriate. They set forth a road map of how to resolve disputes about electors, even after an election as close as this one. That road map foresees resolution of electoral disputes by state courts. See 3 U.S.C. § 5. [But] it nowhere provides for involvement by the United States Supreme Court.

To the contrary, the Twelfth Amendment commits to Congress the authority and responsibility to count electoral votes. A federal statute, the Electoral Count Act, enacted after the close 1876 Hayes-Tilden Presidential election, specifies that, after States have tried to resolve disputes (through "judicial" or other means), Congress is the body primarily authorized to resolve remaining disputes. See Electoral Count Act of 1887, 24 Stat. 373, 3 U.S.C. §§ 5, 6, and 15.

The legislative history of the Act makes clear its intent to commit the power to resolve such disputes to Congress, rather than the courts:

"The two Houses are, by the Constitution, authorized to make the count of electoral votes. They can only count legal votes, and in doing so must determine, from the best evidence to be had, what are legal votes. . . . The power to determine rests with the two Houses, and there is no other constitutional tribunal." H. Rep. No. 1638, 49th Cong., 1st Sess., 2 (1886) (report submitted by Rep. Caldwell, Select Committee on the Election of President and Vice-President). . . .

Given this detailed, comprehensive scheme for counting electoral votes, there is no reason to believe that federal law either foresees or requires resolution of such a political issue by this Court. Nor, for that matter, is there any reason to that think the Constitution's Framers would have reached a different conclusion. Madison, at least, believed that allowing the judiciary to choose the presidential electors "was out of the question." Madison, July 25, 1787 (reprinted in 5 Elliot's Debates on the Federal Constitution 363 (2d ed. 1876)).

The decision by both the Constitution's Framers and the 1886 Congress to minimize this Court's role in resolving close federal presidential elections is as wise as it is clear. However awkward or difficult it may be for Congress to resolve difficult electoral disputes, Congress, being a political body, expresses the people's will far more accurately than does an unelected Court. And the people's will is what elections are about. . . .

[The history of the disputed election of 1876, including] the participation in the work of the electoral commission by five Justices, including Justice Bradley, did not lend that process legitimacy. Nor did it assure the public that the process had worked fairly, guided by the law. Rather, it simply embroiled Members of the Court in partisan conflict, thereby undermining respect for the judicial process. And the Congress that later enacted the Electoral Count Act knew it.

This history may help to explain why I think it not only legally wrong, but also most unfortunate, for the Court simply to have terminated the Florida recount. Those who caution judicial restraint in resolving political disputes have described the quintessential case for that restraint as a case marked, among other things, by the "strangeness of the issue," its "intractability to principled resolution," its "sheer momentousness, . . . which tends to unbalance judicial judgment," and "the inner vulnerability, the self-doubt of an institution which is electorally irresponsible and has no earth to draw strength from [citing A. Bickel, The Least Dangerous Branch 184 (1962)]." Those characteristics mark this case. . . .

I fear that in order to bring this agonizingly long election process to a definitive conclusion, we have not adequately attended to that necessary "check upon our own exercise of power," "our own sense of self-restraint." United States v. Butler, 297 U.S. 1, 79 (1936) (Stone, J., dissenting). Justice Brandeis once said of the Court, "The most important thing we do is not doing." Bickel, supra, at 71. What it does today, the Court should have left undone. I would repair the damage done as best we now can, by permitting the Florida recount to continue under uniform standards.

I respectfully dissent.

Note: *Bush v. Gore*

1. *Standing and the political question doctrine.* The Court's opinion in Bush v. Gore implicates many of the considerations raised in the prior sections' discussions of standing and political questions. On the issue of standing, consider the following: If the injury identified in the per curiam is the exclusion of valid undervotes in some counties because those counties are using a more stringent standard for assessing voter intent and the exclusion of valid overvotes by an incomplete recount process, who has standing to raise these claims?

Does George W. Bush have standing? Why? Bush was not himself a registered voter in Florida who could claim a violation of his equal protection rights.

In this respect, consider Tribe, eroG v. HsuB and Its Disguises: Freeing *Bush v. Gore* from Its Hall of Mirrors, 115 Harv. L. Rev. 170, 229-31 (2001):

> [I]t is hardly credible—indeed, it borders on the fantastic—to argue that Bush himself lacked standing to press an equal protection claim in the Florida lawsuit. . . . [H]e surely had third-party standing. His injury was obvious: the Florida Supreme Court was in essence [replacing the certification he had received with] . . . a recount to be conducted by a process he regarded as an unconstitutional roulette game rigged in favor of his opponent. . . . Bush potentially had standing on this theory to represent at least those who had voted for him and whose votes stood to be devalued during a recount. More generally, he shared with all the voters a sufficiently common interest in protecting the integrity of the vote count to ensure his standing as third-party plaintiff. . . . Because of the sig-

nificant obstacles any individual voter would face in seeking to ensure a fair count, Bush not only had standing but was particularly well placed to assert voters' equal protection rights—even though his ultimate goal was to have some of their votes excluded.

Is "insuring the integrity of the vote count" the kind of "shared individuated right" as to which the Court has traditionally denied standing? Consider in this regard Karlan, Nothing Personal: The Evolution of the Newest Equal Protection from *Shaw v. Reno* to *Bush v. Gore*, 79 N.C.L. Rev. 1345, 1357-60, 1363-64 (2001):

> One striking thing about the Supreme Court's opinion in Bush v. Gore is that it doesn't distinguish [among the different potential claims of injury in fact.] But its general tone seems to focus largely on the claims of individual excluded voters, rather than on voters whose preferred candidate was potentially disadvantaged by the recount the Florida Supreme Court ordered. Perhaps this was a tactical decision by the majority, which sought to avoid having its decision appear partisan: to say that the injury was suffered only by Republican voters whose overall voting strength was diluted by the recount standard would have made explicit that this was a case about partisan outcomes rather than abstract principles. . . .
>
> [George W. Bush] is an especially unlikely candidate for third party standing. It is hard to see George W. Bush as the champion of a claim by undervoters in overwhelmingly Democratic Palm Beach County that they are being denied equal protection because their votes would have been included under the more liberal Broward County standard. Indeed, Bush's third-party complaint . . . alleged, among other things, that the standard used in Broward County was partisan, inconsistent, and unfair. The relief he sought was a declaration that "the illegal votes counted in Broward County under the new rules established after the election should be excluded under the Due Process Clause . . . ." Nothing in that proposed remedy vindicates the rights of excluded voters in Palm Beach County or elsewhere . . . .
>
> The equal protection right of individual voters to participate can really be vindicated only by expanding the scope of the prescribed recount. The only equal protection right that can be vindicated by abolishing recounts altogether is a group-based aggregation interest that depends on the partisan composition of the unrecovered pool, precisely the issue the Supreme Court seemed to want to avoid by couching its discussion in individualistic, atomistic terms. . . .
>
> Whatever interest the Supreme Court's decision vindicated, it was not the interest of an identifiable individual voter. Rather it was a perceived systemic interest in having recounts conducted according to a uniform standard or not at all. . . .

Is Bush an appropriate plaintiff to raise this more systemic claim? Would he be an appropriate plaintiff to raise the Article II claim? For additional discussions of the question of standing, consider Chemerinsky, *Bush v. Gore* Was Not Justiciable, 76 Notre Dame L. Rev. 1093, 1097 (2001) (arguing that Bush lacked first-party standing to raise the equal protection claim because he did not personally suffer an equal protection injury and that he lacked third-party standing because the injured voters could themselves have brought a lawsuit and he lacked the sort of relationship to them that is required to permit him raise their claims); Hoffman, Book Review, 95 Nw. U.L. Rev. 1533, 1548-50 (2001) (suggesting that the deluge of lawsuits filed by individual voters immediately after the election rebut the idea that "Florida voters were unable to raise the equal protection claims on their own" and that Bush should therefore be accorded third-party standing and suggesting that the Court's neglect of the question of standing reflects the doctrine's essential indeterminacy); Levinson and Young, Who's Afraid of the Twelfth Amendment?, 29 Fla. St. U.L. Rev. 925 (2001) (discussing who, if anyone, has standing to raise claims under the Twelfth Amendment); Shane, Disappearing Democracy: How *Bush v. Gore* Undermined the Federal Right to Vote for Presidential Electors, 29 Fla. St. U. L. Rev. 535, 562, n.125 (2001) (suggesting, despite "the prudential rule against so-called third-party standing, which ordinarily bars even injured parties from seeking federal judicial intervention where the cause of their alleged injury is a violation not of their own rights but of another person's," that in Bush v. Gore, "at least three factors argue persuasively for permitting the candidates to litigate their supporters' rights: the close interrelationship of the candidate's and voters' interests, the certainty that the candidates would be vigorous proponents of the voters' rights, and the possibility that direct voter suits might be deterred by uncertainty among the voters as to which of them were specifically affected by the state tabulation practices in dispute"); Tushnet, Renormalizing *Bush v. Gore*: An Anticipatory Intellectual History, 90 Geo. L.J. 113, 120 (2001) (suggesting that the question of standing in Bush v. Gore is complicated by the fact that several of the Justices in the majority had "mounted a major challenge to the entire idea of vote dilution" on the ground that discerning such an injury would require "'federal courts to make decisions based on highly political judgments —judgments that courts are inherently ill-equipped to make'").

On the subject of the political question doctrine, consider whether Article II and the twelfth amendment represent a textual commitment of the question of who is entitled to a state's electoral votes to Congress. Is this an implication of Justice Breyer's dissent? Does this explain the per curiam's decision to rely on the equal protection clause in light of *Baker*'s assurance that the equal protection clause provides judicially enforceable standards for overseeing the political process? See Karlan, Equal Protection: *Bush v. Gore* and The Making of a Precedent, in The Unfinished Election of 2000 (J.N. Rakove ed. 2001). For an extensive discussion of the evolution of the political question doctrine and its relevance to Bush v. Gore, see Issacharoff, Political Judgments, in The Vote, supra. Issacharoff argues that the overall structure of the Electoral Count Act of 1887—the source for 3 U.S.C. § 5— commits the questions raised in the Florida process to political actors. He quotes

The Role of the Supreme Court in the Constitutional Order

Senator John Sherman—coincidentially both one of the sponsors of the act and one of the prime movers behind the equal protection clause—arguing on the floor of the Senate against Supreme Court involvement in presidential election controversies:

> Another plan which has been proposed in the debates at different times and I think also in the constitutional convention, was to allow questions of this kind to be certified at once to the Supreme Court for its decisions in case of a division between the two Houses. If the House should be one way and the Senate the other, then it was proposed to let the case be referred directly to the prompt and summary decision of the Supreme Court. But there is a feeling in this country that we ought not to mingle our great judicial tribunal with political questions, and therefore this proposition has not met with much favor. It would be a very grave fault indeed and a very serious objection to refer a political question in which the people of the country were aroused, about which their feelings were excited, to this great tribunal, which after all has to sit upon the life and property of all the people of the United States. It would tend to bring that court into public odium of one or the other of the two great parties. Therefore that plan may probably be rejected as an unwise provision. I believe, however, that it is the provision made in other countries.

17 Cong. Rec. 817-818 (1886) (Sen. Sherman). Issacharoff argues that had the Electoral Count Act been followed more faithfully, the relevant players in the dispute would have been Florida's governor and its legislature and the newly elected members of Congress. He observes:

> No doubt, this scenario would look to many modern observers like a pure power grab, a partisan circumvention of orderly legal processes. But why is it either surprising or alarming that an electoral deadlock should be resolved by political officials and bodies elected by the same voters? [In] the heated rhetorical battle of Election 2000, no charge was bandied about with greater derision than the claim that one or another group of partisans was engaged in partisanship. But it was, after all, a partisan election that was at stake. It hardly seems an affront to democratic self-governance to channel the ultimate resolution of a true electoral deadlock into other democratically-elected branches of government.

   2. *The merits of the Court's decision.* The Court's decision has been subjected to voluminous scholarly and popular discussion. In general, the scholarship has been scathing in its treatment of the per curiam's equal protection analysis. For representative examples, see, e.g., Klarman, *Bush v. Gore* Through the Lens of Constitutional History, 89 Cal. L. Rev. 1721 (2001); Sunstein, Order without Law, in The Vote, supra. See also infra pages 20-28, 68. Much of the criticism focuses not on the abstract equal protection question of whether a vote should have the same likelihood of being included regardless of where the vote was cast—a sort of "equal protection for

ballots"—but on the question of remedy: Did stopping the manual recount actually protect any voter's equal protection interest? For a defense of the equal protection holding, see Lund, The Unbearable Rightness of *Bush v. Gore*, 23 Cardozo L. Rev. 1219 (2002).

Most defenders of the outcome of Bush v. Gore have defended the case either on the grounds advanced in the Chief Justice's concurrence or on more pragmatic grounds—in Judge Richard Posner's phrase, that it averted a "constitutional trainwreck." For representative samples of this scholarship, see, e.g., Epstein, "In Such Manner as the Legislature Thereof May Direct": The Outcome in *Bush v. Gore* Defended, in The Vote, supra; R.A. Posner, Breaking the Deadlock: The 2000 Election, the Constitution, and the Courts (2001).

Ultimately, despite the per curiam's embrace of an equal protection rationale for finding the ongoing recount unconstitutional, doesn't the per curiam's justification for stopping the recount depend on a weak version of the Article II argument, that is, that the Florida legislature's desire to invoke the safe-harbor provision of 3 U.S.C. § 5 outweighs the state's interest in continuing to recount ballots under a more uniform process?

And with respect to the Article II rationale, what is the Court's basis—and particularly the concurrence's basis—for reading Article II as a grant of special power to a state's legislature? Isn't the legislature a creature of the state constitution?

Consider the exchange between the concurrence and Justice Ginsburg's dissent on the nature of Supreme Court review of state courts' determinations of state law. Does the concurrence's citation of *NAACP* and *Bouie* suggest that the Supreme Court here was overturning Florida law because it thought the Florida Supreme Court was not just mistaken in its interpretation of Florida law but deliberately dishonest? Is the invocation of those cases a sign that the concurrence rested on pragmatic rather than doctrinal grounds?

More generally, the Article II issue raises a question about when a state judicial decision construing state law raises federal questions. Always? How convinced, and with what evidence, must a federal court be that a state judicial decision departs from the legislature's intent and preexisting law? At one end of the spectrum, a state law might be entirely clear, particularly if the situation involved in the current case has arisen before and there are long-standing judicial and administrative interpretations. At the other end, consider a state election statute that has never before been construed by the state courts or interpreted by executive agencies: When the state courts interpret such a statute in the midst of an election, what possible baseline can the federal courts use to assess whether that interpretation is faithful? In such cases, is a federal court doing anything other than simply second-guessing the state court? With respect to the related questions whether the Florida Supreme Court properly interpreted the state's election code, whether its interpretations constituted a change sufficient to violate due process, and the implications of Article II for these questions, consider R. Posner, Breaking the Deadlock: The 2000 Election, the Constitution, and the Courts 152 (2001) (describing the Article II argument and the concurrence's charge that the Florida Supreme Court had changed Florida law as a "respectable" argument); Epstein, "In such Manner as the Legislature Thereof May Direct": The Outcome in *Bush v. Gore* Defended, in The Vote: Bush, Gore and the Supreme Court 13, 19-35 (C.R. Sunstein & R.A. Epstein eds., 2001) (arguing that the Florida Supreme Court adopted a process for conducting election challenges that deviated in substantial respects from the process set out in the state election code and that this shift violated Article II); Klarman, *Bush v. Gore* Through the Lens of Constitutional History, 89 Calif. L. Rev. 1721, 1733-46 (2001) (arguing that nothing in Article II suggests that federal courts should be less deferential to state-court rulings in the context of a presidential election and that nothing in the Florida courts' rulings violated Article II in any event); Krent, Judging Judging: The Problem of Second-Guessing State Judges' Interpretation of State Law in *Bush v. Gore*, 29 Fla. St. U.L. Rev. 493 (2001) (arguing that the Florida Supreme Court's constructions of Florida law were plausible and that the concurrence's "conclusion that the Florida Court's decision was so unforeseeable that it changed law is nothing short of startling"); Kramer, The Supreme Court in Politics in The Unfinished Election of 2000, at 105, 146-47 (J.N. Rakove ed., 2001) (claiming that "with [one] possible exception . . . , the Florida court arguably had better interpretations [of state law] on every issue" than the Supreme Court did); Schapiro, Conceptions and Misconceptions of State Constitutional Law in *Bush v. Gore*, 29 Fla. St. U.L. Rev. 661 (2001) (arguing that the concurrence was plagued by a flawed conception of state constitutionalism and the role of state courts in the state constitutional order).

3. *Questions of institutional respect and institutional competence.* On the more general question of what Bush v. Gore shows about the Supreme Court's role in the constitutional order, consider the following views:

a. Garrett, Institutional Lessons from the 2000 Presidential Election, 29 Fla. St. U.L. Rev. 975, 975-76, 979-80, 982-83 (2001):

> [T]he Bush-Gore election concretely illustrates that institutional design is a crucial consideration in determining which part of the government is best suited to render particular decisions. When institutions must become involved in majoritarian political decisions such as the selection of a President, it may be better to rely largely on the political branches than on the judiciary for several reasons. This allocation of decisionmaking authority is preferable because of the greater democratic credentials of Congress. . . . In addition, there is a less-often recognized advantage of institutional design enjoyed by the legislature. . . . [T]he legislature can adopt procedural frameworks to shape decisionmaking and restrain partisan opportunism before a particular controversy arises. In the case of the 2000 election, the United States Congress actually had a framework in place . . . [The Electoral Count Act long antedated the Bush-Gore election and] would have

ensured that decisions were made transparently so voters could have held politicians accountable both for their ultimate decision and for the manner in which they reached it.

In contrast, . . . the Supreme Court's early intervention into the 2000 election reveals the greater possibility for strategic behavior when an institution acts ex post with relatively full information about how its decisions will affect particular and concrete interests. The presidential election thus provides on the federal level both an example of ex ante rules—the Electoral Count Act—and an example of ex post decisionmaking—the judicial interventions into the political process. While the former contained gaps because its drafters did not foresee all the problems that could arise in a presidential election, the latter provided substantial leeway for opportunistic behavior designed to advance the Justices' preferences. . . .

Although the Constitution's equal protection guarantee was adopted long before the presidential dispute in 2000, it is so open-textured and vague that virtually all the specification occurs when it is applied to particular cases. As an ex ante framework, it is essentially all gap to be filled in the future. Not only did the Court articulate its specification of equal protection for the first time in this case, but it also explicitly limited the doctrine's applicability to the case before it, evading the protection against self-interested decisionmaking that generality in rules can provide. . . .

Others have defended the Supreme Court's repeated intervention into the election contest as a courageous move to save the country from crisis—courageous because the Justices adopted an aggressive role at some risk to the reputations of their institution and themselves. Such fears of a political disaster are overstated, and they reflect an elitist distrust of the relatively messy arena of politics. Congress would not have discharged its responsibility to determine any election contest without some amount of heated rhetoric, opportunistic behavior, and partisan wrangling. However, Congress had the ability to apply [the Electoral Count Act] in a transparent and accountable way.

While others . . . have worried that the Court's decision[s] . . . will damage its long-term reputation, my concern focuses on the damage to the legislative branch. When judges work so hard to keep a case away from our elected representatives, using a novel legal rationale that is not supported with the kind of argument and analysis of precedent that similar holdings have been, their distrust of the political branches is palpable. Furthermore, when those who harshly criticize the Court's opinion as lawless and unprincipled nonetheless defend it as a necessary protection against the chaos that they predict would have consumed the country, this analysis feeds the distrust of Congress already prevalent. . . .

b. Priest, Reanalyzing *Bush v. Gore*: Democratic Accountability and Judicial Overreaching, 72 U. Colo. L. Rev. 953, 963-64 (2001):

The Role of the Supreme Court in the Constitutional Order

[T]he set of events leading up to Bush v. Gore can best be understood as a battle between two courts over the mechanisms of control of the election process in Florida. The Florida Supreme Court . . . claimed through its decisions that it, not the elected Secretary of State, should make the determinative political judgment as to how the Florida election process was to be managed. . . . In Bush v. Gore, the United States Supreme Court reinstated control over the Florida election process to the democratically elected official politically accountable for those decisions, control that had been wrested from that official by the Florida Supreme Court. As a consequence, the United States Supreme Court in Bush v. Gore restored to the citizens of Florida the power to hold politically accountable the official responsible for determining how the election was to proceed.

c. Sunstein, Order Without Law, 68 U. Chi. L. Rev. 757, 758-59 (2001):

The Court's decision in Bush v. Gore did have two fundamental virtues. First, it produced a prompt and decisive conclusion to the chaotic post-election period of 2000. Indeed, it probably did so in a way that carried more simplicity and authority than anything that might have been expected from the United States Congress. The Court might even have avoided a genuine constitutional crisis. Second, the Court's equal protection holding carries considerable appeal. On its face, that holding has the potential to create the most expansive, and perhaps sensible, protection for voting rights since the Court's one-person, one-vote decisions of mid-century. . . .

The Court's decision also had two large vices. First, the Court effectively resolved the presidential election not unanimously, but by a 5-4 vote, with the majority consisting entirely of the Court's most conservative justices. Second, the Court's rationale was not only exceedingly ambitious but also embarrassingly weak. However appealing, its equal protection holding had no basis in precedent or in history. It also raises a host of puzzles for the future, which the Court appeared to try to resolve with its minimalist cry of "here, but nowhere else." . . .

From the standpoint of constitutional order, the Court might well have done the nation a service. From the standpoint of legal reasoning, the Court's decision was very bad. In short, the Court's decision produced order without law. . . .

d. Karlan, Unduly Partial: The Supreme Court and the Fourteenth Amendment in *Bush v. Gore*, 29 Fla. St. U.L. Rev. 587, 600-01 (2001):

[Bush v. Gore] was political, in the broad sense of the word. The Court was trying to wrap its decision in the mantle of its most popularly and jurisprudentially successful intervention into the political process: the one-person, one-vote cases. This is a familiar strategy. Consider Planned Parenthood v. Casey, the case in which the Court reaffirmed the central right to reproductive autonomy recognized in Roe v. Wade. The joint opinion written by Justices O'Connor, Kennedy, and Souter invoked another iconic Equal Protection Clause case, Brown v. Board of Education. It too treated the responsibility of articulating binding principles of constitutional law as an unsought responsibility. And it saw a special dimension "present whenever the Court's interpretation of the Constitution calls the contending sides of a national controversy to end their national division by accepting a common mandate rooted in the Constitution." It identified only two such occasions "in our lifetime, . . . the decisions of Brown and Roe."

Perhaps the Supreme Court saw Bush v. Gore as a third such occasion. Once again, the Court was asking the nation to end its close division by accepting a common mandate rooted in the Constitution and accepting a judicial resolution. And as between the Equal Protection Clause—source of some of the Supreme Court's finest moments—and the other contenders, it was no contest. If the Supreme Court was going to stop the recount, it had to use a constitutional provision with a pedigree. The Equal Protection Clause provided exactly that. Moreover, it allowed the Court to invoke the specter of unfair treatment of voters, whereas the other available constitutional contenders protected either the prerogative of state legislatures (Article II, Section 1) or, even worse, the interests of candidate George W. Bush (the Due Process Clause . . . .)

e. Pildes, Democracy and Disorder, 68 U. Chi. L. Rev. 695, 696-700, 714-15 (2001):

Bush v. Gore is the most dramatic moment in a constitutionalization of the democratic process that has been afoot for nearly forty years, ever since Baker v. Carr dramatically lowered the "political question" barrier to judicial oversight of politics. . . .

[In cases regulating politics,] the formal sources of legal judgment are sufficiently open-textured as not to compel directly a uniquely determinate conclusion. At that point, the implicit understandings of democracy with which all judges necessarily work—whether American democracy is fragile or secure, whether it functioned better or worse at some (partially hypothesized) moment in the past, whether democracy means order and structure or chaos and tumult—have the greatest latitude to operate. . . .

[At the time the Court decided Bush v. Gore, it faced the possibility] of the ultimate resolution emerging from a political struggle within Congress over a possibly competing slate of Florida electors . . . much as Congress was the ultimate dispute resolver in the 1876 Hayes-Tilden election or in the internal civil war in Rhode Island that lay behind Luther v. Borden. . . .

When a justice stares at this kind of political resolution of a disputed presidential election, does that justice see the specter of a "constitutional trainwreck?" A dangerous mechanism to be avoided at nearly all costs, a mechanism that conjures up images of disorder, turbulence, political instability, indeed, "crisis?" Does the very novelty of the Electoral Count Act process, one not invoked for over a hundred years, increase the judicial sense of a system racing to the brink, a race from which judicial rescue is desperately needed? Or does a justice see other disputed presidential elections of 1800 and 1876—elections freighted with profound substantive conflicts genuinely tearing the country apart, unlike in 2000—and yet elections in which political institutions adequately resolved the dispute. . . ? A deep historical sensibility about the elections of 1800 or 1876 is not needed to ask such questions. For we can also ask whether the recent presidential impeachment process was a "constitutional trainwreck" or, again more to the point, whether the constitutional order would have been improved had the Supreme Court determined for the country what constituted "high Crimes and Misdemeanors" within the meaning of the Constitution?

Whether democracy requires order, stability, and channeled, constrained forms of engagement, or whether it requires and even celebrates relatively wide-open competition that may appear tumultuous, partisan, or worse, has long been a struggle in democratic thought and practice (indeed, historically it was one of the defining set of oppositions in arguments about the desirability of democracy itself). . . . [Justices] regularly seem to group themselves into characteristic and recurring patterns of response . . . . These patterned responses suggest that it is something beyond law, or facts, or narrow partisan politics in particular cases, that determine outcomes; it is, perhaps, cultural assumptions and historical interpretations, conscious or not, that inform or even determine these judgments.

f. Yoo, In Defense of the Court's Legitimacy, 68 U. Chi. L. Rev. 775, 776, 779-81 (2001):

[C]oncerns about the Court's legitimacy are overblown. While it is certainly too early to be sure, the Court's actions, and their impact on the political system, come nowhere close to approaching the circumstances that surrounded earlier, real threats to the Court's standing. The Court did not decide any substantive issues—on a par with abortion or privacy rights, for example—that call upon the Court to remain continually at the center of political controversy for years. Instead, the Court issued a fairly narrow decision in a one-of-a-kind case—the procedures to govern presidential election counts—that is not likely to reappear in our lifetimes. Rather than acting hypocritically and lawlessly, the Court's decision to bring the Florida election dispute to a timely, and final, end not only restored stability to the political system but was also consistent with the institutional role the Court has shaped for itself over the last decade. . . .

The Court's authority has come under serious question four times in our history: the Marshall Court, the Taney Court's decision in Dred Scott, the Court's early resistance to the New Deal, and the Warren Court's fight against segregation and its expansion of individual liberties. Close inspection of these periods show that they bear little resemblance to Bush v. Gore. . . .

The defining characteristic of several of these periods was the persistent, central role of the Court in the political disputes of the day. Contrast these periods with Bush v. Gore. In Bush v. Gore, the Court sought to resolve a narrow legal issue involving the selection of presidential electors. The question bears no constitutional implications for the resolution of any significant and ongoing social issues of today—abortion, race relations, education, social security, defense. The decision poses no bar to a society that seeks to use the democratic process to resolve any pressing social problems. While the Democratic party has reason to be dissatisfied with the outcome of Bush v. Gore, it has no interest in challenging the legal reasoning of the decision in the future. It is highly unlikely that the Court will remain a central player in future presidential election contests. . . .

g. Klarman, Bush v. Gore Through the Lens of Constitutional History, 89 Cal. L. Rev. 1721, 1722, 1747-48, 1761-64 (2001):

[H]istory's verdict on a Supreme Court ruling depends more on whether public opinion ultimately supports the outcome than on the quality of the legal reasoning or the craftsmanship of the Court's opinion. . . .

The principal variable influencing the Court's reputation is how popular or unpopular its decisions are. Second, . . . the intensity of that sentiment—how strongly supporters and opponents feel about the underlying issue—influences the Court's standing. Third, [is how convinced opponents are] . . . that the Court decision resolving that issue will be implemented, rather than evaded or even nullified. . . . Fourth, the relative power of the constituencies that support and oppose the Court's rulings may be relevant. . . . Fifth, some constitutional issues linger, while others fade away. Controversial decisions on topics that quickly become obsolete are unlikely to do the Court much long-term harm. Sixth, public opinion changes, often quite dramatically, on some constitutional issues but not others. . . . Seventh, Justices sometimes, but not always, enjoy subsequent opportunities to adjust their original decision, thus modulating results that initially proved controversial. Eighth, contentious constitutional decisions sometimes come in packages. A ruling that might not have significantly impaired the Court's standing had it been an isolated event, may weaken an institution already under siege because of contemporaneous decisions. . . .

Half the country, the half that voted for Al Gore, thinks the result in Bush v. Gore was wrong; many think it was egregiously so. . . . Yet, while nearly all Democrats criticize *Bush*, it is not clear how intense their opposition is. Surely most

Americans are more energized by presidential elections than by flag burning. On the other hand, relatively few Gore supporters seem to have manifested an intensity of commitment for their candidate approaching that displayed by right-to-lifers in opposition to Roe v. Wade. Indeed, a principal reason that Gore found himself in the Florida predicament that he did (recall that all the political scientists' models predicted a relatively comfortable victory for him) was the relative lack of enthusiasm evinced by many Democrats for their party's candidate. Thus one might surmise that many Democrats' opposition to Bush v. Gore will be lukewarm at best. My hunch, however, is that this supposition is mistaken.... This efficacious a ruling, on this divisive an issue, is certain to generate tremendous resentment toward the Court.

As to the relative power of the constituencies impacted by the Court's decision, both Democrats and Republicans have plenty of political and economic clout in American society. Thus, Bush v. Gore is not a case where the Court's critics are relatively disadvantaged in the public relations battle that follows the ruling. On the other hand, it is hard to think of a constitutional issue that is more destined to become obsolete. George W. Bush will be president, possibly as a result of the Supreme Court's ruling, for four years. If he serves eight years, an intervening independent cause, a second electoral victory, will greatly reduce the Court's responsibility for the second term.... Moreover, the Supreme Court's ruling in *Bush*, by design, will have implications for no other constitutional issue.... Memories of what most Democrats will regard as the (at least attempted) judicial theft of a presidential election will survive, but they will be just that—memories....

On the other hand, unlike with racial segregation, where public opinion transformed over time, popular attitudes toward Bush v. Gore probably never will change very much. Democrats are likely always to believe that the Supreme Court intervened in the 2000 presidential election because the conservative Justices preferred George W. Bush for president. Perhaps some attitudes will change if Bush proves to be a particularly good or bad President, but probably not too many. Moreover, unlike with the death penalty, the Supreme Court almost certainly will enjoy no future opportunities to revisit the issue in Bush ... and thus to fix its "mistake." Once elected president, Bush cannot be "unelected."

Finally, from the "basket of issues" perspective, the Rehnquist Court might survive Bush v. Gore reasonably unscathed, because the remainder of the Court's constitutional jurisprudence has been such a political grab bag of results.... While the Rehnquist Court arguably has been the most activist in history, its activism does not manifest a consistent political valence. In recent years, liberals generally have won on issues involving abortion, school prayer, gender discrimination, and freedom of speech. Conservatives, on the other hand, have triumphed on issues such as affirmative action, minority voting districts, public aid to parochial schools, federalism, the death penalty, and (usually) criminal procedure. . . . Perhaps Democratic ire over Bush v. Gore is somewhat ameliorated by the Rehnquist Court's continuing propensity to distribute a substantial share of constitutional victories to liberals.

h. Seidman, What's So Bad About Bush v. Gore? An Essay on Our Unsettled Election, 47 Wayne L. Rev. 953, 958-62, 1024, 1026 (2001):

According to the Official Story, constitutional law settles otherwise destabilizing political disputes through reference to a meta-agreement. . . . This agreement, whether embodied in the constitutional text, or in doctrine and tradition that has glossed it, prevents the community from coming unraveled. Sometimes the agreement is substantive, as for example, when the Constitution directly prohibits certain outcomes like laws depriving people of property without just compensation. More often it is procedural, as when the Constitution allocates decision making authority to a branch of the federal government, the states, or the private sphere. . . .

For this story to make sense, four preconditions must be satisfied. First, there must be agreement on the metalevel. Second, there must be a discourse capable of mediating between the contested political level and the uncontroversial metalevel. Third, there must be an institution capable of engaging in the discourse. And finally, the institution and the discourse it utilizes must be "neutral" in the sense that they must not themselves be caught up in the very political controversy that they are supposed to settle. Conventionally, it is thought that the Constitution provides the area of agreement, that an arcane and specialized form of reasoning—legal reasoning—provides the mediating discourse, that the Supreme Court is uniquely capable of engaging in this discourse, and that both the Court and the discourse are free from political entanglements. . . .

[None of these was true in Bush v. Gore.] The Court's decision does not pass the "straight face" test when judged according to the aspirations for legal analysis required to make the Official Story plausible. There is no reason to take the decision seriously, and it portends precisely nothing with regard to future doctrinal developments. But it is also wrong to condemn the decision because it is political. There simply was no neutral, apolitical way in which the case could have been decided . . . .

All of which suggests that what's gone bad is not the Supreme Court, but instead the Official Story. How is it that the Supreme Court was able to play this role once stripped of the protective covering of legality . . . ?

Three possibilities suggest themselves. First, the Court may have prevailed through deception. Perhaps the decision is parasitic on the reputation for legality or integrity that the Court has built up over the years or on the pseudo-religious imagery that it uses to obscure its exercise of power. . . . The Court's decision had the external trappings of legality, even though it lacked the requisite substance. . . .

A second possibility is that the Supreme Court provided a useful focal point even though its decision was correctly perceived to be partisan rather than legal. Although the country was sharply divided about the election's outcome, there was near unanimity in the desire to get the matter over with. Even if the Supreme Court was acting nonlegally, it was at least able to settle the issue in a peaceful and orderly fashion.

The trouble with this account is that it fails to explain why people were prepared to endorse settlement by the Supreme Court, rather than another institution. After all, the federal judiciary was not the only possible focal point. The 2000 election might have been settled by the Florida Supreme Court, by the Florida Legislature, or, most plausibly, by the United States Congress. . . .

[There is also] a third possibility—one that turns the Official Story inside out. There is a chance that Bush v. Gore may begin a process of laying a more attractive and realistic foundation for constitutionalism than the Official Story provides. The very fact that the Court is not politically independent and that it could not settle the matter in a disinterested, apolitical fashion might set us down a path toward a more mature version of constitutional law. The politically tendentious character of the Court's reasoning demonstrates that our core constitutional commitments are subject to political manipulation. Ironically, public understanding of this malleability makes our politics more, rather than less, inclusive. It does so by suggesting that constitutional law, properly understood, does not settle disputes by ruling certain substantive positions out-of-bounds. . . .

Constitutional law best serves the ends of community when it opens up, rather than closes down, political argument. Nor should the Supreme Court's prestige depend upon its political neutrality. Instead, it earns that prestige when it utilizes concepts and a vocabulary that are sufficiently open-textured to allow the losers, using the same concepts and vocabulary, to claim that the Court's decision is wrong.

With respect to the deluge of academic commentary about Bush v. Gore, consider the analysis offered in Tushnet, Renormalizing Bush v. Gore: An Anticipatory Intellectual History, 90 Geo. L.J. 113, 113-16, 124-25 (2001):

The critical legal studies claim that law, properly understood, was indistinguishable from politics, properly understood, was quite threatening to the self-understanding of legal elites. . . . Legal elites are heavily invested in insisting that there is a real difference between law and politics. They are also invested, though slightly less so, in insisting that judges typically do law rather than politics. These investments . . . meant that something had to be done to take the sting out of the criticisms that [Bush v, Gore] was infected by blatant partisanship. . . . so that we can return to our belief that law is sensibly distinguishable from politics. . . .

I will identify several major techniques of renormalization. The first is simple enough: Ignore the case. Treat it as a unique event in the legal universe, unlikely ever to be repeated. . . . The difficulty that ignoring the case poses for legal elites is precisely that the decision presents itself as law, and for legal elites, judicial decisions are distinguished from executive ones, for example, precisely because executive decisions need have no implications for the future—can be sui generis —in ways that judicial decisions must.

The second renormalization technique . . . acknowledges that the decision in Bush v. Gore cannot really be regarded as an example of courts operating at anywhere near their best and may even be a (hopefully) isolated case in which law was in fact reduced to politics. . . . [T]he Court, and the nation, confronted a chaotic situation implicating both the selection of the nation's most important public official and an impending constitutional crisis. The Court, in this view, was in a position to resolve the crisis in a statesmanlike way. Perhaps the Court's legal theory was thin, but a barely adequate legal theory may be sufficient when invoked to avert a serious constitutional crisis. . . .

[A third] technique of renormalization . . . [tries] to work out the doctrinal implications of the Court's innovations . . . .

A final technique of renormalization is in some ways the most interesting. It involves the generalized invocation of rule-of-law norms, typically in the form of assertions that the Supreme Court's decision, while perhaps incorrect, nonetheless deserves respect because the Court is our nation's voice of the law. . . . Not surprisingly, this creates something of a psychological difficulty, related to, but not quite the same as, the phenomenon of cognitive dissonance. People find it hard to think that decisions with which they disagree are nevertheless justified. People also find it hard to give up on the ideal of the rule of law. The outcome is predictable. As time passes, people come to think that the decisions with which they initially disagreed were actually not wrong. I think we can expect to see, and I think reasonably soon, progressives asserting that, as a matter of fact, Bush v. Gore was correctly decided.

As indeed it was. After all, the equal protection doctrine the case articulated can certainly be turned to progressive uses. . . . And that, to conclude, would be another vindication of a different critical legal studies claim, this one about the indeterminacy of legal doctrine.

2
THE POWERS OF CONGRESS

A. Introduction

Page 142. After Note 5, add the following:

5a. *Enhancing social capital.* Consider the argument of Mazzone, The Social Capital Argument for Federalism, 11 S. Cal. Interdis. L. J. 27, 42, 59 (2001):

[Dividing] authority [increases] the points of political power over which citizens can exert influence in order to achieve their goals. [A] political environment in which there are multiple sites for influence promotes social capital because such an environment is conducive to a large number of interest groups in which citizens actively participate. [Federalism] provides opportunities for smaller groups of active citizens to organize and pursue their goals in a variety of settings rather than relegating vast numbers of citizens to passive roles in a large national advocacy group which pursues its members' interests in Washington. [Decentralization also] increases the sites of political decisionmaking. [In] a decentralized system, however, power ultimately rests in the central authority, providing incentives for citizen groups to seek influence by strengthening their resources at the national level.

5b. *Doctrinal implications?* Assuming that a political system should advance the values of federalism, do the ones listed above provide guidance on what the content of a judicially enforced doctrine of federalism should be?

B. The Basic Issues: Federalism and Judicial Review

Page 157. After Note 4, add the following:

4a. *Political Safeguards and "Horizontal Aggrandizement."* Baker & Young, Federalism and the Double Standard of Review, 51 Duke L.J. 75 (2001), distinguish between "vertical aggrandizement"—the accretion of power to the national government—and "horizontal aggrandizement," which they define as a mechanism "by which a majority of states [imposes] their own policy preferences on a minority of states with different preferences." While skeptical of the effectiveness of political safeguards to protect against vertical aggrandizement, Baker and Young argue that the political safeguards, whether in the form of structural limits built into the Constitution or in the form of the factors Kramer emphasizes, will not guard against horizontal aggrandizement. They identify three circumstances in which horizontal aggrandizement might occur: when "people in some states simply do not approve of certain activities permitted in other states, even though the activity in the other states does not affect them directly," when some states try "to capture a disproportionate share of federal monetary or regulatory largesse" by imposing as a national standard requirements that these states would follow even in the absence of a national rule, and "when states seek federal regulation to avoid externalities [associated] with regulating a particular subject at the state level," as when a local regulation might cause investors to locate in other states. Id. at 118-20.

Do the political safeguards of federalism operate effectively in connection with horizontal aggrandizement? Consider these responses: (1) In the situations described, "[prior] to the adoption of the coercive federal statute there was already a federal law regime in place that constrained state autonomy," and "Congress [was] called upon to [decide] what kind of state autonomy it should promote." Barron, A Localist Critique of the New Federalism, 51 Duke L.J. 377, 418 (2001). What is at stake is the distribution of power among the states to impose their policies on other states, and the Constitution provides no reason to prefer the distribution of power that exists before a particular statute is enacted over the distribution of power that exist afterwards. (2) The Civil War and its outcome demonstrate, or establish, that the Constitution is not concerned about avoiding horizontal aggrandizement.

C. The Evolution of Commerce Clause Doctrine: The Lessons (?) of History

Page 164. After the first paragraph of section 5 of the Note, add the following:

Cushman, Formalism and Realism in Commerce Clause Jurisprudence, 67 U. Chi. L. Rev. 1089 (2000), argues that the Court during this period applied the tests available to it in a principled way, related to its contemporaneous doctrine regarding state power to regulate interstate commerce and dealing with due process limits on state regulatory power. According to Cushman, the Supreme Court confined state regulatory power to businesses affected with a public interest. With respect to the "stream of commerce" test, only those "local" enterprises "affected with a public interest" could be located in a stream of interstate commerce, and with respect to *Shreveport*, that case "recognized federal power to regulate the intrastate rates charged by an interstate business affected with a public interest. So long as the power of Congress to regulate interstate rates remained confined to businesses affected with a public interest, its derivative power to regulate intrastate rates would remain similarly confined." Id. at 1129, 1131.

Page 200. At the end of section 1 of the Note, add the following:

Consider Shane, Federalism's "Old Deal": What's Right and Wrong with Conservative Judicial Activism, 45 Villanova L. Rev. 201, 221 (2000):

Compare [a] national anti-prostitution statute with a hypothetical federal law purporting to mandate compulsory education in some East Asian language as a prerequisite to high school graduation. The first regulates economic activity and the second not. Yet, the second law is obviously grounded in economic motivations that probably do not animate the first. There is no reason consistent with the Commerce Clause why Congress' commerce-driven compulsion of Asian language education should be more suspect than its morally driven regulation of prostitution.

Page 201. After section 2 of the Note, add the following:

2a. *Defining "commercial activities."* Consider Ides, Economic Activity as a Proxy for Federalism: Intuition and Reason in *United States v. Morrison*, 18 Const. Comment. 563, 568, 569 (2002): Relying on law-and-economics analysis, Ides argues that "the rapist [forcibly] takes that to which he has no right. The consequence [is] a forced transfer of wealth [to] the rapist. [In] short, rape is an economic crime, and the act of rape constitutes economic activity." Under this approach, is there anything that is not economic activity? See Choper, Taming Congress's Power Under the Commerce Clause: What Does the Near Future Portend?, 55 Ark. L. Rev. 731, 738, 740 (2003), suggesting that Congress "could enact a nationwide law prohibiting all robbery," and "could make it unlawful to injure any individual or business that carries insurance to cover the economic effects of the criminal act." Nelson and Pushaw, Rethinking the Commerce Clause: Applying First Principles to Uphold Federal Commercial Regulations but Preserve State Control Over Social Issues, 85

Page 201   The Powers of Congress

Iowa L. Rev. 1, 108 (1999), suggest that Congress can regulate commerce defined to include three areas: first, "buying and selling goods; the production of such merchandise; [and] incidents of that production, such as environmental and safety effects"; second, "the compensated provision of services"; and, third, "the means by which commerce is transacted," including negotiable instruments and security interests in property. Note that the latter category would make it permissible for Congress to enact a federal law of mortgages. Choper asks: "Is barring possession or use of marijuana an attempt by Congress to impose a political, moral, cultural, or social view? Or does it seek to regulate an international business?" *Supra* at 742.

After section 3 of the Note, add the following:

3a. *Perverse effects?* Consider Vermeule, Does Commerce Clause Review Have Perverse Effects?, 46 Villanova L. Rev. 1325, 1330, 1334-35 (2001): "The proponent of Commerce Clause review assumes that if Congress enacts policy P and the courts strike it down, the decision has increased decentralization. [But] if the courts' rules allow [Congress] to enact P so long as P is broadened to include some admittedly constitutional policy Q, [the] result of striking down P may [be] to produce a federal statute that mandates *both* P *and* Q." Consider the constitutionality of a federal ban on the possession of machine guns *anywhere*, not just near schools. Vermeule reports that the lower federal courts have upheld such a ban, some arguing that the aggregation principle supports a general ban even when it would not support a narrow one.

Page 202.   At the end of section 5 of the Note, add the following:

Should the Court attempt to develop an interpretation of the commerce clause that takes account of subsequent *constitutional* developments? Should modern notions of equality lead the Court to find an activity within the scope of the power to regulate interstate commerce, even if that activity might not be regulable by Congress absent its implications for equality?

Page 203.   At the end of the Note, add the following:

7. *The commerce clause after Reconstruction.* Consider the argument of Jackson, Holistic Interpretation: *Fitzpatrick v. Bitzer* and Our Bifurcated Constitution, 53 Stan. L. Rev. 1259 (2001), for a "holistic" interpretation of the Constitution, in

which the adoption of the fourteenth amendment (and others) properly should affect the interpretation of the commerce clause. Jackson proposes that "where the special concern or 'central value' of the Fourteenth and subsequent equality-oriented Amendments is at stake—a concern [with] overcoming barriers to full participation in public life, both economic and political, by groups traditionally disadvantaged by a history of government-sponsored discrimination—the federal government's powers across the Constitution should be interpreted in light of the now basic constitutional commitment to equality of treatment for all members of the polity." Id. at 1301-1302. Jackson suggests that this may provide the "articulable limit" the Court seeks on theories that require long chains of causation between the regulated subject and a substantial effect on interstate commerce.

Should we treat the Constitution as an integrated document even though portions were adopted at different times, in the absence of evidence that those who inserted the later portions intended to affect the interpretation of what had been adopted before? Jackson argues that "a sensible reconciliation of constitutionalism (in the sense of precommitment) with democracy is to give greater weight to the constitutional views [of] more contemporary supramajorities as compared with ratifiers who lived many more generations removed." Id. at 1290.

8. *Recent case.* Pierce County v. Guillen, 537 U.S. 129 (2003), upheld under the Commerce Clause a federal statute protecting reports and surveys compiled by state agencies after automobile accidents, as part of a federal program to identify potential accident sites, from discovery in lawsuits in state and federal courts. A federal statute gave state governments funds to improve highways, conditioned on, among other things, their compiling the information. States, fearing liability based on information in the reports, objected to the funding condition. "Congress could reasonably believe that adopting a measure eliminating an unforeseen side effect of the information-gathering requirement [would] result in more diligent efforts to collect the relevant information [and], ultimately, greater safety on our Nation's roads." The statute was "aimed at improving safety in the channels of commerce and increasing protection for the instrumentalities of interstate commerce." The Commerce Clause holding made it unnecessary for the Court to consider whether the statute could be upheld under the Spending Clause.

Page 218. At the bottom of the page, add the following:

Consider whether Sabri v. United States, 541 U.S. ___ (2004), merely restates or modifies the *Dole* standard. The case upheld the constitutionality of a federal statute making it a crime to bribe a state or local official of an entity that receives at least $10,000 in federal funds, without requiring any showing of a connection between the bribe and the federal funds. "Congress has authority under the Spending Clause to appropriate federal monies to promote the general welfare, and it has corresponding authority under the Necessary and Proper Clause to see to it that taxpayer dollars appropriated under that power are in fact spent for the general welfare, and not frittered away in graft or on projects undermined when funds are siphoned off or corrupt public officers are derelict about demanding value for dollars." The statute "addresses the problem at the sources of bribes, by rational means, to safeguard the integrity of the [recipients] of federal dollars." Corruption did not have to be "limited" to the federal money itself "to affect the federal interest. Money is fungible, bribed officials are untrustworthy stewards of federal funds, and corrupt contractors do not deliver dollar-for-dollar value." The "power to keep a watchful eye on expenditures and on the reliability of those who use public money is bound up with congressional authority to spend in the first place." The Court discussed *Dole* in these terms: The criminal statute "is authority to bring federal power to bear directly on individuals who convert public spending into unearned private gain, not a means for bringing federal economic might to bear on a State's own choices of public policy." A footnote to the latter sentence reads, "In enacting [the statute], Congress addressed a legitimate federal concern by licensing federal prosecution in an area historically of state concern." Compare this with the concurring opinion of Justice Kennedy in *Lopez*. Justice Thomas concurred in the judgment, relying on the Commerce Clause as interpreted in Perez v. United States.

D. Other Powers of Congress: Are They More (or Less) Plenary than the Commerce Power?

Page 230. After section 2 of the Note, add the following:

3. *The Court-Congress relation.* Consider these observations:

Boerne assumes that the creation of constitutional meaning is divorced from political and social life. It imagines a world in which the Court pronounces constitutional values and the country merely obeys. . . .

[In contrast,] [i]n the aftermath of *Brown*, the Court invited Congress's participation in vindicating equality norms, both because Congress could secure popular acceptance of the Court's decisions [and] because representative branches of government were an important resource for the Court as it struggled to learn from and speak to the American people about the meaning of the Fourteenth Amendment's guarantee of "equal protection of the laws." In this era, the Court established a relationship with Congress that was fluid and dynamic, and that could not be comprehended by mechanical criteria like "congruence and proportionality." This institutional relationship enabled the Court to interpret the Equal Protection Clause in a manner that was attentive to evolving and contested social norms. The framework of the Court's recent Section 5 decisions represents a fundamental break with the forms of interaction that the Warren and Burger Courts cultivated with Congress.

Post and Siegel, Equal Protection by Law: Federal Antidiscrimination Legislation after *Morrison* and *Kimel*, 110 Yale L.J. 441, 519, 446 (2000). Can "the forms of interaction" used by the Warren and Burger Courts be reconciled with the theory underlying Cooper v. Aaron?

4. *Changing times and prophylactic rules.* Suppose that Congress has before it sufficient evidence to justify adoption of a remedy under section 5 that is proportional to and congruent with constitutional violations but goes beyond providing a remedy for such violations only. Citing cases upholding the Voting Rights Act of 1965, *Boerne* asserts that such prophylactic rules are constitutional. What if, after time passes, the number of direct constitutional violations drops, either because of widespread compliance with the congressional statute or because of changing social norms? Can a statute constitutionally valid when adopted later become disproportionate or incongruent and therefore unconstitutional?

The Supreme Court has held that the fifteenth amendment, guaranteeing a right to vote without regard to race, is violated only by actions that intentionally deprive persons of a right to vote on the basis of race. Section 2 of the Voting Rights Act as amended in 1982 allows relief where voting practices are shown to have a disparate effect on different racial groups. It therefore goes beyond the Constitution's direct requirements. The Court in *Boerne* did not indicate a view on the present constitutionality of section 2 of the Voting Rights Act. For a discussion of section 2's constitutionality after *Boerne*, see Karlan, Two Section Twos and Two Section Fives: Voting Rights and Remedies after *Boerne*, 39 Wm. & Mary L. Rev. 725 (1998); Gerken, Understanding the Right to an Undiluted Vote, 114 Harv. L. Rev. 1663, 1737 (2001).

At the same time, in a series of cases discussed infra at page 552 of the main text, the Court has suggested that compliance with the Act might serve as a compelling state interest sufficient to justify purposefully using race to draw legislative districts. In this light, consider Karlan, Easing the Spring: Strict Scrutiny and Affirmative Action After the Redistricting Cases, 43 Wm. & Mary L. Rev. 1569, 1586 (2002):

> In suggesting that compliance with sections 2 and 5 of the Voting Rights Act can constitute a compelling state interest [sufficient to justify race-specific districting], the Court has raised the possibility that congressional or executive understandings of equality that go beyond what the Constitution itself requires can provide a justification for race-conscious state action.

5. *Garrett.* Board of Trustees of the University of Alabama v. Garrett, 531 U.S. 356 (2000), held that Congress lacked power under section 5 to require that state governments pay monetary damages for their failure to comply with the requirement of the Americans With Disabilities Act that employers take steps to reasonably accommodate employees with disabilities. According to the Court "the legislative record available to Congress did not demonstrate sufficiently widespread violations of the constitutional requirement that states not act arbitrarily in their decisions about persons with disabilities." The record included findings by a congressionally appointed task force that identified instances of disability discrimination, but many of those instances involved discrimination by local governments, not by state governments. Justice Breyer, for four dissenters, criticized the Court for "[r]eviewing the congressional record as if it were an administrative agency record," and noted that there were 300 instances of state government discrimination enumerated in the task force report. Chief Justice Rehnquist's opinion for the Court replied that many of the examples showed a failure to accommodate, but that such failures might not be arbitrary and therefore might not involve constitutional violations.

6. *Applying the* Boerne standard. The Court upheld the constitutionality of Title II of the Americans With Disabilities Act in Tennessee v. Lane, 541 U.S. ___ (2004). Title II provides that "no qualified individual with a disability shall [be] denied the benefits of the services [of] a public entity." Restating prior decisions, Justice Stevens, writing for the Court, said, "When Congress seeks to remedy or prevent unconstitutional discrimination, § 5 authorizes it to enact prophylactic legislation proscribing practices that are discriminatory in effect, if not in intent, to carry out the basic objectives of the Equal Protection Clause." The Court observed that Title II "seeks to enforce" not only constitutional equality requirements but also "a variety of other basic constitutional guarantees, infringements of which are subject to more searching judicial review," such as the right to vote and the right of access to the courts. (Without some accommodations to his disability, Lane was unable to reach the second-floor courtroom in which he was to appear.) Section 5 "authorizes Congress to enact reasonably prophylactic remedial legislation," and "the appropriateness of the remedy turns on the gravity of the harm it seeks to prevent." Title II was enacted "against a backdrop of pervasive unequal treatment in the administration of state services and programs, including systematic deprivations of fundamental rights," which demonstrated "a pattern of unconstitutional treatment in the administration of justice." The "extensive record" compiled prior to the enactment of Title II "makes it clear [that] inadequate provision of public services and access to public facilities was an appropriate subject for prophylactic legislation." Considering only the application of Title II to "the accessibility of judicial services," the Court found its requirement of reasonable accommodation to be "congruent and proportional to [Title II's] object of enforcing the right of access to the courts." (Note the difficulty of defending the constitutionality of Title II as commerce clause legislation.)

Chief Justice Rehnquist, joined by Justices Kennedy and Thomas, dissented, arguing that the evidence of unconstitutional discrimination by state governments against persons with disabilities in the provision of judicial services was insufficient to justify Title II. Justice Scalia also dissented. Concluding that the *Boerne* standard was impossible to administer neutrally, he would confine the prophylactic interpretation of section 5 to the context of race. In other contexts, he would construe section 5 to "create a cause of action" against state violations of Section 1 rights, and to allow Congress to "impose requirements directly relating to the *facilitation* of 'enforcement,'" such as reporting requirements.

Page 231. At the end of the second paragraph, add the following:

Nevada Dept. of Human Resources v. Hibbs, 538 U.S. 721 (2003), rejected a constitutional challenge to the money damages provision of the Family and Medical Leave Act of 1993 as applied to states. Chief Justice Rehnquist wrote the Court's opinion, finding that the history of state-law discrimination based on "invalid gender stereotypes in the employment context" justified a "prophylactic" remedy "that proscribes facially constitutional conduct, in order to prevent and deter unconstitutional conduct." The FMLA satisfied the requirements of congruence and proportionality in part because state laws that discriminate on the basis of gender must survive a higher standard of review than those that discriminate on the basis of age or disability — implying that it is "easier [to] show a pattern of state constitutional violations" — and in part because of limitations on the remedy provided by the FMLA.

Page 254. At the end of Note 6, add the following:

Consider Eid, Federalism and Formalism, 11 Wm. & Mary Bill of Rights J. 1191, 1194-95 (2003):

> The functional approach [is] insufficiently protective of [federalism] values. [The] potential pitfall of any pragmatic balancing approach is that it may devolve simply into an imposition of the judge's personal preferences. This risk [is] particularly great in the federalism context. First and foremost, the Court is a nationalist institution. [Further, a] balancing test does not "cue" Congress [as] well as a line. [Of] course, formalism has its dangers as well. The lines can be too harsh and unyielding. [This] risk has simply not materialized in the New Federalism decisions.

3
JUDICIAL EFFORTS TO PROTECT THE EXPANSION OF THE MARKET AGAINST ASSERTIONS OF LOCAL POWER

A. The Fundamental Framework

Page 261.   At the end of Note 1a, add the following:

Regan, Judicial Review of Member-State Regulation of Trade Within a Federal or Quasi-Federal System: Protectionism and Balancing, *Da Capo*, 99 Mich. L. Rev. 1853, 1889 (2001):

> [P]roviding a neutral perspective [is] what we have judges for. If we had no neutral dispute-settlement organs, then how the regulation appeared to affected foreigners would determine their diplomatic or legislative reaction. [Even] the *appearance* of protectionism would tend to undermine future cooperation. But if there are courts in place, the situation is changed. Trust in the central institutions can to some extent replace trust in the other parties. [The] courts should decide for themselves what the regulating legislature's subjective intent was, not how it appears to the other parties.

C. Facially Neutral Statutes with Effects on Commerce

Page 320. At the end of note 5, add the following:

Stearns, A Beautiful Mend: A Game Theoretical Analysis of the Dormant Commerce Clause Doctrine, 45 Wm. & Mary L. Rev. 1, 82 (2003), suggests that the Court's doctrine aims at identifying "the best available proxies for laws that, if sustained, are likely to provoke a retaliatory response from other states or laws that represent state efforts to appropriate [benefits] that have become available only as a result of other states' pro-commerce [regimes]." He argues that Iowa's law falls into the second category.

Page 321. After section 8 of the Note, add the following:

9. *Regulating the Internet.* A state enacts a statute requiring that all "spam" (multi-receiver, unsolicited commercial) e-mail messages to persons located in the state contain the letters "ADVERT" in the subject line. Does the statute violate the dormant commerce clause? Does such a statute "directly" regulate out-of-state businesses? Does it create a risk of multiple burdens? Are its burdens on interstate commerce excessive relative to its benefits to local e-mail users? See Goldsmith & Sykes, The Internet and the Dormant Commerce Clause, 110 Yale L.J. 785 (2001).

Page 327. At the end of the last paragraph of Section 3 of the Note, add the following:

See also American Insurance Ass'n v. Garamendi, 539 U.S. 396 (2003) (holding that the California Holocaust Victim Insurance Relief Act, which required that insurers licensed to operate in the state disclose the details of insurance policies issued in Europe between 1920 and 1945, was preempted because it conflicted with an executive agreement concluded between the President and Germany, establishing a foundation to compensate victims).

4
THE DISTRIBUTION OF NATIONAL POWERS

A. Introduction

Page 334. At the end of section 2 of the Note, add the following:

Do the efficiency promoting and liberty protecting functions of separation of powers doctrine conflict with each other? Consider Barber, Prelude to the Separation of Powers, 60 Cambridge L. J. 59, 64-65 (2001):

> A reading of the debates of the Federal Convention [does] not support [the] view that the purpose of separation of powers was to slow down government. Madison recognized the need for a division of powers in order to protect the people from tyrannical government; but it should not be assumed that the separation of powers was treated merely as a brake on power. [A] central function of the state was seen to be the promotion of liberty, and the constitution was therefore drafted in a manner that would facilitate this purpose. [The] efficient allocation of functions to institutions was the allocation that best served to protect, and to promote, liberty.

Page 334. At the end of section 3 of the Note, add the following:

For a subtle and interesting criticism of contemporary separation of powers doctrine, see Magill, The Real Separation in Separation of Powers Law, 86 Va. L. Rev. 1127 (2000). Magill argues that despite superficial disagreement, courts and commentators have coalesced around the idea that separation of powers doctrine is designed to prevent a single institution of government from accumulating too much political power. This goal is achieved in two ways: by maintaining "separation of functions" among the three branches, and by maintaining a "balance of power" among them. Magill

Page 334

claims that the standard view is that these two techniques fit together well because the separation of functions will achieve a balance of power. In fact, however,

> Treating these two conceptions as related to one another is a mistake. [The] balance-of-power formulation suggests that courts should invalidate arrangements that undermine a balance among the departments. [Courts] are to be wary of efforts that would dilute tension and competition among the branches. The separation-of-functions conception [suggests] that courts should identify and enforce the allocation of the three functions of government among the departments. [These] doctrinal concerns [can] yield conflicting results.

Id. at 1130-31. Moreover, in Magill's view, when examined individually, neither of these conceptions will withstand analysis.

> The exact reasons why we might wish to keep the exercise of legislative, executive, and judicial power in different departments—reasons other than the failed connection to balancing government power—are rarely specified. When justifications for separated functions are offered, they are inadequate. [Subjecting] the balance-of-power conception to independent analysis likewise reveals serious difficulties with the idea: The meaning of "balance" is obscure and the way in which that balance is maintained is inadequate.

Id. See also Magill, Beyond Powers and Branches in Separation of Powers Law, 150 U. Pa. L. Rev. 603 (2001) (arguing, inter alia, that concern about balance of powers between the branches is misguided because there is no way to measure the distribution of power at any given time and, in any event, intra-branch fragmentation prevents a concentration of power). As you read the rest of the material in this chapter, consider whether these criticisms are justified. How might separation of powers doctrine be reformulated so as to take account of them?

Page 347. Before section 3 of the Note, add the following:

Consider in this connection Bellia, Executive Power in Youngstown's Shadows, 19 Const. Comm. 87, 93 (2002) ("To the extent that Justice Jackson's approach suggests that law has little role to play when Congress is silent, that approach contains the seeds of a misplaced political question doctrine, allowing courts to skirt questions of executive power even when other justiciability requirements are met.").

C. Domestic Affairs

Page 365. Before the Note, add the following:

Consider the possibility that separation of powers doctrine is designed, in part at least, to protect the states from federal overreaching by making it more difficult for branches of the federal government to act, and that the formalism/functionalism debate is influenced by this concern. In Clark, Separation of Powers as a Safeguard of Federalism, 79 Tex. L. Rev. 1321, 1326 (2001), the author argues that the

> debate over formalism and functionalism [affects] the division of power between the federal government and the states. Many of the Court's most prominent decisions employing a formal approach involve enforcement of constitutionally prescribed lawmaking procedures designed to safeguard federalism. Formalism in this context operates to preserve state governance prerogatives by making federal law more difficult to adopt. Decisions taking a functional approach [by] contrast, typically involve potential interference by one branch with the constitutional functions of another rather than attempts to evade federal lawmaking procedures.

Page 367. At the end of section 4a of the Note, add the following:

For a detailed textual argument in favor of the nondelegation doctrine, see Lawson, Delegation and Original Meaning, 88 Va. L. Rev. 327 (2002). Consider Posner & Vermeule, Interring the Nondelegation Doctrine, 69 U. Chi. L. Rev. 1721, 1722-23 (2002):

> [There] just is no constitutional nondelegation rule, nor has there ever been. The nondelegation position lacks any foundation in constitutional text and structure, in standard originalist sources, or in sound economic and political theory....
>
> [We] agree that the Constitution bars the "delegation of legislative power." In our view, however, the content of that prohibition is the following: Neither Congress nor its members may delegate to anyone else the authority to vote on federal statutes or to exercise other de jure powers of federal legislators. [A] statutory grant of authority to the executive isn't a transfer of legislative power, but an exercise of legislative power. Conversely, agents acting within the terms of such a source of statutory grant are exercising executive power, not legislative power.

Page 369. At the end of section 4 of the Note, add the following:

e. In Whitman v. American Trucking Assn., Inc., 531 U.S. 457 (2001), the Court emphatically rejected a nondelegation challenge to the Clean Air Act. Section 109(b)(1) of the act instructs the Environmental Protection Administration (EPA) to set ambient air quality standards "the attainment and maintenance of which [are] requisite to protect the public health [with] an adequate margin of safety." The court of appeals held that the EPA's interpretation of this provision was unconstitutional because it provided no "intelligible principle to guide the agency's exercise of authority." However, instead of holding the provision unconstitutional, the court remanded the matter to the agency in order to allow it to adopt a different construction of the provision.

The Supreme Court, in a unanimous opinion written by Justice Scalia, rejected this approach:

> We have never suggested that an agency can cure an unlawful delegation of legislative power by adopting in its discretion a limiting construction of the statute. [The] idea that an agency can cure an unconstitutionally standardless delegation of power by declining to exercise some of that power seems to us internally contradictory. The very choice of which portion of the power to exercise [would] *itself* be an exercise of the forbidden legislative authority.

The Court then held that the

> scope of discretion § 109(b)(1) allows is [well] within the outer limits of our nondelegation precedents. In the history of the Court we have found the requisite "intelligible principle" lacking in only two statutes, one of which provided literally no guidance for the exercise of our discretion, and the other of which conferred authority to regulate the entire economy on the basis of no more precise a standard than stimulating the economy by assuring "fair competition." [In] short, we have "almost never felt qualified to second-guess Congress regarding the permissible degree of policy judgment that can be left to those executing or applying the law." [Mistretta v. United States, 488 U.S. 361, 416 (1989) (Scalia, J., dissenting).] [Even] in sweeping regulatory schemes we have never demanded, as the Court of Appeals did here, that statutes provide a "determinate criterion" for saying "how much [of the regulated harm] is too much."

Justice Thomas wrote a short concurring opinion:

> I am not convinced that the intelligible principle doctrine serves to prevent all cessions of legislative power. I believe that there are cases in which the principle

is intelligible and yet the significance of the delegated decision is simply too great for the decision to be called anything other than "legislative."

Justice Stevens, joined by Justice Souter, also concurred:

> The Court has two choices. We could choose to articulate our ultimate disposition of this issue by frankly acknowledging that the power delegated to the EPA is "legislative" but nevertheless conclude that the delegation is constitutional because adequately limited by the terms of the authorizing statute. Alternatively, we could pretend, as the Court does, that the authority delegated to EPA is somehow not "legislative power." Despite the fact that there is language in our opinions that supports the Court's articulation of our holding, I am persuaded that it would be both wiser and more faithful to what we have actually done in delegation cases to admit that agency rulemaking authority is "legislative power."

Page 378. At the end of section 3 of the Note, add the following:

In Nourse, Toward a New Constitutional Anatomy, 56 Stan. L. Rev. 835 (2004), the author examines *Chadha* from what she calls a "relational" perspective. Instead of focusing on the function of various branches or on formal definitions, this approach asks how changes in structure affect the relationship between the people and the government.

On this view, it is significant, for example, that the President on the one hand and members of Congress on the other represent different constituencies. "The President does not represent the Third District of Connecticut or the state of Alaska; he represents the nation, just as [the] senator from Oklahoma does not represent the nation."

Nourse believes that this difference has important implications for the legislative veto:

> If Congress had passed a traditional piece of legislation to deport Chadha, the President would have had the opportunity to veto it. [The] Constitution is structured so that a national audience typically has the last say on a piece of legislation (subject to any override by a congressional supermajority). [From] this perspective, the legislative veto is problematic because it shifts the "last say" away from the President and his national constituencies, toward the Congress and its state and locally aggregated [audiences]. . . .
>
> Many self-styled "liberals" have tended to find little troubling in the legislative veto. [Yet], often times, it is these same "liberals" who [view] devolution to the

states with some skepticism, skepticism inspired by the fear that state majorities will oppress minorities. Those two positions are [inconsistent].

56 Stan L. Rev., at 866, 869, 871.

Page 378. At the bottom of the page, add the following:

In Kagan, Presidential Administration, 114 Harv. L. Rev. 2245, 2248-2251 (2001), the author argues that "presidential control of [administrative agencies] expanded dramatically" in recent years. She claims that the expanded use of presidential authority to dictate how administrative agencies should exercise their delegated authority is inconsistent with the "conventional view" that "Congress can insulate discretionary decisions of even removable (that is, executive branch) officials from presidential dictation—and, indeed, that Congress has done so whenever (as is usual) it has delegated power not to the President, but to a specified agency official." In place of this view, she claims that "Congress has left more power in presidential hands than is generally recognized" and that "statutory delegation to an executive agency official—although not to an independent agency head—usually should be read as allowing the President to assert directive authority [over] the exercise of the delegated discretion."

Page 397. At the end of section 2 of the Note, add the following:

Consider the following synthesis:

Chadha is significant not so much for its emphasis on the requirements of bicameralism and presentment as for its implicit recognition of a constitutional principle against congressional self-aggrandizement: Congress may not, by statute, draw to itself, nor confer upon any part of itself, or upon any of its agents, powers that Congress does not already have by virtue of the Constitution. Understanding *Chadha* as embodying a rule against congressional self-aggrandizement explains the mystery of why Congress may delegate to others powers that it may not confer upon its own houses; it also explains why the rule applies even to attempts by Congress to grant itself extra power that it may exercise only through bicameralism and presentment.

Siegel, The Use of Legislative History in a System of Separated Powers, 53 Vand. L. Rev. 1457, 1467-1468 (2000).

D. Foreign Affairs

Page 403. Before Section 1, add the following:

For an argument that "modern scholarship should stop assuming that the Constitution's text says little about foreign affairs and stop treating foreign affairs powers as 'up for grabs' to be resolved by hasty resort to extratextual sources," see Prakash & Ramsey, The Executive Power over Foreign Affairs, 111 Yale L. J. 231, 233 (2001). The authors derive four basic principles from the constitutional text:

> First, and most importantly, the President enjoys a "residual" foreign affairs power under Article II, Section 1's grant of "the executive Power." [The] ordinary eighteenth-century meaning of executive power [included] foreign affairs power....
>
> Second, the President's executive power over foreign affairs is limited by specific allocations of foreign affairs power to other entities—such as the allocation of the power to declare war to Congress. [Third], Congress in addition to its specific foreign affairs powers has a derivative power to legislate in support of the President's executive power over foreign affairs and its own foreign affairs powers. But [Congress] does not have a general and independent authority over all foreign affairs matters. [Fourth], the President's executive power over foreign affairs does not extend to matters that were not part of the traditional executive power, even where they touch upon foreign affairs. In particular, the President cannot claim power over appropriations and lawmaking, even in the foreign affairs arena, by virtue of the executive power.

Page 410. After section 4c of the Note, add the following:

d. *The "war" against terrorism.* On September 18, 2001, Congress enacted a joint resolution, granting the President authority to

> use all necessary and appropriate force against those nations, organizations, or persons he determines planned, authorized, committed, or aided the terrorist attacks that occurred on September 11, 2001, or harbored such organizations or persons, in order to prevent any future acts of international terrorism against the United States by such nations, organizations or persons.

Joint Resolution of Congress Authorizing the Use of Force, Pub. L. No. 107-40, 115 Stat. 224 (2001).

Is the Joint Resolution the constitutional equivalent of a declaration of war? If so, why did Congress fail to adopt an official declaration of war? Compare Turner, The War on Terrorism and the Modern Relevance of the Congressional Power to "Declare War," 25 Harv. J. of Law & Pol. 519, 521 (2002) (quoting Senate Foreign Relations Committee Chairman Joseph Biden as stating that the resolution was "the constitutional equivalent of a declaration of war") with Katyal & Tribe, Waging War, Deciding Guilt: Trying the Military Tribunals, 111 Yale L. J. 1259, 1285 (2002) (quoting Representative Conyers as stating that "[by] not declaring war the resolution preserves our precious civil liberties" and that "[this] is important because declarations of war trigger broad statutes that not only criminalize interference with troops and recruitment but also authorize the President to apprehend 'alien enemies' ").

If the Resolution is the equivalent of a declaration of war, whom is the war being waged against? Traditionally, wars are ended by treaties, subject to ratification by the Senate. Is there some comparable event that will demarcate the end of the war against terrorism? How will we know when the war is over? Consider Paulsen, Youngstown Goes to War, 19 Const. Com. 215 (2002). The author acknowledges that the Joint Resolution constitutes "a truly extraordinary congressional grant to the President of extraordinary discretion in the use of military power for an indefinite period of time." Yet the author also concludes that Congress's position articulated in the Resolution is within the "twilight zone" described in Justice Jackson's *Youngstown* concurrence. Across a broad range of circumstances, Congress's interpretation of the Constitution in support of presidential constitutional power—its view, enacted as part of the 9-18-01 Resolution that 'the President has authority under the Constitution to take action to deter and prevent acts of international terrorism against the United States'—is a legitimate and constitutionally proper one."

Notice that the Resolution authorizes military action only with respect to those involved in the destruction of the World Trade Center. Does the President have constitutional authority to conduct a broader "war" against alleged terrorists not associated with that attack? For an argument that the war power was meant to apply solely to offensive wars and that it is therefore anachronistic under modern conditions, see Turner, supra. See also Delahunty & Yoo, The President's Constitutional Authority to Conduct Military Operations against Terrorist Organizations and the Nations that Harbor or Support Them, 25 Harv. J. of Law & Pol. 488 (2002) (arguing that the President has broad, unilateral authority to act against terrorists). Compare Telman, A Truism that Isn't True? The Tenth Amendment and Executive War Power, 51 Cath. U. L. Rev. 135 (2001) (suggesting that the Tenth Amendment argues against inherent executive authority to wage war without congressional authorization); Ramsey, Textualism and War Powers, 69 U. Chi. L. Rev. 1543 (2002) (concluding that in the eighteenth century the phrase "declare war" was understood to include an armed attack, even without a formal proclamation, and that this understanding "refutes the claim that the President can order military attacks upon foreign powers without Congress's approval so long as no formal declaration is involved") For criticism of Professor Ramsey's view, see Yoo, War and the Constitutional Text, 69 U. Chi. L. Rev. 1639 (2002) (arguing that "the Constitution vests the executive and legislative branches with different powers involving war, which the President and Congress may use to cooperate or to compete for control over war making").

The decision below marks the Court's first response to assertions of Presidential authority to fight the war against terrorism.

HAMDI v. RUMSFELD
542 U.S. ___ (2004)

JUSTICE O'CONNOR announced the judgment of the Court and delivered an opinion, in which THE CHIEF JUSTICE, JUSTICE KENNEDY, and JUSTICE BREYER join.

At this difficult time in our Nation's history, we are called upon to consider the legality of the Government's detention of a United States citizen on United States soil as an "enemy combatant" and to address the process that is constitutionally owed to one who seeks to challenge his classification as such. The United States Court of Appeals for the Fourth Circuit held that petitioner's detention was legally authorized and that he was entitled to no further opportunity to challenge his enemy-combatant label. We now vacate and remand. We hold that although Congress authorized the detention of combatants in the narrow circumstances alleged here, due process demands that a citizen held in the United States as an enemy combatant be given a meaningful opportunity to contest the factual basis for that detention before a neutral decisionmaker.

I

. . .

This case arises out of the detention of a man whom the Government alleges took up arms with the [Taliban]. His name is Yaser Esam Hamdi. Born an American citizen in Louisiana in 1980, Hamdi moved with his family to Saudi Arabia as a child. By 2001, the parties agree, he resided in Afghanistan. At some point that year, he was seized by members of the Northern Alliance, a coalition of military groups opposed to the Taliban government, and eventually was turned over to the United States military. The Government asserts that it initially detained and interrogated Hamdi in Afghanistan before transferring him to the United States Naval Base in Guantanamo Bay in January 2002. In April 2002, upon learning that Hamdi is an American citizen, authorities transferred him to a naval brig in Norfolk, Virginia, where he remained until a recent transfer to a brig in Charleston, South Carolina. The Government contends that Hamdi is an "enemy combatant," and that this status justifies holding him in the United States indefinitely—without formal charges or proceedings—unless and until it makes the determination that access to counsel or further process is warranted. . . .

[This action was a habeas petition brought by Hamdi's father. His father asserted that Hamdi went to Afghanistan to do relief work, that he had been in the country for less than two months before September 11, 2001, that he had not receive military training, and that he was trapped in Afghanistan when the military campaign began.] In response to the petition, the Government filed a declaration from Michael Mobbs, a Special Advisor to the Undersecretary of Defense. The declaration stated that Mobbs had been "substantially involved with matters related to the detention of enemy combatants in the current war against the al Qaeda terrorists and those who support and harbor them (including the Taliban)." He expressed his "familiar[ity]" with Department of Defense and United States military policies and procedures applicable to the detention, control, and transfer of al Qaeda and Taliban personnel, and declared that "[b]ased upon my review of relevant records and reports, I am also familiar with the facts and circumstances related to the capture of . . . Hamdi and his detention by U.S. military forces."

Mobbs then set forth what remains the sole evidentiary support that the Government has provided to the courts for Hamdi's detention. The declaration states that Hamdi "traveled to Afghanistan" in July or August 2001, and that he thereafter "affiliated with a Taliban military unit and received weapons training." It asserts that Hamdi "remained with his Taliban unit following the attacks of September 11" and that, during the time when Northern Alliance forces were "engaged in battle with the Taliban," "Hamdi's Taliban unit surrendered" to those forces, after which he "surrender[ed] his Kalishnikov assault rifle" to them. The Mobbs Declaration also states that, because al Qaeda and the Taliban "were and are hostile forces engaged in armed conflict with the armed forces of the United States," "individuals associated with" those groups "were and continue to be enemy combatants." Mobbs states that Hamdi was labeled an enemy combatant "[b]ased upon his interviews and in light of his association with the Taliban." According to the declaration, a series of "U.S. military screening team[s]" determined that Hamdi met "the criteria for enemy combatants," and "a subsequent interview of Hamdi has confirmed that he surrendered and gave his firearm to Northern Alliance forces, which supports his classification as an enemy combatant." . . .

The District Court found that the Mobbs Declaration fell "far short" of supporting Hamdi's detention. It criticized the generic and hearsay nature of the affidavit, calling it "little more than the government's 'say-so.'" It ordered the Government to turn over numerous materials for *in camera* review . . . .

The Fourth Circuit [reversed]. Concluding that the factual averments in the Mobbs Declaration, "if accurate," provided a sufficient basis upon which to conclude that the President had constitutionally detained Hamdi pursuant to the President's war powers, it ordered the habeas petition dismissed. . . .

We now vacate the judgment below and remand.

II

The threshold question before us is whether the Executive has the authority to detain citizens who qualify as "enemy combatants." [For] purposes of this case, ["enemy] combatant" [is defined as] an individual who, [the government] alleges, was "'part of or supporting forces hostile to the United States or coalition partners'" in Afghanistan and who "'engaged in an armed conflict against the United States'" there. We therefore answer only the narrow question before us: whether the detention of citizens falling within that definition is authorized.

The Government maintains that no explicit congressional authorization is required, because the Executive possesses plenary authority to detain pursuant to Article II of the Constitution. We do not reach the question whether Article II provides such authority, however, because we agree with the Government's alternative position, that Congress has in fact authorized Hamdi's detention, through the [Authorization of Use of Military Force Resolution (AUMF)] [The resolution is reproduced in section d of the Note preceding this case.].

Our analysis on that point, set forth below, substantially overlaps with our analysis of Hamdi's principal argument for the illegality of his detention. He posits that his detention is forbidden by 18 U.S.C. § 4001(a). Section 4001(a) states that "[n]o citizen shall be imprisoned or otherwise detained by the United States except pursuant to an Act of Congress." Congress passed § 4001(a) in 1971 as part of a bill to repeal the Emergency Detention Act of 1950, which provided procedures for executive detention, during times of emergency, of individuals deemed likely to engage in espionage or sabotage. Congress was particularly concerned about the possibility that the Act could be used to reprise the Japanese internment camps of World War II. The Government [maintains] that § 4001(a) is satisfied, because Hamdi is being detained "pursuant to an Act of Congress"—the AUMF. [For] the reasons that follow, we conclude that the AUMF is explicit congressional authorization for the detention of individuals in the narrow category we describe (assuming, without deciding, that such authorization is required), and that the AUMF satisfied § 4001(a)'s requirement that a detention be "pursuant to an Act of Congress" (assuming, without deciding, that § 4001(a) applies to military detentions).

The AUMF authorizes the President to use "all necessary and appropriate force" against "nations, organizations, or persons" associated with the September 11, 2001, terrorist attacks. There can be no doubt that individuals who fought against the United States in Afghanistan as part of the Taliban, an organization known to have supported the al Qaeda terrorist network responsible for those attacks, are individuals Congress sought to target in passing the AUMF. We conclude that detention of individuals falling into the limited category we are considering, for the duration of the particular conflict in which they were captured, is so fundamental and accepted an incident to war as to be an exercise of the "necessary and appropriate force" Congress has authorized the President to use.

The capture and detention of lawful combatants and the capture, detention, and trial of unlawful combatants, by "universal agreement and practice," are "important incident[s] of war." *Ex parte Quirin,* 317 U.S. at 28. The purpose of detention is to prevent captured individuals from returning to the field of battle and taking up arms once again.

There is no bar to this Nation's holding one of its own citizens as an enemy combatant. In *Quirin,* one of the detainees, Haupt, alleged that he was a naturalized United States citizen. We held that "[c]itizens who associate themselves with the military arm of the enemy government, and with its aid, guidance and direction enter this country bent on hostile acts, are enemy belligerents within the meaning of . . . the law of [war]." In light of these principles, it is of no moment that the AUMF does not use specific language of detention. Because detention to prevent a combatant's return to the battlefield is a fundamental incident of waging war, in permitting the use of "necessary and appropriate force," Congress has clearly and unmistakably authorized detention in the narrow circumstances considered here.

Hamdi objects, nevertheless, that Congress has not authorized the *indefinite* detention to which he is now subject. The Government responds that "the detention of enemy combatants during World War II was just as 'indefinite' while that war was being fought." We take Hamdi's objection to be not to the lack of certainty regarding the date on which the conflict will end, but to the substantial prospect of perpetual detention. We recognize that the national security underpinnings of the "war on terror," although crucially important, are broad and malleable. As the Government concedes, "given its unconventional nature, the current conflict is unlikely to end with a formal cease-fire agreement." The prospect Hamdi raises is therefore not far-fetched. If the Government does not consider this unconventional war won for two generations, and if it maintains during that time that Hamdi might, if released, rejoin forces fighting against the United States, then the position it has taken throughout the litigation of this case suggests that Hamdi's detention could last for the rest of his life. . . .

Hamdi contends that the AUMF does not authorize indefinite or perpetual detention. Certainly, we agree that indefinite detention for the purpose of interrogation is not authorized. Further, we understand Congress' grant of authority for the use of "necessary and appropriate force" to include the authority to detain for the duration of the relevant conflict, and our understanding is based on longstanding law-of-war principles. If the practical circumstances of a given conflict are entirely unlike those of the conflicts that informed the development of the law of war, that understanding may unravel. But that is not the situation we face as of this date. Active combat operations against Taliban fighters apparently are ongoing in Afghanistan. If the record establishes that United States troops are still involved in active combat in Afghanistan, those detentions are part of the exercise of "necessary and appropriate force," and therefore are authorized by the AUMF.

Ex parte Milligan, 4 Wall. 2, 125, 18 L. Ed. 281 (1866), does not undermine our holding about the Government's authority to seize enemy combatants, as we define that term today. In that case, the Court made repeated reference to the fact that its inquiry into whether the military tribunal had jurisdiction to try and punish Milligan turned in large part on the fact that Milligan was not a prisoner of war, but a resident of Indiana arrested while at home there. . . .

Moreover, [the] Court in *Ex parte Quirin,* dismissed the language of *Milligan* that the petitioners had suggested prevented them from being subject to military process. . . .

Quirin was a unanimous opinion. It both postdates and clarifies *Milligan,* providing us with the most apposite precedent that we have on the question of whether citizens may be detained in such circumstances. Brushing aside such precedent—particularly when doing so gives rise to a host of new questions never dealt with by this Court—is unjustified and unwise.

To the extent that Justice Scalia accepts the precedential value of *Quirin,* he argues that it cannot guide our inquiry here because "[i]n *Quirin* it was uncontested that the petitioners were members of enemy forces," while Hamdi challenges his classification as an enemy combatant. But it is unclear why, in the paradigm outlined by Justice Scalia, such a concession should have any relevance. Justice Scalia envisions a system in which the only options are congressional suspension of the writ of habeas corpus or prosecution for treason or some other crime. He does not explain how his historical analysis supports the addition of a third option—detention under some other process after concession of enemy-combatant status—or why a concession should carry any different effect than proof of enemy-combatant status in a proceeding that comports with due process. To be clear, our opinion only finds legislative authority to detain under the AUMF once it is sufficiently clear that the individual is, in fact, an enemy combatant; whether that is established by concession or by some other process that verifies this fact with sufficient certainty seems beside the point. . . .

III

Even in cases in which the detention of enemy combatants is legally authorized, there remains the question of what process is constitutionally due to a citizen who disputes his enemy-combatant status. . . .

A

Though they reach radically different conclusions on the process that ought to attend the present proceeding, the parties begin on common ground. All agree that, absent suspension, the writ of habeas corpus remains available to every individual detained within the United States. . . .

The Government recognizes the basic procedural protections required by the habeas statute, but asks us to hold that, given both the flexibility of the habeas mechanism and the circumstances presented in this case, the presentation of the Mobbs Declaration to the habeas court completed the required factual development. It suggests two separate reasons for its position that no further process is due.

B

First, the Government urges the adoption of the Fourth Circuit's holding below—that because it is "undisputed" that Hamdi's seizure took place in a combat zone, the habeas determination can be made purely as a matter of law, with no further hearing or factfinding necessary. This argument is easily rejected. [Under] the definition of enemy combatant that we accept today as falling within the scope of Congress' authorization, Hamdi would need to be "part of or supporting forces hostile to the United States or coalition partners" and "engaged in an armed conflict against the United States" to justify his detention in the United States for the duration of the relevant conflict. The habeas petition states only that "[w]hen seized by the United States Government, Mr. Hamdi resided in Afghanistan." An assertion that one *resided* in a country in which combat operations are taking place is not a concession that one was "*captured* in a zone of active combat operations in a foreign theater of war," and certainly is not a concession that one was "part of or supporting forces hostile to the United States or coalition partners" and "engaged in an armed conflict against the United States." Accordingly, we reject any argument that Hamdi has made concessions that eliminate any right to further process.

C

The Government's second argument requires closer consideration. This is the argument that further factual exploration is unwarranted and inappropriate in light of the extraordinary constitutional interests at stake. Under the Government's most extreme rendition of this argument, "[r]espect for separation of powers and the limited institutional capabilities of courts in matters of military decision-making in connection with an ongoing conflict" ought to eliminate entirely any individual process, restricting the courts to investigating only whether legal authorization exists for the broader detention scheme. At most, the Government argues, courts should review its determination that a citizen is an enemy combatant under a very deferential "some evidence" standard. Under this review, a court would assume the accuracy of the Government's articulated basis for Hamdi's detention, as set forth in the Mobbs Declaration, and assess only whether that articulated basis was a legitimate one. . . .

The District Court, agreeing with Hamdi, apparently believed that the appropriate process would approach the process that accompanies a criminal trial. It therefore disapproved of the hearsay nature of the Mobbs Declaration and anticipated quite extensive discovery of various military affairs. Anything less, it concluded, would not be "meaningful judicial review."

Both of these positions highlight legitimate concerns. And both emphasize the tension that often exists between the autonomy that the Government asserts is necessary in order to pursue effectively a particular goal and the process that a citizen contends he is due before he is deprived of a constitutional right. The ordinary mechanism that we use for balancing such serious competing interests, and for determining the procedures that are necessary to ensure that a citizen is not "deprived of life, liberty, or property, without due process of law," U.S. Const., Amdt. 5, is the test that we articulated in *Mathews v. Eldridge*. [*Mathews* is excerpted on page 930 of the main volume]. *Mathews* dictates that the process due in any given instance is determined by weighing "the private interest that will be affected by the official action" against the Government's asserted interest, "including the function involved" and the burdens the Government would face in providing greater process. The *Mathews* calculus then contemplates a judicious balancing of these concerns, through an analysis of "the risk of an erroneous deprivation" of the private interest if the process were reduced and the "probable value, if any, of additional or substitute safeguards." We take each of these steps in turn.

1

It is beyond question that substantial interests lie on both sides of the scale in this case. Hamdi's "private interest . . . affected by the official action," is the most elemental of liberty interests—the interest in being free from physical detention by one's own government. "We have always been careful not to 'minimize the importance and fundamental nature' of the individual's right to liberty," and we will not do so today.

Nor is the weight on this side of the *Mathews* scale offset by the circumstances of war or the accusation of treasonous behavior, for "[i]t is clear that commitment for *any* purpose constitutes a significant deprivation of liberty that requires due process protection." [The] risk of erroneous deprivation of a citizen's liberty in the absence of sufficient process here is very real. Moreover, as critical as the Government's interest may be in detaining those who actually pose an immediate threat to the national security of the United States during ongoing international conflict, history and common sense teach us that an unchecked system of detention carries the potential to become a means for oppression and abuse of others who do not present that sort of threat. Because we live in a society in which "[m]ere public intolerance or animosity cannot constitutionally justify the deprivation of a person's physical liberty," our starting point for the *Mathews v. Eldridge* analysis is unaltered by the allegations surrounding the particular detainee or the organizations with which he is alleged to have associated. We reaffirm today the fundamental nature of a citizen's right to be free from involuntary confinement by his own government without due process of law, and we weigh the opposing governmental interests against the curtailment of liberty that such confinement entails.

2

On the other side of the scale are the weighty and sensitive governmental interests in ensuring that those who have in fact fought with the enemy during a war do not return to battle against the United States. As discussed above, the law of war and the realities of combat may render such detentions both necessary and appropriate, and our due process analysis need not blink at those realities. Without doubt, our Constitution recognizes that core strategic matters of warmaking belong in the hands of those who are best positioned and most politically accountable for making them.

The Government also argues at some length that its interests in reducing the process available to alleged enemy combatants are heightened by the practical difficulties that would accompany a system of trial-like process. In its view, military officers who are engaged in the serious work of waging battle would be unnecessarily and dangerously distracted by litigation half a world away, and discovery into military operations would both intrude on the sensitive secrets of national defense and result in a futile search for evidence buried under the rubble of war. To the extent that these burdens are triggered by heightened procedures, they are properly taken into account in our due process analysis.

3

Striking the proper constitutional balance here is of great importance to the Nation during this period of ongoing combat. But it is equally vital that our calculus not give short shrift to the values that this country holds dear or to the privilege that is American citizenship. It is during our most challenging and uncertain moments that our Nation's commitment to due process is most severely tested; and it is in those times that we must preserve our commitment at home to the principles for which we fight abroad.

With due recognition of these competing concerns, we believe that neither the process proposed by the Government nor the process apparently envisioned by the District Court below strikes the proper constitutional balance when a United States citizen is detained in the United States as an enemy combatant. . . .

We therefore hold that a citizen-detainee seeking to challenge his classification as an enemy combatant must receive notice of the factual basis for his classification, and a fair opportunity to rebut the Government's factual assertions before a neutral decisionmaker. . . .

At the same time, the exigencies of the circumstances may demand that, aside from these core elements, enemy combatant proceedings may be tailored to alleviate their uncommon potential to burden the Executive at a time of ongoing military conflict. Hearsay, for example, may need to be accepted as the most reliable available evidence from the Government in such a proceeding. Likewise, the Constitution would not be offended by a presumption in favor of the Government's evidence, so long as that presumption remained a rebuttable one and fair opportunity for rebuttal were provided. Thus, once the Government puts forth credible evidence that the habeas petitioner meets the enemy-combatant criteria, the onus could shift to the petitioner to rebut that evidence with more persuasive evidence that he falls outside the criteria. A burden-shifting scheme of this sort would meet the goal of ensuring that the errant tourist, embedded journalist, or local aid worker has a chance to prove military error while giving due regard to the Executive once it has put forth meaningful support for its conclusion that the detainee is in fact an enemy combatant. . . .

We think it unlikely that this basic process will have the dire impact on the central functions of warmaking that the Government forecasts. The parties agree that initial captures on the battlefield need not receive the process we have discussed here; that process is due only when the determination is made to *continue* to hold those who have been seized. The Government has made clear in its briefing that documentation regarding battlefield detainees already is kept in the ordinary course of military affairs. Any factfinding imposition created by requiring a knowledgeable affiant to summarize these records to an independent tribunal is a minimal one. Likewise, arguments that military officers ought not have to wage war under the threat of litigation lose much of their steam when factual disputes at enemy-combatant hearings are limited to the alleged combatant's acts. This focus meddles little, if at all, in the strategy or conduct of war, inquiring only into the appropriateness of continuing to detain an individual claimed to have taken up arms against the United States. While we accord the greatest respect and consideration to the judgments of military authorities in matters relating to the actual prosecution of a war, and recognize that the scope of that discretion necessarily is wide, it does not infringe on the core role of the military for the courts to exercise their own time-honored and constitutionally mandated roles of reviewing and resolving claims like those presented here. . . .

D

In so holding, we necessarily reject the Government's assertion that separation of powers principles mandate a heavily circumscribed role for the courts in such circumstances. Indeed, the position that the courts must forgo any examination of the individual case and focus exclusively on the legality of the broader detention scheme cannot be mandated by any reasonable view of separation of powers, as this approach serves only to *condense* power into a single branch of government. We have long since made clear that a state of war is not a blank check for the President when it comes to the rights of the Nation's citizens. *Youngstown Sheet & Tube.* Whatever power the United States Constitution envisions for the Executive in its exchanges with other nations or with enemy organizations in times of conflict, it most assuredly envisions a role for all three branches when individual liberties are at stake. Likewise, we have made clear that, unless Congress acts to suspend it, the Great Writ of habeas corpus allows the Judicial Branch to play a necessary role in maintaining this delicate balance of governance, serving as an important judicial check on the Executive's discretion in the realm of detentions. Thus, while we do not question that our due process assessment must pay keen attention to the particular burdens faced by the Executive in the context of military action, it would turn our system of checks and balances on its head to suggest that a citizen could not make his way to court with a challenge to the factual basis for his detention by his government, simply because the Executive opposes making available such a challenge. Absent suspension of the writ by Congress, a citizen detained as an enemy combatant is entitled to this process. . . .

[Aside] from unspecified "screening" processes, and military interrogations in which the Government suggests Hamdi could have contested his classification, Hamdi has received no process. An interrogation by one's captor, however effective an intelligence-gathering tool, hardly constitutes a constitutionally adequate factfinding before a neutral decisionmaker. . . .

There remains the possibility that the standards we have articulated could be met by an appropriately authorized and properly constituted military tribunal. [In] the absence of such process, however, a court that receives a petition for a writ of habeas corpus from an alleged enemy combatant must itself ensure that the minimum requirements of due process are achieved. [We] anticipate that a District Court would proceed with the caution that we have indicated is necessary in this setting, engaging in a factfinding process that is both prudent and incremental. We have no reason to doubt that courts faced with these sensitive matters will pay proper heed both to the matters of national security that might arise in an individual case and to the constitutional limitations safeguarding essential liberties that remain vibrant even in times of security concerns.

IV

Hamdi asks us to hold that the Fourth Circuit also erred by denying him immediate access to counsel upon his detention and by disposing of the case without permitting him to meet with an attorney. Since our grant of certiorari in this case, Hamdi has been appointed counsel, with whom he has met for consultation purposes on several occasions, and with whom he is now being granted unmonitored meetings. He unquestionably has the right to access to counsel in connection with the proceedings on remand. No further consideration of this issue is necessary at this stage of the case.

* * *

The judgment of the United States Court of Appeals for the Fourth Circuit is vacated, and the case is remanded for further proceedings.

It is so ordered.

JUSTICE SOUTER, with whom JUSTICE GINSBURG joins, concurring in part, dissenting in part, and concurring in the judgment. . . .

The Government [claims] that Hamdi's incommunicado imprisonment as an enemy combatant seized on the field of battle falls within the Presidents' power as Commander in Chief under the laws and usages of war, and is in any event authorized by two statutes. Accordingly, the Government contends that Hamdi has no basis for any challenge by petition for habeas except to his own status as an enemy combatant; and even that challenge may go no further than to enquire whether "some evidence" supports Hamdi's designation. . . .

The plurality rejects any such limit on the exercise of habeas jurisdiction and so far I agree with its opinion. The plurality does, however, accept the Government's position that if Hamdi's designation as an enemy combatant is correct, his detention (at least as to some period) is authorized by an Act of Congress as required by § 4001(a), that is, by the [AUMF]. Here, I disagree and respectfully dissent. The Government has failed to demonstrate that the Force Resolution authorizes the detention complained of here even on the facts the Government claims. If the Government raises nothing further than the record now shows, the Non-Detention Act entitles Hamdi to be released. . . .

II

The threshold issue is how broadly or narrowly to read the Non-Detention Act, the tone of which is severe: "No citizen shall be imprisoned or otherwise detained by the United States except pursuant to an Act of Congress." Should the severity of the Act be relieved when the Government's stated factual justification for incommunicado detention is a war on terrorism, so that the Government may be said to act "pursuant" to congressional terms that fall short of explicit authority to imprison individuals? With one possible though important qualification, the answer has to be no. . . .

The defining character of American constitutional government is its constant tension between security and liberty, serving both by partial helpings of each. In a government of separated powers, deciding finally on what is a reasonable degree of guaranteed liberty whether in peace or war (or some condition in between) is not well entrusted to the Executive Branch of Government, whose particular responsibility is to maintain security. For reasons of inescapable human nature, the branch of the Government asked to counter a serious threat is not the branch on which to rest the Nation's entire reliance in striking the balance between the will to win and the cost in liberty on the way to victory; the responsibility for security will naturally amplify the claim that security legitimately raises. A reasonable balance is more likely to be reached on the judgment of a different branch, just as Madison said in remarking that "the constant aim is to divide and arrange the several offices in such a manner as that each may be a check on the other—that the private interest of every individual may be a sentinel over the public rights." The Federalist No. 51. Hence the need for an assessment by Congress before citizens are subject to lockup, and likewise the need for a clearly expressed congressional resolution of the competing claims.

III

Under this principle of reading § 4001(a) robustly to require a clear statement of authorization to detain, none of the Government's arguments suffices to justify Hamdi's detention. . . .

C

[There] is one argument for treating the Force Resolution as sufficiently clear to authorize detention of a citizen consistently with § 4001(a). Assuming the argument to be sound, however, the Government is in no position to claim its advantage.

Because the Force Resolution authorizes the use of military force in acts of war by the United States, the argument goes, it is reasonably clear that the military and its Commander in Chief are authorized to deal with enemy belligerents according to the treaties and customs known collectively as the laws of war. Accordingly, the United States may detain captured enemies, and *Ex parte Quirin* may perhaps be claimed for the proposition that the American citizenship of such a captive does not as such limit the Government's power to deal with him under the usages of war. Thus, the Government here repeatedly argues that Hamdi's detention amounts to nothing more than customary detention of a captive taken on the field of battle: if the usages of war are fairly authorized by the Force Resolution, Hamdi's detention is authorized for purposes of § 4001(a).

There is no need, however, to address the merits of such an argument in all possible circumstances. For now it is enough to recognize that the Government's stated legal position in its campaign against the Taliban (among whom Hamdi was allegedly captured) is apparently at odds with its claim here to be acting in accordance with customary law of war and hence to be within the terms of the Force Resolution in its detention of Hamdi. In a statement of its legal position cited in its brief, the Government says that "the Geneva Convention applies to the Taliban detainees." Hamdi presumably is such a detainee, since according to the Government's own account, he was taken bearing arms on the Taliban side of a field of battle in Afghanistan. He would therefore seem to qualify for treatment as a prisoner of war under the Third Geneva Convention, to which the United States is a party.

By holding him incommunicado, however, the Government obviously has not been treating him as a prisoner of war, and in fact the Government claims that no Taliban detainee is entitled to prisoner of war status. This treatment appears to be a violation of the Geneva Convention provision that even in cases of doubt, captives are entitled to be treated as prisoners of war "until such time as their status has been determined by a competent tribunal." The Government answers that the President's determination that Taliban detainees do not qualify as prisoners of war is conclusive as to Hamdi's status and removes any doubt that would trigger application of the Convention's tribunal requirement. But reliance on this categorical pronouncement to settle doubt is apparently at odds with the military regulation, adopted to implement the Geneva Convention, and setting out a detailed procedure for a military tribunal to determine an individual's status. One of the types of doubt these tribunals are meant to settle is whether a given individual may be, as Hamdi says he is, an "[i]nnocent civilian who should be immediately returned to his home or released." [Thus,] there is reason to question whether the United States is acting in accordance with the laws of war it claims as authority.

Whether, or to what degree, the Government is in fact violating the Geneva Convention and is thus acting outside the customary usages of war are not matters I can resolve at this point. What I can say, though, is that the Government has not made out its claim that in detaining Hamdi in the manner described, it is acting in accord with the laws of war authorized to be applied against citizens by the Force Resolution. I conclude accordingly that the Government has failed to support the position that the Force Resolution authorizes the described detention of Hamdi for purposes of § 4001(a). . . .

D

Since the Government has given no reason either to deflect the application of § 4001(a) or to hold it to be satisfied, I need to go no further; the Government hints of a constitutional challenge to the statute, but it presents none here. I will, however, stray across the line between statutory and constitutional territory just far enough to note the weakness of the Government's mixed claim of inherent, extrastatutory authority under a combination of Article II of the Constitution and the usages of war. It is in fact in this connection that the Government developed its argument that the exercise of war powers justifies the detention, and what I have just said about its inadequacy applies here as well. Beyond that, it is instructive to recall Justice Jackson's observation that the President is not Commander in Chief of the country, only of the military. *Youngstown Sheet & Tube Co. v. Sawyer* (concurring opinion); see also *id.,* (Presidential authority is "at its lowest ebb" where the President acts contrary to congressional will.).

There may be room for one qualification to Justice Jackson's statement, however: in a moment of genuine emergency, when the Government must act with no time for deliberation, the Executive may be able to detain a citizen if there is reason to fear he is an imminent threat to the safety of the Nation and its people (though I doubt there is any want of statutory authority.) This case, however, does not present that question, because an emergency power of necessity must at least be limited by the emergency; Hamdi has been locked up for over two years.

Whether insisting on the careful scrutiny of emergency claims or on a vigorous reading of § 4001(a), we are heirs to a tradition given voice 800 years ago by Magna Carta, which, on the barons' insistence, confined executive power by "the law of the land."

IV

Because I find Hamdi's detention forbidden by § 4001(a) and unauthorized by the Force Resolution, I would not reach any questions of what process he may be due in litigating disputed issues in a proceeding under the habeas statute or prior to the habeas enquiry itself. . . .

Since this disposition does not command a majority of the Court, however, the need to give practical effect to the conclusions of eight members of the Court rejecting the Government's position calls for me to join with the plurality in ordering remand on terms closest to those I would impose. Although I think litigation of Hamdi's status as an enemy combatant is unnecessary, the terms of the plurality's remand will allow Hamdi to offer evidence that he is not an enemy combatant, and he should at the least have the benefit of that opportunity.

It should go without saying that in joining with the plurality to produce a judgment, I do not adopt the plurality's resolution of constitutional issues that I would not reach. It is not that I could disagree with the plurality's determinations (given the plurality's view of the Force Resolution) that someone in Hamdi's position is entitled at a minimum to notice of the Government's claimed factual basis for holding him, and to a fair chance to rebut it before a neutral decision maker, nor, of course, could I disagree with the plurality's affirmation of Hamdi's right to counsel. On the other hand, I do not mean to imply agreement that the Government could claim an evidentiary presumption casting the burden of rebuttal on Hamdi, or that an opportunity to litigate before a military tribunal might obviate or truncate enquiry by a court on habeas.

Subject to these qualifications, I join with the plurality in a judgment of the Court vacating the Fourth Circuit's judgment and remanding the case.

JUSTICE SCALIA, with whom JUSTICE STEVENS joins, dissenting. . . .

Where the Government accuses a citizen of waging war against it, our constitutional tradition has been to prosecute him in federal court for treason or some other crime. Where the exigencies of war prevent that, the Constitution's Suspension Clause, Art. I, § 9, cl. 2, allows Congress to relax the usual protections temporarily. Absent suspension, however, the Executive's assertion of military exigency has not been thought sufficient to permit detention without charge. No one contends that the congressional Authorization for Use of Military Force, on which the Government relies to justify its actions here, is an implementation of the Suspension Clause. Accordingly, I would reverse the decision below.

I

The very core of liberty secured by our Anglo-Saxon system of separated powers has been freedom from indefinite imprisonment at the will of the Executive. . . .

The gist of the Due Process Clause, as understood at the founding and since, was to force the Government to follow those common-law procedures traditionally deemed necessary before depriving a person of life, liberty, or property. . . .

To be sure, certain types of permissible *non* criminal detention—that is, those not dependent upon the contention that the citizen had committed a criminal act—did not require the protections of criminal procedure. However, these fell into a limited number of well-recognized exceptions—civil commitment of the mentally ill, for example, and temporary detention in quarantine of the infectious. It is unthinkable that the Executive could render otherwise criminal grounds for detention noncriminal merely by disclaiming an intent to prosecute, or by asserting that it was incapacitating dangerous offenders rather than punishing wrongdoing.

These due process rights have historically been vindicated by the writ of habeas corpus. . . .

II

The allegations here, of course, are no ordinary accusations of criminal activity. Yaser Esam Hamdi has been imprisoned because the Government believes he participated in the waging of war against the United States. The relevant question, then, is whether there is a different, special procedure for imprisonment of a citizen accused of wrongdoing *by aiding the enemy in wartime.*

A

Justice O'Connor, writing for a plurality of this Court, asserts that captured enemy combatants (other than those suspected of war crimes) have traditionally been detained until the cessation of hostilities and then released. That is probably an accurate description of wartime practice with respect to enemy *aliens.* The tradition with respect to American citizens, however, has been quite different. Citizens aiding the enemy have been treated as traitors subject to the criminal process. . . .

B

There are times when military exigency renders resort to the traditional criminal process impracticable. . . .

Our Federal Constitution contains a provision explicitly permitting suspension [of the writ of habeas corpus], but limiting the situations in which it may be invoked: "The privilege of the Writ of Habeas Corpus shall not be suspended, unless when in

Cases of Rebellion or Invasion the public Safety may require it." Art. I, § 9, cl. 2. Although this provision does not state that suspension must be effected by, or authorized by, a legislative act, it has been so understood, consistent with English practice and the Clause's placement in Article I.

The Suspension Clause was by design a safety valve, the Constitution's only "express provision for exercise of extraordinary authority because of a crisis" [*Youngstown* (Jackson, J., concurring)] . . . .

III

. . .

The proposition that the Executive lacks indefinite wartime detention authority over citizens is consistent with the Founders' general mistrust of military power permanently at the Executive's disposal. In the Founders' view, the "blessings of liberty" were threatened by "those military establishments which must gradually poison its very fountain." The Federalist No. 45. No fewer than 10 issues of the Federalist were devoted in whole or part to allaying fears of oppression from the proposed Constitution's authorization of standing armies in peacetime. Many safeguards in the Constitution reflect these concerns. Congress's authority "[t]o raise and support Armies" was hedged with the proviso that "no Appropriation of Money to that Use shall be for a longer Term than two Years." U.S. Const., Art. 1, § 8, cl. 12. Except for the actual command of military forces, all authorization for their maintenance and all explicit authorization for their use is placed in the control of Congress under Article I, rather than the President under Article II. As Hamilton explained, the President's military authority would be "much inferior" to that of the British King: . . .

> A view of the Constitution that gives the Executive authority to use military force rather than the force of law against citizens on American soil flies in the face of the mistrust that engendered these provisions. . . .

V

. . .

It should not be thought [that] the plurality's evisceration of the Suspension Clause augments, principally, the power of Congress. As usual, the major effect of its constitutional improvisation is to increase the power of the Court. Having found a congressional authorization for detention of citizens where none clearly exists; and having discarded the categorical procedural protection of the Suspension Clause; the plurality then proceeds, under the guise of the Due Process Clause, to prescribe what procedural protections *it* thinks appropriate. It "weigh[s] the private interest . . . against the Government's asserted interest," and—just as though writing a new Constitution—comes up with an unheard-of system in which the citizen rather than the Government bears the burden of proof, testimony is by hearsay rather than live witnesses, and the presiding officer may well be a "neutral" military officer rather than judge and jury. It claims authority to engage in this sort of "judicious balancing" from *Mathews v. Eldridge,* a case involving . . . *the withdrawal of disability benefits!* Whatever the merits of this technique when newly recognized property rights are at issue (and even there they are questionable), it has no place where the Constitution and the common law already supply an answer.

Having distorted the Suspension Clause, the plurality finishes up by transmogrifying the Great Writ—disposing of the present habeas petition by remanding for the District Court to "engag[e] in a factfinding process that is both prudent and incremental." "In the absence of [the Executive's prior provision of procedures that satisfy due process], . . . a court that receives a petition for a writ of habeas corpus from an alleged enemy combatant must itself ensure that the minimum requirements of due process are achieved." This judicial remediation of executive default is unheard of. [It] is not the habeas court's function to make illegal detention legal by supplying a process that the Government could have provided, but chose not to. If Hamdi is being imprisoned in violation of the Constitution (because without due process of law), then his habeas petition should be granted; the Executive may then hand him over to the criminal authorities, whose detention for the purpose of prosecution will be lawful, or else must release him.

There is a certain harmony of approach in the plurality's making up for Congress's failure to invoke the Suspension Clause and its making up for the Executive's failure to apply what it says are needed procedures—an approach that reflects what might be called a Mr. Fix-it Mentality. The plurality seems to view it as its mission to Make Everything Come Out Right, rather than merely to decree the consequences, as far as individual rights are concerned, of the other two branches' actions and omissions. Has the Legislature failed to suspend the writ in the current dire emergency? Well, we will remedy that failure by prescribing the reasonable conditions that a suspension should have included. And has the Executive failed to live up to those reasonable conditions? Well, we will ourselves make that failure good, so that this dangerous fellow (if he is dangerous) need not be set free. The problem with this approach is not only that it steps out of the courts' modest and limited role in a democratic society; but that by repeatedly doing what it thinks the political branches ought to do it encourages their lassitude and saps the vitality of government by the people.

VI

Several limitations give my views in this matter a relatively narrow compass. They apply only to citizens, accused of being enemy combatants, who are detained within the territorial jurisdiction of a federal court. This is not likely to be a numerous group; currently we know of only two, Hamdi and Jose Padilla. Where the citizen is captured outside and held outside the United States, the constitutional requirements may be different. Moreover, even within the United States, the accused citizen-enemy combatant may lawfully be detained once prosecution is in progress or in contemplation. The Government has been notably successful in securing conviction, and hence long-term custody or execution, of those who have waged war against the state.

I frankly do not know whether these tools are sufficient to meet the Government's security needs, including the need to obtain intelligence through interrogation. It is far beyond my competence, or the Court's competence, to determine that. But it is not beyond Congress's. If the situation demands it, the Executive can ask Congress to authorize suspension of the writ—which can be made subject to whatever conditions Congress deems appropriate, including even the procedural novelties invented by the plurality today. To be sure, suspension is limited by the Constitution to cases of rebellion or invasion. But whether the attacks of September 11, 2001, constitute an "invasion," and whether those attacks still justify suspension several years later, are questions for Congress rather than this Court. If civil rights are to be curtailed during wartime, it must be done openly and democratically, as the Constitution requires, rather than by silent erosion through an opinion of this Court. . . .

* * *

Many think it not only inevitable but entirely proper that liberty give way to security in times of national crisis—that, at the extremes of military exigency, *inter arma silent leges*. Whatever the general merits of the view that war silences law or modulates its voice, that view has no place in the interpretation and application of a Constitution designed precisely to confront war and, in a manner that accords with democratic principles, to accommodate it. Because the Court has proceeded to meet the current emergency in a manner the Constitution does not envision, I respectfully dissent.

JUSTICE THOMAS, dissenting.

The Executive Branch, acting pursuant to the powers vested in the President by the Constitution and with explicit congressional approval, has determined that Yaser Hamdi is an enemy combatant and should be detained. This detention falls squarely within the Federal Government's war powers, and we lack the expertise and capacity to second-guess that decision. As such, petitioner's habeas challenge should fail, and there is no reason to remand the case. The plurality reaches a contrary conclusion by failing adequately to consider basic principles of the constitutional structure as it relates to national security and foreign affairs and by using the balancing scheme of *Mathews v. Eldridge*. I do not think that the Federal Government's war powers can be balanced away by this Court. Arguably, Congress could provide for additional procedural protections, but until it does, we have no right to insist upon them. But even if I were to agree with the general approach the plurality takes, I could not accept the particulars. The plurality utterly fails to account for the Government's compelling interests and for our own institutional inability to weigh competing concerns correctly. I respectfully dissent.

I

"It is 'obvious and unarguable' that no governmental interest is more compelling than the security of the Nation." But because the Founders understood that they could not foresee the myriad potential threats to national security that might later arise, they chose to create a Federal Government that necessarily possesses sufficient power to handle any threat to the security of the Nation. . . .

The Founders intended that the President have primary responsibility—along with the necessary power—to protect the national security and to conduct the Nation's foreign relations. They did so principally because the structural advantages of a unitary Executive are essential in these domains. . . .

This Court has [held] that the President has *constitutional* authority to protect the national security and that this authority carries with it broad discretion. . . .

Congress, to be sure, has a substantial and essential role in both foreign affairs and national security. But it is crucial to recognize that *judicial* interference in these domains destroys the purpose of vesting primary responsibility in a unitary Executive. . . .

I acknowledge that the question whether Hamdi's executive detention is lawful is a question properly resolved by the Judicial Branch, though the question comes to the Court with the strongest presumptions in favor of the Government. The plurality agrees that Hamdi's detention is lawful if he is an enemy combatant. But the question whether Hamdi is actually an enemy combatant is "of a kind for which the Judiciary has neither aptitude, facilities nor responsibility and which has long been held to belong in the domain of political power not subject to judicial intrusion or inquiry." That is, although it is appropriate for the Court to determine the judicial question whether the President has the asserted authority, we lack the information and expertise to question whether Hamdi is actually an enemy combatant, a question the resolution of which is committed to other branches. . . .

II

"The war power of the national government is 'the power to wage war successfully.'" It follows that this power "is not limited to victories in the field, but carries with it the inherent power to guard against the immediate renewal of the conflict," and quite obviously includes the ability to detain those (even United States citizens) who fight against our troops or those of our allies.

Although the President very well may have inherent authority to detain those arrayed against our troops, I agree with the plurality that we need not decide that question because Congress has authorized the President to do so. . . .

The plurality, however, qualifies its recognition of the President's authority to detain enemy combatants in the war on terrorism in ways that are at odds with our precedent. Thus, the plurality relies primarily on Article 118 of the Geneva Convention (III) Relative to the Treatment of Prisoners of War for the proposition that "[i]t is a clearly established principle of the law of war that detention may last no longer than active hostilities." It then appears to limit the President's authority to detain by requiring that the record establis[h] that United States troops are still involved in active combat in Afghanistan because, in that case, detention would be "part of the exercise of 'necessary and appropriate force.'" But I do not believe that we may diminish the Federal Government's war powers by reference to a treaty and certainly not to a treaty that does not apply. Further, we are bound by the political branches' determination that the United States is at war. And, in any case, the power to detain does not end with the cessation of formal hostilities. . . .

Justice Scalia apparently does not disagree that the Federal Government has all power necessary to protect the Nation. If criminal processes do not suffice, however, Justice Scalia would require Congress to suspend the writ. But the fact that the writ may not be suspended "unless when in Cases of Rebellion or Invasion the public Safety may require it," Art. I, § 9, cl. 2, poses two related problems. First, this condition might not obtain here or during many other emergencies during which this detention authority might be necessary. Congress would then have to choose between acting unconstitutionally and depriving the President of the tools he needs to protect the Nation. Second, I do not see how suspension would make constitutional otherwise unconstitutional detentions ordered by the President. It simply removes a remedy. Justice Scalia's position might therefore require one or both of the political branches to act unconstitutionally in order to protect the Nation. But the power to protect the Nation must be the power to do so lawfully. . . .

IV

Although I do not agree with the plurality that the balancing approach of *Mathews v. Eldridge* is the appropriate analytical tool with which to analyze this case, I cannot help but explain that the plurality misapplies its chosen framework, one that if applied correctly would probably lead to the result I have reached. The plurality devotes two paragraphs to its discussion of the Government's interest, though much of those two paragraphs explain why the Government's concerns are misplaced. But: "It is 'obvious and unarguable' that no governmental interest is more compelling than the security of the Nation." [The] Government seeks to further that interest by detaining an enemy soldier not only to prevent him from rejoining the ongoing fight. Rather, as the Government explains, detention can serve to gather critical intelligence regarding the intentions and capabilities of our adversaries, a function that the Government avers has become all the more important in the war on terrorism.

Additional process, the Government explains, will destroy the intelligence gathering function. It also does seem quite likely that, under the process envisioned by the plurality, various military officials will have to take time to litigate this matter. And though the plurality does not say so, a meaningful ability to challenge the Government's factual allegations will probably require the Government to divulge highly classified information to the purported enemy combatant, who might then upon release return to the fight armed with our most closely held secrets. . . .

Ultimately, the plurality's dismissive treatment of the Government's asserted interests arises from its apparent belief that enemy-combatant determinations are not part of "the actual prosecution of a war" or one of the "central functions of warmaking." This seems wrong: Taking *and holding* enemy combatants is a quintessential aspect of the prosecution of war. Moreover, this highlights serious difficulties in applying the plurality's balancing approach here. First, in the war context, we know neither the strength of the Government's interests nor the costs of imposing additional process.

Second, it is at least difficult to explain why the result should be different for other military operations that the plurality would ostensibly recognize as "central functions of warmaking." [Because] a decision to bomb a particular target might extinguish *life* interests, the plurality's analysis seems to require notice to potential targets. [For example], in November 2002, a Central Intelligence Agency (CIA) Predator drone fired a Hellfire missile at a vehicle in Yemen carrying an al Qaeda leader, a citizen of the United States, and four others. It is not clear whether the CIA knew that an American was in the vehicle. But the plurality's due process would seem to require notice and opportunity to respond here as well. I offer [this example] not because I think the plurality would demand additional process in [this situation] but because it clearly would not. The result here should be the same. . . .

* * *

For these reasons, I would affirm the judgment of the Court of Appeals.

Note: Unanswered Questions

1. *Padilla.* Jose Padilla, an American citizen, was arrested within the United States on a material witness warrant in conjunction with a grand jury investigation into al Quaeda-sponsored terrorism. Shortly before a scheduled hearing at which the government would have been required to establish cause to hold him, the President, relying upon his commander-in-chief authority and the Authorization of Use of Force Resolution, designated Padilla an enemy combatant and ordered that he be taken into

military custody. The President supported his determination with findings that Padilla was "closely associated with alo Quaeda," that he was "engaged in . . . hostile and war-like acts, including . . . preparation for acts of international terrorism" against the United States, that he "possesses intelligence" about al Qaeda that would help prevent attacks, and that he represented "a continuing, present, and grave danger to the national security of the United States."

Padilla then filed a habeas corpus petition. In Rumsfeld v. Padilla, 542 U.S. ___ (2004), the Court, in a 5-4 decision written by Chief Justice Rehnquist, held that Padilla had filed the petition in the wrong venue and that there was therefore no reason to reach the merits of his claim. Does Padilla fit within the definition of "enemy combatant" utilized by the *Hamdi* plurality? Should a judge sitting in an appropriate venue order his release? Consider the following passage from Justice Stevens' dissenting opinion, joined by Justices Souter, Ginsburg, and Breyer:

> Whether respondent is entitled to immediate release is a question that reasonable jurists may answer in different ways. There is, however, only one possible answer to the question whether he is entitled to a hearing on the justification for his detention.
>
> At stake in this case is nothing less than the essence of a free society. Even more important than the method of selecting the people's rulers and their successors is the character of the constraints imposed on the Executive by the rule of law. Unconstrained Executive detention for the purpose of investigating and preventing subversive activity is the hallmark of the Star Chamber. Access to counsel for the purpose of protecting the citizen from official mistakes and mistreatment is the hallmark of due process.
>
> Executive detention of subversive citizens, like detention of enemy soldiers to keep them off the battlefield, may sometimes be justified to prevent persons from launching or becoming missiles of destruction. It may not, however, be justified by the naked interest in using unlawful procedures to extract information. Incommunicado detention for months on end is such a procedure. Whether the information so procured is more or less reliable than that acquired by more extreme forms of torture is of no consequence. For if this Nation is to remain true to the ideals symbolized by its flag, it must not wield the tools of tyrants even to resist an assault by the forces of tyranny.

2. *Guanatanamo*. In the wake of the war in Afghanistan, the United States held approximately six hundred noncitizens allegedly captured on the battlefield at the Guantanamo Bay, Cuba Naval Base, which the United States occupies under a lease and treaty with Cuba. The government claimed that they were not entitled to prisoner of war status but, rather, were enemy combatants. In Rasul v. Bush, 542 U.S. ___ (2004), the Court, in a 6-3 decision written by Justice Kennedy, held that a federal court had habeas corpus jurisdiction to review the legality and conditions of their

confinement. However, the court was silent as to the substantive legal standards a habeas court should utilize. Are these detainees entitled to the protections outlined by the *Hamdi* plurality? Can they be held after American troops withdraw from Afghanistan?

3. *Military tribunals.* In 2001, President Bush signed an executive order establishing military tribunals with jurisdiction to try anyone who is not an American citizen and whom the President determined that there was reason to believe was a member of al Qaida, or had "engaged in, aided or abetted, or conspired to commit, acts of international terrorism, or acts in preparation therefor," or who had knowingly harbored such individuals. The order provided for conviction and sentencing upon concurrence of two-thirds of the members of the tribunal with review of the final decision vested solely in the President or the Secretary of Defense. The order further provided that defendants before the tribunal "shall not be privileged to seek any remedy or maintain any proceeding [in any] court of the United States or any State thereof." Does this order exceed the President's Article II power as Commander in Chief? The power delegated to him by the AUMF? In Ex parte Milligan, 71 U.S. (1 Wall.) 2 (1866), the Court invalidated the conviction of a civilian United States citizen for conspiracy against the United States. The conviction was obtained before a military commission established in Indiana during the Civil War. In a famous passage, the Court held that "[martial] rule can never exist where the courts are open, and in the proper and unobstructed exercise of their jurisdiction." The Court went on to state the following:

> Certainly no part of the judicial power of the country was conferred on [the military commission]; because the Constitution expressly vests it "in one supreme court and such inferior courts as the Congress may from time to time ordain and establish," and it is not pretended that the commission was a court ordained and established by Congress. They cannot justify on the mandate of the President; because he is controlled by law, and has his appropriate sphere of duty, which is to execute, not to make the laws; and there is no unwritten criminal code to which resort can be had as a source of jurisdiction.

Compare *Milligan* to Ex parte Quirin, 317 U.S. 1 (1942), where the Court upheld the conviction before a military tribunal of eight Nazi saboteurs, including a United States citizen, who landed in the United States armed with explosives. The Court noted that the detention and trial "ordered by the President in the declared exercise of his powers as Commander in Chief of the Army in time of war and of grave public danger [are] not to be set aside by the courts without the clear conviction that they are in conflict with the Constitution or laws of Congress constitutionally enacted." It also observed that

> The Constitution [invests] the President as Commander in Chief with the power to wage war which Congress has declared, and to carry into effect all laws passed by

Congress for the conduct of war and for the government and regulation of the Armed Forces and all laws defining and punishing offences against the law of nations, including those which pertain to the conduct of war.

However, the Court found it "unnecessary for present purposes to determine to what extent the President as Commander in Chief has constitutional power to create military commissions without the support of Congressional legislation. For here Congress has authorized trial of offenses against the law of war before such commissions." The Court distinguished *Milligan* on the ground that there, the defendant "was not an enemy belligerent either entitled to the status of a prisoner of war or subject to the penalties imposed upon unlawful belligerents." See also In re Yamashita, 327 U.S. 1 (1946) (upholding the use of a military commission to try the commander of Japanese forces in the Philippines for violation of the laws of war).

In light of *Milligan Quirin*, and *Hamdi*, is the President's Commander in Chief power sufficient to justify President Bush's order? Consider Bradley & Goldsmith, The Constitutional Validity of Military Commissions, 5 Green Bag 2d 249, 252 (2002):

> A strong argument can be made that President Bush has independent power, as Commander in Chief, to establish military commissions to try war crimes violations, even in the absence of affirmative congressional authorization. Presidents have long claimed that their constitutional authority to manage the war effort includes the power to create military commissions, and they have exercised such power throughout U.S. history. The Supreme Court in *Quirin* appeared to agree with this claim in [dicta].

Compare Katyal & Tribe, Waging War, Deciding Guilt: Trying the Military Tribunals, 111 Yale L. J. 1259, 1270 (2002):

> The moment the President moves beyond detaining enemy combatants as war prisoners to actually adjudicating their guilt and meting out punishment [he] has moved outside the perimeter of his role as Commander in Chief of our armed forces and entered a zone that involves judging and punishing alleged violations of the [laws]. In that adjudicatory and punitive zone, the fact that the President entered wearing his military garb should not blind us to the fact that he is now pursuing a different goal — assessing guilt and meting out retrospective justice rather than waging war.

See also Fletcher, On Justice and War: Contradictions in the Proposed Military Tribunals, 25 Harv. J. of L. & Pub. Pol. 635, 637 (2002) (arguing that President Bush's order reflects our "state of collective confusion" about whether our response to September 11 should be grounded in "the ideas of justice or the principles of war").

4. *Torture.* Does the President's commander in chief power allow him to override statutes or treaty obligations prohibiting torture if he determines that doing so is necessary to win the war on terror? In a memorandum prepared for the Counsel to the President, the Justice Department's Office of Legal Counsel reached the following conclusions:

> Even if an interrogation method arguably were to violate [the federal statute implementing the United Nations Convention against Torture and Other Cruel, Inhuman and Degrading Treatment or Punishment], the statute would be unconstitutional if it impermissibly encroached on the President's constitutional power to conduct a military campaign. As Commander-in-Chief, the President has the constitutional authority to order interrogations of enemy combatants to gain intelligence information concerning the military plans of the enemy. The demands of the Commander-in-Chief power are especially pronounced in the middle of a war in which the nation has already suffered a direct attack. In such a case, the information gained from interrogations may prevent future attacks by foreign enemies. Any effort to apply [the statute] in a manner that interferes with the President's direction of such core war matters as the detention and interrogation of enemy combatants thus would be unconstitutional.

In a memorandum signed on February 7, 2002, President Bush stated that he "accept[ed] the legal conclusion of the Attorney General and the department of Justice that I have the authority under the Constitution to suspend [Geneva Accord provisions dealing with the treatment of prisoners] as between the United States and Afghanistan, but I decline to exercise that authority at this time. [I] reserve the right to exercise this authority in this or future conflicts." The memorandum goes on to assert that "our values as a Nation [call] for us to treat detainees hamanely, including those who are not legally entitled to such treatment. [As] a matter of policy, the United States Armed Forces shall continue to treat detainees humanely and, to the extent appropriate and consistent with military necessity, in a manner consistent with the principles of Geneva."

After the Office of Legal Counsel memorandum became public in Spring, 2004, the President disavowed its conclusions.

5. *The relevance of constitutional law.* Suppose that the President determines that Hamdi's continued detention is essential to the national security. Is it plausible that he would obey a judicial order to release him? Should he obey such an order? Consider Justice's Thomas' argument in *Hamdi* that, even if Congress were to suspend the writ of habeas corpus, the President would nonetheless be under a (not judicially enforceable) obligation to obey constitutional commands. If this argument is correct, does it follow that when Justice Scalia claims that national security can be protected by suspension of the writ, he is counseling constitutional disobedience?

In Korematsu v. United States (excerpted at page 501 of the main volume), Justice Jackson dissented from the Court's judgment upholding the conviction of a defendant who had disobeyed the order excluding Japanese Americans from the West Coast during World War II. Unlike the other dissenters, however, Justice Jackson did not argue that the exclusion should not have taken place. Jackson wrote that it would be

> impracticable and dangerous idealism to expect or insist that each specific military command in an area of probable operations will conform to conventional tests of constitutionality. When an area is so beset that it must be put under military control at all, the paramount consideration is that its measures be successful rather than legal.

For Jackson, the crucial question was not whether the exclusion should have taken place, but whether the courts should endorse the exclusion.

> I should hold that a civil court cannot be made to enforce an order which violates constitutional limitations even if it is a reasonable exercise of military authority. The courts can exercise only the judicial power, can apply only law, and must abide by the Constitution, for the case to be civil courts and become instruments of military policy.

Note also Jackson's distinction in *Youngstown* between the President's "paper powers" and "real powers." How would Justice Jackson have voted in *Hamdi*?

Compare Justice Jackson's approach to Gross, Chaos and Rules: Should Responses to Violent Crises Always Be Constitutional?, 112 Yale L.J. 1011, 1022-23 (2003):

> [We] need to reexamine a [fundamental] assumption that underlies the traditional models of emergency powers. The *assumption of constitutionality* tells us that whatever responses are made to the challenges of a particular exigency, such responses are to be found and limited within the confines of the constitution. . . .
>
> [There] may be circumstances where the appropriate method of tackling grave dangers and threats entails going outside the constitutional order, at times even violating otherwise accepted constitutional principles, rules, and norms. . . .
>
> This [model informs] public officials that they may act extralegally when they believe that such action is necessary for protecting the nation and the public in the face of calamity, provided that they openly and publicly acknowledge the nature of their actions. It is then up to the people to decide, either directly or indirectly (e.g., through their elected representatives in the legislature), how to respond to such actions. The people may decide to hold the actor to the wrongfulness of her actions, demonstrating commitment to the violated principles and values. [Alter-

natively,] the people may approve, ex post, the extralegal actions of the public official.

Compare Seidman, The Secret Life of the Political Question Doctrine, 37 John Marshall L. Rev. 441, 475-76 (2004):

> Any [defense of] the Extra Legal Model requires some description of what it is and some norms for when it can be invoked. But as soon as the model is structured in this way, it ceases to be extra-legal. What makes conduct extra-legal is precisely its resistance to rules and norms. Without a recognition of this fact, one is led into an infinite regress. In a *true* emergency, one might ask, are not government officials justified in overriding the rules that Gross establishes for rule violation? [At] the bottom of the chain is the terrifying possibility of unmediated choice that cannot be contained by rules. To describe the circumstances when such choice is appropriate is to insist on the very rules that are being overridden.

Page 413. At the bottom of the page, add the following:

In Currie, Rumors of Wars: Presidential and Congressional War Powers, 1809-1829, 67 U. Chi. L. Rev. 1 (2000), the author concludes that "the express position of every President to address the subject [of warmaking power] during the first forty years of the present Constitution was entirely in line with [the War Powers Resolution]: The President may introduce troops into hostilities only pursuant to a congressional declaration of war or other legislative authorization, or in response to an attack on the United States."

Page 414. At the end of section 2 of the Note, add the following:

Consider the following evaluation in Paulsen, Youngstown Goes to War, 19 Const. Com. 215, 247-48 (2002):

> [In] a constitutional regime in which congressional and presidential war powers are recognized as overlapping and in some respects concurrent, [the] lawfulness of presidential military action [is] affected by Congress's constitutional interpretation of the scope of the President's authority. In this respect, the War Powers Resolution operates, somewhat ironically and probably unintentionally, to provide a constitutional "safe harbor" for certain unilateral presidential actions involving the use of military force—a zone of nearly unchallengeable exercise of presiden-

tial power within the zone of twilight marked by the overlap of congressional and presidential war powers, where Congress has by statute explicitly chosen to accept presidential military initiatives, and where it is not clear that the Constitution of its own force renders such presidential action unlawful.

Page 415. At the end of the Note on the War Powers Resolution, add the following:

4. *The War in Iraq.* On October 16, 2002, Congress enacted the following resolution:

(a) AUTHORIZATION. — The President is authorized to use the Armed Forces of the United States as he determines to be necessary and appropriate in order to —

(1) defend the national security of the United States against the continuing threat posed by Iraq; and

(2) enforce all relevant United Nations Security Council resolutions regarding Iraq.

(b) PRESIDENTIAL DETERMINATION. — In connection with the exercise of the authority granted in subsection (a) to use force the President shall, prior to such exercise or as soon thereafter as may be feasible, but no later than 48 hours after exercising such authority, make available to the Speaker of the House of Representatives and the President pro tempore of the Senate his determination that —

(1) reliance by the United States on further diplomatic or other peaceful means alone either (A) will not adequately protect the national security of the United States against the continuing threat posed by Iraq or (B) is not likely to lead to enforcement of all relevant United Nations Security Council resolutions regarding Iraq; and

(2) acting pursuant to this joint resolution is consistent with the United States and other countries continuing to take the necessary actions against international terrorist and terrorist organizations, including those nations, organizations, or persons who planned, authorized, committed or aided the terrorist attacks that occurred on September 11, 2001.

(c) WAR POWERS RESOLUTION REQUIREMENTS. —

(1) SPECIFIC STATUTORY AUTHORIZATION. — Consistent with section [1547(A)(1)] of the War Powers Resolution, the Congress declares that this section is intended to constitute specific statutory authorization within the meaning of section [1544(B)] of the War Powers Resolution.

(2) APPLICABILITY OF OTHER REQUIREMENTS.—Nothing in this joint resolution supersedes any requirement of the War Powers Resolution.

Authorization for Use of Military Force against Iraq Resolution of 2002, PL 107-243, 116 Stat. 1498 (2002).

Months later, acting pursuant to this authority, the President committed American military forces to Iraq. Does a congressional authorization for military action at some point in the indefinite future constitute a declaration of war within the meaning of Article I § 8? Consider in this regard the material on the nondelegation doctrine at page 365 of the main volume and the implications of United States v. Curtiss-Wright Corp., excerpted at page 403 of the main volume. If the Use of Military Force Resolution is not a declaration of war, does the War Powers Resolution make the President's actions legal? Consider in this regard the effect of §(c)(2) of the Use of Military Force Resolution in conjunction with § 1547(D)(2) of the War Powers Resolution.

Page 418. Before section 3 of the Note, add the following:

For the Court's latest decision on the constitutional effect of executive agreements, see American Insurance Association v. Garamendi, 539 U.S. 396 (2003). In a 5-4 decision the Court, per Justice Souter, invalidated a California statute that required insurers doing business in the state to disclose details of insurance policies issued to persons in Europe which were in effect between 1920 and 1945. The statute was enacted to assist Holocaust victims and their descendants in their efforts to collect the proceeds of insurance policies that were either unpaid by the companies or seized by the Nazi government. The Court held that the state law was preempted by an executive agreement between the United States and Germany. Although the executive agreement did not expressly deal with California's disclosure requirement, the Court held that the agreement's approach, which emphasized voluntary cooperation and settlement of claims through a special fund established by the German government, conflicted with the statute.

With regard to the constitutional power of the President to reach binding executive agreements with foreign states, the Court said the following:

> There is, of course, no question that at some point an exercise of state power that touches on foreign relations must yield to the National Government's [policy]....
>
> Nor is there any question generally that there is executive authority to decide what that policy should be. Although the source of the President's power to act in foreign affairs does not enjoy any textual detail, the historical gloss on the "executive Power" vested in Article II of the Constitution has recognized the President's "vast share of responsibility for the conduct of our foreign relations." [*Youngs-*

town (Frankfurter, J., concurring)]. While Congress holds express authority to regulate public and private dealings with other nations in its war and foreign commerce powers, in foreign affairs the President has a degree of independent authority to act. . . .

At a more specific level, our cases have recognized that the President has authority to make "executive agreements" with other countries, requiring no ratification by the Senate or approval by Congress, this power having been exercised since the early years of the Republic. See [*Dames & Moore*]. [Making] executive agreements to settle claims of American nationals against foreign governments is a particularly longstanding [practice]. Given the fact that the practice goes back over 200 years to the first Presidential administration, and has received congressional acquiescence throughout its history, the conclusion "[t]hat the President's control of foreign relations includes the settlement of claims is indisputable."

In which of Justice Jackson's three categories does the German-American executive agreement fall? Recall that in *Dames & Moore*, the Court stated that it was "crucial" to its decision that "Congress [had] implicitly approved the practice of claim settlement by executive agreement" through the International Claims Settlement Act. Given *Garamendi*, is this fact still "crucial"?

Would a federal statute that specifically disapproved of the executive agreement relied upon in *Garamendi* be constitutional? The *Garamendi* petitioner argued that Congress had authorized state laws of the sort California had enacted, but the Court held that it "need [not] consider the possible significance for preemption doctrine of tension between an Act of Congress and Presidential foreign policy, cf. generally [*Youngstown* (Jackson, J., concurring)]" because the federal statute did not grant such authorization.

Indeed, it is worth noting that Congress has done nothing to express disapproval of the President's policy. Legislation along the lines of [the California statute] has been introduced in Congress repeatedly, but none of the bills has come close to making it into law.

In sum, Congress has not acted on the matter addressed here. Given the President's independent authority "in the areas of foreign policy and national security, . . . congressional silence is not to be equated with congressional disapproval."

Page 419. At the end of section 3 of the Note, add the following:

For a criticism of both the Tribe and Ackerman-Golove positions, see Spiro, Treaties, Executive Agreements, and Constitutional Method, 79 Tex. L. Rev. 961 (2001).

Spiro argues that Tribe's conclusion is "refuted by the broad national acceptance of the manner in which the NAFTA and [World Trade Organization] agreements were effected. [This] constitutional acceptance exposes the flaws of a methodology that does not account for history and practice." Id. at 963. Spiro finds that Ackerman and Golove overstate their case in claiming that there is "full interchangeability" between treaties and congressional-executive agreements. "There remain some types of international agreements for which the treaty process is constitutionally required, and perhaps some for which the congressional-executive agreement is now the only permitted route to international undertakings." Id. at 964.

5
EQUALITY AND THE CONSTITUTION

B. Equal Protection Methodology: Rational Basis Review

Page 483.   After the first paragraph, add the following:

Consider, for example, Fitzgerald v. Racing Association of Central Iowa, 539 U.S. 103 (2003). Iowa law imposed a higher tax on revenues gained from slot machines at racetracks than from slot machines on excursion riverboats. The Iowa Supreme Court held that this differential violated the equal protection clause. It reasoned that the "differential tax completely defeats the [statute's] alleged purpose [of helping] racetracks recover from economic distress" and that there could therefore be "no rational reason for this differential tax." In an opinion written by Justice Breyer, the Supreme Court unanimously reversed:

> [The] Iowa law, like most laws, might predominately serve one general objective, say, helping racetracks, while containing subsidiary provisions that seek to achieve other desirable (perhaps even contrary) ends as well, thereby producing a law that balances objectives but still serves the general objective when seen as a whole. . . .
>
> [The statute's] grant to the racetracks of authority to operate slot machines should help the racetracks economically to some degree—even if its simultaneous imposition of a tax on slot machine adjusted revenue means that the law provides less help than respondents might like. . . .
>
> [The] difference [in taxation rates], harmful to the racetracks, is helpful to the riverboats, which [were] also facing financial peril.

Page 494.   Before section 2 of the Note, add the following:

In connection with the "expressions of animosity" theory, consider the exchange between Justices O'Connor and Scalia in Lawrence v. Texas, 539 U.S. 558 (2003).

At issue was the constitutionality of a Texas criminal statute that prohibited homosexual, but not heterosexual sodomy. The Court's majority invalidated the law on due process grounds. (This portion of the opinion is discussed in the Supplement to page 901 of the main text.) Justice O'Connor concurred in the result on the ground that the distinction between heterosexual and homosexual sodomy violated equal protection:

> We have consistently held [that] some objectives, such as a "bare ... desire to harm a politically unpopular group" are not legitimate state interests. [*Moreno*; *Cleburne*; *Romer*] When a law exhibits such a desire to harm a politically unpopular group, we have applied a more searching form of rational basis review to strike down such laws under the Equal Protection Clause. . . .
>
> Moral disapproval of [homosexuals], like a bare desire to harm the group, is an interest that is insufficient to satisfy rational basis review under the Equal Protection Clause. . . .
>
> Moral disapproval of a group cannot be a legitimate governmental interest under the Equal Protection Clause because legal classifications must not be "drawn for the purpose of disadvantaging the group burdened by the law." [*Romer*]. Texas' invocation of moral disapproval as a legitimate interest proves nothing more than Texas' desire to criminalize homosexual sodomy. But the Equal Protection Clause prevents a State from creating "a classification of persons undertaken for its own sake." [*Romer*]. . . .
>
> That this law as applied to private, consensual conduct is unconstitutional under the Equal Protection Clause does not mean that other laws distinguishing between heterosexuals and homosexuals would similarly fail under rational basis review. Texas cannot assert any legitimate state interest here, such as national security or preserving the traditional institution of marriage. Unlike the moral disapproval of same-sex relations—the asserted state interest in this case—other reasons exist to promote the institution of marriage beyond mere moral disapproval of an excluded group.

Compare Justice Scalia's response in his dissenting opinion:

> [Justice O'Connor's] reasoning leaves on pretty shaky grounds state laws limiting marriage to opposite-sex couples. [She] seeks to preserve them by the conclusory statement that "preserving the traditional institution of marriage" is a legitimate state interest. But "preserving the traditional institution of marriage" is just a kinder way of describing the State's *moral disapproval* of same-sex couples. Texas's interest in [its anti-sodomy statute] could be recast in similarly euphemistic terms: "preserving the traditional sexual mores of our society." In the jurisprudence Justice O'Connor has seemingly created, judges can validate laws by characterizing them as "preserving the traditions of society" (good); or invalidate them by characterizing them as "expressing moral disapproval" (bad).

Equality and the Constitution   Page 505

Page 497.   At the bottom of the page, add the following:

The Court again distinguished *Allegheny Pittsburgh* in Fitzgerald v. Racing Association of Central Iowa, 539 U.S. 103 (2003). Iowa law imposed a heavier tax on revenues gained from slot machines located at racetracks than from slot machines located on riverboats. A unanimous Supreme Court, in an opinion by Justice Breyer, rejected an equal protection challenge to this different treatment.

> In [*Allegheny Pittsburgh*] the Court held that substantial differences in [property tax assessments] violated the Federal Equal Protection Clause. [But the] Court in *Nordlinger* [held] that "*Allegheny Pittsburgh* was the rare case where the facts precluded any plausible inference that the reason for the unequal assessment practice was to achieve the benefits of an acquisition-value scheme." Here, "the facts" do not "preclud[e]" an inference that the reason for the different tax rates was to help the riverboat industry or the river communities.

C. Equal Protection Methodology: Heightened Scrutiny and the Problem of Race

Page 505.   After the first paragraph of the Note, add the following:

In Gudridge, Remember Endo?, 116 Harv. L. Rev. 1933 (2003), the author argues that *Korematsu* should be read together with its companion case, Ex parte Endo, 323 U.S. 283 (1944), which held that the detention (as opposed to the exclusion from the West Coast) of loyal Americans of Japanese descent was illegal. Although formally no more than an interpretation of the power granted by the underlying executive order, the Court's interpretation was influenced by its belief that the detention "touch[ed] the sensitive area of rights specifically guaranteed by the Constitution" and by the Court's practice of favoring "that interpretation of legislation which gives it the greater chance of surviving the test of constitutionality."

Gudridge argues that when *Endo* and *Korematsu* are read together, they produce a "doubled legal consciousness."

> *Korematsu* posited a gap open to military [improvisers]. *Endo* did not close the gap, but rather ignored it, proceeded as though there was no possibility that constitutional law was a less than universal language. *Endo* shows *Korematsu* to be marginal—even as, of course, *Korematsu* also shows *Endo* to be marginal. . . .
>
> Especially in circumstances in which judicial review is unavailable, reluctant, or likely to be too late to be relevant, executive or legislative appreciation and ex-

pression of this alternation may be the only telling manifestation of constitutional law. Thus, in a Justice Department or Defense Department under stress, challenged, doubled perspectives evident in instruments or acts, signs that both emergency responses and ordinary senses of limitation are or were subject to question, may be the only readable signs of the continuing impact of constitutional sensibility, of at least the elementary patterns of constitutional law.

Page 510. Before section 7 of the Note, add the following:

What implications does the antisubordination argument hold regarding strict scrutiny of racial classifications? In Harris, Equality Trouble: Sameness and Difference in Twentieth-Century Law, 88 Cal. L. Rev. 1923 (2000), the author argues that twentieth-century race law has moved from a conception of constitutional equality that encompassed the notion of inherent racial difference to a conception that made racial sameness "the foundation of common sense." However,

> [both] equality as sameness and equality as difference have a way of obscuring questions such as "who sets the standard for equality?" The fact that both equality as sameness and equality as difference can coexist with relations of dominance begins to explain why many of today's antiracists denounce colorblindness. It also begins to explain how we may not have made as much progress over the past century as it might initially appear.

Id. at 1929.

Consider also Siegal, Equality Talk: Antisubordination and Anticlassification Values in Constitutional Struggles over Brown, 117 Harv. L. Rev. 1470, 1475 (2004):

> Standing alone, the principle that it is wrong to classify on the basis of race neither states a norm of conduct nor articulates a complex of values that can account for the path along which equal protection law has developed. Instead, [application] of the [anticlassification] principle varies over time and across social practices because the principle is in fact applied to vindicate different kinds of social concerns. [At] some points in our history, courts have employed claims about the wrongs of racial classification to express and to mark constitutional concerns about practices that enforce second-class citizenship for members of relatively powerless social groups—and at other points in our history, courts have employed claims about the wrongs of racial classification to block, diffuse, and limit constitutional expression of such concerns.

Page 512. After the first two lines on the page, add the following:

8. *A synthesis.* For a detailed and insightful "unified framework" for strict scrutiny, see Rubin, Reconnecting Doctrine and Purpose: A Comprehensive Approach to Strict Scrutiny after *Adarand* and *Shaw*, 149 U. Penn. L. Rev. 1 (2000). Rubin provides a taxonomy of the risks and harms that may accompany the use of race as a classificatory principle:

1. The risk that race is being used "to harm an unpopular group [or] to indicate that the members of that group are unfit to partake of something given to others [and] to convey in this way the community's judgment about the inherent worth of people of different kinds."
2. The risk that the classification "reflects nothing more than racial politics, a desire to reward the members of [one's] own racial group."
3. The risk that a racial classification "[reflects] nothing more than erroneous stereotypes."
4. The risk that racial classifications, even if related to a legitimate purpose, may perpetuate a negative racial stereotype.
5. The risk that decisionmaking based on race may "[deny] a person treatment as an individual in a way that other sorting mechanisms do not."
6. The risk that "the very use of race to identify people [will] [have] some divisive effect on the races by reinforcing the belief in inherent racial differences, regardless of [correlation] with traditional stereotypes."
7. The risk that the use of race will "cause a dignitary harm to individuals [regardless] of whether anyone is disadvantaged on the basis of their racial identity."

Id. at 20-23. Rubin goes on to argue in considerable detail that "strict scrutiny must be flexible enough to recognize that different uses of race pose different risks and impose different harms. To determine what risks and harms are present requires a careful examination of the factual circumstances and social contexts in which the use of race by government has taken place." Id. at 25-26. Consider the extent to which this flexibility undermines the advantages of having formally distinct levels of review in the first place.

9. *Abandoning special scrutiny?* Although in recent years, the Supreme Court has continued to insist upon strict scrutiny for racial classifications, it has also suggested that this scrutiny need not be "fatal in fact." Adarand Constructors Inc. v. Pena, 515 U.S. 200, 202 (1995). Thus, in the context of affirmative action it has suggested that narrowly tailored measures designed to remedy specific acts of prior discrimination

might satisfy strict scrutiny. See id. Similarly, in the context of racial districting, the Court has held that the use of race is permissible so long as it is not "the predominant factor motivating the legislature's decision to place a significant number of voters within or without a particular district." Miller v. Johnson, 515 U.S. 900, 916 (1995). (These cases are considered in more detail at pp. 545 and 574 of the main volume.) Consider whether these decisions constitute a dilution or abandonment of strict scrutiny, in fact if not in name. Karlan, Easing the Spring: Strict Scrutiny and Affirmative Action After the Redistricting Cases, 43 Wm. & Mary L. Rev. 1569 (2002), argues that these cases suggest that "strict scrutiny may be strict in theory, but . . . rather pliable in practice." Id. at 1573.

In Griffin, Judicial Supremacy and Equal Protection in a Democracy of Rights, 4 U. Pa. J. of Con. L. 281 (2002), the author argues that the Court should formally abandon strict scrutiny for racial classifications. From a strategic point of view, Professor Griffin contends, recent decisions make clear that minorities gain little from such scrutiny. As Griffin puts it, "if you are a member of a racial minority, the Supreme Court is not your friend." Id. at 282. Moreover, "the protection against unjust discrimination all Americans receive from civil rights statutes is plainly superior to the protection provided by the Equal Protection Clause." Id. The abandonment of strict scrutiny is also normatively desirable: This is so, Griffin argues, because we presently live in a "democracy of rights," which "connects rights with democratic deliberation." In a democracy of this sort, "government actors take it for granted that it is desirable to create, enforce, and promote individual constitutional and legal rights. Hence, the political branches of government (not just the courts) are seeking constantly to maintain and extend the system of rights they have created through democratic means." Id. Do you agree? If the Supreme Court announced tomorrow that racial classifications were no longer subject to strict scrutiny, would the announcement make any practical difference?

Page 551. At the end of section 1 of the Note, add the following:

Does the Court's conception of harm match its restrictive standing rule? Compare Ely, Standing to Challenge Pro-Minority Gerrymanders, 111 Harv. L. Rev. 576, 594 (1997) (arguing that white voters "have standing basically because they've been deprived of a meaningful shot at helping to elect a representative whose race is the same as theirs") with Issacharoff & Karlan, Standing and Misunderstanding in Voting Rights Law, 111 Harv. L. Rev. 2276 (1998) (arguing that the Court's standing doctrine is completely incoherent because it fails to explain the dividing line between those voters who have standing and those who lack standing and that the plaintiffs in the race-specific districting cases deliberately declined to claim vote dilution or the inability to elect their preferred candidates).

For a particularly dramatic example of the formal bite and substantive emptiness of the Court's standing doctrine, consider Sinkfield v. Kelley, 531 U.S. 28 (2000). The plaintiffs lived in several majority-white state legislative districts that were adjacent to deliberately-created majority black legislative districts. Taking *Hays* at its word, they challenged the majority-white districts in which they lived: an inevitable consequence of having to redraw those districts would be the need also to redraw the adjacent majority-black districts. The Supreme Court, in a per curiam opinion, directed the district court to dismiss the complaint for lack of standing.

"[The voters'] position here is essentially indistinguishable from that of the appellees in *Hays*. Appellees are challenging their own majority-white districts as the product of unconstitutional racial gerrymandering under a redistricting plan whose purpose was the creation of majority-minority districts, some of which border appellees' districts. Like the appellees in *Hays*, they have neither alleged nor produced any evidence that any of them was assigned to his or her district as a direct result of having 'personally been subjected to a racial classification.'...

"The shapes of appellees' districts, however, were necessarily influenced by the shapes of the majority-minority districts upon which they border, and appellees have produced no evidence that anything other than the deliberate creation of those majority-minority districts is responsible for the districting lines of which they complain. Appellees' suggestion thus boils down to the claim that an unconstitutional use of race in drawing the boundaries of majority-minority districts necessarily involves an unconstitutional use of race in drawing the boundaries of neighboring majority-white districts. We rejected that argument in *Hays* . . . ."

Page 552. At the end of section 2 of the Note, add the following:

EASLEY v. CROMARTIE, 532 U.S. 234 (2001). This case involved a challenge to a redrawn version of North Carolina's Twelfth Congressional District, the district challenged originally in Shaw v. Reno, 509 U.S. 630 (1993) (discussed supra page 544 of the main text), and struck down as unjustifiably race conscious in Shaw v. Hunt, 517 U.S. 899 (1996). This time around, the Court held that the district court had erred in finding that race, rather than politics, drove the legislature's districting decision.

Justice Breyer's opinion for the Court sharpened the distinction between race "simply hav[ing] been '*a* motivation for the drawing of a majority minority district'" —which would be permissible—and race being the "predominant factor," the showing that would trigger strict scrutiny. Justice Breyer cautioned against concluding that race was the predominant factor in situations "where the State has articulated a legitimate political explanation for its districting decision, and the voting population is one in which race and political affiliation are highly correlated."

Justice Breyer's opinion performed a painstakingly thorough review of the record, going beyond the district court's findings to examine the entire testimony of the expert witness on whom the trial court had relied. It also discounted the direct evidence relied on by the district court. One of the leaders of the redistricting process, State Senator Roy Cooper, testified before the legislative committee considering the plan "'overall it provides for a fair, geographic, racial and partisan balance throughout the State of North Carolina. . . .'" Justice Breyer "agree[d] that one can read the statement about 'racial . . . balance' as the District Court read it—to refer to the current congressional delegation's racial balance. But even as so read, the phrase shows that the legislature considered race, along with other partisan and geographic considerations; and as so read it says little or nothing about whether race played a predominant role comparatively speaking. . . .

"We can put the matter more generally as follows: In a case such as this one where majority-minority districts (or the approximate equivalent) are at issue and where racial identification correlates highly with political affiliation, the party attacking the legislatively drawn boundaries must show at the least that the legislature could have achieved its legitimate political objectives in alternative ways that are comparably consistent with traditional districting principles. That party must also show that those districting alternatives would have brought about significantly greater racial balance."

Justice Thomas, joined by the Chief Justice and Justices Scalia and Kennedy, dissented: "The issue for this Court is simply whether the District Court's factual finding—that racial considerations [predominated in drawing the district]—was clearly erroneous. . . . [P]erhaps the best evidence that the Court has emptied clear error review of meaningful content in the redistricting context . . . is the Court's foray into the minutiae of the record. I do not doubt this Court's ability to sift through volumes of facts or to argue its interpretation of those facts persuasively. But I do doubt the wisdom, efficiency, increased accuracy, and legitimacy of an extensive review that is any more searching than clear error review. . . .

"If I were the District Court, I might have reached the same conclusion that the Court does, that 'the evidence taken together . . . does not show that racial considerations predominated in the drawing of District 12's boundaries.' But I am not the trier of fact, and it is not my role to weigh evidence in the first instance. The only question that this Court should decide is whether the District Court's finding of racial predominance was clearly erroneous. In light of the direct evidence of racial motive and the inferences that may be drawn from the circumstantial evidence, I am satisfied that the District Court's finding was permissible, even if not compelled by the record."

And Justice Thomas "assume[d] because the District Court did, that the goal of protecting incumbents is legitimate, even where, as here, individuals are incumbents by virtue of their election in an unconstitutional racially gerrymandered district. No doubt this assumption is a questionable proposition. Because the issue was not

Equality and the Constitution

presented in this action, however, I do not read the Court's opinion as addressing it."

In light of *Easley*, consider Karlan, Easing the Spring: Strict Scrutiny and Affirmative Action After the Redistricting Cases, 43 Wm. & Mary L. Rev. 1569, 1586, 1602-03 (2002):

> [The Supreme Court's recognition that] the legislature "considered" race is, of course, not precisely the same thing as saying that the legislature was "aware" of race—the state of mind described in Shaw v. Reno and *Miller*.] The former at least suggests some level of volition as to the consequences of its decision, whereas the latter need not. Put in *Feeney* terms, it seems quite clear that the Supreme Court is prepared to conclude that North Carolina selected the challenged plan "at least in part 'because of,' not merely 'in spite of,'" the racial composition of the districts. Yet the Court did not apply strict scrutiny....
>
> [T]he redistricting cases suggest there is definitely more than one kind of strict scrutiny. Faced with the prospect of applying a form of strict scrutiny that threatened to resegregate state legislatures and congressional delegations, the Supreme Court has been unwilling to apply strict scrutiny strictly. It has constricted the domain in which strict scrutiny comes into play, permitting race to be taken into account when it is one factor among many and its inclusion produces districts that do not deviate too obviously from the sorts of districts created for other groups. It has also broadened the interests that can justify race-conscious redistricting, by holding that compliance with the Voting Rights Act's results tests can serve as a compelling state interest. The understanding of political equality embodied in the Act goes beyond what the Constitution itself demands. It requires states to arrange their electoral institutions to minimize the lingering effects of prior un-constitutional discrimination not otherwise chargeable to them, as well as to mitigate the impact of racially polarized voting that involves otherwise constitutionally protected private choice. In short, the theory of strict scrutiny yielded to the need for an electoral system that is equally open to members of minority groups.

Page 552. Before section 3 of the Note, add the following:

Might some government actions be shielded from improper purpose review because they are "mandatory" or "ministerial" rather than "discretionary"? Consider City of Cuyahoga Falls, Ohio v. Buckeye Community Hope Foundation, 538 U.S. 188 (2003). The City Council enacted legislation authorizing construction of a low-income housing complex to be built by Buckeye. Before construction began, opponents of the project mounted a referendum petition campaign. At public meetings, some of the opponents claimed that the project would cause crime and drug activity to escalate, that families with children would move in, and that the complex would attract a population similar to the one in the City's only African-American neighborhood.

The campaign culminated in a formal petition filed with the City requesting that the ordinance be repealed or submitted to a popular vote. Pursuant to a provision of the City Charter, the filing stayed the implementation of the project. Buckeye thereupon sought relief from a state court, claiming that the proposed referendum violated the Ohio Constitution. While this lawsuit was pending, Buckeye's request for a building permit was denied on the ground that the City Council ordinance could not take effect because of the petition. Eventually, Ohio voters passed the referendum, but the Ohio Supreme Court agreed with Buckeye that the referendum violated state law. Although Buckeye was then allowed to begin construction, it filed suit in federal court arguing that the City had violated the equal protection clause by delaying the project. The court of appeals held that Buckeye had produced enough evidence to survive summary judgment on the allegation that the City, by allowing the referendum petition to stay construction, gave effect to racial bias reflected in public opposition to the project. The Supreme Court, in an opinion by Justice O'Connor, unanimously reversed:

> [The court of appeals] erred in relying on cases in which we have subjected enacted, discretionary measures to equal protection scrutiny and treated decisionmakers' statements as evidence of such intent. . . .
>
> By placing the referendum on the ballot, the City did not enact the referendum and therefore cannot be said to have given effect to voters' allegedly discriminatory [motives]. Similarly, the city engineer, in refusing to issue the building permits while the referendum was pending, performed a nondiscretionary, ministerial act. [Respondents] point to no evidence suggesting that these official acts were themselves motivated by racial animus.

According to the Court, the fact that individuals who supported the petition drive may have done so for racially motivated reasons did not change this conclusion:

> [Statements] made by private individuals in the course of a citizen-driven petition drive, while sometimes relevant to equal protection analysis [do] not, in and of themselves, constitute state action for the purpose of the Fourteenth Amendment. . . .
>
> [By] adhering to charter procedures, city officials enabled public debate on the referendum to take place, thus advancing significant First Amendment interests. [Our] well established First Amendment admonition that "government may not prohibit the expression of an idea simply because society finds the idea itself offensive or disagreeable," [citing Texas v. Johnson, discussed at page 1314 of the

main text] dovetails with the notion that all citizens, regardless of the content of their ideas, have the right to petition their government.

If the Ohio Court had allowed the referendum result to stand, would discriminatory motives by private citizens who supported it make it vulnerable to constitutional challenge? According to Justice O'Connor, "statements by decisionmakers or referendum sponsors during deliberation over the referendum may constitute relevant evidence of discriminatory intent in a challenge to an ultimately enacted initiative. [But] respondents do not challenge an enacted referendum." Can this observation be reconciled with the First Amendment concerns quoted above? If it could be shown that voters supported a candidate for public office for racially discriminatory reasons, is the candidate's election unconstitutional? If the discriminatory motives of referendum sponsors can vitiate the legal effect of the enacted referendum (e.g., a permanent prohibition of the proposed project), why do not similar motives on the part of petition sponsors vitiate the legal effect of the petition (e.g., a temporary prohibition of the proposed project)?

In connection with equal protection standards appropriate when evaluating the results of referenda, consider Washington v. Seattle School District No. 1 at page 535 of the main text and Romer v. Evans at page 638 of the main text.

Page 552. At the end of section 3a of the Note, add the following:

Consider Karlan, Easing the Spring: Strict Scrutiny and Affirmative Action After the Redistricting Cases, 43 Wm. & Mary L. Rev. 1569, 1586 (2002):

In suggesting that compliance with sections 2 and 5 of the Voting Rights Act can constitute a compelling state interest [sufficient to justify race-specific districting], the Court has raised the possibility that congressional or executive understandings of equality that go beyond what the Constitution itself requires can provide a justification for race-conscious state action.

Is this suggestion consistent with the Court's current approach to section 5 of the fourteenth amendment (discussed supra at pages 224-30 of the main text)?

Page 590. Before subsection b of the Note, add the following:

Given the Supreme Court's recent affirmative action jurisprudence, what is the constitutional status of statutes prohibiting race-neutral practices that have a disproportionate racial impact? Recall that Washington v. Davis holds that government employers are under no *constitutional* obligation to refrain from using such practices. However, the Supreme Court has interpreted Title VII of the Civil Rights Act of 1964 to create a a *statutory* limitation on such practices. In Griggs v. Duke Power Co., 401 U.S. 424 (1971), the Court interpreted Title VII to prohibit race neutral employment criteria that have statistically disparate effects on different racial groups unless the criteria are adequately justified. Notice that the statute may require these employers to engage in what might be thought to amount to affirmative action. Thus, an employer using a race-neutral criterion must, in some circumstances, abandon it so as to avoid statistical underrepresentation of particular racial groups. Do *Croson* and *Adarand* mean that Title VII must now survive strict scrutiny?

In Primus, Equal Protection and Disparate Impact: Round Three, 117 Harv. L. Rev. 493, 585 (2003), the author argues that statutory disparate impact analysis can be made to cohere with current equal protection doctrine by treating it as "an evidentiary dragnet for hidden deliberate discrimination or present subconscious discrimination."

> But mediation of the tension between equal protection and disparate impact in this way would empty disparate impact doctrine of much of the content that makes it valuable. [Disparate impact doctrine] preserve[s] some awareness that existing racial hierarchies are products of past discrimination and that a level-playing-field approach today could help those hierarchies perpetuate themselves indefinitely. If disparate impact law is limited to issues of present states of mind, that structural and historical orientation will be lost. [That] would not be a good development.

Page 590. At the end of subsection b of the Note, add the following:

For criticism of the diversity argument, see Lawrence, Two Views of the River: A Critique of the Liberal Defense of Affirmative Action, 101 Colum. 928 (2001). Professor Lawrence argues that

> liberal supporters of affirmative action have used the diversity argument to defend affirmative action at elite universities and law schools without questioning the ways that traditional admissions criteria continue to perpetuate race and class privilege. [As] diversity has emerged as the dominant defense of affirmative action in the university setting, it has pushed other more radical substantive defenses to the background. These more radical arguments focus on the need to remedy

past discrimination, address present discriminatory practices, and reexamine traditional notions of merit and the role of universities in the reproduction of elites.

See also Bell, Diversity's Distractions, 103 Colum. L. Rev. 1622 (2003).

Page 590. Before subsection c of the Note, add the following:

GRUTTER v. BOLLINGER
539 U.S. 306 (2003)

JUSTICE O'CONNOR delivered the opinion of the Court.

This case requires us to decide whether the use of race as a factor in student admissions by the University of Michigan Law School [is] unlawful.

I

[The Law School's admission policy required admissions officials to evaluate each applicant based upon the entire file, including a personal statement, letters of recommendation, and an essay. Admissions officers were directed to take into account undergraduate grades and LSAT scores, but the policy made clear that no score led to either automatic admission or rejection. Instead, officials also looked to "soft variables" such as the enthusiasm of recommenders or the areas and difficulty of undergraduate course selection. The policy also emphasized diversity of various sorts. In this connection, the policy reaffirmed the Law School's commitment to "one particular type of diversity" that is "racial and ethnic diversity with special reference to the inclusion of students from groups which have been historically discriminated against, like African-Americans, Hispanics and Native Americans, who without this commitment might not be represented in our student body in meaningful numbers."

[Grutter, a white Michigan resident whose application to the Law School was denied, claimed that she was rejected because the Law School used race as a predominant factor in violation of the equal protection clause. The trial court heard testimony from the Law School's director of admissions, who said that he did not direct his staff to admit a particular percentage or number of minority students, but rather to consider an applicant's race along with all other factors. He further testified that at the height of the admissions season, he would frequently consult the "daily reports" indicating the racial and ethnic composition of the class in order to ensure that a "critical mass" of underrepresented minority students would be reached so as to realize the educational benefits of a diverse student body. He stressed, however, that he did not seek to admit any particular number or percentage of minority students.

[The Dean of the Law School also testified. He stated that "critical mass" meant numbers such that underrepresented minority students did not feel isolated or like spokespersons for their race. When asked about the extent to which race was considered, he stated that it varied from one applicant to another. In some cases, an applicant's race might play no role, while in others it might be a determinative factor.

[An expert witness testifying for Grutter examined data obtained from the Law School and concluded that membership in certain minority groups "is an extremely strong factor in the decision for acceptance" and that applicants from these groups "are given an extremely large allowance for admission." An expert testifying for the Law School predicted that if race were eliminated as a factor, the change would have a "very dramatic" negative effect on minority admissions.

[The District Court concluded that the Law School's use of race was unlawful, but the Court of Appeals reversed].

II

A

We last addressed the use of race in public higher education over 25 years ago. In the landmark *Bakke* case, we reviewed a racial set-aside program that reserved 16 out of 100 seats in a medical school class for members of certain minority groups. . . .

Since this Court's splintered decision in *Bakke*, Justice Powell's opinion announcing the judgment of the Court has served as the touchstone for constitutional analysis of race-conscious admissions policies. Public and private universities across the Nation have modeled their own admissions programs on Justice Powell's views on permissible race-conscious policies. . . .

[For] the reasons set out below, today we endorse Justice Powell's view that student body diversity is a compelling state interest that can justify the use of race in university admissions.

B

We have held that all racial classifications imposed by government "must be analyzed by a reviewing court under strict scrutiny." [*Adarand*]. . . .

Although all governmental uses of race are subject to strict scrutiny, not all are invalidated by it. [When] race-based action is necessary to further a compelling governmental interest, such action does not violate the constitutional guarantee of equal protection so long as the narrow-tailoring requirement is also satisfied.

Context matters when reviewing race-based governmental action under the Equal Protection Clause. [Not] every decision influenced by race is equally objectionable and strict scrutiny is designed to provide a framework for carefully examining the

III

A

With these principles in mind, we turn to the question whether the Law School's use of race is justified by a compelling state interest. [The] Law School asks us to recognize, in the context of higher education, a compelling state interest in student body diversity.

We first wish to dispel the notion that the Law School's argument has been foreclosed, either expressly or implicitly, by our affirmative-action cases decided since *Bakke*. [We] have never held that the only governmental use of race that can survive strict scrutiny is remedying past discrimination. Nor, since *Bakke*, have we directly addressed the use of race in the context of public higher education. Today, we hold that the Law School has a compelling interest in attaining a diverse student body.

The Law School's educational judgment that such diversity is essential to its educational mission is one to which we defer. The Law School's assessment that diversity will, in fact, yield educational benefits is substantiated by respondents and their *amici*. Our scrutiny of the interest asserted by the Law School is no less strict for taking into account complex educational judgments in an area that lies primarily within the expertise of the university. Our holding today is in keeping with our tradition of giving a degree of deference to a university's academic decisions, within constitutionally prescribed limits.

We have long recognized that, given the important purpose of public education and the expansive freedoms of speech and thought associated with the university environment, universities occupy a special niche in our constitutional tradition.

As part of its goal of "assembling a class that is both exceptionally academically qualified and broadly diverse," the Law School seeks to "enroll a 'critical mass' of minority students." The Law School's interest is not simply "to assure within its student body some specified percentage of a particular group merely because of its race or ethnic origin." [*Bakke* (opinion of Powell, J.)]. That would amount to outright racial balancing, which is patently unconstitutional.... Rather, the Law School's concept of critical mass is defined by reference to the educational benefits that diversity is designed to produce.

These benefits are substantial. As the District Court emphasized, the Law School's admissions policy promotes "cross-racial understanding," helps to break down racial stereotypes, and "enables [students] to better understand persons of different races." These benefits are "important and laudable," because "classroom discussion is livelier, more spirited, and simply more enlightening and interesting" when the students have "the greatest possible variety of backgrounds."

The Law School's claim of a compelling interest is further bolstered by its *amici*, who point to the educational benefits that flow from student body diversity. . . .

These benefits are not theoretical but real, as major American businesses have made clear that the skills needed in today's increasingly global marketplace can only be developed through exposure to widely diverse people, cultures, ideas, and viewpoints. Brief for 3M et al. as *Amici Curiae*; Brief for General Motors Corp. as *Amicus Curiae*. What is more, high-ranking retired officers and civilian leaders of the United States military assert that, "[b]ased on [their] decades of experience," a "highly qualified, racially diverse officer corps . . . is essential to the military's ability to fulfill its principle mission to provide national security." Brief for Julius W. Becton, Jr. et al. as *Amici Curiae*. The primary sources for the Nation's officer corps are the service academies and the Reserve Officers Training Corps (ROTC) the latter comprising students already admitted to participating colleges and universities. At present, "the military cannot achieve an officer corps that is *both* highly qualified *and* racially diverse unless the service academies and the ROTC used limited race-conscious recruiting and admissions policies." (emphasis in original). . . .

We have repeatedly acknowledged the overriding importance of preparing students for work and citizenship, describing education as pivotal to "sustaining our political and cultural heritage" with a fundamental role in maintaining the fabric of society. Plyler v. Doe, 457 U.S. 202, 221 (1982). . . .

Moreover, universities, and in particular, law schools, represent the training ground for a large number of our Nation's leaders. Sweatt v. Painter, 339 U.S. 629, 634 (1950) (describing law school as a "proving ground for legal learning and practice"). Individuals with law degrees occupy roughly half the state governorships, more than half the seats in the United States Senate, and more than a third of the seats in the United States House of Representatives. The pattern is even more striking when it comes to highly selective law schools. A handful of these schools accounts for 25 of the 100 United States Senators, 74 United States Courts of Appeals judges, and nearly 200 of the more than 600 United States District Court judges.

In order to cultivate a set of leaders with legitimacy in the eyes of the citizenry, it is necessary that the path to leadership be visibly open to talented and qualified individuals of every race and ethnicity. All members of our heterogeneous society must have confidence in the openness and integrity of the educational institutions that provide this training. As we have recognized, law schools "cannot be effective in isolation from the individuals and institutions with which the law interacts." See Sweatt v. Painter. Access to legal education (and thus the legal profession) must be inclusive of talented and qualified individuals of every race and ethnicity, so that all members of our heterogeneous society may participate in the educational institutions that provide the training and education necessary to succeed in America.

The Law School does not premise its need for critical mass on "any belief that minority students always (or even consistently) express some characteristic minority viewpoint on any issue." To the contrary, diminishing the force of such stereotypes is both a crucial part of the Law School's mission, and one that it cannot accomplish with only token numbers of minority students. Just as growing up in a particular region or having particular professional experiences is likely to affect an individual's views, so too is one's own, unique experience of being a racial minority in a society, like our own, in which race unfortunately still matters. The Law School has determined, based on its experience and expertise, that a "critical mass" of underrepresented minorities is necessary to further its compelling interest in securing the educational benefits of a diverse student body.

B

To be narrowly tailored, a race-conscious admissions program cannot use a quota system—it cannot "insulat[e] each category of applicants with certain desired qualifications from competition with all other applicants." *Bakke* (opinion of Powell, J.). Instead, a university may consider race or ethnicity only as a "'plus' in a particular applicant's file, without 'insulat[ing]' the individual from comparison with all other candidates for the available seats." *Id.* In other words, an admissions program must be "flexible enough to consider all pertinent elements of diversity in light of the particular qualifications of each applicant, and to place them on the same footing for consideration, although not necessarily according them the same weight." *Ibid.*

We find that the Law School's admissions program bears the hallmarks of a narrowly tailored plan. . . .

We are satisfied that the Law School's admissions program, like the Harvard plan described by Justice Powell, does not operate as a quota. Properly understood, a "quota" is a program in which a certain fixed number or proportion of opportunities are "reserved exclusively for certain minority groups." Richmond v. J. A. Croson Co., (plurality opinion). [In] contrast, "a permissible goal . . . require[s] only a good-faith effort . . . to come within a range demarcated by the goal itself," and permits consideration of race as a "plus" factor in any given case while still ensuring that each candidate "compete[s] with all other qualified applicants". . . .

The Law School's goal of attaining a critical mass of underrepresented minority students does not transform its program into a quota. As the Harvard plan described by Justice Powell recognized, there is of course "some relationship between numbers and achieving the benefits to be derived from a diverse student body, and between numbers and providing a reasonable environment for those students admitted." [*Bakke*]. "[S]ome attention to numbers," without more, does not transform a flexible admissions system into a rigid quota. *Ibid.* Nor, as Justice Kennedy posits, does the Law School's consultation of the "daily reports," which keep track of the racial and ethnic composition of the class (as well as of residency and gender), "suggest[ ] there was no further attempt at individual review save for race itself" during the final stages of the admissions process. To the contrary, the Law School's admissions officers testified without contradiction that they never gave race any more or less weight based on the information contained in these reports. Moreover, as Justice Kennedy concedes, between 1993 and 2000, the number of African-American, Latino, and Native-American students in each class at the Law School varied from 13.5 to 20.1 percent, a range inconsistent with a quota.

The Chief Justice believes that the Law School's policy conceals an attempt to achieve racial balancing, and cites admissions data to contend that the Law School discriminates among different groups within the critical mass. But, as The Chief Justice concedes, the number of underrepresented minority students who ultimately enroll in the Law School differs substantially from their representation in the applicant pool and varies considerably for each group from year to year.

That a race-conscious admissions program does not operate as a quota does not, by itself, satisfy the requirement of individualized consideration. When using race as a "plus" factor in university admissions, a university's admissions program must remain flexible enough to ensure that each applicant is evaluated as an individual and not in a way that makes an applicant's race or ethnicity [dispositive].

Here, the Law School engages in a highly individualized, holistic review of each applicant's file, giving serious consideration to all the ways an applicant might contribute to a diverse educational environment. The Law School affords this individualized consideration to applicants of all races. There is no policy, either *de jure* or *de facto*, of automatic acceptance or rejection based on any single "soft" variable. Unlike the program at issue in Gratz v. Bollinger, the Law School awards no mechanical, predetermined diversity "bonuses" based on race or ethnicity. . . .

We also find that, like the Harvard plan Justice Powell referenced in *Bakke*, the Law School's race-conscious admissions program adequately ensures that all factors that may contribute to student body diversity are meaningfully considered alongside race in admissions decisions. With respect to the use of race itself, all underrepresented minority students admitted by the Law School have been deemed qualified. By virtue of our Nation's struggle with racial inequality, such students are both likely to have experiences of particular importance to the Law School's mission, and less likely to be admitted in meaningful numbers on criteria that ignore those experiences.

The Law School does not, however, limit in any way the broad range of qualities and experiences that may be considered valuable contributions to student body diversity. To the contrary, the 1992 policy makes clear "[t]here are many possible bases for diversity admissions," and provides examples of admittees who have lived or traveled widely abroad, are fluent in several languages, have overcome personal adversity and family hardship, have exceptional records of extensive community service, and have had successful careers in other fields. . . .

What is more, the Law School actually gives substantial weight to diversity factors besides race. The Law School frequently accepts nonminority applicants with grades and test scores lower than underrepresented minority applicants (and other nonminority applicants) who are rejected.

Petitioner and the United States argue that the Law School's plan is not narrowly tailored because race-neutral means exist to obtain the educational benefits of student body diversity that the Law School seeks. We disagree. Narrow tailoring does not require exhaustion of every conceivable race-neutral alternative. Nor does it require a university to choose between maintaining a reputation for excellence or fulfilling a commitment to provide educational opportunities to members of all racial groups. Narrow tailoring does, however, require serious, good faith consideration of workable race-neutral alternatives that will achieve the diversity the university seeks.

We agree with the Court of Appeals that the Law School sufficiently considered workable race-neutral alternatives. The District Court took the Law School to task for failing to consider race-neutral alternatives such as "using a lottery system" or "decreasing the emphasis for all applicants on undergraduate GPA and LSAT scores." But these alternatives would require a dramatic sacrifice of diversity, the academic quality of all admitted students, or both.

The Law School's current admissions program considers race as one factor among many, in an effort to assemble a student body that is diverse in ways broader than race. Because a lottery would make that kind of nuanced judgment impossible, it would effectively sacrifice all other educational values, not to mention every other kind of diversity. So too with the suggestion that the Law School simply lower admissions standards for all students, a drastic remedy that would require the Law School to become a much different institution and sacrifice a vital component of its educational mission. The United States advocates "percentage plans," recently adopted by public undergraduate institutions in Texas, Florida, and California to guarantee admission to all students above a certain class-rank threshold in every high school in the State. The United States does not, however, explain how such plans could work for graduate and professional schools. Moreover, even assuming such plans are race-neutral, they may preclude the university from conducting the individualized assessments necessary to assemble a student body that is not just racially diverse, but diverse along all the qualities valued by the university. We are satisfied that the Law School adequately considered race-neutral alternatives currently capable of producing a critical mass without forcing the Law School to abandon the academic selectivity that is the cornerstone of its educational mission. . . .

We are mindful, however, that "[a] core purpose of the Fourteenth Amendment was to do away with all governmentally imposed discrimination based on race." Palmore v. Sidoti. Accordingly, race-conscious admissions policies must be limited in time. This requirement reflects that racial classifications, however compelling their goals, are potentially so dangerous that they may be employed no more broadly than the interest demands. Enshrining a permanent justification for racial preferences would offend this fundamental equal protection principle. We see no reason to exempt race-conscious admissions programs from the requirement that all governmental use of race must have a logical end point. The Law School, too, concedes that all "race-conscious programs must have reasonable durational limits."

In the context of higher education, the durational requirement can be met by sunset provisions in race-conscious admissions policies and periodic reviews to determine whether racial preferences are still necessary to achieve student body diversity. Universities in California, Florida, and Washington State, where racial preferences in admissions are prohibited by state law, are currently engaged in experimenting with a wide variety of alternative approaches. Universities in other States can and should draw on the most promising aspects of these race-neutral alternatives as they develop.

The requirement that all race-conscious admissions programs have a termination point "assure[s] all citizens that the deviation from the norm of equal treatment of all racial and ethnic groups is a temporary matter, a measure taken in the service of the goal of equality itself." Richmond v. J. A. Croson Co. (plurality opinion).

We take the Law School at its word that it would "like nothing better than to find a race-neutral admissions formula" and will terminate its race-conscious admissions program as soon as practicable. It has been 25 years since Justice Powell first approved the use of race to further an interest in student body diversity in the context of public higher education. Since that time, the number of minority applicants with high grades and test scores has indeed increased. We expect that 25 years from now, the use of racial preferences will no longer be necessary to further the interest approved today.

IV

In summary, the Equal Protection Clause does not prohibit the Law School's narrowly tailored use of race in admissions decisions to further a compelling interest in obtaining the educational benefits that flow from a diverse student body. [The] judgment of the Court of Appeals for the Sixth Circuit, accordingly, is affirmed.

JUSTICE GINSBURG, with whom JUSTICE BREYER joins, concurring. . . .

The Court [observes] that "[i]t has been 25 years since Justice Powell [first] approved the use of race to further an interest in student body diversity in the context of public higher education." For at least part of that time, however, the law could not fairly be described as "settled," and in some regions of the Nation, overtly race-conscious admissions policies have been proscribed. Moreover, it was only 25 years before *Bakke* that this Court declared public school segregation unconstitutional, a declaration that, after prolonged resistance, yielded an end to a law-enforced racial caste system, itself the legacy of centuries of slavery.

It is well documented that conscious and unconscious race bias, even rank discrimination based on race, remain alive in our land, impeding realization of our highest values and ideals. As to public education, data for the years 2000-2001 show that 71.6% of African-American children and 76.3% of Hispanic children attended a school in which minorities made up a majority of the student body. And schools in predominantly minority communities lag far behind others measured by the educational resources available to them.

However strong the public's desire for improved education systems may be, it remains the current reality that many minority students encounter markedly inadequate and unequal educational opportunities. Despite these inequalities, some minority students are able to meet the high threshold requirements set for admission to the country's finest undergraduate and graduate educational institutions. As lower school education in minority communities improves, an increase in the number of such students may be anticipated. From today's vantage point, one may hope, but not firmly forecast, that over the next generation's span, progress toward nondiscrimination and genuinely equal opportunity will make it safe to sunset affirmative action.

CHIEF JUSTICE REHNQUIST, with whom JUSTICE SCALIA, JUSTICE KENNEDY, and JUSTICE THOMAS join, dissenting.

I agree with the Court that, "in the limited circumstance when drawing racial distinctions is permissible," the government must ensure that its means are narrowly tailored to achieve a compelling state interest. I do not believe, however, that the University of Michigan Law School's [means] are narrowly tailored to the interest it asserts. The Law School claims it must take the steps it does to achieve a "critical mass" of underrepresented minority students. But its actual program bears no relation to this asserted goal. Stripped of its "critical mass" veil, the Law School's program is revealed as a naked effort to achieve racial balancing. . . .

Although the Court recites the language of [strict] scrutiny analysis, its application of that review is unprecedented in its deference. . . .

In practice, the Law School's program bears little or no relation to its asserted goal of achieving "critical mass." Respondents explain that the Law School seeks to accumulate a "critical mass" of *each* underrepresented minority group. But the record demonstrates that the Law School's admissions practices with respect to these groups differ dramatically and cannot be defended under any consistent use of the term "critical mass."

From 1995 through 2000, the Law School admitted between 1,130 and 1,310 students. Of those, between 13 and 19 were Native American, between 91 and 108 were African-Americans, and between 47 and 56 were Hispanic. If the Law School is admitting between 91 and 108 African-Americans in order to achieve "critical mass," thereby preventing African-American students from feeling "isolated or like spokespersons for their race," one would think that a number of the same order of magnitude would be necessary to accomplish the same purpose for Hispanics and Native Americans. Similarly, even if all of the Native American applicants admitted in a given year matriculate, which the record demonstrates is not at all the case, how can this possibly constitute a "critical mass" of Native Americans in a class of over 350 students? In order for this pattern of admission to be consistent with the Law School's explanation of "critical mass," one would have to believe that the objectives of "critical mass" offered by respondents are achieved with only half the number of Hispanics and one-sixth the number of Native Americans as compared to African-Americans. But respondents offer no race-specific reasons for such disparities. Instead, they simply emphasize the importance of achieving "critical mass," without any explanation of why that concept is applied differently among the three underrepresented minority groups.

These different numbers, moreover, come only as a result of substantially different treatment among the three underrepresented minority groups, as is apparent in an example offered by the Law School and highlighted by the Court: The school asserts that it "frequently accepts nonminority applicants with grades and test scores lower than underrepresented minority applicants (and other nonminority applicants) who are rejected." Specifically, the Law School states that "[s]ixty-nine minority applicants were rejected between 1995 and 2000 with at least a 3.5 [Grade Point Average (GPA)] and a [score of] 159 or higher on the [Law School Admissions Test (LSAT)]" while a number of Caucasian and Asian-American applicants with similar or lower scores were admitted.

Review of the record reveals only 67 such individuals. Of these 67 individuals, 56 were Hispanic, while only 6 were African-American, and only 5 were Native American. This discrepancy reflects a consistent practice. . . .

[Respondents] have *never* offered any race-specific arguments explaining why significantly more individuals from one underrepresented minority group are needed in order to achieve "critical mass" or further student body diversity. They certainly have not explained why Hispanics, who they have said are among "the groups most isolated by racial barriers in our country," should have their admission capped out in this manner. [The] Law School's disparate admissions practices with respect to these minority groups demonstrate that its alleged goal of "critical mass" is simply a sham. [Surely] strict scrutiny cannot permit these sort of disparities without at least some explanation.

Only when the "critical mass" label is discarded does a likely explanation for these numbers emerge. . . .

[The] correlation between the percentage of the Law School's pool of applicants who are members of the three minority groups and the percentage of the admitted applicants who are members of these same groups is far too precise to be dismissed as merely the result of the school paying "some attention to [the] numbers." [From] 1995 through 2000 the percentage of admitted applicants who were members of these minority groups closely tracked the percentage of individuals in the school's applicant pool who were from the same groups. . . .

For example, in 1995, when 9.7% of the applicant pool was African-American, 9.4% of the admitted class was African-American. By 2000, only 7.5% of the applicant pool was African-American, and 7.3% of the admitted class was African-American. This correlation is striking. [The] tight correlation between the percentage of applicants and admittees of a given race, therefore, must result from careful race based planning by the Law School. It suggests a formula for admission based on the aspirational assumption that all applicants are equally qualified academically, and therefore that the proportion of each group admitted should be the same as the proportion of that group in the applicant pool.

Not only do respondents fail to explain this phenomenon, they attempt to obscure it. See [the Law School's brief] ("The Law School's minority enrollment percentages . . . diverged from the percentages in the applicant pool by as much as 17.7% from 1995-2000"). But the divergence between the percentages of underrepresented minorities in the applicant pool and in the *enrolled* classes is not the only relevant comparison. In fact, it may not be the most relevant comparison. The Law School cannot precisely control which of its admitted applicants decide to attend the university. But it can and, as the numbers demonstrate, clearly does employ racial preferences in extending offers of admission. Indeed, the ostensibly flexible nature of the Law School's admissions program that the Court finds appealing, appears to be, in practice, a carefully managed program designed to ensure proportionate representation of applicants from selected minority groups. . . .

Finally, I believe that the Law School's program fails strict scrutiny because it is devoid of any reasonably precise time limit on the Law School's use of race in admissions. . . .

The Court suggests a possible 25-year limitation on the Law School's current program. Respondents, on the other hand, remain more ambiguous, explaining that "the Law School of course recognizes that race- conscious programs must have reasonable durational limits, and the Sixth Circuit properly found such a limit in the Law School's resolve to cease considering race when genuine race-neutral alternatives become available." These discussions of a time limit are the vaguest of assurances. In truth, they permit the Law School's use of racial preferences on a seemingly permanent basis. Thus, an important component of strict scrutiny—that a program be limited in time—is casually subverted.

The Court, in an unprecedented display of deference under our strict scrutiny analysis, upholds the Law School's program despite its obvious flaws. We have said that when it comes to the use of race, the connection between the ends and the means used to attain them must be precise. But here the flaw is deeper than that; it is not merely a question of "fit" between ends and means. Here the means actually used are forbidden by the Equal Protection Clause of the Constitution.

JUSTICE KENNEDY, dissenting.

The separate opinion by Justice Powell in *Regents of Univ. of Cal. v. Bakke* is based on the principle that a university admissions program may take account of race as one, nonpredominant factor in a system designed to consider each applicant as an individual, provided the program can meet the test of strict scrutiny by the judiciary.

This is a unitary formulation. If strict scrutiny is abandoned or manipulated to distort its real and accepted meaning, the Court lacks authority to approve the use of race even in this modest, limited way. . . .

It is unfortunate, however, that the Court takes the first part of Justice Powell's rule but abandons the second. Having approved the use of race as a factor in the admissions process, the majority proceeds to nullify the essential safeguard Justice Powell insisted upon as the precondition of the approval. The safeguard was rigorous judicial review, with strict scrutiny as the controlling standard. . . .

The Court, in a review that is nothing short of perfunctory, accepts the University of Michigan Law School's assurances that its admissions process meets with constitutional requirements. The majority fails to confront the reality of how the Law School's admissions policy is implemented. The dissenting opinion by The Chief Justice, which I join in full, demonstrates beyond question why the concept of critical mass is a delusion used by the Law School to mask its attempt to make race an automatic factor in most instances and to achieve numerical goals indistinguishable from quotas. . . .

The Law School has not demonstrated how individual consideration is, or can be, preserved [given] the instruction to attain what it calls critical mass. In fact the evidence shows otherwise. There was little deviation among admitted minority students during the years from 1995 to 1998. The percentage of enrolled minorities fluctuated only by 0.3%, from 13.5% to 13.8%. The number of minority students to whom offers were extended varied by just a slightly greater magnitude of 2.2%, from the high of 15.6% in 1995 to the low of 13.4% in 1998.

[Admittedly,] there were greater fluctuations among enrolled minorities in the preceding years, 1987-1994, by as much as 5 or 6%. The percentage of minority offers, however, at no point fell below 12%, historically defined by the Law School as the bottom of its critical mass range. The greater variance during the earlier years, in any event, does not dispel suspicion that the school engaged in racial balancing. The data would be consistent with an inference that the Law School modified its target only twice, in 1991 (from 13% to 19%), and then again in 1995 (back from 20% to 13%). The intervening year, 1993, when the percentage dropped to 14.5%, could be an aberration, caused by the school's miscalculation as to how many applicants with offers would accept or by its redefinition, made in April 1992, of which minority groups were entitled to race-based preference. . . .

The narrow fluctuation band raises an inference that the Law School subverted individual determination, and strict scrutiny requires the Law School to overcome the inference. . . .

The Court's refusal to apply meaningful strict scrutiny will lead to serious consequences. By deferring to the law schools' choice of minority admissions programs, the courts will lose the talents and resources of the faculties and administrators in devising new and fairer ways to ensure individual consideration. Constant and rigorous judicial review forces the law school faculties to undertake their responsibilities as state employees in this most sensitive of areas with utmost fidelity to the mandate of the Constitution. Dean Allan Stillwagon, who directed the Law School's Office of Admissions from 1979 to 1990, explained the difficulties he encountered in defining racial groups entitled to benefit under the School's affirmative action policy. He testified that faculty members were "breathtakingly cynical" in deciding who would qualify as a member of underrepresented minorities. An example he offered was faculty debate as to whether Cubans should be counted as Hispanics: One professor objected on the grounds that Cubans were Republicans. Many academics at other law schools who are "affirmative action's more forthright defenders readily concede that diversity is merely the current rationale of convenience for a policy that they prefer to justify on other grounds." Schuck, Affirmative Action: Past, Present, and Future, 20 Yale L. & Pol'y Rev. 1, 34 (2002) (citing Levinson, Diversity, 2 U. Pa. J. Const. L. 573, 577-578 (2000); Rubenfeld, Affirmative Action, 107 Yale L. J. 427, 471 (1997)). This is not to suggest the faculty at Michigan or other law schools do not pursue aspirations they consider laudable and consistent with our constitutional traditions. It is but further evidence of the necessity for scrutiny that is real, not feigned, where the corrosive category of race is a factor in decisionmaking. . . .

It is difficult to assess the Court's pronouncement that race-conscious admissions programs will be unnecessary 25 years from now. If it is intended to mitigate the damage the Court does to the concept of strict scrutiny, neither petitioners nor other rejected law school applicants will find solace in knowing the basic protection put in place by Justice Powell will be suspended for a full quarter of a century. Deference is antithetical to strict scrutiny, not consistent with it.

As to the interpretation that the opinion contains its own self-destruct mechanism, the majority's abandonment of strict scrutiny undermines this objective. Were the courts to apply a searching standard to race-based admissions schemes, that would force educational institutions to seriously explore race-neutral alternatives. The Court, by contrast, is willing to be satisfied by the Law School's profession of its own good faith. . . .

It is regrettable the Court's important holding allowing racial minorities to have their special circumstances considered in order to improve their educational opportunities is accompanied by a suspension of the strict scrutiny which was the predicate of allowing race to be considered in the first place. If the Court abdicates its constitutional duty to give strict scrutiny to the use of race in university admissions, it negates my authority to approve the use of race in pursuit of student diversity. The Constitution cannot confer the right to classify on the basis of race even in this special context absent searching judicial review. For these reasons, though I reiterate my approval of giving appropriate consideration to race in this one context, I must dissent in the present case.

JUSTICE SCALIA, with whom JUSTICE THOMAS joins, concurring in part and dissenting in part. . . .

The "educational benefit" that the University of Michigan seeks to achieve by racial discrimination consists, according to the Court, of "cross-racial understanding," and "better prepar[ation of] students for an increasingly diverse workforce and society," all of which is necessary not only for work, but also for good "citizenship," This is not, of course, an "educational benefit" on which students will be graded on their Law School transcript (Works and Plays Well with Others: B+) or tested by the bar examiners (Q: Describe in 500 words or less your cross-racial understanding). For it is a lesson of life rather than law—essentially the same lesson taught to (or rather learned by, for it cannot be "taught" in the usual sense) people three feet shorter and twenty years younger than the full-grown adults at the University of Michigan Law School, in institutions ranging from Boy Scout troops to public-school kindergartens. If properly considered an "educational benefit" at all, it is surely not one that is either uniquely relevant to law school or uniquely "teachable" in a formal educational setting. *And therefore:* If it is appropriate for the University of Michigan Law School to use racial discrimination for the purpose of putting together a "critical mass" that will convey generic lessons in socialization and good citizenship, surely it is no less appropriate—indeed, *particularly* appropriate—for the civil service system of the State of Michigan to do so. There, also, those exposed to "critical masses" of certain races will presumably become better Americans, better Michiganders, better civil servants. And surely private employers cannot be criticized—indeed, should be praised—if they also "teach" good citizenship to their adult employees through a patriotic, all-American system of racial discrimination in hiring. The nonminority individuals who are deprived of a legal education, a civil service job, or any job at all by reason of their skin color will surely understand.

Unlike a clear constitutional holding that racial preferences in state educational institutions are impermissible, or even a clear anticonstitutional holding that racial preferences in state educational institutions are OK, today's *Grutter-Gratz* split double header seems perversely designed to prolong the controversy and the litigation. Some future lawsuits will presumably focus on whether the discriminatory scheme in question contains enough evaluation of the applicant "as an individual," and sufficiently avoids "separate admissions tracks" to fall under *Grutter* rather than *Gratz*. Some will focus on whether a university has gone beyond the bounds of a "good faith effort" and has so zealously pursued its "critical mass" as to make it an unconstitutional *de facto* quota system, rather than merely "a permissible goal." Other lawsuits may focus on whether, in the particular setting at issue, any educational benefits flow from racial diversity. (That issue was not contested in *Grutter*; and while the opinion accords "a degree of deference to a university's academic decisions," "deference does not imply abandonment or abdication of judicial review," Miller-El v. Cockrell, 537 U.S. 322, 340 (2003).) Still other suits may challenge the bona fides of the institution's expressed commitment to the educational benefits of diversity that immunize the discriminatory scheme in *Grutter*. (Tempting targets, one would suppose, will be those universities that talk the talk of multiculturalism and racial diversity in the courts but walk the walk of tribalism and racial segregation on their campuses—through minority-only student organizations, separate minority housing opportunities, separate minority student centers, even separate minority-only graduation ceremonies.) And still other suits may claim that the institution's racial preferences have gone below or above the mystical *Grutter*-approved "critical mass." Finally, litigation can be expected on behalf of minority groups intentionally short changed in the institution's composition of its generic minority "critical mass." I do not look forward to any of these cases. The Constitution proscribes government discrimination on the basis of race, and state-provided education is no exception.

JUSTICE THOMAS, with whom JUSTICE SCALIA joins as to Parts I-VII, concurring in part and dissenting in part.

Frederick Douglass, speaking to a group of abolitionists almost 140 years ago, delivered a message lost on today's majority:

> [I]n regard to the colored people, there is always more that is benevolent, I perceive, than just, manifested towards us. What I ask for the negro is not benevolence, not pity, not sympathy, but simply *justice*. The American people have always been anxious to know what they shall do with us. . . . I have had but one answer from the beginning. Do nothing with us! Your doing with us has already played the mischief with us. Do nothing with us! If the apples will not remain on the tree of their own strength, if they are worm-eaten at the core, if they are early ripe and disposed to fall, let them fall! . . . And if the negro cannot stand on his own legs, let him fall also. All I ask is, give him a chance to stand on his own legs! Let him alone! . . . [Y]our interference is doing him positive injury.

What the Black Man Wants: An Address Delivered in Boston, Massachusetts, on 26 January 1865, reprinted in 4 The Frederick Douglass Papers 59, 68 (J. Blassingame & J. McKivigan eds. 1991) (emphasis in original).

Like Douglass, I believe blacks can achieve in every avenue of American life without the meddling of university administrators. Because I wish to see all students succeed whatever their color, I share, in some respect, the sympathies of those who sponsor the type of discrimination advanced by the University of Michigan Law School (Law School). The Constitution does not, however, tolerate institutional devotion to the status quo in admissions policies when such devotion ripens into racial discrimination. Nor does the Constitution countenance the unprecedented deference the Court gives to the Law School, an approach inconsistent with the very concept of "strict scrutiny."

No one would argue that a university could set up a lower general admission standard and then impose heightened requirements only on black applicants. Similarly, a university may not maintain a high admission standard and grant exemptions to favored races. The Law School, of its own choosing, and for its own purposes, maintains an exclusionary admissions system that it knows produces racially disproportionate results. Racial discrimination is not a permissible solution to the self-inflicted wounds of this elitist admissions policy.

The majority upholds the Law School's racial discrimination not by interpreting the people's Constitution, but by responding to a faddish slogan of the cognoscenti. Nevertheless, I concur in part in the Court's opinion. First, I agree with the Court insofar as its decision, which approves of only one racial classification, confirms that further use of race in admissions remains unlawful. Second, I agree with the Court's holding that racial discrimination in higher education admissions will be illegal in 25 years. I respectfully dissent from the remainder of the Court's opinion and the judgment, however, because I believe that the Law School's current use of race violates the Equal Protection Clause and that the Constitution means the same thing today as it will in 300 months.

I

The majority agrees that the Law School's racial discrimination should be subjected to strict scrutiny. Before applying that standard to this case, I will briefly revisit the Court's treatment of racial classifications. [Justice Thomas summarizes the Court's cases upholding and invalidating racial classifications based on strict scrutiny.] . . .

Where the Court has accepted only national security, [*Korematsu*] and rejected even the best interests of a child, [Palmore v. Sidoti] as a justification for racial discrimination, I conclude that only those measures the State must take to provide a bulwark against anarchy, or to prevent violence, will constitute a "pressing public necessity."

The Constitution abhors classifications based on race, not only because those classifications can harm favored races or are based on illegitimate motives, but also because every time the government places citizens on racial registers and makes race relevant to the provision of burdens or benefits, it demeans us all. . . . .

II

Unlike the majority, I seek to define with precision the interest being asserted by the Law School before determining whether that interest is so compelling as to justify racial discrimination. The Law School maintains that it wishes to obtain "educational benefits that flow from student body diversity." This statement must be evaluated carefully, because it implies that both "diversity" and "educational benefits" are components of the Law School's compelling state interest. Additionally, the Law School's refusal to entertain certain changes in its admissions process and status indicates that the compelling state interest it seeks to validate is actually broader than might appear at first glance.

Undoubtedly there are other ways to "better" the education of law students aside from ensuring that the student body contains a "critical mass" of underrepresented minority students. . . .

One must also consider the Law School's refusal to entertain changes to its current admissions system that might produce the same educational benefits. The Law School adamantly disclaims any race-neutral alternative that would reduce "academic selectivity," which would in turn "require the Law School to become a very different institution, and to sacrifice a core part of its educational mission." In other words, the Law School seeks to improve marginally the education it offers without sacrificing too much of its exclusivity and elite status.

The proffered interest that the majority vindicates today, then, is not simply "diversity." Instead the Court upholds the use of racial discrimination as a tool to advance the Law School's interest in offering a marginally superior education while maintaining an elite institution. Unless each constituent part of this state interest is of pressing public necessity, the Law School's use of race is unconstitutional. I find each of them to fall far short of this standard.

III. . . .

B

Under the proper standard, there is no pressing public necessity in maintaining a public law school at all and, it follows, certainly not an elite law school. Likewise, marginal improvements in legal education do not qualify as a compelling state interest.

1

While legal education at a public university may be good policy or otherwise laudable, it is obviously not a pressing public necessity when the correct legal standard is applied. Additionally, circumstantial evidence as to whether a state activity is of pressing public necessity can be obtained by asking whether all States feel compelled to engage in that activity. [In] this sense, the absence of a public, American Bar Association (ABA) accredited, law school in Alaska, Delaware, Massachusetts, New Hampshire, and Rhode Island, provides further evidence that Michigan's maintenance of the Law School does not constitute a compelling state interest.

2

[Still,] even assuming that a State may, under appropriate circumstances, demonstrate a cognizable interest in having an elite law school, Michigan has failed to do so here.

This Court has limited the scope of equal protection review to interests and activities that occur within that State's jurisdiction. . . .

The only cognizable state interests vindicated by operating a public law school are, therefore, the education of that State's citizens and the training of that State's lawyers. . . .

The Law School today, however, does precious little training of those attorneys who will serve the citizens of Michigan. [Less] than 16% of the Law School's graduating class elects to stay in Michigan after law school. . . .

It does not take a social scientist to conclude that it is precisely the Law School's status as an elite institution that causes it to be a way-station for the rest of the country's lawyers, rather than a training ground for those who will remain in Michigan. The Law School's decision to be an elite institution does little to advance the welfare of the people of Michigan or any cognizable interest of the State of Michigan. . . .

IV. . . .

With the adoption of different admissions methods, such as accepting all students who meet minimum qualifications, the Law School could achieve its vision of the racially aesthetic student body without the use of racial discrimination. The Law School concedes this, but the Court holds, implicitly and under the guise of narrow tailoring, that the Law School has a compelling state interest in doing what it wants to do. I cannot agree. First, under strict scrutiny, the Law School's assessment of the benefits of racial discrimination and devotion to the admissions status quo are not entitled to any sort of deference, grounded in the First Amendment or anywhere else. Second, even if its "academic selectivity" must be maintained at all costs along with racial discrimination, the Court ignores the fact that other top law schools have succeeded in meeting their aesthetic demands without racial discrimination.

A

The Court bases its unprecedented deference to the Law School—a deference antithetical to strict scrutiny—on an idea of "educational autonomy" grounded in the First Amendment. In my view, there is no basis for a right of public universities to do what would otherwise violate the Equal Protection Clause. . . .

B

1

The Court's deference to the Law School's conclusion that its racial experimentation leads to educational benefits will, if adhered to, have serious collateral consequences. The Court relies heavily on social science evidence to justify its deference.

The Court never acknowledges, however, the growing evidence that racial (and other sorts) of heterogeneity actually impairs learning among black students. [Justice Thomas cites studies showing that black students attending historically black colleges (HBCs) report higher academic achievement than those attending predominantly white colleges.] . . . .

The majority grants deference to the Law School's "assessment that diversity will, in fact, yield educational benefits." It follows, therefore, that an HBC's assessment that racial homogeneity will yield educational benefits would similarly be given deference. An HBC's rejection of white applicants in order to maintain racial homogeneity seems permissible, therefore, under the majority's view of the Equal Protection Clause. But see United States v. Fordice. (Thomas, J., concurring) ("Obviously, a State cannot maintain . . . traditions by closing particular institutions, historically white or historically black, to particular racial groups"). Contained within today's majority opinion is the seed of a new constitutional justification for a concept I thought long and rightly rejected—racial segregation. . . .

C

The sky has not fallen at Boalt Hall at the University of California, Berkeley. Prior to Proposition 209's adoption of Cal. Const., Art. 1, § 31(a), which bars the State from "grant[ing] preferential treatment . . . on the basis of race . . . in the operation of . . . public education," Boalt Hall enrolled 20 blacks and 28 Hispanics in its first-year class for 1996. In 2002, without deploying express racial discrimination in admissions, Boalt's entering class enrolled 14 blacks and 36 Hispanics. Total underrepresented minority student enrollment at Boalt Hall now exceeds 1996 levels. Apparently the Law School cannot be counted on to be as resourceful. The Court is willfully blind to the very real experience in California and elsewhere, which raises the inference that institutions with "reputation[s] for excellence," rivaling the Law School's have satisfied their sense of mission without resorting to prohibited racial discrimination.

V

Putting aside the absence of any legal support for the majority's reflexive deference, there is much to be said for the view that the use of tests and other measures to "predict" academic performance is a poor substitute for a system that gives every applicant a chance to prove he can succeed in the study of law. The rallying cry that in the absence of racial discrimination in admissions there would be a true meritocracy ignores the fact that the entire process is poisoned by numerous exceptions to "merit." For example, in the national debate on racial discrimination in higher education admissions, much has been made of the fact that elite institutions utilize a so-called "legacy" preference to give the children of alumni an advantage in admissions.

This, and other, exceptions to a "true" meritocracy give the lie to protestations that merit admissions are in fact the order of the day at the Nation's universities. The Equal Protection Clause does not, however, prohibit the use of unseemly legacy preferences or many other kinds of arbitrary admissions procedures. What the Equal Protection Clause does prohibit are classifications made on the basis of race. So while legacy preferences can stand under the Constitution, racial discrimination cannot. I will not twist the Constitution to invalidate legacy preferences or otherwise impose my vision of higher education admissions on the Nation. The majority should similarly stay its impulse to validate faddish racial discrimination the Constitution clearly forbids.

In any event, there is nothing ancient, honorable, or constitutionally protected about "selective" admissions. The University of Michigan should be well aware that alternative methods have historically been used for the admission of students, for it brought to this country the German certificate system in the late-19th century . . . Under this system, a secondary school was certified by a university so that any graduate who completed the course offered by the school was offered admission to the university. The certification regime supplemented, and later virtually replaced (at least in the Midwest), the prior regime of rigorous subject-matter entrance examinations. The facially race-neutral "percent plans" now used in Texas, California, and Florida are in many ways the descendents of the certificate system.

Certification was replaced by selective admissions in the beginning of the 20th century, as universities sought to exercise more control over the composition of their student bodies. Since its inception, selective admissions has been the vehicle for racial, ethnic, and religious tinkering and experimentation by university administrators. The initial driving force for the relocation of the selective function from the high school to the universities was the same desire to select racial winners and losers that the Law School exhibits today. Columbia, Harvard, and others infamously determined that they had "too many" Jews, just as today the Law School argues it would have "too many" whites if it could not discriminate in its admissions process.

Columbia employed intelligence tests precisely because Jewish applicants, who were predominantly immigrants, scored worse on such tests. Thus, Columbia could claim (falsely) that "[w]e have not eliminated boys because they were Jews and do not propose to do so. We have honestly attempted to eliminate the lowest grade of applicant [through the use of intelligence testing] and it turns out that a good many of the low grade men are New York City Jews." In other words, the tests were adopted with full knowledge of their disparate impact.

Similarly no modern law school can claim ignorance of the poor performance of blacks, relatively speaking, on the Law School Admissions Test (LSAT). Nevertheless, law schools continue to use the test and then attempt to "correct" for black underperformance by using racial discrimination in admissions so as to obtain their aesthetic student body. The Law School's continued adherence to measures it knows produce racially skewed results is not entitled to deference by this Court. The Law

School itself admits that the test is imperfect, as it must, given that it regularly admits students who score at or below 150 (the national median) on the test. . . .

Having decided to use the LSAT, the Law School must accept the constitutional burdens that come with this decision. The Law School may freely continue to employ the LSAT and other allegedly merit-based standards in whatever fashion it likes. What the Equal Protection Clause forbids, but the Court today allows, is the use of these standards hand-in-hand with racial discrimination. An infinite variety of admissions methods are available to the Law School. Considering all of the radical thinking that has historically occurred at this country's universities, the Law School's intractable approach toward admissions is striking. . . .

VI

The absence of any articulated legal principle supporting the majority's principal holding suggests another rationale. I believe what lies beneath the Court's decision today are the benighted notions that one can tell when racial discrimination benefits (rather than hurts) minority groups, and that racial discrimination is necessary to remedy general societal ills. This Court's precedents supposedly settled both issues, but clearly the majority still cannot commit to the principle that racial classifications are *per se* harmful and that almost no amount of benefit in the eye of the beholder can justify such classifications.

Putting aside what I take to be the Court's implicit rejection of *Adarand*'s holding that beneficial and burdensome racial classifications are equally invalid, I must contest the notion that the Law School's discrimination benefits those admitted as a result of it. The Court spends considerable time discussing the impressive display of *amicus* support for the Law School in this case from all corners of society. But nowhere in any of the filings in this Court is any evidence that the purported "beneficiaries" of this racial discrimination prove themselves by performing at (or even near) the same level as those students who receive no preferences.

The silence in this case is deafening to those of us who view higher education's purpose as imparting knowledge and skills to students, rather than a communal, rubber-stamp, credentialing process. The Law School is not looking for those students who, despite a lower LSAT score or undergraduate grade point average, will succeed in the study of law. The Law School seeks only a facade—it is sufficient that the class looks right, even if it does not perform right.

The Law School tantalizes unprepared students with the promise of a University of Michigan degree and all of the opportunities that it offers. These overmatched students take the bait, only to find that they cannot succeed in the cauldron of competition. And this mismatch crisis is not restricted to elite institutions. Indeed, to cover the tracks of the aestheticists, this cruel farce of racial discrimination must continue—in selection for the Michigan Law Review, see University of Michigan Law School Student Handbook 2002-2003, pp. 39-40 (noting the presence of a "diversity

129

plan" for admission to the review), and in hiring at law firms and for judicial clerkships—until the "beneficiaries" are no longer tolerated. While these students may graduate with law degrees, there is no evidence that they have received a qualitatively better legal education (or become better lawyers) than if they had gone to a less "elite" law school for which they were better prepared. And the aestheticists will never address the real problems facing "underrepresented minorities," instead continuing their social experiments on other people's children. . . .

It is uncontested that each year, the Law School admits a handful of blacks who would be admitted in the absence of racial discrimination. Who can differentiate between those who belong and those who do not? The majority of blacks are admitted to the Law School because of discrimination, and because of this policy all are tarred as undeserving. This problem of stigma does not depend on determinacy as to whether those stigmatized are actually the "beneficiaries" of racial discrimination. When blacks take positions in the highest places of government, industry, or academia, it is an open question today whether their skin color played a part in their advancement. The question itself is the stigma—because either racial discrimination did play a role, in which case the person may be deemed "otherwise unqualified," or it did not, in which case asking the question itself unfairly marks those blacks who would succeed without discrimination. Is this what the Court means by "visibly open"? . . .

VII . . .

For the immediate future, [the] majority has placed its *imprimatur* on a practice that can only weaken the principle of equality embodied in the Declaration of Independence and the Equal Protection Clause. "Our Constitution is color-blind, and neither knows nor tolerates classes among citizens." *Plessy v. Ferguson* (Harlan, J., dissenting). It has been nearly 140 years since Frederick Douglass asked the intellectual ancestors of the Law School to "[d]o nothing with us!" and the Nation adopted the Fourteenth Amendment. Now we must wait another 25 years to see this principle of equality [vindicated].

GRATZ v. BOLLINGER, 539 U.S. 244 (2003). In this companion case to *Grutter,* the Court invalidated the affirmative action plan used by the undergraduate college of liberal arts and sciences at the University of Michigan. The University ranked college applicants according to a 150 point scale. Students receiving over 100 points were generally admitted, while those receiving under 75 points were generally delayed or rejected. Applicants received points based upon factors like high school grade point average, standardized test scores, the academic quality of an applicant's high school, in-state residency and alumni relationships. Up to 110 points could be assigned for academic performance, and up to 40 points could be assigned for the other, nonacademic factors. Michigan residents, for example, received 10 points, and children of alumni received 4. Counselors could assign an outstanding essay up to 3 points and could award up to 5 points for an applicant's personal achievement, leadership, or public service. An applicant automatically received a 20 point bonus if he or she possesses any one of the following "miscellaneous" factors: membership in an underrepresented minority group; attendance at a predominantly minority or disadvantaged high school; or recruitment for athletics.

This point system was supplemented by the review of some applications by an Admissions Review Committee (ARC). Under this system, some applications were "flagged" for review by the Committee if it was determined that the applicant was academically prepared to succeed at the University, had received a minimum index score, and possessed characteristics important to the University's composition of its freshman class, such as high class rank, unique life experiences, challenges, circumstances, interests or talents, socioeconomic disadvantage, and underrepresented race, ethnicity, or geography. The Committee reviewed "flagged" applications and determined whether to admit or deny each applicant.

Chief Justice Rehnquist delivered the opinion of the Court: "Justice Powell's opinion in *Bakke* emphasized the importance of considering each particular applicant as an individual, assessing all of the qualities that individual possesses, and in turn, evaluating that individual's ability to contribute to the unique setting of higher education. . . .

"The [challenged] policy does not provide such individualized consideration. The [policy] automatically distributes 20 points to every single applicant from an 'underrepresented minority' group, as defined by the University. The only consideration that accompanies this distribution of points is a factual review of an application to determine whether an individual is a member of one of these minority groups. Moreover, unlike Justice Powell's example, where the race of a 'particular black applicant' could be considered without being decisive, see *Bakke*, the [University's] automatic distribution of 20 points has the effect of making 'the factor of race . . . decisive' for virtually every minimally qualified underrepresented minority applicant.

"Respondents emphasize the fact that the [college] has created the possibility of an applicant's file being flagged for individualized consideration by the ARC. . . .

"But the fact that the 'review committee can look at the applications individually and ignore the points,' once an application is flagged, is of little comfort under our strict scrutiny analysis. The record does not reveal precisely how many applications are flagged for this individualized consideration, but it is undisputed that such consideration is the exception and not the [rule]. Additionally, this individualized review is only provided *after* admissions counselors automatically distribute the University's version of a 'plus' that makes race a decisive factor for virtually every minimally qualified underrepresented minority applicant.

"Respondents contend that '[t]he volume of applications and the presentation of applicant information make it impractical for [the College] to use the . . . admissions system' upheld by the Court today in *Grutter*. But the fact that the implementation of a program capable of providing individualized consideration might present administrative challenges does not render constitutional an otherwise problematic system."

Justice O'Connor wrote a concurring opinion: "Although the Office of Undergraduate Admissions does assign 20 points to some 'soft' variables other than race, the points available for other diversity contributions, such as leadership and service, personal achievement, and geographic diversity, are capped at much lower levels. Even the most outstanding national high school leader could never receive more than five points for his or her accomplishments—a mere quarter of the points automatically assigned to an underrepresented minority solely based on the fact of his or her race. Of course, as Justice Powell made clear in *Bakke*, a university need not 'necessarily accor[d]' all diversity factors 'the same weight,' and the 'weight attributed to a particular quality may vary from year to year depending on the "mix" both of the student body and the applicants for the incoming class.' But the selection index, by setting up automatic, predetermined point allocations for the soft variables, ensures that the diversity contributions of applicants cannot be individually assessed. This policy stands in sharp contrast to the law school's admissions plan, which enables admissions officers to make nuanced judgments with respect to the contributions each applicant is likely to make to the diversity of the incoming class."

Justices Thomas and Breyer also wrote concurring opinions.

Justice Souter, joined by Justice Ginsburg, dissented: "The record does not describe a system with a quota like the one struck down in *Bakke*, which 'insulate[d]' all nonminority candidates from competition from certain seats. [The] *Bakke* plan 'focused *solely* on ethnic diversity' and effectively told nonminority applicants that '[n]o matter how strong their qualifications, quantitative and extracurricular, including their own potential for contribution to educational diversity, they are never afforded the chance to compete with applicants from the preferred [groups].'

"The plan here, in contrast, lets all applicants compete for all places and values an applicant's offerings for any place not solely on the grounds of [race]. A nonminority applicant who scores highly in [other] categories can readily garner a selection index exceeding that of a minority applicant who gets the 20-point bonus. . . .

"The very nature of a college's permissible practice of awarding value to racial diversity means that race must be considered in a way that increases some applicants' chances for admission. Since college admission is not left entirely to inarticulate intuition, it is hard to see what is inappropriate in assigning some stated value to a relevant characteristic, whether it be reasoning ability, writing style, running speed, or minority race. [The] college simply does by a numbered scale what the law school accomplishes in its 'holistic review'; the distinction does not imply that applicants to the undergraduate college are denied individualized consideration or a fair chance to compete on the basis of all the various merits their applications may disclose. . . .

"[In] contrast to the college's forthrightness in saying just what plus factor it gives for membership in an underrepreseted minority, it is worth considering the character of one alternative thrown up as preferable, because supposedly not based on race. Drawing on admissions systems used at public universities in California, Florida, and Texas, the United States contends that Michigan could get student diversity [by] guaranteeing admission to a fixed percentage of the top students from each high school in Michigan.

"While there is nothing unconstitutional about such a practice, it nonetheless suffers from a serious disadvantage. It is the disadvantage of deliberate obfuscation. The 'percentage plans' are just as race conscious as the point system (and fairly so), but they get their racially diverse results without saying directly what they are doing or why they are doing it. In contrast, Michigan states its purpose directly and, if this were a doubtful case for me, I would be tempted to give Michigan an extra point of its own for its frankness. Equal protection cannot become an exercise in which the winners are the ones who hide the ball."

Justice Ginsburg, joined by Justice Souter, also dissented: "The stain of generations of racial oppression is still visible in our society, and the determination to hasten its removal remains vital. One can reasonably anticipate, therefore, that colleges and universities will seek to maintain their minority enrollment—and the networks and opportunities thereby opened to minority graduates—whether or not they can do so in full candor through adoption of affirmative action plans of the kind here at issue. Without recourse to such plans, institutions of higher education may resort to camouflage. For example, schools may encourage applicants to write of their cultural traditions in the essays they submit, or to indicate whether English is their second language. Seeking to improve their chances for admission, applicants may highlight the minority group associations to which they belong, or the Hispanic surnames of their mothers or grandparents. In turn, teachers' recommendations may emphasize who a student is as much as what he or she has accomplished. If honesty is the best policy, surely Michigan's accurately described, fully disclosed College affirmative action program is preferable to achieving similar numbers through winks, nods, and disguises."

In an opinion joined by Justice Souter, Justice Stevens dissented on the ground that the plaintiffs lacked standing.

Page 592. Before section 3 of the Note, add the following:

Consider in this connection Katz, Race and the Right to Vote after *Rice v. Cayetano*, 99 Mich. L. Rev. 491, 503 (2000):

> *Rice* [accepts] the Indian analogy but nevertheless insists that the OHA's electoral restriction rests on a racial classification. It holds that aboriginal Hawaiians may well enjoy a special legal or political status when receiving employment

preferences or other benefits. [But] once Hawaii's native people compose an exclusive electorate for a state agency [they] are transformed (at least for purposes of judicial review) into a racial group....

The decision accordingly conceives of race not as an immutable physical characteristic, but instead as a legal conclusion reached when the State organizes a group for some activities, but not others.

For an examination of the equal protection problems posed by defining membership in Indian tribes based upon racial criteria, see Gould, Mixing Bodies and Beliefs: The Predicament of Tribes, 101 Colum. L. Rev. 702 (2001).

D. *Equal Protection Methodology: Heightened Scrutiny and the Problem of Gender*

Page 608. At the end of section 2c of the Note, add the following:

For a criticism of the Court's reliance on the race analogy, see Siegel, She the People: The Nineteenth Amendment, Sex Equality, Federalism, and the Family, 115 Harv. L. Rev. 949, 960 (2002). Siegel argues that seeing gender discrimination through the lens of race

> [obscures] the extent to which gender status regulation had its own constitutional and common law history and distinctive social forms. Doctrinal effacement of this history [has] two important consequences. By enjoining sex discrimination on the ground that it resembled race discrimination prohibited by the Fourteenth Amendment, the Court suggested that the new body of sex discrimination doctrine lacked independent grounding in our constitutional history. At the same time, the Court's effort to reason by analogy deflected attention from the ways that race and gender status regulation intersect and [differ].

Instead of focusing on the fourteenth amendment alone, Siegel advocates a "synthetic" approach that reads the fourteenth amendment against the backdrop of the struggle to attain women's suffrage, which culminated in the nineteenth amendment. (For a more general defense of an approach that attempts to integrate language from different parts of the constitutional text, see Amar, Intratextualism, 112 Harv. L. Rev. 748 (1999).) Of course, on its face, the nineteenth amendment does no more than guarantee women the right to vote. But Siegel argues that its adoption constituted a rejection of two interrelated arguments: that men adequately represented women within the family, and that the family, as so understood, was immune from federal regulation. Rejection of these arguments, in turn, should be read back into the fourteenth amendment conception of equality.

What practical difference would this regrounding of gender discrimination doctrine make? Siegel argues that her approach would extend equal protection review beyond suspicion of gender-based classifications:

> [Sex] discrimination doctrine grounded in a synthetic interpretation of the Fourteenth and Nineteenth Amendments, and in an understanding of the history of the woman suffrage campaign might accord heightened scrutiny to state action regulating the family that denies women "full citizenship stature" or that perpetuates the "legal, social, and economic inferiority of women."

Id. at 1044 (quoting United States v. Virginia, 518 U.S. 532, 534 (1996)).

Given that the language of the Nineteenth Amendment more nearly tracks the language of the Fifteenth Amendment, which has been given an extremely narrow reading (protecting against racial discrimination only in formal participation in the political process), does reading the Nineteenth Amendment in tandem with the Fourteenth Amendment instead raise interpretive problems?

Page 610. At the end of section 3 of the Note, add the following:

May a state permit the establishment of a gender-segregated charter school? For an analysis, see Brown-Nagin, Toward a Pragmatic Understanding of Status-Consciousness: The Case of Deregulated Education, 50 Duke L.J. 753, 802-831 (2000).

Page 619. At the end of section 1 of the Note, add the following:

In Hasday, The Principle and Practice of Women's "Full Citizenship": A Case Study of Sex-Segregated Public Education, 101 Mich. L. Rev. 755, 757-58 (2002), the author points out that "[the] practice of sex-segregated public education [has] historically been entangled in both racial and class stratification" and suggests that "a decisionmaker regulating single-sex public schools [would] be well-advised to consider whether some or all of those schools have different consequences for different groups of women." The author also argues that historically "the differences [between] sex-segregated and coeducational public education [may be] relatively unimportant in terms of their substantive impact on women's status." If this remains true, "it is hard to see why a jurisprudence committed to women's 'full citizenship' would want to emphasize form by absolutely prohibiting sex-segregated public schooling, or how transferring all public school students to coeducational schools would advance women's 'full citizenship stature' and fight their 'inferiority.'"

Page 624. Before the Note, add the following:

In the case that follows, the Court answered the question that *Miller* left unresolved.

NGUYEN v. IMMIGRATION AND NATURALIZATION SERVICE, 533 U.S. 33 (2001). Nguyen was a nonmarital child, born in Vietnam to his father, who was a U.S. citizen, and his mother, a citizen of Vietnam. When he was six, he came to the United States, became a lawful permanent resident, and was raised by his father. At age 22, he was convicted of two counts of sexual assault on a child. The Immigration and Naturalization Service thereupon initiated deportation proceedings against him as an alien who had been convicted of crimes of moral turpitude. While the matter was pending, the father obtained an order of parentage from state court based on a DNA test that conclusively demonstrated paternity. The Board of Immigration Appeals nonetheless rejected Nguyen's claim to U.S. citizenship because he failed to meet the requirements of citizenship for nonmarital children born abroad to a citizen father and noncitizen mother. (The requirements are set out on pages 621-622 of the main volume.) Both Nguyen and his father challenged the constitutionality of this determination.

In a five-to-four decision, the Court, in an opinion written by Justice Kennedy, held that the statute was consistent with the constitutional guarantee of equal protection.

Justice Kennedy began his analysis by noting the familiar requirements that gender-based classifications serve important governmental objectives and be substantially related to the achievement of those objectives. "The first governmental interest to be served [by the statute] is the importance of assuring that a biological parent-child relationship exists. In the case of the mother, the relation is verifiable from the birth itself. . . .

"In the case of the father, the uncontestable fact is that he need not be present at the birth. If he is present, furthermore, that circumstance is not incontrovertible proof of fatherhood. . . .

"Petitioners argue that the requirement of [the statute] that a father provide clear and convincing evidence of parentage is sufficient to achieve the end of establishing paternity, given the sophistication of modern DNA tests. [The statute] does not actually mandate a DNA test, however. The Constitution, moreover, does not require that Congress elect one particular mechanism from among many possible methods of establishing paternity, even if that mechanism arguably might be the most scientifically advanced method. With respect to DNA testing, the expense, reliability, and availability of such testing in various parts of the world may have been a particular concern of Congress. . . .

"[To] require Congress to speak without reference to the gender of the parent with regard to its objective of ensuring a blood tie between parent and child would be to insist on a hollow neutrality.

"[Congress] could have required both mothers and fathers to provide parenthood within 30 days or, for that matter, 18 years, of the child's birth. Given that the mother is always present at birth, but that the father need not be, the facially neutral rule would sometimes require fathers to take additional affirmative steps which would not be required of [mothers]. Just as neutral terms can mark discrimination that is unlawful, gender specific terms can mark a permissible distinction. [Here,] the use of gender specific terms takes into account a biological difference between the parents. The differential treatment is inherent in a sensible statutory scheme, given the unique relationship of the mother to the event of birth.

"The second important governmental interest furthered in a substantial manner by [the statute] is the determination to ensure that the child and the citizen parent have some demonstrated opportunity or potential to develop not just a relationship that is recognized, as a formal matter, by the law, but one that consists of the real, everyday ties that provide a connection between child and citizen parent and, in turn, the United States. In the case of a citizen mother and a child born overseas, the opportunity for a meaningful relationship between citizen parent and child inheres in the very event of birth, an event so often critical to our constitutional and statutory understandings of citizenship. The mother knows that the child is in being and is hers and has an initial point of contact with him. There is at least an opportunity for mother and child to develop a real, meaningful relationship.

"The same opportunity does not result from the event of birth, as a matter of biological inevitability, in the case of the unwed father. Given the 9-month interval between conception and birth, it is not always certain that a father will know that a child was conceived, nor is it always clear that even the mother will be sure of the father's identity. This fact takes on particular significance in the case of a child born overseas and out of wedlock. One concern in this context has always been with young people, men for the most part, who are on duty with the Armed Forces in foreign countries.

"[The] passage of time has produced additional and even more substantial grounds to justify the statutory distinction. The ease of travel and the willingness of Americans to visit foreign countries have resulted in numbers of trips abroad that must be of real concern when we contemplate the prospect of accepting petitioners' argument, which would mandate, contrary to Congress' wishes, citizenship by male parentage subject to no condition save the father's previous length of residence in this country. . . .

"The importance of the governmental interest at issue here is too profound to be satisfied merely by conducting a DNA test. [Scientific] proof of biological paternity does nothing, by itself, to ensure contact between father and child during the child's minority. . . .

"[This] difference does not result from some stereotype, defined as a frame of mind resulting from irrational or uncritical analysis. There is nothing irrational or improper in the recognition that at the moment of birth—the critical event in the statutory scheme and in the whole tradition of citizenship law—the mother's knowledge of the child and the fact of parenthood have been established in a way not guaranteed in the case of the unwed father. This is not a stereotype. . . .

"[The] question remains whether the means Congress chose to further its objective—the imposition of certain additional requirements upon an unwed father—substantially relate to [the ends of the statute].

"[It] should be unsurprising that Congress decided to require that an opportunity for a parent-child relationship occur during the formative years of the child's minority. . . .

"[Petitioners] assert that, although a mother will know of her child's birth, 'knowledge that one is a parent, no matter how it is acquired, does not guarantee a relationship with one's child.' They thus maintain that imposition of the additional requirements of [the statute] only on the children of citizen fathers must reflect a stereotype that women are more likely than men to actually establish a relationship with their children.

"[Congress] would of course be entitled to advance the interest of ensuring an actual, meaningful relationship in every case before citizenship is conferred. Or Congress could excuse compliance with the formal requirements when an actual father-child relationship is proved. It did neither here, perhaps because of the subjectivity, intrusiveness, and difficulties of proof that might attend an inquiry into any particular bond or tie. Instead, Congress enacted an easily administered scheme to promote the different but still substantial interest of ensuring at least an opportunity for a parent-child relationship to develop. . . .

"To fail to acknowledge even our most basic biological differences—such as the fact that a mother must be present at birth but the father need not be—risks making the guarantee of equal protection superficial, and so disserving it. Mechanistic classification of all our differences as stereotypes would operate to obscure those misconceptions and prejudices that are real. The distinction embodied in the statutory scheme here at issue is not marked by misconception and prejudice, nor does it show disrespect for either class. The difference between men and women in relation to the birth process is a real one, and the principle of equal protection does not forbid Congress to address the problem at hand in a manner specific to each gender."

JUSTICE O'CONNOR, joined by JUSTICES SOUTER, GINSBURG, and BREYER, dissented:
"While the Court invokes heightened scrutiny, the manner in which it explains and applies this standard is a stranger to our precedents. . . .

"Sex-based statutes, even when accurately reflecting the way most men or women behave, deny individuals opportunity. Such generalizations must be viewed not in isolation, but in the context of our nation's 'long and unfortunate history of sex discrimination' [quoting *Frontiero*]. . . .

"It is [difficult] to see how [the statute's] limitation of the time allowed for obtaining proof of paternity substantially furthers the assurance of a blood relationship. Modern DNA testing, in addition to providing accuracy unmatched by other methods of establishing a biological link, essentially negates the evidentiary significance of the passage of time. . . .

"[Petitioners'] argument does not depend on the idea that one particular method of establishing paternity is constitutionally required. Petitioners' argument rests instead on the fact that, if the goal is to obtain proof of paternity, the existence of a statutory provision governing such proof, coupled with the efficacy and availability of modern technology, is highly relevant to the sufficiency of the tailoring between [the statute's] sex-based classification and the asserted end. . . .

"In our prior cases, the existence of comparable or superior sex-neutral alternatives has been a powerful reason to reject a sex-based classification. The majority, however, turns this principle on its head by denigrating as 'hollow' the very neutrality that the law requires. While the majority trumpets the availability of superior sex-neutral alternatives as confirmation of [the statute's] validity, our precedents demonstrate that this fact is a decided strike against the law. Far from being 'hollow,' the avoidance of gratuitous sex-based distinctions is the hallmark of equal protection. . . .

"The [majority's] discussion [demonstrates] that, at most, differential impact will result from the fact that '[f]athers and mothers are not similarly situated with regard to the proof of biological parenthood.' [But] facially neutral laws that have a disparate impact are a different animal for purposes of constitutional analysis than laws that specifically provide for disparate treatment. . . .

"Assuming as the majority does, that Congress was actually concerned about ensuring a 'demonstrated opportunity' for a relationship, it is questionable whether such an opportunity qualifies as an 'important' governmental interest apart from the existence of an actual relationship. [It] is difficult to see how [anyone] profits from a 'demonstrated opportunity' for a relationship in the absence of the fruition of an actual tie. . . .

"Even if it is important 'to require that an opportunity for a parent-child relationship occur during the formative years of the child's minority,' it is difficult to see how the requirement that proof of such opportunity be obtained before the child turns 18 substantially furthers the asserted interest. . . .

"Moreover, available sex-neutral alternatives would at least replicate, and could easily exceed, whatever fit there is between [the statute's] discriminatory means and the majority's asserted end. [Congress] could simply substitute for [the statute] a requirement that the parent be present at birth or have knowledge of birth. Congress could at least allow proof of such presence or knowledge to be one way of demonstrating an opportunity for a relationship. [Indeed], the idea that a mother's presence at birth supplies adequate assurance of an opportunity to develop a relationship while a father's presence at birth does not would appear to rest only on an overbroad sex-based generalization. . . .

"The claim that [the statute] substantially relates to the achievement of the goal of a 'real practical relationship' thus finds support not in biological differences but instead in a stereotype. . . .

"The majority asserts that a 'stereotype' is 'defined as a frame of mind resulting from irrational or uncritical analysis.' This Court has long recognized, however, that an impermissible stereotype may enjoy empirical support and thus be in a sense 'rational.' . . .

"Nor do stereotypes consist only of those overbroad generalizations that the reviewing court considers to 'show disrespect' for a class. [Indeed], arbitrary distinction between the sexes may rely on no identifiable generalization at all but may simply be a denial of opportunity out of pure caprice. Such a distinction, of course, would nonetheless be a classic equal protection violation."

Page 625. At the conclusion of section 1 of the Note, add the following:

With regard to the "naturalness" of gender differences, consider the possibility that current constitutional doctrine does not deal adequately with "people for whom gender and anatomical birth sex in some way diverge." Flynn, *Trans*forming the Debate: Why We Need to Include Transgender Rights in the Struggles for Sex and Sexual Orientation Equality, 101 Colum. L. Rev. 392, 394 (2001). Flynn argues that this problem leads to the

> failure to remedy much of the discrimination experienced by women and sexual minorities, specifically the discrimination based on gender nonconformity. This failure is premised on a prevalent juridical assumption that the law should target discrimination based on sex (i.e., whether a person is anatomically male or female), rather than gender (i.e., whether a person has qualities that society considers masculine or feminine). In both law and life, though, conceptions of sex and gender are so firmly cemented together that courts' frequent refusals to address gender-based inequalities mean that much discrimination against women and sexual minorities goes unremedied.

Id. at 394-395. For a discussion of the relationship between gender discrimination and discrimination based on sexual orientation, see page 656 of the main volume.

Page 626. Before section 3 of the Note, add the following:

In connection with these issues, consider Nevada Department of Human Resources v. Hibbs, 538 U.S. 721 (2003). At issue was whether Congress could constitutionally authorize private suits for damages against state governments under the Family and Medical Leave Act. The act authorized eligible employees to take up to 12 weeks of unpaid leave annually for the onset of a "serious health condition" in the employee's spouse, child, or parent. Congress used its powers under § 5 of the fourteenth amendment to apply this prohibition to state governments. Section 5 authorizes Congress to enforce the amendment with appropriate legislation. In previous cases, the Court had held that Congress could not use its § 5 powers to change substantive equal protection rights, but that it could adopt prophylactic remedial measures that proscribed facially constitutional conduct in order to prevent and deter unconstitutional conduct so long as these remedial measures were "congruent and proportional." (For a discussion of these cases, see page 220 of the main text.)

In a 6-3 decision, the Court, per Chief Justice Rehnquist, used this test to uphold Hibbs' claim for damages.

> According to evidence that was before Congress, [States] continue to rely on invalid gender stereotypes in the employment context, specifically in the administration of leave benefits. . . .
>
> Congress [heard] testimony that "[p]arental leave for fathers . . . is rare. Even . . . [w]here child-care leave policies do exist, men, *both in the public and private sectors*, receive notoriously discriminatory treatment in their requests for such leave." [Many] States offer women extended "maternity" leave that far exceeded the typical 4- to 8-week period of physical disability due to pregnancy and childbirth, but very few States grant men a parallel [benefit]. This and other differential leave policies were not attributable to any differential physical needs of men and women, but rather to the pervasive sex-role stereotype that caring for family members is women's work.

Given the social roles commonly played by men and women, are the state practices upon which the Court relies evidence of gender discrimination or are they, instead, efforts to respond to gender discrimination? According to Chief Justice Rehnquist,

> [Mutually] reenforcing stereotypes [that women have domestic responsibilities and men do not] created a self-fulfilling cycle of discrimination that forced women to continue to assume the role of primary family caregiver, and fostered employers' stereotypical views about women's commitment to work and their value as employees . . . .
>
> By creating an across-the-board routine employment benefit for all eligible employees, Congress sought to ensure that family-care leave would no longer be

stigmatized as an inordinate drain on the workplace caused by female employees, that the employers could not evade leave obligations simply by hiring men.

In the Court's view, a simple requirement that states administer leave benefits in a gender neutral fashion would not solve this problem:

> Such a law would allow States to provide for no family leave at all. Where "[t]wo thirds of the nonprofessional caregivers for older, chronically ill, or disabled persons are working women" and state practices continue to reinforce the stereotype of women as caregivers, such a policy would exclude far more women than men from the workplace.

Why is this fact relevant? Isn't this mode of analysis in tension with the Court's own conclusion that official recognition of different social roles performed by men and women serves to reenforce stereotypes about those roles? In light of the statistics cited by the Court, would it be constitutional for Congress to mandate caretaker leave for women but not for men?

E. Equal Protection Methodology: The Problem of Sexual Orientation

Page 652. Before subsection b of the Note, add the following:

The Court overruled *Bowers* in Lawrence v. Texas, 539 U.S. 558 (2003). The opinion is excerpted at the Supplement to page 901 of the main text.

Page 657. At the end of section 4 of the Note, add the following:

For a skeptical examination of the gender discrimination argument, see Stein, Evaluating the Sex Discrimination Argument for Lesbian and Gay Rights, 49 UCLA L. Rev. 471 (2001).

In Flynn, *Trans*forming the Debate: Why We Need to Include Transgender Rights in the Struggles for Sex and Sexual Orientation Equality, 101 Colum. L. Rev. 392 (2001), the author argues that the law should focus on "transgendered" individuals. People are "transgendered" when their "appearance, behavior, or other personal characteristics differ from traditional gender norms." Id. at 392. Flynn argues that focusing on transgender discrimination addresses a rather astonishing gap in sex and sexual orientation equality jurisprudence: The failure to remedy much of the discrimination experienced by women and sexual minorities [based] on gender nonconformity. [Transgender] rights cases [challenge] the sex system by presenting the courts with people for whom gender and anatomical birth sex in some way diverge. The typical conceptualization of sex, a doctor's peek at a newborn's genitals, is simply a form of shorthand that [is] [an] oversimplification that fails to capture the multitude of factors that constitute sex. Most crucially, this shorthand overlooks a person's gender identification, one's internal sense of being male or female.

Id. at 394.

F. Equal Protection Methodology: Other Candidates for Heightened Scrutiny

Page 668. At the end of section 1 of the Note, add the following:

In the wake of September 11, the President ordered the establishment of military tribunals with jurisdiction to try aliens, but not American citizens, for, inter alia, engaging in acts of "international terrorism." (The order is discussed at greater length in the supplement to page 352 of the main volume). In light of *Mathews*, is there a plausible argument that the order unconstitutionally discriminates against noncitizens? Consider Katyal & Tribe, Waging War, Deciding Guilt: Trying the Military Tribunals, 111 Yale L. J. 1259, 1300-01 (2002):

[Deferential] review of federal distinctions between citizens and aliens [has] its roots in the wide berth accorded the political branches "in the area of immigration and naturalization" [citing *Mathews*]. When a categorical preference for American citizens cannot be justified in terms of immigration and naturalization policy or as an adjunct to our international bargaining posture, the basis for relaxing the scrutiny otherwise applicable to discrimination against aliens as a class [evaporates].
    Even more important, the decisions manifesting relaxed [scrutiny] of federal discrimination [have] involved nothing beyond the preferential availability to our own citizens of government employment or other socioeconomic benefits that do not touch the raw never of equal justice under [law]. Crucially, the Military Order curtails rights that, at least when made available to others similarly situated, have long been deemed too fundamental to be dispensed with on a merely rational basis. For a more general criticism of the government's treatment of aliens in the

wake of the World Trade Center attack, see Cole, Enemy Aliens, 54 Stan. L. Rev. 953 (2002).

Page 681. At the end of section 1 of the Note, add the following:

Does the broader category of the physically and mentally disabled constitute a suspect class? In Tennessee v. Lane, 541 U.S. ___ (2004), the Court rejected a constitutional attack on Title II of the Americans with Disabilities Act of 1990 (which prohibits qualified persons with disabilities from being "excluded from participation or denied the benefits of the services, programs or activities of a public entity") as applied to physically disabled individuals who claimed that their disabilities prevented them from gaining access to state courthouses. Tennessee argued that the measure exceeded Congress' power under section 5 of the fourteenth amendment to enforce the prohibitions of that amendment. (For a general discussion of Congress' section 5 powers, see pages 220-30 of the main text.) In the course of rejecting this argument, Justice Stevens, writing for the Court, stated the following:

> Congress enacted Title II against a backdrop of pervasive unequal treatment in the administration of state services and programs, including systematic deprivations of fundamental rights. For example, "[a]s of 1979, most States . . . categorically disqualified 'idiots' from voting, without regard to individual capacity." The majority of these laws remain on the books, and have been the subject of legal challenge as recently as 2001. Similarly, a number of States have prohibited and continue to prohibit persons with disabilities from engaging in activities such as marrying and serving as jurors. The historical experience that Title II reflects is also documented in this Court's cases, which have identified unconstitutional treatment of disabled persons by state agencies in a variety of settings, including unjustified commitment; the abuse and neglect of persons committed to state mental health hospitals; and irrational discrimination in zoning decisions. The decisions of other courts, too, document a pattern of unequal treatment in the administration of a wide range of public services, programs, and activities, including the penal system, public education, and voting.

In light of this history, should disability discrimination be subject to heightened scrutiny? In *Lane*, the Court was not required to answer this question because it found that the Americans with Disabilities Act, as applied, was a permissible congressional effort to enforce the access to courts guaranteed by due process of law. Note that the Americans with Disabilities Act in some circumstances requires

Equality and the Constitution

"reasonable accommodation" of persons with disabilities. If disability constituted a suspect class, would this requirement be constitutionally vulnerable under the Court's affirmative action jurisprudence? Conversely, if disability were a suspect class, would governments be constitutionally required to accommodate the disabled? Consider in this regard the Court's treatment of classifications that are facially neutral, discussed on pages 514-33 of the main text.

Page 683. At the end of section 2 of the Note, add the following:

Consider the accuracy of the following description of how the Court goes about deciding which groups to protect:

> [The] present Court [is] reluctant to strike down particular discriminations so long as the minority group is totally marginalized and powerless. [Once] an historically excluded group shows political clout and cultural and economic resonance, however, the Court becomes sensitive to discriminations against the group and increasingly willing to nullify some such discriminations at the retail level, but remains unenthusiastic about insisting on radical, or wholesale, revisions. Such revisions would be risky for the Court, because people whose status or values depend on discriminating against the minority group will be riled by any big constitutional entitlement for the group. The Court's current strategy is to send up trial balloons and to see what happens.

Eskridge, Destabilizing Due Process and Evolutive Equal Protection, 47 UCLA L. Rev. 1183, 1216-17 (2000).

Page 683. Before section 3 of the Note, add the following:

Consider the suggestion in Dorf, Equal Protection Incorporation, 88 Va. L. Rev. 951 (2002), that the Court can give the strict scrutiny doctrine principled content by "incorporating" other provisions of the Constitution into equal protection analysis. Under this approach, the first, fourteenth and nineteenth amendments make discrimination based upon religion, race, color, previous condition of servitude, and sex presumptively unconstitutional. Moreover, the twenty sixth amendment raises important questions about the constitutionality of age discrimination. For another discussion of how the equal protection and due process clauses inform on another, see Karlan, Equal Protection, Due Process, and the Stereoscopic Fourteenth Amendment, 33 McGeorge L. Rev. 473 (2002).

6
IMPLIED FUNDAMENTAL RIGHTS

E. Fundamental Interests and the Equal Protection Clause

Page 744. At the end of the Note, add the following:

3a. *Bush v. Gore.* In connection with the putative "fundamental" character of the right to vote, consider the Supreme Court's decision that brought to a conclusion the disputed presidential election of 2000. (The decision is excerpted at greater length in the material supplementing page 135 of the main volume). With the presidential candidates separated by no more than a few hundred votes and the deadline for the casting of electoral ballots fast approaching, the Florida Supreme Court ordered a state-wide, manual recount of all ballots on which the voting machines had failed to detect a vote for president. In Bush v. Gore, 531 U.S. 98 (2000), the Supreme Court, in a five-to-four decision, reversed. In a per curiam opinion, joined by five justices, the Court held that the failure of the Florida Court to specify standards for determining which votes would count violated the equal protection clause:

> When the state legislature vests the right to vote for President in its people, the right to vote as the legislature has prescribed is fundamental; and one source of its fundamental nature lies in the equal weight accorded to each vote and the equal dignity owned to each voter. . . .
> The right to vote is protected in more than the initial allocation of the franchise. Equal protection applies as well to the manner of its exercise. Having once granted the right to vote on equal terms, the State may not, by later arbitrary and disparate treatment, value one person's vote over that of another. . . .
> The recount mechanisms implemented in response to the decisions of the Florida Supreme Court do not satisfy the minimum requirement for non-arbitrary treatment of voters necessary to secure the fundamental right. [The] problem inheres in the absence of specific standards to ensure [equal] application. The for-

mulation of uniform rules to determine intent based on [recurring] circumstances is practicable and, we conclude, necessary. . . .

Our consideration is limited to the present circumstances, for the problem of equal protection in election processes generally presents many complexities.

The question before the Court is not whether local entities, in the exercise of their expertise, may develop different systems for implementing elections. Instead, we are presented with a situation where a state court with the power to assure uniformity has ordered a statewide recount with minimal procedural safeguards. When a court orders a statewide remedy, there must be at least some assurance that the rudimentary requirements of equal treatment and fundamental fairness are satisfied.

The Court went on to hold that it was impossible to conduct a recount satisfying equal protection standards before the deadline specified in 3 U.S.C. § 5, which made conclusive state resolutions of election controversies if the determination was made at least six days prior to the date for the casting of electoral votes. (By the time the Court rendered its decision, this deadline was only hours away). The Court also determined that the Florida legislature intended to take advantage of this "safe harbor." Accordingly, the Court held that the recount could not proceed. Chief Justice Rehnquist, joined by Justices Scalia and Thomas, wrote a concurring opinion. Justices Souter and Breyer both wrote opinions in which they agreed with the majority that the absence of uniform standards for the recount created constitutional difficulties. However, both would have remanded the case to the Florida court so that it could formulate such standards. Justices Ginsburg and Stevens also wrote dissenting opinions.

Page 755. At the end of Note 6b, add the following:

The Supreme Court's inability to confront directly problems of excessive partisanship in the redistricting process has put substantial pressure on the 10 percent safe harbor of cases like *White*, *Gaffney*, and *Brown*.

In Cox v. Larios, 542 U.S. ___ (2004), the Supreme Court summarily affirmed a three-judge district court's decision striking down a Georgia state legislative redistricting plan in which the deviations were 9.98 percent. Justice Stevens, in a concurrence joined by Justice Breyer, explained that the Court's recent decision in Vieth v. Jubelirer, 541 U.S. ___ (2004) (excerpted in the supplement to pages 118-20 and 764-68 of the main text), in which four Justices had voted to make claims of political gerrymandering nonjusticiable altogether and a fifth Justice had left open the possibility that such claims might be justiciable under some as-yet unidentified test while declining to articulate any standard that could currently be applied, meant that "the equal-population principle remains the only clear limitation on improper districting practices, and we must be careful not to dilute its strength. [T]he District Court's detailed factual findings regarding appellees' equal protection claim confirm that an impermissible partisan gerrymander is visible to the judicial eye and subject to judicially manageable standards." In particular, Justice Stevens emphasized the challenged plan's "selective incumbent protection"—in which Republican incumbents were paired against one another while Democratic incumbents were given underpopulated districts as evidence of its unconstitutionality.

Justice Scalia, the author of the plurality opinion in *Vieth* that would have held claims of unconstitutional political gerrymandering nonjusticiable, would have set the case for oral argument:

> A substantial case can be made that Georgia's redistricting plan *did* comply with the Constitution. Appellees do not contend that the population deviations—all less than 5% from the mean—were based on race or some other suspect classification. They claim only impermissible *political* bias . . . .
>
> The problem with this analysis is that it assumes "politics as usual" is not *itself* a "traditional" redistricting criterion. . . . It is not obvious to me that a legislature goes too far when it stays within the 10% disparity in population our cases allow. To say that it does is to invite allegations of political motivation whenever there is population disparity, and thus to destroy the 10% safe harbor our cases provide. Ferreting out political motives in minute population deviations seems to me more likely to encourage politically motivated litigation than to vindicate political rights.

Page 763. After Note 4, add the following:

5. *Bush v. Gore.* The Supreme Court's per curiam opinion in Bush v. Gore relies heavily on the Court's one-person, one-vote jurisprudence in holding that the recount ordered by the Florida Supreme Court violated the equal protection clause. (The decision is excerpted in the material supplementing page 135 of the main volume.) To what extent do these cases support the Court's result? Consider, for example, Karlan, Equal Protection: *Bush v. Gore* and the Making of a Precedent, in The Unfinished Election of 2000, at 159, 189 (J.N. Rakove ed., 2001) (suggesting that "the problem in *Gray* and *Reynolds* was not the random, one-time-only differential weighting of individuals' votes," in the context of an unprecedented and unanticipated recount that served to decrease, rather than heighten, inequalities in treatment, "but the systematic degradation of identifiable blocs of citizens' votes" and that the remedy of stopping the recount ignored the fundamental rights strand of the Court's earlier equal protection cases, which would have suggested that such a recount might be required); Lund, The Unbearable Rightness of *Bush v. Gore*, 23 Cardozo L. Rev. 1219 (2002) (arguing that the situation in Florida resembled the "paradigmatic" and

long-established equal protection violation that results from the stuffing of ballot boxes because there is no real distinction between adding illegal votes to the vote total and adding legal votes selectively as the recount ordered by the Florida Supreme Court would have done); Seidman, What's So Bad About Bush v. Gore? An Essay on Our Unsettled Election, 47 Wayne L. Rev. 953, 973, 984 (2001) (suggesting that the Court failed "to utilize any of the normal machinery of equal protection analysis" because it did not "[discuss] the relevant classes, [articulate] the appropriate level of review, ... [determine] whether a "purpose" or "effects" test is appropriate, [or weigh] the countervailing state interest supporting the classification"); Tribe, eroG v. HsuB and Its Disguises: Freeing Bush v. Gore from Its Hall of Mirrors, 115 Harv. L. Rev. 170, 223 (2001) (arguing that the per curiam's analysis fails to comprehend that "*Reynolds* and its progeny have become increasingly sensitive to the political dimensions of the voting process, finding in the rough and tumble of party politicking over the composition of voting districts a set of 'neutral' justifications" and thus that "'one person, one vote' is not the place to find an antidote to partisanship [that would demand] ... the sort of mechanistic, formula-driven methods of vote tabulation required by the Court in Bush v. Gore").

Page 768. Before Section C, add the following:

VIETH v. JUBELIRER, 541 U.S. ___ (2004). After the 2000 census, Pennsylvania was entitled to nineteen congressional seats. Republicans controlled both houses of the state legislature as well as the governorship. Prominent national figures in the Republican Party urged state officials to adopt a redistricting that would punish Democrats for having enacted what they saw as pro-Democrat redistricting plans in other states. The Republicans drew a plan that paired two sets of incumbent Democratic representatives against one another, and relocated a fifth Democrat into a decisively Republican district, pairing him against a Republican incumbent. The plan split cohesive communities and contained districts with highly irregular borders. Based on *Bandemer*, the district court dismissed the plaintiffs' political gerrymandering claim, finding that Democratic voters in Pennsylvania could not show consistent degradation of their influence on the political process as a whole.

On appeal, the Supreme Court affirmed. Justice Scalia's plurality opinion (joined by Chief Justice Rehnquist and Justices O'Connor and Thomas) would have overruled *Bandemer* and held political gerrymandering claims nonjusticiable. (That opinion is discussed in Chapter 1 supra.)

The other five Justices all abandoned the *Bandemer* plurality test. Justice Kennedy, who concurred in the judgment, expressed some doubt that the equal protection clause would provide a judicially manageable standard for assessing claims of unconstitutional political gerrymandering. But he suggested a different doctrinal avenue:

"The First Amendment may be the more relevant constitutional provision in future cases that allege unconstitutional partisan gerrymandering. After all, these allegations involve the First Amendment interest of not burdening or penalizing citizens because of their participation in the electoral process, their voting history, their association with a political party, or their expression of political views. See Elrod v. Burns, 427 U.S. 347 (1976) (plurality opinion). [*Elrod* and the other cases limiting political patronage are discussed at pages 1349-50 of the main text.] Under general First Amendment principles those burdens in other contexts are unconstitutional absent a compelling government interest.... As these precedents show, First Amendment concerns arise where a State enacts a law that has the purpose and effect of subjecting a group of voters or their party to disfavored treatment by reason of their views. In the context of partisan gerrymandering, that means that First Amendment concerns arise where an apportionment has the purpose and effect of burdening a group of voters' representational rights.

"The plurality suggests there is no place for the First Amendment in this area. The implication is that under the First Amendment any and all consideration of political interests in an apportionment would be invalid.... That misrepresents the First Amendment analysis. The inquiry is not whether political classifications were used. The inquiry instead is whether political classifications were used to burden a group's representational rights....

"Where it is alleged that a gerrymander had the purpose and effect of imposing burdens on a disfavored party and its voters, the First Amendment may offer a sounder and more prudential basis for intervention than does the Equal Protection Clause.... The analysis allows a pragmatic or functional assessment that accords some latitude to the States....

"The ordered working of our Republic, and of the democratic process, depends on a sense of decorum and restraint in all branches of government, and in the citizenry itself. Here, one has the sense that legislative restraint was abandoned. That should not be thought to serve the interests of our political order. Nor should it be thought to serve our interest in demonstrating to the world how democracy works. Whether spoken with concern or pride, it is unfortunate that our legislators have reached the point of declaring that, when it comes to apportionment, 'We are in the business of rigging elections.' J. Hoeffel, Six Incumbents Are a Week Away from Easy Election, Winston-Salem Journal, Jan. 27, 1998, p. B1 (quoting a North Carolina state senator).

"Still, the Court's own responsibilities require that we refrain from intervention in this instance. The failings of the many proposed standards for measuring the burden a gerrymander imposes on representational rights make our intervention improper. If workable standards do emerge to measure these burdens, however, courts should be prepared to order relief."

Justice Stevens continued to adhere to the position taken by Justice Powell in *Bandemer*: "In my view, when partisanship is the legislature's sole motivation—

when any pretense of neutrality is forsaken unabashedly and all traditional districting criteria are subverted for partisan advantage—the governing body cannot be said to have acted impartially.

"The judicial standards applicable to gerrymandering claims are deeply rooted in decisions that long preceded *Bandemer* and have been refined in later cases. Among those well-settled principles is the understanding that a district's peculiar shape might be a symptom of an illicit purpose in the line-drawing process. . . .

"The Court has made use of all three parts of Justice Powell's standard in its recent racial gerrymandering jurisprudence. In those cases, the Court has examined claims that redistricting schemes violate the equal protection guarantee where they are 'so highly irregular' on their face that they 'rationally cannot be understood as anything other than an effort' to segregate voters by race, Shaw v. Reno, 509 U.S. 630 (1993) (Shaw I), or where 'race for its own sake, and not other districting principles, was the legislature's dominant and controlling rationale in drawing its district lines.' Miller v. Johnson, 515 U.S. 900 (1995). . . .

"Undergirding the *Shaw* cases is the premise that racial gerrymanders effect a constitutional wrong when they disrupt the representational norms that ordinarily tether elected officials to their constituencies as a whole. . . . Gerrymanders subvert that representative norm because the winner of an election in a gerrymandered district inevitably will infer that her success is primarily attributable to the architect of the district rather than to a constituency defined by neutral principles. The *Shaw* cases hold that this disruption of the representative process imposes a cognizable 'representational harm.' . . .

"The risk of representational harms identified in the *Shaw* cases is equally great, if not greater, in the context of partisan gerrymanders. *Shaw I* was borne of the concern that an official elected from a racially gerrymandered district will feel beholden only to a portion of her constituents, and that those constituents will be defined by race. The parallel danger of a partisan gerrymander is that the representative will perceive that the people who put her in power are those who drew the map rather than those who cast ballots, and she will feel beholden not to a subset of her constituency, but to no part of her constituency at all. . . .

"In sum, in evaluating a challenge to a specific district, I would apply the standard set forth in the *Shaw* cases and ask whether the legislature allowed partisan considerations to dominate and control the lines drawn, forsaking all neutral principles. Under my analysis, if no neutral criterion can be identified to justify the lines drawn, and if the only possible explanation for a district's bizarre shape is a naked desire to increase partisan strength, then no rational basis exists to save the district from an equal protection challenge. Such a narrow test would cover only a few meritorious claims, but it would preclude extreme abuses . . . and it would perhaps shorten the time period in which the pernicious effects of such a gerrymander are felt. This test would mitigate the current trend under which partisan considerations are becoming the be-all and end-all in apportioning representatives."

Justice Souter, joined by Justice Ginsburg, would have thrown out the *Bandemer* test and made a "fresh start." He proposed a five-element prima facie case:

"First, the resident plaintiff would identify a cohesive political group to which he belonged, which would normally be a major party, as in this case and in *Davis*. There is no reason in principle, however, to rule out a claimant from a minor political party . . . or from a different but politically coherent group whose members engaged in bloc voting, as a large labor union might do. . . .

"Second, a plaintiff would need to show that the district of his residence paid little or no heed to those traditional districting principles whose disregard can be shown straightforwardly: contiguity, compactness, respect for political subdivisions, and conformity with geographic features like rivers and mountains. . . .

"Third, the plaintiff would need to establish specific correlations between the district's deviations from traditional districting principles and the distribution of the population of his group. For example, one of the districts to which appellants object most strongly in this case is District 6, which they say 'looms like a dragon descending on Philadelphia from the west, splitting up towns and communities throughout Montgomery and Berks Counties.' To make their claim stick, they would need to point to specific protuberances on the draconian shape that reach out to include Democrats, or fissures in it that squirm away from Republicans. They would need to show that when towns and communities were split, Democrats tended to fall on one side and Republicans on the other. . . .

"Fourth, a plaintiff would need to present the court with a hypothetical district including his residence, one in which the proportion of the plaintiff's group was lower (in a packing claim) or higher (in a cracking one) and which at the same time deviated less from traditional districting principles than the actual district. . . .

"Fifth, and finally, the plaintiff would have to show that the defendants acted intentionally to manipulate the shape of the district in order to pack or crack his group. . . . I would . . . treat any showing of intent in a major-party case as too equivocal to count unless the entire legislature were controlled by the governor's party (or the dominant legislative party were vetoproof). . . .

"I would then shift the burden to the defendants to justify their decision by reference to objectives other than naked partisan advantage. They might show by rebuttal evidence that districting objectives could not be served by the plaintiff's hypothetical district better than by the district as drawn, or they might affirmatively establish legitimate objectives better served by the lines drawn than by the plaintiff's hypothetical.

"The State might, for example, posit the need to avoid racial vote dilution. It might plead one person, one vote, a standard compatible with gerrymandering but in some places perhaps unattainable without some lopsided proportions. The State might adopt the object of proportional representation among its political parties through its districting process.

"This is not, however, the time or place for a comprehensive list of legitimate objectives a State might present. The point here is simply that the Constitution should not petrify traditional districting objectives as exclusive, and it is enough to say that the State would be required to explain itself, to demonstrate that whatever reasons it gave were more than a mere pretext for an old-fashioned gerrymander."

Justice Breyer also dissented:

"I start with a fundamental principle. 'We the People,' who 'ordained and established' the American Constitution, sought to create and to protect a workable form of government that is in its 'principles, structure, and whole mass,' basically democratic. In a modern Nation of close to 300 million people, the workable democracy that the Constitution foresees must mean more than a guaranteed opportunity to elect legislators representing equally populous electoral districts. There must also be a method for transforming the will of the majority into effective government.

"This Court has explained that political parties play a necessary role in that transformation. At a minimum, they help voters assign responsibility for current circumstances, thereby enabling those voters, through their votes for individual candidates, to express satisfaction or dissatisfaction with the political status quo. . . . A party-based political system that satisfies this minimal condition encourages democratic responsibility. It facilitates the transformation of the voters' will into a government that reflects that will.

"Why do I refer to these elementary constitutional principles? Because I believe they can help courts identify at least one abuse at issue in this case. To understand how that is so, one should begin by asking why single-member electoral districts are the norm, why the Constitution does not insist that the membership of legislatures better reflect different political views held by different groups of voters. History, of course, is part of the answer, but it does not tell the entire story. The answer also lies in the fact that a single-member-district system helps to assure certain democratic objectives better than many 'more representative' (i.e., proportional) electoral systems. Of course, single-member districts mean that only parties with candidates who finish 'first past the post' will elect legislators. That fact means in turn that a party with a bare majority of votes or even a plurality of votes will often obtain a large legislative majority, perhaps freezing out smaller parties. But single-member districts thereby diminish the need for coalition governments. And that fact makes it easier for voters to identify which party is responsible for government decisionmaking (and which rascals to throw out), while simultaneously providing greater legislative stability. . . .

"If single-member districts are the norm, however, then political considerations will likely play an important, and proper, role in the drawing of district boundaries. . . .

"More important for present purposes, the role of political considerations reflects a surprising mathematical fact. Given a fairly large state population with a fairly large congressional delegation, districts assigned so as to be perfectly random in respect to politics would translate a small shift in political sentiment, say a shift from 51% Republican to 49% Republican, into a seismic shift in the makeup of the legislative delegation, say from 100% Republican to 100% Democrat. Any such exaggeration of tiny electoral changes—virtually wiping out legislative representation of the minority party—would itself seem highly undemocratic....

"[R]eference back to these underlying considerations helps to explain why the legislature's use of political boundary drawing considerations ordinarily does not violate the Constitution's Equal Protection Clause. The reason lies not simply in the difficulty of identifying abuse or finding an appropriate judicial remedy. The reason is more fundamental: Ordinarily, there simply is no abuse. The use of purely political boundary-drawing factors, even where harmful to the members of one party, will often nonetheless find justification in other desirable democratic ends, such as maintaining relatively stable legislatures in which a minority party retains significant representation.

"At the same time, these considerations can help identify at least one circumstance where use of purely political boundary-drawing factors can amount to a serious, and remediable, abuse, namely the unjustified use of political factors to entrench a minority in power. By entrenchment I mean a situation in which a party that enjoys only minority support among the populace has nonetheless contrived to take, and hold, legislative power. By unjustified entrenchment I mean that the minority's hold on power is purely the result of partisan manipulation and not other factors....

"Courts need not intervene often to prevent the kind of abuse I have described, because those harmed constitute a political majority, and a majority normally can work its political will. Where a State has improperly gerrymandered legislative or congressional districts to the majority's disadvantage, the majority should be able to elect officials in statewide races—particularly the Governor—who may help to undo the harm that districting has caused the majority's party, in the next round of districting if not sooner. And where a State has improperly gerrymandered congressional districts, Congress retains the power to revise the State's districting determinations.

"Moreover, voters in some States, perhaps tiring of the political boundary-drawing rivalry, have found a procedural solution, confiding the task to a commission that is limited in the extent to which it may base districts on partisan concerns. According to the National Conference of State Legislatures, 12 States currently give 'first and final authority for [state] legislative redistricting to a group other than the legislature.' A number of States use a commission for congressional redistricting: Arizona, Hawaii, Idaho, Montana, New Jersey, and Washington, with Indiana using a commission if the legislature cannot pass a plan and Iowa requiring the district-drawing body not to consider political data. Indeed, where state governments have been unwilling or unable to act, "an informed, civically militant electorate," Baker v. Carr, 369 U.S. 186, 270 (1962) (Frankfurter, J., dissenting), has occasionally taken matters into its own hands, through ballot initiatives or referendums. Arizona voters, for example, passed Proposition 106, which amended the State's Constitution and created an independent redistricting commission to draw legislative and congressional districts. . . .

"But we cannot always count on a severely gerrymandered legislature itself to find and implement a remedy. The party that controls the process has no incentive to change it. And the political advantages of a gerrymander may become ever greater in the future. The availability of enhanced computer technology allows the parties to redraw boundaries in ways that target individual neighborhoods and homes, carving out safe but slim victory margins in the maximum number of districts, with little risk of cutting their margins too thin. By redrawing districts every 2 years, rather than every 10 years, a party might preserve its political advantages notwithstanding population shifts in the State. The combination of increasingly precise map-drawing technology and increasingly frequent map drawing means that a party may be able to bring about a gerrymander that is not only precise, but virtually impossible to dislodge. Thus, court action may prove necessary. . . .

"[C]ourts can identify a number of strong indicia of abuse. The presence of actual entrenchment, while not always unjustified (being perhaps a chance occurrence), is such a sign, particularly when accompanied by the use of partisan boundary drawing criteria in the way that Justice Stevens describes, i.e., a use that both departs from traditional criteria and cannot be explained other than by efforts to achieve partisan advantage. . . . The more permanently entrenched the minority's hold on power becomes, the less evidence courts will need that the minority engaged in gerrymandering to achieve the desired result. . . ."

F. Modern Substantive Due Process

Page 901. Before the Note, add the following:

LAWRENCE v. TEXAS
539 U.S. 558 (2003)

JUSTICE KENNEDY delivered the opinion of the Court.

Liberty protects the person from unwarranted government intrusions into a dwelling or other private places. In our tradition the State is not omnipresent in the home. And there are other spheres of our lives and existence, outside the home, where the State should not be a dominant presence. Freedom extends beyond spatial bounds. Liberty presumes an autonomy of self that includes freedom of thought, belief, expression, and certain intimate conduct. The instant case involves liberty of the person both in its spatial and more transcendent dimensions.

I

The question before the Court is the validity of a Texas statute making it a crime for two persons of the same sex to engage in certain intimate sexual conduct.

In Houston, Texas, officers of the Harris County Police Department were dispatched to a private residence in response to a reported weapons disturbance. They entered an apartment where one of the petitioners, John Geddes Lawrence, resided. The right of the police to enter does not seem to have been questioned. The officers observed Lawrence and another man, Tyron Garner, engaging in a sexual act. The two petitioners were arrested, held in custody overnight, and charged and convicted before a Justice of the Peace.

The complaints described their crime as "deviate sexual intercourse, namely anal sex, with a member of the same sex (man)." The applicable state law is Tex. Penal Code Ann. § 21.06(a) (2003). It provides: "A person commits an offense if he engages in deviate sexual intercourse with another individual of the same sex." The statute defines "[d]eviate sexual intercourse" as follows:

> "(A) any contact between any part of the genitals of one person and the mouth or anus of another person; or
> "(B) the penetration of the genitals or the anus of another person with an object."
> § 21.01(1)....

We granted certiorari, 537 U.S. 1044 (2002), to consider three questions:

> "1. Whether Petitioners' criminal convictions under the Texas "Homosexual Conduct" law—which criminalizes sexual intimacy by same-sex couples, but not identical behavior by different-sex couples—violate the Fourteenth Amendment guarantee of equal protection of laws?

> "2. Whether Petitioners' criminal convictions for adult consensual sexual intimacy in the home violate their vital interests in liberty and privacy protected by the Due Process Clause of the Fourteenth Amendment?

> "3. Whether Bowers v. Hardwick, 478 U.S. 186 (1986), should be overruled?"

The petitioners were adults at the time of the alleged offense. Their conduct was in private and consensual.

II

We conclude the case should be resolved by determining whether the petitioners were free as adults to engage in the private conduct in the exercise of their liberty under the Due Process Clause of the Fourteenth Amendment to the Constitution. For this inquiry we deem it necessary to reconsider the Court's holding in *Bowers*.

There are broad statements of the substantive reach of liberty under the Due Process Clause in earlier cases, including Pierce v. Society of Sisters, 268 U.S. 510 (1925), and Meyer v. Nebraska, 262 U.S. 390 (1923); but the most pertinent beginning point is our decision in Griswold v. Connecticut, 381 U.S. 479 (1965).

In *Griswold* the Court invalidated a state law prohibiting the use of drugs or devices of contraception and counseling or aiding and abetting the use of contraceptives. The Court described the protected interest as a right to privacy and placed emphasis on the marriage relation and the protected space of the marital bedroom.

After *Griswold* it was established that the right to make certain decisions regarding sexual conduct extends beyond the marital relationship. In Eisenstadt v. Baird, 405 U.S. 438 (1972), the Court invalidated a law prohibiting the distribution of contraceptives to unmarried persons. The case was decided under the Equal Protection Clause, but with respect to unmarried persons, the Court went on to state the fundamental proposition that the law impaired the exercise of their personal rights. It quoted from the statement of the Court of Appeals finding the law to be in conflict with fundamental human rights, and it followed with this statement of its own:

> It is true that in *Griswold* the right of privacy in question inhered in the marital relationship. . . . If the right of privacy means anything, it is the right of the *individual*, married or single, to be free from unwarranted governmental intrusion into matters so fundamentally affecting a person as the decision whether to bear or beget a child.

The opinions in *Griswold* and *Eisenstadt* were part of the background for the decision in Roe v. Wade, 410 U.S. 113 (1973). . . . *Roe* recognized the right of a woman to make certain fundamental decisions affecting her destiny and confirmed once more that the protection of liberty under the Due Process Clause has a substantive dimension of fundamental significance in defining the rights of the person.

In Carey v. Population Services Int'l, 431 U.S. 678 (1977), the Court confronted a New York law forbidding sale or distribution of contraceptive devices to persons under 16 years of age. Although there was no single opinion for the Court, the law was invalidated. Both *Eisenstadt* and *Carey*, as well as the holding and rationale in *Roe*, confirmed that the reasoning of *Griswold* could not be confined to the protection of rights of married adults. This was the state of the law with respect to some of the most relevant cases when the Court considered Bowers v. Hardwick. . . .

The Court began its substantive discussion in *Bowers* as follows: "The issue presented is whether the Federal Constitution confers a fundamental right upon homosexuals to engage in sodomy and hence invalidates the laws of the many States that still make such conduct illegal and have done so for a very long time." That statement, we now conclude, discloses the Court's own failure to appreciate the extent of the liberty at stake. To say that the issue in *Bowers* was simply the right to engage in certain sexual conduct demeans the claim the individual put forward, just as it would demean a married couple were it to be said marriage is simply about the right to have sexual intercourse. The laws involved in *Bowers* and there are, to be sure, statutes that purport to do no more than prohibit a particular sexual act. Their penalties and purposes, though, have more far-reaching consequences, touching upon the most private human conduct, sexual behavior, and in the most private of places, the home. The statutes do seek to control a personal relationship that, whether or not entitled to formal recognition in the law, is within the liberty of persons to choose without being punished as criminals.

This, as a general rule, should counsel against attempts by the State, or a court, to define the meaning of the relationship or to set its boundaries absent injury to a person or abuse of an institution the law protects. It suffices for us to acknowledge that adults may choose to enter upon this relationship in the confines of their homes and their own private lives and still retain their dignity as free persons. When sexuality finds overt expression in intimate conduct with another person, the conduct can be but one element in a personal bond that is more enduring. The liberty protected by the Constitution allows homosexual persons the right to make this choice.

Having misapprehended the claim of liberty there presented to it, and thus stating the claim to be whether there is a fundamental right to engage in consensual sodomy, the *Bowers* Court said: "Proscriptions against that conduct have ancient roots." In academic writings, and in many of the scholarly amicus briefs filed to assist the Court in this case, there are fundamental criticisms of [this statement.] We need not enter this debate in the attempt to reach a definitive historical judgment, but the following considerations counsel against adopting the definitive conclusions upon which *Bowers* placed such reliance.

At the outset it should be noted that there is no longstanding history in this country of laws directed at homosexual conduct as a distinct matter. Beginning in colonial times there were prohibitions of sodomy derived from the English criminal laws passed in the first instance by the Reformation Parliament of 1533. . . . The absence of legal prohibitions focusing on homosexual conduct may be explained in part by noting that according to some scholars the concept of the homosexual as a distinct category of person did not emerge until the late 19th century. See, e.g., J. Katz, The Invention of Heterosexuality 10 (1995); J. D'Emilio & E. Freedman, Intimate Matters: A History of Sexuality in America 121 (2d ed. 1997) ("The modern terms homosexuality and heterosexuality do not apply to an era that had not yet articulated these distinctions"). Thus early American sodomy laws were not directed at homosexuals as such but instead sought to prohibit nonprocreative sexual activity more generally. This does not suggest approval of homosexual conduct. It does tend to show that this particular form of conduct was not thought of as a separate category from like conduct between heterosexual persons.

Laws prohibiting sodomy do not seem to have been enforced against consenting adults acting in private. A substantial number of sodomy prosecutions and convictions for which there are surviving records were for predatory acts against those who could not or did not consent, as in the case of a minor or the victim of an assault. As to these, one purpose for the prohibitions was to ensure there would be no lack of coverage if a predator committed a sexual assault that did not constitute rape as defined by the criminal law. Thus the model sodomy indictments presented in a 19th-century treatise, addressed the predatory acts of an adult man against a minor girl or minor boy. Instead of targeting relations between consenting adults in private, 19th-century sodomy prosecutions typically involved relations between men and minor girls or minor boys, relations between adults involving force, relations between adults implicating disparity in status, or relations between men and animals.

To the extent that there were any prosecutions for the acts in question, 19th-century evidence rules imposed a burden that would make a conviction more difficult to obtain even taking into account the problems always inherent in prosecuting consensual acts committed in private. . . . In all events that infrequency makes it difficult to say that society approved of a rigorous and systematic punishment of the consensual acts committed in private and by adults. The longstanding criminal prohibition of homosexual sodomy upon which the *Bowers* decision placed such reliance is as consistent with a general condemnation of nonprocreative sex as it is with an established tradition of prosecuting acts because of their homosexual character.

The policy of punishing consenting adults for private acts was not much discussed in the early legal literature. We can infer that one reason for this was the very private nature of the conduct. Despite the absence of prosecutions, there may have been periods in which there was public criticism of homosexuals as such and an insistence that the criminal laws be enforced to discourage their practices. But far from possessing "ancient roots," *Bowers*, 478 U.S., at 192, American laws targeting same-sex couples did not develop until the last third of the 20th century. The reported decisions concerning the prosecution of consensual, homosexual sodomy between adults for the years 1880-1995 are not always clear in the details, but a significant number involved conduct in a public place.

It was not until the 1970's that any State singled out same-sex relations for criminal prosecution, and only nine States have done so. Post-*Bowers* even some of these States did not adhere to the policy of suppressing homosexual conduct. Over the course of the last decades, States with same-sex prohibitions have moved toward abolishing them.

In summary, the historical grounds relied upon in *Bowers* are more complex than the majority opinion and the concurring opinion by Chief Justice Burger indicate. Their historical premises are not without doubt and, at the very least, are overstated.

It must be acknowledged, of course, that the Court in *Bowers* was making the broader point that for centuries there have been powerful voices to condemn homosexual conduct as immoral. The condemnation has been shaped by religious beliefs, conceptions of right and acceptable behavior, and respect for the traditional family. For many persons these are not trivial concerns but profound and deep convictions accepted as ethical and moral principles to which they aspire and which thus determine the course of their lives. These considerations do not answer the question before us, however. The issue is whether the majority may use the power of the State to enforce these views on the whole society through operation of the criminal law. . . .

Chief Justice Burger joined the opinion for the Court in *Bowers* and further explained his views as follows: "Decisions of individuals relating to homosexual conduct have been subject to state intervention throughout the history of Western civilization. Condemnation of those practices is firmly rooted in Judeao-Christian moral and ethical standards." As with Justice White's assumptions about history, scholarship casts some doubt on the sweeping nature of the statement by Chief Justice Burger as it pertains to private homosexual conduct between consenting adults. In all events we think that our laws and traditions in the past half century are of most relevance here. These references show an emerging awareness that liberty gives substantial protection to adult persons in deciding how to conduct their private lives in matters pertaining to sex. "[H]istory and tradition are the starting point but not in all cases the ending point of the substantive due process inquiry." County of Sacramento v. Lewis, 523 U.S. 833, 857 (1998) (Kennedy, J., concurring).

This emerging recognition should have been apparent when *Bowers* was decided. In 1955 the American Law Institute promulgated the Model Penal Code and made clear that it did not recommend or provide for "criminal penalties for consensual sexual relations conducted in private." ALI, Model Penal Code § 213.2, Comment 2, p. 372 (1980). It justified its decision on three grounds: (1) The prohibitions undermined respect for the law by penalizing conduct many people engaged in; (2) the statutes regulated private conduct not harmful to others; and (3) the laws were arbitrarily enforced and thus invited the danger of blackmail. ALI, Model Penal Code, Commentary 277-280 (Tent. Draft No. 4, 1955). In 1961 Illinois changed its laws to conform to the Model Penal Code. Other States soon followed. . . .

The sweeping references by Chief Justice Burger to the history of Western civilization and to Judeo-Christian moral and ethical standards did not take account of other authorities pointing in an opposite direction. A committee advising the British Parliament recommended in 1957 repeal of laws punishing homosexual conduct. The Wolfenden Report: Report of the Committee on Homosexual Offenses and Prostitution (1963). Parliament enacted the substance of those recommendations 10 years later. Sexual Offences Act 1967, § 1.

Of even more importance, almost five years before *Bowers* was decided the European Court of Human Rights considered a case with parallels to *Bowers* and to today's case. An adult male resident in Northern Ireland alleged he was a practicing homosexual who desired to engage in consensual homosexual conduct. The laws of Northern Ireland forbade him that right. He alleged that he had been questioned, his home had been searched, and he feared criminal prosecution. The court held that the laws proscribing the conduct were invalid under the European Convention on Human Rights. Dudgeon v. United Kingdom, 45 Eur. Ct. H. R. (1981) ¶52. Authoritative in all countries that are members of the Council of Europe (21 nations then, 45 nations now), the decision is at odds with the premise in *Bowers* that the claim put forward was insubstantial in our Western civilization.

In our own constitutional system the deficiencies in *Bowers* became even more apparent in the years following its announcement. The 25 States with laws prohibiting the relevant conduct referenced in the *Bowers* decision are reduced now to 13, of which 4 enforce their laws only against homosexual conduct. In those States where sodomy is still proscribed, whether for same-sex or heterosexual conduct, there is a pattern of nonenforcement with respect to consenting adults acting in private. The State of Texas admitted in 1994 that as of that date it had not prosecuted anyone under those circumstances.

Two principal cases decided after *Bowers* cast its holding into even more doubt. In Planned Parenthood of Southeastern Pa. v. Casey, 505 U.S. 833 (1992), the Court reaffirmed the substantive force of the liberty protected by the Due Process Clause. The *Casey* decision again confirmed that our laws and tradition afford constitutional protection to personal decisions relating to marriage, procreation, contraception, family relationships, child rearing, and education. In explaining the respect the Constitution demands for the autonomy of the person in making these choices, we stated as follows:

> These matters, involving the most intimate and personal choices a person may make in a lifetime, choices central to personal dignity and autonomy, are central to the liberty protected by the Fourteenth Amendment. At the heart of liberty is the right to define one's own concept of existence, of meaning, of the universe, and of the mystery of human life. Beliefs about these matters could not define the attributes of personhood were they formed under compulsion of the State.

Persons in a homosexual relationship may seek autonomy for these purposes, just as heterosexual persons do. The decision in *Bowers* would deny them this right.

The second post-*Bowers* case of principal relevance is Romer v. Evans, 517 U.S. 620 (1996). There the Court struck down class-based legislation directed at homosexuals as a violation of the Equal Protection Clause. . . .

As an alternative argument in this case, counsel for the petitioners and some amici contend that *Romer* provides the basis for declaring the Texas statute invalid under the Equal Protection Clause. That is a tenable argument, but we conclude the instant case requires us to address whether *Bowers* itself has continuing validity. Were we to hold the statute invalid under the Equal Protection Clause some might question whether a prohibition would be valid if drawn differently, say, to prohibit the conduct both between same-sex and different-sex participants.

Equality of treatment and the due process right to demand respect for conduct protected by the substantive guarantee of liberty are linked in important respects, and a decision on the latter point advances both interests. If protected conduct is made criminal and the law which does so remains unexamined for its substantive validity, its stigma might remain even if it were not enforceable as drawn for equal protection reasons. When homosexual conduct is made criminal by the law of the State, that declaration in and of itself is an invitation to subject homosexual persons to discrimination both in the public and in the private spheres. The central holding of *Bowers* has been brought in question by this case, and it should be addressed. Its continuance as precedent demeans the lives of homosexual persons.

The stigma this criminal statute imposes, moreover, is not trivial. The offense, to be sure, is but a class C misdemeanor, a minor offense in the Texas legal system. Still, it remains a criminal offense with all that imports for the dignity of the persons charged. The petitioners will bear on their record the history of their criminal convictions. . . . We are advised that if Texas convicted an adult for private, consensual homosexual conduct under the statute here in question the convicted person would come within the registration laws of at least four States were he or she to be subject to their jurisdiction. This underscores the consequential nature of the punishment and the state-sponsored condemnation attendant to the criminal prohibition. Furthermore, the Texas criminal conviction carries with it the other collateral consequences always following a conviction, such as notations on job application forms, to mention but one example.

The foundations of *Bowers* have sustained serious erosion from our recent decisions in *Casey* and *Romer*. When our precedent has been thus weakened, criticism from other sources is of greater significance. In the United States criticism of *Bowers* has been substantial and continuing, disapproving of its reasoning in all respects, not just as to its historical assumptions. The courts of five different States have declined to follow it in interpreting provisions in their own state constitutions parallel to the Due Process Clause of the Fourteenth Amendment.

To the extent *Bowers* relied on values we share with a wider civilization, it should be noted that the reasoning and holding in *Bowers* have been rejected elsewhere. The European Court of Human Rights has followed not *Bowers* but its own decision in Dudgeon v. United Kingdom. Other nations, too, have taken action consistent with an affirmation of the protected right of homosexual adults to engage in intimate, consensual conduct. The right the petitioners seek in this case has been accepted as an integral part of human freedom in many other countries. There has been no showing that in this country the governmental interest in circumscribing personal choice is somehow more legitimate or urgent.

The doctrine of stare decisis is essential to the respect accorded to the judgments of the Court and to the stability of the law. It is not, however, an inexorable command. In *Casey* we noted that when a Court is asked to overrule a precedent recognizing a constitutional liberty interest, individual or societal reliance on the existence of that liberty cautions with particular strength against reversing course. The holding in *Bowers*, however, has not induced detrimental reliance comparable to some instances where recognized individual rights are involved. Indeed, there has been no individual or societal reliance on *Bowers* of the sort that could counsel against overturning its holding once there are compelling reasons to do so. *Bowers* itself causes uncertainty, for the precedents before and after its issuance contradict its central holding.

The rationale of *Bowers* does not withstand careful analysis. In his dissenting opinion in *Bowers* Justice Stevens came to these conclusions:

> Our prior cases make two propositions abundantly clear. First, the fact that the governing majority in a State has traditionally viewed a particular practice as immoral is not a sufficient reason for upholding a law prohibiting the practice; neither history nor tradition could save a law prohibiting miscegenation from constitutional attack. Second, individual decisions by married persons, concerning the intimacies of their physical relationship, even when not intended to produce offspring, are a form of "liberty" protected by the Due Process Clause of the Fourteenth Amendment. Moreover, this protection extends to intimate choices by unmarried as well as married persons.

Justice Stevens' analysis, in our view, should have been controlling in *Bowers* and should control here.

Bowers was not correct when it was decided, and it is not correct today. It ought not to remain binding precedent. Bowers v. Hardwick should be and now is overruled.

The present case does not involve minors. It does not involve persons who might be injured or coerced or who are situated in relationships where consent might not easily be refused. It does not involve public conduct or prostitution. It does not involve whether the government must give formal recognition to any relationship that homosexual persons seek to enter. The case does involve two adults who, with full and mutual consent from each other, engaged in sexual practices common to a homosexual lifestyle. The petitioners are entitled to respect for their private lives. The State cannot demean their existence or control their destiny by making their private sexual conduct a crime. Their right to liberty under the Due Process Clause gives them the full right to engage in their conduct without intervention of the government. The Texas statute furthers no legitimate state interest which can justify its intrusion into the personal and private life of the individual.

Had those who drew and ratified the Due Process Clauses of the Fifth Amendment or the Fourteenth Amendment known the components of liberty in its manifold possibilities, they might have been more specific. They did not presume to have this insight. They knew times can blind us to certain truths and later generations can see that laws once thought necessary and proper in fact serve only to oppress. As the Constitution endures, persons in every generation can invoke its principles in their own search for greater freedom....

Implied Fundamental Rights

JUSTICE O'CONNOR, concurring in the judgment.

The Court today overrules Bowers v. Hardwick, 478 U.S. 186 (1986). I joined *Bowers*, and do not join the Court in overruling it. Nevertheless, I agree with the Court that Texas' statute banning same-sex sodomy is unconstitutional. Rather than relying on the substantive component of the Fourteenth Amendment's Due Process Clause, as the Court does, I base my conclusion on the Fourteenth Amendment's Equal Protection Clause. . . .

This case raises a different issue than *Bowers*: whether, under the Equal Protection Clause, moral disapproval is a legitimate state interest to justify by itself a statute that bans homosexual sodomy, but not heterosexual sodomy. It is not. Moral disapproval of this group, like a bare desire to harm the group, is an interest that is insufficient to satisfy rational basis review under the Equal Protection Clause. Indeed, we have never held that moral disapproval, without any other asserted state interest, is a sufficient rationale under the Equal Protection Clause to justify a law that discriminates among groups of persons.

Moral disapproval of a group cannot be a legitimate governmental interest under the Equal Protection Clause because legal classifications must not be "drawn for the purpose of disadvantaging the group burdened by the law." Texas' invocation of moral disapproval as a legitimate state interest proves nothing more than Texas' desire to criminalize homosexual sodomy. But the Equal Protection Clause prevents a State from creating "a classification of persons undertaken for its own sake." And because Texas so rarely enforces its sodomy law as applied to private, consensual acts, the law serves more as a statement of dislike and disapproval against homosexuals than as a tool to stop criminal behavior. . . .

A State can of course assign certain consequences to a violation of its criminal law. But the State cannot single out one identifiable class of citizens for punishment that does not apply to everyone else, with moral disapproval as the only asserted state interest for the law. The Texas sodomy statute subjects homosexuals to "a lifelong penalty and stigma. . . .

A law branding one class of persons as criminal solely based on the State's moral disapproval of that class and the conduct associated with that class runs contrary to the values of the Constitution and the Equal Protection Clause, under any standard of review. I therefore concur in the Court's judgment that Texas' sodomy law banning "deviate sexual intercourse" between consenting adults of the same sex, but not between consenting adults of different sexes, is unconstitutional.

JUSTICE SCALIA, with whom THE CHIEF JUSTICE and JUSTICE THOMAS join, dissenting.

[I] begin with the Court's surprising readiness to reconsider a decision rendered a mere 17 years ago in Bowers v. Hardwick. I do not myself believe in rigid adherence to stare decisis in constitutional cases; but I do believe that we should be consistent rather than manipulative in invoking the doctrine. Today's opinions in support of reversal do not bother to distinguish—or indeed, even bother to mention—the paean to stare decisis coauthored by three Members of today's majority in Planned Parenthood v. Casey....

Today's approach to stare decisis invites us to overrule an erroneously decided precedent (including an "intensely divisive" decision) if: (1) its foundations have been "eroded" by subsequent decisions; (2) it has been subject to "substantial and continuing" criticism; and (3) it has not induced "individual or societal reliance" that counsels against overturning. The problem is that *Roe* itself—which today's majority surely has no disposition to overrule—satisfies these conditions to at least the same degree as *Bowers*....

I do not quarrel with the Court's claim that Romer v. Evans, 517 U.S. 620 (1996), "eroded" the "foundations" of *Bowers*' rational-basis holding. But *Roe* and *Casey* have been equally "eroded" by Washington v. Glucksberg, 521 U.S. 702, 721 (1997), which held that only fundamental rights which are "'deeply rooted in this Nation's history and tradition'" qualify for anything other than rational basis scrutiny under the doctrine of "substantive due process." *Roe* and *Casey*, of course, subjected the restriction of abortion to heightened scrutiny without even attempting to establish that the freedom to abort was rooted in this Nation's tradition.

Bowers, the Court says, has been subject to "substantial and continuing [criticism], disapproving of its reasoning in all respects, not just as to its historical assumptions." [Of] course, *Roe* too (and by extension *Casey*) had been (and still is) subject to unrelenting criticism, including criticism from the two commentators cited by the Court today.

That leaves, to distinguish the rock-solid, unamendable disposition of *Roe* from the readily overrulable *Bowers*, only the third factor. "[T]here has been," the Court says, "no individual or societal reliance on *Bowers* of the sort that could counsel against overturning its holding . . . ." It seems to me that the "societal reliance" on the principles confirmed in *Bowers* and discarded today has been overwhelming. Countless judicial decisions and legislative enactments have relied on the ancient proposition that a governing majority's belief that certain sexual behavior is "immoral and unacceptable" constitutes a rational basis for regulation. . . . State laws against bigamy, same-sex marriage, adult incest, prostitution, masturbation, adultery, fornication, bestiality, and obscenity are likewise sustainable only in light of *Bowers*' validation of laws based on moral choices. Every single one of these laws is called into question by today's decision; the Court makes no effort to cabin the scope of its decision to exclude them from its holding. The impossibility of distinguishing homosexuality from other traditional "morals" offenses is precisely why *Bowers* rejected the rational-basis challenge. . . .

What a massive disruption of the current social order, therefore, the overruling of *Bowers* entails. Not so the overruling of *Roe*, which would simply have restored the regime that existed for centuries before 1973, in which the permissibility of and restrictions upon abortion were determined legislatively State-by-State....

To tell the truth, it does not surprise me, and should surprise no one, that the Court has chosen today to revise the standards of stare decisis set forth in *Casey*. It has thereby exposed *Casey*'s extraordinary deference to precedent for the result-oriented expedient that it is....

Texas Penal Code Ann. § 21.06(a) (2003) undoubtedly imposes constraints on liberty. So do laws prohibiting prostitution, recreational use of heroin, and, for that matter, working more than 60 hours per week in a bakery. But there is no right to "liberty" under the Due Process Clause, though today's opinion repeatedly makes that claim. The Fourteenth Amendment expressly allows States to deprive their citizens of "liberty," so long as "due process of law" is provided:

> No state shall ... deprive any person of life, liberty, or property, *without due process of law*." Amdt. 14 (emphasis added).

Our opinions applying the doctrine known as "substantive due process" hold that the Due Process Clause prohibits States from infringing fundamental liberty interests, unless the infringement is narrowly tailored to serve a compelling state interest. We have held repeatedly, in cases the Court today does not overrule, that only fundamental rights qualify for this so-called "heightened scrutiny" protection—that is, rights which are "'deeply rooted in this Nation's history and tradition.'" All other liberty interests may be abridged or abrogated pursuant to a validly enacted state law if that law is rationally related to a legitimate state interest.

The Court's description of "the state of the law" at the time of *Bowers* only confirms that *Bowers* was right. The Court points to Griswold v. Connecticut, 381 U.S. 479, 481-482 (1965). But that case expressly disclaimed any reliance on the doctrine of "substantive due process," and grounded the so-called "right to privacy" in penumbras of constitutional provisions other than the Due Process Clause. Eisenstadt v. Baird, 405 U.S. 438 (1972), likewise had nothing to do with "substantive due process"; it invalidated a Massachusetts law prohibiting the distribution of contraceptives to unmarried persons solely on the basis of the Equal Protection Clause. Of course *Eisenstadt* contains well known dictum relating to the "right to privacy," but this referred to the right recognized in *Griswold*—a right penumbral to the specific guarantees in the Bill of Rights, and not a "substantive due process" right....

After discussing the history of antisodomy laws, the Court proclaims that, "it should be noted that there is no longstanding history in this country of laws directed at homosexual conduct as a distinct matter." This observation in no way casts into doubt the "definitive [historical] conclusion," on which *Bowers* relied: that our Nation has a longstanding history of laws prohibiting sodomy in general—regardless of whether it was performed by same-sex or opposite-sex couples....

It is (as *Bowers* recognized) entirely irrelevant whether the laws in our long national tradition criminalizing homosexual sodomy were "directed at homosexual conduct as a distinct matter." Whether homosexual sodomy was prohibited by a law targeted at same-sex sexual relations or by a more general law prohibiting both homosexual and heterosexual sodomy, the only relevant point is that it was criminalized—which suffices to establish that homosexual sodomy is not a right "deeply rooted in our Nation's history and tradition." The Court today agrees that homosexual sodomy was criminalized and thus does not dispute the facts on which *Bowers* actually relied.

Next the Court makes the claim, again unsupported by any citations, that "[l]aws prohibiting sodomy do not seem to have been enforced against consenting adults acting in private." The key qualifier here is "acting in private"—since the Court admits that sodomy laws were enforced against consenting adults (although the Court contends that prosecutions were "infrequent"). I do not know what "acting in private" means; surely consensual sodomy, like heterosexual intercourse, is rarely performed on stage.... *Bowers*' conclusion that homosexual sodomy is not a fundamental right "deeply rooted in this Nation's history and tradition" is utterly unassailable.

Realizing that fact, the Court instead says: "[W]e think that our laws and traditions in the past half century are of most relevance here. These references show *an emerging awareness* that liberty gives substantial protection to adult persons in deciding how to conduct their private lives *in matters pertaining to sex*." (emphasis added). Apart from the fact that such an "emerging awareness" does not establish a "fundamental right," the statement is factually false. States continue to prosecute all sorts of crimes by adults "in matters pertaining to sex": prostitution, adult incest, adultery, obscenity, and child pornography. Sodomy laws, too, have been enforced "in the past half century," in which there have been 134 reported cases involving prosecutions for consensual, adult, homosexual sodomy....

In any event, an "emerging awareness" is by definition not "deeply rooted in this Nation's history and tradition[s]," as we have said "fundamental right" status requires. Constitutional entitlements do not spring into existence because some States choose to lessen or eliminate criminal sanctions on certain behavior. Much less do they spring into existence, as the Court seems to believe, because foreign nations decriminalize conduct.... The Court's discussion of these foreign views (ignoring, of course, the many countries that have retained criminal prohibitions on sodomy) is therefore meaningless dicta....

I turn now to the ground on which the Court squarely rests its holding: the contention that there is no rational basis for the law here under attack. This proposition is so out of accord with our jurisprudence—indeed, with the jurisprudence of any society we know—that it requires little discussion.

The Texas statute undeniably seeks to further the belief of its citizens that certain forms of sexual behavior are "immoral and unacceptable"—the same interest furthered by criminal laws against fornication, bigamy, adultery, adult incest, bestiality, and obscenity. *Bowers* held that this was a legitimate state interest. The Court today reaches the opposite conclusion. The Texas statute, it says, "furthers no legitimate state interest which can justify its intrusion into the personal and private life of the individual." The Court embraces instead Justice Stevens' declaration in his *Bowers* dissent, that "the fact that the governing majority in a State has traditionally viewed a particular practice as immoral is not a sufficient reason for upholding a law prohibiting the practice." This effectively decrees the end of all morals legislation. If, as the Court asserts, the promotion of majoritarian sexual morality is not even a legitimate state interest, none of the above-mentioned laws can survive rational-basis review....

Today's opinion is the product of a Court, which is the product of a law-profession culture, that has largely signed on to the so-called homosexual agenda, by which I mean the agenda promoted by some homosexual activists directed at eliminating the moral opprobrium that has traditionally attached to homosexual conduct....

One of the most revealing statements in today's opinion is the Court's grim warning that the criminalization of homosexual conduct is "an invitation to subject homosexual persons to discrimination both in the public and in the private spheres." It is clear from this that the Court has taken sides in the culture war, departing from its role of assuring, as neutral observer, that the democratic rules of engagement are observed. Many Americans do not want persons who openly engage in homosexual conduct as partners in their business, as scoutmasters for their children, as teachers in their children's schools, or as boarders in their home. They view this as protecting themselves and their families from a lifestyle that they believe to be immoral and destructive. The Court views it as "discrimination" which it is the function of our judgments to deter. So imbued is the Court with the law profession's anti-anti-homosexual culture, that it is seemingly unaware that the attitudes of that culture are not obviously "mainstream"; that in most States what the Court calls "discrimination" against those who engage in homosexual acts is perfectly legal; that proposals to ban such "discrimination" under Title VII have repeatedly been rejected by Congress; that in some cases such "discrimination" is mandated by federal statute, see 10 U.S.C. § 654(b)(1) (mandating discharge from the armed forces of any service member who engages in or intends to engage in homosexual acts); and that in some cases such "discrimination" is a constitutional right, see Boy Scouts of America v. Dale, 530 U.S. 640 (2000).

Let me be clear that I have nothing against homosexuals, or any other group, promoting their agenda through normal democratic means. Social perceptions of sexual and other morality change over time, and every group has the right to persuade its fellow citizens that its view of such matters is the best. That homosexuals have achieved some success in that enterprise is attested to by the fact that Texas is one of the few remaining States that criminalize private, consensual homosexual acts. But persuading one's fellow citizens is one thing, and imposing one's views in absence of democratic majority will is something else. I would no more require a State to criminalize homosexual acts—or, for that matter, display any moral disapprobation of them—than I would forbid it to do so. What Texas has chosen to do is well within the range of traditional democratic action, and its hand should not be stayed through the invention of a brand-new "constitutional right" by a Court that is impatient of democratic change. . . .

One of the benefits of leaving regulation of this matter to the people rather than to the courts is that the people, unlike judges, need not carry things to their logical conclusion. The people may feel that their disapprobation of homosexual conduct is strong enough to disallow homosexual marriage, but not strong enough to criminalize private homosexual acts—and may legislate accordingly. The Court today pretends that it possesses a similar freedom of action, so that we need not fear judicial imposition of homosexual marriage, as has recently occurred in Canada (in a decision that the Canadian Government has chosen not to appeal). See Halpern v. Toronto, 2003 WL 34950 (Ontario Ct. App.); Cohen, Dozens in Canada Follow Gay Couple's Lead, Washington Post, June 12, 2003, p. A25. At the end of its opinion—after having laid waste the foundations of our rational-basis jurisprudence—the Court says that the present case "does not involve whether the government must give formal recognition to any relationship that homosexual persons seek to enter." Do not believe it. More illuminating than this bald, unreasoned disclaimer is the progression of thought displayed by an earlier passage in the Court's opinion, which notes the constitutional protections afforded to "personal decisions relating to marriage, procreation, contraception, family relationships, child rearing, and education," and then declares that "[p]ersons in a homosexual relationship may seek autonomy for these purposes, just as heterosexual persons do." Today's opinion dismantles the structure of constitutional law that has permitted a distinction to be made between heterosexual and homosexual unions, insofar as formal recognition in marriage is concerned. If moral disapprobation of homosexual conduct is "no legitimate state interest" for purposes of proscribing that conduct and if, as the Court coos (casting aside all pretense of neutrality), "[w]hen sexuality finds overt expression in intimate conduct with another person, the conduct can be but one element in a personal bond that is more enduring"; what justification could there possibly be for denying the benefits of marriage to homosexual couples exercising "[t]he liberty protected by the Constitution." Surely not the encouragement of procreation, since the sterile and the elderly are allowed to marry. This case "does not involve" the issue of homosexual marriage only if one entertains the belief that principle and logic have nothing to do with the decisions of this Court. . . .

JUSTICE THOMAS, dissenting.

I join Justice Scalia's dissenting opinion. I write separately to note that the law before the Court today "is . . . uncommonly silly." Griswold v. Connecticut, 381 U.S. 479, 527 (1965) (Stewart, J., dissenting). If I were a member of the Texas Legislature, I would vote to repeal it. Punishing someone for expressing his sexual preference through noncommercial consensual conduct with another adult does not appear to be a worthy way to expend valuable law enforcement resources.

Notwithstanding this, I recognize that as a member of this Court I am not empowered to help petitioners and others similarly situated. My duty, rather, is to "decide cases 'agreeably to the Constitution and laws of the United States.'" And, just like Justice Stewart, I "can find [neither in the Bill of Rights nor any other part of the Constitution a] general right of privacy," or as the Court terms it today, the "liberty of the person both in its spatial and more transcendent dimensions."

Page 920. After section 3 of the Note, add the following:

4. *Crane.* An interesting substantive due process issue was resolved in Kansas v. Crane, 534 U.S. 407 (2002). The Kansas Sexually Violent Predator Act allows civil detention of certain sex offenders. Crane, a previously convicted sex offender, was found (by at least one of the state's psychiatric witnesses) to suffer from antisocial personality disorder and exhibitionism. A court ordered his confinement, but without finding that Crane was completely unable to control his conduct. The Supreme Court held that the due process clause did not require such a finding. At the same time, the Court required some kind of "lack-of-control determination." In the Court's view, "there must be proof of serious difficulty in controlling behavior." This difficulty might be shown by "such features of the case as the nature of the psychiatric diagnosis, and the severity of the mental abnormality itself." Without such a finding, the civil confinement would be unconstitutional. Justice Scalia, joined by Justice Thomas, disagreed, urging that it was sufficient to find that "the person previously convicted . . . is suffering from a mental abnormality or personality disorder" and that this condition "renders him likely to commit future acts of sexual violence."

5. *State Farm.* For a striking due process ruling, with strong substantive due process overtones, see State Farm Mutual Automobile Insurance Co. v. Campbell, 538 U.S. 408 (2003). At issue was a $145 million punitive damage award against an insurer for bad faith refusal to settle. The Court held that the award violated the due process clause. The Court said that in general, a state cannot punish a defendant for "unlawful acts committed outside of the State's jurisdiction" — and hence that a punitive damage award cannot be justified as a way of punishing a range of misconduct, some of which occurred outside the state. The Court also said that "courts must ensure that the measure of punishment is both reasonable and proportionate to the amount of harm to the plaintiff and to the general damages suffered" — an idea that would support "single digit multipliers" of the compensatory award as "more likely to comply with due process" than higher numbers. Thus the Court seemed to suggest that the due process clause would severely discipline punitive damage awards from

juries, requiring a reasonable ratio, judicially policed, between those awards and compensatory awards.

State Farm is part of a series of cases in which the Court has confronted the question whether the Constitution imposes any substantive limit on the size of punitive damages awards. In Browning-Ferris Industries v. Kelco Disposal, Inc., 492 U.S. 257 (1989), the Court held that the Eighth Amendment's excessive fines clause did not apply to punitive damages awards in civil cases involving private parties. In Pacific Mutual Life Insurance Co. v. Haslip, 499 U.S. 1 (1991), the Court held that the due process clause imposes both a procedural and a substantive limit on the size of punitive damages awards. The procedural component requires that juries be properly instructed on the purposes of punitive damages and the factors to be taken into account in deciding whether and what amount of punitive damages to award. It also requires appellate review of jury awards to ensure reasonableness. The substantive component requires that the award in fact *be* reasonable, rather than "grossly excessive" or disproportionate. In ensuing cases, the Court reviewed awards of punitive damages, upholding some, see TXO Production Corporation v. Alliance Resources Corporation, 509 U.S. 443 (1993) (upholding a $10 million punitive damages award in a case where the plaintiff recovered $19,000 in compensatory damages), and striking down others, see B.M.W. of North America v. Gore, 517 U.S. 559 (1996) (rejecting a punitive damages award of $2 million in a case where the plaintiff recovered roughly $3000 in compensatory damages).

Why is the Court so willing to use substantive due process to control punitive damage awards if it is so reluctant to control other forms of arbitrariness? For two recent comparisons of the Court's robust substantive due process jurisprudence of disproportionality in the area of punitive damages with its deferential jurisprudence of disproportionality under the eighth amendment, see Chemerinsky, The Constitution and Punishment, 56 Stan. L. Rev. 1049 (2004); Karlan, "Pricking the Lines: The Due Process Clause, Punitive Damages, and Criminal Punishment," 88 Minn. L. Rev. 880 (2004).

G. Procedural Due Process

Page 939. After section 4 of the Note add the following:

4a. *Matthews and the war on terror.* For an application of the *Matthews* test in the context of enemy combatants held during the war on terror, see Hamdi v. Rumsfeld, 542 U.S. ___ (2004), excerpted at the Supplement to page 410 of the main text.

H. The Contracts and Takings Clauses

Page 992. At the bottom of the page, add the following:

PALAZZOLO v. RHODE ISLAND
533 U.S. 606 (2001)

JUSTICE KENNEDY delivered the opinion of the Court.

Petitioner Anthony Palazzolo owns a waterfront parcel of land in the town of Westerly, Rhode Island. Almost all of the property is designated as coastal wetlands under Rhode Island law. After petitioner's development proposals were rejected by respondent Rhode Island Coastal Resources Management Council (Council), he sued in state court, asserting the Council's application of its wetlands regulations took the property without compensation in violation of the Takings Clause of the Fifth Amendment, binding upon the State through the Due Process Clause of the Fourteenth Amendment. . . .

I

The town of Westerly is on an edge of the Rhode Island coastline. The town's western border is the Pawcatuck River, which at that point is the boundary between Rhode Island and Connecticut. . . . In later times Westerly's coastal location had a new significance: It became a popular vacation and seaside destination. . . . Westerly today has about 20,000 year-round residents, and thousands of summer visitors come to enjoy its beaches and coastal advantages.

One of the more popular attractions is Misquamicut State Beach, a lengthy expanse of coastline facing Block Island Sound and beyond to the Atlantic Ocean. The primary point of access to the beach is Atlantic Avenue, a well-traveled 3-mile stretch of road running along the coastline within the town's limits. At its western end, Atlantic Avenue is something of a commercial strip, with restaurants, hotels, arcades, and other typical seashore businesses. The pattern of development becomes more residential as the road winds eastward onto a narrow spine of land bordered to the south by the beach and the ocean, and to the north by Winnapaug Pond, an intertidal inlet often used by residents for boating, fishing, and shellfishing.

In 1959 petitioner, a lifelong Westerly resident, decided to invest in three undeveloped, adjoining parcels along this eastern stretch of Atlantic Avenue. To the north, the property faces, and borders upon, Winnapaug Pond; the south of the property faces Atlantic Avenue and the beachfront homes abutting it on the other side, and beyond that the dunes and the beach. To purchase and hold the property, petitioner and associates formed Shore Gardens, Inc. (SGI). After SGI purchased the property petitioner bought out his associates and became the sole shareholder. In the first decade of SGI's ownership of the property the corporation submitted a plat to the town subdividing the property into 80 lots; and it engaged in various transactions that left it with 74 lots, which together encompassed about 20 acres. During the same period SGI also made initial attempts to develop the property and submitted intermittent applications to state agencies to fill substantial portions of the parcel. Most of the property was then, as it is now, salt marsh subject to tidal flooding. The wet ground and permeable soil would require considerable fill—as much as six feet in some places—before significant structures could be built. SGI's proposal, submitted in 1962 to the Rhode Island Division of Harbors and Rivers (DHR), sought to dredge from Winnapaug Pond and fill the entire property. The application was denied for lack of essential information. A second, similar proposal followed a year later. A third application, submitted in 1966 while the second application was pending, proposed more limited filling of the land for use as a private beach club. These latter two applications were referred to the Rhode Island Department of Natural Resources, which indicated initial assent. The agency later withdrew approval, however, citing adverse environmental impacts. SGI did not contest the ruling.

No further attempts to develop the property were made for over a decade. Two intervening events, however, become important to the issues presented. First, in 1971, Rhode Island enacted legislation creating the Council, an agency charged with the duty of protecting the State's coastal properties. Regulations promulgated by the Council designated salt marshes like those on SGI's property as protected "coastal wetlands," on which development is limited to a great extent. Second, in 1978 SGI's corporate charter was revoked for failure to pay corporate income taxes; and title to the property passed, by operation of state law, to petitioner as the corporation's sole shareholder.

In 1983 petitioner, now the owner, renewed the efforts to develop the property. An application to the Council, resembling the 1962 submission, requested permission to construct a wooden bulkhead along the shore of Winnapaug Pond and to fill the entire marsh land area. The Council rejected the application, noting it was "vague and inadequate for a project of this size and nature." The agency also found that "the proposed activities will have significant impacts upon the waters and wetlands of Winnapaug Pond," and concluded that "the proposed alteration . . . will conflict with the Coastal Resources Management Plan presently in effect." Petitioner did not appeal the agency's determination.

Petitioner went back to the drawing board, this time hiring counsel and preparing a more specific and limited proposal for use of the property. The new application, submitted to the Council in 1985, echoed the 1966 request to build a private beach club. The details do not tend to inspire the reader with an idyllic coastal image, for the proposal was to fill 11 acres of the property with gravel to accommodate "50 cars with boat trailers, a dumpster, port-a-johns, picnic tables, barbecue pits of concrete, and other trash receptacles."

The application fared no better with the Council than previous ones. Under the agency's regulations, a landowner wishing to fill salt marsh on Winnapaug Pond needed a "special exception" from the Council. In a short opinion the Council said the beach club proposal conflicted with the regulatory standard for a special exception. To secure a special exception the proposed activity must serve "a compelling public purpose which provides benefits to the public as a whole as opposed to individual or private interests." . . .

Petitioner filed an inverse condemnation action in Rhode Island Superior Court, asserting that the State's wetlands regulations, as applied by the Council to his parcel, had taken the property without compensation in violation of the Fifth and Fourteenth Amendments.

[We] hold [that] the owner is not deprived of all economic use of his property because the value of upland portions is substantial. We remand for further consideration of the claim under the principles set forth in *Penn Central*.

II

[Since] *Mahon*, we have given some, but not too specific, guidance to courts confronted with deciding whether a particular government action goes too far and effects a regulatory taking. First, we have observed, with certain qualifications, that a regulation which "denies all economically beneficial or productive use of land" will require compensation under the Takings Clause. Where a regulation places limitations on land that fall short of eliminating all economically beneficial use, a taking nonetheless may have occurred, depending on a complex of factors including the regulation's economic effect on the landowner, the extent to which the regulation interferes with reasonable investment-backed expectations, and the character of the government action. *Penn Central*. . . .

[The Court held that the takings issue was ripe for review.] While a landowner must give a land-use authority an opportunity to exercise its discretion, once it becomes clear that the agency lacks the discretion to permit any development, or the permissible uses of the property are known to a reasonable degree of certainty, a takings claim is likely to have ripened. The case is quite unlike those upon which respondents place principal reliance, which arose when an owner challenged a land-use authority's denial of a substantial project, leaving doubt whether a more modest submission or an application for a variance would be accepted. . . . The rulings of the Council interpreting the regulations at issue, and the briefs, arguments, and candid statements by counsel for both sides, leave no doubt on this point: On the wetlands there can be no fill for any ordinary land use. There can be no fill for its own sake; no fill for a beach club, either rustic or upscale; no fill for a subdivision; no fill for any likely or foreseeable use. And with no fill there can be no structures and no development on the wetlands. Further permit applications were not necessary to establish this point.

We turn to the second asserted basis for declining to address petitioner's takings claim on the merits. When the Council promulgated its wetlands regulations, the disputed parcel was owned not by petitioner but by the corporation of which he was sole shareholder.... The theory underlying the argument that postenactment purchasers cannot challenge a regulation under the Takings Clause seems to run on these lines: Property rights are created by the State. See, e.g., Phillips v. Washington Legal Foundation, 524 U.S. 156, 163 (1998). So, the argument goes, by prospective legislation the State can shape and define property rights and reasonable investment-backed expectations, and subsequent owners cannot claim any injury from lost value. After all, they purchased or took title with notice of the limitation.

The State may not put so potent a Hobbesian stick into the Lockean bundle. The right to improve property, of course, is subject to the reasonable exercise of state authority, including the enforcement of valid zoning and land-use restrictions. The Takings Clause, however, in certain circumstances allows a landowner to assert that a particular exercise of the State's regulatory power is so unreasonable or onerous as to compel compensation. Just as a prospective enactment, such as a new zoning ordinance, can limit the value of land without effecting a taking because it can be understood as reasonable by all concerned, other enactments are unreasonable and do not become less so through passage of time or title. Were we to accept the State's rule, the postenactment transfer of title would absolve the State of its obligation to defend any action restricting land use, no matter how extreme or unreasonable. A State would be allowed, in effect, to put an expiration date on the Takings Clause. This ought not to be the rule. Future generations, too, have a right to challenge unreasonable limitations on the use and value of land.

Nor does the justification of notice take into account the effect on owners at the time of enactment, who are prejudiced as well. Should an owner attempt to challenge a new regulation, but not survive the process of ripening his or her claim (which, as this case demonstrates, will often take years), under the proposed rule the right to compensation may not by asserted by an heir or successor, and so may not be asserted at all. The State's rule would work a critical alteration to the nature of property, as the newly regulated landowner is stripped of the ability to transfer the interest which was possessed prior to the regulation. The State may not by this means secure a windfall for itself. The proposed rule is, furthermore, capricious in effect. The young owner contrasted with the older owner, the owner with the resources to hold contrasted with the owner with the need to sell, would be in different positions. The Takings Clause is not so quixotic. A blanket rule that purchasers with notice have no compensation right when a claim becomes ripe is too blunt an instrument to accord with the duty to compensate for what is taken.

Implied Fundamental Rights   Page 992

Direct condemnation, by invocation of the State's power of eminent domain, presents different considerations than cases alleging a taking based on a burdensome regulation. In a direct condemnation action, or when a State has physically invaded the property without filing suit, the fact and extent of the taking are known. In such an instance, it is a general rule of the law of eminent domain that any award goes to the owner at the time of the taking, and that the right to compensation is not passed to a subsequent purchaser. . . .

We have no occasion to consider the precise circumstances when a legislative enactment can be deemed a background principle of state law or whether those circumstances are present here. It suffices to say that a regulation that otherwise would be unconstitutional absent compensation is not transformed into a background principle of the State's law by mere virtue of the passage of title. This relative standard would be incompatible with our description of the concept in *Lucas,* which is explained in terms of those common, shared understandings of permissible limitations derived from a State's legal tradition, see [*Lucas*]. A regulation or common-law rule cannot be a background principle for some owners but not for others. The determination whether an existing, general law can limit all economic use of property must turn on objective factors, such as the nature of the land use proscribed. A law does not become a background principle for subsequent owners by enactment itself. For reasons we discuss next, the state court will not find it necessary to explore these matters on remand in connection with the claim that all economic use was deprived; it must address, however, the merits of petitioner's claim under *Penn Central.* That claim is not barred by the mere fact that title was acquired after the effective date of the state-imposed restriction.

III

[Petitioner] accepts the Council's contention and the state trial court's finding that his parcel retains $200,000 in development value under the State's wetlands regulations. He asserts, nonetheless, that he has suffered a total taking and contends the Council cannot sidestep the holding in *Lucas* "by the simple expedient of leaving a landowner a few crumbs of value."

Assuming a taking is otherwise established, a State may not evade the duty to compensate on the premise that the landowner is left with a token interest. This is not the situation of the landowner in this case, however. A regulation permitting a landowner to build a substantial residence on an 18-acre parcel does not leave the property "economically idle." *Lucas.*

In his brief submitted to us petitioner attempts to revive this part of his claim by reframing it. He argues, for the first time, that the upland parcel is distinct from the wetlands portions, so he should be permitted to assert a deprivation limited to the latter. This contention asks us to examine the difficult, persisting question of what is the proper denominator in the takings fraction. Some of our cases indicate that the extent of deprivation effected by a regulatory action is measured against the value of the parcel as a whole, see, e.g., Keystone Bituminous Coal Assn. v. DeBenedictis; but we have at times expressed discomfort with the logic of this rule, see *Lucas,* a sentiment echoed by some commentators, see, e.g., Epstein, Takings: Descent and Resurrection, 1987 Sup. Ct. Rev. 1, 16-17 (1987); Fee, Unearthing the Denominator in Regulatory Takings Claims, 61 U. Chi. L. Rev. 1535 (1994). Whatever the merits of these criticisms, we will not explore the point here. Petitioner did not press the argument in the state courts, and the issue was not presented in the petition for certiorari. The case comes to us on the premise that petitioner's entire parcel serves as the basis for his takings claim, and, so framed, the total deprivation argument fails. . . .

For the reasons we have discussed, the State Supreme Court erred in finding petitioner's claims were unripe and in ruling that acquisition of title after the effective date of the regulations barred the takings claims. The court did not err in finding that petitioner failed to establish a deprivation of all economic value, for it is undisputed that the parcel retains significant worth for construction of a residence. The claims under the *Penn Central* analysis were not examined, and for this purpose the case should be remanded.

The judgment of the Rhode Island Supreme Court is affirmed in part and reversed in part, and the case is remanded for further proceedings not inconsistent with this opinion.

It is so ordered.

JUSTICE O'CONNOR, concurring.

I join the opinion of the Court but with my understanding of how the issues discussed in Part II of the opinion must be considered on remand.

Part II of the Court's opinion addresses the circumstance, present in this case, where a takings claimant has acquired title to the regulated property after the enactment of the regulation at issue. As the Court holds, the Rhode Island Supreme Court erred in effectively adopting the sweeping rule that the preacquisition enactment of the use restriction ipso facto defeats any takings claim based on that use restriction. Accordingly, the Court holds that petitioner's claim under Penn Central Transp. Co. v. New York City "is not barred by the mere fact that title was acquired after the effective date of the state-imposed restriction."

The more difficult question is what role the temporal relationship between regulatory enactment and title acquisition plays in a proper *Penn Central* analysis. Today's holding does not mean that the timing of the regulation's enactment relative to the acquisition of title is immaterial to the *Penn Central* analysis. Indeed, it would be just as much error to expunge this consideration from the takings inquiry as it would be to accord it exclusive significance. Our polestar instead remains the principles set forth in *Penn Central* itself and our other cases that govern partial regulatory takings. Under these cases, interference with investment-backed expectations is one of a number of factors that a court must examine. Further, the regulatory regime in place at the time the claimant acquires the property at issue helps to shape the reasonableness of those expectations.

If investment-backed expectations are given exclusive significance in the *Penn Central* analysis and existing regulations dictate the reasonableness of those expectations in every instance, then the State wields far too much power to redefine property rights upon passage of title. On the other hand, if existing regulations do nothing to inform the analysis, then some property owners may reap windfalls and an important indicium of fairness is lost. As I understand it, our decision today does not remove the regulatory backdrop against which an owner takes title to property from the purview of the *Penn Central* inquiry. It simply restores balance to that inquiry. Courts properly consider the effect of existing regulations under the rubric of investment-backed expectations in determining whether a compensable taking has occurred. As before, the salience of these facts cannot be reduced to any "set formula." *Penn Central* (internal quotation marks omitted). The temptation to adopt what amount to per se rules in either direction must be resisted. The Takings Clause requires careful examination and weighing of all the relevant circumstances in this context. The court below therefore must consider on remand the array of relevant factors under *Penn Central* before deciding whether any compensation is due.

JUSTICE SCALIA, concurring.

I write separately to make clear that my understanding of how the issues discussed in Part II of the Court's opinion must be considered on remand is not Justice O'Connor's.

The principle that underlies her separate concurrence is that it may in some (unspecified) circumstances be "[un]fai[r]," and produce unacceptable "windfalls," to allow a subsequent purchaser to nullify an unconstitutional partial taking (though, inexplicably, not an unconstitutional total taking) by the government. The polar horrible, presumably, is the situation in which a sharp real estate developer, realizing (or indeed, simply gambling on) the unconstitutional excessiveness of a development restriction that a naïve landowner assumes to be valid, purchases property at what it would be worth subject to the restriction, and then develops it to its full value (or resells it at its full value) after getting the unconstitutional restriction invalidated.

This can, I suppose, be called a windfall—though it is not much different from the windfalls that occur every day at stock exchanges or antique auctions, where the knowledgeable (or the venturesome) profit at the expense of the ignorant (or the risk averse). There is something to be said (though in my view not much) for pursuing abstract "fairness" by requiring part or all of that windfall to be returned to the naïve original owner, who presumably is the "rightful" owner of it. But there is nothing to be said for giving it instead to the government—which not only did not lose something it owned, but is both the cause of the miscarriage of "fairness" and the only one of the three parties involved in the miscarriage (government, naïve original owner, and sharp real estate developer) which acted unlawfully—indeed unconstitutionally. Justice O'Connor would eliminate the windfall by giving the malefactor the benefit of its malefaction. It is rather like eliminating the windfall that accrued to a purchaser who bought property at a bargain rate from a thief clothed with the indicia of title, by making him turn over the "unjust" profit to the thief.

In my view, the fact that a restriction existed at the time the purchaser took title (other than a restriction forming part of the "background principles of the State's law of property and nuisance," Lucas v. South Carolina Coastal Council), should have no bearing upon the determination of whether the restriction is so substantial as to constitute a taking. The "investment-backed expectations" that the law will take into account do not include the assumed validity of a restriction that in fact deprives property of so much of its value as to be unconstitutional. Which is to say that a *Penn Central* taking, see Penn Central Transp. Co. v. New York City, no less than a total taking, is not absolved by the transfer of title.

[Justices Ginsburg and Breyer wrote separate opinions, dissenting on ripeness grounds.]

JUSTICE STEVENS, concurring in part and dissenting in part.

[I] have no doubt that [a property owner] has standing to challenge the restriction's validity whether she acquired title to the property before or after the regulation was adopted. For, as the Court correctly observes, even future generations "have a right to challenge unreasonable limitations on the use and value of land."

It by no means follows, however, that, as the Court assumes, a succeeding owner may obtain compensation for a taking of property from her predecessor in interest. A taking is a discrete event, a governmental acquisition of private property for which the state is required to provide just compensation. Like other transfers of property, it occurs at a particular time, that time being the moment when the relevant property interest is alienated from its owner....

[To] the extent that the adoption of the regulations constitute the challenged taking, petitioner is simply the wrong party to be bringing this action. If the regulations imposed a compensable injury on anyone, it was on the owner of the property at the moment the regulations were adopted. Given the trial court's finding that petitioner did not own the property at that time, in my judgment it is pellucidly clear that he has no standing to claim that the promulgation of the regulations constituted a taking of any part of the property that he subsequently acquired.

[At] oral argument, petitioner contended that the taking in question occurred in 1986, when the Council denied his final application to fill the land. Though this theory, to the extent that it was embraced within petitioner's actual complaint, complicates the issue, it does not alter my conclusion that the prohibition on filling the wetlands does not take from Palazzolo any property right he ever possessed.

The title Palazzolo took by operation of law in 1978 was limited by the regulations then in place to the extent that such regulations represented a valid exercise of the police power. For the reasons expressed above, I think the regulations barred petitioner from filling the wetlands on his property. At the very least, however, they established a rule that such lands could not be filled unless the Council exercised its authority to make exceptions to that rule under certain circumstances.

[If] the existence of valid land-use regulations does not limit the title that the first postenactment purchaser of the property inherits, then there is no reason why such regulations should limit the rights of the second, the third, or the thirtieth purchaser. Perhaps my concern is unwarranted, but today's decision does raise the spectre of a tremendous—and tremendously capricious—one-time transfer of wealth from society at large to those individuals who happen to hold title to large tracts of land at the moment this legal question is permanently resolved.

In the final analysis, the property interest at stake in this litigation is the right to fill the wetlands on the tract that petitioner owns. Whether either he or his predecessors in title ever owned such an interest, and if so, when it was acquired by the State, are questions of state law. If it is clear—as I think it is and as I think the Court's disposition of the ripeness issue assumes—that any such taking occurred before he became the owner of the property, he has no standing to seek compensation for that taking. On the other hand, if the only viable takings claim has a different predicate that arose later, that claim is not ripe and the discussion in [the] Court's opinion is superfluous dictum. In either event, the judgment of the Rhode Island Supreme Court should be affirmed in its entirety.

Question: What, exactly, is the "Lockean" bundle involved in this case? How can we know what the property right is at the time of acquisition without knowing what the state's law says at that time?

Page 992. After section 5 of the Note, add the following:

6. *Temporary takings*? Is the government permitted to impose a moratorium on economic development? What if the moratorium deprives the property owner of all valuable use of the property? In Tahoe-Sierra Preservation Council, Inc. v. Tahoe Regional Planning Agency, 535 U.S. 302 (2002), the Court held that a moratorium, imposed during a period for studying the impact of development on Lake Tahoe, would not be treated as a categorical taking, subject to a per se requirement of compensation. The Court stressed that the case did not involve a physical taking, and concluded that the rules for physical takings should not be used for "regulatory tak-

ings." Hence the *Penn Central* test, involving balancing, would be appropriate. The Court emphasized that *Lucas* involved a permanent taking, not a taking for a mere thirty-two months. The Court refused to accept the view "that we can effectively sever a 32-month segment from the remainder of each landowner's fee simple estate and then ask whether that segment has been taken in its entirety" by the moratorium. Hence the Court concluded that it was appropriate to rely on "the familiar *Penn Central* approach when deciding cases like this, rather than by attempting to craft a new categorical rule." Chief Justice Rehnquist dissented, in an opinion joined by Justices Scalia and Thomas.

7
FREEDOM OF EXPRESSION

A. Introduction

Page 997. At the end of section 4 of the Note, add the following:

The framers themselves were unsure what a constitutional guarantee of "freedom of the speech or of the press" would mean. Benjamin Franklin observed, for example, that "Few of us, I believe, have distinct ideas of its nature and extent," and Alexander Hamilton asked "Who can give it any definition which would not leave the utmost latitude for evasion?" See Meyerson, The Neglected History of the Prior Restraint Doctrine, 34 Ind. L. Rev. 295, 320 (2001).

Page 998. In section 6 of the Note, before the citation to R. Nye, add the following:

M. Curtis, Free Speech, "The People's Darling Privilege" (2000) (focusing on the Sedition Act of 1798, suppression of abolitionist speech and suppression of speech during the Civil War); D. Rabban, Free Speech in its Forgotten Years: 1870-1920 (1997);

After the citation to Rabban, add the following:

Stone, Abraham Lincoln's First Amendment, 78 N.Y.U. L. Rev. 1 (2003).

Page 1002. Before section 3 of the Note, add the following:

e. Post, Reconciling Theory and Doctrine in First Amendment Jurisprudence, in L. Bollinger & G. Stone, Eternal Vigilance: Free Speech in the Modern Era 153, 165-167 (2002):

[Under Meiklejohn's view, the] First Amendment is understood to protect the communicative processes necessary to disseminate the information and ideas required for citizens to vote in a fully informed and intelligent way. [Under this view,] the state is imagined as a moderator, [and] speech [that is] inconsistent with "responsible and regulated discussion" can and should be suppressed....

The alternative account of democracy, which I shall call the "participatory" theory, does not locate self-governance in mechanisms of decisionmaking, but rather in the processes through which citizens come to identify a government as their own. [This] account postulates that it is a necessary precondition [that] a state be constitutionally prohibited from preventing its citizens from participating in the communicative processes relevant to the formation of democratic public opinion.

[This] approach views the function of the First Amendment to be the safeguarding of public discourse from regulations that are inconsistent with democratic legitimacy. State restrictions on public discourse can be inconsistent with democratic legitimacy in two distinct ways. To the extent that the state cuts off particular citizens from participation in public discourse, it *pro tanto* negates its claim to democratic legitimacy with respect to such citizens. To the extent that the state regulates public discourse so as to reflect the values and priorities of some vision of collective identity, it preempts the very democratic process by which collective identity is to be determined.

[The] Meiklejohnian and participatory perspectives [differ] in at least two fundamental respects. First, the Meiklejohnian approach interprets the First Amendment primarily as a shield against the "mutilation of the thinking process of the community," whereas the participatory approach understands the First Amendment [as] safeguarding the ability of individual citizens to participate in the formation of public opinion. The Meiklejohnian theory thus stresses the quality of public debate, whereas the participatory perspective emphasizes the autonomy of individual citizens.

Second, the Meiklejohnian perspective imagines the state [as] a neutral moderator, capable of saving public discourse from "mutilation" by distinguishing between relevant and irrelevant speech, abusive and nonabusive speech.... The participatory approach, in contrast, denies that there can be any possible neutral position within public discourse, because public discourse is precisely the site of political contention about the nature of collective identity, and it is only by reference to some vision of collective identity that speech can be categorized as relevant or irrelevant, abusive or nonabusive....

Page 1003. At the end of section 4 of the Note, add the following:

c. *Free speech and character.* Consider Blasi, Free Speech and Good Character: From Milton to Brandeis to the Present, in L. Bollinger & G. Stone, Eternal Vigilance: Free Speech in the Modern Era 61, 62, 84-85 (2002):

Freedom of Expression

[A] culture that prizes and protects expressive liberty nurtures in its members certain character traits such as inquisitiveness, distrust of authority, willingness to take initiative, and the courage to confront evil. Such character traits are valuable [for] their instrumental contribution to the collective well-being, social as well as political. . . .

The most important [consequence] of protecting free speech is the intellectual and moral pluralism, and thus disorder in a sense, thereby engendered. In matters of belief, conventional structures of authority are weakened, rebellion is facilitated, closure is impaired. Persons who live in a free-speech regime are forced to cope with persistent, and frequently intractable, differences of understanding. For most of us that is a painful challenge. . . . Being made to take account of such differences shapes our character.

Page 1004. At the end of section 5 of the Note, add the following:

On the other hand, consider Post, Reconciling Theory and Doctrine in First Amendment Jurisprudence, in L. Bollinger & G. Stone, Eternal Vigilance: Free Speech in the Modern Era 153, 153 (2002): "Doctrine becomes confused when [it] is required to articulate the implications of inconsistent theories. First Amendment doctrine has unfortunately suffered from [this difficulty]."

6. *First Amendment decisionmaking.* Given what you have read about the history and philosophy underlying the first amendment, is it possible to decide in a principled manner whether the first amendment protects nude dancing in bars, or a $50,000 campaign contribution to a political candidate, or commercial advertising of toothpaste? Is first amendment decisionmaking realistically about anything "other than a particular set of social, political, and ideological moves that are available at a particular point in time?" Schauer, First Amendment Opportunism, in L. Bollinger & G. Stone, Eternal Vigilance: Free Speech in the Modern Era 175, 195 (2002).

Consider Strauss, Freedom of Speech and the Common-Law Constitution, in L. Bollinger & G. Stone, Eternal Vigilance: Free Speech in the Modern Era 33, 59 (2002):

[The] story of the development of the American system of freedom of expression is not a story about the text of the First Amendment. That text was part of the Constitution for a century and a half before the central principles of the American regime of free speech [became] established in the law. Nor is it a story about the wisdom of those who drafted the First Amendment. There is a habit of attributing to the framers [great] foresight about freedom of expression as well as other subjects. But the actual views of the drafters and ratifiers of the First Amendment are in many ways unclear; and to the extent we can determine their views, they did not think they were establishing a system of free expression resembling what we have today. [In fact, the] central principles of the American system of freedom of expression were hammered out mostly over the course of the twentieth century, in fits and starts, in a series of judicial decisions and extrajudicial developments. The story of the emergence of the American constitutional law of free speech is a story of evolution and precedent, trial and error. . . .

[Our current free speech jurisprudence] emerged fitfully by a process in which principles were tried and sometimes abandoned, sometimes modified, in light of experience and of an explicit assessment of whether they were good principles as a matter of policy and political morality. The law of the First Amendment is one of the great creations of the law, and it is a creation of the common-law Constitution.

7. *Our Democratic Constitution.* Consider Justice Breyer's approach to constitutional interpretation. How would this approach shape the analysis of such issues as the constitutionality of campaign finance reform or the regulation of commercial advertising? Breyer, Our Democratic Constitution, 77 N.Y.U. L. Rev. 245, 247-249 (2002):

[T]he Constitution, considered as a whole, creates a framework for a certain kind of government. Its general objectives can be described abstractly as including: (1) democratic self-government; (2) dispersion of power (avoid concentration of too much power in too few hands); (3) individual dignity (through protection of individual liberties); (4) equality before the law (through equal protection of the law); and (5) the rule of law itself. [In interpreting specific provisions of the Constitution, the Court] must consider the document as a whole. . . .

[T]he real-world consequences of a particular interpretive decision, valued in terms of [these] basic constitutional purposes, [should] play an important role in constitutional decisionmaking. To that extent, my approach differs from that of judges who would place near exclusive interpretive weight upon language, history, tradition, and precedent. [The] more literal judges may hope to find, in language, history, tradition, and precedent, objective interpretive standards; they may seek to avoid an interpretive subjectivity that could confuse a judge's personal idea of what is good for that which the Constitution demands; and they may believe that these "original" sources more readily will yield rules that can guide other institutions, including lower courts. These objectives are desirable, but I do not think the literal approach will achieve them, and, in any event, the constitutional price is too high. [It] is important to place greater weight upon constitutionally valued consequences. . . .

B. Content-Based Restrictions: Dangerous Ideas and Information

Page 1011. At the end of section 1 of the Note, add the following:

For the arguments that Judge Hand correctly interpreted the Espionage Act of 1917 and that the bad tendency test distorted not only the Espionage Act but the common law understanding of "attempt," see Stone, Judge Learned Hand and the Espionage Act of 1917: A Mystery Unraveled, 70 U. Chi. L. Rev. 335 (2003); Stone, The Origins of the "Bad Tendency" Test: Free Speech in Wartime, 2002 Sup. Ct. Rev. 411.

Page 1013. After the second paragraph of section 4 of the Note, add the following:

Should the government be required to prove *both* clear and present danger *and* that the speaker intended to create a clear and present danger? Consider Alexander, Incitement and Freedom of Speech, in D. Kretzmer & F. Hazan, Freedom of Speech and Incitement Against Democracy 101, 107-108 (2000):

[N]either the value [nor] the danger of the speech [turns] on the speaker's purpose. [Suppose, for example,] the government interdicts a shipment of pamphlets written without any purpose to incite to violence but which are quite likely to do so. [The] question the government faces is not whether to prosecute but whether to destroy the pamphlets. Solely as a matter of freedom of speech, [it] is difficult to see why the answer to that question should turn on the authors' intention. . . .

Page 1028. After the citation to Blasi in section 1 of the Note, add the following:

Consider Blasi, Free Speech and Good Character: From Milton to Brandeis to the Present, in L. Bollinger & G. Stone, Eternal Vigilance: Free Speech in the Modern Era 61, 83 (2002): "To Brandeis, the measure of courage in the civic realm is the capacity to experience change [without] losing perspective or confidence. [The] character conducive to the maintenance of that [capacity] is what he considered the principal benefit of a robust freedom of speech."

Page 1030. At the end of section 7 of the Note, add the following:

Although there were no major Supreme Court decisions concerning subversive advocacy during World War II, there were several prosecutions of individuals under both the Espionage Act of 1917 and the Smith Act of 1940. Most often, these were prosecutions of individuals who were leaders of fascist organizations in the United States. See R. Steele, Free Speech in the Good War (1999); M. St. George & L. Dennis, The Great Sedition Trial of 1944 (1946).

Page 1035. At the end of section 1 of the Note, add the following:

Who are the "real" targets of the prosecutions in cases like *Schenck*, *Abrams*, *Gitlow*, *Whitney* and *Dennis*? Consider M. St. George & L. Dennis, A Trial on Trial: The Great Sedition Trial of 1944 41-42 (1946):

> [True agitators] are never intimidated by sedition trials. The blood of martyrs is the seed of the Church. The people who are intimidated by sedition trials are the people who have not enough courage [ever] to say or do anything that would get them involved in a sedition trial. And it is mainly for the purpose of intimidating these more prudent citizens that sedition trials are held. The cautious, of course, would be the last persons in the world to see this.

Page 1036. At the end of section 2 of the Note, add the following:

Consider Posner, The Speech Market and the Legacy of *Schenck*, in L. Bollinger and G. Stone, Eternal Vigilance: Free Speech in the Modern Era 121, 125-126 (2002):

> If the benefits of challenged speech are given by B; the cost (a fire, desertion, riot, rebellion, and so on) if the speech is allowed by H (for harm) or O (for offensiveness); the probability that the cost will actually materialize if the speech is allowed by p; the rate at which future costs or benefits are discounted to the present by d (like p a number between 0 and 1); the number of years [or other unit of time] between when the speech occurs and the harm from the speech materializes or is likely to occur if the speech is allowed by n; then the speech should be allowed if but only if $B \geq pH/(1+d)^n + O - A$ [the cost of administering the ban], which, in

words, is if but only if the benefits of the speech equal or exceed its costs discounted by their probability and by their futurity, and reduced by the costs of administering the ban.

But consider also Posner, Pragmatism versus Purposivism in First Amendment Analysis, 54 Stan. L. Rev. 737, 744 (2002):

[A] shortcoming of the pragmatic approach is that the costs of freedom of expression are often more salient than the benefits, and their salience may cause the balance to shift too far toward suppression. [Doubt] is the engine of progress, but because people hate being in a state of doubt they may prefer to silence the doubters rather than to alter their beliefs. [Because] the cost of heterodox speech is immediate and its benefit deferred, the benefit may be slighted. All this must be kept steadily in mind by judges called upon to uphold the suppression of expression. . . .

Page 1037. After section 4 of the Note, add the following:

5. *Understanding* Dennis. Consider Wiecek, The Legal Foundations of Domestic Anticommunism: The Background of *Dennis v. United States*, 2001 Sup. Ct. Rev. 375, 377-379, 417, 428-429:

In the 1927-47 period, and then again a decade later, the Court's speech decisions consistently expanded freedom to [communicate]. The 1950-56 decisions interrupted that trend. In those years, the Court regressed to the spirit of the 1919-1927 [era]. [The reason for this phenomenon] is found in the dominant outlook and anxieties of contemporary anticommunism. This outlook produced an image of Communists that depicted them as unscrupulous traitors controlled by Moscow, committed to subverting American freedom. [This] image of Communists was an artifact of the preceding eighty years of anticommunism. [The Justices] were not exempt from the fears and beliefs of other Americans. [Indeed, it] was natural for the Justices to employ the anticommunist image as a kind of general template to make sense of legal issues coming before them in cases implicating the liberties of Communists. . . .

[The] half-century that followed World War II was not merely a string of relatively low-level crises [*e.g.*, Berlin blockade, the fall of China, the Soviet atomic bomb, the Korean War, etc.], but a slow-motion hot war, conducted on the periphery of rival empires, sometimes by the principals themselves, sometimes by their proxies. It threatened to escalate to nuclear conflict at any time. Seeing the period of the Cold War [as] a nightmare from which we could not disengage

Page 1037

[that] threatened our annihilation at any moment [helps] us to understand the fears and reactions of another time. . . .

The [anticommunist] crusade after World War II [demonized] Communists, endowing them with extraordinary powers and malignity, making them both covert and ubiquitous. [Communists] became The Other. Popular culture, in movies like *On the Waterfront* [and] *Invasion of the Body Snatchers,* effectively delivered this image to a mass audience. [The] manufactured image of the domestic Communist, cultivated and propagated by J. Edgar Hoover, the Catholic Church, the American Legion, and political opportunists, made of Communists something less than full humans, full [citizens]. [To] resist the ideological and emotional pressures of the Cold War era would have required superhuman wisdom and equanimity. Whatever else might be said of the Justices of the *Dennis* Court, the majority of them did not have those qualities.

Does this seem right? Keep it in mind as you think in the present about the War on Terrorism.

Page 1044. At the end of section 4 of the Note, add the following:

d. Is the private solicitation of murder protected by *Brandenburg*? Consider Greenawalt, "Clear and Present Danger" and Criminal Speech, in L. Bollinger & G. Stone, Eternal Vigilance: Free Speech in the Modern Era 97, 116-119 (2002):

Such a solicitation differs importantly from public speech in which the speaker urges a specific crime for political reasons. [But this] distinction should not be grounded on the view that free speech is [only] about speech in public. . . . [Most] people discuss political, social, and moral issues [in private conversations, and it] would be paradoxical [to] say that the government may freely regulate what is said in these private settings. . . .

As Justice Brandeis emphasized, a crucial assumption about free speech concerns countervailing speech. If one person or group urges people to do one thing, others are free to urge the opposite. . . . Another aspect of public speech is that officials know what has been said; they may be able to take precautions to lessen the chance of a crime being successfully committed. However, when one person [privately] urges another to commit a crime, there is opportunity neither for directly countervailing speech nor for official precautions. [In] such circumstances, imminence and likelihood provide too much protection for dangerous speech. [This] sort of solicitation should receive First Amendment protection only if [the] speaker reasonably believes that the remark will not have a serious effect on the listener.

5. *From* Schenck *to* Brandenburg, *and beyond*. Consider the following views:

a. Stone, Dialogue, in L. Bollinger & G. Stone, Eternal Vigilance: Free Speech in the Modern Era 1, 4 (2002):

[In] its initial efforts to make sense of the First Amendment, the [Court] seemed rather innocently to believe that the government could effectively excise from public debate only those views that could be said to be "dangerous," without threatening free speech more generally. But over time the Court came increasingly to understand that although each generation's effort to suppress *its* idea of "dangerous speech" (antiwar speech during World War I; syndicalist expression during the 1920s; Communist advocacy during the 1950s) seemed warranted at the time, each seemed with the benefit of hindsight an exaggerated [response] to a particular political or social problem. The Court came to understand that there is a natural tendency of even well-meaning citizens, legislators, and judges to want to suppress ideas they find offensive or misguided, to inflate the potential dangers of such expression, and to undervalue the costs of its suppression.

b. Stone, Dialogue, in L. Bollinger & G. Stone, Eternal Vigilance: Free Speech in the Modern Era 1, 7-8 (2002):

Earlier, I offered a very rosy view of the evolution of First Amendment jurisprudence. . . . There is, however, a more cynical view of this process. [During] World War I the Court enunciated the seemingly speech-protective "clear and present danger" test, but then construed the test in such a way as to uphold the convictions of those who protested against the war. . . . In the 1920s, the Court looked back on the World War I cases with some dismay, and embraced a more speech-protective interpretation of the First Amendment [that] presumably would have reversed the convictions of the earlier era, but that enabled the Court to uphold the convictions of the syndicalists. In the 1950s, the Court strengthened its protection of free speech in such a way as to call into question both the World War I cases and the syndicalist decisions of the 1920s, while enabling it to uphold the convictions of the leaders of the Communist Party. [So], one might say that the Court learns just enough to correct the mistakes of the past, but never quite enough to avoid the mistakes of the present.

c. Posner, Pragmatism versus Purposivism in First Amendment Analysis, 54 Stan. L. Rev. 737, 741 (2002):

[W]hen the country feels very safe the Justices [can] without paying a large political cost plume themselves on their fearless devotion to freedom of speech and professors can deride the cowardice of the *Dennis* decision. But they are likely to change their tune when next the country feels endangered. The word "feels" is important here. The country may have exaggerated the danger that Communism posed. But the fear of Communism was a brute fact that judges who wanted to preserve their power had to consider.

d. Bollinger, Epilogue, in L. Bollinger & G. Stone, Eternal Vigilance: Free Speech in the Modern Era 1, 312-313 (2002):

The question for the future [is] whether the scope of First Amendment rights articulated in the *Brandenburg* era reflects the distilled wisdom of historical experience, which makes it more likely to survive in future periods of social upheaval, or whether the *Brandenburg* era will turn out to be just one era among many, in which the freedom of speech varies widely and more or less according to the sense of security and tolerance prevailing in the nation at the time. The fact that the last thirty years since *Brandenburg* have been remarkably peaceful and prosperous means that the understandings we now have about the meaning of free speech have not really been tested. By the standards we now apply (that is, through the eyes of *Brandenburg*), just about every time the country has felt seriously threatened the First Amendment has retreated.

Page 1048. At the end of section 6 of the Note, add the following:

After September 11, may the government refuse to employ as an airport screener any person who, in the past five years, has been a member of, or contributed to, any organization on the government's list of Islamic terrorist organizations?

Page 1055. At the end of section 3 of the Note, add the following:

In the actual Nuremberg Files case, the web site was established after an unrelated individual had murdered three abortion providers after distributing similar posters naming them as "Wanted" persons. Is this relevant?

In Planned Parenthood v. American Coalition of Life Activists, 290 F.3d 1058 (9th Cir. 2002), cert. denied, 539 U.S. 958 (2003), the Court of Appeals, in a six-to-five *en banc* decision, held that the Nuremberg Files web site could be held liable in damages and enjoined because it constituted an unprotected threat:

> If ACLA had merely endorsed or encouraged the violent actions of others, its speech would be protected. [Citing *Brandenburg*.] However, while advocating

violence is protected, threatening a person with violence is not. [Although the] posters contain no language that is [literally] a threat, whether a particular statement may properly be considered to be a threat is governed by an objective standard—whether a reasonable person would foresee that the statement would be interpreted by those to whom the maker communicates the statement as a serious expression of intent to harm or assault. [It] is not necessary that the defendant intend to, or be able to carry out his threat; the only intent requirement for a true threat is that the defendant intentionally or knowingly communicate the [threat] *with the intent to intimidate.* [It] is making a threat to intimidate that makes ACLA's conduct unlawful. . . .

The true threats analysis [in this case] turns on the poster pattern. [The Website does not contain] any language that is overtly threatening. [It] is use of the "Wanted"-type format in the context of the poster pattern—poster followed by murder—that constitutes the threat. Because of the pattern, a "Wanted"-type poster naming a specific doctor who provides abortions was perceived by physicians, who are providers of reproductive health services, as a serious threat of death or bodily harm. [The] posters are a true threat because, [like] burning crosses, they connote something they do not literally say, yet both the actor and the recipient get the message. To the doctor who performs abortions, these posters meant "You'll be shot or killed."

[As] a direct result of having [a] poster out on them, physicians wore bulletproof vests and took other extraordinary security measures to protect themselves and their families. ACLA had every reason to foresee that its expression [would] elicit this reaction. Physicians' fear did not simply happen; ACLA intended to intimidate them from doing what they do. This [is] conduct that [lacks] any protection under the First Amendment. Violence is not a protected value. Nor is a true threat of violence with intent to intimidate.

The dissenting judges argued as follows:

[I]t is not illegal—and cannot be made so—merely to say things that would frighten or intimidate the listener. For example, when a doctor says, "You have cancer and will die within six months," it is not a threat, even though you almost certainly will be frightened. [By] contrast, "If you don't stop performing abortions, I'll kill you" is a true threat and surely illegal. The difference between a true threat and protected expression is this: A true threat warns of violence or other harm that the speaker controls. . . .

[As the majority argues,] because context matters, the statements [in this case] could reasonably be interpreted as an effort to intimidate plaintiffs into ceasing their abortion-related activities. If that were enough to strip the speech of First Amendment protection, there would be nothing left to decide. But the Supreme Court has told us that "[s]peech does not lose its protected character ... simply because it may embarrass others *or coerce them into action.*" [*Claiborne Hardware.*] In other words, some forms of intimidation enjoy constitutional protection.

The majority does not point to any statement by defendants that they intended to inflict bodily harm on plaintiffs, nor is there any evidence that defendants took any steps whatsoever to plan or carry out physical violence against anyone. Rather, the majority relies on the fact that "the poster format itself had acquired currency as a death threat for abortion providers." [But none of the doctors who were killed were killed by anyone connected with this web page.]

The majority tries to fill this gaping hole in the record by noting that defendants "kn[ew] the fear generated among those in the reproductive health services community who were singled out for identification on a 'wanted'-type poster." But a statement does not become a true threat because it instills fear in the listener; as noted above, many statements generate fear in the listener, yet are not true threats and therefore may not be punished or enjoined consistent with the First Amendment. In order for the statement to be a threat, it must send the message that the speakers themselves—or individuals acting in concert with them—will engage in physical violence. [Yet] the opinion points to no evidence that defendants [would] have been understood by a reasonable listener as saying that *they* will cause the harm.

From the point of view of the victims, it makes little difference whether the violence against them will come from the makers of the posters or from unrelated third parties; bullets kill their victims regardless of who pulls the trigger. But it makes a difference for the purpose of the First Amendment. Speech—especially political speech, as this clearly was—may not be punished or enjoined unless it falls into one of the narrow categories of unprotected speech recognized by the Supreme Court: true threat, incitement, fighting words, etc.

[The] posters can be viewed, at most, as a call to arms for *other* abortion protesters to harm plaintiffs. However, the Supreme Court made it clear that under *Brandenburg*, encouragement or even advocacy of violence is protected by the First Amendment [unless the harm is both likely and imminent]. . . .

The Nuremberg Files website is clearly an expression of a political point of view. The posters and the website are designed both to rally political support for the views espoused by defendants, and to intimidate plaintiffs and others like them into desisting abortion related activities. This political agenda may not be to the liking of many people—political dissidents are often unpopular—but the speech, including the intimidating message, does not constitute a direct threat because there is no evidence [that] the speakers intend to resort to physical violence if their threat is not heeded.

We have recognized that statements communicated directly to the target are much more likely to be true threats than those, as here, communicated as part of a public protest. [In] deciding whether the coercive speech is protected, it makes a big difference whether it is contained in a private communication—a face-to-face confrontation, a telephone call, a dead fish wrapped in newspaper—or is made during the course of public discourse. The reason for this distinction is obvious: Private speech is aimed only at its target. Public speech, by contrast, seeks to move public opinion and to encourage those of like mind. Coercive speech that is part of public discourse enjoys far greater protection than identical speech made in a purely private context.

In this case, defendants said nothing remotely threatening, yet they find themselves crucified financially. Who knows what other neutral statements a jury might imbue with a menacing meaning based on the activities of unrelated parties. . . .

See also Rothman, Freedom of Speech and True Threats, 25 Harv. J. L. & Pub. Pol. 283 (2001) (to prove a "true" threat, the prosecution must prove (a) that the speaker knowingly or recklessly made a statement that would frighten or intimidate the victim with the threat of harm; (b) that the speaker knowingly or recklessly suggested that the threat would be carried out by the speaker or his co-conspirators; and (c) that a reasonable person who heard the statement would conclude that it was meant to threaten the victim with harm). In what circumstances, if any, might the display of a swastika or a burning cross constitute a "true threat"?

Page 1056. At the end of the sentence immediately before *Cantwell*, add the following:

Consider Posner, The Speech Market and the Legacy of *Schenck*, in L. Bollinger & G. Stone, Eternal Vigilance: Free Speech in the Modern Era 121, 136 (2002):

There [is] a pragmatic argument against putting much weight on offensiveness as a ground for restricting freedom of speech. Offensiveness is often a by-product of challenging the values and beliefs that are important to people, and these challenges are an important part of the market in ideas and opinions. People get upset when their way of life is challenged, yet that upset may be the beginning of doubt and lead eventually to change. Think of all the currently conventional ideas and opinions that were deeply offensive when first voiced. Perhaps, therefore, a condition of being allowed to hear and utter ideas that may challenge other people's values and beliefs should be the willingness to extend that same right to others and thus agree that offensiveness will not be a permissible ground for punishing expression.

Page 1064. At the end of section 1 of the Note, add the following:

On the problem of cross-burning as a "threat," see Virginia v. Black, 538 U.S. 343 (2003), section D6 infra, this Supplement.

Page 1086. At the end of section 5 of the Note, add the following:

Suppose a newspaper gains information as a result of a third party's unlawful act, such as theft of a document or an illegal wiretap. Can the newspaper be enjoined, criminally punished, or held civilly liable for invasion of privacy for publishing the information? See Bartnicki v. Vopper, 532 U.S. 514 (2001), in which the Court held that federal and state antiwiretap statutes cannot constitutionally be applied to a radio station that broadcasts the tape of an unlawfully intercepted telephone call, where the subject of the call was a matter of public concern and the broadcaster did not participate directly in the unlawful wiretap, even though the broadcaster knew that the material had been obtained unlawfully.

Page 1090. Before *Note: Dangerous Ideas and Information— Final Thoughts*, add the following:

Note: Terrorism and the First Amendment

1. *September 11.* To what extent do any of the events following September 11 raise significant first amendment concerns? Consider the following:

(a) Several days after the September 11 attack, New York City police arrested a man who was picketing at the site of the former World Trade Center carrying a placard with a large photograph of Osama bin Laden. The man was charged with attempting to incite a breach of the peace.

(b) In testimony before the Senate Judiciary Committee, Attorney General John Ashcroft accused critics of the administration's policies in the war on terrorism of being "fearmongers" who give "aid" to our enemies. Suppose he had described such critics as "traitors"? Suppose he said they should be "stifled"?

(c) The federal government seized the assets of a charitable organization that was sending funds to the Middle East. The government alleged that at least some of these funds were being used to support terrorism.

(d) The federal government refused to disclose to the press the names of hundreds of individuals of Middle Eastern descent who were arrested and detained for alleged immigration violations in the wake of September 11 and it insisted on closed legal proceedings against such individuals.

(e) The federal government refused to permit representatives of the press to observe combat missions or to inspect combat sites during the war in Afghanistan.

2. *Intelligence activities.* Suppose in an investigation of alleged Communist infiltration of the NAACP, an FBI informant infiltrates the organization's leadership and reports regularly on its membership and activities. Or suppose a government official photographs all persons attending a public NOW rally. In what circumstances, if any, are these and similar forms of surveillance limited by the first amendment? The question is hardly hypothetical. Consider the 1976 findings of the Senate Select Committee to Study Governmental Operations with Respect to Intelligence Activities:

> The Government has often undertaken the secret surveillance of citizens on the basis of their political beliefs, even when those beliefs posed no threat of violence or illegal acts on behalf of a hostile foreign power. The Government, operating primarily through secret informants, [has] swept in vast amounts of information about the personal lives, views, and associations of American citizens. Investigations of groups deemed potentially dangerous—and even of groups suspected of associating with potentially dangerous organizations—have continued for decades, despite the fact that those groups did not engage in unlawful activity. [FBI] headquarters alone has developed over 500,000 domestic intelligence files. [The] targets of intelligence activity have included political adherents of the right and the left, ranging from activist to casual supporters.
>
> [Although] the FBI has admitted that the Socialist Workers Party has committed no criminal acts, [it] has investigated the [SWP] for more than three decades on the basis of its revolutionary rhetoric [and] its claimed international links. [As] part of their effort to collect information which "related even remotely" to people or groups "active" in communities which had "the potential" for civil disorder, Army intelligence agencies took such steps as: sending agents to a Halloween party for elementary school children [because] they suspected a local "dissident" might be present; monitoring protests of welfare mothers' organizations in Milwaukee; infiltrating a coalition of church youth groups in Colorado; and sending agents to a priests' conference in Washington, D.C., held to discuss birth control measures. [In] 1970 the FBI ordered investigations of every member of the Students for a Democratic Society and of "every Black Student Union and similar group regardless of their past or present involvement in disorders."

Senate Select Committee to Study Governmental Operations with Respect to Intelligence Activities, Final Report, Intelligence Activities and the Rights of Americans,

Book II, S. Doc. No. 13133-4, 94th Cong., 2d Sess. 5-9 (1976). See generally F. Donner, The Age of Surveillance (1980); A. Theoharis, Spying on Americans (1978); Symposium, National Securities and Civil Liberties, 69 Cornell L. Rev. 685 (1984). See also Laird v. Tatum, 408 U.S. 1 (1972) (plaintiffs have no standing to challenge army's "surveillance of lawful political activities" on ground that their first amendment rights are "chilled" where there is no evidence of "objective" harm).

In 1976, Attorney General Edward Levi promulgated a series of guidelines that sharply curtailed the FBI's authority to infiltrate or investigate political and religious organizations. In 1983, Attorney General William French Smith issued a new and less restrictive set of guidelines. The Smith Guidelines provided that "[a] domestic security/terrorism investigation may be initiated when facts or circumstances reasonably indicate that two or more persons are engaged in an enterprise for the purpose of furthering political or social goals wholly or in part through activities that involve force or violence and a violation of the criminal laws of the United States." Although the Levi guidelines had prohibited any investigation based on constitutionally protected expression, the Smith guidelines expressly authorize the FBI to open an investigation "when statements advocate criminal activity."

In May of 2002, Attorney General John Ashcroft granted the FBI broad new authority to monitor political rallies, religious services and Internet chat rooms for indications of terrorist activity, and to search commercial databases that maintain detailed information on consumers such as their magazine subscriptions, book purchases, charitable contributions, and travel itineraries. The only limit the new guidelines place on such monitoring is that it be "for the purpose of detecting or preventing terrorist activities." Attorney General Ashcroft tied the new powers to the FBI's efforts to transform itself from a law-enforcement organization into a domestic security agency dedicated to preventing future terrorist attacks. In what circumstances, if any, would the new guidelines violate the first amendment?

C. *Overbreadth, Vagueness, and Prior Restraint*

Page 1104. At the end of the section 1 of the Note, add the following:

Suppose a permit scheme provides that the official "may" deny a permit only in certain clearly specified circumstances. Does the word "may" render the scheme "standardless"? See Thomas v. Chicago Park District, 534 U.S. 316 (2002) (rejecting this argument because on this theory every law regulating expression "contains a constitutional flaw, since it merely permits, but does not require, prosecution").

Page 1106. After the citations to Blasi and Monaghan in section 5 of the Note, add the following:

See Thomas v. Chicago Park District, 534 U.S. 316 (2002) (a content-neutral licensing scheme regulating the time, place and manner of use of a public forum need not employ the procedural safeguards required by *Freedman* because such a scheme "does not authorize a licensor to pass judgment on the content of speech").

Page 1106. At the end of the first paragraph of section 5 of the Note, add the following:

On the requirement of a "prompt final judicial decision," see Littleton v. Z. J. Gifts D-4, L.L.C. 541 U.S. ___ (2004).

Page 1110. At the end of section 3 of the Note, add the following:

For a general analysis of the collateral bar rule, see Palmer, Collateral Bar and Contempt: Challenging a Court Order After Disobeying It, 88 Cornell L. Rev. 215 (2002).

Page 1112. After the citation to Scordato, add the following:

Meyerson, The Neglected History of the Prior Restraint Doctrine, 34 Ind. L. Rev. 295 (2001) (suggesting that the prior restraint doctrine can best be understood as an extension of concerns about the separation of powers).

D. Content-Based Restrictions: "Low" Value Speech

Page 1120. At the end of section 4 of the Note, add the following:

e. BeVier, The Invisible Hand of the Marketplace of Ideas, in L. Bollinger & G. Stone, Eternally Vigilant: Free Speech in the Modern Era 233, 235 (2002):

[The] political information industry—the press—is the only major industry in the U.S. economy [that] is not routinely held accountable for the harms that defects in its products cause, either to the electorate as a whole or to particular victimized individuals. [The arguable explanation is] that the private market fails to produce [political information] in optimal amounts. [Because] property rights in [information] are so difficult to establish and maintain, those who gather information [encounter] systematic difficulty in appropriating the full social benefits of their efforts. Since the "investment they make in producing information will benefit others as well as themselves," they will tend [to] underproduce it relative to its social value. This general tendency of markets to underproduce information [is] regarded as an important source of "failure" in [the] market for political information, [and thus a reason to support *New York Times v. Sullivan* as a form of subsidy to offset this market failure].

Page 1128. Before section 1 of the Note, add the following:

1a. *False ideas*. Do you agree with Justice Powell that "under the First Amendment there is no such thing as a false idea"? Consider Stone, Dialogue, in L. Bollinger & G. Stone, Eternal Vigilance: Free Speech in the Modern Era 29-31 (2002):

[Perhaps] the Supreme Court's single most important [statement] on the freedom of speech [was] its declaration in *Gertz* that "under the First Amendment there is no such thing as a false idea." [In effect, the Court announced that] the First Amendment places out of bounds any law that attempts to freeze public opinion at a particular moment in time. A majority of the People, acting through their government, may decide an issue of policy for themselves, but they have no power irrevocably to decide that issue by preventing continuation of the debate.

[But why] should that be so? [The] explanation is that we [are] balancing two competing risks. On the one hand, there is the risk that, if permitted to consider all ideas, the People will not always act wisely and will sometimes embrace bad ideas.... On the other hand, there is the risk that, if given the power to censor "bad" ideas, the People will not always act wisely and will sometimes prohibit the consideration of "good" ideas.

In choosing between these risks, [we] must consider the nature of human nature. History teaches that people are prone to undue certitude, intolerance [and] even fanaticism. [We] have a deep need to believe that we are right, [to] silence others who disagree with us, and in the words of Justice Holmes to "sweep away all opposition." If we empower the People to act on this instinct, there is every danger that they will do so. It is not inherent in human nature to be skeptical, self-doubting, and tolerant of others. We are not naturally inclined to abide ideas "we loathe and believe to be fraught with death." The First Amendment, on this view, cuts against human nature. It demands of us that we be better than we would be.

[For] the Supreme Court to declare that "under the First Amendment there is no such thing as a false idea" is, in effect, to insist on doubt.

Page 1139. At the end of section 3 of the Note, add the following:

Consider Gewirtz, Privacy and Speech, 2001 Sup. Ct. Rev. 139, 179, 185-189:

> Publicizing a rape victim's name is a cruel invasion of privacy concerning a matter of great sensitivity to the victim. Furthermore, in most cases, why is the name of a rape victim a matter of legitimate public concern? The fact of the rape or even the name of the alleged perpetrator is one thing, but the victim's name is ordinarily not something the public profits from knowing....
>
> The flavor of the Court's [opinions] is that [it] will find any conceivable escape hatch for media liability. The Court gives only token recognition to the value of implementing legal protections of privacy. This extreme solicitude for [speech] and sharply limited solicitude for [privacy should] be reversed....
>
> Supreme courts and constitutional courts in most other democracies give greater weight to values of privacy [when] they conflict with free speech claims [citing cases from Great Britain, Germany, India and Canada]. Although the constitutional rules in these countries are somewhat different, the press is vibrant and robust. [To] other countries, our current free speech doctrines seem to have become quite extreme....

4. *Information of public concern.* In Bartnicki v. Vopper, 532 U.S. 514 (2001), the Court held that federal and state anti-wiretap statutes cannot constitutionally be applied to a radio station that broadcasts the tape of an unlawfully intercepted telephone call, where the subject of the call was a matter of public concern (collective-bargaining negotiations between a union representing teachers at a public high school and the local school board) and where the broadcaster did not participate directly in the unlawful wiretap, even though the broadcaster knew that the material had been obtained unlawfully. Without deciding whether there might be some circumstances in which the privacy interest is "strong enough to justify the application" of the statute, such as when there is disclosure of "domestic gossip [of] purely private concern," the Court held that the enforcement of the statute in this case "implicates core purposes of the First Amendment because it imposes sanctions on the publication of truthful information of public concern." In such circumstances, "privacy concerns give way when balanced against the interest in publishing matters of public importance." Was the information disclosed in *Cox Broadcasting* and *Florida Star* "of public importance"? Suppose the newspaper in *Bartnicki* had intercepted the phone call. Should that lead to a different result?

Page 1157. Before the Note, add the following:

THOMPSON v. WESTERN STATES MEDICAL CENTER, 535 U.S. 357 (2002). Drug compounding is a process by which a pharmacist combines ingredients to create a medication tailored to the needs of an individual patient. Compounding is typically used to prepare medications that are not commercially available. It is a traditional component of the practice of pharmacy. The federal Food, Drug and Cosmetic Act of 1938 prohibits any person to manufacture or sell any "new drug" without prior FDA approval. Until the early 1990s, the FDA essentially left the regulation of drug compounding to the States. In the early 1990s, however, the FDA became increasingly concerned that the practice of drug compounding was occurring largely outside the scope of the FDCA's testing standards. Thus, in 1997 Congress enacted the Food and Drug Administration Modernization Act which, among other things, expressly exempted compounded drugs from the FDA's standard drug approval requirements, but only if the providers of those drugs do not advertise or otherwise promote the use of specific compounded drugs. The Court, in a five-to-four decision, held that this restriction of advertising violates the First Amendment.

Justice O'Connor delivered the opinion of the Court: "In *Virginia Pharmacy*, [we] recognized that a 'particular consumer's interest in the free flow of commercial information ... may be as keen [as] his interest in the day's most urgent political debate.' [Although] several Members of the Court have expressed doubts about [whether our] *Central Hudson* analysis [is sufficient to protect that interest], *Central Hudson,* as applied in our more recent commercial speech cases, provides an adequate basis for decision [of this case].

"[T]he Government [notes] that the FDCA's [general] drug approval requirements are critical to the public health [because the safety] of a new drug needs to be established by rigorous, scientifically valid clinical studies, [rather than by the] impressions of individual doctors, who cannot themselves compile sufficient [data]. [But] 'because obtaining FDA approval for a new drug is a costly process, requiring [such] approval of all drug products compounded by pharmacies for the particular needs of an individual patient would, as a practical matter, eliminate the practice of compounding, and thereby eliminate availability of compounded drugs for those patients who have no alternative treatment.' [Thus], the Government needs to be able to draw a line between small-scale compounding and large-scale drug manufacturing. That line must distinguish compounded drugs produced on such a small scale that they could not [realistically] undergo [costly] safety and efficacy testing from drugs produced and sold on a large enough scale that they could undergo such testing and therefore must do so.

"The Government argues that the FDAMA's speech-related provisions provide just such a line [because they] use advertising as the trigger for requiring FDA ap-

Freedom of Expression   **Page 1157**

proval—essentially, as long as pharmacists do not advertise particular compounded drugs, they may sell [them] without first [obtaining] FDA approval. If they advertise their compounded drugs, however, FDA approval is required. [The] Government argues [that] Congress' decision to limit the FDAMA's compounding exemption to pharmacies that do not engage in promotional activity was 'rationally calculated' to avoid creating "'a loophole that would allow unregulated drug manufacturing to occur under the guise of pharmacy compounding.'"

"Assuming [that] drugs cannot be marketed on a large scale without advertising, the FDAMA's prohibition on advertising compounded drugs might indeed 'directly advanc[e]' the Government's interests. [But] the Government has failed to demonstrate that the speech restrictions are 'not more extensive than is necessary to serve [those] interest[s].' In previous cases [we] have made clear that if the Government could achieve its interests in a manner that does not restrict speech, or that restricts less speech, the Government must do so. [Citing *Rubin* and *44 Liquormart*.]

"Several non-speech related means of drawing a line between compounding and large-scale manufacturing might be possible here. [For] example, the Government could ban the use of 'commercial scale manufacturing [for] compounding drug products.' It could prohibit pharmacists from compounding more drugs in anticipation of receiving prescriptions than in response to prescriptions already received. It could prohibit pharmacists from '[o]ffering compounded drugs at wholesale to other state licensed [entities] for resale.' [It could cap] the amount of any particular compounded drug [that] a pharmacist may make or sell in a given period of time. [The] Government has not offered any reason why these possibilities, alone or in combination, would be insufficient to prevent compounding from occurring on such a scale as to undermine the new drug approval process. . . .

"The dissent describes another governmental interest—an interest in prohibiting the sale of compounded drugs to 'patients who may not clearly need them.' Nowhere in its briefs, however, does the Government argue that this interest motivated the advertising ban. [We] have generally sustained statutes on the basis of hypothesized justifications when reviewing [them] merely to determine whether they are rational. [The] *Central Hudson* test is significantly stricter than the rational basis test, however. . . .

"Even if the Government had argued that the FDAMA's speech-related restrictions were motivated by a fear that advertising compounded drugs would put people who do not need such drugs at risk by causing them to convince their doctors to prescribe the drugs anyway, that fear would fail to justify the restrictions. Aside from the fact that this concern rests on the questionable assumption that doctors would prescribe unnecessary medications, [this] concern amounts to a fear that people would make bad decisions if given truthful information about compounded drugs. We have previously rejected the notion that the Government has an interest in preventing the dissemination of truthful commercial information in order to prevent

203

members of the public from making bad decisions with the information. [Citing *Virginia Pharmacy* and *44 Liquormart*.]

"If the Government's failure to justify its decision to regulate speech were not enough to convice us that the FDAMA's advertising provisions were unconstitutional, the amount of beneficial speech prohibited by the FDAMA would be. Forbidding the advertisement of compounded drugs would affect pharmacists other than those interested in producing drugs on a large scale. It would prevent pharmacists [who] serve clienteles with special medical needs from telling [doctors] about the alternative drugs available through compounding. For example, [this law] would prohibit a pharmacist from posting a notice informing customers that if their children refuse to take medications because of the taste, the pharmacist could change the flavor. The fact that the FDAMA would prohibit such seemingly useful speech even though doing so does not appear to directly further any asserted governmental objective confirms our belief that the prohibition is unconstitutional."

Justice Breyer, joined by Chief Justice Rehnquist and Justices Stevens and Ginsburg, dissented: "[The] exemption from testing requirements inherently creates risks simply by placing untested drugs in the hands of the consumer. Where an individual has a specific medical need for a specially tailored drug those risks are likely offset. But where an untested drug is a convenience, not a necessity, that offset is unlikely to be present. [The FDAMA reflects] the view that individualized consideration is more likely present, and convenience alone is more likely absent, when the demand for a compounding prescription originates with a doctor, not an advertisement. The restrictions try to assure that demand is generated doctor-to-patient-to-pharmacist, not pharmacist-to-patient-to-doctor. And they do so in order to diminish the likelihood that those who do not genuinely need untested compounded drugs will not receive them.

"[No one can] deny that [the] risks associated with the untested combination of ingredients [can] for some patients mean infection, serious side effects, or even death. [There] is considerable evidence that consumer oriented advertising will create strong consumer-driven demand for a particular drug, [and] there is strong evidence that doctors will often respond affirmatively to a patient's request for a specific drug that the patient has seen advertised. . . .

"Congress could [not] have achieved its safety objectives in significantly less restrictive ways. [The alternatives suggested by the Court do not] assure the kind of individualized doctor-patient need determination that the statute [was] designed to help achieve, [and they do not] successfully distinguish traditional compounding from unacceptable manufacturing.

"It is an oversimplification to say that the Government 'fear[s]' that doctors or patients 'would make bad decisions if given truthful information.' Rather, the Government fears the safety consequences of multiple compound-drug prescription decisions initiated not by doctors but by pharmacist-to-patient advertising. Those consequences flow from the adverse cumulative effects of multiple individual decisions each of which may seem perfectly reasonable considered on its own. The Government fears that, taken together, these apparently rational individual decisions will undermine the safety testing system, thereby producing overall a net balance of harm. . . .

"I do not deny that the statute restricts the circulation of some truthful information. [Nonetheless], this Court has not previously held that commercial advertising restrictions automatically violate the First Amendment. Rather, the Court has applied a more flexible test. [It] has done so because it has concluded that, from a constitutional perspective, commercial speech does not warrant application of the Court's strictest speech-protective tests. And it has reached this conclusion in part because restrictions on commercial speech do not often repress individual self-expression; they rarely interfere with the functioning of democratic political processes; and they often reflect a democratically determined governmental decision to regulate a commercial venture in order to protect, for example, the consumer.

"[The] Court, in my view, gives insufficient weight [in this case] to the Government's regulatory rationale, and too readily assumes the existence of practical alternatives. It thereby applies the commercial speech doctrine too strictly. [An] overly rigid 'commercial speech' doctrine will transform what ought to be a legislative or regulatory decision about the best way to protect the health and safety of the American public into a constitutional decision prohibiting the legislature from enacting necessary protections. As history in respect to the Due Process Clause shows, any such transformation would involve a tragic constitutional misunderstanding."

Page 1158. At the end of section 1 of the Note, add the following:

LORILLARD TOBACCO CO. v. REILLY, 533 U.S. 525 (2001). In 1999, the Attorney General of Massachusetts promulgated comprehensive regulations governing the advertising and sale of cigarettes, smokeless tobacco products, and cigars. These regulations prohibited (a) outdoor advertising of such products within 1,000 feet of a public playground or elementary or secondary school; (b) point-of-sale advertising that is placed lower than five feet from the floor of any retail establishment located within 1,000 feet of a public playground or elementary or second school; and (c) placing such products within a retail establishment within reach of consumers. The purpose of these regulations was "to address the incidence" of tobacco use "by children." Petitioners—a group of cigarette, smokeless tobacco, and cigar manufacturers and retailers—challenged the constitutionality of these regulations.

The Court, in an opinion by Justice O'Connor, held that the outdoor advertising and point-of-sale advertising regulations were preempted by federal law with respect to cigarettes. The Court held that those regulations violated the first amendment with respect to advertising of both cigars and smokeless tobacco products. The Court found it unnecessary to discuss the continuing validity of *Central Hudson* because it found these regulations unconstitutional even under the *Central Hudson* standard.

"The final step of the *Central Hudson* analysis [requires] a reasonable fit between the means and ends of the regulatory scheme. The Attorney General's regulations [with respect to outdoor advertising and point-of-sale advertising] do not meet this standard. The broad sweep of the regulations indicate that the Attorney General did not 'carefully calculat[e] the costs and benefits associated with the burden on speech imposed' by the regulations.

"The outdoor advertising regulations [would] prevent advertising in 87% to 91% of Boston. [Indeed], in some geographical areas, these regulations would constitute nearly a complete ban on the communication of truthful information about smokeless tobacco and cigars to adult consumers. The breadth and scope of the regulations [do] not demonstrate a careful calculation of the speech interests involved. [The] effect of [these] regulations will vary based on whether a locale is rural, suburban, or urban. The uniformly broad sweep of the geographical limitation demonstrates a lack of tailoring.

"In addition, the range of communications restricted seems unduly broad. [A] ban on all signs of any size seems ill suited to target the problem of highly visible billboards, as opposed to smaller signs. To the extent that studies have identified particular advertising and promotion practices that appeal to youth, tailoring would involve targeting those practices while permitting others. . . .

"The State's interest in preventing underage tobacco use is substantial, and even compelling, but it is no less true that the sale and use of tobacco products by adults is a legal activity. [Tobacco] retailers and manufacturers have an interest in conveying truthful information about their products to adults, and adults have a corresponding interest in receiving truthful information about tobacco products. [The] Attorney General has failed to show that [these regulations] are not more extensive than necessary to advance the State's substantial interest in preventing underage tobacco use."

The Court similarly found the point-of-sale regulation invalid under *Central Hudson*: "[The] State's goal is to prevent minors from using tobacco products and to curb demand for that activity by limiting youth exposure to advertising. The 5 foot rule does not seem to advance that goal. Not all children are less than 5 feet tall, and those who are certainly have the ability to look up. [Massachusetts] may wish to target tobacco advertisements and displays that entice children, much like floor-level candy displays in a convenience store, but the blanket height restriction does not constitute a reasonable fit with that goal."

Finally, the Court upheld the regulations that barred the "use of self-service displays" and required "that tobacco products be placed out of the reach of all consumers in a location accessible only to salespersons." The Court explained that these regulations did not require the application of *Central Hudson* because they restricted conduct "for reasons unrelated to the communication of ideas." Thus, they were constitutional because "the State has demonstrated a substantial interest in preventing access to tobacco products by minors and has adopted an appropriately narrow means of advancing that interest." The Court reasoned that "unattended displays of tobacco products present an opportunity for access without the proper age verification provided by law," that the regulations "leave open ample channels of communication" and "do not significantly impede adult access to tobacco products," and that "retailers have other means of exercising any cognizable speech interest in the presentation of their products," such as by placing "empty tobacco packaging on open display."

In a concurring opinion, Justice Thomas argued that "there is no 'philosophical or historical basis for asserting that "commercial" speech is of "lower value" than "noncommercial" speech.'" Thus, the "asserted government interest in keeping people ignorant by suppressing expression 'is per se illegitimate and can no more justify regulation of "commercial" speech than it can justify regulation of "noncommercial" speech.'" Moreover, with respect to the specifics of these regulations, he added that "the theory that public debate should be limited in order to protect impressionable children has a long historical pedigree: Socrates was condemned for being 'a doer of evil, inasmuch as he corrupts the youth.' [Speech] 'cannot be suppressed solely to protect the young from ideas or images that a legislative body thinks unsuitable for them.'"

Justice Stevens, joined by Justices Ginsburg and Breyer, concurred in part and dissented in part. With respect to the outdoor advertising regulation, Justice Stevens argued that "when calculating whether a child-direction location restriction goes too far in regulating adult speech, one crucial question is whether the regulatory scheme leaves available sufficient 'alternative avenues of communication.'" Justice Stevens concluded that the record did not contain "sufficient information to enable us to answer that question." He therefore advocated a remand "for trial on that issue."

Justice Stevens agreed with the Court that the sales practice regulations prohibiting self-service sales of tobacco products were consistent with the first amendment: "[These restrictions] are best analyzed as regulating conduct, not speech. While the decision how to display one's products no doubt serves a marginal communicative function, the same can be said of virtually any human activity performed with the hope or intention of evoking the interest of others. This Court has long recognized the need to differentiate between legislation that targets expression and legislation that targets conduct for legitimate non-speech-related reasons but imposes an incidental burden on expression. [Citing United States v. O'Brien, page 1302 of the main text]. [Laws] requiring that stores maintain items behind counters and prohibiting self-service displays fall squarely on the conduct side of the line. [I] see nothing the least bit constitutionally problematic in requiring individuals to ask for the assistance of a salesclerk in order to examine or purchase a handgun, a bottle of penicillin, or a package of cigarettes." Justice Stevens reached the same conclusion with respect to the five-foot regulation.

Consider M. Redish, Money Talks, 57-60 (2001):

The arguments against First Amendment protection for tobacco advertising [underscore] every one of the theoretical flaws underlying the commercial speech distinction. No one could seriously dispute that smoking is a social and political issue of enormous intensity and import. [In] order to demonstrate that point, one need only inquire whether full First Amendment protection would extend to the commentary of anti-tobacco activists either asserting the scientific case for the link between smoking and illness or directly urging individuals not to smoke. [Even] the most ardent advocate of a narrow, politically based First Amendment would have to concede that such expression lies at the core of free speech protection. [But] if this is true for the expression of those advocating that individuals refrain from smoking, it [must] be equally true of speech on the other side of the issue. [To] uphold such a restriction would allow government to skew the democratic process in order to achieve an externally preordained result. It would, moreover, reflect government's paternalistic mistrust of its citizens' ability to make lawful choices on the basis of free and open debate. . . .

It could be argued [of course] that tobacco advertisements [do not make] a real contribution to the debate. [But] far from failing to contribute to a public debate, the advertisements [urge] individuals to risk the possibility of future health injury in order to obtain certain largely intangible social or personal benefits. [It] would be difficult to distinguish appeals made in tobacco advertisements from [other appeals that] promote lawful lifestyle choices available to the individual. [Regulation of tobacco advertising] takes on the ominous character of government orchestrated suppression, manipulation, and mind control—the epitome of the type of expressive regulation the First Amendment precludes.

Page 1158. Before section 2 of the Note, add the following:

1a. *Regulating truthful commercial adverstising.* Consider Post, The Constitutional Status of Commercial Speech, 48 UCLA L. Rev. 1, 2-4, 14, 49, 53-54 (2000):

[C]ommercial speech doctrine [is] a notoriously unstable and contentious domain of First Amendment jurisprudence. . . . Although the Court has persistently adjudged commercial speech to be "subordinate," it has never explained why this might be true. [In my view], core First Amendment protections extend to those forms of communication that are deemed necessary to ensure that a democratic state remains responsive to the views of its citizens. [Commercial] speech, by contrast, consists of communication about commercial matters that conveys information necessary for public decision making, but that does not itself form part of public discourse. Commercial speech differs from public discourse because it is constitutionally valued merely for the information it disseminates, rather than for being itself a valuable way of participating in democratic self-determination. . . .

This focus on information introduces an important point of difference from the First Amendment protections that apply to public discourse. It is a necessary condition for democratic legitimacy that citizens have free access to public discourse, because censoring a citizen's ability to contribute to public opinion renders the government, with respect to that citizen, "heteronomous and nondemocratic." From a constitutional point of view, the censorship of commercial speech does not endanger the process of democratic legitimation. [Instead] it merely jeopardizes the circulation of information relevant to "the voting of wise decisions.". . .

The reason why the First Amendment prohibits the state from suppressing public discourse on the grounds of its persuasiveness is that participation within democratic self-governance [assumes that] speakers seek to persuade others of their point of view and in this way to make the state responsive to their perspective; for the state deliberately to disrupt this communicative relationship is to negate the very constitutional raison d'etre of public discourse. This analysis, however, is not applicable to commercial speech, which is protected [only] to ensure "the free flow of information." [Thus, in] the particular environment of commercial speech, [the doctrine ought to focus not on whether the regulation is paternalistic, but on] whether the "informational function" of commercial speech has been unacceptably compromised. [A] workable rule of thumb might well be that government regulations entirely eliminating a category of truthful information are good candidates for heightened constitutional suspicion.

Page 1160. After section 8 of the Note, add the following:

9. *Other forms of compelled commercial advertising.* In what circumstances may government compel commercial firms to pay assessments to support common advertising programs? Compare Glickman v. Wileman Brothers & Elliott, Inc., 512 U.S. 1145 (1997) (upholding an order of the Secretary of Agriculture requiring California agricultural producers to pay assessments to help defray the costs of generic advertising of California fruits, noting that the advertising at issue does not promote any "message other than encouraging consumers to buy California tree fruit," that the order does "not compel the producers to endorse or to finance any political or

ideological views," and that "the mere fact that the objectors believe their money is not being well spent "does not mean [that] they have a First Amendment complaint'"), with United States v. United Foods, 533 U.S. 405 (2001) (invalidating a federal statute requiring producers of fresh mushrooms to fund a common advertising program promoting mushroom sales, and distinguishing *Glickman* on the ground that the compelled assessments in *Glickman* were ancillary to a comprehensive regulatory scheme of government-mandated collective action, whereas the compelled assessments in *United Foods* were not part of such a comprehensive scheme, other than a program "to generate the very speech to which some of the producers object"). For more on compelled speech, see pages 1159-1164 of the main text.

Page 1165. Before section 2 of the Note, add the following:

1b. *The freedom of imagination*. Consider Rubenfeld, The Freedom of Imagination: Copyright's Constitutionality, 112 Yale L. J. 1, 35-38 (2002):

Why does American law rebel at state aesthetic censors? [A] society with state control over art might never have known Pollock's great abstractions, Schoenberg's tone poems, or Carroll's captivating Jabberwocky. [It] is simply confusion to think that constitutional protection of [Britney Spears] depends on the quality of her singing or dancing, [or] on the fact that she actually spurs a great deal of conversation on "matters of public concern." [The] art/entertainment distinction has no place in First Amendment law. [It] would be better to dispense with the idea that the First Amendment protects works of high aesthetic, cultural, political, or individually-expressive value. We should say rather that the First Amendment protects—the freedom of imagination....

This should be a First Amendment bedrock.... The freedom of imagination means the freedom to explore the world not present, creatively and communicatively. [It] means the freedom to explore, without state penalty, any thought, any image, any emotion, any melody, as far as the imagining mind may take it.

Page 1180. After section 4 of the Note, add the following:

4a. *Community standards on the Internet*. In Ashcroft v. American Civil Liberties Union, 535 U.S. 564 (2002), the Court held that a federal statute (the Child Online Protection Act) regulating obscene material on the Internet is not invalid on its face because it applies local community standards in determining whether particular material is obscene, even though an individual posting sexually explicit material on the

Internet has no control over the geographic areas in which the material is accessible. The Court of Appeals had invalidated the use of local community standards because, in the special context of the Internet, such a test "would effectively force all speakers on the Web to abide by the 'most puritan' community's standards."

In a plurality opinion, Justice Thomas reasoned that the Internet is not sufficiently different from other media of communication, such as the mail, to "justify adopting a different approach than that set forth in *Hamling*." Moreover, "if a publisher chooses to send its material into a particular community, [it] is the publisher's responsibility to abide by that community's standards. If a publisher wishes for its material to be judged only by the standards of particular communities, then it need only take the simple step of utilizing a medium that enables it to target the release of its material into [only] those communities." Finally, Justice Thomas observed that the statute is not unconstitutionally overbroad because those challenging the statute had failed to demonstrate with "objective evidence" that local community standards differ *substantially* from one community to another.

Although concurring in the judgment that the statute was not unconstitutional on its face, Justice O'Connor observed that "given Internet speakers' inability to control the geographic location of their audience, expecting them to bear the burden of controlling the recipients of their speech [may] be entirely too much to ask, and would potentially suppress an inordinate amount of expression. For these reasons, adoption of a national standard is necessary [for] any reasonable regulation of Internet obscenity."

In another concurring opinion, Justice Breyer argued that "Congress intended the statutory word 'community' to refer to the Nation's adult community taken as a whole, not to geographically separate local areas." He added that "to read the statute as adopting the community standards of every locality in the United States would provide the most puritan of communities with a heckler's Internet veto affecting the rest of the Nation."

Justice Kennedy, joined by Justices Souter and Ginsburg, also filed a concurring opinion: "Unlike Justice Thomas, [I] would not assume that the Act is narrow enough to render the national variation in community standards unproblematic. [The] economics and technology of Internet communication differ in important ways from those of [other means of communication, and] it is no answer to say that the speaker should 'take the simple step of utilizing a [different] medium.' [The] nation variation in community standards constitutes a particular burden on Internet speech." Nonetheless, Justice Kennedy agreed with the plurality that the act was not unconstitutional on its face.

Justice Stevens dissented: "[In] light of [the] fundamental difference in technologies, the rules applicable to the mass mailing of an obscene montage [should] not be used to judge the legality of messages on the World Wide Web. [Because] communities differ widely in their attitudes toward sex, [the] Court of Appeals was correct to conclude that [applying] local community standards to the Internet will restrict a substantial amount of protected speech that would not be considered [obscene] in many communities. [It] is quite wrong to allow the standards of a minority consisting of the least tolerant communities to regulate access to relatively harmless messages in this burgeoning market."

Page 1181. After section 6 of the Note, add the following:

7. *Violence.* Suppose a city enacts an ordinance regulating the freedom of minors to play video games that "appeal predominantly to the morbid interest of minors in violence, are patently offensive to prevailing adult standards about what is suitable for minors, lack serious literary, artistic, political or scientific value for minors, and contain graphic depictions of violence, such as decapitation, dismemberment, mutilation, maiming and bloodshed."

Consider American Amusement Machine Assn. v. Kendrick, 244 F.3d 572 (7th Cir.), *cert. denied,* 534 U.S. 994 (2001)), in which the court, in an opinion by Judge Richard Posner, invalidated such an ordinance:

> Violence and obscenity are distinct categories of objectionable depiction. [The] main worry about obscenity [is] that it is offensive. [But] offensiveness is not the basis on which [the challenged ordinance] seeks to regulate violent video games. [The] basis of the ordinance, rather, is a belief that violent video games cause temporal harm by engendering aggressive attitudes and behavior, which might lead to violence. [To restrict speech on this basis], a state would have to present a compelling basis for believing that [such] harms were actually caused [by the expression].
>
> No doubt the City would concede this point if the question were whether to forbid children to read [the] *Odyssey,* with its graphic descriptions of Odysseus's grinding out the eye of Polyphemus with a heated, sharpened stake, [or] the *Divine Comedy,* with its graphic descriptions of the tortures of the damned, [or] *War and Peace,* with its graphic descriptions [of] death from war wounds. [Violence] has always been and remains a central interest of humankind and a recurrent, even obsessive theme of culture both high and low. It engages the interest of children from an early age, as anyone familiar with the classic fairy tales [is] aware. To shield children right up to the age of 18 from exposure to violent descriptions and images would not only be quixotic, but deforming; it would leave them unequipped to cope with the world as we know it. . . .
>
> Most of the video games in the record of this case [are] stories. Take "The House of the Dead." The player is armed with a gun—most fortunately, because he is being assailed by a seemingly unending succession of hideous axe-wielding zombies, the living dead conjured back to life by voodoo. [Zombies] are supernatural beings, therefore difficult to kill. Repeated shots are necessary to stop

Freedom of Expression Page 1183

them as they rush headlong toward the player. He must not only be alert to the appearance of zombies from any quarter, he must be assiduous about reloading his gun periodically, lest he be overwhelmed. . . .

Self-defense, protection of others, dread of the "undead," fighting against overwhelming odds—these are all age-old themes of literature, and ones particularly appealing to the young. "The House of the Dead" is not distinguished literature. [We] are in the world of kids' popular culture. But it is not lightly to be suppressed.

7a. *Video games as "speech."* Are video games "speech" within the meaning of the first amendment? Are games such as bingo, blackjack, chess and baseball "speech" within the meaning of the first amendment? See Saunders, Regulating Youth Access to Violent Video Games: Three Responses to First Amendment Concerns, 2003 L. Rev. M.S.U.-D.C.L. 51, 99 ("Where there is no intent to or likelihood of passing information or communicating a message, even the principle that entertainment is protected [speech] does not apply.").

7b. *Internet filters for public libraries.* Can a public library use filters on its internet terminals designed to preclude patrons from accessing obscene web-sites? Suppose the filter is imprecise and inevitably will block access to non-obscene as well as obscene web-sites? See United States v. American Library Association, 539 U.S. 194 (2003), section E.2, *infra* this Supplement.

Page 1183. At the end of the first full paragraph after the decision in *Ferber*, add the following:

Does it make sense under the first amendment to prohibit X from showing a movie because Y committed an unlawful act to create the movie? Consider Bartnicki v. Vopper, 532 U.S. 514 (2001), in which the Court held that federal and state anti-wiretap statutes cannot constitutionally be applied to a radio station that broadcasts the tape of an unlawfully intercepted telephone call, where the subject of the call was a matter of public concern and the broadcaster did not participate directly in the unlawful wiretap, even though the broadcaster knew that the material had been obtained unlawfully. The Court expressly distinguished *Ferber* on the ground that *Ferber* involved speech "considered of minimal value."

Page 1183. At the end of the second full paragraph after the decision in *Ferber*, add the following:

Consider Adler, Inverting the First Amendment, 149 U. Pa. L. Rev. 921, 996 (2001):

Congress significantly broadened the scope of child pornography laws in 1996 when it passed [the] Child Pornography Prevention Act ("CPPA"). [The] CPPA responded to a technological innovation, the development of wholly computer-generated or "virtual" child pornography, [by outlawing] materials that *appear* to be (but are not) depictions of children engaged in sexual conduct. According to Congress, such material [must] be prevented because [it] "inflames the desires of child molesters, pedophiles, and child pornographers" and it "encourages a societal perception of children as sexual objects." [The] CPPA is a total departure from *Ferber*, which was premised on preventing the abuse of children in the production of the material. [CPPA] has, in effect, enacted Catherine MacKinnon's theory of speech into law.

Page 1184. Before Section 5, add the following:

For the argument that, by unwittingly perpetuating and escalating the sexual representation of children, child pornography laws may perversely "reinforce the very problem they are designed to attack," see Adler, The Perverse Law of Child Pornography, 101 Colum. L. Rev. 209 (2001) ("sexual prohibitions invite their own violation by increasing the sexual allure of what they forbid" and child pornography laws may thus generate "a vast realm of discourse in which the image of the child as sexual is preserved and multiplied").

ASHCROFT v. THE FREE SPEECH COALITION, 535 U.S. 234 (2002). The Court invalidated the Child Pornography Prevention Act of 1996 (CPPA), which extended the prohibition against child pornography to sexually explicit images that *appear* to depict minors, but were in fact produced without using real children—either by computer imaging or by using adults who look like children. Justice Kennedy delivered the opinion of the Court:

"By prohibiting child pornography that does not depict an actual child, the statute goes beyond *Ferber*, which distinguished child pornography from other sexually explicit speech because of the State's interest in protecting the children exploited by the production process. [Although the statute] captures a range of depictions [that] do not [harm] any children in the production process[, Congress] decided the materials threaten children in other, less direct, ways. Pedophiles might use the materials to encourage children to participate in sexual activity [or they] might 'whet their own sexual appetites' with the pornographic images, 'thereby increasing the creation and distribution of child pornography and the sexual abuse and exploitation of actual children.' Under these rationales, harm flows from the content of the images, not from the means of their production. In addition, Congress [was concerned that the existence of] computer-generated images [can] can make it harder to prosecute pornographers who [use] real minors. As imaging technology improves, Congress found, it becomes more difficult to prove that a particular picture was produced using actual children. To ensure that defendants possessing child pornography using real minors cannot evade prosecution, Congress extended the ban to virtual child pornography. . . .

"The sexual abuse of a child is a most serious crime and an act repugnant to the moral instincts of a decent people. [Congress] may pass valid laws to protect children from abuse, and it has. The prospect of crime, however, by itself does not justify laws suppressing protected speech. See *Kingsley Pictures*. ('Among free men, the deterrents ordinarily to be applied to prevent crime are education and punishment for violations of the law, not abridgment of the rights of free speech'). . . .

"As a general principle, the First Amendment bars the government from dictating what we see or read or speak or hear. The freedom of speech has its limits; it does not embrace certain categories of speech, including defamation, incitement, obscenity, and pornography produced with real children. While these categories may be prohibited without violating the First Amendment, none of them includes the speech prohibited by the CPPA. . . .

"[T]he CPPA [does not deal with] obscenity. Under *Miller*, the Government must prove that the work, taken as a whole, appeals to the prurient interest, is patently offensive in light of community standards, and lacks serious literary, artistic, political, or scientific value. The CPPA, however, [applies] without regard to the *Miller* requirements. . . .

"[The] statute proscribes the visual depiction of an idea—that of teenagers engaging in sexual activity—that is a fact of modern society and has been a theme in art and literature throughout the ages. [Citing, e.g., Romeo and Juliet; and the movies Traffic and American Beauty.] If [such works] contain a single graphic depiction of sexual activity within the statutory definition, the possessor [or distributor] would be subject to severe punishment without inquiry into the work's redeeming value. This is inconsistent with an essential First Amendment rule: The artistic merit of a work does not depend on the presence of a single explicit scene. Under *Miller*, the First Amendment requires that redeeming value be judged by considering the work as a whole. . . .

"The Government seeks to address this deficiency by arguing that speech prohibited by the CPPA is virtually indistinguishable from child pornography, which may be banned without regard to whether it depicts works of value. See *Ferber*. Where the images are themselves the product of child sexual abuse, *Ferber* recognized that the State had an interest in stamping it out without regard to any judgment about its content. The production of the work, not its content, was the target of the statute. The fact that a work contained serious literary, artistic, or other value did not excuse the harm it caused to its child participants. [*Ferber*] upheld a prohibition on the distribution and sale of child pornography, as well as its production, because these acts were 'intrinsically related' to the sexual abuse of children in two ways. First, as a permanent record of a child's abuse, the continued circulation itself would harm the child who had participated. Like a defamatory statement, each new publication of the speech would cause new injury to the child's reputation and emotional well-being. Second, because the traffic in child pornography was an economic motive for its production, the State had an interest in closing the distribution network. [Under] either rationale, the speech had what the Court in effect held was a proximate link to the crime from which it came. . . .

"In contrast to the speech in *Ferber*, [the] CPPA prohibits speech that records no crime and creates no victims by its production. Virtual child pornography is not 'intrinsically related' to the sexual abuse of children, as were the materials in *Ferber*. While the Government asserts that the images can lead to actual instances of child abuse, the causal link is contingent and indirect. The harm does not necessarily follow from the speech, but depends upon some unquantified potential for subsequent criminal acts.

"The Government says these indirect harms are sufficient because, as *Ferber* acknowledged, child pornography rarely can be valuable speech. This argument, however, suffers from two flaws. First, *Ferber*'s judgment about child pornography was based upon how it was made, not on what it communicated. [Second,] *Ferber* did not hold that child pornography is by definition without value. On the contrary, the Court recognized some works in this category might have significant value, but relied on virtual images—the very images prohibited by the CPPA—as an alternative and permissible means of expression. *Ferber*, then, not only referred to the distinction between actual and virtual child pornography, it relied on it as a reason supporting its holding. *Ferber* provides no support for a statute that eliminates the distinction and makes the alternative mode criminal as well.

"The CPPA [is thus] inconsistent with *Miller* and finds no support in *Ferber*. The Government seeks to justify its prohibitions in other ways. It argues that the CPPA is necessary because pedophiles may use virtual child pornography to seduce children. There are many things innocent in themselves, however, such as cartoons, video games, and candy, that might be used for immoral purposes, yet we would not expect those to be prohibited because they can be misused. The Government, of course, may punish adults who provide unsuitable materials to children, see *Ginsberg*, and it may enforce criminal penalties for unlawful solicitation. The precedents establish, however, that speech within the rights of adults to hear may not be silenced completely in an attempt to shield children from it. [Here, the] evil in question depends upon the actor's unlawful conduct, conduct defined as criminal quite apart from any link to the speech in question. This establishes that the speech ban is not narrowly drawn. The objective is to prohibit illegal conduct, but this restriction goes well beyond that interest by restricting the speech available to law-abiding adults.

"The Government submits further that virtual child pornography whets the appetites of pedophiles and encourages them to engage in illegal conduct. This rationale cannot sustain the provision in question. The mere tendency of speech to encourage unlawful acts is not a sufficient reason for banning it. [The] Court's First Amendment cases draw vital distinctions between words and deeds, between ideas and conduct. The government may not prohibit speech because it increases the chance an unlawful act will be committed 'at some indefinite future time.' [The] Government has shown no more than a remote connection between speech that might encourage thoughts or impulses and any resulting child abuse. Without a significantly stronger, more direct connection, the Government may not prohibit speech on the ground that it may encourage pedophiles to engage in illegal conduct. . . .

"Finally, the Government says that the possibility of producing images by using computer imaging makes it very difficult for it to prosecute those who produce pornography by using real children. Experts, we are told, may have difficulty in saying whether the pictures were made by using real children or by using computer imaging. The necessary solution, the argument runs, is to prohibit both kinds of images. The argument, in essence, is that protected speech may be banned as a means to ban unprotected speech. This analysis turns the First Amendment upside down. The Government may not suppress lawful speech as the means to suppress unlawful speech. Protected speech does not become unprotected merely because it resembles the latter."

Justice Thomas filed a concurring opinion in which he observed that "if technological advances" eventually reach a point where they actually (as opposed to speculatively) "thwart prosecution of 'unlawful speech,' the Government may well have a compelling interest [in] regulating some narrow category of 'lawful speech' in order to enforce effectively laws against pornography made through the abuse of real children."

Justice O'Connor, joined in part by Chief Justice Rehnquist and Justice Scalia, dissented in part. Justice O'Connor concluded that the CPPA was unconstitutional insofar as it restricts material created by using youthful-looking adults, but that it was constitutional insofar as it restricts virtual-child pornography. With respect to the latter, with which Chief Justice Rehnquist and Justice Scalia agreed, Justice O'Connor argued that if the CPPA is narrowly construed to limit only computer-generated images that are "virtually indistinguishable" from real child pornography, it would satisfy "strict scrutiny" because it would then be narrowly-tailored to serve the compelling governmental interest in eliminating real child pornography. She also noted that if any work falling within this category in fact has serious social, political, literary or scientific value, the possible "overbreadth" of the law in that regard could be considered in an "as applied" challenge. On the other hand, Justice O'Connor concurred with the Court in invalidating the law insofar as it restricts material created with youthful-looking adults because such material would not pose the same problem to the enforcement of the prohibition on actual child pornography as material created using computer images.

Chief Justice Rehnquist, with whom Justice Scalia joined, dissented. Chief Justice Rehnquist argued that the Court should interpret the CPPA narrowly, as extending

217

the definition of child pornography only to computer-generated images that are "virtually indistinguishable" from real children engaged in sexually explicit conduct. So construed, he would uphold the statute for the reasons offered by Justice O'Connor.

Another provision of the CPPA, not at issue in this case, prohibits the use of computer morphing to alter the images of real children so they appear to be engaged in sexual activity. Is this different from the issues addressed in *Ashcroft*? The Court noted in passing that because such morphed images "implicate the interests of real children" they are closer to the issue considered in *Ferber*. Might this better be analyzed as a form of libel?

Suppose Congress re-enacted the CPPA verbatim, but recognized an affirmative defense to enable the defendant to prove that the image had been created without the abuse of a real child. Would that satisfy the first amendment?

What do you suppose is the "real" motivation underlying laws like the CPPA? Is it the concern that the existence of virtual child pornography will increase pedophilia? That it will make it more difficult to prosecute actual child pornography? That the images are themselves so offensive that they should not be tolerated? Of course, the answer must be some mix of the three. But to the extent the most candid answer is the third, the Court made clear its view of this in *Ashcroft*: "[S]peech may not be prohibited because it concerns subjects offending our sensibilities."

Page 1204. At the end of section 1 of the Note, add the following:

1a. *Solving the problems of the CDA.* After the Court's decision in *Reno*, Congress enacted the Child Online Protection Act, which was designed to address the problems the Court found with the CDA. COPA prohibits any person from knowingly making "any communication for commercial purposes" on the World Wide Web that is "available to any minor and that includes any material that is harmful to minors." Thus, unlike the CDA, COPA applies only to material displayed on the World Wide Web (and not to e-mail); only to material made for commercial purposes; and only to material that is "harmful to minors" (*i.e.*, "obscene for minors," as recognized in *Ginsberg*). COPA defines material that is "harmful to minors" as any communication that "the average person, applying contemporary community standards, would find, taking the material as a whole and with respect to minors, is designed to appeal [to] the prurient interest"; that depicts in "a manner patently offensive with respect to minors, an actual or simulated sexual act [or] lewd exhibition of the genitals"; and that "taken as a whole, lacks serious literary, artistic, politi-

Freedom of Expression   Page 1204

cal, or scientific value for minors." Like the CDA, COPA provides an affirmative defense if the defendant "in good faith has restricted access by minors to material that is harmful to minors by requiring the use of a credit card, debit account, adult access code, or adult personal identification number." Is COPA constitutional? Cf. Ashcroft v. American Civil Liberties Union, 535 U.S. 564 (2002) (holding that COPA is not unconstitutional on its face because it uses local community standards to determine whether material is "harmful to minors," but not otherwise addressing the constitutionality of COPA). Approximately 40% of all sexually explicit web sites are placed on the Internet by individuals not in the United States. Given the nature of the Internet, and the way search engines work, is there anything to be gained by a law like COPA, which cannot reach individuals not within the jurisdiction of the United States?

    1b. *The moral faculties of children.* Consider Tubbs, Conflicting Images of Children in First Amendment Jurisprudence, 30 Pepperdine L. Rev. 1, 51 (2002): "Perhaps the most distressing thing about the majority opinion in *Playboy Entertainment* is [its] cavalier indifference toward the vulnerability of the young [and its assumption] that the moral faculties of children are indistinguishable from those of adults."

ASHCROFT v. AMERICAN CIVIL LIBERTIES UNION, 542 U.S. ___ (2004).
This decision revisits the constitutionality of COPA, which Congress enacted in an effort to solve the constitutional problems in the Communications Decency Act, which the Court invalidated in *Reno*. COPA imposes criminal penalties of a $50,000 fine and six months in prison for the knowing posting, for "commercial purposes," of World Wide Web content that is "harmful to minors."

    COPA defines material that is "harmful to minors" as: "any communication, picture, image, graphic image file, article, recording, writing, or other matter of any kind that is obscene or that (A) the average person, applying contemporary community standards, would find, taking the material as a whole and *with respect to minors*, is designed to appeal to, or is designed to pander to, the prurient interest; (B) depicts, describes, or represents, in a manner patently offensive *with respect to minors*, an actual or simulated sexual act or sexual contact, an actual or simulated normal or perverted sexual act, or a lewd exhibition of the genitals or post-pubescent female breast; and (C) taken as a whole, lacks serious literary, artistic, political, or scientific value for minors." (Emphasis added.)

    COPA defines "minor" as "any person under 17 years of age" and specifies that a person acts for "commercial purposes" only if he "makes a communication, or offers to make a communication, by means of the World Wide Web, that includes any material that is harmful to minors, . . . as a regular course of such person's trade or business, with the objective of earning a profit as a result of such activities."

    COPA recognizes an affirmative defense for those who attempt to prevent minors from gaining access to the prohibited materials "(A) by requiring use of a credit card,

219

debit account, adult access code, or adult personal identification number; (B) by accepting a digital certificate that verifies age; or (C) by any other reasonable measures that are feasible under available technology."

In a five-to-four decision, the Court held that the federal district court did not "abuse its discretion" in entering a preliminary injunction against enforcement of COPA. In its opinion, written by Justice Kennedy, the Court explained that the district court had issued the preliminary injunction because it found that there "are plausible, less restrictive alternatives to COPA." The Court continued:

"The primary alternative considered by the District Court was blocking and filtering software. [Filters] are less restrictive than COPA. They impose selective restrictions on speech at the receiving end, not universal restrictions at the source. Under a filtering regime, adults without children may gain access to speech they have a right to see without having to identify themselves or provide their credit card information. Even adults with children may obtain access to the same speech on the same terms simply by turning off the filter on their home computers. . . .

"Filters also may well be more effective than COPA. First, a filter can prevent minors from seeing all pornography, not just pornography posted to the Web from America. The District Court noted [that] 40% of harmful-to-minors content comes from overseas. COPA does not prevent minors from having access to those foreign harmful materials. That alone makes it possible that filtering software might be more effective in serving Congress' goals. [It] is not an answer to say that COPA reaches some amount of materials that are harmful to minors; the question is whether it would reach more of them than less restrictive alternatives. In addition, the District Court found that verification systems may be subject to evasion and circumvention, for example by minors who have their own credit cards. [The] Commission on Child Online Protection, a blue-ribbon commission created by Congress, unambiguously found that filters are more effective than age-verification requirements. . . .

"Filtering software, of course, is not a perfect solution to the problem of children gaining access to harmful-to-minors materials. It may block some materials that are not harmful to minors and fail to catch some that are. Whatever the deficiencies of filters, however, the Government failed to introduce specific evidence proving that existing technologies are less effective than the restrictions in COPA. In the absence of a showing as to the relative effectiveness of COPA and the alternatives proposed by respondents, it was not an abuse of discretion for the District Court to grant the preliminary injunction. . . .

"One argument to the contrary is worth mentioning—the argument that filtering software is not an available alternative because Congress may not require it to be used. That argument carries little weight, because Congress undoubtedly may act to encourage the use of filters. We have held that Congress can give strong incentives to schools and libraries to use them. *United States v. American Library Assn.* [The] need for parental cooperation does not automatically disqualify a proposed less restrictive alternative. *Playboy Entertainment.* [By] enacting programs to promote use of filtering software, Congress could give parents that ability without subjecting protected speech to severe penalties. [The] reasoning of *Playboy Entertainment*, and the holdings and force of our precedents require us to affirm the preliminary injunction."

Justice Breyer, joined by Chief Justice Rehnquist and Justice O'Connor, dissented: "Like the Court, I would subject the Act to 'the most exacting scrutiny.' [But] my examination of (1) the burdens the Act imposes on protected expression, (2) the Act's ability to further a compelling interest, and (3) the proposed 'less restrictive alternatives' convinces me that the Court is wrong. . . .

"[The] Act, properly interpreted, imposes a burden on protected speech that is no more than modest. [A] comparison of this Court's definition of unprotected, 'legally obscene,' material with the Act's definitions makes [clear that the] only significant difference between the present statute and *Miller*'s definition consists of the addition of the words 'with respect to minors.' [The] addition of these words to a definition that would otherwise cover only obscenity expands the statute's scope only slightly. That is because [material] that appeals to the 'prurient interest[s]' of some group of adolescents [will] almost inevitably appeal to the 'prurient interest[s]' of some group of adults as well, [and] because one cannot easily imagine material that has serious literary, artistic, political, or scientific value for a significant group of adults, but lacks such value for any significant group of minors. Thus, the statute, [insofar] as it extends beyond the legally obscene, could reach only borderline cases. . . .

"These limitations on the statute's scope answer many of the concerns raised by those who attack its constitutionality. [They] fear prosecution for the Internet posting of [such material as] an essay about a young man's experience with masturbation and sexual shame; 'a serious discussion about birth control practices, homosexuality, . . . or the consequences of prison rape'; an account by a 15-year-old, written for therapeutic purposes, of being raped when she was 13; [or] a graphic illustration of how to use a condom. . . . [But such] materials are *not* both (1) 'designed to appeal to, or . . . pander to, the prurient interest' of significant groups of minors *and* (2) lacking in 'serious literary, artistic, political, or scientific value' for significant groups of minors. Thus, they fall outside the statute's definition of the material that it restricts. . . .

"[Moreover, the] Act does not censor the material it covers. Rather, it requires providers of the 'harmful to minors' material to restrict minors' access to it by verifying age. [In] this way, the Act requires creation of an internet screen that minors, but not adults, will find difficult to bypass. [I] recognize that the screening requirement imposes some burden on adults who seek access to the regulated material, as well as on its providers. The [burden] is, in part, monetary [and, in part, the fear of embarrassment caused by the identification requirement]. Both monetary costs and potential embarrassment can deter potential viewers and, in that sense, the statute's requirements may restrict access to a site. But this Court has held that in the context of congressional efforts to protect children, restrictions of this kind do not automatically violate the Constitution. [Citing *United States v. American Library Assn*].

"I turn next to the question of 'compelling interest,' that of protecting minors from exposure to commercial pornography. No one denies that such an interest is 'compelling.' Rather, the question here is whether the Act, given its restrictions on adult access, significantly advances that interest. In other words, is the game worth the candle? [The] majority argues that it is not, because of the existence of 'blocking and filtering software.' The majority refers to the presence of that software as a 'less restrictive alternative.' But that is a misnomer [because] the presence of filtering software is not an *alternative* legislative approach to the problem of protecting children from exposure to commercial pornography. Rather, it is part of the status quo, *i.e.*, the backdrop against which Congress enacted the present statute. It is always true, by definition, that the status quo is less restrictive than a new regulatory law. It is always less restrictive to do *nothing* than to do *something*. But 'doing nothing' does not address the problem Congress sought to address—namely that, despite the availability of filtering software, children were still being exposed to harmful material on the Internet.

"Thus, the relevant constitutional question [posits] a comparison of (a) a status quo that includes filtering software with (b) a change in that status quo that adds to it an age-verification screen requirement. Given the existence of filtering software, does the problem Congress identified remain significant? Does the Act help to address it? These are questions about the relation of the Act to the compelling interest. Does the Act, compared to the status quo, significantly advance the ball? [The] answers to these [questions] are clear: Filtering software, as presently available, does not solve the 'child protection' problem. It suffers from four serious inadequacies that prompted Congress to pass legislation instead of relying on its voluntary use. First, its filtering is faulty, allowing some pornographic material to pass through without hindrance. [Second], filtering software costs money. Not every family has the $40 or so necessary to install it. Third, filtering software depends upon parents willing to decide where their children will surf the Web and able to enforce that decision. As to millions of American families, that is not a reasonable possibility. [Fourth], software blocking lacks precision, with the result that those who wish to use it to screen out pornography find that it blocks a great deal of material that is valuable. [Thus], Congress could reasonably conclude that a system that relies entirely upon the use of such software is not an effective system. And a law that adds to that system an age-verification screen requirement significantly increases the system's efficacy. That is to say, at a modest additional cost to those adults who wish to obtain access to a screened program, that law will bring about better, more precise blocking, both inside and outside the home. . . .

"I turn, then, to the actual 'less restrictive alternatives' that the Court proposes. The Court proposes [that] the Government might 'act to encourage' the use of blocking and filtering software. The problem is that any argument that rests upon this alternative proves too much. If one imagines enough government resources devoted to the [problem], then, of course, the use of software might become as effective and less restrictive. Obviously, the Government could give all parents, schools, and Internet cafes free computers with filtering programs already installed, hire federal employees to train parents and teachers on their use, and devote millions of dollars to the development of better software. The result might be an alternative that is extremely effective. But the Constitution does not, because it cannot, require the Government to disprove the existence of magic solutions, *i.e.,* solutions that, put in general terms, will solve any problem less restrictively but with equal effectiveness. [Perhaps] that is why no party has argued seriously that additional expenditure of government funds to encourage the use of screening is a 'less restrictive alternative.'"

Justice Scalia also dissented: "Both the Court and Justice Breyer err [in] subjecting COPA to strict scrutiny. '[C]ommercial activities which engage in "the sordid business of pandering" by "deliberately emphasiz[ing] the sexually provocative aspects of [their nonobscene products], in order to catch the salaciously disposed," engage in constitutionally unprotected behavior.' [There] is no doubt that the commercial pornography covered by COPA fits this description. [Since] this business could, consistent with the First Amendment, be banned entirely, COPA's lesser restrictions raise no constitutional concern."

Page 1209. After *Renton*, add the following:

CITY OF LOS ANGELES v. ALAMEDA BOOKS, 535 U.S. 425 (2002). In 1977, the city of Los Angeles conducted a study that concluded that concentrations of adult entertainment establishments are associated with higher crimes rates. Accordingly, it enacted an ordinance prohibiting such establishments within 1,000 feet of each other or within 500 feet of a religious institution, school or public park. In 1983, to close a "loophole" in the original ordinance, the city amended the ordinance to prohibit "more than one adult entertainment business in the same building." Alameda Books, which operates a combined adult book store and adult video arcade in a single location, challenged the amendment on the ground that there was no evidence that combining these two activities in a single location causes higher crime rates. The lower court granted summary judgment to Alameda Books. The Supreme Court reversed.

Justice O'Connor, joined by Chief Justice Rehnquist and Justices Scalia and Thomas, delivered the plurality opinion: "[In *Renton,*] we stated that the ordinance would be upheld so long as the city [showed] that [it] was designed to serve a substantial government interest and that reasonable alternative avenues of communication remained available. [We agree with Justice Kennedy's observation in his concurring opinion in this case that a zoning] ordinance warrants intermediate scrutiny only if it is a time, place, and manner regulation and not a ban.

"[Although the 1977 study did not specifically consider the problem addressed by the 1983 amendment, it was] rational for the city to infer that reducing the concentration of adult operations in a neighborhood, whether within separate establishments or in one large establishment, will reduce crime rates. [We] conclude that the city, at this [very early] stage of the litigation, has [sufficiently] complied with the evidentiary requirement in *Renton* [to withstand a motion for summary judgment]."

Justice Kennedy concurred in the judgment: "If a city can decrease the crime and blight associated with certain speech by the traditional exercise of its zoning power, and at the same time leave the quantity and accessibility of the speech substantially undiminished, there is no First Amendment objection. This is so even if the measure identifies the problem outside by reference to the speech inside—that is, even if the measure is in that sense content-based. [But] the purpose and effect of [such] a zoning ordinance must be to reduce secondary effects and not to reduce speech.

"[In *Renton*,] the Court designated the restriction 'content neutral.' [This] was something of a fiction. [Whether] a statute is content-based or content neutral is something that can be determined on the face of it; if the statute describes speech by content then it is content based. [This ordinance is] content based and we should call [it] so. [Nevertheless], the central holding of *Renton* is sound: [zoning] regulations do not automatically raise the specter of impermissible content discrimination, even if they are content based, [because the] zoning context provides a built-in legitimate rationale, which rebuts the usual presumption that content-based restrictions are unconstitutional. [But] the necessary rationale for applying intermediate [rather than strict] scrutiny is the promise that zoning ordinances like this one may reduce the costs of secondary effects without substantially reducing speech. [It] is no trick to reduce secondary effects by reducing speech or its audience; but a city may not attack secondary effects [by] attacking speech.

"[If] two adult businesses are under the same roof, an ordinance requiring them to separate will have one of two results: One business will either move elsewhere or close. The city's premise cannot be the latter. [In] this case the proposition to be shown is supported by [the] 1977 study and common experience. [If respondent can prove otherwise] at trial, then the ordinance might not withstand intermediate scrutiny. [But it does] survive summary judgment."

Justice Souter, joined by Justices Stevens, Ginsburg and Breyer, dissented: "Because content-based regulation applies to expression by very reason of what is said, it carries a high risk that expressive limits are imposed for the sake of suppressing a message that is disagreeable to listeners or readers, or the government. [The regulation at issue here], though called content-neutral [in *Renton*, would better be] called content-correlated. [This] would not only describe it for what it is, but keep alert to a risk of content-based regulation that it poses. The risk lies in the fact that when a law applies selectively only to speech of particular content, the more precisely the content is identified, the greater is the opportunity for government censorship. [The] capacity of zoning regulations to address the [secondary effects] without eliminating the speech [is] the only possible excuse for [treating them] as akin to time, place and manner regulations.

"In this case, [the] government has not shown that bookstores containing viewing booths [increase] negative secondary effects, [and] we are thus left without substantial justification for viewing the [restriction as content neutral]. [If] we take the city's breakup policy at its face, enforcing it will mean that in every case two establishments will operate instead of [one]. Since the city presumably does not wish merely to multiply adult establishments, it makes sense to ask what offsetting gain the city may obtain from [its] breakup policy. The answer may lie in the fact that two establishments in place of one will entail two [overheads] in place of one. [Every] month business will be more expensive than it used to be. [That] sounds like a good strategy for driving out expressive adult businesses. In sounds, in other words, like a policy of content-based regulation."

Page 1218. After section g of the Note, add the following:

gg. R. Kennedy, Nigger 151, 154, 158-59 (2002):

[P]roponents of enhanced hate-speech regulation have typically failed to establish persuasively the asserted predicate for their campaign—that is, that verbal abuse [is] a "rising" [development] demanding countermeasures. Regulationists do cite racist incidents [but] too often the dramatic retelling of an anecdote is permitted to substitute for a more systematic, quantitative analysis. [An] examination of the substance of the regulationists' proposals turns up suggested reforms that are puzzlingly narrow, frighteningly broad, or disturbingly susceptible to discriminatory manipulation. . . .

The cumulative effect of [the Supreme Court's] speech-protective doctrines is a conspicuous toleration of speech [that] many people—in some instances the vast majority of people—find deeply, perhaps even viscerally, obnoxious, including flag burning, pornography, Nazis' taunting of Holocaust survivors, a jacket emblazoned with the phrase "Fuck the Draft," *The Satanic Verses, The Birth of a Nation, The Last Temptation of Christ*. And just as acute wariness [of] censorship has long furthered struggles for freedom of expression in all its many guises, so has resistance against censorship always been an important and positive feature of the great struggles against racist tyranny in the United States, from the fight against slavery to the fight against Jim Crow. For this reason, we may count ourselves fortunate that the anti-hate-speech campaign [has] fizzled and largely subsided. This [effort] was simply not worth the various costs that success would have exacted.

ggg. A. Tsesis, Destructive Messages 180, 192 (2002):

A general consensus among nations holds that hate propaganda [threatens] both outgroup participation in democracy and minority rights. Countries that have enacted laws penalizing the dissemination of hate speech include Austria, Belgium, Brazil, Canada, Cyprus, England, France, Germany, India, Israel, Italy, Netherlands, and Switzerland. [These] international examples demonstrate that the United States's pure speech jurisprudence is anomalous. A broad consensus holds that inciting others to hatred is detrimental to society. Democracies generally recognizes that preserving human rights supersedes a bigot's desire to spread venomous messages. [The] history of racism in the United States, from Native American dislocations, to slavery, to Japanese internment, makes clear that here, as in other democracies, intolerance and persecution can exist in spite of socially held ideals of fairness and equality. Safeguards against the realistic effects of hate speech should be enacted to prevent the forces of bigotry from harnessing resources to strengthen socially regressive movements.

Page 1226. Before section 3 of the Note, add the following:

d. After *R.A.V.*, would the following law be constitutional: No person may incite "others to discriminate, persecute, oppress, or commit any similar acts against members of an identifiable group [where] it is substantially probable or reasonably foreseeable, based on the content and context of the message, that its dissemination will elicit such acts [and] where the speaker specifically intended the message to promote destructive behavior, [provided that no] one shall be convicted under this law [if] the statement was uttered as an expression of opinion on a neutral scientific, academic, or religious subject and/or the statement was made to eliminate the incidence of hatred toward an identifiable group." A. Tsesis, Destructive Messages 208-09 (2002).

Page 1228. Before the Note on *Pornography and the Victimization of Women*, add the following:

VIRGINIA v. BLACK
538 U.S. 343 (2003)

JUSTICE O'CONNOR announced the judgment of the Court and delivered the opinion of the Court with respect to Parts I, II, and III, and an opinion with respect to Parts IV and V, in which THE CHIEF JUSTICE, JUSTICE STEVENS, and JUSTICE BREYER join.

In this case we consider whether the Commonwealth of Virginia's statute banning cross burning with "an intent to intimidate a person or group of persons" violates the First Amendment. Va. Code Ann. § 18.2-423 (1996). We conclude that while a State, consistent with the First Amendment, may ban cross burning carried out with the intent to intimidate, the provision in the Virginia statute treating any cross burning as prima facie evidence of intent to intimidate renders the statute unconstitutional. . . .

I

Respondents Barry Black, Richard Elliott, and Jonathan O'Mara were convicted separately of violating Virginia's cross-burning statute, § 18.2-423. That statute provides:

> It shall be unlawful for any person or persons, with the intent of intimidating any person or group of persons, to burn, or cause to be burned, a cross on the property of another, a highway or other public place. . . . Any such burning of a cross shall be prima facie evidence of an intent to intimidate a person or group of persons.

On August 22, 1998, Barry Black led a Ku Klux Klan rally in Carroll County, Virginia. Twenty-five to thirty people attended this gathering, which occurred on private property with the permission of the owner, who was in attendance. The property was located on an open field. . . .

When the sheriff of Carroll County learned that a Klan rally was occurring in his county, he went to observe it from the side of the road. During the approximately one hour that the sheriff was present, about 40 to 50 cars passed the site, a "few" of which stopped to ask the sheriff what was happening on the property. [Rebecca] Sechrist, who was related to the owner of the property where the rally took place, "sat and watched to see wha[t] [was] going on" from the lawn of her in-laws' house. She looked on as the Klan prepared for the gathering and subsequently conducted the rally itself.

During the rally, Sechrist heard Klan members speak about "what they were" and "what they believed in." The speakers "talked real bad about the blacks and the Mexicans." One speaker told the assembled gathering that "he would love to take a .30/.30 and just random[ly] shoot the blacks." The speakers also talked about "President Clinton and Hillary Clinton," and about how their tax money "goes to . . . the black people." Sechrist testified that this language made her "very . . . scared."

At the conclusion of the rally, the crowd circled around a 25- to 30-foot cross. The cross was between 300 and 350 yards away from the road. According to the sheriff, the cross "then all of a sudden . . . went up in a flame." As the cross burned, the Klan played Amazing Grace over the loudspeakers. Sechrist stated that the cross burning made her feel "awful" and "terrible."

227

When the sheriff observed the cross burning, he informed his deputy that they needed to "find out who's responsible and explain to them that they cannot do this in the State of Virginia." The sheriff then went down the driveway, entered the rally, and asked "who was responsible for burning the cross." Black responded, "I guess I am because I'm the head of the rally." The sheriff then told Black, "[T]here's a law in the State of Virginia that you cannot burn a cross and I'll have to place you under arrest for this."

Black was charged with burning a cross with the intent of intimidating a person or group of persons, in violation of § 18.2-423. At his trial, the jury was instructed that "intent to intimidate means the motivation to intentionally put a person or a group of persons in fear of bodily harm. Such fear must arise from the willful conduct of the accused rather than from some mere temperamental timidity of the victim." The trial court also instructed the jury that "the burning of a cross by itself is sufficient evidence from which you may infer the required intent." [The] jury found Black guilty, and fined him $2,500. The Court of Appeals of Virginia affirmed Black's conviction.

On May 2, 1998, respondents Richard Elliott and Jonathan O'Mara, as well as a third individual, attempted to burn a cross on the yard of James Jubilee. Jubilee, an African-American, was Elliott's next-door neighbor in Virginia Beach, Virginia. Four months prior to the incident, Jubilee and his family had moved from California to Virginia Beach. Before the cross burning, Jubilee spoke to Elliott's mother to inquire about shots being fired from behind the Elliott home. Elliott's mother explained to Jubilee that her son shot firearms as a hobby, and that he used the backyard as a firing range.

On the night of May 2, respondents drove a truck onto Jubilee's property, planted a cross, and set it on fire. Their apparent motive was to "get back" at Jubilee for complaining about the shooting in the backyard. Respondents were not affiliated with the Klan. The next morning, as Jubilee was pulling his car out of the driveway, he noticed the partially burned cross approximately 20 feet from his house. After seeing the cross, Jubilee was "very nervous" because he "didn't know what would be the next phase," and because "a cross burned in your yard . . . tells you that it's just the first round."

Elliott and O'Mara were charged with attempted cross burning and conspiracy to commit cross burning. O'Mara pleaded guilty to both counts, reserving the right to challenge the constitutionality of the cross-burning statute. The judge sentenced O'Mara to 90 days in jail and fined him $2,500. The judge also suspended 45 days of the sentence and $1,000 of the fine. At Elliott's trial, the judge [instructed] the jury that the Commonwealth must prove that "the defendant intended to commit cross burning," that "the defendant did a direct act toward the commission of the cross burning," and that "the defendant had the intent of intimidating any person or group of persons." The court did not instruct the jury on the meaning of the word "intimidate," nor on the prima facie evidence provision of § 18.2-423. The jury

Freedom of Expression Page 1228

found Elliott guilty of attempted cross burning and acquitted him of conspiracy to commit cross burning. It sentenced Elliott to 90 days in jail and a $2,500 fine. The Court of Appeals of Virginia affirmed the convictions of both Elliott and O'Mara. O'Mara v. Commonwealth, 33 Va. App. 525, 535 S.E. 2d 175 (2000).

Each respondent appealed to the Supreme Court of Virginia, arguing that § 18.2-423 is facially unconstitutional. The Supreme Court of Virginia consolidated all three cases, and held that the statute is unconstitutional on its face. 262 Va. 764, 553 S.E. 2d 738 (2001). It held that the Virginia cross-burning statute "is analytically indistinguishable from the ordinance found unconstitutional in [R.A.V. v. St. Paul]. The Virginia statute, the court held, discriminates on the basis of content since it "selectively chooses only cross burning because of its distinctive message." The court also held that the prima facie evidence provision renders the statute overbroad because "[t]he enhanced probability of prosecution under the statute chills the expression of protected speech." . . .

II

Cross burning originated in the 14th century as a means for Scottish tribes to signal each other. [Cross] burning in this country, however, long ago became unmoored from its Scottish ancestry. Burning a cross in the United States is inextricably intertwined with the history of the Ku Klux Klan.

The first Ku Klux Klan began in Pulaski, Tennessee, in the spring of 1866. Although the Ku Klux Klan started as a social club, it soon changed into something far different. The Klan fought Reconstruction and the corresponding drive to allow freed blacks to participate in the political process. Soon the Klan imposed "a veritable reign of terror" throughout the South. The Klan employed tactics such as whipping, threatening to burn people at the stake, and murder. The Klan's victims included blacks, southern whites who disagreed with the Klan, and "carpetbagger" northern whites.

The activities of the Ku Klux Klan prompted legislative action at the national level. In 1871, [Congress] passed what is now known as the Ku Klux Klan Act (now codified at 42 U.S.C §§ 1983, 1985, and 1986). President Grant used these new powers to suppress the Klan [and by] the end of Reconstruction in 1877, the first Klan no longer existed.

The genesis of the second Klan began in 1905, with the publication of Thomas Dixon's The Clansmen: An Historical Romance of the Ku Klux Klan. Dixon's book was a sympathetic portrait of the first Klan, depicting the Klan as a group of heroes "saving" the South from blacks and the "horrors" of Reconstruction. Although the first Klan never actually practiced cross burning, Dixon's book depicted the Klan burning crosses to celebrate the execution of former slaves. Cross burning thereby became associated with the first Ku Klux Klan. When D.W. Griffith turned Dixon's book into the movie The Birth of a Nation in 1915, the association between cross

229

burning and the Klan became indelible. [Soon] thereafter, in November 1915, the second Klan began.

From the inception of the second Klan, cross burnings have been used to communicate both threats of violence and messages of shared ideology. The first initiation ceremony occurred on Stone Mountain near Atlanta, Georgia. While a 40-foot cross burned on the mountain, the Klan members took their oaths of loyalty. [The] new Klan's ideology did not differ much from that of the first Klan. As one Klan publication emphasized, "We avow the distinction between [the] races, . . . and we shall ever be true to the faithful maintenance of White Supremacy and will strenuously oppose any compromise thereof in any and all things." Violence was also an elemental part of this new Klan. . . .

Often, the Klan used cross burnings as a tool of intimidation and a threat of impending violence. For example, in 1939 and 1940, the Klan burned crosses in front of synagogues and churches. After one cross burning at a synagogue, a Klan member noted that if the cross burning did not "shut the Jews up, we'll cut a few throats and see what happens." In Miami in 1941, the Klan burned four crosses in front of a proposed housing project, declaring, "We are here to keep niggers out of your town . . . . When the law fails you, call on us." These cross burnings embodied threats to people whom the Klan deemed antithetical to its goals. And these threats had special force given the long history of Klan violence. [The] Klan continued to use cross burnings to intimidate after World War II. [These] incidents of cross burning, among others, helped prompt Virginia to enact its first version of the cross-burning statute in 1950.

The decision of this Court in Brown v. Board of Education, along with the civil rights movement of the 1950's and 1960's, sparked another outbreak of Klan violence. These acts of violence included bombings, beatings, shootings, stabbings, and mutilations. Members of the Klan burned crosses on the lawns of those associated with the civil rights movement, assaulted the Freedom Riders, bombed churches, and murdered blacks as well as whites whom the Klan viewed as sympathetic toward the civil rights movement.

Throughout the history of the Klan, cross burnings have also remained potent symbols of shared group identity and ideology. The burning cross became a symbol of the Klan itself and a central feature of Klan gatherings. [The] Klan has often published its newsletters and magazines under the name The Fiery Cross. [At] Klan gatherings across the country, cross burning became the climax of the rally or the initiation. [Throughout] the Klan's history, the Klan continued to use the burning cross in their ritual ceremonies. [For] its own members, the cross was a sign of celebration and ceremony. . . .

To this day, regardless of whether the message is a political one or whether the message is also meant to intimidate, the burning of a cross is a "symbol of hate." And while cross burning sometimes carries no intimidating message, at other times the intimidating message is the *only* message conveyed. For example, when a cross burning is directed at a particular person not affiliated with the Klan, the burning cross often serves as a message of intimidation, designed to inspire in the victim a fear of bodily harm. Moreover, the history of violence associated with the Klan shows that the possibility of injury or death is not just hypothetical. The person who burns a cross directed at a particular person often is making a serious threat, meant to coerce the victim to comply with the Klan's wishes unless the victim is willing to risk the wrath of the Klan. Indeed, as the cases of respondents Elliott and O'Mara indicate, individuals without Klan affiliation who wish to threaten or menace another person sometimes use cross burning because of this association between a burning cross and violence.

In sum, while a burning cross does not inevitably convey a message of intimidation, often the cross burner intends that the recipients of the message fear for their lives. And when a cross burning is used to intimidate, few if any messages are more powerful.

III

A

The protections afforded by the First Amendment [are] not absolute, and we have long recognized that the government may regulate certain categories of expression consistent with the Constitution. The First Amendment permits "restrictions upon the content of speech in a few limited areas, which are 'of such slight social value as a step to truth that any benefit that may be derived from them is clearly outweighed by the social interest in order and morality.'" [*R.A.V.*, quoting *Chaplinsky*]. . . .

Thus, for example, a State may punish [a] "true threat." [*Watts*.] "True threats" encompass those statements where the speaker means to communicate a serious expression of an intent to commit an act of unlawful violence to a particular individual or group of individuals. The speaker need not actually intend to carry out the threat. Rather, a prohibition on true threats "protect[s] individuals from the fear of violence" and "from the disruption that fear engenders," in addition to protecting people "from the possibility that the threatened violence will occur." Intimidation in the constitutionally proscribable sense of the word is a type of true threat, where a speaker directs a threat to a person or group of persons with the intent of placing the victim in fear of bodily harm or death. Respondents do not contest that some cross burnings fit within this meaning of intimidating speech, and rightly so. As noted in Part II, *supra*, the history of cross burning in this country shows that cross burning is often intimidating, intended to create a pervasive fear in victims that they are a target of violence.

B

The Supreme Court of Virginia ruled that in light of *R.A.V.*, even if it is constitutional to ban cross burning in a content-neutral manner, the Virginia cross-burning statute is unconstitutional because it discriminates on the basis of content and viewpoint. It is true [that] the burning of a cross is symbolic expression. The reason why the Klan burns a cross at its rallies, or individuals place a burning cross on someone else's lawn, is that the burning cross represents the message that the speaker wishes to communicate. Individuals burn crosses as opposed to other means of communication because cross burning carries a message in an effective and dramatic manner.

The fact that cross burning is symbolic expression, however, does not resolve the constitutional question. [In] *R.A.V.*, we held that a local ordinance that banned certain symbolic conduct, including cross burning, when done with the knowledge that such conduct would "'arouse anger, alarm or resentment in others on the basis of race, color, creed, religion or gender'" was unconstitutional. We held that the ordinance did not pass constitutional muster because it discriminated on the basis of content by targeting only those individuals who "provoke violence" on a basis specified in the law. The ordinance did not cover "[t]hose who wish to use 'fighting words' in connection with other ideas—to express hostility, for example, on the basis of political affiliation, union membership, or homosexuality." This content-based discrimination was unconstitutional because it allowed the city "to impose special prohibitions on those speakers who express views on disfavored subjects."

We did not hold in *R.A.V.* that the First Amendment prohibits *all* forms of content-based discrimination within a proscribable area of speech. Rather, we specifically stated that some types of content discrimination did not violate the First Amendment:

> When the basis for the content discrimination consists entirely of the very reason the entire class of speech at issue is proscribable, no significant danger of idea or viewpoint discrimination exists. Such a reason, having been adjudged neutral enough to support exclusion of the entire class of speech from First Amendment protection, is also neutral enough to form the basis of distinction within the class.

Indeed, we noted that it would be constitutional to ban only a particular type of threat: "[T]he Federal Government can criminalize only those threats of violence that are directed against the President . . . since the reasons why threats of violence are outside the First Amendment . . . have special force when applied to the person of the President." And a State may "choose to prohibit only that obscenity which is the most patently offensive *in its prurience—i.e.,* that which involves the most lascivious displays of sexual activity." Consequently, while the holding of *R.A.V.* does not permit a State to ban only obscenity based on "offensive *political* messages," or "only those threats against the President that mention his policy on aid to inner cities," the First Amendment permits content discrimination "based on the very reasons why the particular class of speech at issue . . . is proscribable."

Similarly, Virginia's statute does not run afoul of the First Amendment insofar as it bans cross burning with intent to intimidate. Unlike the statute at issue in *R.A.V.*, the Virginia statute does not single out for opprobrium only that speech directed toward "one of the specified disfavored topics." It does not matter whether an individual burns a cross with intent to intimidate because of the victim's race, gender, or religion, or because of the victim's "political affiliation, union membership, or homosexuality." Moreover, as a factual matter it is not true that cross burners direct their intimidating conduct solely to racial or religious minorities. . . .

The First Amendment permits Virginia to outlaw cross burnings done with the intent to intimidate because burning a cross is a particularly virulent form of intimidation. Instead of prohibiting all intimidating messages, Virginia may choose to regulate this subset of intimidating messages in light of cross burning's long and pernicious history as a signal of impending violence. Thus, just as a State may regulate only that obscenity which is the most obscene due to its prurient content, so too may a State choose to prohibit only those forms of intimidation that are most likely to inspire fear of bodily harm. A ban on cross burning carried out with the intent to intimidate is fully consistent with our holding in *R.A.V.* and is proscribable under the First Amendment.

IV

The Supreme Court of Virginia ruled in the alternative that Virginia's cross-burning statute was unconstitutionally overbroad due to its provision stating that "[a]ny such burning of a cross shall be prima facie evidence of an intent to intimidate a person or group of persons." [The] Supreme Court of Virginia has . . . stated that "the act of burning a cross alone, with no evidence of intent to intimidate, [will] suffice for arrest and prosecution and will insulate the Commonwealth from a motion to strike the evidence at the end of its case-in-chief." . . .

The prima facie evidence provision . . . renders the statute unconstitutional. [The] prima facie provision strips away the very reason why a State may ban cross burning with the intent to intimidate. The prima facie evidence provision permits a jury to convict in every cross-burning case in which defendants exercise their constitutional right not to put on a defense. And even where a defendant [presents] a defense, the prima facie evidence provision makes it more likely that the jury will find an intent to intimidate regardless of the particular facts of the case. The provision permits the Commonwealth to arrest, prosecute, and convict a person based solely on the fact of cross burning itself.

It is apparent that the provision as so interpreted "'would create an unacceptable risk of the suppression of ideas.'" The act of burning a cross may mean that a person is engaging in constitutionally proscribable intimidation. But that same act may mean only that the person is engaged in core political speech. The prima facie evidence provision in this statute blurs the line between these two meanings of a burning cross. As interpreted by the jury instruction, the provision chills constitutionally protected political speech because of the possibility that a State will prosecute—and potentially convict—somebody engaging only in lawful political speech at the core of what the First Amendment is designed to protect.

As the history of cross burning indicates, a burning cross is not always intended to intimidate. Rather, sometimes the cross burning is a statement of ideology, a symbol of group solidarity. It is a ritual used at Klan gatherings, and it is used to represent the Klan itself. Thus, "[b]urning a cross at a political rally would almost certainly be protected expression." . . .

The prima facie provision makes no effort to distinguish among these different types of cross burnings. It does not distinguish between a cross burning done with the purpose of creating anger or resentment and a cross burning done with the purpose of threatening or intimidating a victim. It does not distinguish between a cross burning at a public rally or a cross burning on a neighbor's lawn. It does not treat the cross burning directed at an individual differently from the cross burning directed at a group of like-minded believers. It allows a jury to treat a cross burning on the property of another with the owner's acquiescence in the same manner as a cross burning on the property of another without the owner's permission. . . .

It may be true that a cross burning, even at a political rally, arouses a sense of anger or hatred among the vast majority of citizens who see a burning cross. But this sense of anger or hatred is not sufficient to ban all cross burnings. [The] prima facie evidence provision in this case ignores all of the contextual factors that are necessary to decide whether a particular cross burning is intended to intimidate. The First Amendment does not permit such a shortcut. . . .

JUSTICE STEVENS, concurring.

Cross burning with "an intent to intimidate" unquestionably qualifies as the kind of threat that is unprotected by the First Amendment. For the reasons stated in the separate opinions that Justice White and I wrote in *R.A.V.*, that simple proposition provides a sufficient basis for upholding the basic prohibition in the Virginia statute even though it does not cover other types of threatening expressive conduct. With this observation, I join Justice O'Connor's opinion.

JUSTICE THOMAS, dissenting.

In every culture, certain things acquire meaning well beyond what outsiders can comprehend. That goes for both the sacred, see *Texas v. Johnson* [section E3 *infra*] (describing the unique position of the American flag in our Nation's 200 years of history), and the profane. I believe that cross burning is the paradigmatic example of the latter.

Although I agree with the majority's conclusion that it is constitutionally permissible to "ban . . . cross burning carried out with intent to intimidate," I believe that the majority errs in imputing an expressive component to the activity in question. . . .

A

[The] majority's brief history of the Ku Klux Klan [reinforces the] understanding of the Klan as a terrorist organization, which, in its endeavor to intimidate, or even eliminate those its dislikes, uses the most brutal of methods. Such methods typically include cross burning—"a tool for the intimidation and harassment of racial minorities, Catholics, Jews, Communists, and any other groups hated by the Klan." For those not easily frightened, cross burning has been followed by more extreme measures, such as beatings and murder. [Indeed], the connection between cross burning and violence is well ingrained. . . . In our culture, cross burning has almost invariably meant lawlessness and understandably instills in its victims well-grounded fear of physical violence.

B

That in the early 1950s the people of Virginia viewed cross burning as creating an intolerable atmosphere of terror is not surprising. . . . [At] the time the statute was enacted, racial segregation was not only the prevailing practice, but also the law in Virginia. And, just two years after the enactment of this statute, Virginia's General Assembly embarked on a campaign of "massive resistance" in response to Brown v. Board of Education. [It] strains credulity to suggest that a state legislature that adopted a litany of segregationist laws self-contradictorily intended to squelch the segregationist message. [The] ban on cross burning with intent to intimidate demonstrates that even segregationists understood the difference between intimidating and terroristic conduct and racist expression. . . .

Accordingly, this statute prohibits only conduct, not expression. And, just as one cannot burn down someone's house to make a political point and then seek refuge in the First Amendment, those who hate cannot terrorize and intimidate to make their point. In light of my conclusion that the statute here addresses only conduct, there is no need to analyze it under any of our First Amendment tests.

II

Even assuming that the statute implicates the First Amendment, in my view, the fact that the statute permits a jury to draw an inference of intent to intimidate from the cross burning itself presents no constitutional problems. Therein lies my primary disagreement with the plurality. . . .

The plurality [is] troubled by the presumption because this is a First Amendment case. The plurality laments the fate of an innocent cross-burner who burns a cross, but does so without an intent to intimidate. The plurality fears the chill on expression because, according to the plurality, the inference permits "the Commonwealth to arrest, prosecute and convict a person based solely on the fact of cross burning itself." [But] the inference is rebuttable [and] Virginia law still requires the jury to find the existence of each element, including intent to intimidate, beyond a reasonable doubt. [The] plurality strikes down the statute because one day an individual might wish to burn a cross, but might do so without an intent to intimidate anyone. That cross burning subjects its targets [to] extreme emotional distress, and is virtually never viewed merely as "unwanted communication," but rather, as a physical threat, is of no concern to the plurality. Henceforth, under the plurality's view, physical safety will be valued less than the right to be free from unwanted communications. . . .

Because I would uphold the validity of this statute, I respectfully dissent.

JUSTICE SCALIA, with whom JUSTICE THOMAS joins as to Parts I and II, concurring in part, concurring in the judgment in part, and dissenting in part.

I agree with the Court that, under our decision in *R.A.V.*, a State may, without infringing the First Amendment, prohibit cross burning carried out with the intent to intimidate. Accordingly, I join Parts I-III of the Court's opinion. I also agree that we should vacate and remand the judgment of the Virginia Supreme Court so that that Court can have an opportunity authoritatively to construe the prima-facie-evidence provision of Va. Code Ann. § 18.2-423 (1996). I write separately, however, to describe what I believe to be the correct interpretation of § 18.2-423, and to explain why I believe there is no justification for the plurality's apparent decision to invalidate that provision on its face.

I

Section 18.2-423 provides that the burning of a cross in public view "shall be prima facie evidence of an intent to intimidate." In order to determine whether this component of the statute violates the Constitution, it is necessary, first, to establish precisely what the presentation of prima facie evidence accomplishes.

Typically, "prima facie evidence" is defined as:

"Such evidence as, in the judgment of the law, is sufficient to establish a given fact . . . and which if not rebutted or contradicted, will remain sufficient. [Such evidence], if unexplained or uncontradicted, is sufficient to sustain a judgment in favor of the issue which it supports, but [it] may be contradicted by other evidence." Black's Law Dictionary 1190 (6th ed. 1990).

The Virginia Supreme Court has, in prior cases, embraced this canonical understanding of the pivotal statutory language. [That] is, presentation of evidence that a defendant burned a cross in public view is automatically sufficient, on its own, to support an inference that the defendant intended to intimidate *only until* the defendant comes forward with some evidence in rebuttal.

II

The question presented, then, is whether, given this understanding of the term "prima facie evidence," the cross-burning statute is constitutional. [We] have never held that the mere threat that individuals who engage in protected conduct will be subject to arrest and prosecution suffices to render a statute overbroad. Rather, our overbreadth jurisprudence has consistently focused on whether *the prohibitory terms* of a particular statute extend to protected conduct; that is, we have inquired whether individuals who engage in protected conduct can be *convicted* under a statute, not whether they might be subject to arrest and prosecution. [The plurality] notes that "[t]he prima facie evidence provision permits a jury *to convict* in every cross-burning case in which defendants exercise their constitutional right not to put on a defense." [And] this, according to the plurality, is constitutionally problematic because "a burning cross is not always intended to intimidate," and nonintimidating cross burning cannot be prohibited. [The] plurality is correct in all of this—and it means that some individuals who engage in protected speech may, because of the prima-facie-evidence provision, be subject to conviction. Such convictions, assuming they are unconstitutional, could be challenged on a case-by-case basis. The plurality, however, with little in the way of explanation, leaps to the conclusion that the *possibility* of such convictions justifies facial invalidation of the statute.

[W]e have noted that "[i]n a facial challenge to the overbreadth . . . of a law, a court's first task is to determine whether the enactment reaches a substantial amount of constitutionally protected conduct." [But here, as] the plurality concedes, the only persons who might impermissibly be convicted [because of the prima facie evidence provision] are those who adopt a particular trial strategy, to wit, abstaining from the presentation of a defense.

The plurality is thus left with a strikingly attenuated argument to support the claim that Virginia's cross-burning statute is facially invalid. The class of persons that the plurality contemplates could impermissibly be convicted under § 18.2-423 includes only those individuals who (1) burn a cross in public view, (2) do not intend to intimidate, (3) are nonetheless charged and prosecuted, and (4) refuse to present a

237

defense. [Conceding] (quite generously, in my view) that this class of persons exists, it cannot possibly give rise to a viable facial challenge, not even with the aid of our First Amendment overbreadth doctrine. For this Court has emphasized repeatedly that "where a statute regulates expressive conduct, the scope of the statute does not render it unconstitutional unless its overbreadth is not only real, but *substantial* as well, judged in relation to the statute's plainly legitimate sweep refused." . . .

JUSTICE SOUTER, with whom JUSTICE KENNEDY and JUSTICE GINSBURG join, concurring in the judgment in part and dissenting in part.

I agree with the majority that the Virginia statute makes a content-based distinction within the category of punishable intimidating or threatening expression, the very type of distinction we considered in *R.A.V.* I disagree that any exception should save Virginia's law from unconstitutionality under the holding in *R.A.V.* or any acceptable variation of it.

I

The ordinance struck down in *R.A.V.*, as it had been construed by the State's highest court, prohibited the use of symbols (including but not limited to a burning cross) as the equivalent of generally proscribable fighting words, but the ordinance applied only when the symbol was provocative "'on the basis of race, color, creed, religion or gender.'" Although the Virginia statute in issue here contains no such express "basis of" limitation on prohibited subject matter, the specific prohibition of cross burning with intent to intimidate selects a symbol with particular content from the field of all proscribable expression meant to intimidate. To be sure, that content often includes an essentially intimidating message, that the cross burner will harm the victim, most probably in a physical way, given the historical identification of burning crosses with arson, beating, and lynching. But even when the symbolic act is meant to terrify, a burning cross may carry a further, ideological message of white Protestant supremacy. The ideological message not only accompanies many threatening uses of the symbol, but is also expressed when a burning cross is not used to threaten but merely to symbolize the supremacist ideology and the solidarity of those who espouse it. . . .

The issue is whether the statutory prohibition restricted to this symbol falls within one of the exceptions to *R.A.V.*'s general condemnation of limited content-based proscription within a broader category of expression proscribable generally. Because of the burning cross's extraordinary force as a method of intimidation, the *R.A.V.* exception most likely to cover the statute is the first of the three mentioned there, which the *R.A.V.* opinion called an exception for content discrimination on a basis that "consists entirely of the very reason the entire class of speech at issue is proscribable." This is the exception the majority speaks of here as covering statutes prohibiting "particularly virulent" proscribable expression.

I do not think that the Virginia statute qualifies for this virulence exception as *R.A.V.* explained it. The statute fits poorly with the illustrative examples given in *R.A.V.*, none of which involves communication generally associated with a particular message, and in fact, the majority's discussion of a special virulence exception here moves that exception toward a more flexible conception than the version in *R.A.V.* ...

II

R.A.V. defines the special virulence exception to the rule barring content-based subclasses of categorically proscribable expression this way: prohibition by subcategory is nonetheless constitutional if it is made "entirely" on the "basis" of "the very reason" that "the entire class of speech at issue is proscribable" at all. The Court explained that when the subcategory is confined to the most obviously proscribable instances, "no significant danger of idea or viewpoint discrimination exists." ...

The first example of permissible distinction is for a prohibition of obscenity unusually offensive "in its prurience." [Distinguishing] obscene publications on this basis does not suggest discrimination on the basis of the message conveyed. The opposite is true, however, when a general prohibition of intimidation is rejected in favor of a distinct proscription of intimidation by cross burning. The cross may have been selected because of its special power to threaten, but it may also have been singled out because of disapproval of its message of white supremacy, either because a legislature thought white supremacy was a pernicious doctrine or because it found that dramatic, public espousal of it was a civic embarrassment. Thus, there is no kinship between the cross-burning statute and the core prurience example.

Nor does this case present any analogy to the statute prohibiting threats against the President, the second of *R.A.V.*'s examples of the virulence exception and the one the majority relies upon. The content discrimination in that statute relates to the addressee of the threat and reflects the special risks and costs associated with threatening the President. Again, however, threats against the President are not generally identified by reference to the content of any message that may accompany the threat, let alone any viewpoint, and there is no obvious correlation in fact between victim and message. Millions of statements are made about the President every day on every subject and from every standpoint; threats of violence are not an integral feature of any one subject or viewpoint as distinct from others. Differential treatment of threats against the President, then, selects nothing but special risks, not special messages. A content-based proscription of cross burning, on the other hand, may be a subtle effort to ban not only the intensity of the intimidation cross burning causes when done to threaten, but also the particular message of white supremacy that is broadcast even by nonthreatening cross burning.

I thus read *R.A.V.*'s examples of the particular virulence exception as covering prohibitions that are not clearly associated with a particular viewpoint, and that are consequently different from the Virginia statute. On that understanding of things, I necessarily read the majority opinion as treating *R.A.V.*'s virulence exception in a more flexible, pragmatic manner than the original illustrations would suggest. Actually, another way of looking at today's decision would see it as a slight modification of *R.A.V.*'s third exception, which allows content-based discrimination within a proscribable category when its "nature" is such "that there is no realistic possibility that official suppression of ideas is afoot." The majority's approach could be taken as recognizing an exception to *R.A.V.* when circumstances show that the statute's ostensibly valid reason for punishing particularly serious proscribable expression probably is not a ruse for message suppression, even though the statute may have a greater (but not exclusive) impact on adherents of one ideology than on others.

III

[N]o content-based statute should survive . . . without a high probability that no "official suppression of ideas is afoot." I believe the prima facie evidence provision stands in the way of any finding of such a high probability here.

Virginia's statute provides that burning a cross on the property of another, a highway, or other public place is "prima facie evidence of an intent to intimidate a person or group of persons. [The primary effect of this provision] is to skew jury deliberations toward conviction in cases where the evidence of intent to intimidate is relatively weak and arguably consistent with a solely ideological reason for burning. [This] provision will encourage a factfinder to err on the side of a finding of intent to intimidate when the evidence of circumstances fails to point with any clarity either to the criminal intent or to the permissible one. . . . To the extent the prima facie evidence provision skews prosecutions, then, it skews the statute toward suppressing ideas. . . .

Page 1232. Before section 3 of the Note, add the following:

i. Posner, The Speech Market and the Legacy of *Schenck*, in L. Bollinger & G. Stone, Eternal Vigilance: Free Speech in the Modern Era 121, 136-137 (2002):

In the case of both pornography and hate speech, [one] has the sense that the desire to crack down on these forms of speech has little to do with demonstrable harms [but] with an ideological project—[that] of denying or occluding the existence of deep-seated differences between groups (in particular men and women, and blacks and whites). Hate speakers are vociferous deniers of equality, and pornography caters primarily to a specifically male interest in women as sexual playthings for men. . . . Insofar as campaigns for the regulation of hate speech and pornography have the purpose and effect of correcting ideological or political "error," giving them the backing of the law interferes arbitrarily with the market in ideas and opinions.

E. *Content-Neutral Restrictions: Limitations on the Means of Communication and the Problem of Content-Neutrality*

Page 1240. After *NAACP v. Alabama,* add the following:

BARTNICKI v. VOPPER, 532 U.S. 514 (2001). During contentious collective-bargaining negotiations between a union representing teachers at a public high school and the local school board, an unidentified person intercepted and recorded a cell phone conversation between the union negotiator and the union president. Vopper, a radio commentator, played a tape of the intercepted conversation on his public affairs talk show in connection with news reports about the settlement. The Court held that Vopper could not be held liable for damages under federal or state wiretap laws for broadcasting the unlawfully recorded phone call.

Justice Stevens delivered the opinion of the Court. The Court accepted that the information on the tapes had been obtained unlawfully by an unknown party, that Vopper had played no part in the illegal interception, that he knew or should have known that the phone call had been intercepted unlawfully, and that "the subject matter of the conversation was a matter of public concern."

The Court then explained that the relevant statutes, which prohibited the unauthorized disclosure of unlawfully intercepted communications, were "content-neutral" laws of general applicability. The Court then defined the issue as follows: "Where the punished publisher of information has obtained the information [in] a manner lawful in itself but from a source who has obtained it unlawfully, may the government punish the ensuing publication of that information?" The Court explained that, as a general proposition, "'if a newspaper unlawfully obtains truthful information about a matter of public significance then [government] officials may not constitutionally punish publication of the information, absent a need of the highest order'" [quoting Smith v. Daily Mail Publishing Co.].

The Court identified "two interests served by the statutes—first, the interest in removing an incentive for parties to intercept private conversations, and second, the interest in minimizing the harm to persons whose conversations have been illegally intercepted." With respect to the first of these interests, the Court reasoned that "the normal method of deterring unlawful conduct is to impose an appropriate punishment on the person who engages in it. If the sanctions that presently attach to [these unlawful acts] do not provide sufficient deterrence, perhaps those sanctions should be made more severe. But it would be quite remarkable to hold that speech by a law-abiding possessor of information can be suppressed in order to deter conduct by a non-law abiding third party."

The Court conceded that the second interest "is considerably stronger" because "privacy of communications is an important interest" and "the fear of public disclosure of private conversations might well have a chilling effect on private speech." Without deciding whether there might be some circumstances in which the privacy interest is "strong enough to justify the application" of the statutes, such as when there is disclosure of a trade secret or "domestic gossip [of] purely private concern," the Court held that the enforcement of the statutes in this case "implicates core purposes of the First Amendment because it imposes sanctions on the publication of truthful information of public concern." In such circumstances, "privacy concerns give way when balanced against the interest in publishing matters of public importance."

Justice Breyer, joined by Justice O'Connor, filed a concurring opinion: "I would ask whether the statutes strike a reasonable balance between their speech-restricting and speech-enhancing consequences. [What] this Court has called 'strict scrutiny' [is] normally out of place where, as here, important competing constitutional interests are implicated. [The] statutory restrictions before us directly enhance private speech. [The] assurance of privacy helps to overcome our natural reluctance to discuss private matters when we fear that our private conversations may become public. . . .

"But the statutes, as applied in these circumstances, do not reasonably reconcile the competing constitutional interests. Rather, they disproportionately interfere with media freedom. For one thing, the broadcasters here engaged in no unlawful activity other than the ultimate publication of the information. . . . For another thing, the speakers had little or no *legitimate* interest in maintaining the privacy of the particular conversation, [which] involved a suggestion [about] 'doing some work on some of these guys.' [Further], the speakers themselves [were] 'limited public figures,' for they voluntarily engaged in a public controversy. [Given these circumstances,] the speakers' legitimate privacy interests are unusually low and the public interest in defeating those expectations is unusually high."

Chief Justice Rehnquist, joined by Justices Scalia and Thomas, dissented: "[The] Court's decision diminishes, rather than enhances, the purposes of the First Amendment: chilling the speech of the millions of Americans who rely upon electronic

Freedom of Expression Page 1243

technology to communicate each day. [These] are 'content-neutral laws of general applicability' which serve recognized interests of the highest order."

Chief Justice Rehnquist then argued that the *Smith v. Daily Mail* line of cases was irrelevant: "Each of the laws at issue in the *Daily Mail* cases regulated the content [of] speech. This fact alone was enough to trigger strict scrutiny. [These] laws are content-neutral; they only regulate information that was illegally obtained; they do not restrict republication of what is already in the public domain; they impose no special burdens upon the media; they have a scienter requirement to provide fair warning; and they promote the privacy and free speech of those using cellular telephones. [It] distorts our precedents to review these statutes under the often fatal standard of strict scrutiny. These laws should [be] upheld if they further a substantial governmental interest unrelated to the suppression of free speech, and they do."

Consider Gewirtz, Privacy and Speech, 2001 Sup. Ct. Rev. 139, 149-151:

> Illegal conduct that yields stolen information can be every bit as wrongful and offensive as illegal conduct that yields stolen goods, and there is no reason why deterrence of the former should be disfavored any more than deterrence of the latter. [If] someone breaks into my home and steals my diary or personal letters, of course that person can be sanctioned for publishing the diary's or the letter's contents. This is usually a rule of government-created intellectual property law, and nothing in the First Amendment prohibits it. Similarly, nothing in the First Amendment should prohibit the government from creating an analogous rule of privacy law [in the wiretap statute].

Page 1242. At the end of section 2(e) of the Note, add the following:

Do you agree that there can be "no such thing as a free speech immunity based on the claim that someone wants to break an otherwise constitutional law for expressive purposes." Rubenfeld, The First Amendment's Purpose, 53 Stan. L. Rev. 767, 769 (2001) (arguing that "when a law is otherwise constitutional, and when an actor has not been singled out because of his expression, the actor has no free speech claim").

Page 1243. At the end of section 1 of the Note, add the following:

Consider Rubenfeld, The First Amendment's Purpose, 53 Stan. L. Rev. 767, 777 (2001):

> Whether a person is being punished for speaking [depends] on the kind [of] harm that the state seeks to prevent. Some harms arising out of our actions are inde-

243

pendent of whatever we might be expressing through those actions. [But] other harms are communicative; the communicativeness of the action is a but-for cause of the harm. There are many kinds of harm [that] arise out of communication. The message communicated might be said to be immoral. Or the message might annoy or alarm its audience. Or the communication might be effective and lead others to take actions harmful either to themselves or others. The First Amendment is implicated when the government makes communicative harm the basis for liability. [Indeed] this is why the distinction between "content-based" and "content-neutral" regulations is so important to First Amendment law.

Page 1244. At the end of Section 2 of the Note, add the following:

In City of Los Angeles v. Alameda Books, 535 U.S. 425 (2002), the Court revisited the issue of content-neutrality and secondary effects. Like *Renton*, *Alameda Books* concerned the constitutionality of a zoning ordinance that regulated the location of adult establishments. Although there was no majority opinion, four Justices expressly rejected the notion that such regulations should be characterized as "content-neutral." Justice Kennedy described as a "fiction" *Renton*'s designation of such ordinances as "content-neutral" and explained that "whether a statute is content neutral or content based is something that can be determined on the face of it; if the statute describes speech by content, then it is content based."

Justice Souter, joined by Justices Stevens and Ginsburg, observed that "this kind of regulation [occupies] a kind of limbo between full-blown, content-based restrictions and regulations that apply without any reference to the substance of what is said." He added that "it would in fact make sense to give this kind of zoning regulation a First Amendment label of its own, and if we called it content correlated, we would not only describe it for what it is, but keep alert to a risk of content-based regulation that it poses." Justice Souter explained that "when a law applies selectively only to speech of particular content, the more precisely the content is identified, the greater is the opportunity for government censorship."

Page 1248. Before *Schneider v. State*, add the following:

Consider C. Sunstein, republic.com 30-32 (2001):

[The public forum doctrine promotes three important goals. First, it ensures that speakers can have access to a wide array of people. [It allows speakers] to press their concerns that might otherwise be ignored by their fellow citizens. [Second,

Freedom of Expression

the doctrine] allows speakers [to have access] to specific people and specific institutions with whom they have a complaint. [The] public forum doctrine ensures that you can make your views heard by legislators, for example, by protesting in front of the state legislature. [Third, the doctrine] increases the likelihood that people generally will be exposed to a wide variety of people and views. [It] tends to ensure a range of experiences that are widely shared [and] a set of exposures to diverse views. [These] exposures can help promote understanding.

Page 1255. At the end of section 1 of the Note, add the following:

See also Thomas v. Chicago Park District, 534 U.S. 316 (2002) (a content-neutral licensing scheme regulating the time, place and manner of use of a public forum need not employ the *Freedman* safeguards because such a scheme "does not authorize a licensor to pass judgment on the content of speech").

If a city can use a "time, place and manner" based licensing scheme for individuals who want to parade on public streets, can it also use such a licensing scheme for speakers who want to go door-to-door to speak with homeowners and distribute literature? In Watchtower Bible & Tract Society v. Village of Stratton, 536 U.S. 150 (2002), the Court, in an eight-to-one decision, held such a scheme unconstitutional. Although acknowledging that the Village's interests in preventing fraud, preventing crime and protecting privacy are "important," the Court nonetheless held that the effect of the licensing scheme on the interests of speakers who want to maintain their anonymity, the administrative burden the scheme imposes on speakers, and the potential impact of the licensing requirement on "spontaneous speech" rendered the ordinance unconstitutional. The Court indicated that such a scheme limited to commercial activities and the solicitation of funds might not be invalid.

1a. *Overbreadth*. Suppose X is convicted of vandalizing a public park and is fined $100. The park district provides by regulation that anyone convicted of this offense is banned from the public park for three months from the date of conviction. A week after his conviction, X enters the public park in order to play basketball. He is arrested for trespass. Can X challenge the constitutionality of the park district regulation on the ground that it is overbroad—that is, on the ground that the regulation could not constitutionally be applied to a "banned" person who wants to enter the park for the purpose of speech? Should X lose because the regulation is not "substantially" overbroad? Suppose X enters the public park a week after his conviction in order to participate in a political rally. Is the regulation unconstitutional as applied? See Virginia v. Hicks, 539 U.S. ___ (2003), in which the Court rejected an overbreadth challenge to a regulation prohibiting any individual who had previously trespassed on the grounds of a public housing development from later entering the grounds of that development. The Court explained that the regulation was not "substantially" overboard and that "rarely, if ever, will an overbreadth challenge succeed against a law or regulation that is not specifically addressed to speech or conduct necessarily associated with speech (such as picketing or demonstrating)."

Page 1285. After section 4 of the Note, add the following:

4a. *Religious speech as viewpoint discrimination: another look.* In Good News Club v. Milford Central School, 533 U.S. 98 (2001), the school district authorized district residents to use school buildings after school hours for "instruction in education, learning, or the arts" and for "social, civic, recreational, and entertainment uses pertaining to the community welfare" but not for "religious purposes." The school district denied a request by the Good News Club, a private Christian organization for children ages six to twelve, to use school property to "sing songs, hear Bible lessons, memorize scripture and pray" on the ground that this constituted "religious purposes."

The Court, in a six-to-three decision, held that this was unconstitutional viewpoint discrimination in a limited public forum. In his opinion for the Court, Justice Thomas explained that "the Club seeks to address a subject otherwise permitted under the rule, the teaching of morals and character, from a religious standpoint." He therefore concluded that this case was indistinguishable from *Lamb's Chapel* and *Rosenberger*.

In dissent, Justice Stevens argued that "speech for 'religious purposes' may reasonably be understood to encompass three different categories. First, there is religious speech that is simply speech about a particular topic from a religious point of view. [Second], there is religious speech that amounts to worship. [Third], there is [speech] that is aimed principally at proselytizing or inculcating a belief in a particular religious faith." In Justice Stevens's view, "the question is whether a school can [create] a limited public forum that admits the first type of religious speech without allowing the other two." He concluded that "just as a school may allow meetings to discuss current events from a political perspective without also allowing organized political recruitment, so too can a school allow discussion of topics such as moral development from a religious (or nonreligious) perspective without thereby opening its forum to religious proselytizing or worship."

In a separate dissenting opinion, Justice Souter, joined by Justice Ginsburg, argued that this case was distinguishable from *Lamb's Chapel* and *Rosenberger* because "Good News intends to use the public school premises not for the mere discussion of a subject from a particular, Christian point of view, but for an evangelical service of worship calling children to commit themselves in an act of Christian conversion." He maintained that the majority's position stands "for the remarkable proposition that any public school opened for civic meetings must be opened for use as a church, synagogue, or mosque."

In a concurring opinion, Justice Scalia responded to the dissenters: "The dissenters emphasize that the religious speech [of the Club is] 'aimed principally at proselytizing or inculcating belief in a particular religious faith.' [But this] does not distinguish the Club's activities from those of [political, social, and cultural organizations that also] may seek to inculcate children with their beliefs [and try to] 'recruit others to join their respective groups.'"

Page 1288. At the end of Forbes, add the following:

Consider Fiss, The Censorship of Television, in L. Bollinger & G. Stone, Eternally Vigilant: Free Speech in the Modern Era 257, 278 (2001):

[Justice Kennedy's argument that access must] be granted to overcome an exclusion based on disagreement with the candidate's views [does not seem] sensible. [Justice] Kennedy explained that such viewpoint discrimination would inevitably skew the electoral debate. [But] every exclusion [will] have this same effect. The only difference between a viewpoint-based exclusion and a viewpoint-neutral exclusion is the justification. [Suppose], for instance, that a station excludes a candidate not because it disagrees with the candidate's view, but because it believes the candidate is not popular, or is not likely to win, or does not have the economic resources needed to mount an effective campaign. [All] of these rationales strike me [as] insufficient to justify the skew that the exclusion will produce.

Page 1291. At the end of the material after *Pico*, add the following:

See also Nadel, The First Amendment's Limitations on the Use of Internet Filtering in Public and School Libraries, 78 Tex. L. Rev. 1117 (2000).

Most states permit individuals to purchase "vanity" license plates. May a state refuse to sell license plates that contain the following words or messages: "GODIZDED," "PRAY," "ARYAN," "FUK" and "DAGO"? See Jacobs, The Public Sensibilities Forum 95 Nw. U. L. Rev. 1357 (2001).

Page 1291. After the citation to *Loudoun*, add the following:

But see United States v. American Library Ass'n, 539 U.S. 194 (2003) (upholding the federal Children's Internet Protection Act, which required the use of filtering software by public libraries as a condition of the receipt of federal funding). On the issue of prior restraint, consider the fact that when a filter is used either some individual or some machine is screening material in advance, determining that it is "obscene," or whatever, and then denying it to the prospective user without any judicial determination.

In thinking about the use of filters, it may be useful to know that there are more than 2 billion Web pages on the Internet and that 10,000 new Web pages are added each hour. In this context, can filters possibly "work"? Consider R. Thornburgh & H. Lin (eds.), Youth, Pornography and the Internet (2002):

> In practice, the volume of material on the Internet is so large that it is impractical for human beings to evaluate every discrete piece of information for inappropriateness. Moreover, the content of some existing Web pages changes very quickly, and new Web pages appear at a rapid rate. Thus, identifying inappropriate material must rely either on an automated, machine-executable process for determining inappropriate content or on a presumption that everything that is not explicitly identified by a human being as appropriate is inappropriate. An approach based on machine-executable rules abstracted from human judgments inevitably misses nuances in those human judgments, which reduces the accuracy of this approach compared to that of humans, while the presumption-based approach necessarily identifies a large volume of appropriate material as inappropriate.

Is public education consistent with the First Amendment? Is there a danger that in structuring what individuals learn the government will engage in "thought control"? Are there circumstances in which the nature of public education may itself violate the First Amendment? Consider Redish & Finnerty, What Did You Learn in School Today? Free Speech, Values Inculcation, and the Democratic-Educational Paradox, 88 Corn. L. Rev. 62, 67-70 (2002):

> The problem [is] that by means of the public educational process, the state is able to engage is a dangerous form of political, social, or moral thought control that potentially interferes with a citizen's subsequent exercise of individual autonomy. [By] selectively instilling in students a predetermined set of normative values and empirical assumptions, the state effectively favors certain viewpoints over others. . . .
>
> [Although it] would be both practically and theoretically impossible to completely prevent the governmental values inculcation that occurs in the educational process, [it] is possible [for] the judiciary to reasonably police the educational process in order to restrict values inculcation to that essential minimum degree required for the educational process to function. [Under this view, the public school may] convey only those values that are both substantially related and incidental to the educational process. . . .

Page 1298. At the end of the Note, add the following:

LEGAL SERVICES CORP. v. VELAZQUEZ, 531 U.S. 533 (2001). In 1974, Congress established the Legal Services Corporation (LSC), whose mission is to distribute funds appropriated by Congress to eligible local grantee organizations "for the purpose of providing financial support for legal assistance in noncriminal proceedings . . . to persons financially unable to afford legal assistance." LSC grantees consist of hundreds of local organizations governed by local boards of directors. In many instances, the grantees are funded by a combination of LSC funds and other public or private sources. The grantee organizations hire and supervise lawyers to provide free legal assistance to indigent clients.

In a five-to-four decision, the Court distinguished *Rust* and held unconstitutional a congressionally imposed restriction prohibiting LSC-funded attorneys from challenging the legality or constitutionality of existing welfare laws. Justice Kennedy delivered the opinion of the Court: "The Court in *Rust* did not place explicit reliance on the rationale that the counseling activities of the doctors under Title X amounted to governmental speech; when interpreting the holding in later cases, however, we have explained *Rust* on this understanding. We have said that viewpoint-based funding decisions can be sustained in instances in which the government is itself the speaker, or instances, like *Rust*, in which the government 'used private speakers to transmit information pertaining to its own program.' As we said in *Rosenberger*, "[w]hen the government disburses public funds to private entities to convey a governmental message, it may take legitimate and appropriate steps to ensure that its message is neither garbled nor distorted by the grantee.' . . .

"[But] '[i]t does not follow . . . that viewpoint-based restrictions are proper when the [government] does not itself speak or subsidize transmittal of a message it favors but instead expends funds to encourage a diversity of views from private speakers.' *Rosenberger*. Although the LSC program differs from the program at issue in *Rosenberger* in that its purpose is not to 'encourage a diversity of views,' the salient point is that, like the program in *Rosenberger*, the LSC program was designed to facilitate private speech, not to promote a governmental message. Congress funded LSC grantees to provide attorneys to represent the interests of indigent clients. [In] this vital respect this suit is distinguishable from *Rust*.

"The private nature of the speech involved here, and the extent of LSC's regulation of private expression, are indicated further by the circumstance that the Government seeks to use an existing medium of expression and to control it, in a class of cases, in ways which distort its usual functioning. Where the government uses or attempts to regulate a particular medium, we have been informed by its accepted usage in determining whether a particular restriction on speech is necessary for the program's purposes and limitations. [Citing FCC v. League of Women Voters; Arkansas Educational Television Commn. v. Forbes; and *Rosenberger*.]

"[Restricting] LSC attorneys in advising their clients and in presenting arguments and analyses to the courts distorts the legal system by altering the traditional role of the attorneys in much the same way broadcast systems or student publication networks were changed in the limited forum cases we have cited. Just as government in those cases could not elect to use a broadcasting network or a college publication structure in a regime which prohibits speech necessary to the proper functioning of those systems, it may not design a subsidy to effect this serious and fundamental restriction on advocacy of attorneys and the functioning of the judiciary. . . .

"Interpretation of the law and the Constitution is the primary mission of the judiciary when it acts within the sphere of its authority to resolve a case or controversy. Under [the challenged statute], however, cases would be presented by LSC attorneys who could not advise the courts of serious questions of statutory validity. The disability is inconsistent with the proposition that attorneys should present all the reasonable and well-grounded arguments necessary for proper resolution of the case. By seeking to prohibit the analysis of certain legal issues and to truncate presentation to the courts, the enactment under review prohibits speech and expression upon which courts must depend for the proper exercise of the judicial power. Congress cannot wrest the law from the Constitution which is its source. . . .

"It is no answer to say the restriction on speech is harmless because, under LSC's interpretation of the Act, its attorneys can withdraw. This misses the point. The statute is an attempt to draw lines around the LSC program to exclude from litigation those arguments and theories Congress finds unacceptable but which by their nature are within the province of the courts to consider.

"The restriction on speech is even more problematic because in cases where the attorney withdraws from a representation, the client is unlikely to find other counsel. [Thus], with respect to the litigation services Congress has funded, there is no alternative channel for expression of the advocacy Congress seeks to restrict. This is in stark contrast to *Rust*. There, a patient could receive the approved Title X family planning counseling funded by the Government and later could consult an affiliate or independent organization to receive abortion counseling. Unlike indigent clients who seek LSC representation, the patient in *Rust* was not required to forfeit the Government-funded advice when she also received abortion counseling through alternative channels. Because LSC attorneys must withdraw whenever a question of a welfare statute's validity arises, an individual could not obtain joint representation so that the constitutional challenge would be presented by a non-LSC attorney, and other, permitted, arguments advanced by LSC counsel.

"Finally, LSC and the Government maintain that [this restriction] is necessary to define the scope and contours of the federal program, a condition that ensures funds can be spent for those cases most immediate to congressional concern. [In the Government's] view, the restriction operates neither to maintain the current welfare system nor insulate it from attack; rather, it helps the current welfare system function in a more efficient and fair manner by removing from the program complex challenges to existing welfare laws.

"The effect of the restriction, however, is to prohibit advice or argumentation that existing welfare laws are unconstitutional or unlawful. Congress cannot recast a condition on funding as a mere definition of its program in every case, lest the First Amendment be reduced to a simple semantic exercise. Here, notwithstanding Congress' purpose to confine and limit its program, the restriction operates to insulate current welfare laws from constitutional scrutiny and certain other legal challenges, a condition implicating central First Amendment concerns. [There] can be little doubt that the LSC Act funds constitutionally protected expression; and in the context of this statute there is no programmatic message of the kind recognized in *Rust* and which sufficed there to allow the Government to specify the advice deemed necessary for its legitimate objectives. . . .

"Congress was not required to fund an LSC attorney to represent indigent clients; and when it did so, it was not required to fund the whole range of legal representations or relationships. The LSC and the United States, however, in effect ask us to permit Congress to define the scope of the litigation it funds to exclude certain vital theories and ideas. The attempted restriction is designed to insulate the Government's interpretation of the Constitution from judicial challenge. The Constitution does not permit the Government to confine litigants and their attorneys in this manner. We must be vigilant when Congress imposes rules and conditions which in effect insulate its own laws from legitimate judicial challenge."

Justice Scalia, joined by Chief Justice Rehnquist and Justices O'Connor and Thomas, dissented: "The LSC Act is a federal subsidy program, not a federal regulatory program, and '[t]here is a basic difference between [the two].' Regulations directly restrict speech; subsidies do not. [In *Rust*, the Court upheld] a statutory scheme that is in all relevant respects indistinguishable from [the provision challenged in this case]. The LSC Act, like the scheme in *Rust*, does not [discriminate] on the basis of viewpoint, since it funds neither challenges to nor defenses of existing welfare law. The provision simply declines to subsidize a certain class of litigation, and under *Rust* that decision 'does not infringe the right' to bring such litigation. . . . The Court's repeated claims that [the Act] 'restricts' and 'prohibits' speech, and 'insulates' laws from judicial review, are simply baseless. No litigant who, in the absence of LSC funding, would bring a suit challenging existing welfare law is deterred from doing so by [the Act]. *Rust* thus controls [this case] and compels the conclusion that [the Act] is constitutional.

"The Court contends that *Rust* is different because the program at issue subsidized government speech, while the LSC funds private speech. This is so unpersuasive it hardly needs response. If the private doctors' confidential advice to their patients at issue in *Rust* constituted 'government speech,' it is hard to imagine what subsidized speech would not be government speech. Moreover, the majority's contention that the subsidized speech in these cases is not government speech because the lawyers have a professional obligation to represent the interests of their clients founders on the reality that the doctors in *Rust* had a professional obligation to serve the interests of their patients....

"The Court further asserts that these cases are different from *Rust* because the welfare funding restriction 'seeks to use an existing medium of expression and to control it . . . in ways which distort its usual functioning.' This is wrong on both the facts and the law. It is wrong on the law because there is utterly no precedent for the novel and facially implausible proposition that the First Amendment has anything to do with government funding that—though it does not actually abridge anyone's speech —'distorts an existing medium of expression.' None of the three cases cited by the Court mentions such an odd principle. [The] Court's 'nondistortion' principle is also wrong on the facts, since there is no basis for believing that [the challenged provision], by causing 'cases [to] be presented by LSC attorneys who [can]not advise the courts of serious questions of statutory validity,' will distort the operation of the courts. It may well be that the bar of [the Act] will cause LSC-funded attorneys to decline or to withdraw from cases that involve statutory validity. But that means at most that fewer statutory challenges to welfare laws will be presented to the courts because of the unavailability of free legal services for that purpose. So what? The same result would ensue from excluding LSC-funded lawyers from welfare litigation entirely....

"Finally, the Court is troubled 'because in cases where the attorney withdraws from a representation, the client is unlikely to find other counsel.' That is surely irrelevant, since it leaves the welfare recipient in no worse condition than he would have been in had the LSC program never been enacted. [*Rust*] rejected a similar argument.... There is no legitimate basis for declaring [this law] unconstitutional."

Page 1301. At the end of *Finley*, add the following:

Consider Chemerinsky, Content Neutrality as a Central Problem of Freedom of Speech, 74 S. Cal. L. Rev. 49, 56, 59 (2000):

> The determination of whether a law is viewpoint based [is] crucial in determining its constitutionality. Two recent [decisions—*Forbes* and *Finley*]—are important because each [compromises] the protection against content-based regulation by adopting an unduly restrictive definition of viewpoint discrimination. [In] *Forbes*, the Court concluded that excluding a minor party candidate from a debate is viewpoint neutral. But the entire difference between minor party and major party candidates revolves around their views. In *Finley*, the Court said that a federal law that authorized the NEA to consider "decency and respect" for values

was viewpoint neutral. Yet these terms are all about government examination of the viewpoint expressed. [The] Court has erred by adopting such an unduly restrictive definition of viewpoint discrimination in these cases.

Consider also Bezanson & Buss, The Many Faces of Government Speech, 86 Iowa L. Rev. 1377, 1382-1383, 1487 (2001):

> The imperative of government speaking, and the roles occupied by government when it speaks, are vastly multiplied in the modern state. [Government is] a creator [of] programs, a manager of economic and social relationships, a vast employer and purchaser, an educator, investor, curator, librarian, historian [and patron]. [It] taxes and spends, subsidizes and penalizes, encourages and discourages. None of these undertakings [could] be successfully pursued without speech by government....
>
> [In *Velazquez*], the Court drew upon the now established dichotomy between the *Rust* and *Rosenberger* paradigms: "... viewpoint-based funding decisions can be sustained [when] the government is itself the speaker [or uses] private speakers to transmit information pertaining to its own programs" [but not when the government] "expends funds to encourage a diversity of views from private speakers." [This distinction] rests on an incoherent theoretical premise [and] has left unanswered many important [questions]. For example, what [is] government "speech"? [Must] the message be specific [or] might [it] consist of nothing more than tacit government agreement with private messages that the government prefers? [Can the government speak] through private speakers whose messages [are] favored by subsidy or reward? [Can] it speak through exclusion of private speech as well as inclusion? [Is] government speaking when it acts as educator, [as] curator of a museum, as librarian, or as a patron of artistic [work]? Does it speak when it acts as a manager of [physical spaces]?...
>
> We conclude that government speech should receive little or no immunity from the [ordinary requirement of viewpoint neutrality] when the government's speech creates a monopoly for a particular point of view, when it distorts the marketplace of ideas, and [when there is] government deception.

How would you apply "monopoly," "distortion" and "deception" to such cases as *Rosenberger*, *Mosley*, *Rust*, *Forbes*, *Finley*, *Pico* and *Velazquez*? Are these the right factors to consider in deciding these cases?

UNITED STATES v. AMERICAN LIBRARY ASSOCIATION, 539 U.S. 194 (2003). Two federal programs provide funds to public libraries to help them expand access to the Internet. The Children's Internet Protection Act (CIPA), however, forbids public libraries to receive federal under these programs unless they install software to block obscenity and child pornography and prevent minors from accessing material that is "harmful of minors." A group of libraries, library patrons and Web site publishers brought suit challenging CIPA's filtering provisions. A statutorily mandated three-judge district court held CIPA unconstitutional, but the Supreme Court reversed.

Chief Justice Rehnquist, joined by Justices O'Connor, Scalia and Thomas, authored a plurality opinion: "Even before Congress enacted CIPA, almost 17% of public libraries used such software on at least some of their Internet terminals, and 7% had filters on all of them. When a patron tries to view a site that falls within [a prohibited] category, a screen appears indicating that the site is blocked. [A] filter set to block pornography may sometimes block other sites that present neither obscene nor pornographic [material]. To minimize this problem, a library can [delete] specific sites from a blocking category, and [CIPA] permits [a library] library to 'disable' the filter 'to enable access for bona fide research or other lawful purposes. . . . '

"Congress has wide latitude to attach conditions to the receipt of federal assistance in order to further its policy objectives. But Congress may not 'induce' the recipient 'to engage in activities that would themselves be unconstitutional." To determine whether libraries would violate the First Amendment by employing the filtering software that CIPA requires, we must [examine] the role of libraries in our society. Public libraries pursue the worthy missions of facilitating learning and cultural enrichment. [To] fulfill [these] missions, public libraries must have broad discretion to decide what material to provide to their patrons. Although they seek to provide a wide array of information, their goal has never been to provide 'universal coverage.' Instead, public libraries seek to provide materials 'that would be of the greatest direct benefit or interest to the community.' To this end, libraries collect only those materials deemed to have 'requisite and appropriate quality.' . . .

"We have held in two analogous contexts that the government has broad discretion to make content-based judgments in deciding what private speech to make available to the public. [Citing *Forbes* and *Finley*.] Just as forum analysis and heightened judicial scrutiny are incompatible with the role of public television stations and the role of the NEA, they are also incompatible with the discretion that public libraries must have to fulfill their traditional missions. . . .

". . . Most libraries already exclude pornography from their print collections because they deem it inappropriate for inclusion. We do not subject these decisions to heightened scrutiny; it would make little sense to treat libraries' judgments to block online pornography any differently, when these judgments are made for just the same reason. . . .

"[The] dissents fault the tendency of filtering software to 'overblock' — that is, to erroneously block access to constitutionally protected speech that falls outside the categories that software users intend to block. [Assuming] that such erroneous blocking presents constitutional difficulties, any such concerns are dispelled by the ease with which patrons may have the filtering software disabled. When a patron encounters a blocked site, he need only ask a librarian to unblock it, [and CIPA] ex-

Freedom of Expression   **Page 1301**

pressly authorizes library officials to 'disable' a filter altogether 'to enable access for bona fide research or other lawful purposes.' The Solicitor General confirmed that a [patron] would not 'have to explain . . . why he was asking a site to be unblocked or the filtering to be disabled.' The District Court viewed unblocking and disabling as inadequate because some patrons may be too embarrassed to request them. But the Constitution does not guarantee the right to acquire information at a public library without any risk of embarrassment.

"Appellees urge us to affirm the District Court's judgment on the alternative ground that CIPA imposes an unconstitutional condition on the receipt of federal assistance. Under this doctrine, 'the government may not deny a benefit to a person on a basis that infringes his constitutionally protected . . . freedom of speech even if he has no entitlement to that benefit.' Appellees argue that CIPA imposes an unconstitutional condition on libraries that receive [federal] subsidies by requiring them, as a condition on their receipt of federal funds, to surrender their First Amendment right to provide the public with access to constitutionally protected speech. The Government counters that this claim fails because Government entities do not have First Amendment rights. . . .

"We need not decide this question because, even assuming that appellees may assert an 'unconstitutional conditions' claim, this claim would fail on the merits. Within broad limits, 'when the Government appropriates public funds to establish a program it is entitled to define the limits of that program.' [Citing *Rust*.] The [Internet subsidy] programs were intended to help public libraries fulfill their traditional role of obtaining material of requisite and appropriate quality for educational and informational purposes. Congress may certainly insist that these 'public funds be spent for the purposes for which they were authorized.' Especially because public libraries have traditionally excluded pornographic material from their other collections, Congress could reasonably impose a parallel limitation on its Internet assistance programs. As the use of filtering software helps to carry out these programs, it is a permissible condition under *Rust*.

"Justice Stevens [asserts] that '[a] federal statute penalizing a library for failing to install filtering software on every one of its Internet-accessible computers would unquestionably violate [the First] Amendment.' But—assuming again that public libraries have First Amendment rights—CIPA does not 'penalize' libraries that choose not to install such software, or deny them the right to provide their patrons with unfiltered Internet access. Rather, CIPA simply reflects Congress' decision not to subsidize their doing so. To the extent that libraries wish to offer unfiltered access, they are free to do so without federal assistance. 'A refusal to fund protected activity, without more, cannot be equated with the imposition of a "penalty" on that activity.' *Rust.*

"Appellees mistakenly contend, in reliance on [*Velazquez*] that CIPA's filtering conditions '[d]istor[t] the [u]sual [f]unctioning of [p]ublic [l]ibraries.' In *Velazquez,* the Court concluded that [the] restriction on advocacy [in] welfare disputes would distort the usual functioning of the legal profession and the federal and state courts

255

before which the lawyers appeared. Public libraries, by contrast, have no comparable role that pits them against the Government, and there is no comparable assumption that they must be free of any conditions that their benefactors might attach to the use of donated funds. . . .

"Relying on *Velazquez*, Justice Stevens argues mistakenly that *Rust* is inapposite because that case 'only involved and only applies to . . . situations in which the government seeks to communicate a specific message,' and unlike the Title X program in *Rust*, the [public library subsidy] programs 'are not designed to foster or transmit any particular governmental message.' But he misreads our cases discussing *Rust* [and] misapprehends the purpose of providing Internet terminals in public libraries. *Velazquez* held only that viewpoint-based restrictions are improper 'when the [government] does not itself speak or subsidize transmittal of a message it favors *but instead expends funds to encourage a diversity of views from private speakers.*' [But] public libraries do not install Internet terminals to provide a forum for Web publishers to express themselves, but rather to provide patrons with online material of requisite and appropriate quality.

"Because public libraries' use of Internet filtering software does not violate their patrons' First Amendment rights, CIPA does not induce libraries to violate the Constitution, and is a valid exercise of Congress' spending power. Nor does CIPA impose an unconstitutional condition on public libraries."

Justice Kennedy concurred in the judgment: "If, on the request of an adult user, a librarian will unblock filtered material or disable the Internet software filter without significant delay, there is little to this case. The Government represents this is indeed the fact. [If] some libraries do not have the capacity to unblock specific Web sites or to disable the filter or if it is shown that an adult user's election to view constitutionally protected Internet material is burdened in some other substantial way, that would be the subject for an as-applied challenge, not the facial challenge made in this case. There are, of course, substantial Government interests at stake here. The interest in protecting young library users from material inappropriate for minors is legitimate, and even compelling, as all Members of the Court appear to agree. Given this interest, and the failure to show that the ability of adult library users to have access to the material is burdened in any significant degree, the statute is not unconstitutional on its face."

Justice Breyer also concurred in the judgment: "I would apply a form of heightened scrutiny, examining the statutory requirements in question with special care. The Act directly restricts the public's receipt of information. And it does so through limitations imposed by outside bodies (here Congress) upon two critically important sources of information—the Internet as accessed via public libraries. For that reason, we should not examine the statute's constitutionality as if it raised no special First Amendment concern—as if, like tax or economic regulation, the First Amendment demanded only a 'rational basis' for imposing a restriction. . . .

"At the same time, in my view, the First Amendment does not here demand application [of] 'strict scrutiny.' The statutory restriction in question is, in essence, a kind of 'selection' restriction (a kind of editing). It affects the kinds and amount of materials that the library can present to its patrons. And libraries often properly engage in the selection of materials, either as a matter of necessity (*i.e.*, due to the scarcity of resources) or by design (*i.e.*, in accordance with collection development policies). To apply 'strict scrutiny' to the 'selection' of a library's collection [would] unreasonably interfere with the discretion necessary to create, maintain, or select a library's 'collection' (broadly defined to include all the information the library makes available). . . .

". . . I would examine [the] Act's restrictions here as the Court has examined speech-related restrictions in other contexts where circumstances call for heightened, but not 'strict,' scrutiny—where, for example, complex, competing constitutional interests are potentially at issue or speech-related harm is potentially justified by unusually strong governmental interests. Typically the key question in such instances is one of proper fit. [Citing *Denver Area*; *Red Lion, infra* section F.4; *Turner Broadcasting, infra* section F.4]. In such cases the Court has asked whether the harm to speech-related interests is disproportionate in light of both the justifications and the potential alternatives. It has considered the legitimacy of the statute's objective, the extent to which the statute will tend to achieve that objective, whether there are other, less restrictive ways of achieving that objective, and ultimately whether the statute works speech-related harm that, in relation to that objective, is out of proportion. . . .

"The Act's restrictions satisfy these constitutional demands. The Act seeks to restrict access to obscenity, child pornography, and, in respect to access by minors, material that is comparably harmful. These objectives are 'legitimate,' and indeed often 'compelling.' [Citing *Miller*; *Ferber*]. As the District Court found, software filters 'provide a relatively cheap and effective' means of furthering these goals. Due to present technological limitations, however, the software filters both 'overblock' [and] 'underblock.' [But] no one has presented any clearly superior or better fitting alternatives.

"At the same time, the Act contains an important exception that limits the speech-related harm that 'overblocking' might cause. As the plurality points out, the Act allows libraries to permit any adult patron access to an 'overblocked' Web site; the adult patron need only ask a librarian to unblock the specific Web site or, alternatively, ask the librarian, 'Please disable the entire filter.' The Act does impose upon the patron the burden of making this request. But it is difficult to see how that burden (or any delay associated with compliance) could prove more onerous than traditional library practices associated with segregating library materials in, say, closed stacks, or with interlibrary lending practices that require patrons to make requests that are not anonymous and to wait while the librarian obtains the desired materials from elsewhere. [Given] the comparatively small burden that the Act imposes upon the library patron seeking legitimate Internet materials, I cannot say that any speech-related harm that the Act may cause is disproportionate when considered in relation to the Act's legitimate objectives."

Justice Stevens dissented: "I agree with the plurality that it is neither inappropriate nor unconstitutional for a local library to experiment with filtering software as a means of curtailing children's access to Internet Web sites displaying sexually explicit images. I also agree with the plurality that the 7% of public libraries that decided to use such software on *all* of their Internet terminals in 2000 did not act unlawfully. Whether it is constitutional for the Congress of the United States to impose that requirement on the other 93%, however, raises a vastly different question. Rather than allowing local decisionmakers to tailor their responses to local problems, [CIPA] operates as a blunt nationwide restraint on adult access to 'an enormous amount of valuable information' that individual librarians cannot possibly review. Most of that information is constitutionally protected speech. In my view, this restraint is unconstitutional.

"... Because the software relies on key words or phrases to block undesirable sites, it does not have the capacity to exclude a precisely defined category of images. [Image] recognition technology is immature, ineffective, and unlikely to improve substantially in the near future. [Given] the quantity and ever-changing character of Web sites offering free sexually explicit material, it is inevitable that a substantial amount of such material will never be blocked. Because of this 'underblocking,' the statute will provide parents with a false sense of security without really solving the problem that motivated its enactment. Conversely, the software's reliance on words to identify undesirable sites necessarily results in the blocking of thousands of pages that 'contain content that is completely innocuous.' [A] statutory blunderbuss that mandates this vast amount of 'overblocking' abridges the freedom of speech. ...

"... Neither the interest in suppressing unlawful speech nor the interest in protecting children from access to harmful materials justifies this overly broad restriction on adult access to protected speech. 'The Government may not suppress lawful speech as the means to suppress unlawful speech.' [Quoting *Ashcroft v. Free Speech Coalition*].

"[T]he District Court expressly found that a variety of less restrictive alternatives are available at the local level: '[P]ublic libraries may enforce Internet use policies that make clear to patrons that the library's Internet terminals may not be used to access illegal speech. [They may require] parental consent [for] unfiltered access, or [restrict] minors' unfiltered access to terminals within view of library staff. [And] privacy screens, recessed monitors, and placement of unfiltered Internet terminals outside of sight-lines provide less restrictive alternatives for libraries to prevent patrons from being unwillingly exposed to sexually explicit content on the Internet.' [Such] local decisions tailored to local circumstances are more appropriate than a mandate from Congress.

"The plurality does not reject any of those findings. Instead, [it] relies on [the] assurance that the statute permits individual librarians to disable filtering mechanisms whenever a patron so requests. [This] does not cure the constitutional infirmity in the statute. Until a blocked site [is] unblocked, a patron is unlikely to know what is being hidden and therefore whether there is any point in asking for the filter to be removed. It is as though the statute required a significant part of every library's reading materials to be kept in unmarked, locked rooms or cabinets, which could be opened only in response to specific requests. Some curious readers would in time obtain access to the hidden materials, but many would not. [Unless] we assume that the statute is a mere symbolic gesture, we must conclude that it will create a significant prior restraint on adult access to protected speech. . . .

"The plurality incorrectly argues that the statute does not impose 'an unconstitutional condition on public libraries.' On the contrary, it impermissibly conditions the receipt of Government funding on the restriction of significant First Amendment rights. The plurality explains the 'worthy missions' of the public library in facilitating 'learning and cultural enrichment.' It then asserts that in order to fulfill these missions, 'libraries must have broad discretion to decide what material to provide to their patrons.' Thus the selection decision is the province of the librarians, a province into which we have hesitated to enter. [We] have always assumed that libraries have discretion when making decisions regarding what to include in, and exclude from, their collections. That discretion is comparable to the "'business of a university . . . to determine for itself on academic grounds who may teach, what may be taught, how it shall be taught, and who may be admitted to study.'" Given our Nation's deep commitment 'to safeguarding academic freedom' and to the 'robust exchange of ideas,' a library's exercise of judgment with respect to its collection is entitled to First Amendment protection.

"A federal statute penalizing a library for failing to install filtering software on every one of its Internet-accessible computers would unquestionably violate [the First] Amendment. I think it equally clear that the First Amendment protects libraries from being denied funds for refusing to comply with an identical rule. An abridgment of speech by means of a threatened denial of benefits can be just as pernicious as an abridgment by means of a threatened penalty.

"The plurality argues that [*Rust*] requires rejection of [the] unconstitutional conditions claim. But, as subsequent cases have explained, *Rust* only involved and only applies to instances of governmental speech—that is, situations in which the government seeks to communicate a specific message. The [subsidies] involved in this case do not subsidize any message favored by the Government. As Congress made clear, these programs were designed '[t]o help public libraries provide their patrons with Internet access [to] a vast amount and wide variety of private speech. They are not designed to foster or transmit any particular governmental message. [This] Court should not permit federal funds to be used to enforce this kind of broad restriction of First Amendment rights. . . ."

Justice Souter, joined by Justice Ginsburg, also dissented: "I agree [with] Justice Stevens that the blocking requirements of [CIPA] impose an unconstitutional condition on the Government's subsidies to local libraries for providing access to the Internet. I also [conclude that] the blocking rule [is] invalid in the exercise of the spending power under Article I, § 8 [because it] mandates action by recipient libraries that would violate the First Amendment's guarantee of free speech if the libraries took that action entirely on their own. . . .

". . . I have no doubt about the legitimacy of governmental efforts to put a barrier between child patrons of public libraries and the raw offerings on the Internet otherwise available to them there, and if the only First Amendment interests raised here were those of children, I would uphold application of the Act. [Nor] would I dissent if I agreed with the majority of my colleagues that an adult library patron could, consistently with the Act, obtain an unblocked terminal simply for the asking. I realize the Solicitor General represented this to be the Government's policy, and if that policy were communicated to every affected library as unequivocally as it was stated to us at argument, local librarians might be able to indulge the unblocking requests of adult patrons to the point of taking the curse off the statute. [But] the Federal Communications Commission, in its order implementing the Act, pointedly declined to set a federal policy on when unblocking by local libraries would be appropriate under the statute. [Moreover,] the District Court expressly found that 'unblocking may take days, and may be unavailable, especially in branch libraries, which are often less well staffed than main libraries.'

"In any event, we are here to review a statute, and the unblocking provisions simply cannot be construed [to] say that a library must unblock upon adult request, no conditions imposed and no questions asked. [We] have to take the statute on the understanding that adults will be denied access to a substantial amount of nonobscene material harmful to children but lawful for adult examination, and a substantial quantity of text and pictures harmful to no one. [This] is the inevitable consequence [of] current filtering mechanisms, which screen out material to an extent known only by the manufacturers of the blocking software.

"We likewise have to examine the statute on the understanding that the restrictions on adult Internet access have no justification in the object of protecting children. Children could be restricted to blocked terminals, and [screened] from casual glances. And of course the statute could simply have provided for unblocking at adult request, with no questions asked. The statute could, in other words, have protected children without blocking access for adults or subjecting adults to anything more than minimal inconvenience, just the way (the record shows) many librarians had been dealing with obscenity and indecency before imposition of the federal conditions. Instead, the Government's funding conditions engage in overkill. . . .

"The question for me, then, is whether a local library could itself constitutionally impose these restrictions on the content otherwise available to an adult patron through an Internet connection, at a library terminal provided for public use. The answer is no. A library that chose to block an adult's Internet access to material harmful to children (and whatever else the undiscriminating filter might interrupt) would be imposing a content-based restriction on communication of material in the library's control that an adult could otherwise lawfully see. This would simply be censorship. True, the censorship would not necessarily extend to every adult, for [an] Internet user might convince a librarian that he was a true researcher or had a 'lawful purpose' to obtain everything the library's terminal could provide. But as to those who did not qualify for discretionary unblocking, the censorship would be complete and, like all censorship by an agency of the Government, presumptively invalid owing to strict scrutiny in implementing [the] First Amendment....

"The [plurality] does not treat blocking affecting adults as censorship, but chooses to describe a library's act in filtering content as simply an instance of the kind of selection from available material that every library [must] perform. But this position does not hold up. Public libraries are indeed selective in what they acquire to place in their stacks, as they must be. There is only so much money and so much shelf space, and the necessity to choose some material and reject the rest justifies the effort to be selective with an eye to demand, quality, and the object of maintaining the library as a place of civilized enquiry by widely different sorts of people. Selectivity is thus necessary and complex, and these two characteristics explain why review of a library's selection decisions must be limited: the decisions are made all the time, and only in extreme cases could one expect particular choices to reveal impermissible reasons (reasons even the plurality would consider to be illegitimate), like excluding books because their authors are Democrats or their critiques of organized Christianity are unsympathetic. [Citing *Pico*]. Review for rational basis is probably the most that any court could conduct, owing to the myriad particular selections that might be attacked by someone, and the difficulty of untangling the play of factors behind a particular decision.

"At every significant point, however, the Internet blocking here defies comparison to the process of acquisition. Whereas traditional scarcity of money and space require a library to make choices about what to acquire, and the choice to be made is whether or not to spend the money to acquire something, blocking is [a] choice made after the money for Internet access has been spent or committed. Since it makes no difference to the cost of Internet access whether an adult calls up material harmful for children or the Articles of Confederation, blocking (on facts like these) is not necessitated by scarcity of either money or space. [The] proper analogy therefore is not to passing up a book that might have been bought; it is either to buying a book and then keeping it from adults lacking an acceptable 'purpose,' or to buying an encyclopedia and then cutting out pages with anything thought to be unsuitable for all adults. . . .

"The plurality claims to find support for its conclusions in the 'traditional missio[n]' of the public library. The plurality thus argues, in effect, that the traditional responsibility of public libraries has called for denying adult access to certain books, or bowdlerizing the content of what the libraries let adults see. But, in fact, [the history of the public library in this nation over the past half-century offers] not a word about barring requesting adults from any materials in a library's collection, or about limiting an adult's access based on evaluation of his purposes in seeking materials. . . .

"There is no good reason [to] treat blocking of adult enquiry as anything different from the censorship [it] is. For this reason, I would hold in accordance with conventional strict scrutiny that a library's practice of blocking would violate an adult patron's [First] Amendment right to be free of Internet censorship, when unjustified (as here) by any legitimate interest in screening children from harmful material. On that ground, the Act's blocking requirement in its current breadth calls for unconstitutional action by a library recipient, and is itself unconstitutional."

Page 1310. After the citation of Kagan in section 6 of the Note, add the following:

Rubenfeld, The First Amendment's Purpose, 53 Stan. L. Rev. 767, 769 (2001) ("there is no such thing as a free speech immunity based on the claim that someone wants to break an otherwise constitutional law for expressive purposes");

Page 1311. At the end of section 6 of the Note, add the following:

For a more recent example, see Boy Scouts of America v. Dale, at page 1356 of the main text.

Page 1322. At the end of *Pap's*, add the following:

Consider Leahy, The First Amendment Gone Awry, 150 U. Pa. L. Rev. 1021, 1059 (2002): "The *Pap's* decision is irreconcilable with [*Schad,* supra page 1210 of the main text, which held that a ban on all live entertainment in a town is unconstitutional]. Erie's nudity law in effect does exactly what [*Schad*] admonished could not be allowed, but the *Pap's* plurality was simply willing to ignore this. . . ." Is there a principled way to reconcile *Pap's* with *Schad*?

Page 1323. After the Note on Political Boycotts, add the following:

Note: Computer Code

Another interesting, and increasingly important, example of symbolic speech involves the use of computer code. The Digital Millenium Copyright Act, 17 U.S.C. § 1201 *et seq.*, provides that no person shall distribute any technology that is "primarily designed" to circumvent any technological measure that "effectively controls access to a work protected" by copyright. In Universal City Studios, Inc. v. Corley, 273 F.3d 429 (2d Cir. 2001), the Court of Appeals upheld an order enjoining the defendant, publisher of *The Hacker Quarterly*, from posting on his web site a decryption program known as DeCSS. DeCSS is an algorithm that enables users to circumvent the encryption scheme that protects movies on DVDs from limitless copying. DeCSS was developed by a Norwegian teenager who reverse-engineered the encryption system used by DVD producers.

Analogizing the code to a recipe or a music score, the Court of Appeals held that a computer code is "speech" for purposes of the first amendment. The court then noted that DeCSS combines "nonspeech and speech elements, *i.e.* functional and expressive elements." On the one hand, the code is like a recipe or a blueprint, which conveys information to a user. On the other hand, "unlike a blueprint or a recipe, which cannot yield any functional result without human comprehension of its content, human decision-making and human action, computer code can instantly cause a computer to accomplish tasks and instantly render the results of those tasks available throughout the world via the Internet."

Turning to the specific issue, the court noted that "the essential purpose of encryption code is to prevent unauthorized access. Owners of all property rights are entitled to prohibit access to their property by unauthorized persons." Here, the encryption code is "like a lock on a homeowner's door" or "a combination to a safe." Thus, "one might think that Congress has as much authority to regulate the distribution of a computer code to decrypt DVD movies as it has to regulate distribution of skeleton keys" or "combinations to safes." But "DeCSS differs from a skeleton key in one important respect: it not only is capable of performing the function of unlocking the encrypted DVD movie, it also is a form of communication, albeit written in a language not understood by the general public."

The court concluded that the prohibition on posting DeCSS on a web-site is a content-neutral restriction because it targets "the nonspeech" or "functional" capability of DeCSS to decrypt the DVD security code. In this sense, the court reasoned, DeCSS is merely a "skeleton key," and its regulation thus has only an "incidental effect" on speech. Applying *O'Brien*, the court then upheld the Act as applied.

Do you agree with this analysis? As the court observed, posting DeCSS has (at least) two effects. It is information that can be studied by people who are interested in understanding computer codes, and it is a device that can be downloaded to circumvent an encryption code. If the regulation is aimed at the second effect, is its "incidental impact" on the first effect permissible under *O'Brien*? Is a law aimed at the second effect analytically different under the First Amendment than a law restricting a book on how to make dynamite?

Page 1324. After the citation to *International Society for Krishna Consciousness v. Lee*, add the following:

See also Illinois ex rel. Madigan v. Telemarketing Associates, Inc., 538 U.S. 600 U.S. (2003), in which a non-profit organization retained Telemarketing Associates to solicit donations to aid Vietnam veterans. Under its contract with the non-profit organization, Telemarketing Associates was to keep 85% of the gross receipts. The state initiated an action for fraud on the ground that Telemarketing Associates had made false representations to donors about the percent of their contributions that would actually benefit Vietnam veterans. The Court distinguished *Schaumburg* and held that such an action is consistent with the First Amendment because under Illinois law the state must prove by clear and convincing evidence that the defendant knowingly made false representations of fact in order to mislead prospective donors and that the misrepresentations did mislead such donors.

Page 1333. At the end of the first paragraph of section 1 of the Note, add the following:

Is this precept consistent with other aspects of first amendment jurisprudence? Consider Tushnet, Copyright as a Model for Free Speech Law, 42 B.C. L. Rev. 1, 2-3 (2000):

> When one speaker wishes to use another's words, [the] government may tell her that she cannot. [If] we believe standard First Amendment theory, then we should believe that copyright is unconstitutional because it is designed to suppress some speech to generate other speech, a result the Supreme Court condemned in [*Buckley*]. But that would be silly: copyright is constitutional, in large part because it does encourage speech by the people it protects. The problem is with the standard theory: Government is already involved in shaping available speech, and that's a good thing. Our objections to particular government regulations [must] be to their bias or ineffectiveness, not to the mere fact of government action.

Page 1343. Before section 1 of the Note, add the following:

1a. *Advocacy corporations.* North Carolina Right to Life, a non-profit advocacy corporation that counsels pregnant women how to deal with unwanted pregnancies without resorting to abortion, challenged the constitutionality of 2 U.S.C. § 441, which prohibits corporations from making political contributions directly to candidates for federal office, but permits them to establish, administer and solicit contributions to separately created PACs, which can themselves make such contributions. In Federal Election Commission v. Beaumont, 539 U.S. 146 (2003), the Court upheld § 441, even as applied to non-profit advocacy corporations. In an opinion by Justice Souter, the Court noted that non-profit advocacy corporations, like for-profit corporations, benefit from state-created advantages and may thus be able to amass substantial political war chests. Moreover, § 441 helps to prevent individuals and organizations from circumventing the contribution limits upheld in *Buckley*. Because restrictions on political contributions are "merely 'marginal' speech restrictions," and "lie closer to the edges than to the core of political expression," they are constitutional if they are "closely drawn" to serve a "sufficiently important interest," a test the Court held was satisfied in this case. Justice Thomas, joined by Justice Scalia, dissented.

Page 1344. At the end of section 2 of the Note, add the following:

In order to prevent circumvention of the contribution limits, if an individual or organization makes campaign expenditures in *coordination* with a candidate, those expenditures ordinarily are treated not as independent expenditures but as contributions under both the Federal Election Campaign Act and the first amendment. But suppose a political party makes such coordinated expenditures on behalf of its electoral candidates? Should those expenditures also be treated as contributions, and thus be subjected to the limitations of the act? Would such an approach make sense, in light of the special nature and purpose of political parties?

In Federal Election Commission v. Colorado Republican Federal Campaign Committee, 533 U.S. 431 (2001) (*Colorado II*), the Court rejected the claim that a political party's *coordinated* expenditures on behalf of its electoral candidates should be treated as expenditures rather than contributions. The Court explained that "a party's right to make unlimited expenditures coordinated with a candidate would induce individual and other nonparty contributors to give to the party in order to finance coordinated spending for a favored candidate beyond the contribution limits, [and thus bypass the very limits] that *Buckley* upheld."

Page 1345. After section 4 of the Note, add the following:

4a. *Regulating the speech of judicial candidates.* Minnesota elects its judges. It prohibits candidates for judicial office from announcing their views of any disputed legal issues that might come before them as judges. In Republican Party of Minnesota v. White, 536 U.S. 735 (2002), the Court, in a five-to-four decision, held that this prohibition (known as the "announce clause") violated the first amendment. (Minnesota has a separate provision, not challenged in this case, which prohibits candidates for judicial office from making "promises or pledges of conduct in office.")

Justice Scalia delivered the opinion of the Court. At the outset, Justice Scalia reasoned that because the "announce clause both prohibits speech on the basis of its content and burdens a category of speech that is 'at the very core of our First Amendment freedoms' — speech about the qualifications for public office," the State must "prove that the announce clause is (1) narrowly tailored, to serve (2) a compelling state interest." Justice Scalia then observed that the State had asserted two interests: "preserving the impartiality of the state judiciary and preserving the appearance of the impartiality of the state judiciary." Defining the interest in "impartiality" as meaning that a judge should not have "a preconception in favor or against a particular legal view," Justice Scalia said that "it is virtually impossible to find a judge who does not have preconceptions about the law," and "pretending otherwise by attempting to preserve the 'appearance' of that type of impartiality can hardly be a compelling interest."

Justice Scalia also considered another version of impartiality: "openmindedness." This "sort of impartiality seeks to guarantee each litigant, not an *equal* chance to win the legal points in the case, but at least *some* chance of doing so." Justice Scalia conceded that impartiality and the appearance of impartiality in this sense "may well be . . . desirable in the judiciary" and that the announce clause serves these interests "because it relieves a judge from pressure to rule a certain way in order to maintain consistency with statements the judge has previously made. Justice Scalia nonetheless concluded, that "statements in election campaigns are such an infinitesimal portion of the public commitments to legal positions that judges (or judges to be) undertake, that this object of the prohibition is implausible." Justice Scalia offered as examples of such other statements rulings in earlier cases, statements made in classes judges teach, statements made in books, articles, speeches and so on.

Justice Scalia also rejected the argument that "statements made in an election campaign pose a special threat to openmindedness because the candidate, when elected judge, will have a *particular* reluctance to contradict them. Justice Scalia agreed that "that might be plausible [with] regard to campaign *promises*." But, he observed, Minnesota has "a separate prohibition on campaign 'pledges or promises' [by judicial candidates] which is not challenged here." Beyond that, Justice Scalia reasoned that "the proposition that judges feel significantly greater compulsion [to] maintain consistency with *nonpromissory* statements made during a judicial campaign than with such statements made before or after the campaign is not self-evidently true," and does not carry "the burden imposed by our strict-scrutiny test."

Responding to Justice Ginsburg's argument in dissent that "the announce clause must be constitutional because due process would be denied if an elected judge sat in a case involving an issue on which he had previously announced his view," Justice Scalia argued that elected judges "*always*" face the pressure of an electorate who might disagree with their ruling and therefore vote them off the bench. Surely the judge who frees Timothy McVeigh places his job much more at risk than the judge who (horror of horrors!) reconsiders his previously announced view on a disputed legal view."

Finally, Justice Scalia concluded that the practice of restricting the speech of judicial candidates under the "announce clause," which for the most part developed since the 1920s and is not followed in four of the 31 states with elected judges, is not so "universal and long-established" that there should be any special "presumption" of constitutionality for that reason. Justices O'Connor and Kennedy filed concurring opinions.

Justice Stevens, joined by Justices Souter, Ginsburg and Breyer, dissented:

By obscuring the fundamental distinction between campaigns for the judiciary and the political branches, [the] Court defies any sensible notion of the judicial office and the importance of impartiality in that context. [The] very purpose of most statements prohibited by the announce clause is to convey the message that the candidate's mind is not open on a particular issue.

Justice Ginsburg, joined by Justices Stevens, Souter and Breyer, also dissented:

Legislative and executive officials act on behalf of the voters who placed them in office; 'judge[s] represen[t] the Law.' Unlike their counterparts in the political branches, judges are expected to refrain from catering to particular constituencies or committing themselves on controversial issues in advance of adversarial presentation. [I] would differentiate elections for political offices, in which the First Amendment holds full sway, from elections designed to select those who office it is to administer justice without respect to persons. Minnesota's choice to elect its judges [does] not preclude [it] from installing an election process geared to the judicial office. [The] rationale underlying unconstrained speech in elections for political office—that representative government depends on the public's ability to choose agents who will act at its behest—does not carry over to campaigns for the bench.

All parties to this case agree that [the] State may constitutionally prohibit judicial candidates from pledging or promising certain results. [This is so because when] a judicial candidate promises to rule a certain way on an issue that may later reach the courts, the potential for due process violations is [grave]. If successful in her bid for office, [the judge] will be under pressure to resist the pleas of litigants who advance positions contrary to her pledges on the campaign trail. [A] judge in this position therefore may be thought to have a "direct, personal, substantial, [and] pecuniary interest" in ruling against certain litigants. [Given] this grave danger to litigants from judicial campaign promises, States are justified in barring expressing of such commitments. . . .

The announce clause [is] equally vital to achieving these compelling ends, for without it, the pledges or promises provision would be feeble. [Uncoupled] from the announce clause, the ban on pledges or promises is easily circumvented. By prefacing a campaign commitment with the caveat, "although I cannot promise anything," [a] candidate could declare with impunity how she would decide specific issues. Semantic sanitizing of the candidate's commitment would not, however, diminish its pernicious effects on actual and perceived judicial impartiality.

Page 1346. Before the Note on Regulating the Activities of Public Employees, add the following:

Note: *The Bipartisan Campaign Finance Reform Act of 2002*

1. *The Supreme Court's Decision*

McCONNELL v. FEDERAL ELECTION COMM'N, 540 U.S. ___ (2003). The Bipartisan Campaign Reform Act of 2002 (BCRA), which amended the Federal Election Campaign Act of 1971 (FECA), sought to address three important developments in the years since *Buckley*: the increased importance of "soft money," the proliferation of "issue ads," and the disturbing findings of a Senate investigation into campaign practices related to the 1996 federal elections.

Prior to BCRA, FECA's contribution limitations extended only to so-called "hard money" contributions made for the purpose of influencing an election for federal office. Political parties and candidates were able to contribute "soft money"—money unregulated under FECA—to support activities intended to influence state or local elections, for mixed-purpose activities such as get-out-the-vote (GOTV) drives and generic party advertising, and for legislative advocacy advertisements, even if they mentioned a federal candidate's name, so long as the ads did not expressly advocate the candidate's election or defeat. Parties and candidates were also free to use soft-money to pay for "issue ads" that advocated positions on substantive issues, as long as they did not expressly endorse or oppose particular candidates. In BCRA, Congress sought to close these soft-money "loopholes" on the premise that they facilitated widespread circumvention of FECA's requirements.

Justices Stevens and O'Connor, joined by Justices Souter, Ginsburg, and Breyer, delivered the opinion of the Court with respect to Titles I and II of BCRA, which dealt with soft money and with corporate and union use of general treasury funds for election-related communication. "The solicitation, transfer, and use of soft money [has] enabled parties and candidates to circumvent FECA's limitations on the source and amount of contributions in connection with federal elections. [In] *Buckley* we construed FECA's [requirements] 'to reach only funds used for communications that expressly advocate the election or defeat of a clearly identified candidate.' As a result of that strict reading of the statute, the use or omission of 'magic words' such as 'Elect John Smith' or 'Vote Against Jane Doe' marked a bright statutory line separating 'express advocacy' from 'issue advocacy.' Express advocacy was subject to FECA's limitations and could be financed only using hard money. [Political parties could] not use soft money to sponsor ads that used any magic words, and corporations and unions could not fund such ads out of their general treasuries. So-called issue ads, on the other hand, not only could be financed with soft money, but could be aired without disclosing the identity of, or any other information about, their sponsors.

"While the distinction between 'issue' and express advocacy seemed neat in theory, the two categories of advertisements proved functionally identical in important respects. [Little] difference existed, for example, between an ad that urged viewers to 'vote against Jane Doe' and one that condemned Jane Doe's record on a particular issue before exhorting viewers to 'call Jane Doe and tell her what you think.' [Corporations] and unions spent hundreds of millions of dollars of their general funds to pay for these ads, and those expenditures, like soft-money donations to the political parties, were unregulated under FECA. [As] with soft-money contributions, political parties and candidates used the availability of so-called issue ads to circumvent FECA's limitations, asking donors who contributed their permitted quota of hard money to give money to nonprofit corporations to spend on 'issue' advocacy.

"In 1998 the Senate Committee on Governmental Affairs issued a six-volume report summarizing the results of an extensive investigation into the campaign practices in the 1996 federal elections. The report gave particular attention to the effect of soft money on the American political system, including elected officials' practice of granting special access in return for political contributions. [The report concluded] that both parties promised and provided special access to candidates and senior Government officials in exchange for large soft-money contributions. . . .

"[BCRA's] central provisions are designed to address Congress' concerns about the increasing use of soft money and issue advertising to influence federal elections. [Title I] is Congress' effort to plug the soft-money loophole. The cornerstone of Title

I [is] § 323(a), which prohibits national party committees and their agents from soliciting, receiving, directing, or spending any soft money. In short, § 323(a) takes national parties out of the soft-money business.

"In *Buckley* and subsequent cases, we [have] recognized that contribution limits, unlike limits on expenditures, 'entai[l] only a marginal restriction upon the contributor's ability to engage in free communication.' [The] less rigorous standard of review we have applied to contribution limits [shows] proper deference to Congress' ability to weigh competing constitutional interests in an area in which it enjoys particular expertise. [Like] the contribution limits we upheld in *Buckley*, § 323's restrictions have only a marginal impact on the ability of contributors, candidates, officeholders, and parties to engage in effective political speech. Complex as its provisions may be, § 323, in the main, does little more than regulate the ability of wealthy individuals, corporations, and unions to contribute large sums of money to influence federal elections, federal candidates, and federal officeholders. . . .

"The core of Title I [is] § 323(a), which provides that 'national committee[s] of a political party . . . may not solicit, receive, or direct to another person a contribution, donation, or transfer of funds or any other thing of value, or spend any funds, that are not subject to the limitations, prohibitions, and reporting requirements of this Act.' [Before the enactment of this provision], national parties were able to use vast amounts of soft money in their efforts to elect federal candidates. Consequently, as long as they directed the money to the political parties, donors could contribute large amounts of soft money for use in activities designed to influence federal elections. New § 323(a) is designed to put a stop to that practice.

"The Government defends § 323(a)'s ban on national parties' involvement with soft money as necessary to prevent the actual and apparent corruption of federal candidates and officeholders. Our cases have made clear that the prevention of corruption or its appearance constitutes a sufficiently important interest to justify political contribution limits. [The] idea that large contributions to a national party can corrupt or, at the very least, create the appearance of corruption of federal candidates and officeholders is neither novel nor implausible. . . .

"The question for present purposes is whether large *soft-money* contributions to national party committees have a corrupting influence or give rise to the appearance of corruption. Both common sense and the ample record in these cases confirm Congress' belief that they do. [The] evidence in the record shows that candidates and donors alike [have] exploited the soft-money loophole, the former to increase their prospects of election and the latter to create debt on the part of officeholders, with the national parties serving as willing intermediaries. . . .

"For their part, lobbyists, CEOs, and wealthy individuals alike all have candidly admitted donating substantial sums of soft money to national committees not on ideological grounds, but for the express purpose of securing influence over federal officials. [Particularly] telling is the fact that, in 1996 and 2000, more than half of the top 50 soft-money donors gave substantial sums to *both* major national parties, leaving room for no other conclusion but that these donors were seeking influence, or avoiding retaliation, rather than promoting any particular ideology. [We] reject the plaintiffs' First Amendment challenge [to] § 323(a).

"In constructing a coherent scheme of campaign finance regulation, Congress recognized that, given the close ties between federal candidates and state party committees, BCRA's restrictions on national committee activity would rapidly become ineffective if state and local committees remained available as a conduit for soft-money donations. Section 323(b) is designed to foreclose wholesale evasion of § 323(a)'s anticorruption measures by sharply curbing state committees' ability to use large soft-money contributions to influence federal elections.

"The core of § 323(b) is a straightforward contribution regulation: It prevents donors from contributing [soft-money] to state and local party committees to help finance 'Federal election activity.' The term 'Federal election activity' encompasses four distinct categories of electioneering: (1) voter registration activity during the 120 days preceding a regularly scheduled federal election; (2) voter identification, get-out-the-vote (GOTV), and generic campaign activity that is 'conducted in connection with an election in which a candidate for Federal office appears on the ballot'; (3) any 'public communication' that 'refers to a clearly identified candidate for Federal office' and 'promotes,' 'supports,' 'attacks,' or 'opposes' a candidate for that office; and (4) the services provided by a state committee employee who dedicates more than 25% of his or her time to 'activities in connection with a Federal election.'...

"[In] addressing the problem of soft-money contributions to state committees, Congress both drew a conclusion and made a prediction. Its conclusion, based on the evidence before it, was that the corrupting influence of soft money does not insinuate itself into the political process solely through national party committees. Rather, state committees function as an alternate avenue for precisely the same corrupting forces. [Congress] also made a prediction. Having been taught the hard lesson of circumvention by the entire history of campaign finance regulation, Congress knew that soft-money donors would react to § 323(a) by scrambling to find another way to purchase influence. [We] 'must accord substantial deference to the predictive judgments of Congress.' [Preventing] corrupting activity from shifting wholesale to state committees and thereby eviscerating FECA clearly qualifies as an important governmental interest. [Because] voter registration, voter identification, GOTV, and generic campaign activity all confer substantial benefits on federal candidates, the funding of such activities creates a significant risk of actual and apparent corruption. Section 323(b) is a reasonable response to that risk."

The Court also upheld other sections of Title I, including § 323(d), which prohibits political parties from soliciting and donating funds to tax-exempt organizations that engage in electioneering activities; § 323(e), which restricts federal candidates and officeholders from receiving, spending, or soliciting soft money in connection with federal elections and limits their ability to do so in connection with state and local elections; and § 323(f), which prohibits state and local candidates from raising and spending soft money to fund advertisements and other public communications that promote or attack federal candidates.

The Court then turned to Title II of BCRA: "The first section of Title II, § 201, [coins] a new term, 'electioneering communication,' to replace the narrowing construction of FECA's [provisions] adopted by this Court in *Buckley*. [The] term 'electioneering communication' [is] defined to encompass any 'broadcast, cable, or satellite communication' that [refers to a clearly identified candidate for Federal office, is made within 60 days before a general election or 30 days before a primary election, and is targeted to the relevant electorate. BCRA specifies] significant disclosure requirements for persons who fund electioneering communications [and] restricts corporations' and labor unions' funding of electioneering communications.

"The major premise of [the] challenge to BCRA's use of the term 'electioneering communication' is that *Buckley* drew a constitutionally mandated line between express advocacy and so-called issue advocacy, and that speakers possess an inviolable First Amendment right to engage in the latter category of speech. [That] position misapprehends our prior decisions, for the express advocacy restriction was an endpoint of statutory interpretation, not [a] principle of constitutional law. [Nor] are we persuaded, independent of our precedents, that the First Amendment erects a rigid barrier between express advocacy and so-called issue advocacy. [Indeed,] the unmistakable lesson from the record in this litigation [is] that *Buckley*'s magic-words requirement is functionally meaningless. Not only can [speakers] easily evade the line by eschewing the use of magic words, but they would seldom choose to use such words even if permitted. And although the resulting advertisements do not urge the viewer to vote for or against a candidate in so many words, they are no less clearly intended to influence the election. *Buckley*'s express advocacy line, in short, has not aided the legislative effort to combat real or apparent corruption, and Congress enacted BCRA to correct the flaws it found in the existing system....

"[Congress'] power to prohibit corporations and unions from using funds in their treasuries to finance advertisements expressly advocating the election or defeat of candidates in federal elections has been firmly embedded in our law. The ability to [form] separate segregated funds [has] provided corporations and unions with a constitutionally sufficient opportunity to engage in express advocacy. [Section 203 extends] this rule [to] all 'electioneering communications.' [Plaintiffs] argue that the justifications that adequately support the regulation of express advocacy do not apply [to] electioneering communications. [This] argument fails [because] corporations and unions may finance genuine issue ads [by] simply avoiding any specific reference to federal candidates, or in doubtful cases by paying for the ad from a segregated fund.

"Plaintiffs also argue that FECA § 316(b)(2)'s segregated-fund requirement for electioneering communications is underinclusive because it does not apply to advertising in the print media or on the Internet. The records developed in this litigation and by the Senate Committee adequately explain the reasons for this legislative choice. Congress found that corporations and unions used soft money to finance a virtual torrent of televised election-related ads during the periods immediately preceding federal elections, and that remedial legislation was needed to stanch that flow of money. As we held in *Buckley,* 'reform may take one step at a time, addressing itself to the phase of the problem which seems most acute to the legislative mind.' . . .

"In addition to arguing that § 316(b)(2)'s segregated-fund requirement is underinclusive, some plaintiffs contend that it unconstitutionally discriminates in favor of media companies. FECA § 304(f)(3)(B)(i) excludes from the definition of electioneering communications any 'communication appearing in a news story, commentary, or editorial distributed through the facilities of any broadcasting station, unless such facilities are owned or controlled by any political party, political committee, or candidate.' Plaintiffs argue this provision gives free rein to media companies to engage in speech without resort to PAC money. Section 304(f)(3)(B)(i)'s effect, however, is much narrower than plaintiffs suggest. The provision excepts news items and commentary only. . . . The statute's narrow exception is wholly consistent with First Amendment principles. 'A valid distinction . . . exists between corporations that are part of the media industry and other corporations that are not involved in the regular business of imparting news to the public.' *Austin.*

"Section 204 of BCRA applies the prohibition on the use of general treasury funds to pay for electioneering communications to not-for-profit corporations [such as the ACLU, the NRA, and NOW]. Prior to the enactment of BCRA, FECA required such corporations, like business corporations, to pay for their express advocacy from segregated funds rather than from their general treasuries. Our recent decision in *Federal Election Comm'n v. Beaumont*, 539 U.S. ___ (2003), confirmed that the requirement was valid, [and the broader BCRA requirement is valid as well]."

Chief Justice Rehnquist delivered the opinion of the Court with respect to § 318 of the BCRA, which prohibited individuals 17 years old or younger from making contributions to candidates or political parties. The Court invalidated this provision: "Minors enjoy the protection of the First Amendment. [The] Government asserts that the provision protects against corruption by conduit; that is, donations by parents through their minor children to circumvent contribution limits applicable to the parents. But the Government offers scant evidence of this form of evasion. [Absent] a more convincing case of the claimed evil, this interest is simply too attenuated for § 318 to withstand heightened scrutiny."

Justice Scalia concurred in part and dissented in part: "This is a sad day for the freedom of speech. Who could have imagined that the same Court which, within the past four years, has sternly disapproved of restrictions upon such inconsequential forms of expression as virtual child pornography, *Ashcroft v. Free Speech Coalition,* tobacco advertising, *Lorillard Tobacco,* [and] sexually explicit cable programming, *Playboy Entertainment,* would smile with favor upon a law that cuts to the heart of

273

what the First Amendment is meant to protect: the right to criticize the government. For that is what the most offensive provisions of this legislation are all about. We are governed by Congress, and this legislation prohibits the criticism of Members of Congress by those entities most capable of giving such criticism loud voice: national political parties and corporations, both of the commercial and the not-for-profit sort. . . .

"To be sure, the legislation is evenhanded: It similarly prohibits criticism of the candidates who oppose Members of Congress in their reelection bids. But as everyone knows, this is an area in which evenhandedness is not fairness. [If] incumbents and challengers are limited to the same quantity of electioneering, incumbents are favored. [Beyond] that, however, the present legislation *targets* for prohibition certain categories of campaign speech that are particularly harmful to incumbents. Is it accidental, do you think, that incumbents raise about three times as much 'hard money'—the sort of funding generally *not* restricted by this legislation—as do their challengers? Or that lobbyists [give] 92 percent of their money in 'hard' contributions? [Is] it mere happenstance [that] national-party funding, which is severely limited by the Act, is more likely to assist cash-strapped challengers than flush-with-hard-money incumbents? . . .

"I wish to address three fallacious propositions that might be thought to justify some or all of the provisions of this legislation—only the last of which is explicitly embraced by the principal opinion for the Court, but all of which underlie [its] approach to these cases. [First, it] was said by congressional proponents of this legislation that since this legislation regulates nothing but the expenditure of money for speech, as opposed to speech itself, the burden it imposes is not subject to full First Amendment scrutiny; the government may regulate the raising and spending of campaign funds just as it regulates other forms of conduct, such as burning draft cards, see *O'Brien,* or camping out on the National Mall, see *Clark.* [But] what good is the right to print books without a right to buy works from authors? Or the right to publish newspapers without the right to pay deliverymen? The right to speak would be largely ineffective if it did not include the right to engage in financial transactions that are the incidents of its exercise. [This] is not to say that *any* regulation of money is a regulation of speech. The government may apply general commercial regulations to those who use money for speech if it applies them evenhandedly to those who use money for other purposes. But where the government singles out money used to fund speech as its legislative object, it is acting against speech as such, no less than if it had targeted the paper on which a book was printed or the trucks that deliver it to the bookstore. . . .

"Another proposition which could explain at least some [of] today's opinion is that the First Amendment [does] not include the right to combine with others in spending money for speech. [But the] freedom to associate with others for the dissemination of ideas—not just by singing or speaking in unison, but by pooling financial resources for expressive purposes—is part of the freedom of speech. [The] constitutional right of association explicated in *NAACP v. Alabama* stemmed from the Court's recognition that '[e]ffective advocacy of both public and private points of view, particularly controversial ones, is undeniably enhanced by group association.'....

"The last proposition that might explain at least some of today's casual abridgment of free-speech rights is this: that the particular form of association known as a corporation does not enjoy full First Amendment protection. The Court [embraced this view in *Austin*.] I dissented in that case, and remain of the view that it was error. In the modern world, giving the government power to exclude [both for-profit and not-for-profit] corporations from the political debate enables it effectively to muffle the voices that best represent the most significant segments of the economy and the most passionately held social and political views....

"But what about the danger to the political system posed by 'amassed wealth'? [The] use of corporate wealth (like individual wealth) to speak to the electorate is unlikely to 'distort' elections—*especially* if disclosure requirements *tell* the people where the speech is coming from. The premise of the First Amendment is that the American people are neither sheep nor fools, and hence fully capable of considering both the substance of the speech presented to them and its proximate and ultimate source. If that premise is wrong, our democracy has a much greater problem to overcome than merely the influence of amassed wealth. Given the premises of democracy, there is no such thing as *too much* speech."

Chief Justice Rehnquist, joined by Justices Scalia and Kennedy, dissented in part: "The issue presented by Title I is not, as the Court implies, whether Congress can [seek] to eliminate corruption in the political process. [Certainly] 'infusions of money into [candidates'] campaigns' can be regulated, but § 323(a) does not regulate only donations given to influence a particular federal election; it regulates *all donations* to national political committees, no matter the use to which the funds are put. [For] sure, national political party committees exist in large part to elect federal candidates, but [they] also promote coordinated political messages and participate in public policy debates unrelated to federal elections. [When] political parties engage in pure political speech that has little or no potential to corrupt their federal candidates and officeholders, the government cannot constitutionally burden their speech any more than it could burden the speech of individuals engaging in these same activities....

"By untethering its inquiry from corruption or the appearance of corruption, the Court has removed the touchstone of our campaign finance precedent and has failed to replace it with any logical limiting principle. [Sections] 323(a), (b), (d), and (f) are vastly overinclusive. [Every] campaign finance law [will] reduce *some* appearance of corruption. [But it] is precisely because broad laws are likely to nominally further a legitimate interest that we require Congress to tailor its restrictions; requiring all federal candidates to self-finance their campaigns would surely reduce the appearance of donor corruption, but it would hardly be constitutional. In allowing Congress to rely on general principles such as 'affecting a federal election' or 'prohibiting the circumvention of existing law,' the Court all but eliminates the 'closely drawn' tailoring requirement and meaningful judicial review."

Justice Kennedy, joined in part by Chief Justice Rehnquist and Justices Scalia and Thomas, filed an opinion concurring in part and dissenting in part: "Today's decision [replaces] respected First Amendment principles with new, amorphous, and unsound rules, rules which dismantle basic protections for speech. [A] few examples show how BCRA reorders speech rights and codifies the Government's own preferences for certain speakers. BCRA would have imposed felony punishment on Ross Perot's 1996 efforts to build the Reform Party. BCRA makes it a felony for an environmental group to broadcast an ad, within 60 days of an election, exhorting the public to protest a Congressman's impending vote to permit logging in national forests. BCRA escalates Congress' discrimination in favor of the speech rights of giant media corporations and against the speech rights of other corporations, both profit and nonprofit.

"To the majority, all this is not only valid under the First Amendment but also is part of Congress' 'steady improvement of the national election laws.' We should make no mistake. It is neither. [It] is an effort by Congress to ensure that civic discourse takes place only through the modes of its choosing. [Our] precedents teach, above all, that Government cannot be trusted to moderate its own rules for suppression of speech. The dangers posed by speech regulations have led the Court to insist upon principled constitutional lines and a rigorous standard of review. The majority now abandons these distinctions and limitations. . . .

"In *Buckley,* the Court held that one, and only one, interest justified the significant burden on the right of association involved there: eliminating, or preventing, actual corruption or the appearance of corruption stemming from contributions to candidates. [*Buckley*] made clear [that] the corruption interest only justifies regulating candidates' and officeholders' receipt of what we can call the '*quids*' in the *quid pro quo* formulation. The Court rested its decision on the principle that campaign finance regulation that restricts speech without requiring proof of particular corrupt action withstands constitutional challenge only if it regulates conduct posing a demonstrable *quid pro quo* danger. . . .

"The Court ignores these constitutional bounds and in effect interprets the anticorruption rationale to allow regulation not just of 'actual or apparent *quid pro quo* arrangements,' but of any conduct that wins goodwill from or influences a Member of Congress. [The] very aim of *Buckley*'s standard [was] to define undue influence by reference to the presence of *quid pro quo* involving the officeholder. The Court, in contrast, concludes that access, without more, proves influence is undue. Access, in the Court's view, has the same legal ramifications as actual or apparent corruption of officeholders. This new definition of corruption sweeps away all protections for speech that lie in its path. . . .

"Access in itself [shows] only that in a general sense an officeholder favors someone or that someone has influence on the officeholder. There is no basis, in law or in fact, to say favoritism or influence in general is the same as corrupt favoritism or influence in particular. By equating vague and generic claims of favoritism or influence with actual or apparent corruption, the Court adopts a definition of corruption that dismantles basic First Amendment rules, permits Congress to suppress speech in the absence of a *quid pro quo* threat, and moves beyond the rationale that is *Buckley*'s very foundation. . . .

"The majority attempts to mask its extension of *Buckley* under claims that BCRA prevents the appearance of corruption, even if it does not prevent actual corruption, since some assert that any donation of money to a political party is suspect. Under *Buckley*'s holding that Congress has a valid 'interest in stemming the reality or appearance of corruption,' however, the inquiry does not turn on whether some persons assert that an appearance of corruption exists. Rather, the inquiry turns on whether the Legislature has established that the regulated conduct has inherent corruption potential, thus justifying the inference that regulating the conduct will stem the appearance of real corruption. *Buckley* was guided and constrained by this analysis. . . .

"The majority [also] permits a new and serious intrusion on speech when it upholds § 203, [which] prohibits corporations and labor unions from using money from their general treasury to fund electioneering communications. The majority compounds the error made in *Austin*, and silences political speech central to the civic discourse that sustains and informs our democratic processes. Unions and corporations, including nonprofit corporations, now face severe criminal penalties for broadcasting advocacy messages that 'refe[r] to a clearly identified candidate' in an election season. . . .

"[The] Government is unwilling to characterize § 203 as a ban, citing the possibility of funding electioneering communications out of a separate segregated fund. This option, though, does not alter the categorical nature of the prohibition. '[T]he corporation *as a corporation* is prohibited from speaking. What the law allows—permitting the corporation 'to serve as the founder and treasurer of a different association of individuals that can endorse or oppose political candidates' — 'is not speech by the corporation.' [Moreover, our] cases recognize the practical difficulties [individuals and corporations] face when they are limited to communicating through PACs. [PACs must appoint a treasurer; ensure the treasurer keeps an account of every contribution; preserve all records for three years; file a statement containing the name of its custodian of records, and its banks or other depositories; and file detailed regular reports with the FEC. PACs may solicit contributions only from their "members," which does not include individuals who have merely contributed to or indicated support for the organization in the past.] These regulations [create] major disincentives for speech, with the effect falling most heavily on smaller entities that often have the most difficulty bearing the costs of compliance. Even worse, for an organization that has not yet set up a PAC, spontaneous speech that 'refers to a clearly identified candidate for Federal office' becomes impossible, even if the group's vital interests are threatened by a piece of legislation pending before Congress on the eve of a federal election. [In short,] PACs are inadequate substitutes."

Justice Thomas, joined in part by Justice Scalia, concurred in part and dissented in part: "[At] root, the *Buckley* Court was concerned that bribery laws could not be effectively enforced [and] it approved the $1,000 contribution ceiling on this ground. [Section 323(a)] is intended to prevent [circumvention of that] contribution ceiling, [and] the remaining provisions [of] § 323 are [intended to prevent] circumvention of § 323(a). [It] is not difficult to see where this leads. Every law has limits, and there will always be behavior [easily] characterized as 'circumventing' the law's prohibition. Hence, speech regulation will again expand to cover new forms of 'circumvention,' only to spur supposed circumvention of the new regulations, and so forth. Rather than permit this never-ending and self-justifying process, I would require that the Government explain why proposed speech restrictions are needed in light of actual Government interests, and, in particular, why the bribery laws are not sufficient. . . .

"The chilling endpoint of the Court's reasoning is not difficult to foresee: outright regulation of the press. None of [the] reasoning employed by the Court exempts the press. [Media] companies can run procandidate editorials as easily as nonmedia corporations can pay for advertisements. Candidates can be just as grateful to media companies as they can be to corporations and unions. In terms of 'the corrosive and distorting effects' of wealth accumulated by corporations, [there] is no distinction between a media corporation and a nonmedia corporation. [What] is to stop a future Congress from determining that the press is 'too influential,' and that the 'appearance of corruption' is significant when media organizations endorse candidates or run 'slanted' or 'biased' news stories in favor of candidates or parties? [The] press now operates at the whim of Congress."

2. *Voting with dollars.* Consider B. Ackerman & I. Ayres, Voting with Dollars 4-8, 156-157 (2002):

[The Bipartisan Campaign Reform Act of 2002 follows] the traditional reform repertoire [by attempting] to limit the amount of private money flowing into campaigns. [This effort] is positively misguided. If reformers ever succeeded in convincing the Court to change its mind [about limitations on campaign expenditures], they would not improve our democracy but degrade it further—making it even easier for incumbents to assure their endless reelection without serious challenge. [We] have something to fear from entrenched politicians as well as entrenched wealth; [reformers] should not be eager to exchange one master for another in the struggle for democracy. . . .

[Instead,] the American citizen should [be] given a more equal say in [campaign] funding decisions. Just as he receives a ballot on election day, he should also receive a special credit card to finance his favorite candidate. [Suppose] that Congress seeded every voter's account with fifty [dollars, which each voter could allocate among the candidates for federal office as he sees fit]. If the 100 million Americans who came to the polls in 2000 [each had fifty such dollars], their combined contributions would have amounted to $5 billion—overwhelming the $3 billion provided by private donors. [This approach] makes campaign finance into a new occasion for citizen sovereignty. . . .

[Additional private contributions should be permitted, but contributors should] be barred from giving money directly to candidates. They [should] instead pass their checks through a blind trust [so candidates] won't be able to identify who provided the funds. [There] are lots of reasons for contributing to campaigns, and this [approach] undercuts only one of them—the desire to obtain a quid pro quo from a victorious candidate. . . .

[This two-pronged approach] promises an effective increase in both political equality *and* political expression.

For a discussion of Ackerman and Ayres' proposal, see Karlan, Elections and Change Under "Voting with Dollars," 91 Cal. L. Rev. 706 (2003) (suggesting some contradictions between first amendment theory and the proposal's reliance on anonymous donation).

Page 1358. At the end of section 4 of the Note, add the following:

Consider the following views of *Dale*:

a. Note, Freedom of Expressive Association—Antidiscrimination Laws, 114 Harv. L. Rev. 259, 263-265 (2000):

First Amendment jurisprudence draws a sharp distinction between direct and indirect burdens on speech. [This distinction] is practically and theoretically unavoidable, in part because its elimination would open the floodgates to First Amendment challenges to the incidental burdens that nearly all laws [impose] on speech. [To] avoid opening the floodgates, [the Court has taken a highly deferential approach to incidental restrictions except] when the effect on expression [is] substantial. . . .

The problem with the [Court's analysis in *Dale* was] its failure to recognize that "merely engag[ing] in expressive activity" cannot be a sound basis for invoking the right of association when the burdened message relates only tangentially to an organization's broader purposes. [BSA's] freedom of association claim [might] have failed as insubstantial had the Court looked to the centrality, rather than to the mere existence, of the organization's anti-homosexual views.

b. Epstein, The Constitutional Perils of Moderation: The Case of the Boy Scouts, 74 S. Cal. L. Rev. 119, 120, 139-140 (2000):

[The] majority reached the right decision [in *Dale*]. But its grounds for decision were too narrow. [The] right outcome in this case should not depend on a delicate balance of what kinds of organizations count as expressive organizations under the First Amendment. Rather, any proper decision must recognize that the state has no interest in counteracting discrimination by private associations that do not possess monopoly power. [All] private associations, regardless of their internal structure and stated purposes, should receive the same freedom afforded the Boy Scouts. . . .

If the reasoning underlying *Dale* is applied correctly, then Title VII is flatly unconstitutional. [The] core illustration of a nonexpressive organization has to be the profit-making corporation that ships goods [and] cares only for its bottom line. But it is sheer fantasy to assume that any successful organization fits this odd caricature of the firm, and is wholly indifferent to how it is perceived in the external world or by its own staff. [A] business firm that refuses to hire workers that have criminal records, or who lack certain religious affiliations, also makes a statement as to how it views itself. [If] the First Amendment applies [so] long as the organization "merely engage[s] in expressive activity that could be impaired," then it follows that every organization engages in expressive activity when it projects itself to its own members and to the rest of the world. [The] short, unhappy truth is that the phrase "expressive association" [cannot] bear the weight that is thrown onto its fragile shoulders.

c. Rubenfeld, The First Amendment's Purpose, 53 Stan. L. Rev. 767, 768-769 (2001):

[The] Boy Scouts claim was a simple one. The Scouts wanted [to] discriminate for expressive reasons. If they could not exclude homosexuals, they would not be able effectively—or as effectively—to express their sincerely held anti-homosexual views. [But] people constantly want to violate laws for expressive reasons. Every person and every organization that wants to discriminate probably has good expressive reasons for doing so. Discrimination is profoundly expressive. It is by far the most effective way most people have of expressing their view of the superiority of their own group and the inferiority of others.

Title VII has "significantly affected" the ability of countless employers to express their views about race or sex. Indeed, it has forced them to "send a message" of equality that many presumably oppose (or would oppose if permitted to do so), in the same way that New Jersey's law forced the Boy Scouts to do so. Should racist and sexist employers be able to come to court with First Amendment challenges to Title VII, demanding that judges accord them the same strict scrutiny that the Boy Scouts received? [Should] a person who can prove that he genuinely holds anti-government views, and that refusing to pay taxes is his most effective or only effective means of communicating these views, be exempt from the income tax?

The answer to all these questions is no, and the reason is that there is no such thing as a free speech immunity based on the claim that someone wants to break an otherwise constitutional law for expressive purposes. [When] a law is otherwise constitutional, and when an actor has not been singled out *because of* his expression, the actor has no free speech claim. The Boy Scouts were not singled out in this way. As a result, the Scouts' claim should have been taken no more seriously than that of a tax protestor or that of a racist employer who demanded an exemption from Title VII on the theory that he wanted to discriminate for expressive, rather than merely commercial, reasons.

d. Sunder, Cultural Dissent, 54 Stan. L. Rev. 495, 498-501, 508, 557 (2001):

[C]ultures now more than ever are characterized by cultural dissent: challenges by individuals within a community to modernize, or broaden, the traditional terms of cultural membership. [For example,] Gay Irish-Americans want to march in a St. Patrick's Day parade [and] Muslim feminists reinterpret the Koran and emphasize women's right [to] equality. [One response to] the rise of internal cultural debates [has] been to turn to law to protect against the dilution of cultural traditions. . . .

In seeking to protect the Boy Scouts' expressive message against dilution, the Court [in *Dale*] ignored internal dissent in the Scouts over homosexuality and treated Boy Scouts culture like a "thing" that is static, homogeneous, bounded, and distinct. [The decision therefore] ends up authorizing the exclusion of cultural dissenters because their speech conflicts with the speech of a cultural association's leaders. [A better approach would] recognize the plurality of meanings within a culture. [Where] law finds substantial disagreement over a culture's norms, law should be wary of uncritically granting [associational] leaders [the right] of private censorship.

e. Johnson, Expressive Association and Organizational Autonomy, 85 Minn. L. Rev. 1639, 1648-49 (2001):

> There is little doubt that different scouts disagree over whether to permit gay men to serve in leadership roles. The problem with accepting this argument, however, is that it would permit dissenting factions to circumvent an organization's established means of effecting internal change. [If] there is insufficient internal support for change, that suggests that those who dissent from the Scouts' official position are just that—dissenters—and courts should be wary of concluding that an organization's leadership does not speak for the organization as a whole. [One] aspect of associational freedom is the freedom to decide who decides. . . .

Page 1364. In section 8 of the Note, after the citation to *Glickman,* add the following:

United States v. United Foods, 533 U.S. 405 (2001) (invalidating a federal statute requiring producers of fresh mushrooms to fund a common advertising program promoting mushroom sales, and distinguishing *Glickman* on the ground that the compelled assessments in *Glickman* were ancillary to a comprehensive regulatory scheme of government-mandated collective action, whereas the compelled assessments in *United Foods* were not part of such a comprehensive scheme, other than a program "to generate the very speech to which some of the producers object").

F. Freedom of the Press

Page 1373. After the first paragraph of section 5 of the Note, add the following:

Is copyright protection consistent with the First Amendment? Consider Netanel, Locating Copyright Within the First Amendment, 54 Stan. L. Rev. 1, 39, 47-49, 81 (2001):

> Copyright is often characterized as a property right. As such, to some, copyright "doesn't sound like censorship, just people enforcing their lawful property rights." To be certain, rights in real property do enjoy at least qualified First Amendment immunity. One cannot generally trespass on privately-owned land in order to speak. But that, in First Amendment terms, is because real property rights are general regulations that impose only isolated and incidental burdens on speech. [Property rights in information or expression, on the other hand,] are

more properly characterized as speech regulations. [Moreover,] even if much slavish copying [is] properly viewed as the mere misappropriation of the economic value of copyrighted expression, [some] copyright regulation may have a chilling effect on speech that is protected under the First Amendment. . . .

[Some] commentators have suggested that copyright is content-based speech regulation [because] "[c]opyright liability turns on the content of what is published." But the fact that copyright law is content-sensitive does not mean that it is "content-based." [Copyright's] purpose is to provide an economic incentive for the creation and dissemination of original expression. Its target is not the viewpoint, subject matter, or even communicative impact [of the speech]. In enacting a copyright law, the government takes no position on the viewpoint or subject matter of restricted expression.

First Amendment challenges to copyright law [should] focus on whether the regulation leaves open "ample alternative channels" for communication of the burdened speech. [Consider], for example, Alan Cranston's translation, with critical commentary, of substantial portions of Hitler's *Mein Kampf*, which [a court in 1939] held to infringe the copyright in the original work. [Cranston] undertook his translation in order to counter the innocuous impression that the heavily edited official English translation had sought to impart. [Cranston] did not absolutely need to publish his own translation in order to covey his message. He might merely have drafted a critical review of the original *Mein Kampf*, [but] his publication of critical review [would have been] significantly less effective. . . .

Page 1373. Before the citation to Volokh and McDonnell in section 5 of the Note, add the following:

Rubenfeld, The Freedom of Imagination: Copyright's Constitutionality, 112 Yale L.J. 1 (2002); R. Tushnet, Copyright as a Model for Free Speech Law, 42 B.C. L. Rev. 1 (2000).

Page 1373. Before section 6 of the Note, add the following:

5a. *Copyright and the First Amendment.* In Eldred v. Ashcroft, 537 U.S. 186 (2003), the Court upheld the 1998 Copyright Term Extension Act, which extended the duration of existing copyrights by an additional twenty years. The Court rejected the argument that the CTEA violated the first amendment because it limited the public's ability to use previously copyrighted material without serving a substantial government purpose:

The Copyright Clause and First Amendment were adopted close in time. This proximity indicates that, in the Framers' view, copyright's limited monopolies are compatible with free speech principles. Indeed, copyright's purpose is to *promote* the creation and publication of free expression. As *Harper & Row* observed: "[T]he Framers intended copyright itself to be the engine of free expression. By establishing a marketable right to the use of one's expression, copyright supplies the economic incentive to create and disseminate ideas."

In addition to spurring the creation and publication of new expression, copyright law contains built-in First Amendment accommodations. First, it distinguishes between ideas and expression and makes only the latter eligible for copyright protection. [As] we said in *Harper & Row*, this "idea/expression dichotomy strike[s] a definitional balance between the First Amendment and the Copyright Act by permitting free communication of facts while still protecting an author's expression." Due to this distinction, every idea, theory, and fact in a copyrighted work becomes instantly available for public exploitation at the moment of publication.

Second, the "fair use" defense allows the public to use not only facts and ideas contained in a copyrighted work, but also expression itself in certain circumstances. [The] defense provides: "[T]he fair use of a copyrighted work, including such use by reproduction in copies . . . , for purposes such as criticism, comment, news reporting, teaching (including multiple copies for classroom use), scholarship, or research, is not an infringement of copyright." The fair use defense affords considerable "latitude for scholarship and comment," and even for parody.

The CTEA itself supplements these traditional First Amendment safeguards. First, it allows libraries, archives, and similar institutions to "reproduce" and "distribute, display, or perform in facsimile or digital form" copies of certain published works "during the last 20 years of any term of copyright . . . for purposes of preservation, scholarship, or research" if the work is not already being exploited commercially and further copies are unavailable at a reasonable price. Second, Title II of the CTEA [exempts] small businesses, restaurants, and like entities from having to pay performance royalties on music played from licensed radio, television, and similar facilities. . . .

. . . The CTEA [protects] authors' original expression from unrestricted exploitation. [The] First Amendment securely protects the freedom to make—or decline to make—one's own speech; it bears less heavily when speakers assert the right to make other people's speeches. To the extent such assertions raise First Amendment concerns, copyright's built-in free speech safeguards are generally adequate to address them. . . .

As we read the Framers' instruction, the Copyright Clause empowers Congress to determine the intellectual property regimes that, overall, in that body's judgment, will serve the ends of the Clause. Beneath the facade of their inventive constitutional interpretation, petitioners forcefully urge that Congress pursued very bad policy in prescribing the CTEA's long terms. The wisdom of Congress' action, however, is not within our province to second guess. . . .

Page 1384. At the very beginning of the Note, add the following:

1a. *Detainees in deportation proceedings relating to the "War on Terrorism."* To what extent, if any, does the press have a right to information about individuals who are being detained by the Immigration and Naturalization Service and/or a right to attend deportation hearings? In New Jersey Media Group, Inc. v. Ashcroft, 205 F. Supp. 2d 288 (D.N.J. 2002), federal district judge John Bissell held unconstitutional an order issued by Chief Immigration Judge Michael Creppy on September 21, 2001, informing all immigration judges that "the Attorney General had implemented additional security procedures for certain cases in Immigration Court." Among these new "security procedures" that the immigration judges were to employ in proceedings involving "special interest" cases were that the hearings were to be closed to the public and the judges were to avoid "disclosing any information about the case to anyone outside the Immigration Court." The order explained further that the determination of which cases would be deemed "special interest" for the purposes of these new "security procedures" would be made by the Attorney General. The plaintiff, an association of New Jersey newspapers, filed this suit to enjoin the continued enforcement of this new policy. The government moved to dismiss the complaint for failure to state a claim. Judge Bissell rejected the government's argument that the judiciary has no jurisdiction over such procedural matters because the political branches have "plenary" authority over matters of immigration.

Judge Bissell then concluded that the principle recognized in *Richmond Newspapers* applied in this context because there has been a long "history of openness in deportation proceedings" and there "is no doubt that deportation hearings inherently involve a governmental process that affects a person's liberty interest and . . . must comport with constitutional guarantees of due process." Thus, Judge Bissell concluded that the government may "inhibit the disclosure of sensitive information in this context" only upon a showing "that denial is necessitated by a compelling governmental interest, and is narrowly tailored to serve that interest." The government asserted two interests in support of its policy of closing access to these proceedings: (1) avoidance of setbacks to the terrorism investigation caused by open hearings, and (2) prevention of stigma or harm to detainees that might result if hearings were open. Judge Bissell held that these interests did not justify the sweeping nature of the closure order. With respect to the first interest, he determined that it could be dealt with by "a more narrow method of in camera disclosure of sensitive evidence" to enable a judicial determination of the necessity for closure. The second interest should be a matter of election for the individual detainee. Judge Bissell therefore held the policy unconstitutional. The United States Court of Appeals for the Third Circuit reversed, in a two-to-one decision. See Ashcroft v. New Jersey Media Group, 308 F. 3d 178 (3d Cir. 2002). See also Detroit Free Press v. Ashcroft, 195 F. Supp. 2d 937 (E.D. Mich. 2002) (reaching the same result as the District Court in *New Jersey Media Group*), aff'd, 303 F. 3d 68 (6th Cir. 2002).

Page 1407. After section 2c of the Note, add the following:

d. Kreimer, Technologies of Protest: Insurgent Social Movements and the First Amendment in the Era of the Internet, 150 U. Penn. L. Rev. 119, 122, 124, 143, 162, 168, 171 (2001):

Given the structure of twentieth-century communications media, established or well-financed contenders in the public arena [had] a built-in advantage: the cost of disseminating arguments or information to a broad audience threatened effectively to exclude outsiders from public debate. [The Internet] has changed this dynamic, for [almost] any social movement can put up a website. [From] neo-Nazism and Christian Identity to gay liberation and disability rights, [the Internet] facilitates challenges to the status quo. . . .

Does this mean the twenty-first century brings nothing but millennial prospects for insurgent social movements? Unfortunately, no. [As] sources of information proliferate, the constant stock of audience attention becomes the object of increased competition, [and] established groups are likely to hold a substantial advantage over insurgents in the production of expensive graphics, the purchase of online and offline advertising, and the paid placement of links on attractive websites. [Moreover, for] an insurgent social movement, transparency is not an unmixed blessing. Precisely the qualities of the Internet which enable insurgents to reach previously unaffiliated constituencies allow opponents to track [insurgent] activities. [A] First Amendment jurisprudence aimed at facilitating the potential of the Internet for "the poorly financed causes of little people" will [attend] both to the scarcity of attention and the vulnerabilities to surveillance which shadow the prospects of online activism.

e. C. Sunstein, republic.com 8-9, 16, 54, 65, 71, 86 (2001):

[A] well-functioning system of free expression must meet two distinctive requirements. First, people should be exposed to materials that they would not have chosen in advance. Unplanned [encounters] are central to democracy [and people should] often come across views and topics that they have not specifically selected. Second, [citizens] should have a range of common experiences. Without shared experiences, [people may] find it hard to understand one another. [There] are serious dangers in a system in which individuals [restrict] themselves to opinions and topics of their own choosing. . . .

The specialization of Websites [and discussion groups] is obviously important here. [For example], there are hundreds of Websites created [by] hate groups and extremist organizations [which] provide links to one another. [Such Websites] are being used [to] reinforce existing convictions. [They are] permitting people [to] spread rumors, many of them paranoid and hateful. [This is an example of group polarization, which] refers to something very simple: After deliberation, people are likely to move toward a more extreme point in the direction to which the group's members were originally inclined. . . .

With respect to the Internet, [the] implication is that groups of like-minded people, engaged in discussion with one another, will end up thinking the same thing that they thought before—but in more extreme form. [Group] polarization is unquestionably occurring on the Internet, [which] is serving as a breeding ground for extremism. [For] citizens of a heterogeneous democracy, a fragmented communications market creates considerable dangers.

Page 1408. At the end of section 3 of the Note, add the following:

Should local community standards apply in deciding whether sexually explicit material posted on the Internet is "obscene"? See Ashcroft v. American Civil Liberties Union, section D4 supra this Supplement.

8
THE CONSTITUTION AND RELIGION

A. Introduction

Page 1418. At the end of section 4 of the Note, add the following:

In Zelman v. Simmons-Harris, 536 U.S. 639 (2002), criticizing the Court's decision upholding a school voucher program that allowed vouchers to be used at religiously affiliated schools, Justice Souter discussed how, in his view, the risk that religion would be corrupted by government aid was "already being realized." He pointed to statutory provisions meaning that "the school may not give admission preferences to children who are members of the patron faith," suggesting that "a participating religious school may [be] forbidden to choose a member of its own clergy to serve as teacher or principal over a layperson of a different religion claiming equal qualification for the job," and suggesting that participating schools might not be allowed to "[teach] traditionally legitimate articles of faith as to the error, sinfulness, or ignorance of others, if they want government money for their schools." What basis is there for a constitutional rule that protects religious institutions from making decisions that judges believe to be contrary to the institutions' long-term interests?

Page 1419. At the end of section 5 of the Note, add the following:

Justice Thomas discussed the federalism interpretation and its relationship to incorporation in his opinion concurring in the judgment in Elk Grove Unified School District v. Newdow, 542 U.S. ___ (2004). He would interpret the Fourteenth Amendment to protect a "liberty interest of being free from coercive state establishments," and observed that such an interpretation might imply that "anything that would violate the incorporated Establishment Clause would actually violate the Free

Exercise Clause, further calling into doubt the utility of incorporating the Establishment Clause."

Page 1421. After the quotation from Widmar v. Vincent, insert the following:

In Zelman v. Simmons-Harris, 536 U.S. 639 (2002), Justice Souter's dissenting opinion argued that "[religious] teaching at taxpayer expense simply cannot be cordoned from taxpayer politics, and every major religion currently espouses social positions that provoke intense opposition. Not all taxpaying Protestant citizens [will] be content to underwrite the teaching of the Roman Catholic Church condemning the death penalty. Nor will all of America's Muslims acquiesce in paying for the endorsement of the religious Zionism taught in many religious Jewish schools, which combines 'a nationalistic sentiment' in support of Israel with a 'deeply religious' element. Nor will every secular taxpayer be content to support Muslim views on differential treatment of the sexes, or, for that matter, to fund the espousal of a wife's obligation of obedience to her husband, presumably taught in any schools adopting the articles of faith of the Southern Baptist Convention. Views like these, and innumerable others, have been safe in the sectarian pulpits and classrooms of this Nation not only because the Free Exercise Clause protects them directly, but because the ban on supporting religious establishment has protected free exercise, by keeping it relatively private. With the arrival of vouchers in religious schools, that privacy will go, and along with it will go confidence that religious disagreement will stay moderate." Consider whether the combination of religious and political pluralism might combine to moderate disagreement, either through compromises that allow each religious institution to receive public assistance while maintaining its own views or through compromises that restrict all religious institutions. (Would the latter compromises violate the Free Exercise or Free Speech Clause?)

B. *The Establishment Clause*

Page 1437. At the end of section 3 of the Note, add the following:

Feldman, The Intellectual Origins of the Establishment Clause, 77 N.Y.U. L. Rev. 346, 351, 424 (2002), argues that "[liberty] of conscience [was] the central value invoked by the states that proposed constitutional amendments on the question of religion, and the purpose that underlay the Establishment Clause when it was enacted," and that "the Constitution never suggested that individual liberty of conscience should be protected from government actions that on their face have nothing to do with religion. [It] protects liberty of conscience [only] in the sphere of government action that relates *specifically to religion*." What does the establishment clause understood in this way add to the free exercise and free speech clauses?

Page 1437. At the end of section 4 of the Note, add the following:

Does the distinction between permissible private speech and arguably impermissible government speech make sense in the contexts of *Lee* and *Santa Fe*? Consider the suggestion in Brady, The Push to Private Religious Expression: Are We Missing Something?, 70 Fordham L. Rev. 1147, 1199 (2002), that "the most promising approach is for students of all perspectives to 'opt in' to the educational process by voicing and defending differing views" in these contexts. Would school authorities have to develop guidelines setting out the limits beyond which student speech could not go in these contexts? If so, would those guidelines convert private into government speech? Would school authorities be barred from developing such guidelines by free speech principles?

Page 1446. At the end of section 2 of the Note, add the following:

Consider the argument in Feldman, From Liberty to Equality: The Transformation of the Establishment Clause, 90 Calif. L. Rev. 673, 677, 718 (2002), that the non-endorsement principle rests on a mistaken reduction of the establishment clause to a principle of equality: "Religious minorities are not uniquely vulnerable to political inequality, and religious discrimination in the United States has not been noticeably worse than discrimination on the basis of political ideology, immigrant status, or language. [The] political-equality approach [cannot] provide a compelling answer to the question 'what is special about religion?'" [The] harms associated with [exclusion] are no worse than the harms associated with other sorts of second-class citizenship and identity."

Page 1466. Before *Note: Purpose and Effect in Aid to Nonpublic Education — Benevolent Neutrality*, add the following:

ZELMAN v. SIMMONS-HARRIS, 536 U.S. 639 (2002). In an opinion by Chief Justice Rehnquist, the Court upheld a school voucher program with the following characteristics, as described in the syllabus to the Court's opinion. The program "gives educational choices to families in any Ohio school district that is under state control pursuant to a federal court order. The program provides tuition aid for certain students in the Cleveland City School District, the only covered district, to attend participating public or private schools of their parent's choosing and tutorial aid for students who choose to remain enrolled in public school. Both religious and nonreligious schools in the district may participate, as may public schools in adjacent school districts. Tuition aid is distributed to parents according to financial need, and where the aid is spent depends solely upon where parents choose to enroll their children. The number of tutorial assistance grants provided to students remaining in public school must equal the number of tuition aid scholarships. In the 1999-2000 school year, 82% of the participating private schools had a religious affiliation, none of the adjacent public schools participated, and 96% of the students participating in the scholarship program were enrolled in religiously affiliated schools. [Cleveland] schoolchildren also have the option of enrolling in community schools, which are funded under state law but run by their own school boards and receive twice the per-student funding as participating private schools, or magnet schools, which are public schools emphasizing a particular subject area, teaching method, or service, and for which the school district receives the same amount per student as it does for a student enrolled at a traditional public school."

Finding "no dispute that the program [was] enacted for the valid secular purpose of providing educational assistance to poor children in a demonstrably failing public school system, "the Court said that "[the] question presented is whether the Ohio program [has] the forbidden 'effect' of advancing or inhibiting religion." Relying on *Mueller*, *Witters*, and *Zobrest*, it concluded that it did not have such an effect. Those cases, the Court said, "make clear that where a government aid program is neutral with respect to religion, and provides assistance directly to a broad class of citizens who, in turn, direct government aid to religious schools wholly as a result of their own genuine and independent private choice, the program is not readily subject to challenge under the Establishment Clause. A program that shares these features permits government aid to reach religious institutions only by way of the deliberate choices of numerous individual recipients. The incidental advancement of a religious mission, or the perceived endorsement of a religious message, is reasonably attributable to the individual recipient, not to the government, whose role ends with the disbursement of benefits."

It continued, "[the] Ohio program is neutral in all respects toward religion. It is part of a general and multifaceted undertaking by the State of Ohio to provide educational opportunities to the children of a failed school district. It confers educational assistance directly to a broad class of individuals defined without reference to religion, *i.e.*, any parent of a school-age child who resides in the Cleveland City School District. The program permits the participation of *all* schools within the district, religious or nonreligious. Adjacent public schools also may participate and have a financial incentive to do so. Program benefits are available to participating families on neutral terms, with no reference to religion. The only preference stated anywhere in the program is a preference for low-income families, who receive greater assistance and are given priority for admission at participating schools.

"There are no 'financial incentives' that 'skew' the program toward religious schools. [*Witters*]. Such incentives '[are] not present . . . where the aid is allocated on the basis of neutral, secular criteria that neither favor nor disfavor religion, and is made available to both religious and secular beneficiaries on a nondiscriminatory basis.' [*Agostini*]. The program here in fact creates financial *dis*incentives for religious schools, with private schools receiving only half the government assistance given to community schools and one-third the assistance given to magnet schools. Adjacent public schools, should any choose to accept program students, are also eligible to receive two to three times the state funding of a private religious school. Families too have a financial disincentive to choose a private religious school over other schools. Parents that choose to participate in the scholarship program and then to enroll their children in a private school (religious or nonreligious) must copay a portion of the school's tuition. Families that choose a community school, magnet school, or traditional public school pay nothing. Although such features of the program are not necessary to its constitutionality, they clearly dispel the claim that the program 'creates . . . financial incentives for parents to choose a sectarian school.' [*Zobrest*]."

On whether the program gave "genuine opportunities for Cleveland parents to select secular educational options for their school-age children," the Court argued that "Cleveland schoolchildren enjoy a range of educational choices: They may remain in public school as before, remain in public school with publicly funded tutoring aid, obtain a scholarship and choose a religious school, obtain a scholarship and choose a nonreligious private school, enroll in a community school, or enroll in a magnet school. That 46 of the 56 private schools now participating in the program are religious schools does not condemn it as a violation of the Establishment Clause. The Establishment Clause question is whether Ohio is coercing parents into sending their children to religious schools, and that question must be answered by evaluating *all* options Ohio provides Cleveland schoolchildren, only one of which is to obtain a program scholarship and then choose a religious school."

Relying on *Mueller*, the Court rejected the argument that "we should attach constitutional significance to the fact that 96% of scholarship recipients have enrolled in religious schools. They claim that this alone proves parents lack genuine choice, even if no parent has ever said so. We need not consider this argument in detail, since it was flatly rejected in *Mueller*, where we found it irrelevant that 96% of parents taking deductions for tuition expenses paid tuition at religious schools." Explaining why it rejected the argument, the Court pointed out that "[the] 96% figure [discounts] entirely (1) the more than 1,900 Cleveland children enrolled in alternative community schools, (2) the more than 13,000 children enrolled in alternative magnet schools, and (3) the more than 1,400 children enrolled in traditional public schools with tutorial assistance. Including some or all of these children in the denominator of children enrolled in nontraditional schools during the 1999-2000 school year drops the percentage enrolled in religious schools from 96% to under 20%. The 96% figure also represents but a snapshot of one particular school year. In the 1997-1998 school year, by contrast, only 78% of scholarship recipients attended religious schools."

Justices O'Connor and Thomas wrote concurring opinions. Justices Stevens, Souter, Ginsburg, and Breyer dissented. Justice Souter's dissent asserted that "the espoused criteria of neutrality in offering aid, and private choice in directing it, [are] nothing but examples of verbal formalism." To apply the neutrality test, he argued, "it makes sense to focus on a category of aid that may be directed to religious as well as secular schools, and ask whether the scheme favors a religious direction. Here, one would ask whether the voucher provisions [were] written in a way that skewed the scheme toward benefiting religious schools. [The] majority looks not to the provisions for tuition vouchers, but to every provision for educational [opportunity]. The majority then finds confirmation that 'participation of *all* schools' satisfies neutrality by noting that the better part of total state educational expenditure goes to public schools, thus showing there is no favor of religion. The illogic is patent. If regular, public schools (which can get no voucher payments) 'participate' in a voucher scheme with schools that can, and public expenditure is still predominantly on public schools, then the majority's reasoning would find neutrality in a scheme of vouchers available for private tuition in districts with no secular private schools at all. 'Neutrality' as the majority employs the term is, literally, verbal and nothing more." Justice Souter also criticized the Court for what he described as its abandonment of the previously enforced limitation on provision of "substantial" aid to religious institutions.

Page 1466. Replace section 1 of the Note with the following:

1. *Vouchers*. What, if any, limits does the Establishment Clause place on voucher programs? What are the criteria for determining whether a program allows participants to exercise "genuine choice" among secular and religious options? Justice O'Connor's concurring opinion in *Zelman* argued that choice should be determined by "consider[ing] all reasonable educational alternatives to religious schools that are available to parents," and pointed out that "[when] one considers the option to attend community schools, the percentage of students enrolled in religious schools falls to 62.1 percent. If magnet schools are included, [this] percentage falls to 16.5 percent."

Justice Souter's dissent criticized this focus as "confused" because it "ignores the reason for having a private choice criterion in the first place. [It] is a criterion for deciding whether indirect aid to a religious school is legitimate because it passes through private hands that can spend or use the aid in a secular school. The question is whether the private hand is genuinely free to send the money in either a secular direction or a religious one. The majority now has transformed this question [into] a question about selecting from examples of state spending (on education) including direct spending on magnet and community public schools that goes through no private hands and could never reach a religious school under any circumstance. When the choice test is transformed from where to spend the money to where to go to school, it is cut loose from its very purpose." He concluded, "If 'choice' is present whenever there is any educational alternative to the religious school to which vouchers can be endorsed, then there will always be a choice and the voucher can always be constitutional, even in a system in which there is not a single private secular school as an alternative to the religious school."

For an analysis of the fiscal and political limits on voucher programs, see Ryan & Heise, The Political Economy of School Choice, 111 Yale L.J. 2043 (2002).

1a. *Locke v. Davey.* Locke v. Davey, 540 U.S. ___ (2004), upheld against a Free Exercise challenge a Washington State program that awarded merit scholarships to college students, but excluded students pursuing degrees in "devotional theology." Chief Justice Rehnquist noted that the religion clauses allowed some "play in the joints," and that the Washington program involved that consideration. "[We] can think of few areas in which a State's antiestablishment interests come more into play.... Given the historic and substantial state interest at issue, we [cannot] conclude that the denial of funding for vocational religious instruction alone is inherently constitutionally suspect." Justice Scalia, joined by Justice Thomas, dissented, arguing that "[when] the State makes a public benefit generally available, that benefit becomes part of the baselines against which burdens on religion are measured; and when the State withholds that benefit from some individuals solely on the basis of religion, it violates the Free Exercise Clause no less than if it had imposed a special tax." Here, "[no] field of study but religion is singled out for disfavor. [The student] seeks only *equal* treatment." The majority responded: "[Training] for religious professions and training for secular professions are not fungible. [The] subject of religion is one in which [the Constitution] embod[ies] distinct views [that] find no counterpart with respect to other callings or professions."

What implications does *Locke* have for voucher programs that *exclude* religious schools from participation? The Court observed that the Washington program "goes a long way toward including religion in its benefits, allowing scholarships to be used at accredited "pervasively" religious schools, and allowing scholarship recipients to *take* devotional theology classes. Justice Scalia's dissent described this point as identifying "the lightness of" the burden the exclusion placed on students.

1b. *Further questions about vouchers.* The Court in *Locke* rejected in a footnote the argument that the exclusion was an unconstitutional viewpoint restriction, saying that the scholarship program "is not a forum for speech." Its "purpose [is] to assist

295

students [with the cost of postsecondary education, not to 'encourage a diversity of views from private speakers.'"

Many proposed voucher programs bar the use of vouchers at schools that discriminate in admissions or employment on the basis of race, gender, religion, or sexual orientation, or at schools that do not offer particular subjects. As applied to schools that discriminate because of religious belief (for example, the belief that women with children should not be employed outside the home) or refuse to teach some subject (for example, evolutionary theory) because of religious belief, are such provisions violations of the First Amendment right of expressive association, or the Free Exercise Clause? For discussions, see Tushnet, Vouchers After *Zelman*, 2002 Supreme Court Rev. 1; Berg, Vouchers and Religious Schools: The New Constitutional Questions, 72 U. Cin. L. Rev. 151 (2003).

Page 1468. After section 6 of the Note, add the following:

7. *Neutrality, steering, and "real choice."* What considerations are relevant in determining whether a neutral program offers participants a real choice or steers them towards religious institutions? Lupu & Tuttle, Sites of Redemption: A Wide Angle Look at Government Vouchers and Sectarian Service Providers, 18 J. L. & Politics 537, 561, 565 (2002), suggest the following considerations: the extent to which participants are constrained in choosing the religious provider rather than not participating in the program at all; the extent to which there are nonreligious institutions providing the services and able to accept the vouchers; the ease with which new providers can start up, making the market more or less dynamic in response to demand; and the degree to which the government's purpose is connected to a character change itself tied to religious transformation. How might these factors bear on voucher programs for the provision of child care services? For the provision of drug treatment programs offered as alternatives to incarceration?

Page 1469. Before Section C, add the following:

Lupu, Government Messages and Government Money: *Santa Fe, Mitchell v. Helms,* and the Arc of the Establishment Clause, 42 Wm. & Mary L. Rev. 771, 801 (2001), argues that

> [i]ssues involving government resources in support of religion quite frequently [are] truly about "church." [When] the state provides resources to such entities, it typically does so on the theory that churches may effectively assist in the state's

secular work. [Government] message cases [are] very different in their character: [They] involve officials of the state doing the work of faith institutions—that is, preaching, proselytizing, [and] generally spreading the Word or respect for the Word. [Government] message cases are not about institutional connection between agencies of government and agencies of faith. [They are] about the political misappropriation of religious themes.

Does the distinction between money and message cases account for differences in the outcomes of the cases you have studied?

Page 1484. At the end of section 2(a) of the Note, add the following:

Consider Brownstein, Protecting Religious Liberty: The False Messiahs of Free Speech Doctrine and Formal Neutrality, 18 J. L. & Politics 119, 191-92 (2002): Under the individualized determination exception, "religion is granted something like most favored nation status. If any secular interest can justify an exemption from a law, then the state must recognize that religious interests also deserve to be exempt from the law. [But an] extraordinary range of laws contain exemptions to their application, including most civil rights laws [and] even homicide statutes. [This] militates against such an understanding." See also Duncan, Free Exercise is Dead, Long Live Free Exercise: *Smith, Lukumi,* and the General Applicability Requirement, 3 U. Pa. J. Const. L. 850, 868 (2001): "[A] law burdening religious conduct is underinclusive, with respect to any particular government interest, if the law fails to pursue that interest uniformly against other conduct that causes similar damage to that government interest." Does this meet Brownstein's concerns?

Page 1485. At the end of section 2(b) of the Note, add the following:

Consider Brownstein, Protecting Religious Liberty: The False Messiahs of Free Speech Doctrine and Formal Neutrality, 18 J. L. & Politics 119, 191-92 (2002): "A hybrid rights situation involves a neutral law of general applicability that substantially burdens the exercise of religion and sufficiently burdens some other constitutionally protected interested to invoke the application of the requisite standard of review [short] of strict scrutiny." Brownstein argues that this idea is coherent but inconsistent with "basic constitutional intuitions." He uses the example of an informed-consent requirement for abortion: If the requirement is "applied to a woman seeking an abortion for secular reasons, the regulation is reviewed under the undue burden standard and is upheld. If the woman is seeking an abortion for religious reasons, this application of the law will be reviewed under strict scrutiny and invalidated." Brownstein says that this is an "odd conclusion" because "it justifies treating people differently with regard to their exercise of fundamental rights. Hybrid rights analysis suggests that religious people should be treated preferentially with regard to the exercise of fundamental rights when their religious beliefs influence the way they exercise their rights. [That] cannot be right. There is an equality dimension to liberty rights. [Religious] people do not get special treatment with respect to these basic freedoms. No one does."

D. Permissible Accommodation

Page 1497. At the conclusion of the first paragraph of section 1 of the Note, add the following:

The Court followed *Lamb's Chapel* in Good News Club v. Milford Central School, 533 U.S. 98 (2001), which involved a club that would conduct prayer meetings and Bible lessons after school hours in a room at a school attended by children from kindergarten through the twelfth grade. Again finding that excluding the club would amount to viewpoint discrimination, the Court concluded that parents, who had to give permission for their children to attend the club's meetings, would not be coerced into participating or "confused about whether the school was endorsing religion." Nor did the evidence support the claim that students not attending the club's meetings would perceive endorsement. Indeed, "we cannot say the danger that children would misperceive the endorsement of religion is any greater than the danger that they would perceive a hostility toward religious viewpoint if the Club were excluded from the public forum. [We] decline to employ Establishment Clause jurisprudence using a modified heckler's veto, in which a group's religious activity can be proscribed on the basis of what the youngest members of the audience might misperceive."

Page 1500. After the first paragraph of the Note, add the following:

Sullivan, The New Religion and the Constitution, 116 Harv. L. Rev. 1397 (2003), develops a taxonomy of ways of understanding the relation between religious associations and government. "(1) Religion as Quasi-Government: Here religious associations are seen "as unique in their power to interpret the world and express shared understandings," and "exert a quasi-sovereign authority over their members." Sullivan argues that this view "favors weak judicial enforcement of the Free Exercise Clause and strong judicial enforcement of the Establishment Clause. If religion poses the danger of quasi-sovereign competition with government, then judges [should] not afford religious groups special exemptions from general laws [nor] should they permit public subsidies to flow to religious activities." (2) "Religion as Private Expressive Association": Here religious associations are "on a continuum with other forms of private expressive association," but "with the twist that government is uniquely disabled [from] speaking in a religious voice." This view calls for "strong enforcement" of both religion clauses. "[Courts] would review strictly both government refusals to exempt religious associations from general laws that inhibit their collective expressive practices, and government inclusion of religious organizations within the scope of public subsidies." (3) "Religion as Discrete and Insular Minority": Here religion associations "are entitled not only to protection from unequal treatment, but also to preferential treatment in order to offset historical and structural disadvantages. [The] judicial prescription that follows [consists] of strong enforcement of the Free Exercise Clause but weak enforcement of the Establishment Clause." (4) "Religion as Ordinary Interest Group": Here religious associations "are best conceived as ordinary interest groups that may participate freely in politics but should expect no particular judicial solicitude from courts interpreting either of the Religion Clauses." Descriptively, which position do today's justices take? Prescriptively, on what basis should a judge choose among these approaches?

9
THE CONSTITUTION, BASELINES, AND THE PROBLEM OF PRIVATE POWER

C. Constitutionally Impermissible Departures from Neutrality: State Subsidization, Approval, and Encouragement

Page 1544. Before Section D, add the following:

BRENTWOOD ACADEMY v. TENNESSEE SECONDARY SCHOOL ATHLETIC ASSOCIATION
531 U.S. 288 (2001)

JUSTICE SOUTER delivered the opinion of the Court.

The issue is whether a statewide association incorporated to regulate interscholastic athletic competition among public and private secondary schools may be regarded as engaging in state action when it enforces a rule against a member school. The association in question here includes most public schools located within the State, acts through their representatives, draws its officers from them, is largely funded by their dues and income received in their stead, and has historically been seen to regulate in lieu of the State Board of Education's exercise of its own authority. We hold that the association's regulatory activity may and should be treated as state action owing to the pervasive entwinement of state school officials in the structure of the association, there being no offsetting reason to see the association's acts in any other way.

I

Respondent Tennessee Secondary School Athletic Association (Association) is a not-for-profit membership corporation organized to regulate interscholastic sport among the public and private high schools in Tennessee that belong to it. No school is forced to join, but without any other authority actually regulating interscholastic athletics, it enjoys the memberships of almost all the State's public high schools (some 290 of them or 84% of the Association's voting membership), far outnumbering the 55 private schools that belong. A member school's team may play or scrimmage only against the team of another member, absent a dispensation.

The Association's rulemaking arm is its legislative council, while its board of control tends to administration. The voting membership of each of these nine-person committees is limited under the Association's bylaws to high school principals, assistant principals, and superintendents elected by the member schools, and the public school administrators who so serve typically attend meetings during regular school hours. Although the Association's staff members are not paid by the State, they are eligible to join the State's public retirement system for its employees. Member schools pay dues to the Association, though the bulk of its revenue is gate receipts at member teams' football and basketball tournaments, many of them held in public arenas rented by the Association.

The constitution, bylaws, and rules of the Association set standards of school membership and the eligibility of students to play in interscholastic games. Each school, for example, is regulated in awarding financial aid, most coaches must have a Tennessee state teaching license, and players must meet minimum academic standards and hew to limits on student employment. Under the bylaws, "in all matters pertaining to the athletic relations of his school," the principal is responsible to the Association, which has the power "to suspend, to fine, or otherwise penalize any member school for the violation of any of the rules of the Association or for other just cause."

Ever since the Association was incorporated in 1925, Tennessee's State Board of Education (State Board) has (to use its own words) acknowledged the corporation's functions "in providing standards, rules and regulations for interscholastic competition in the public schools of Tennessee." More recently, the State Board cited its statutory authority, Tenn. Code Ann. § 49-1-302 (App. 220), when it adopted language expressing the relationship between the Association and the Board. Specifically, in 1972, it went so far as to adopt a rule expressly "designat[ing]" the Association as "the organization to supervise and regulate the athletic activities in which the public junior and senior high schools in Tennessee participate on an interscholastic basis." [That] same year, the State Board specifically approved the Association's rules and regulations, while reserving the right to review future changes. Thus, on several occasions over the next 20 years, the State Board reviewed, approved, or reaffirmed its approval of the recruiting Rule at issue in this case. In 1996, however, the State Board dropped the original Rule expressly designating the Association as regulator; it substituted a statement "recogniz[ing] the value of participation in interscholastic athletics and the role of [the Association] in coordinating interscholastic athletic competition," while "authoriz[ing] the public schools of the state to voluntarily maintain membership in [the Association]."

The action before us responds to a 1997 regulatory enforcement proceeding brought against petitioner, Brentwood Academy, a private parochial high school member of the Association. The Association's board of control found that Brentwood violated a rule prohibiting "undue influence" in recruiting athletes, when it wrote to incoming students and their parents about spring football practice. The Association accordingly placed Brentwood's athletic program on probation for four years, declared its football and boys' basketball teams ineligible to compete in playoffs for two years, and imposed a $3,000 fine. When these penalties were imposed, all the voting members of the board of control and legislative council were public school administrators.

Brentwood sued the Association and its executive director in federal court under Rev. Stat. § 1979, 42 U.S.C. § 1983 claiming that enforcement of the Rule was state action and a violation of the First and Fourteenth Amendments. . . .

II

A

Our cases try to plot a line between state action subject to Fourteenth Amendment scrutiny and private conduct (however exceptionable) that is not. [*Tarkanian; Jackson.*] The judicial obligation is not only to "'preserv[e] an area of individual freedom by limiting the reach of federal law' and avoi[d] the imposition of responsibility on a State for conduct it could not control" [*Tarkanian* (quoting *Lugar*)], but also to assure that constitutional standards are invoked "when it can be said that the State is responsible for the specific conduct of which the plaintiff complains" [*Blum*]. If the Fourteenth Amendment is not to be displaced, therefore, its ambit cannot be a simple line between States and people operating outside formally governmental organizations, and the deed of an ostensibly private organization or individual is to be treated sometimes as if a State had caused it to be performed. Thus, we say that state action may be found if, though only if, there is such a "close nexus between the State and the challenged action" that seemingly private behavior "may be fairly treated as that of the State itself."

What is fairly attributable is a matter of normative judgment, and the criteria lack rigid simplicity. From the range of circumstances that could point toward the State behind an individual face, no one fact can function as a necessary condition across the board for finding state action; nor is any set of circumstances absolutely sufficient, for there may be some countervailing reason against attributing activity to the government.

Page 1544   The Constitution, Baselines, and the Problem of Private Power

Our cases have identified a host of facts that can bear on the fairness of such an attribution. We have, for example, held that a challenged activity may be state action when it results from the State's exercise of "coercive power" [*Blum*], when the State provides "significant encouragement, either overt or covert," ibid., or when a private actor operates as a "willful participant in joint activity with the State or its agents" [*Lugar* (internal quotation marks omitted)]. We have treated a nominally private entity as a state actor when it is controlled by an "agency of the State," Pennsylvania v. Board of Directors of City Trusts of Philadelphia, 353 U.S. 230, 231 (1957) (per curiam), when it has been delegated a public function by the State, cf., e.g., [West v. Atkins]; Edmonson v. Leesville Concrete Co., 500 U.S. 614, 627-628 (1991), when it is "entwined with governmental policies" or when government is "entwined in [its] management or control," Evans v. Newton, 382 U.S. 296, 299, 301 (1966).

Amidst such variety, examples may be the best teachers, and examples from our cases are unequivocal in showing that the character of a legal entity is determined neither by its expressly private characterization in statutory law, nor by the failure of the law to acknowledge the entity's inseparability from recognized government officials or agencies. Lebron v. National Railroad Passenger Corporation, 513 U.S. 374 (1995), held that Amtrak was the Government for constitutional purposes, regardless of its congressional designation as private; it was organized under federal law to attain governmental objectives and was directed and controlled by federal appointees. Pennsylvania v. Board of Directors of City Trusts of Philadelphia held the privately endowed Gerard College to be a state actor and enforcement of its private founder's limitation of admission to whites attributable to the State, because, consistent with the terms of the settlor's gift, the college's board of directors was a state agency established by state law. Ostensibly the converse situation occurred in Evans v. Newton, which held that private trustees to whom a city had transferred a park were nonetheless state actors barred from enforcing racial segregation, since the park served the public purpose of providing community recreation, and "the municipality remain[ed] entwined in [its] management [and] control."

These examples of public entwinement in the management and control of ostensibly separate trusts or corporations foreshadow this case, as this Court itself anticipated in *Tarkanian*. *Tarkanian* arose when an undoubtedly state actor, the University of Nevada, suspended its basketball coach, Tarkanian, in order to comply with rules and recommendations of the National Collegiate Athletic Association (NCAA). The coach charged the NCAA with state action, arguing that the state university had delegated its own functions to the NCAA, clothing the latter with authority to make and apply the university's rules, the result being joint action making the NCAA a state actor.

To be sure, it is not the strict holding in *Tarkanian* that points to our view of this case, for we found no state action on the part of the NCAA. We could see, on the one hand, that the university had some part in setting the NCAA's rules, and the Supreme Court of Nevada had gone so far as to hold that the NCAA had been delegated the

304

university's traditionally exclusive public authority over personnel. But on the other side, the NCAA's policies were shaped not by the University of Nevada alone, but by several hundred member institutions, most of them having no connection with Nevada, and exhibiting no color of Nevada law. Since it was difficult to see the NCAA, not as a collective membership, but as surrogate for the one State, we held the organization's connection with Nevada too insubstantial to ground a state action claim.

But dictum in *Tarkanian* pointed to a contrary result on facts like ours, with an organization whose member public schools are all within a single State. "The situation would, of course, be different if the [Association's] membership consisted entirely of institutions located within the same State, many of them public institutions created by the same sovereign." To support our surmise, we approvingly cited two cases: Clark v. Arizona Interscholastic Assn., 695 F.2d 1126 (CA9 1982), cert. denied, 464 U.S. 818 (1983), a challenge to a state high school athletic association that kept boys from playing on girls' interscholastic volleyball teams in Arizona; and Louisiana High School Athletic Assn. v. St. Augustine High School, 396 F.2d 224 (CA5 1968), a parochial school's attack on the racially segregated system of interscholastic high school athletics maintained by the athletic association. In each instance, the Court of Appeals treated the athletic association as a state actor.

B

Just as we foresaw in *Tarkanian*, the "necessarily fact-bound inquiry" [*Lugar*], leads to the conclusion of state action here. The nominally private character of the Association is overborne by the pervasive entwinement of public institutions and public officials in its composition and workings, and there is no substantial reason to claim unfairness in applying constitutional standards to it.

The Association is not an organization of natural persons acting on their own, but of schools, and of public schools to the extent of 84% of the total. Under the Association's bylaws, each member school is represented by its principal or a faculty member, who has a vote in selecting members of the governing legislative council and board of control from eligible principals, assistant principals and superintendents.

Although the findings and prior opinions in this case include no express conclusion of law that public school officials act within the scope of their duties when they represent their institutions, no other view would be rational, the official nature of their involvement being shown in any number of ways. Interscholastic athletics obviously play an integral part in the public education of Tennessee, where nearly every public high school spends money on competitions among schools. Since a pickup system of interscholastic games would not do, these public teams need some mechanism to produce rules and regulate competition. The mechanism is an organization overwhelmingly composed of public school officials who select representatives (all of them public officials at the time in question here), who in turn adopt and enforce the rules that make the system work. Thus, by giving these jobs to the Association, the 290 public schools of Tennessee belonging to it can sensibly be seen as exercising their own authority to meet their own responsibilities. Unsurprisingly, then, the record indicates that half the council or board meetings documented here were held during official school hours, and that public schools have largely provided for the Association's financial support. A small portion of the Association's revenue comes from membership dues paid by the schools, and the principal part from gate receipts at tournaments among the member schools. Unlike mere public buyers of contract services, whose payments for services rendered do not convert the service providers into public actors, see [*Rendell-Baker*], the schools here obtain membership in the service organization and give up sources of their own income to their collective association. The Association thus exercises the authority of the predominantly public schools to charge for admission to their games; the Association does not receive this money from the schools, but enjoys the schools' moneymaking capacity as its own.

In sum, to the extent of 84% of its membership, the Association is an organization of public schools represented by their officials acting in their official capacity to provide an integral element of secondary public schooling. There would be no recognizable Association, legal or tangible, without the public school officials, who do not merely control but overwhelmingly perform all but the purely ministerial acts by which the Association exists and functions in practical terms. Only the 16% minority of private school memberships prevents this entwinement of the Association and the public school system from being total and their identities totally indistinguishable.

To complement the entwinement of public school officials with the Association from the bottom up, the State of Tennessee has provided for entwinement from top down. State Board members are assigned ex officio to serve as members of the board of control and legislative council, and the Association's ministerial employees are treated as state employees to the extent of being eligible for membership in the state retirement system.

It is, of course, true that the time is long past when the close relationship between the surrogate association and its public members and public officials acting as such was attested frankly. [But] the removal of the designation language from Rule 0520-1-2-.08 affected nothing but words. Today the State Board's member-designees continue to sit on the Association's committees as nonvoting members, and the State continues to welcome Association employees in its retirement scheme. The close relationship is confirmed by the Association's enforcement of the same preamendment rules and regulations reviewed and approved by the State Board (including the recruiting Rule challenged by Brentwood), and by the State Board's continued willingness to allow students to satisfy its physical education requirement by taking part in interscholastic athletics sponsored by the Association. The most one can say on the evidence is that the State Board once freely acknowledged the Association's official character but now does it by winks and nods.

[The] entwinement down from the State Board is therefore unmistakable, just as the entwinement up from the member public schools is overwhelming. Entwinement will support a conclusion that an ostensibly private organization ought to be charged with a public character and judged by constitutional standards; entwinement to the degree shown here requires it.

C

Entwinement is also the answer to the Association's several arguments offered to persuade us that the facts would not support a finding of state action under various criteria applied in other cases. These arguments are beside the point, simply because the facts justify a conclusion of state action under the criterion of entwinement, a conclusion in no sense unsettled merely because other criteria of state action may not be satisfied by the same facts.

The Association places great stress, for example, on the application of a public function test, as exemplified in Rendell-Baker v. Kohn. There, an apparently private school provided education for students whose special needs made it difficult for them to finish high school. The record, however, failed to show any tradition of providing public special education to students unable to cope with a regular school, who had historically been cared for (or ignored) according to private choice. It was true that various public school districts had adopted the practice of referring students to the school and paying their tuition, and no one disputed that providing the instruction aimed at a proper public objective and conferred a public benefit. But we held that the performance of such a public function did not permit a finding of state action on the part of the school unless the function performed was exclusively and traditionally public, as it was not in that case. The Association argues that application of the public function criterion would produce the same result here, and we will assume, arguendo, that it would. But this case does not turn on a public function test, any more than *Rendell-Baker* had anything to do with entwinement of public officials in the special school.

For the same reason, it avails the Association nothing to stress that the State neither coerced nor encouraged the actions complained of. "Coercion" and "encouragement" are like "entwinement" in referring to kinds of facts that can justify characterizing an ostensibly private action as public instead. Facts that address any of these criteria are significant, but no one criterion must necessarily be applied. When, therefore, the relevant facts show pervasive entwinement to the point of largely overlapping identity, the implication of state action is not affected by pointing out that the facts might not loom large under a different test.

D

This is not to say that all of the Association's arguments are rendered beside the point by the public officials' involvement in the Association, for after application of the entwinement criterion, or any other, there is a further potential issue, and the Association raises it. Even facts that suffice to show public action (or, standing alone, would require such a finding) may be outweighed in the name of some value at odds with finding public accountability in the circumstances. In [Polk County v. Dodson, 454 U.S. 312 (1981)], a defense lawyer's actions were deemed private even though she was employed by the county and was acting within the scope of her duty as a public defender. Full-time public employment would be conclusive of state action for some purposes, see West v. Atkins, accord, *Lugar,* but not when the employee is doing a defense lawyer's primary job; then, the public defender does "not ac[t] on behalf of the State; he is the State's adversary." *Polk County.* The state-action doctrine does not convert opponents into virtual agents.

The assertion of such a countervailing value is the nub of each of the Association's two remaining arguments, neither of which, however, persuades us. The Association suggests, first, that reversing the judgment here will somehow trigger an epidemic of unprecedented federal litigation. Even if that might be counted as a good reason for a *Polk County* decision to call the Association's action private, the record raises no reason for alarm here. Save for the Sixth Circuit, every Court of Appeals to consider a statewide athletic association like the one here has found it a state actor. [No] one, however, has pointed to any explosion of § 1983 cases against interscholastic athletic associations in the affected jurisdictions. [If] Brentwood's claim were pushing at the edge of the class of possible defendant state actors, an argument about the social utility of expanding that class would at least be on point, but because we are nowhere near the margin in this case, the Association is really asking for nothing less than a dispensation for itself. Its position boils down to saying that the Association should not be dressed in state clothes because other, concededly public actors are; that Brentwood should be kept out of court because a different plaintiff raising a different claim in a different case may find the courthouse open. Pleas for special treatment are hard to sell, although saying that does not, of course, imply anything about the merits of Brentwood's complaint; the issue here is merely whether Brentwood properly names the Association as a § 1983 defendant, not whether it should win on its claim.

The judgment of the Court of Appeals for the Sixth Circuit is reversed, and the case is remanded for further proceedings consistent with this opinion.

It is so ordered.

JUSTICE THOMAS, with whom THE CHIEF JUSTICE, JUSTICE SCALIA, and JUSTICE KENNEDY join, dissenting.

We have never found state action based upon mere "entwinement." Until today, we have found a private organization's acts to constitute state action only when the organization performed a public function; was created, coerced, or encouraged by the government; or acted in a symbiotic relationship with the government. The majority's holding—that the Tennessee Secondary School Athletic Association's (TSSAA) enforcement of its recruiting rule is state action—not only extends state-action doctrine beyond its permissible limits but also encroaches upon the realm of individual freedom that the doctrine was meant to protect. I respectfully dissent.

I

Like the state-action requirement of the Fourteenth Amendment, the state-action element of 42 U.S.C. § 1983 excludes from its coverage "merely private conduct, however discriminatory or wrongful." American Mfrs. Mut. Ins. Co. v. Sullivan, 526 U.S. 40, 50 (1999) (internal quotation marks omitted). "Careful adherence to the 'state action' requirement" thus "preserves an area of individual freedom by limiting the reach of federal law and federal judicial power." [*Lugar.*] The state-action doctrine also promotes important values of federalism, "avoid[ing] the imposition of responsibility on a State for conduct it could not control." [*Tarkanian.*] Although we have used many different tests to identify state action, they all have a common purpose. Our goal in every case is to determine whether an action "can fairly be attributed to the State." [*Blum.*] *American Mfrs.,* supra, at 52.

A

Regardless of these various tests for state action, common sense dictates that the TSSAA's actions cannot fairly be attributed to the State, and thus cannot constitute state action. The TSSAA was formed in 1925 as a private corporation to organize interscholastic athletics and to sponsor tournaments among its member schools. Any private or public secondary school may join the TSSAA by signing a contract agreeing to comply with its rules and decisions. Although public schools currently compose 84% of the TSSAA's membership, the TSSAA does not require that public schools constitute a set percentage of its membership, and, indeed, no public school need join the TSSAA. The TSSAA's rules are enforced not by a state agency but by its own board of control, which comprises high school principals, assistant principals, and superintendents, none of whom must work at a public school. Of course, at the time the recruiting rule was enforced in this case, all of the board members happened to be public school officials. However, each board member acts in a representative capacity on behalf of all the private and public schools in his region of Tennessee, and not simply his individual school.

The State of Tennessee did not create the TSSAA. The State does not fund the TSSAA and does not pay its employees. In fact, only 4% of the TSSAA's revenue comes from the dues paid by member schools; the bulk of its operating budget is derived from gate receipts at tournaments it sponsors. The State does not permit the TSSAA to use state-owned facilities for a discounted fee, and it does not exempt the TSSAA from state taxation. No Tennessee law authorizes the State to coordinate interscholastic athletics or empowers another entity to organize interscholastic athletics on behalf of the State. The only state pronouncement acknowledging the

TSSAA's existence is a rule providing that the State Board of Education permits public schools to maintain membership in the TSSAA if they so choose.

Moreover, the State of Tennessee has never had any involvement in the particular action taken by the TSSAA in this case: the enforcement of the TSSAA's recruiting rule prohibiting members from using "undue influence" on students or their parents or guardians "to secure or to retain a student for athletic purposes." There is no indication that the State has ever had any interest in how schools choose to regulate recruiting. In fact, the TSSAA's authority to enforce its recruiting rule arises solely from the voluntary membership contract that each member school signs, agreeing to conduct its athletics in accordance with the rules and decisions of the TSSAA.

B

Even approaching the issue in terms of any of the Court's specific state-action tests, the conclusion is the same: The TSSAA's enforcement of its recruiting rule against Brentwood Academy is not state action.

[The] TSSAA has not performed a function that has been "traditionally exclusively reserved to the State." [*Jackson*.] The organization of interscholastic sports is neither a traditional nor an exclusive public function of the States. [Certainly,] in Tennessee, the State did not even show an interest in interscholastic athletics until 47 years after the TSSAA had been in existence and had been orchestrating athletic contests throughout the State. Even then, the State Board of Education merely acquiesced in the TSSAA's actions and did not assume the role of regulating interscholastic athletics. Cf. *Blum* ("Mere approval of or acquiescence in the initiatives of a private party is not sufficient to justify holding the State responsible for those initiatives . . ."); see also [*Flagg Brothers*]. The TSSAA no doubt serves the public, particularly the public schools, but the mere provision of a service to the public does not render such provision a traditional and exclusive public function. See [*Rendell-Baker*].

It is also obvious that the TSSAA is not an entity created and controlled by the government for the purpose of fulfilling a government objective, as was Amtrak in Lebron v. National Railroad Passenger Corporation. See also Pennsylvania v. Board of Directors of City Trusts of Philadelphia (per curiam) (holding that a state agency created under state law was a state actor). Indeed, no one claims that the State of Tennessee played any role in the creation of the TSSAA as a private corporation in 1925.

[In] addition, the State of Tennessee has not "exercised coercive power or . . . provided such significant encouragement [to the TSSAA], either overt or covert" [*Blum*] that the TSSAA's regulatory activities must in law be deemed to be those of the State. The State has not promulgated any regulations of interscholastic sports, and nothing in the record suggests that the State has encouraged or coerced the TSSAA in enforcing its recruiting rule. To be sure, public schools do provide a small portion of the TSSAA's funding through their membership dues, but no one argues that these dues are somehow conditioned on the TSSAA's enactment and enforcement of recruiting rules. Likewise, even if the TSSAA were dependent on state funding to the extent of 90%, as was the case in *Blum*, instead of less than 4%, mere financial dependence on the State does not convert the TSSAA's actions into acts of the State.

Finally, there is no "symbiotic relationship" between the State and the TSSAA. [The] TSSAA provides a service—the organization of athletic tournaments—in exchange for membership dues and gate fees, just as a vendor could contract with public schools to sell refreshments at school events. Certainly the public school could sell its own refreshments, yet the existence of that option does not transform the service performed by the contractor into a state action. Also, there is no suggestion in this case that, as was the case in *Burton,* the State profits from the TSSAA's decision to enforce its recruiting rule.

Because I do not believe that the TSSAA's action of enforcing its recruiting rule is fairly attributable to the State of Tennessee, I would affirm.

II

Although the TSSAA's enforcement activities cannot be considered state action as a matter of common sense or under any of this Court's existing theories of state action, the majority presents a new theory. Under this theory, the majority holds that the combination of factors it identifies evidences "entwinement" of the State with the TSSAA, and that such entwinement converts private action into state action. The majority does not define "entwinement," and the meaning of the term is not altogether clear. But whatever this new "entwinement" theory may entail, it lacks any support in our state-action jurisprudence.

[Because] the majority never defines "entwinement," the scope of its holding is unclear. If we are fortunate, the majority's fact-specific analysis will have little bearing beyond this case. But if the majority's new entwinement test develops in future years, it could affect many organizations that foster activities, enforce rules, and sponsor extracurricular competition among high schools—not just in athletics, but in such diverse areas as agriculture, mathematics, music, marching bands, forensics, and cheerleading. Indeed, this entwinement test may extend to other organizations that are composed of, or controlled by, public officials or public entities, such as firefighters, policemen, teachers, cities, or counties. I am not prepared to say that any private organization that permits public entities and public officials to participate acts as the State in anything or everything it does, and our state-action jurisprudence has never reached that far. The state-action doctrine was developed to reach only those actions that are truly attributable to the State, not to subject private citizens to the control of federal courts hearing § 1983 actions.

I respectfully dissent.

GRUPHEL, Phase One

GENDER RESEARCH on URBANIZATION, PLANNING, HOUSING and EVERYDAY LIFE

EDITED BY:
Sylvia Sithole-Fundire, Agnes Zhou, Anita Larsson and Ann Schlyter

LIBRARY
Michigan State
University

GENDER RESEARCH

ON

URBANIZATION, PLANNING,

HOUSING AND EVERYDAY LIFE

GRUPHEL, Phase One

EDITED BY:

Sylvia Sithole-Fundire, Agnes Zhou,
Anita Larsson and Ann Schlyter

Gender Research on Urbanization, Planning, Housing and Everyday Life
GRUPHEL, Phase One

Published by:
Zimbabwe Women's Resource Centre & Network
288c Herbert Chitepo Avenue
P.O. Box 2192
Harare
Zimbabwe

ISBN   0-7974-1495-9

Copyright © rests with the researchers who have contributed to this publication, 1995

Multiple copying of the contents or parts thereof without permission is a breach of copyright. Applications for the copyright holders' written permission to reproduce, transmit or store in a retrieval system any part of this publication should be addressed to the publisher.

Editorial and Publishing Manager: Lesley Humphrey

Computer Typesetting: Fontline, Harare

Printing: AT & T Systemedia, Harare

The first phase of GRUPHEL and the ultimate publication of these papers was funded by the Swedish Agency for Research Cooperation with Developing Countries (SAREC), for which the respective researchers are grateful.

Whilst the research for this publication was housed and administered by the Zimbabwe Women's Resource Centre and Network (ZWRCN), it should be noted that the respective authors are responsible for their papers. The views presented in this publication are not necessarily those of the ZWRCN.

CONTENTS

INTRODUCTION

1. Gender Research on Urbanization, Planning, Housing and Everyday Life
   ANN SCHLYTER and AGNES ZHOU 7

2. Approaches to Women and Housing in Development Policy
   ANN SCHLYTER 20

3. Theoretical and Methodological Considerations
   ANITA LARSSON 30

RESEARCH PAPERS

4. Women as 'Home-makers' and Men as 'Heads' of Households: Who is Responsible for Housing Improvements?
   NOLULAMO N. GWAGWA 42

5. Basotho Women's Role in Urban Housing: The Case of Maseru
   TIISETSO MATETE-LIEB 61

6. Credit Facilities for Housing for Women: A Case Study of Maseru, Lesotho
   SYMPHOROSA REMBE 82

7. Women on Co-operative Mines in Zimbabwe
   HENRY CHIWAWA 92

8. Gender Issues amongst Dombo Tombo Lodgers: A Case Study Approach
   SYLVIA SITHOLE-FUNDIRE 115

9. Women in Micro-Enterprises: The Case of Mbare, Zimbabwe
   DIANA NACHUDWA 135

10 Ideologies on Everyday Life amongst Finalists
   at the University of Zimbabwe
   SIBUSISIWE NCUBE 145

11 Women's Access to Trading Space at
   Growth Points in Zimbabwe: A Case Study of Mataga
   AGNES ZHOU 163

12 Social and Physical Living Conditions
   of Nannies in High Cost Residential Areas of Lusaka, Zambia
   MUBIANA MACWAN'GI 185

13 The Choice of Law: Theoretical Perspectives on
   Urbanization and Women's Rights to Property
   MULELA MARGARET MUNALULA 195

14 Changing Gender Contracts and Housing Conflicts
   ANITA LARSSON and ANN SCHLYTER 212

REFERENCES 232

CONTRIBUTORS 239

INTRODUCTION

Chapter One

Gender Research on Urbanization, Planning, Housing and Everyday Life

Ann Schlyter and Agnes Zhou

From the early eighties, the impact of gender relations has become increasingly topical in social development analysis. In Southern Africa, women are faced with many socio-economic problems traceable to unbalanced gender relations. Their access to the law, to resources and social amenities are sometimes restricted by either written laws or social conventions. Many key issues arising from such constraints encountered by women do not readily receive priority in research agenda for development planning. A challenge for researchers in the region has therefore been to establish networks that document and analyze these issues from a gender perspective. This publication is an attempt to meet such a challenge. It provides an overview of women's position and status in Southern Africa within the context of gender relations, institutional frameworks, intra-household approaches and wider development strategies.

The research papers in this collection are the output of the GRUPHEL theme and research network. GRUPHEL is the acronym for Gender Research on Urbanization, Planning, Housing and Everyday Life. The theme focuses on the concept of gender as a term which describes social, economic and cultural values, ideas and beliefs which a given society attaches to the biological differences between men and women. The researchers adopt the view of gender as a mental and social construct which influences power relations between men and women. Based on this common definition, development problems and issues in the sectors of housing, urbanization, planning and everyday life are studied.

In this introduction we will point out some important achievements in terms of empirical findings, and also discuss them in the light of conceptual development and theoretical generalizations. First, however, some reflections on the production of knowledge. McFadden (1993) has noted that the 'fundamental problem of modern social science is not only that it appears gender-blind and gender-insensitive, but more that it is premised on the gendered construction and definition of what knowledge is and who the knowers in our society are.'

What knowledge?

GRUPHEL is a gender research programme and aims at producing knowledge on and understanding of gender issues within the field of urbanization, planning and housing. Gender research is a newly established, very potent and active research area. There are ongoing international debates on the definition of this research subject as well as on conceptual and theoretical issues. The definition of gender mentioned above is very close to the one given by Ruth Meena in the book *Gender in Southern Africa* (1992): 'Gender has been defined as socially constructed culturally variable rules that men and women play in their daily lives. It refers to a structural relationship of inequality between men and women.'

Gender research focuses on the relationship between men and women. In single studies the focus can be on men only or on women only given that their situation is analyzed within a structural gender relationship. Many of the studies in the GRUPHEL programme focus on women, a thing that can easily be defended given the fact the urban and housing research historically has been severely biased. For example, there has been a bias in the choice of research issues and formulation of research problems.

African towns are facing tremendous problems. The deterioration of urban service affects women most as issues related to water, fuel, and food, are largely women's responsibilities. However, these issues have not been prioritized on the research agenda. In a Gender Statement adopted at the African Urban Forum in Nairobi in December 1992, women and poverty, women and the management of public services, women's access to land and housing, and changing social roles are defined as four research areas of priority.

In the GRUPHEL programme most studies are concerned with poor women's conditions, some deal with aspects of public service, some with access to land and housing, and, taken together, they all elucidate changing gender relations.

Who are the knowers?

McFadden points at the fact that it is usually men that are defined as the knowers whether within the research community itself or within the researched communities. To define women in the researched communities as knowers and to find research methods to allow for their knowledge to be uncovered are among the main challenges of the GRUPHEL programme.

Meena (1992) states that 'women have as much a right to participate in the production of knowledge as they have the right to be part of that knowledge'. Women are under-represented among the producers of knowledge, a fact that influences the content and quality of the product. In GRUPHEL women researchers are over-represented. But for the future it is important that there are also male researchers engaged in gender research. Gender research has to be included in the main stream of research efforts and tendencies to isolation must be counteracted.

All researchers in the programme are not permanently based within the academic world, but represent links towards planning and applied research. Most of the studies combine two perspectives, that of the planner and that of men and women affected in the process of planning and urbanization.

In the GRUPHEL programme women as well as men are recognized as carriers of knowledge. In many of the papers the experiences of women are seriously considered. The process of extracting the knowledge carried by women and of reaching an understanding of their experiences leads us to the question of research methodology.

On research methodology

Studies in urbanization, planning and housing have, in Southern Africa, as in other parts of the world, not only been male dominated, they have also been biased by the domination of a survey methodology emphasizing quantitative information. Of course, numbers are important in planning, but in addition to the question of how many, there are questions of how and why to be addressed.

Studies aiming at an understanding of underlying structures of ideological or institutional levels need a qualitative research methodology. For a new understanding of a phenomenon, new concepts and new categories need to be created. These new concepts and categories should be grounded in empirical work.

The researchers in the GRUPHEL programme have used both quantitative and qualitative methods in their studies. While some researchers had wide experience, others had no experience of qualitative studies and the GRUPHEL research has been a period of learning. The strategic selection of informants and other issues in relation to the collection of data have been thoroughly discussed in the seminars. The importance of concepts and the need for the development of new concepts and new categories within the research process have been acknowledged. The change from a quantitative to a qualitative analytical perspective has been a great challenge, and so has the presentation of qualitative information as research findings.

Challenging household gender contracts

A gender contract is defined as an unwritten and invisible social contract according to which men and women act in the belief that this is what the society expects from them. The concept 'head of household' is central in the dominating gender contract as identified by Larsson and Schlyter. However, the actual meaning of this concept is not static but under constant negotiation. There are different opinions whether it is related to breadwinning, to house ownership, or just to the biological fact of being male. These ideas are reflected by Gwagwa looking at the assumptions of household headship and the responsibility for housing improvement which have been based on existing gender contracts. She points out the value systems that help perpetuate gender contracts in societies stating that, although women may seem to 'passively' accept the contracts, they are increasingly challenging them with the management strategies they develop. Fundire deals with the same theme indicating different levels of opposition to the existing gender contracts.

Ncube's paper on housing aspirations of university students illustrates that among the younger, educated groups some men and women are seeking to shift the boundaries imposed by the significant divergence of opinion regarding perceived gender roles between men and women. However, what now exists is a pragmatic acceptance of the need to be flexible in operationalizing the roles. For example, a number of men and women were willing to share chores and the burden of developing their homes with their partner.

Chiwawa deals with the male breadwinner concept. He points out that women are challenging the boundaries of this gender contract. Their input in the co-operative mining sector is quite significant yet the criteria for selection of mine workers overtly discriminates against them. Challenges to alter existing gender contracts lead to conflicts, particularly in housing.

Usually married women try to negotiate the meaning of gender contracts without coming to open conflict. In housing the wife is often the most active of the spouses, taking initiatives such as finding plots and organizing the building. Still, the men as heads of the household hold the ownership and the formal power, as demonstrated in Lieb's paper.

The fact that in poor societies breadwinning is a joint responsibility, or that it often lies heavily on the woman, is confirmed by the papers in this volume. The husband as a head having the ultimate power in the household is still acknowledged by many women (as Ncube's paper shows). But, as shown in the paper by Larsson and Schlyter, there are also poor women challenging the concept.

Living conditions and access problems

A number of research reports deal specifically with women's living conditions and access problems. Such papers include Chiwawa's paper on women's living conditions on co-operative mines in Zimbabwe, Macwan'gi's research on living conditions of nannies in Lusaka, Zhou's study on women's access to trading space at growth points in Zimbabwe, Fundire's paper on gender issues amongst lodgers and Rembe's paper on poor women's credit facilities.

These studies highlight gender specific problems that women encounter when forced into an urbanized lifestyle. In all case studies, researchers explored more than one theme in order to tell the complete story and to correctly represent the problem. They confirm that, despite legal improvements in the situation of women in Southern Africa, it is still necessary to empower them to access and utilize these provisions. As Zhou's paper reflects, the presence of laws that allow women to access trading space in growth points in Zimbabwe did not ensure that they actually got allocations. There were issues of attitudes and institutional procedures which created barriers to women's access to resources.

Fundire's paper further explains this point using cases of women's constraints in getting housing allocations within urban local authorities. For Macwan'gi, the social situation and living conditions of nannies indicate that, due to factors such as poor educational background and lack of awareness, women often operate with very few options. The physical and mental health of the nannies studied is affected by their living conditions because they are unable to access better housing facilities in proximity to their places of work. Many of them have no space whatsoever which they can call their own.

Rembe investigates the informal credit facilities in Lesotho, which are more often utilized by women than by men. She confirms what has been found in other countries, that poor people and married women do not have access to formal credit facilities. Instead, women create their own informal ones, such as saving clubs and burial societies. Such clubs and societies give loans, most frequently for immediate domestic needs, but some also give credit for house building and housing improvements.

Intra-household strategies and urbanization

The theme of urbanization is central to all studies in this collection. The rural urban dichotomy is viewed here as a 'pedagogic' construct. In reality, the two are inter-related components of the same system. Urbanization as both a spatial phenomenon and as a way of living has taken root in Southern Africa as in many other parts of the world. Initially externally imposed in the region, the urbanization tradition was selective until after independence. The labour migrations absorbed men only and legally prevented women from coming to the urban centres. Most of the women therefore remained in the village with the responsibilities (but not the rights to resources) for farming and food production in those areas. In almost all these countries, the urbanization of women is more recent and most families still maintain two homes, one rural and the other urban. The experiences of such societies need to be analyzed at the local level and some of the studies in this collection attempt to do so.

How have these experiences affected men's and women's roles in the socio-economic and cultural spheres at both micro and macro levels? This theme was explored in Chiwawa's paper looking at the exclusion of women from profitable mining activities while they are expected to live on mine compounds in the capacity of wives or welfare workers in a somewhat urbanized setting. Securing the welfare of the assumed principal wage earners (the men) was their part in the contract, but they were increasingly asking for more stake in actual mining and related services.

Munalula's paper also traces the disadvantages that women face in the urbanization process. She views urbanization as detrimental to women's progress, their rights to property and the law. Her study depicts the struggles of women to maintain their housing and property rights. She mostly uses the testimonies of women who have been through a legal aid clinic to illustrate the choice of law and alternatives which women may have in their fight for housing rights.

Women and men as actors

In the introduction of the GRUPHEL programme, a conceptual framework was suggested, but was in no way made compulsory for all the studies. It was regarded as important to keep an open view to a variety of theoretical approaches.

Some of the contributions are mainly empirical and do not explicitly discuss their theoretical base. In common is the view of gender as a socially constructed role. Few papers take the analysis further into how the roles are constructed within structural gender relationships. Much is left implicit in the analyses of women's actions and conditions. At the final GRUPHEL seminar, the participants agreed that it is possible to generalize their findings in the suggested conceptual framework of gender system and gender contracts.

In the suggested theoretical framework, women are recognized as actors and the gender system is seen as a structural relationship that is continuously reconstructed or changed. Early theories on the structural relationships between men and women concentrated on the male power structure. Hartmann (1981) defined patriarchy as men's struggle and organization to keep or achieve privileges. She built her theories on studies of the labour market in developed countries, mainly the USA. Studies within this theoretical framework produced many interesting results, but were also criticized for not fully recognizing women as actors. Women are too often identified as victims of male superiority only.

Nevertheless, it can be very fruitful to focus on men's actions and men's organization to keep or achieve privileges in formal and informal ways. Chiwawa shows how women are out-defined or marginalized in the mining sector. Zhou takes a step further in revealing how men act informally to excluded women from land for production although they have formal rights to ownership. This is revealed although Zhou's focus is on women's own activities.

Separation and subordination

According to a theory developed by Hirdman and presented by Larsson, the gender system has two major logics, one of separation and one of subordination. The working of these logics can be studied on any of three analytical levels: the level of ideologies and cultural images; the level of institutions; and the level of inter-personal relationships. Some papers concentrate on one level, while most others show an overlap of the levels.

Ncube's paper concentrates on the ideological level in looking into the attitudes of students, the elite of tomorrow. The female students, as much as the male, feel a need for maintaining, at least in public, a separation between male and female tasks – leaving housework to women, even if both spouses have degrees. It seems as if women's identity as women and wives is close connected to caring for the husband. The logic of separation is reproduced in new forms.

Chiwawa's paper looks at women who have entered a previously male sector, the mining sector. It shows how separation can be overcome but also how it is recreated according to new definitions of special male tasks and special female tasks. Zhou's paper also illustrates how separation is coming in as a logic on the institutional level, although not according to regulation. Lieb finds more positive experiences among women in construction. Generally, contractors had good experiences of women workers; she finds only one contractor who maintains that the presence of women at the working site distracts the male workers by appealing to their sexual desires.

The logic of the relative subordination of women is obvious in Ncube's paper by the male students' desire to have a wife of lower education. Only a few male students wished to marry women with degrees. Even these believed that their wife would find it disturbing if their husband was not superior: 'She will not have a superiority complex because I am a doctor'. Most female students, however, wanted to marry someone they considered their equal.

In the dominating gender contract the logics of separation and subordination are often, especially at household level, presented as benign and complementary: the husband is the head and the breadwinner; the wife is the homemaker. Gwagwa finds in a Durban township that women provide the income but the men provide security and dignity. The role of the male head of the household is thus reduced to fulfilling a woman's need for protection. This need is created by the risk of being subjected to accusations of prostitution, and the risk of being subjected to violence from thieves or sexual abusers.

Differences among women

There is always a danger in talking about women as one category. Women have different conditions and interests related to class or race, to mention two major analytical categories. Important in housing studies is the contradiction between homeowners and lodgers. Fundire shows that the landladies are often relatively poor women. The lodgers aspire to become landladies themselves.

The class differences are more clear and definite in the relationship between domestic workers and their employers. Domestic work is the single largest category of employment in Southern Africa and it is the wife that takes on the role as employer of the domestic worker or nanny. According to the gender contract, the wife is responsible for the running of the home.

Domestic workers in Zambia are often men, but male nannies are exceptions. The nanny's situation is often experienced as a woman exploiting another woman. Macwan'gi's paper on nannies in Lusaka explores this relationship, showing how powerless the nanny is.

Ncube's paper touches on this relationship from the viewpoint of the wife-to-be. It shows a complicated relationship between the wife and the domestic worker. The domestic worker is the underdog, but the wife, subordinate to her husband, finds herself in an uneasy in-between situation which can be threatening to her own identity as a wife caring for her husband.

Negotiations and struggle

Many of the contributions to this volume illustrate how old gender contracts are renegotiated. Imposed by changing conditions, the gendered division of labour and responsibility is changing. Men and women elaborate arguments in the negotiation. The concept of gender struggle has been used by Thorbek (1993) in which she emphasizes that changes to the gender contract are not easily obtained. Women struggle in their daily work to extend their space of action, while men often struggle to maintain their privileges.

The concept of gender struggle is an abstract concept in the same way as class struggle. It refers to the efforts of changing or maintaining the gender system. Women as individuals may support male superiority. It is, for example, not unusual that the mother-in-law is the one who advocates her daughter-in-law's total subordination under the husband. Sometimes, however, individual men may support struggle for changes in the gender contract in order to benefit women. The struggle should not be seen as necessarily violent, although violence against women can be seen as an ultimate expression of the gender struggle.

Another tool in the gender struggle used by men (and women) against women is to depict women who are taking independent actions as immoral. Fundire notes that women lodgers are often depicted as prostitutes. Unmarried women have, with few exceptions, equal legal rights to men, but are prevented from using them in several ways. Women's sexuality is made a tool in the negotiations around the definitions of what a woman should do. The definition of a decent woman is used to keep women out of public life.

Impact of state policy

Looking at the women's actions and strategies, it becomes obvious that restrictions posed by planning, housing policy, legal frameworks and other state responsibilities on their possibility of improving their everyday life are severe.

There are several papers that show how important the role of the state is in giving the framework for the gender contracts. By not ensuring women's status as major persons in law or in practice the state is supporting a gender contract which limits women's space of manoeuvre. Social contracts can never be imposed by one party, not even the state. But the state provides new frameworks for negotiation; for example, new laws. Munalula puts forward the need for informal support to women negotiating their rights. She argues against an optimistic belief that new laws bring about rapid changes in the gender contract.

If women had more influence in policy-making and planning it is likely that, for example, urban services such as water, fuel and land for growing of food would be higher on the list of priorities within local authorities.

The papers of Zhou and Rembe have documented that women meet difficulties whether wanting access to productive land or to credit. Efforts of participatory planning procedures are reported in two papers. Nachudwa studied the planning of a central market, where any different interests between men and women seem to be overshadowed by differences in interests between formal and informal traders and between differences depending on the sector of trade.

Many of the papers have documented poor women's living conditions. These can be read as testimonies with a direct message to policy makers. Macwan'gi's description of the lack of privacy, respect and free time for nannies calls for new measures in labour policy. Fundire's description of the situation for lodgers, many of them renting only one room for the whole family calls for consideration in formulating so-called ownership housing policies.

For planners, the case studies in this book confirm the need to reconstruct gender ideologies to provide more development space for women. Housing provision must therefore look towards adequate provision for households headed by both men and women. From the conclusions of the studies, a gender awareness in development approaches is needed to overcome some of the problems highlighted in the different studies.

GRUPHEL – achievements and prospects

When initiated, the objective of the GRUPHEL programme was to stimulate and support gender research within the areas of urbanization, planning, housing and everyday life. This has, as this book bears witness, been achieved. Young researchers and planners in Southern Africa have, thanks to the programme, embarked on gender studies. A network has been established. In three working seminars, concepts and research methods as well as results and techniques for presentation have been discussed.

The papers in this volume contribute to the knowledge of how the urbanizing societies in Southern Africa are gendered. They provide a qualitative understanding which is a type of knowledge that is not often found in applied urban or housing research. The step to making recommendations to policy-makers and other actors in the sector is, in some papers, quite explicit. There is a need to further develop qualitative research methods to be used in complement to surveys in any research on urbanization, planning and housing. This book presents the results of efforts in that direction.

Southern Africa is in a period of continuously rapid urban growth, and local governments will face tremendous planning problems. The further impoverishment of the urban poor population has direct effects on the everyday life of women. A feminization of poverty is predicted and has to be counteracted. In many countries the system for state rule is under transformation and democracy has to find forms that include women as well as men.

This book has only touched on some of the problems following with this development. Obviously, a great deal of gender-aware urban research has to be done. Questions such as what strategies have women devised to extend their decision space and whether women are content with incremental changes at local levels or opt for more confrontational approaches to empowerment are pertinent. The future need of knowledge and understanding is tremendous, and there is a need to further develop the research area.

Chapter Two

Approaches to Women and Housing in Development Policy

(This paper was given as an introduction to the first GRUPHEL seminar in Harare, 29 March to 2 April 1992)

Ann Schlyter

In this introduction I will present research approaches to women and housing in a context of development policy. Aims and motives for doing research vary over time, and certainly within the GRUPHEL programme we will come to discuss our own role and the relationship between research and development policy. This historical background might be of some help in such a discussion, although our theme is wider than women and housing.

Women in development is established as a research theme with its own theoretical and methodological discourse. Research on women in development is usually applied research linked to planning and aid projects. This is a feature it shares with most other research on housing. A comparison is therefore easily made.

Gender research differs from research on women in development by focusing on the relationship between women and men, on how they themselves form their physical and cultural space. Gender research has developed independently from the development aid perspective. This presentation will conclude with a few comments on perspectives and theories in gender research. In *World Development* Caroline Moser (1989) gave an overview of different policy approaches to Third World women. She drew from Buvinic who had identified three policy approaches towards women: welfare, equity and anti-poverty, and added two: efficiency and empowerment. I will, with special reference to Southern Africa, review some of Moser's points and draw parallels to policy approaches in housing. I will also add another policy approach: market adaptation.

An overview like this is not possible in a short paper without bold generalizations, approximations and a blind eye to contradictions. Still, I hope it will not confuse more than it helps.

These five policy approaches have been applied by UN organizations and other international organizations, governments, and funders of aid projects. The main streams of the research in the field developed in interaction with the policy approaches. Much research has been carried out directly for appraisal or monitoring of aid projects. However, independent research has also been carried out within the same dominating discourse, though there have been counter currents and critiques of these approaches.

The welfare/modernization approach

In Southern Africa, the colonial administrations originally maintained that the welfare of women was best protected if they stayed in the rural areas and cultivated the land, a view that fitted well into the organization of labour by migrant work.

During the fifties, the welfare approach was integrated into the dominating paradigm of modernization. From the need for a permanent labour force in the cities, followed the construction of family housing and the right of women to live in town.

The modernization paradigm was not restricted to the economy but extended to cultural issues. A modern family was a nuclear family. An urban woman's role in development was to be a good mother and home-maker. Welfare projects aimed at educating her to fulfil these roles. Research was used to find the scientific knowledge on which mothering should be based. Nutrition and family planning were basic issues.

In projects as well as in research, men and women were seen to have separate but functional roles. The drastic change of the African women's roles imposed by urbanization was seldom regarded as problematic. In the modernization paradigm the societies and the gender roles were rapidly to become similar to those in the 'modern' northern societies.

Housing is central in welfare policies. As in most countries, the target group of welfare policy in Southern Africa was the workforce. More explicitly than in other parts of the world, welfare aimed at a rational reproduction of the working force. Housing was tied to employment, and very few women managed to get formal employment.

Large scale employers such as the mine companies or the state, whether colonial or not, were regarded as the functional provider of housing. Quite a lot of research was carried out to design optimal low cost infrastructure and housing. Most research was on technical issues. In South Africa the settlement, township and housing policy were part of the implementation of apartheid. The Anglophone neighbours followed suit in the development of urban policies.

During the fifties and sixties in Lusaka and Harare, some research was carried out on 'social issues' related to housing and urban living. There were even some isolated examples of studies on housing preferences. Sociological surveys mapped out the social composition of the growing urban areas. These studies were designed to provide material for welfare planning as well as for control. There were also studies of urban life in the anthropological tradition of studying people, not problems. A few of these studies paid attention to the changes in women's roles brought about by urbanization.

In African countries decolonized in the sixties, the dream of rapid development and modernization was strong. In Latin America, the paradigm of modernization was already under criticism, though still dominant. Despite a relatively high level of economic growth, the benefits of industrialization failed to reach large parts of the population. Instead, poverty increased and became visible in the urban shantytowns.

Modernization of housing through bulldozing of shanties and construction of conventional housing benefited only the growing middle class.

The equity/participation approach

Researchers on housing as well as on women increasingly focused on the impoverished part of the population, and arguments for participation approaches and upgrading of shantytowns and squatter areas were nourished by a 'from below' perspective. As a student in 1968, I myself argued for upgrading in Lusaka. But long before upgrading, self-help housing in the form of site-and-service was accepted. In practice, however, a rather limited number of houses were actually constructed.

In Africa, family-based, home-ownership schemes dominated. Participation was mainly in the form of a house owner managing the construction of his (almost never her) own house. In Latin America many projects built on the idea of community-based mutual aid. According to the new approach, people were not seen as mere recipients but as participators in the creation of their environment. Their productive role was extended to include the production of their own house. However, the state continued to be regarded as the functional, albeit too poor, provider of housing.

Research was carried out in connection with large scale housing projects, such as those carried out by the World Bank and the USAID. Many studies focused on the participatory processes, while relatively few included research for adequate plans, houses and technical solutions.

The educational character of many women's welfare projects had always meant some form of participation. Therefore, the concept of participation did not bring much change to women's projects, while in women's studies a break with the modernization paradigm, especially the welfare approach, meant a new focus on women as actors.

In 1970, Boserup published her book, *Women's Role in Economic Development*, emphasizing the role of Third World women in production, especially in agriculture. She pointed out negative impacts of modernization on women's status, and this effect was confirmed by several studies all over the world. First World women engaged in aid policy to make aid projects more gender aware. Women's conditions within the productive sphere had to be improved. Women should not be discriminated against but given access to employment and the means of earning a livelihood. The question of equity became central.

In research this perspective led to studies that criticized the paradigm of modernization and that compared women's rights to men's. Gender roles were questioned and the character of women's subordination identified. As a result, women tended to be regarded as victims rather than as creators of their own conditions, and in reaction to this tendency research grew around ideas on consciousness raising and on participation.

The pushing of the equity approach met resistance, not only among Third World men decision makers, but also among Third World women. For example, at the 1975 International Women's Year conference, these women identified their problem as poverty, and for them development was the answer. They also maintained the view of specific women's roles, and felt that the equity approach was drawn from First World experiences and did not take due cognisance of their culture.

The anti-poverty/basic needs approach

In women's studies the anti-poverty approach grew strong in response to Third World critique of the equity approach and to reports of growing poverty and income differences. Theories of modernization had failed to understand the growing so-called informal sector. Aid projects targeted the poor. To eradicate poverty, production had to be supported, and women were first and foremost regarded as producers. Education and employment programmes were to reduce income inequalities.

While research within the equity approach, when focusing on production' was at risk of reducing women's lives so that family and children were defined as hindrances, research within the anti-poverty approach saw the needs also of human reproduction.

The anti-poverty approach emphasized basic needs. Housing was defined as a basic need together with food, health, and education. Housing was put on the list of priorities, but below the other mentioned sectors. In many countries, quantitative surveys were conducted to assess the housing needs. Numerical and computerized models were elaborated to simulate figures reliably.

In the seventies upgrading of existing slum and squatter areas was put on the agenda. The World Bank and other powerful aid and funding organizations supported large scale upgrading and projects targeting the poor. In reality though, most projects were not affordable for the quarter of the population with the lowest income. Site and service schemes remained middle-class housing, with few exceptions, while the poor in upgraded areas did not pay the rates and the condition of cost recovery was not met.

Though several studies confirmed that upgrading benefited the poorest, the policy did not continue. For the funders, upgrading projects were not replicable as they did not reach the goal of cost recovery. The anti-poverty approach in housing faded.

The efficiency approach

The shift from the anti-poverty approach to the efficiency approach is not clear cut. Efficiency had always been important, but in the eighties the approach became dominant, which resulted in fewer efforts to reach the poorest. In housing, self help projects continued but with less emphasis on the poor as the target group. Evaluations conducted during the seventies show that projects aimed at low-income groups regularly reached middle-income groups. Predictably, there was a better efficiency in projects that avoided the poorest. A gender difference is worth mentioning here: low-income women regularly managed better in building a house and were better debt payers than low-income men.

There was a good deal of manipulation with the definition of housing for various income groups. For example, in Zambia, 98 percent of the population was in the two income groups called low and very low, while four income groups were distinguished among the remaining two percent of the population: lower-middle, middle, higher-middle and higher. About half of the governmental investments in housing were directed to the one or one-and-a-half per cent of the population with the highest income (Schlyter, 1988).

A key word in the terminology of the efficiency approach is management, and research focuses on management. Aid for housing was no longer provided through funding of actual housing projects. Instead experts were paid to work within local authorities and housing ministries. Projects tended to be isolated and thus not efficient in the long run. On the other hand, development aid to management of housing tended to result in housing policies but no houses. In women's projects economic participation in development remained in focus. The approach coincided with economic deterioration in Southern Africa. It became obvious that life could continue through all the work done outside the formal economy. In order to make the formal economy more efficient, a lot of necessary but unprofitable tasks were moved from state responsibility to households themselves.

In research the interest for the so-called informal sector continued, and in women's studies the sharp boundary between women's life in production and in reproduction faded.

The enabling/empowerment approach

The enabling and the empowerment approaches became very popular in the late eighties but they had always existed as counter currents to dominating approaches. There is usually a mix of two or more of the approaches in research, as well as in development projects and policy formulations. In presenting a chronological list of approaches there is a risk that the first ones appear outdated in all respects. This is not necessarily so, as experiences from the welfare approach might, for example, be highly valid in a new context.

Enabling has been an important element in equity and participation, even in welfare approaches. The more radical vision of empowerment has been a counter current in development theory since the beginning of the seventies. It has been more common in research than in implemented projects. Many researchers in women's studies and in housing studies have held the view of empowerment in their hearts and tried to show its necessity in their research.

The use of concepts as control of resources and assets led also to the concept of power in the main stream of thinking. The concept empowerment was picked up by powerful organizations and became common among housing project planners, especially when targeting neighbourhoods. While most of the talk about enabling and empowerment remained in the thin air of ideas, the approaches may have had some impact on local projects.

The market adaptation approach

In my view, the enabling/empowerment approach was never dominant, though very popular in discourse; it has rather been used as a complementary approach to what I would like to label the market adaptation approach.

There are clear overlaps with what was called the efficiency approach, but it is still a distinct approach. While efficiency could be calculated and disputed in terms of effectiveness, units of calculation, time perspective, etc., the market adaptation approach is presented more ideologically as the only way. In fact, it is more antagonistic towards previous approaches as it is not only supportive to market solutions, but aggressively negative to public solutions.

Consequently, governmental structures for intervention in housing are dismantled. In *Zimbabwe: A Framework for Economic Reform* (1991) it is expected that government will 'achieve significant savings in the urban sector' by giving the private sector responsibility for financing low-income housing, and by making local authorities financially independent. This will minimize the central financing of capital works for urban services. It is recognized that there will be negative effects on the everyday life of the poor and vulnerable. In the sectors of health and education an income threshold for payment according to the cost recovery policy is discussed, but in housing and urban services no measures are suggested.

Research within this approach has largely focused on how poor men and women will be able to cope with the consequences. People have to be enabled to act on the market by themselves. This approach needs the enabling approach as a complement.

Perspectives in gender research

In the review above I discussed how women have been viewed in development policy. Women in Development, WID, has become an established concept. Why is it then that we are holding a workshop on gender research? The concepts 'women in development' and 'women's studies' imply a research focus on women. Indeed, it is important to make women visible and to conduct research with a consistent women's perspective.

The concept of gender was introduced into social sciences to replace sex which is defined biologically. As a social concept it has to do with a relationship. Gender research does not necessarily focus on women, but the research problems look at the relations between women and men. Women's and men's different conditions can be described, but questions should also be put as to why the conditions are different and how they are differentiated. In other words, the very gendering of the society is the object of investigation.

Gender research is still a new research area, and there are many views on concepts and definitions. Often the term gender has just replaced the term sex. To clarify one may say that gender is to sex, what ethnicity is to race. Gender and ethnicity are socially and culturally created, while sex and race refer to biology, to nature. Racists and sexists in common defend social inequalities with reference to nature.

In all thoughts on gender there is a dialectic between two basic perspectives: one that emphasizes the sameness, the basic similarities, between men and women and therefore demands equity; another that emphasizes the differences and the particular qualities of women and women's culture, and therefore demands respect and recognition. The dialectic between the equity and difference perspectives cannot be avoided but has to be considered in any conceptual framework. It has a direct bearing on the application of research, and on women's political strategies.

The main critique of the welfare approach generated by the equity perspective was not against the notion of welfare as such, but against the fact that welfare reforms and projects were based on an analysis of gender roles from a difference perspective, directing the welfare to women exclusively in their roles as home-makers and mothers. In the anti-poverty and efficiency approaches, there is a mix of the two perspectives. In demands for income-generating activities and for putting a higher value on women's work, an equity perspective may dominate, while if priority is on efficiency, a different perspective is often appropriate. Reforms or projects that demand changes in the gendering of the society, which an equity perspective most often does, are likely to take time and be inefficient from the funders' perspective. The concept of gender roles also met criticism from a difference perspective. Researchers found the role concept too shallow; it was not for an individual just to choose which role she wanted to play. In studies of societies with a strict gendering of work, it was easy to define separate spheres for men and women. In the early seventies in Nordic research the concept of women's culture became important. It can be traced to Berit Ås (Jonasdottir, 1984). Ås had read Myrdal's studies of Indian society in which he defined a dominant and a subordinated culture and analyzed them according to five dimensions: language, tools and resources, organization, self-estimation and finally conceptions of time and planning. Ås found it fruitful to draw parallels to women's conditions, and she defined a women's subordinated culture.

The concept women's culture can easily be confusing if applied in multi-cultural societies or in international comparative studies. Therefore, we do not want to use it, but we can acknowledge that it generated dynamic and fruitful Nordic research for a period. In this perspective the importance of house and home became visible. Studies on women's culture resulted in a consciousness (among researchers) of women's traditional skills and of motherhood. The criticism that followed claimed that there were tendencies to idealization of a subordinated culture, that studies focusing exclusively on women would never help to explain the gendering of the society, and that women from different classes did not have the same culture.

Another old but continuing debate is on differences among women. The choice of perspective has a direct impact on women's political strategies. What do all women have in common? What unites them? In the socialist traditions women from different classes are seen to have very little in common, and the classic Marxist approaches are gender-blind. Many feminist researchers worked to find a conceptual framework which includes class as well as gender.

Without denying differences caused by class, ethnicity, religion or other factors, gender research concentrates on exploring how the differences between men and women are created. It is a great challenge to embark on a programme for gender research in the fields of urbanization, planning housing and everyday life.

Chapter Three

Theoretical and Methodological Considerations

(This paper was given as an introduction to the first GRUPHEL seminar in Harare, 29 March to 2 April 1992)

Anita Larsson

Some key concepts

This presentation will discuss Gender Research, the first words of the umbrella programme's theme.

Gender is a concept used to distinguish culture from biology. While the term sex is derived from biology, gender refers to what has been created by culture. The concept of gender describes the relationship between women and men. It allows us to understand, explore and analyze what is considered male and female in a specific context. Although the concept includes both women and men, it has developed out of a concern for women, out of women's studies. It is the intention of GRUPHEL to focus on gender relationships in the context of the different research projects.

Structures and individuals

In the housing studies by Ann Schlyter and myself (Larsson 1989, Schlyter 1988 and 1989), a major point of departure was the recognition of a mutual inter-dependence between human agency and structures. The structures of social systems provide the means by which people act. At the same time, those structures are the outcome of people's actions. It is thus an approach which lets neither the actions of human beings nor the structural properties alone provide explanations. Instead, the interaction between human beings and structures is in focus. Structures provide both constraints and opportunities. This approach was developed, by Giddens (1986) among others, who named his theory the structuration theory. He argues that there is a duality, not a dichotomy, between structure and agents. Although Giddens' theory is not easy to use as a tool in the analysis of collected data, it provides an essential basic platform when developing research concepts and methods.

The way the concepts 'gender system' and 'gender contracts' will be explained fits well into Giddens' way of approaching the duality of structure and agents. In the review of gender-related concepts I will, however, start with what a focus on women has meant in our studies on women householders and their strategies to acquire a house of their own. There are several reasons for looking specifically at women in their role as householders. This is not a place where it is necessary to defend our points of departure, but still it can be useful to outline the reasons.

Why a focus on women householders?

The very basic argument is that unless a gender-aware perspective is used, male heads of households constitute the norm, both in policy making and in research approaches. A focus on women householders is a means to make women visible, which implies that women are different and/or have different claims to men householders. There is an important difference between men and women householders; women as householders are the sole breadwinners at the same time as they have the responsibility for child-rearing and for domestic work. Many married women perform these three duties as well, but as a rule they are supported by their husbands.

There are many more poor women than there are poor men. This is because of the difficulties women face on the labour market, and due to their many duties. Besides being marginalized on the labour market, women are restricted when developing their survival strategies. Women lack or have poor access to cattle, to land in rural areas and to other important means of production. A network of relatives which provides support traditionally is rare in the urban setting. In addition, there may be legal obstacles for women to get access to housing, to business activities and the like.

Another important argument for focusing on women householders is that although women householders constitute a minority group, the proportion is increasing. The global average is roughly one third of all households. The figures for African urban areas are often higher, for instance in Gaborone it is now estimated to be 45 percent.

There are many reasons to focus on all categories of women, including married ones. In such cases, the need for a gender perspective becomes more obvious as these women are more often in some way or other under the control of a father, a husband or another male relative. The implications of focusing on women householders, and the approaches we used in earlier studies, will constitute the point of departure for the gender perspective developed here.

Women's strategies

When women and their everyday lives are made visible and understood, it is possible to make gender sensitive policies, that is, policies which take their interests and claims into consideration. Women's studies offer a means to move away from discrimination and a subordinate position in society, whether in Africa or Europe.

Despite the fact that women's generally subordinate position in relation to men is recognized, women should be considered active subjects, not objects. They actively participate in shaping their everyday life, although there are several constraints. Such an approach allows us to make use of the concept 'strategies'. In the space for action allowed by society, women develop strategies to improve their lives. They may not necessarily be actions based on explicit intentions and arguments like, 'If I do that and that, I will achieve that and that'.

Instead, the actions may be based on a general awareness of what is possible, a kind of common sense, what Giddens calls 'practical consciousness'. These strategies were identified in our research on women householders, when we found similar patterns of actions among many women in similar circumstances.

The fact that women constantly have to adapt their behaviour to circumstances beyond their control made us talk about strategies of adaptation. We also use the concept survival strategies, although it poses some difficulties. It may appear too broad as it could include everything, and too narrow, as it may lead to including only material aspects and excluding emotional and symbolic values.

In our housing studies we have found that to get a house 'of my own' is not just an aim in itself. We also found that such a house is a means in women's strategies to form a household on their terms, to generate income, to develop networks together with neighbours, to be urban and to achieve security in old age.

The concept 'strategy' can of course be used in relation to any actor. In our analysis of the housing situation of women householders, the concept 'strategies' was also used in relation to government actions. The strategies of government and of women may, however, not coincide. In that case the government identifies failure; the women identify obstacles. The concept 'strategy' can of course also be used in relation to men householders and to married women.

Household and head of household

Another concept important to elaborate on in this context is household. The household is often the smallest unit in large scale surveys. Although there are many advantages in using it, there are some pitfalls, such as how a household is defined. There is no single definition of that concept.

In housing studies household is often defined in relation to housing, that is, a household comprises the people who share the dwelling and carry out the unpaid work to cater for the immediate needs of the group. For other purposes other criteria for defining the household may have to be used. The household may be studied primarily as an economic unit comprising people living in different places but tied together through different kinds of economic transactions. The large scale survey of migration in Botswana defined the household as a group related by blood or marriage, with economic and social ties, and often making joint decisions. Generally, households identified in that study had many different places of living, located in both urban and rural areas.

Whatever type of definition is used, it does not, as a rule account, for changes over time. Relatives may come and stay for rather long periods and be catered for by the core household. These people may belong to some other household as well, perhaps in rural areas. There may also be absent household members, gone to work somewhere else and living in hostels. There may be people in the dwelling who are relatives and who cook their own food but are not paying tenants. There is no easy way to overcome the problem. The researcher has to listen to the informants and note how they describe their household compositions in relation to the theme of the study. Often pragmatic decisions have to be taken. If it is desirable to make comparisons with other studies or use supplementary data, it may be necessary to adjust the chosen definition to the ones used in these studies.

Another pitfall when the household is used as the smallest unit is that one may take for granted that decisions are shared by all members of the household, and that all have been involved in taking them. When, however, gender relations within the household are problematized, it becomes obvious that this is seldom the case. Both sex and age of the members play an important role when constituting the household's hierarchy.

It may also be difficult to identify the head of the household. It is often the oldest man, or in case of household lacking grown-up men, the oldest woman. In our studies we let the statements from our informants decide. As a rule, the plot holder was also the head of the household, even if an older person stayed in the house. Power to make decisions is often coupled to the achievement of becoming a plot holder, and such a position often overrules positions defined by age.

A model for analyzing gender relations

In order to reveal the impact of power structures on individual actions within the marriage, a broader theoretical framework is needed, a theoretical framework which can be applied to actions between individuals and to customs of marriage and property, to legislation, and to state policy. Yvonne Hirdman (1991), a Swedish historian, has developed an analytic model which fits such purposes. Her basic concepts **gender contract** and **gender system** will be described below together with her arguments for using them.

Yvonne Hirdman, in her development of a gender theory, has tried to create a category which incorporates power structures, that is, a category of the same status as class. She criticizes theories based on gender roles because she considers they avoid power relations. Instead the concept of gender roles creates a functional dichotomy indirectly derived from biology. In that way women are made into a category with less resources, and they are themselves responsible. The dichotomy allows for women's inferior position on the labour market and in politics to be explained by traditions instead of asking why certain traditions survive and others not.

Hirdman argues that the complicated process by which people are shaped into males and females must be understood. This process has institutional, cultural and even biological consequences. For instance, inequalities and differences are created in the process. Hirdman's gender theory not only emphasizes the power relationship, it also tries to understand how women's subordination is recreated again and again. She has identified two characteristic patterns – or logics – in the changeable picture of gender shaping that history demonstrates. They are firstly, the logic of separation between the sexes, and secondly, the logic of the male norm, that is, higher value is automatically given to masculine things.

Gender contracts

To find a way to study these rationalities systematically, Hirdman introduced the concept gender contract. Contract in this context is a broad concept that allows us to analyze the space between men and women, together with the ideas, rules and norms about places, tasks and qualities of men and women in a society which are generated by this space. The gender contracts (or 'contracts' between sexes) can be distinguished as more or less abstract phenomena at different levels, and taken together they create a gender system. The gender system in turn creates a number of 'irrefutabilities', obvious statements about how things are, and should be.

Hirdman points out that the contracts can be found on three levels in society: the abstract level of cultural images, the institutionalized level (the concrete level of work, politics and culture), and the interpersonal level. On the second and third level, class structure, family relations, and age operate and contribute to shaping the gender contracts. As I see it, these levels can be broken down further, especially the level of institutions. There is the level high up in the hierarchy of politics where policy decisions are taken, the level at the bottom where these policies are implemented by people in the field, and often one or more levels in between.

At all these levels more or less easily identified contracts are at work, whether or not the words men and women are mentioned. Changes in contracts on one level have an impact on contracts on other levels. The contracts are often hidden by the two logics, the one of male norm and the one of separation between the sexes. Thus, if the aim is to carry out a gender analysis, the researcher must investigate what is embedded 'between' the lines in policy documents and what is hidden in men's and women's everyday statements.

A gender concept which includes gender contracts allows us to consider changeability and historicity; it allows us to discuss variations among women related to class, age, family status, etc.; it allows us to include the relationship between men and women, 'maleness' and 'femaleness' and puts into focus the fact that this gender shaping relationship plays a fundamental social, economic and political role. Changes occur because the system is open to disturbances and can be questioned. The gender system is a dynamic system. The dialectic process is, however, not necessarily a change from oppression to emancipation; it may also result in an ideological reinforcement of abstract meanings of 'he' and 'she'.

Particular gender contracts, i.e. a concretization of the gender system, are specific in time and setting. These specific gender contracts provides the point of departure for women's strategies as well as for men's responses, sometimes in the shape of almost conspiratorial resistance.

Modernity and democracy

In her analysis of Western history Hirdman argues that the breakthrough of modernity meant the development of strong sex-integrating impulses. One such impulse was that the capitalist system ignored earlier systems. Instead, it chose the cheapest labour, often female labour. Another impulse, and perhaps more important, was the democratic concept, that is, ideas about equality of human beings regardless of race, social position and sex. These ideas of democracy grew and were in principle shared by most people. Thus the sex-integrating rules and the existing 'traditional' gender system's rules of segregation and gender-hierarchies worked against each other. In this process the male positions, tasks and qualities grew, while the female positions shrank. 'This did not merely happen; it was created through human acts,' Hirdman postulates.

In the development of Western modern societies, assumptions about conflicting dichotomies between the sexes began to play important and legitimizing roles. For instance, a distinction between productive and reproductive economies was made; so was a distinction between the public, male sphere and the private, female, subordinate sphere. The public and productive spheres became the 'big world' or 'big life' which were allowed to expand in different ways. In contrast the 'little world' of women became 'a subordinate, unproblematized (forgotten) "prerequisite" '.

Although such an analysis refers to Western societies, I can see similar transformations in Southern Africa countries. Independence, and consequently also democracy, came later in these countries, where the conflict between sex-integrating forces and the gender system's segregating rules is of a later date. This conflict becomes obvious when the constitutions of the new independent countries are studied. Most, if not all, constitutions include a declaration that human rights apply to all citizens regardless of sex, race, etc. Nonetheless, sex is excluded from the criteria specified for illegal discrimination in the constitutions of some countries. Also, a number of laws, such as the marriage law, are excluded from the general prohibition of illegal discrimination. Hirdman has developed her theories further. With the emergence of democracy a triangle can be distinguished; two sides are made up by the integrative forces she calls capitalism/industrialism and democracy and the base is 'the segregative logics of the gender system'. In the middle of the triangle there is the built-in conflict between the sexes over issues of work, places and interpretation of reality. This built-in conflict insists upon the continual creation and re-creation of new gender contracts. They in turn create a modernized gender system which helps shape society in a mutual process.

This process is indeed a distinguishing feature of modernization in line with Marx's famous characterization, 'all that is solid melts into air'. Furthermore, the process of recreating gender contracts fits well into the theory of structuration as developed by Giddens.

In the case of former colonies I argue that another triangle was at work before independence, namely, the one constituted by capitalism/industrialism, colonialism and the indigenous gender system. Capitalism/industrialism and colonialism cannot, in this situation, be labelled strong integrative forces. They were, rather, strong interfering forces, and the outcome varies from country to country. I think it is important to be aware of the impact of colonialism on the gender system and the gender contracts at different levels. Such an awareness helps us to understand the contracts' construction at the time of independence. The impact of colonization can, for instance, be studied in how indigenous laws and rules regarding marriage and inheritance were transformed by the colonial power.

Likeness and sameness

In today's societies, the conflict caused by capitalism and democracy becomes increasingly acute the more sex-integrated a society becomes, Hirdman argues. The reason is that today's conflict between sex-integrating forces and the existing gender system comprises two opposing aspects: the 'conflict of sameness' and 'the conflict of differences'. When women move into male-dominated areas, do male jobs, demand male rights, etc., this is allowed because of the principle of 'sameness of the sexes'. At the same time the mixing of men and women in the same arena threatens the rule of the male norm. This situation creates the 'conflict of sameness'. At the same time the conflicts escalate because the integration of men and women reveals their differences. In this 'conflict of difference' it becomes obvious that various institutions in society are modelled on the male norm, and the biological differences become a source of provocation. For instance, child-bearing becomes an illness and a deviation.

As a result, women in modern societies are trapped into an insoluble unfruitful definition of their own nature. Are women primarily people and secondarily women, or vice versa? It is also women who are forced to formulate the problem.

The model's applicability

Hirdman has offered what she calls a theoretical blueprint for understanding the gender dynamics in society and how the relations between men and women are constantly changing as a result of negotiations and contracts. I consider it a very useful model, although it may not be easy to use in the analysis of empirical data or to make interviews that reveal the existing gender contracts which can be summarized into a gender system. This model, constructed by a historian, is perhaps more easily used if changes over long periods are the researcher's main interest.

The model's main significance within the GRUPHEL project is that it offers a means to be aware of the forces at work in the relationship between men and women. Men and women are perceived as actors shaping their lives, and the structural obstacles and opportunities caused by the gender system can be explored. We deal with a process; the system is being created and recreated all the time, and the process takes place at all levels of society and in different ways: in the way laws are written, judgements, policy documents and regulations are formulated, in the way men and women act as politicians, as administrators, as supervisors, as parents, as spouses, etc. The gender contracts may not be congruent at different levels; the normal case is probably the opposite. This fact allows us to understand a seemingly contradictory reality. With the theoretical model in the back of our heads, we can develop our proposals, analyze our data and draw conclusions.

Methodological considerations

The methodology used in a study should be the result of the type of questions formulated and the theoretical framework chosen for developing the study. A major distinction is made between qualitative and quantitative methods. If we want to understand processes and why and how people act under certain conditions, that is, if we want to focus on men and women as actors and as negotiators in society, qualitative methods have many advantages. It is not easy to get answers to these questions through quantitative methods. Quantitative methods correspond to questions like how often? with what frequency? and is there a relation between income and house investments?

There is not enough space to discuss qualitative methods in detail here; just a few comments will be given. Qualitative methods comprise many ways of working. In-depth interviews are frequently used within the GRUPHEL project. Instead of a statistical sample, a limited number of strategically selected people constitute the informants. It is important that the considerations which led up to the selection of informants are presented in the report. It is also important to discuss the influence the researcher may have had on the interviews.

A research project can make use of both methods if the two types of questions are posed. Instead of collecting quantitative data oneself to get an overall picture of, for instance, the frequency of women householders, data from large scale surveys can be used.

In our housing studies Ann and I have made use of existing quantitative surveys. The data obtained from such surveys supplemented the findings derived from interviews analyzed according to qualitative methods. We have not had time or money for large scale surveys; nonetheless, we wanted to put our findings in a context which appeals to policy makers. For example, if we find that a certain group of women develops a certain kind of strategy, policy makers want to know some characteristics of the group, such as its size and average age. When deciding on policy, they will know what target group will be reached. It is our experience that there exist quite a number of quantitative surveys for such purposes. At the same time there is a lack of studies based on qualitative methods, which allow us to understand processes and people's actions.

When making use of existing quantitative surveys, one must be cautious. As pointed out previously, there are a number of pitfalls when using concepts such as 'household' and 'head of household'. These pitfalls become obvious when you start to look closely at census and similar data. One must be very careful and very critical when using figures from surveys compiled by others. Whether or not the data relate properly to the new project's questions, and whether or not 'household', etc. are defined in accordance with the new project are just some of the issues that must be investigated. It is very important the that shortcomings of data presentations are honestly discussed.

RESEARCH PAPERS

Chapter Four

Women as 'Home-makers' and Men as 'Heads' of Households: Who is Responsible for Housing Improvements?

Nolulamo N. Gwagwa

Introduction

The household, as a basic unit of society, forms the basis for a number of social and economic policies. However, the dominant approach has been to look at the household as a unit rather than examining more closely what happens inside it. Fundamental to this neglect are three basic assumptions about the household. Firstly, that households are nuclear in structure with a wife, husband and children. Therefore there is no need to understand different household structures. Secondly, is the notion of a unified household whose members pool resources and services to the equal benefit and wellbeing of the household. Thirdly, is the assumption of a clear sexual division of labour within the household, with the husband as the breadwinner responsible for the economic wellbeing, and the wife as a home-maker looking after the social wellbeing of the household (Moser, 1993).

This paper seeks to add to the body of literature that critiques these assumptions and therefore 'enters' the household to examine its internal dynamics. Central to this literature is the enquiry into gender issues within the household, how these impact on relations within the household, and, hence, to the functioning of the household as a unit. To accomplish this three very closely related issues are addressed in this paper, both explicitly and implicitly.

First, the validity of the above assumptions is explored. Second, meanings attached by different household members to some of the key concepts behind these assumptions are probed. Third, how these different meanings affect the way households respond to constraints and opportunities available to them, is explored.

To achieve these three objectives the paper analyzes home ownership as a particular housing policy. It asserts that the very notion of home ownership is based on certain implicit assumptions about the household and relations within it. In the housing literature, relationships are often drawn between home ownership and household investment in housing. This, however, remains at a descriptive level, and as such fails to form a useful basis for any penetrating evaluation of the effects of the policy on recipients. The paper therefore suggests a need for an understanding of the actual experiences of men and women within the household (both as individuals *and* as a collective).

Case study

In South Africa, as in many developing countries, site and service has been adopted as a particular strategy to deliver home ownership and security of tenure to low income communities. To examine the issues explained above, a site and service project was chosen. Three points justify this choice.

With site and service, householders have to make critical choices about investment right from the beginning of the process. Also, the history of the project suggests that the majority of households did not have security of tenure in their previous housing. Lastly, as outlined in the next section, the settlement is now twelve years old and therefore ripe for an evaluation.

Inanda Newtown (hereafter known as Newtown) is located north of the Umngeni river in Durban and was established as a response to a cholera outbreak at Amawoti in early 1980. The settlement was laid out as a site and service scheme, and proclaimed as a township in terms of Proclamation 293 of 1962. This gave people access to Deeds of Grant, which is a form of secure tenure. To date approximately 4 690 sites have been developed in Newtown.

The project began with rudimentary services like standpipes at 60 metre intervals, no hot water, pit latrines, gravel roads, or stormwater earth drains, and no electricity.

As for water, approximately 900 households have been connected and a further 700 applications were being processed by the township office. Connection in this case means a standpipe on site, and this costs the household R80.

In 1990 the Durban Metropolitan Transport Advisory Board (DMTAB) estimated the use of pit latrines in Newtown at 98 percent. Thus only a few households use septic tanks and they pay R8 for drainage as and when need arises.

The most common form of access to electricity in Newtown is what is commonly known as the prepaid 'card system'. Through this system households pay R137 connection fee, and a further fee for internal reticulation which varies according to household requirements.

Households were initially permitted to erect temporary structures. For the construction of permanent structures, they were offered choices in the form of assistance in the building process and house type. The Urban Foundation operated an advice centre and material supply yards. The majority of households opted for full technical advice. This involved the Urban Foundation taking the full responsibility of supervising building works and handing over keys with a township manager's certificate to the prospective owner. The owner would, thus, pay for a completed house for which s/he would have specified to the Urban Foundation housing type and finish.

With regard to house type, the advice office had a set of building plans from which people could choose. These differed in size and finish from a simple shell to a five-room house, in order to cater for different affordability levels. The majority of households opted for a shell house. A typical house, therefore, had unplastered cement block walls, cement floated floor, trench foundation, asbestos roof, and no ceiling. As in the case of infrastructure, it was envisaged that households would upgrade their houses in time.

In summary, how much households invested in their housing (house and infrastructure) was determined by the household itself.

This was a function of house type (therefore loan) and level of service. Therefore, householders had to make decisions, on the one hand, on where and how to allocate the resources towards the various components of their housing, and, on the other, between housing and other expenses. This paper examines how these decisions were made and subsequently implemented.

Because of the complexity and sensitivity of issues being researched, due consideration was given to methodological strategies. The following section, therefore, outlines the research methodology followed.

Research methodology

Unquantifiable concepts like relations and decision making processes do not lend themselves well to conventional research methods. The same applies to sensitive questions like income and investment. A two-pronged research strategy was thus adopted. Stage one involved a structured questionnaire survey whose purpose was to establish a broad socio-economic profile of Newtown. More importantly, the survey also provided a sampling frame for the second and main stage of the research. Various authorities, agents, organizations and individuals involved in the project were interviewed to ascertain background information on the project. Relevant plans, maps and aerial photos were also collected.

An attempt was made to inform the Newtown Civic Association about the study. However, because of organizational problems in the area at the time, it was not possible to achieve this. The survey was thus done without informing the community, but no difficulties were experienced in the field because of this omission.

Because of resource constraints, instead of a simple random sample, a multi-cluster one was used. With the use of 1991 1:11 000 aerial photos blown up four times, the township was divided into the three existing sections. Although the sections differ in size, this was not viewed as significant since the Newtown population is fairly homogeneous in character. Having decided on a 220 household sample, these were spread equally amongst the three sections.

Because there were eight assistant researchers, each section was further divided into eight districts. Houses to be targeted within each district were then randomly selected and marked on the aerial photos. Experienced interviewers, including the researcher, conducted the survey. They were first briefed and a pilot of two questionnaires per interviewer administered in section B. The pilot led to the decision to undertake the survey over weekends in order to maximize response. The questionnaire was given to the head of the household or his/her partner, if applicable.

A total of 211 households (96%) were successfully interviewed: 70 from section A; 67 from section B; and 74 from section C. Data was then coded by the researcher with the assistance of four interviewers. A statsgraphics programme was used to manipulate and analyze the data, and the results will be discussed in the next section (see Gwagwa, 1993, for a more detailed analysis of the socio-economic survey).

The second stage and main focus of the research was done after analyzing the socio-economic survey, and identifying main patterns. The following criteria was used to identify households for in-depth study: household structure; household income; number of earners; and person under whose name the title is registered. Although there are many households with a combined income of less than R500, a balance had to be struck between households that are too poor to have money to improve their houses, and those that are too well-off to worry about money. In looking at the number of earners, it was also important to explore situations where different household members are working, that is, husbands, wives, daughters and sons. The same applied to title holder.

Table 1 gives a profile of the criteria for the seven households studied.

In all the seven households, except one, all the earners were interviewed. In one case, an unemployed daughter, whose brother is working, was interviewed. All interviews were conducted individually. It was the intention to bring all adult household members together in a combined household interview, but unforeseen constraints prevented this. All interviews were taped and later transcribed. Analysis was done continuously to identify emerging themes and develop them with further interviews. It was interesting to note that all the men interviewed were very keen and did not present any problems or reservations about the questions asked. On the other hand women, except in two cases (a household head, and a daughter), were very reluctant in the beginning. However, in the end

Table 1: Profile of Households Studied

House No.	Household Structure	Household Income	No. of Earners	Title
A	Nuclear	R1 760	2	Wife
B	Woman Headed	R1 200	3	Head
C	Extended Male Headed	R1 600	2	Head
D	Extended Woman Headed	R1 300	2	Head
E	Nuclear	R 800	1	Head
F	Woman Headed	R2 500	2	Head
G	Extended Woman Headed	R1 303	2	Head

the longest interviews were with women because they provided more elaborate answers even with limited probing.

The purpose of the in-depth interviews was not to get a representative sample of the households, but rather to explore and understand more deeply identified issues.

Socio-economic patterns in Newtown

Whilst Newtown was primarily established for cholera victims from Amawoti (Inanda informal settlement), only a third (29,4%) of the households in fact lived in Greater Inanda before moving to Newtown. Approximately half (48%) came from Durban townships, in particular KwaMashu. Whilst a significant majority (79,6%) own their houses in Newtown, only 30% owned their previous house. This suggests that generally households did not have secure tenure before moving to Newtown. It can thus, be asserted that the settlement presents conducive conditions, and for most households, the first opportunity to invest in their housing in a substantial way.

Not surprisingly, the majority (71,5%) of the houses are registered in the household head's name, and of these 42,6% and 28,9% are male and female heads, respectively. Of particular importance is the 6,1% of cases where houses are registered in wives' names. In all these cases it was reported that the reason had been that the male head was unemployed at the time the loan was applied for. The key question is whether this has any bearing on how and where these households improve their houses, and also on gender relations within the household.

Whilst not a single house is registered in a daughter's name, 0,9% are registered in sons' names. Although insignificant in statistical terms, this raises important gender questions. Similarly is the meaning of 14,2% non-responses. Registration of the house is perceived as a sensitive issue because it implicitly deals with inheritance questions. There is also a set of power relations embedded in property ownership.

The survey also tried to establish who pays for the house. The results show a very close correlation between who owns and who pays for the house. It is worth pursuing this question later. The purpose would be to test the extent to which the 'who pays for the house' responses are in fact socially desirable ones.

Literature on households generally works with three generic household structures: nuclear, woman headed, and extended. Whilst the researcher started with the same categorization, the survey results pointed to the necessity of a further disaggregation. As such five categories were adopted: nuclear (32,2%), single woman headed (13,7%), single male headed (1,4%); extended woman headed (29,8%), extended male headed (20,8%).

Of the total number of households, 3,3% have no cash income at all. A significant proportion of the households, 31,7%, have a combined household income of less than R1 000. This figure, however, needs to be looked at in relation to the 45% no response/unknown category. The survey was thus not immune to the general difficulties of establishing incomes through questionnaire methods.

Despite these limitations, cross-tabulating income with household structure clearly shows nuclear households as having higher incomes. For instance, half of the households with a household income of more than R2 000 are nuclear. The fact that the second largest category are male headed extended households is indicative of the level of male incomes in relation to other members of the household. Extended woman headed households, on the other hand, are the poorest, being 42,8% and 39,3% of the total number of householders with a household income of zero and between R1 and R500, respectively. The question is to what extent does the dominance of male incomes translate into their contribution towards housing improvement?

In discussing incomes, it is also useful to introduce number of earners per household. At issue is whether there is necessarily a correlation between the number of earners and the level of household income. The fact that nuclear households have the lowest number of earners whilst having the highest overall household incomes, suggests that individual income is a stronger determinant of household income than number of earners per se.

The second reason for addressing the question of number of earners is to explore to what extent source of income affects gender relations within the household. For instance, would there be a significant difference between two households with the same structure and household income, but differences in the number and sex of the individuals who are earning that income? Moreover, would that have any impact on the nature and level of household investment in their housing?

At the heart of this research is an exploration of the relationship between household investment in housing and gender relations within the household. Two main indicators were used to measure investment: physical improvement to the house, and furniture bought by the household.

As explained in section two of this paper, households had a choice over housing type and building assistance, and most households chose a shell house built by the Urban Foundation. In essence, households had a basic shelter to start with and it was up to them to decide on the nature and level of improvement and according to what priorities. The rest of these sections therefore present how different households responded to this challenge.

Almost all households have divided their shell house. The general pattern is one lounge, two bedrooms and one kitchen. What is interesting is the small size of kitchens, which are even smaller than the standard township kitchen. People seem to trade off small kitchen for a bigger lounge, at least in relative terms.

After dividing walls (in numbers) which could be translated to improvements to privacy, most households have opted for the finishes. For example, 79,6% and 69,7% of the households have plastered and painted their houses, respectively. Of those households who have not plastered or painted the whole house, the lounge and the kitchen seem to get more priority, respectively. Bedrooms are generally the most neglected rooms. Many (62,5%) of the households have improved their floors. The majority have opted for concrete floors, while a small percentage have put in carpets and/or tiles.

Electricity has been installed by 71,1% of the households. It is, however, surprising that only 14,2% of the household have brought water on site. The connection cost cannot be said to be a deterrent because it costs a household R80 as opposed to R137 for electricity.

Very few households have increased their space through extensions and outside rooms. These are 14,9% and 9,9%, respectively. The latter largely correlates with households that have working sons.

In terms of furniture bought since households moved to Newtown, the following pieces were used as indicators: stove, fridge, television, video, and lounge suite. The basis for choosing these particular items is that they represent generic rooms in a house. Questions were also asked about bedroom suites, but interviewers confused bedroom suites and beds. As an indicator it was thus dropped in the analysis because of the unreliable data.

A high percentage, 60,2%, of households using electric stoves in fact have two-plate stoves supplied with the electricity connection. Therefore, they did not necessarily make the choice to buy it. Of those with electricity, 19,9% households still use paraffin stoves. The most common paraffin stove in the area is a one-plate primus stove. Thus households have generally not invested in cooking facilities. Furthermore, only 47,8% of the households have fridges. Only 56,8% of those with electricity in fact have fridges. Taking into account the number of households with televisions (51,1%) and videos (39,3%), the cost of a fridge cannot be a significant enough factor. Television ownership in the area is higher than that of fridges. Lounge suite ownership is also higher than that of electric stoves. A number of gender conclusions can be deduced from these patterns.

To conclude this section, a presentation of results on who, within the household, has paid for what investment will be outlined. Because the research is concerned specifically with gender relations, household members will be defined in terms of their relationship to the household head, which in itself has gender connotations. It is important to acknowledge the limitations of data obtained on this theme. Because questions raised are sensitive, the possibility of socially desirable answers is increased.

The survey suggests that heads of households generally pay for investments, and this applies to both physical improvements and furniture. It is interesting to note that what is reported as joint payment tends to correlate with households where men are unemployed. Of significance also is the difference between what daughters and sons pay for. Sons seem to pay for physical improvements to the house, whilst daughters pay for finishes. Whether this is indicative of the cost of improvements in relation to incomes or gender differences, needs further exploration. Taking into account inheritance practices in this particular culture one would be tempted to emphasize the latter.

A comparison of who pays for what physical improvements and who has paid for what piece of furniture, as illustrated in Table 2, suggests a more compelling argument for a gender explanation of these patterns.

Table 2: Furniture: Who pays?			
Furniture	Wife	Daughter	Son
Stove	20,9	3,0	0,0
Fridge	19,2	7,4	1,7
Television	13,3	5,4	6,7
Video	14,3	7,9	9,5
Lounge suite	17,1	6,1	7,1

In relation to their total contributions towards furniture, wives seem to invest more in cooking facilities like stoves and fridges. They also invest in lounge suites. On the other hand, daughters' contributions seem to be mediated by age as indicated, for instance, by more emphasis on fridges than stoves. However, they still invest more than their brothers in kitchen facilities. Higher investment in videos, lounge suite and television, whilst investing nothing in stoves strongly suggests that sons' investment decisions are mediated by both gender and generation.

Interesting patterns emerge when cross-tabulating improvements with household structure. Whilst extended women headed households, on average, have the lowest incomes, they score the highest percentage as far as making physical improvement to houses is concerned. Nuclear households, on the other hand, feature highest in building outside rooms. Investment in furniture in extended women headed households is almost at the same level as in nuclear. Extended women households are also, on average, the biggest in size. It is perhaps important to state how these households are constituted. It is all those households that are headed by women who stay with people other than their own children.

This section has described the investment patterns of different households in Newtown. Whilst it begins to present interesting gender and generation patterns, we still do not understand what gender processes are at play within these households. With the use of case study material collected, the next section of the paper, therefore, enters some of these households to explore these emerging patterns further.

Internal household dynamics

Housing improvements are a sociological statement about what the household deems essential for its functioning. Whilst this is also mediated by the amount of resources available to the household, this paper shows that how these are allocated within the household is also critical. What became apparent in the in-depth study is that there are distinct gender differences on what is perceived as essential. More importantly though, are gender differences on motivations and explanations, even where both men and women identified the same improvement as essential.

Water
Although very few households have connected water, women within studied households stressed its importance.

Phile, an employed wife in nuclear household, told me that: 'Water is important. Women have to collect water all the time. There are long queues, sometimes the tap is not working. Water is life, we use it often. Also, my children suffer because they have to help me collect water'.

Yanga, an unemployed wife in an extended male headed household, said that 'I rely on my neighbour's children to collect water for me. It is far for me. I am old and sickly'.

On the other hand, whilst also arguing that water is important, men did not identify distance from standpipes as a factor, nor did they raise the reliability question. Instead, they insisted that electricity was more important than water.

Bhoji, a working husband in a nuclear household, contends that 'Electricity is more important than water. We use it for many things like TV, radio, stove and lighting. Before we had electricity we used batteries.'

Electricity

All interviewed women also emphasized the centrality of electricity to their housework. Cooking and ironing was reported as faster, cleaner and easier with electricity. Electricity was also declared a cheaper source of energy.

Phile emphasized: 'I use a hot plate to cook. Also I have an electric iron and kettle. The kettle is broken at the moment. I bought all these appliances myself because my husband was not interested. I realized that electricity is better, it is fast ... Paraffin is expensive, electricity is 100%. Candles are expensive and dangerous.'

Fridge

Both men and women agreed on the usefulness of fridges. However, probing further it became evident that women prioritized it more than men.

The advantage of bulk-buying was mentioned, but it became apparent that it meant different things to men and women. For men, bulk-buying is associated with reduction of costs, therefore financial savings.

Mngce, a working husband (Yanga's husband) said: 'With a fridge I can buy meat in bulk, and that works out cheaper.'

For women, bulk buying presents an opportunity to access more money from husbands on pay day. Consequently it limits the number of occasions they have to ask for additional money towards the end of the month. Secondly, women see the fridge as opening possibilities for controlling their husbands' liquor consumption level, thus limiting amount of 'household money' spent on liquor.

Laughing Phile told me: 'I thought he might be motivated to buy the fridge as he can also use it to store his beer. I even suggested it to him indirectly. He did not even look at me. I have given up and I have to buy it myself because we need it.'

Also, drinking from home is seen by women as being safer for their husbands who would otherwise come home late from shebeens.

Thirdly, the fridge is an important income generating tool for women. Most women were selling iced-drinks and cold drinks to extend their incomes.

Asanda, a working mother in a woman headed household told: 'Right now we have iced cold drinks in the fridge which we sell. This helps us quite a lot. We also keep food, like leftovers, especially in summer'.

Lounge

The lounge is an important room in most houses. It houses the television and hi-fi. Despite acknowledgements of space shortages by all interviews, the lounge is not used as a sleeping space.

Phile insisted, 'It is not correct to sleep in the lounge because visitors might arrive early or late and find people sleeping. That is not nice, I don't like it.'

For Kholeka, a working mother in an extended woman headed household: 'The main thing for me is using the lounge for prayer meetings, when fellow Christians visit me. Well, the kids use it more often, for the TV and music.'

Men, on the other hand, see the lounge as a place to entertain visitors, and where they, themselves, relax and read the paper.

Bhoji said: 'I use the lounge when I read the paper. My wife is usually in the kitchen. I watch TV or play cassettes. I sit with my friends in the lounge.'

The above discussion shows that within households, there are conflicting notions of what is essential improvement. Meaning put to improvements also differs. The question then is what are the implications of this for men and women within the household, and also for their respective spending patterns?

Space needs

An interesting dilemma confronts women in terms of their space needs. At one level is the desire for bigger and better equipped kitchens as they spend a lot of time in them. On the other hand, these women also view the lounge as essential space for their children and visitors.

Thenji, working mother in a woman headed household, said: 'They (children) usually sit in the lounge, listening to music, watching TV and chatting. I also sit there if there are visitors, but I normally sit in the kitchen or in my bedroom.'

Women, especially working mothers, explicitly admit that they themselves do not have time to spend in the lounge.

Phile told me: 'I spend little time in the lounge. When I come back from work, I go to the kitchen. I drink tea, then I cook. When everybody has eaten I clean the house. Children watch TV in the lounge, I go to sleep'.

Natasha, an unemployed daughter in a woman headed household, confirmed that 'When my mother comes home from work she is tired, maybe she only watches the seven o'clock news. Otherwise she is somewhere between the kitchen and her bedroom. I watch the TV most. My brother spends a lot of time with his drinking friends, like all drinking people.'

Therefore, trying to ascertain who benefits from what improvements is quite complex. It can be argued that for these women satisfying their children' needs is a much more important benefit than their immediate needs for bigger kitchens. Small kitchens in both female headed and male headed households seems to suggest this conclusion.

Implications of different priorities

For any household to get approval from the township manager to extend the house or to build an outside room, and to bring water on site, they must have paid in full for the site. Also, the title holder must sign the application form. The fact that men, who are title holders, do not prioritize water means that fulfilling these requirements is not essential for them.

Phile told me: 'I started with electricity because I had a problem with water. When I went to the office they said my husband must come personally. I told him, even tried to talk nicely to him. He did not respond. I reported this to the office, and they told me everything depends on him because the house is registered in his name. I thought let me wait and see if I can't be patient with him. I am still waiting, what else can I do.'

Yanga stated: 'Water is a problem. We have not paid for the site. My husband can try to pay slowly even if it is R100,00 per month. I asked the office and they said it is okay. You know, he does not have any accounts, so he can do it. If I was working I would have paid for the site ... Women are not like men, they see things differently. I don't want to expose family problems. But it is true that women work for a better home, also they like good things. Men just don't care, I don't know why. I stopped working long ago because of diabetes. That was the end of good things in this family. We were sleeping on the floor so I saved and bought a bed with my pension. He doesn't care'.

Loli had another story: 'I am paying arrears on rates. I used to pay and then told him it's his turn to pay, the house is his anyway. He was still working then. Of course, he did not pay until it accumulated. Now the office says they can't connect water because we owe money. Guess what, I am paying his arrears now. I am the one who is suffering because of water.'

An important result of different priorities within households is an increase in the workload of most women. Because they do not control the allocation of household income they have to devise alternative income generating strategies.

Yanga said: 'I sell chips and other small things to get money for food. He gives me little money and insists that it must last the whole month. I do make a profit, but I also have to pay for electricity, the house and bread for the children. When he (husband) runs short of tobacco he also demands this money ... I don't know how much he earns. He works shifts and overtime. He got a bonus but did not give me any extra money. I just kept quiet, it is better that way ... I have told myself I will save and start plastering the house. I can't wait for him, he will never do anything.'

Therefore, over and above their formal employment and reproductive roles, these women have to engage in informal activities, including 'stokfels' to extend household income. They, in fact, argue that it is a luxury for a mother to have one source of income. This is the money they use to buy fridges, repay arrears, and feed the whole household.

Fuquza, working wife to Bhoji, argues: 'It's a problem to rely on men. As a woman you must also get money from somewhere else. It is difficult to get money from him ... Fathers, fathers, do what? I don't want to lie. This new generation, nowadays they don't care about the home, they don't care for children. They are just fathers by name. It's true.'

Men as heads of households

Despite the disagreements over essentials and consequently over the allocation of resources within households and the implications thereof for housing improvement, it is instructive to note that women see a critical role for their husbands in these households. They acknowledge that regardless of the size of their incomes, men are not the main determinants of the household's economic wellbeing. However, men as heads of households bring with them dignity to the household.

Phile said: 'He does not contribute (money) to the house. So, I ask myself what use is he to my children? On the other hand, his presence gives the home some dignity. This is important to me and the children.'

Kholeka added: 'People outside, especially drunk people, don't just come and do as they please if there's a man. So he does bring that dignity ... Also, a father's love is important to the children. They can have me, but there is always that gap for their father even if he does not buy them anything. I believe that.'

Fuquza argued: 'Children without a father, it's a problem. Even if he doesn't do anything for them, just the name that they have a father. It makes a difference. There is that dignity if he is there. Women don't have that dignity.'

This observation is supported by men who see themselves as heads of households, with the role being conferred on them by nature and tradition. They further insist that women headed households lack this status. In addition, and despite what women say about them, men still perceive themselves as main providers for their households.

Bhoji insists: 'My neighbour, there is no man there. They come to me if they have a problem. If there is a traditional feast or a custom to be done, they need a man to serve the traditional beer. Women can't do that. You see, the man is the head of the home. I am the head of this house, the person who looks after this home. The man is the head even if he is not working. This house is registered in her name. It does not matter. I'm still the head, therefore it is my house and she is my wife. This is law of people – the man is the head, he is responsible for everything in the home, all problems and shortages. This is how people live, it's life'.

In conclusion, lessons learnt from this research will be outlined. The main purpose is to redefine some key concepts in analyzing gender processes within households.

Conclusion

Several feminist writers insist that there is no household interest, need or priority. Rather, the household is composed of interests, needs and priorities that are gender and generation specific, reflecting different obligations and responsibilities (Moser & Chant, 1985; Guyer, 1988; Chant, 1991, etc.). These are normatively defined (Mencher, 1988; Bruce, 1989, Wilson, 1987; Moock, 1986), and most rigid in Africa (Bruce, 1989; Guyer, 1986). A cursory look at the results of both the socio-economic survey and in-depth interviews in Inanda Newtown would seem to concur with this assertion.

Feminist literature also suggests that gender division of responsibility is more or less similar across culture (for example, Wilson, 1987, on London; Munochonga, 1988, on Zambia; Fapohunda, 1988, on Nigeria; Chant, 1991, on Mexico). Men are largely responsible for major one-off expenditures like housing, education, health and consumer durables, whilst women are responsible for food, child care and children's clothing.

It is further proposed that these gender specific responsibilities translate into different expenditure priorities, hence the struggle over resources. An increase in income means that an individual increases expenditure on their socially allocated areas and not necessarily the general standard of living of other members (Fapohunda, 1988).

In her seminal work on gender planning, Moser (1993) writes that 'of the three planning stereotypes, the most problematic is the third, which relates to gender division of labour within the household' (p.27). The contentious point embedded in this stereotype is the assumption that this division is benign and complementary. Most problematic for this paper are the unproblematized concepts of 'homemaker', 'breadwinner' and 'head' of household, associated with gender division of labour within households.

The gender specific responsibilities assigned to men and women within households are closely linked to a particular understanding of women as 'home-makers' and men as 'breadwinners' and as 'heads' of households. The content and tasks associated with these titles is hardly analyzed. It is important to note, as this research clarifies, that content includes both concrete and ideological meanings.

A close examination of 'who pays' for what housing investment in Newtown, reveals that whilst housing might not be their traditional area of responsibility, women invest in it substantially (in relation to resources available to them). Whilst this point is raised by Sorock *et al.* (1984), Nimpuno-Parente (1987) and Moser and Chant (1985), this research underlines the centrality of women's *indirect* investment in housing. This includes 'helping' their husbands pay off arrears on housing loans, and paying for sites.

This 'helping out' is not insignificant both in terms of quantity of resources involved and frequency of 'help'. Central to an effective dissection of gender processes within households, is a disaggregation of concepts of women as 'home-makers' and men as 'heads' of household. Such a redefinition improves our understanding of investment behaviours of men and women within households, and underlying struggles over resources.

Women are perceived as home-makers both by themselves and by men. This perception is the same regardless of household type. The content that is given to this role means that women play this role whether they are in male headed households or they head households. Home-making is therefore performed independent of men, although male financial contribution might enhance it. Central to this role is providing for the household, but more especially for children. Invariably this compels women to earn formally, informally or through social networks. In most cases they tap on a combination of these three sources. A 'good home-maker' therefore provides for and ensures good food, a good home, a TV, water on site. To what extent can this role be defined as maternal altruism? Is it simultaneously maternal self-interest? More importantly, in male headed households home-making requires constantly negotiating and sustaining a state of equilibrium within the household. Also, home-making provides that equilibrium as Phile, Loli and Yanga in this research have shown. However, another critical component of this equilibrium encompasses the notion of a male 'head' who brings dignity to the household. In concrete terms for women this dignity means discipline to children and physical protection from public violence. In fact, some women argue that it is precisely when men do not guarantee this task, rather than when they do not contribute financially, that the state of equilibrium gets threatened and they are jettisoned from the household.

The concept of dignity, however, seems to fundamentally encompass an ideological component, as Fuquza aptly puts it. It is useful to note that this notion is upheld by women in all household structures. This raises interesting theoretical questions about the role of women headed households in challenging, fundamentally, gender division of labour within households and in society generally.

What this paper suggests, therefore, is that gender division of labour within households is a reality. What has changed is the *content* of roles played by men and women. 'Home-making' has been substantially extended to centrally take on board breadwinning. On the other hand, the content of male roles has shifted from breadwinning to emphasize 'heading' households. The concrete content of this role is not very clear, hence reification of its ideological content. This paper concludes that herein lies the basis for understanding the investment behaviour of men and women within households. At the end of the day, men's position within the household is not measured by their provisioning for the household, but by their status as a head. It, therefore, does not necessarily and fundamentally include investing in housing. For further research it will be useful to trace historically the origins and changing content of these concepts.

Chapter Five

Basotho Women's Role in Urban Housing: The Case of Maseru

Tiisetso Matere-Lieb

Introduction

The importance of housing in a society cannot be overemphasized. It plays very closely interrelated physical, social and economic functions. The physical functions of housing in any society are to protect its occupants and their belongings from the harshness of the elements e.g. rains, storms, winds, dust, the heat of the sun and the cold. Housing also provides its occupants with privacy and offers them general security and comfort.

The social functions of housing are to provide a framework within which individuals, households, and/or communities undergo the development process into becoming fully-fledged human beings, a home being a place in which parents bring up their children and perform all other activities required in the process of socialization of a person. A home is also a place to socialize with friends, neighbours, relatives and visitors.

The direct economic functions of housing may be realized in its form as an investment to a household, for example, whereby a house is rented out thereby earning its owner some rental income; in a case where a house is being pledged as security in support of some financial transaction as in cases of loans and mortgages and/or whereby it provides some space within which an economic activity is being undertaken. The indirect economic functions of housing may be realized when it is adequately sheltering its occupants in a manner that enhances their social, physical and psychological development thereby facilitating their effective participation in other sectors of the economy.

What is of relevance to this study is to point out the gender dynamics within these functions. As a general rule, women, when compared to men, spend more time at home due to the nature of the domestic responsibilities that society assigns to them. One may therefore argue that women are more affected by housing their conditions are men. Women face immediate consequences in situations of physical housing inadequacies.

Again, it is a fact that women, more than men, carry the largest share of the responsibility for raising children and guiding their socialization process that leads them into adulthood. It is therefore women more than men who feel the pressure when the social environment provided by housing is not adequate.

A gender perspective on the direct economic function of housing basically raises legal issues, while a gender perspective on the indirect economic functions raises environmental issues. A healthy and stimulating home environment contributes much to the state of an individual's wellbeing and motivation in life in general thereby enhancing the individual's participation in other fields of life.

A brief review of laws and policies on women and housing

Four pieces of legislation govern all rights over property in Lesotho, namely the two marriage laws – Customary Law and Common Law (the latter is sometimes referred to as Roman Dutch Law), the Land Act of 1979 and the Deeds Registry Act of 1967. Lesotho's draft national housing policy of 1987 is also relevant to the discussions of women and housing.

Under Customary Law a woman is a minor for her whole life, always under the guardianship of her male family lineage. A woman may not be allocated land in her own right. Only men can acquire land. Widows, however, have user rights but they may neither sell nor transfer the property to anybody as it legally belongs to family heirs, usually the eldest son or, where there are no sons, the senior uncle or any male relative so designated by the family.

Under Common Law unmarried women of 21 years or over, widows, divorcees and women married out of Community of Property (sometimes referred to as ante-nuptial) all have a right to acquire property/land. They may dispose of it in any manner they deem fit. However, women married in Community of Property are minors. (This is the most common type of marriage, estimated at over 95% of the cases). Community of Property connotes that all property and rights of spouses which belonged to either of them at the time of marriage and those acquired during the marriage form part of the joint estate, with both spouses having an equal share to their joint property but with the husband as the sole administrator of the estate. Women married in Community of Property may therefore not get into any dealings involving the property except with their husbands' consent.

The Land Act of 1979 simply states that all qualifying citizens of Lesotho are entitled to acquire and transfer land. The Act does not in itself discriminate against women but the marriage laws cited above and the Deeds Registry Act explained below guide its operation. Under the Land (Amendment) Order no. 6 of 1992 Section 8 of the Land Act has been amended to give even rural widows full rights to the land that formed part of the joint estate.

The Deeds Registry Act of 1967 on the other hand stipulates that no immovable property may be registered or transferred in the name of a woman married in Community of Property. Subsequent to allocation of land under the provisions of the Land Act, in order to secure title to that land it must be registered. Furthermore, in order to **put forward property as security for a loan from** the formal financial institutions one needs to prove one's ownership of such property by way of a title. In a way this Act defeats the spirit embodied in the Land Act.

The scenario described above clearly identifies two things: firstly, that there are contradictions in the laws governing women's access to housing and, secondly, that marriage, except under ante-nuptial, is a dominant factor placing women in a subordinated position with respect to property as an economic tool. A woman married under

Customary Law has nothing to her name, irrespective of how much she is contributing towards the family welfare and the one married in Community of Property has limited access to land as she depends on the goodwill of her husband. She has no independent property rights even to use as security for obtaining a loan to develop her own housing; even if such a woman were to have financial means to develop housing, that house would not exclusively belong to her in the end as it would have to form part of the joint estate and, in most cases, be registered in the husband's name. Any benefit from it would be derived only with the husband's consent. Women married out of Community of Property, adult single females, divorcees and common law widows are legal majors.

The research findings that follow attempt to illustrate to what extent the law is a factor in women's role in housing in practice and what other factors warrant recognition.

Objectives of the research

The research seeks to determine the following:
a) The extent to which urban Basotho women are involved throughout the process of housing provision, specifically in planning for and designing their houses; in the actual construction of those houses and in their management.
b) The factors, if any, which constrain women's participation in the provision of housing in general.
c) What have actually been the experiences and strategies of women house owners in acquiring housing and of women working in housing related professions in dealing with both male colleagues and the general public?

Methodology

It is important here to bear in mind that the emphasis is on qualitative methods of research. I have therefore tended to look for validity rather than reliability and replicability which characterize quantitative research. I am seeking to understand the motives and beliefs behind the actions of my subjects as well as their own perspectives of the situation; hence the modest sample size and limited statistical evidence which under quantitative methods would justifiably be condemned as unconvincing.

The study was carried out in the urban area of Maseru, the capital of Lesotho, the reasons being that of easy access as I also live there and, most importantly, Maseru being the biggest urban area, I felt I could get the most varying situations likely to depict what can be obtained in any of the other urban areas. I personally conducted all the interviews and the discussions.

Urban Maseru was classified into three categories based on three distinct land allocation/acquisition procedures.

1) *The public formal housing areas* which cover sites-and-services project areas and 'turnkey' housing schemes that are implemented by the Lesotho Housing and Land Development Corporation. In general, the project areas are adequately serviced with basic infrastructure to varying levels, depending on the income groups that they are undertaken for.

2) *The private formal housing areas* which are concentrated within the inner city. Under the provisions of the 1979 Land Act these areas are professionally planned and surveyed. The Commissioner of Lands then publicizes the sites in the government gazette and newspapers. Power to grant titles is vested in the Urban Land Allocation Committee. They are relatively the best serviced with roads, electricity supply, sewerage and water connections hooked to the city's main lines.

3) *The private informal housing areas* which cover peri-urban areas. Before the 1979 Land Act, these areas had been administered as traditional areas with no planning provisions at all and up until now still lack basic infrastructure and services like access roads, electricity, clean drinking water and hygienic sanitary facilities as they are not connected to the main city lines.

Some house owners were picked from within each of the above classifications and an effort was made to cover the four categories of women house owners i.e. married women, widows, divorcees and single women since the law treats them differently.

The area of Phahameng was chosen as an example of a public formal housing area. The beneficiary lists were organized to allow the identification of women house owners according to their marital status.

For the private formal housing areas, a number of households were chosen from records of mortgagors at the Lesotho Building Finance Corporation as well as records of property owners at the Department of Lands, Surveys and Physical Planning. From the location given to the property, it was possible to choose only those that fall under the classification of formal since a lot of mortgagors and other property owners also came from informal areas but have by now formalized their tenurial titles into leases.

For the private informal housing areas, a research method termed 'snow-balling' was used. I used people that I know in those areas to identify the categories of households I was interested in and these were visited. I conducted structured interviews with the chosen owners of houses asking what their role had been throughout the whole process of obtaining a house which included securing a site, designing the house, arranging the necessary finance, securing building materials, finding a builder, supervising the actual construction and, lastly, the managing of a house after completion.

In cases of husband/wife households an attempt was made to interview them both, and separately if they so chose, but I should confess that it was not often that I found both at home at the same time. A total of 45 households were interviewed, 15 in each area.

I also held discussions with some house building contractors and building-materials producing establishments. I wished to discover whether they had any female employees and, if so, what roles they played, and which factors determined those roles, etc.

Some organizations handling housing related services like water supply, carpentry workshops, steel works, etc. were visited. Discussions held with both men and women working there focusing on experiences from interacting with one another and with clients.

In addition to the above, discussions were held with government and parastatal organizations officials dealing with housing policy, physical planning, land allocation, housing finance, housing development and technical/vocational education for a better understanding of the research topic. An analytical review of their documents as well as that of the relevant literature to include books, journals, conference/workshop/seminar papers and newspapers was also undertaken.

Women house owners and their role in housing

In this paper women house owners are classified into four categories based on their marital status. This is a factor which has been laid out in the review of women and the law and plays a determinant role in their access to housing. The importance of other variables such as income, education level and age, etc. was appreciated but they were not part of this research analysis.

Public formal housing areas
Firstly, I shall report on the experiences of women in a public formal setting at Phahameng. I found that at the application intake stage of the project, for the male headed households, the men themselves had to apply. In cases where the male household head was not present the wife could apply in the husband's name but she had to produce sufficient proof that the husband had given her permission. This was a requirement by the Lower Income Housing Company, the then executing agency for low income housing projects commonly known as LEHCO-OP. All the other households where husbands were present at the time of application and had applied directly simply reported that this was in order as husbands were heads of households. The titles for sites in all these cases were registered in husbands' names as per the provisions of the Deeds Registry Act.

Widows applied in their own right and registered titles in their names. They were required to prove their widowhood by producing a copy of the death certificate or any valid written proof. In one case, a widow had produced a letter from her rural chief certifying her marital status and recommending that since she was fully responsible for her household she should be considered for allocation of a site in her own right. This letter was taken as legitimate proof of her widowhood.

Single beneficiaries applied and registered titles in their own right. One of them told me that it had been easier to enrol in the project than try to find a site on the private market where she had to compete with married couples which are the society's model of a household. For a long time she had tried to get a site through the Ministry responsible for land and from the chiefs but had failed. Another single woman reported that the chiefs had said as she was single she should remain a child in her parents' home all her life. This is a concept that underlies the Sesotho customary law and that can obviously be expected from a traditional institution of chieftainship. She found this very unfair as she was over 40 years old.

Divorced women too had applied for sites and some had them registered in their own names. A striking point though was that the divorced respondents had only been separated (not divorced) at the time of application. One woman, for example, said her marriage was at a breaking point, with the divorce case already in court. As she was keen to have a house of her own, she presented her story to LEHCO-OP and she was accepted when it seemed clear that by the time site allocations would be made her divorce case would be through.

Another said that her father-in-law wrote a letter in her favour which confirmed that his son had abandoned his wife and children many years before and giving his blessings to the idea of her being given a site in her own right.

There were also beneficiaries who were still under the 'separated' category. One said she had to produce an affidavit proving that she and her children were long separated from the husband and that therefore she was fully responsible for her household, with full guardianship over the children. She said, for her, divorce was not possible as her religion did not allow it. The other separated beneficiary had to do everything in the name of husband. She had been considered as still legally married since her divorce proceedings were not yet advanced at the time of application. Fortunately, the husband had been co-operative in signing papers on her behalf. As he had not shown any interest in the house until that time, she hoped that after their divorce, which according to her should be soon, she should be in a position to pay off her loan and also change the registration of the site title into her own name.

It is clear, therefore, that management sometimes took upon itself the right to arbitrarily act in favour of long deserted women by giving them sites in their own right on the merit of their stories after they had been subjected to verification or based on written evidence and requests from the in-laws or chiefs who are traditional authorities.

As Phahameng beneficiaries were provided with house plans, both husbands, wives, and the other classifications of women house owners had no role in designing their original structures. Also, at the construction stage, beneficiaries had been provided with the services of a project supervisor who saw to it that builders did their job well. Beneficiaries had to employ builders and sign out for building materials from LEHCO-OP stores. Husbands and wives participated in securing builders and husbands had to authorize wives when they could not come to sign out materials. Women heads of households authorized their sons when they could not come. In general, women reported that they visited building sites more regularly than husbands to check on progress.

Many households have by now extended their structures and what is reported below on women owners role in the two other area classifications also applies to house owners in public formal housing areas at the time of house extensions.

Private informal areas

The research findings reveal that it was often women who took the lead in initiating the process of acquiring sites. Women kept their ears open for news/information about sites' availability. As soon as they heard about the possibility of acquiring a site married women had to urge the husbands to meet with the relevant authorities, in this case, chiefs and/or field owners. If they thought the husbands were delaying they took it upon themselves to conduct the negotiations up to the point of agreeing on and/or paying a price. Occasionally they would be asked why the husbands were not the ones coming. The reasons given were that husbands were not working in Maseru at the time or were busy with other things. But, through probing, I found out that mostly it was that husbands were there but did not consider the acquisition of a site a priority. At times they were not even interested in engaging in such a commitment-demanding undertaking as the building of a house. The wives would then inform the husbands about their meetings with chiefs or field owners as the case might be, and the husbands were usually supportive from then on.

One wife told me that her husband was the kind of person who would just not take the initiative to embark on such major projects as housing but that once she started he became very supportive. She regretted that she had not realized this early on as she now felt she could have long undertaken many house improvements as her husband would have supported her.

Even when the wives were the ones who met with chiefs and/or field owners in all cases they used the husbands' names for the registration of sites. An interesting point to note here was that almost all of the wives were not even aware that there existed a legal provision which actually prohibited the registration of sites in their own names. Asked why they did not try to register the sites in their names some wives said in the Sesotho culture husbands were the heads of households so it was only logical to undertake household's business in husbands' names. Others said they did not like to appear selfish to start doing things in their own names just because the husbands had not been able to be personally there. This latter response was in cases where husbands were working away from Maseru and they had to leave the wives in charge of household affairs.

Single women, widows and divorcees could go through the whole process of acquiring a house in their own right as the law allows them. Progress, however, depended on the attitude of the land authorities who were often sympathetic to widows and to some extent divorcees, especially when they had dependants; but were sometimes negative to single women, as traditionally they are their families' responsibility forever.

House building in the informal areas was financed through the households' own savings, and where husbands and wives were both working, both contributed. Actual house construction was done by casual labour and it was the responsibility of house owners to hire builders and to see to it that materials were brought on site. In most cases the house owners had accumulated building materials over time so as to avoid having to take up loans. Either husband or wife arranged for the purchase and transport of the materials, depending on which of them had the time off from work or was nearer the shops. Also both husbands and wives visited the sites to oversee construction progress and they discussed with the construction supervisor anything that needed discussing. In general, house owners had cordial relations with their builders, however, there were cases where women on their own felt builders did not respect them. In one instance, a woman reported that she had to go to her site with a male relative in order to get the builders to listen to what she was asking of them, otherwise they were not willing to take orders from a woman who, according to culture, is their subordinate.

Here again women said that they visited the sites most as they were more anxious to see their households finally settle somewhere.

Literature documents that 'The fact that women do make a generally greater contribution to participatory development projects than men by no means signifies that they have more time available, merely that they are possibly willing to make more sacrifices because of vested interests in improving the welfare and living conditions of their families.' (Brydon & Chant, 1989, p.227.)

Private formal areas

As in the other area classifications, women were generally the ones who got news of sites being advertised or under direct grant by the minister. Single, divorced, and widowed women applied whereas married ones had to urge husbands to go and apply or apply on their behalf when they were given written consent. In the case of married couples, husbands were the ones interviewed on the grounds that they were expected to have full information about households' affairs. These interviews were to try to gauge whether households had the means to develop sites and that they did not already have many other sites.

Some women on their own sometimes felt that allocations were biased against them as the male dominated committee arbitrarily exercised their cultural attitudes. For example, there was a case of a divorced woman who told me that she had filled site application forms for herself and her brother. They then individually attended interviews and when the results came out her brother, and not she, had been successful. The woman felt that the committee had thought since traditionally she was her brother's dependent there should be no harm in giving priority to the brother over her. Also, some single women felt that where a choice had to be made between married applicants and themselves preference was often for the former as these conformed with the culturally conceived household norm, i.e. that which came about as a result of marriage.

After securing the sites, house owners had to submit building plans for approval by the City Council following consultation with some services agencies. Generally, women reported more follow up on this process although one woman told me that she had relied on her husband in this matter as she had thought that men in relevant offices might not have taken her seriously. However, the same woman also told me that in the process of their house building she had left for overseas studies and two years latter when she returned she found there had been no progress on construction during her absence simply because her husband had not bothered to keep an eye on progress.

Houses in these areas were usually financed by bank loans as they were of better standard and more expensive. In cases of spouses, both contributed towards financing but the banks contracted with the husbands and only with married women if their husbands so consented. Widows, divorcees and single women obtained loans in their own names. The bank, however, reported that there were sometimes reservations with lending to single women as it worried over the women's continued ability to repay their loans after marriage. Males, be they spouses, friends or relatives had better contacts with contractors through work or friendship. However, women reported more regular visits to the sites over the construction period.

In concluding this section the following similarities in all three classifications of housing areas were noted:

Husbands and wives both played a part in designing their houses, i.e. if they were not bought 'turnkey' or project specific designs. They usually sat together with the drafts-person and discussed what structures they wanted or they agreed on a readily available plan chosen from the drafts-person's collection. Where any changes were necessary husbands and wives discussed them together and finally agreed. Factors that seemed to determine the level of involvement by spouses were the house size and the amount of money that was being invested in the structure. For example, where a house was just a simple and cheap two-room unit neither husband nor wife bothered if only one of them decided on the design, but for big family houses which required substantial amounts of money they both got involved. Even in cases where one of them worked away from home the other waited to consult during weekends or holidays.

In one case the husband was a qualified building engineer but he gave his wife the opportunity to participate fully in the house design discussions and he mostly just gave advice based on his work experience. There were, however, cases where husbands did not consider their wives' wishes. One wife said that her husband did not take her participation in the design discussions seriously. He had let her talk but afterwards he had simply done as he pleased and ignored her concerns. She, however, said that this was not only peculiar to housing but to all other matters of everyday life and she complained that this was an unhealthy environment for a family relationship.

In the case of married couples, property was registered in husbands' names and only husbands had to sign for tenurial documents and bank mortgages even when wives had been the ones to initiate the house building projects. Some wives, including those employed by the bank, got loans through housing schemes at their jobs but still their husbands had to sign the relevant papers.

The general upkeep and maintenance of houses were the full responsibility of owners, both husbands and wives. The wives, however, reported that by virtue of their being home managers, they were more exposed to the day-to-day conditions of the units. They had to cook in those houses, sweep, clean and decorate them, so they were the ones with the highest chances of noticing first when anything went wrong or needed improving. For example, when roofs leaked, plumbing work leaked, doors, wardrobes or cupboards could not close, etc. Overall, the women felt their role was greater in this phase. This seemed to be consistent with an observation stated by Muller and Vos: 'The upkeep of the dwellings is largely the task of women. It is estimated that in Africa 30% of the building and 50% of the maintenance of homes is carried out by women'. (UNCHS 'Habitat' Report, 1988, p. 62.) There were, however, noticeable differences in the women's outlook towards their achievements.

Some married women felt that having husbands always involved consultation and that this sometimes put them at a disadvantage, especially when husbands had no interest in owning houses. Other women felt husbands had been sources of strength and inspiration. They did not believe they could have achieved as much as they had without husbands' assistance.

Some single women said it was good they were on their own and could do as they pleased. Some felt they could have achieved more if they had husbands as partners in the process of acquiring houses.

Some widows felt they would have been in a position to achieve something better if husbands had been around to assist financially. Others were only too happy that at last they were free to act as they pleased as now they had majority status. They said that they had long wished to own houses of their own and, in some instances, they even had chances, through housing loan schemes at their places of work, but they had lost those chances when husbands were either irresponsible, not interested in owning a house or preferred allocated sites which they described as hard to get by comparison to those in the informal areas. Their husbands had refused to sign any papers which were required as a formality and therefore households' chances of owning houses had been lost.

With divorcees, all were happy to also finally have majority status and therefore be in a position to have houses in their own right. Most of them reported that their ex-husbands, wherever they were, still did not own any houses. Even those husbands with sites acquired during marriage but were now divorced had still not managed to develop them on their own, perhaps proving true a Sesotho saying that 'Lelapa ke la mosali' (a woman is the spouse with managerial powers to set up a proper home). Most divorcees described their ex-husbands either as irresponsible, not at all serious about life, not able to think so far ahead as to worry about important things like owning a house, etc.

One divorced woman in particular told me that now, looking back, she was actually appreciative of what her husband's irresponsibility had done to her life. She had come into marriage at a very young age thinking all would go well. After her dreams were shattered, she had actually derived a source of strength from that experience and learnt to do things for herself even to the point of acquiring a house.

Literature again documents that 'The hypothesis that male control over women's involvement in household budgeting and housing decisions was a crucial factor determining quality of dwelling was substantiated by the fact that many women who headed households began to improve their housing only after their husbands had died or deserted them. Contrary to the stereotype, households headed by men were living in inferior dwellings to those headed by women, despite having higher earnings.' (Brydon & Chant, 1989, p 42.)

The role of women working in the construction and the housing related services sectors

For the purpose of the analysis, construction and housing related services include brick-laying and masonry, plumbing, electrical wiring carpentry and some steel work.

None of the house owners visited during the course of this research reported the presence of female labour at the construction phase of their house. Also, none of the building contractors, which were another source of information on the role women played in housing construction, had women on their field staff. Women within the construction firms, who ranged in numbers between one and four at some of the firms that were contacted, were there basically as secretaries or typists, accounts clerks/bookkeepers, store keepers and office cleaners. The latter, in some cases, were used to clean clients houses at the end of the construction period, just before those houses were handed over to owners. Men in the construction industry's workforce were plumbers, carpenters, masons, bricklayers, electricians, machine operators, drivers and unskilled labourers who underwent on-the-job training.

Contractors' views

Most of the contractors contacted said they would have no problem employing women qualified in construction skills, the reasons why they had no women was simply that no such women came to them in search of jobs. They felt this situation could be attributed to the poor levels of enrolment figures of females in these fields in the technical/vocational institutions.

Some contractors went further to say that this marginalization of women in this sector could be explained by the prevailing cultural beliefs that technical jobs are physically heavy and even rough and therefore are men's, and not women's, jobs. Some others reported that women were usually a bit slow and therefore not good to have in jobs that entailed meeting set time targets.

In one case, there was information that the company directors had resolved never to hire women workers as, some years ago when they had hired them, they experienced a lack of seriousness of duty on the part of male staff. With women around, the men were not doing their work efficiently and some even started to have love affairs. Supervisors would find them relaxing in the rooms with the women when it was work time. Women were being perceived as trouble makers on construction sites in as far as they appealed to men's sexual desires and disturbed the seriousness with which they should do their work.

Some contractors raised the issue of the relative immobility of women owing to their several household responsibilities. They argued that by nature construction work involved moving from place to place as it was subject to locational demand. Sometimes the locations could be far, meaning workers had to be away from home for long periods of time depending on the size of the job. They also said that often accommodation in remote places was not comfortable therefore not suitable for women and that as workers often had to share rooms it would not be economical both in financial and spatial terms to have to worry about one or just a few women.

One contractor was particularly eager to see an increase in women's participation in the construction sector. He had, in fact, recently worked on a construction project in one urban centre where he had, among other things, taken it upon himself to train women labourers in paint mixing, painting of walls and ceilings, window-glazing and carpet tiles fitting. His view was that once women were interested in a discipline and their confidence was built up they became easily trainable and at times even ended up better skilled than men. For example, he found that the women were very good with paint mixing and he thought they definitely had better taste for colours. This contractor would have liked to see more women qualify in carpentry as they were good with making wardrobes and cupboards and mostly had better taste and style in the designs and workmanship. He was, however, the one who said most women were afraid of heights, so according to him their chances of building high walls and taking part in roofing were limited.

Views of building materials producers

The following findings were made during visits to a brick producing company called Loti Brick and to a pan tile producing company called Nala Roofing.

At Loti Brick, out of a total of about 147 employees, there were no women working on the production line. In fact, only three women worked for the company, one as a secretary, two as accounts clerks. The absence of women's participation was attributed to the nature of the work, described to me by management as dirty i.e. wet and muddy during the rainy season and dusty during the dry season. Actually, no women had even come asking for jobs on the production line. Management, however, felt that with the technological production improvements which were being presently undertaken women might eventually be attracted to this job. This would be highly supported they said, as they believed in principle that women were neat and reliable. Management went further to report that with big groups of male labour, there were always problems of high turnover of staff, especially after payday at the end of the month. Often the men went drinking. Since they felt that women in general were more responsible, having them in this job would provide more stability in the workforce.

At Nala Roofing there were six men and two women working on the production line and one male carpenter whose job was to assist clients to do their roofing. In the process of the discussions it was made clear that the two women worked on the tiles during the men's lunch break, their real job was basically to cut fibre and clean plastics used in tile production. When asked why the women were not full-time tile producers, after it became clear that workers only acquired the skill through on-the-job-training, a male worker replied that he felt women were a bit slow and that they could not take the physical strain of standing up the whole day whereas the men endured this strain.

Views of educators

The thinking within the Technical and Vocational Division of the Ministry of Education as well as at the Lerotholi Polytechnic, Lesotho's main technical institute, was that social attitudes were working to dissuade women from developing a keen interest in technical/vocational fields. Technical/vocational work is considered heavy and dirty and therefore only suitable for men and women in Sotho society are considered frail, delicate and symbols of cleanliness.

Another view expressed by the Polytechnic management was that the promotion of women's participation in technical/vocational education should better be handled by women already in those fields. It was, however, noted that often women were not in a position to attend workshops and/or training sessions which should equip them because they were either pregnant at any given time or young mothers. They also were full-time household managers even when they were in other jobs so, at times, husbands simply did not allow them to be absent from home.

Concerning the trainability of women in technical/vocational fields, some instructors said that they thought the problem was with the way children were brought up in the homes. From the early stages of upbringing, boys were familiarized with the technical world, for example, they had cars for toys; whereas girls were familiarized with the home, for example, they had dolls and dishes for toys. When women later decided to enrol in technical/vocational fields they found themselves confronted with a completely new world. So at the beginning they were scared compared to men but after about half a year they overcame their fears and some even became the best students.

The instructors said women really made an effort to listen, understand and perform well as they knew the men they competed with were already familiar with the fields of study. That helped them to be good once they were confident. The instructors believed that women were equally trainable like men and sometimes even better. They did not all play the sort of female-weakness games like society always tries to portray. They took their work seriously and they should therefore be encouraged.

I was told about the situation that the one female bricklayer graduate encountered when she went on attachment some years ago: Her employer was very reluctant at the beginning to have her. He was doubtful as to whether a female could perform well in bricklaying which he regarded as a male skill. The compromise was to allow her to work on the inside walls of the building. Within a short time she proved herself very good and she was allowed to work also on outside walls with male colleagues. She turned out to be very precise with keeping straight and sticking to measurements. From then on she was looked upon as an asset for precision by the colleagues.

The present female bricklayer student told me that she was attracted to that field because she would like to be able to build her own house and not have to pay builders whom she felt were very expensive. Also, she liked to challenge the thinking that building was a low valued job. She said she felt accepted by her male classmates and she even liked the idea of being the only woman among men as she felt often woman-to-woman interactions resulted in clashes. While she admitted that some of the roles were physically heavy, like carrying bags of cement, she said she always tried to do as much as her physical strength permitted and only thereafter she allowed the male colleagues to help her. Her skills development were as good as that of any student and her instructors even felt that since brick-laying was a decorative job she as a woman was doing it with excellent neatness.

Women workers' views

From the discussions held with some women working in the housing-related-services establishments there were no reports of significant physical advantages for men over women. Also, in general, these women related well with their male colleagues. In fact, in one case a woman told me that she preferred to work with men rather than with other women. She said that whenever she started in a new job she always found men colleagues more willing to share their knowledge and experiences. And, when men were new at her workplace they showed more willingness to learn from her or any other woman colleague who was experienced than was the case with women newcomers. There were, however, also reports of male colleagues who had a bad attitude towards 'women meddling in their territory'. In one organization dealing mainly with carpentry and steel works, I had earlier talked to a man who had told me he felt the work they were doing was very heavy, and if things were to go his way he would allow a maximum of 10 years for women to be in that job as he believed it was not good for their health. I later got to hear from some of his women colleagues that they regarded him as one of those who did not like the idea of 'women meddling in men's fields'. The women themselves felt there was no reason why, under the same working conditions, women's health should deteriorate more quickly than men's. Some of them had already been in their jobs for over 15 years and they still liked it.

In concluding this section I should remark that, in general, within the housing-related-services establishments the women put a lot of emphasis on having self-confidence. They said as long as they had it, they never felt that any of their clients doubted their skills in doing as good a job as male colleagues. They did not look for special treatment in their jobs – they liked being treated as equals by male colleagues.

The women also reported that they felt encouraged by the attitudes of clients, most of whom praised their courage for venturing into the fields termed 'male domain' and viewed this as a positive indicator for the nation's mental development. A point was at times made by women themselves to the effect that women work force was more stable in their jobs than men. In the words of one of the women, 'The men often shuttled between jobs in search of something lighter'. On the whole, women in these fields advocated more female participation.

Conclusion

It is clearly evident that Basotho women are active participants in housing provision and that they are the primary users of housing yet their full participation remains jeopardised.

Women's involvement in own housing

The law remains prejudiced against women's full participation, in as far as it denies some categories of women direct access to land and financial resources as well as final decisions making. It gives men the right to dominate site registration, contracting with banks, signing all sorts of documentation and generally having absolute administrative powers over property.

Where the law facilitates and/or is not prescriptive against women's full participation, there exist deeply rooted cultural/traditional practices that marginalize the women's role. For example, although the law says single women are majors traditional attitudes still view them as children within their families of origin and this sometimes impacts negatively on their chances of securing housing where a choice has to be made between them and the married couples.

Traditional institutions like chieftainship and in-laws' family are strong authorities when it comes to certifying women's marital status and/or relationship with husbands.

Women on their own and wives side by side with husbands participate in designing their houses. However, women are often the ones who take a lead in initiating site acquisition process and are more anxious throughout the construction phase, visiting their sites to oversee progress. There are still cases, though, where women feel dependent on husbands or male relatives and friends especially when it involves contact with formal establishments run mainly by men, like building contractors and government departments.

Women's involvement in housing as professionals

The socialization of females is still, to a large extent, directed away from the technical/vocational fields as they are still looked upon as male fields. Consequently, women lack the education and training in skills that would enhance their participation in housing. For the scanty numbers of women who are in housing related professions there persists a conflict in as far as their role is perceived. One view describes them as reliable, stable in their jobs, having taste for colours and designs, being precise with measuring things and arranging them and, indeed, being trainable. An opposing view describes them as immobile, physically weak, vulnerable to strain, needing comfort and levels of cleanliness not permissible by the nature of construction work and sometimes even distracting men's attention at work in as far as they appeal to their sexual desires. The latter view seems to find support in modern construction resulting in women being 'relegated to "invisible", supportive roles characteristic of their routine domestic duties (servicing male participants by providing them with refreshments or clearing up after them, for example)'. (Brydon & Chant, 1989, p. 228.)

Chapter Six

Credit Facilities for Housing for Women: A Case Study of Maseru, Lesotho

Symphorosa Rembe

Introduction

Women's access to shelter involves not only the right to build, buy or rent a house, but also participation in policy and decision making in the housing sector and in construction employment as professionals, managers, entrepreneurs and workers. This includes access to land and housing finance. Women's access to information also plays an important role. They need to be informed of opportunities in the housing sector: finance and eligibility criteria for housing schemes. Adequate finance is very crucial in the provision of housing for the urban population. However, the majority of the urban poor, mostly women, lack proper shelter because of financial constraints. They cannot obtain housing loans from financial institutions and housing projects, because their income levels are below the requirements and policies of the institutions. It is evident that poor women in the urban areas have to struggle for a long period before they can acquire their own shelter.

Over the past ten years, the population in the urban areas of Lesotho has increased rapidly. The cause of the increase can be attributed to rural-urban migration. Due to lack of arable land in the rural areas, as well as the increase in unemployment, people have been moving to the urban areas in search of jobs and a better life. While they are in the urban areas, these people are confronted with the problem of securing employment and shelter. The housing policies adopted by the government theoretically recognizes the problem of housing and the need to provide shelter for all the income groups in the urban areas. Practically almost all the low income groups (and women are the majority in this group) have been left out because of their economic position.

Objective and Methodology

The study examines credit facilities for housing for women with low income in the urban Maseru.

Qualitative and quantitative methods were used to collect data. Unstructured interviews were held with officials from financial institutions and housing projects, members of 55 informal financial associations and five credit unions. A questionnaire was administered to 60 low income households (30 headed by men and 30 headed by women) which were selected randomly from a list of households from the suburbs of Maseru.

Formal financial institutions

The Lesotho Housing Corporation (LHC) was established in 1971 to supply housing to all income groups. Since the houses were very expensive, only those in the high income group were catered for in this scheme. For example, the cheapest housing unit provided by LHC until 1978 had an area of 40 square metres at a cost of M8 000,00. To qualify for such a unit, the prospective buyer had to be able to repay this amount over a period of 15 years at an interest rate of 12% without exceeding his total income. This meant a monthly instalment of M106 which very few people could afford since only 5% of the total population earned annual incomes exceeding M5 000.00 at that time. (Hattings, *et al.*). Therefore, all the women in the low income group were left out.

In 1975, the government reviewed its housing policy to include low cost housing in order to cater for the low income groups in the urban areas. The Lesotho Lower Income Housing Company (LEHCO-OP) was established for that purpose. Housing was provided through sites and services scheme under which families built their own houses through self help construction methods. They received loans (ranging from M1 829 to M2 880) for building materials and construction was done on a co-operative basis with advice from LEHCO-OP. Beneficiaries paid a deposit of 5% of the loan and had eight months to build before they started paying back the loan.

However, it was very few women in the low income brackets who benefited. The reason was that the majority of the poor women, many of whom are de facto heads of households, could not afford to participate in the project. The two corporations (LHC and LEHCO-OP) merged to form the Lesotho Housing and Land Development Corporation (LHLDC). Because of its policies of cost recovery and profit making, the corporation (LHLDC) develops sites and sells them to people of all income levels. The costs per plot range from M1 500 to M35 000 and the applicants are required to pay 10% as down payment and the balance is repaid over a period of 2 years. The applicant can then apply for a building loan from the bank using the serviced plot as security. Many of the low income women have not been able to make use of the services of the corporation because the cost of the plots is beyond their means. Furthermore, they do not qualify for housing loans from the bank because they cannot afford the deposits and the high interest rates charged thereafter.

The Lesotho Building Finance (LBFC) was established in 1976 to mobilize finances for housing development and to provide long term mortgages for housing. Theoretically, all the people could get loans for housing from LBFC provided they met the requirements. Practically, the operation of LBFC has excluded the majority of women. This is revealed when we examine requirements for one to qualify for a housing loan. For an individual to qualify for a housing loan from LBFC, the following are required: a lease, a plan, a building permit, quotations and a deposit. In order to obtain all these documents, one has to go through long and complicated procedures which are very expensive for the women in the low income brackets. First, a large number might not have leases, taking into consideration that they have acquired land through informal allocations. Second, they cannot afford deposits because of their low incomes. It is also evident that they will have to incur other expenses in the process, namely, payment for production of plans. Often building regulations might require them to conform with certain building standards which might not be possible because it is beyond their financial levels.

As well as having lengthy, complicated and expensive procedures, LBFC provides housing loans for a plot and housing unit package but not for a plot only. This obviously excludes the majority of the women in the low income brackets.

The Maseru Municipal Council was supposed to develop a revenue base from property rates and service charges. These funds would have been used in housing development programmes. At the time of data collection, the programme had not been implemented. However, even if it is implemented, many women in the low income brackets might not benefit because of profit making and cost recovery policies which will be applied.

Commercial banking institutions such as Lesotho Bank, Standard Bank and Barclays Bank provide housing loans for their employees. Theoretically, all the employees, regardless of their levels of income, are entitled to these loans. Practically, it is only those in the higher and middle positions who benefit from these loans. Those who are in the lower positions, the majority of whom are women, are discouraged from securing such loans because of high interest rates and high instalments. Moreover, many do not meet the specified criteria which favour those in the higher positions.

The laws which operate in the country discriminate against women. According to the laws of Lesotho, a woman is regarded as a minor and any woman married in Community of Property cannot enter into a contract without the consent of the husband. These laws are put into practice by financial institutions when they consider women for credit facilities for different purposes including housing. This puts women, especially those who are separated and abandoned, in a very difficult position.

Informal financial associations

It is evident that the majority of women in the low income brackets in the urban areas of Lesotho are unable to secure housing loans from financial institutions, housing schemes and housing projects. The findings revealed that these women have resorted to informal financial associations as a way of acquiring credit for housing.

A number of informal financial associations exist and most of their members are women. For poor women, these informal associations are a survival strategy. They provide a basis for changes in their living conditions. They might not be able to afford what is required by the formal financial institutions, but poor women are able to make some form of indirect savings in the informal financial associations. This was acknowledged by some of the women who were interviewed. They said that they have managed to build their own houses and secure other household necessities because of saving in the informal financial associations. People are not afraid of joining informal financial associations because the subscriptions are fixed at a level which even the poorest person can afford to pay.

The most common informal financial associations are burial societies. Members of these societies are assisted in meeting funeral expenses of their families and relatives in case of bereavement. Membership of burial societies is large, and is mostly composed of people of all income levels. It was discovered that people can become members of as many burial societies as they like, provided that they are able to pay their monthly subscriptions. The 15 burial societies which were surveyed had close to 3 500 members of whom 65% were women. Membership fees for the burial societies ranged from M15 to M100 depending on the income level of most of the members. Monthly subscriptions ranged from M5 to M20. They all had bank accounts, constitutions and members of committees who are entrusted with the operations of the societies. The amount which a member received in times of bereavement ranged from M400 to M2 000 depending on the subscriptions and the savings in the bank.

Most of the burial societies are doing fund raising activities, namely, renting out tents and household appliances to individuals or groups, selling foods and holding concerts. Money raised in these activities is kept in the bank accounts and members' monthly subscriptions are reduced. However, in many of these burial societies, members can take loans for financing other activities. The money is repaid within a period of three to six months with a small interest. Some of the members who participated in our discussions, mainly women, had benefited from these type of loans. They used the loans for a number of activities, namely, renovating their houses, buying building materials, buying furniture, etc. A number had used the loan to start small businesses. The return from businesses was used to purchase building materials, to buy building sites from field owners and other activities related to improving their households. At the time of the interview, some had finished repaying the loans and were contemplating taking additional loans and others were still repaying. Although burial societies started for a specific purpose, they have been flexible and accommodate other activities like extending loans for businesses and housing, something which is not done by formal financial institutions.

Other types of informal financial associations are formed by people in the informal sector. The 25 associations included in the study had about 2 000 members, the majority of whom were women. In some of these associations members were contributing a certain amount of money (M10 to M20) at the beginning of each week. At the end of the week, the total amount of the money contributed was given to one member to buy stock. Any other member could apply for a loan from the amount contributed, provided that it was repaid before the end of the week. The loan was not repaid with interest. It was discovered that the members were able to maintain their businesses and had reasonable savings. The majority of members were living in their own houses which they built by using the money which was saved indirectly in the informal financial associations. Some of them might have taken very long to build those houses because they built piecemeal.

In other informal associations, members would contribute money and, at the end of each month, one member receives the whole amount. Although the women who were interviewed said that members were free to use the money for any project of their own, it was discovered that all the beneficiaries had used the money either to buy building materials or to renovate their old houses. With other informal associations, members contribute money each month (M50 to M200) and it is saved in the bank. During this period members can take loans from the association for different activities. The loan is repaid with a small interest ranging from 2% to 5%. The money is repaid within 12 months. Members also share a certain amount from their savings at the end of the year. Most of the members use the money for household improvements, that is, buying furniture, completing unfinished houses, renovating their houses and paying school fees at the beginning of the new year.

In two associations, members built houses for each other. Members of these associations are women who engage in income generating activities. They contribute a portion of their income each month to purchase building materials. After stockpiling enough building materials for a house, they engage a builder. However, this researcher noticed that there were fewer members (10 and 20) compared to other associations. Members were engaged in activities which gave high returns (from M500 to M850 per month).

Many of the women who are working in the formal sector (public and private) have their own informal financial associations. Membership is small. The 15 informal financial associations included in the sample had a total of only 200 members. Their contributions are higher and, unlike those in the informal sector, they are able to secure higher loans from the associations or bigger sums as their shares. Some contribute an amount of M100 to M300 per month and receive M2 000 as their share. They can also take loans and repay with 5% interest. The repayment period is 12 months. From the discussions, some associations specify what one can buy with the money. Some specify building materials, furniture and kitchen appliances while many provide the money for down payments or deposits for a housing loan from the housing institutions.

Responses from questionnaires which were administered to selected men and women headed low income households confirmed the importance of informal financial associations in housing for women in the low income brackets. The majority of the women had built their houses with small loans and savings from informal financial associations. Although building was piecemeal and it took along time, others had managed to extend their houses using the same sources for loans and savings to accommodate tenants. In this way they were getting additional incomes for their families.

Many of the men had skills and could secure piece jobs which paid well. However, the majority of spouses of those who were married were members of informal financial associations. Their savings and loans from the informal financial associations were used for household expenses while the money from piece jobs was used for building the houses. Evidently, in both types of households, informal financial associations played a part in providing money for building purposes. It was also discovered that men had their own way of raising money. They hold feasts where foods and drinks are sold to people and there is singing and dancing. Usually the group fixes an entrance fee. The money made from each function is given to each member in turn. It should be noted that the men's associations are loose and members do not have a strong bond. This is different to women's informal associations. They also do not save as they do in women's associations and, similarly, their associations do not give out loans. Unlike women, very few men are members of informal associations or participate in raising funds as a group. One could attribute this to the fact that many can easily secure piece jobs which pay more and a number of them have skills and can get employment. Because of cultural and social orientations, some men look down on informal financial associations as women's activities. Therefore, they would not easily join hands with women in the same associations because other men would not approve. In other words, it is either the wife or the mother who should be a member of an informal financial association and not the husband or the father.

Credit Unions

Credit Unions have assisted women in the low income brackets in shelter finance. Credit Unions were established in the early 1960s for the purpose of assisting poor people in both the urban and rural areas in saving money and raising income for themselves. All the Credit Unions are formally registered and they have their own constitutions. They have their own finances which come from membership contributions and often they conduct their own income generating activities in order to raise funds. Membership in the Credit Unions is 75% women and 25% men. Members can save any amount of money depending on their financial ability and they can take loans which they repay with a small interest.

All the five Credit Unions which were surveyed had granted their members housing loans. One had extended over M20 000 as housing loans to 34 of its members in 1991. Of the 34 members, 25 were women and 9 were men. In the discussions the beneficiaries said that loans extended by Credit Unions were not much, but they enabled them to purchase building materials. They then repaid the loans after which they were able to take second loans and then started building. The process was repeated until they completed their houses. Others had taken loans for other activities and the profits were used to build their own houses.

With Credit Unions, there are no legal obstacles to married, separated or abandoned women. If a woman is a member and requests a loan, she will qualify like anybody else provided she meets the criteria which is set for loan applicants. In other words, if she is a married or separated woman, Credit Unions do not necessarily require consent of the husband. Consent is only sought when a married woman pledges things in the household as security.

From our findings, Credit Unions have assisted many poor women who had no means of building their houses to do so. Although it took a long time for the houses to be completed due to the fact that Credit Unions have not got a strong financial base to give big loans, they are potential sources of credit for housing for poor women.

Concluding remarks

The findings revealed that women in the low income groups are excluded from acquiring credit for housing from formal financial institutions because of their income level. Consequently, informal financial associations provide alternative ways of enabling poor women to secure their own homes. Because these associations are made up of people who know each other and often friends, their functioning has been very smooth, with no embezzlement or misappropriation of funds. Being on the same economical level, the members have mutual trust of each other and they feel more secure. They are not only able to save money and obtain small loans, but they can also get advice from other members on how to build and the cheaper way of doing so. Informal financial associations are flexible and they can accommodate anybody. This means one is able to save any amount depending on their income level. To get a loan from informal financial associations, one is not required to pay a deposit and the interest charged is very small. Repayment is over a period which a beneficiary can manage. This means poor women are able to maintain their households while they are building their own houses.

Although informal financial associations do not have strong financial bases, their importance and the role they play in assisting women in the low income brackets need to be recognized. The Structural Adjustment programme and other related policies which are purported to improve the economy of the country, have tightened all the avenues whereby low income groups could secure any form of financial assistance. Many people in the low income brackets have been retrenched from their jobs. This has affected many women, mostly because they are in the low positions. Therefore, informal associations are the only options for them since they have to engage in income generating activities to maintain their households and to acquire their own shelter. With some help and a little more capital, some of the informal financial associations might eventually grow into big financial associations like the 'stokvels' in South Africa. These also started as small informal financial associations and eventually as membership increased and with more capital and contributions they grew into big financial associations assisting mainly the poor people.

Chapter Seven

Women on Co-operative Mines in Zimbabwe

Henry Chiwawa

Introduction

The most influential justification for the discrimination against women in mining has been the resort to biological accounts of sex differences in order to reinforce and maintain traditional sexual division of labour. The use of biology has a long history dating back to the colonial period in Zimbabwe when contract labour was recruited and imported from neighbouring countries. According to Clarke (1974), the contract workers who were all male, were screened, allocated to white employers and paid on 'medical' grounds. There were four 'medical' categories, A, B, C and D, based on the arrival weight and height of the recruit. The crude grading system arbitrarily dictated 'the type of work that the recruit was physically able to perform (p. 53)'. Mining was considered heavy work, and only contract workers in the top two categories (A and B) were eligible. Yet there was nothing 'medical' about this exercise. Just looking at a healthy person's height and weight is not medical – it is biological.

This approach has persisted for many years in the mining sector, and decision makers at all levels – the central planning level, sectoral level, enterprise level, household and individual levels – have continued to believe in the anti-feminist perspective that sexual equality in industry is a reproductive hazard. The general thinking has been that because of biological factors, sexual equality can be achieved only at great cost to women's health, particularly the damage of their reproductive physiology (Sayers, 1982). Consequently, colonial hang-over and subscription to the biological approach and its anti-feminist implications have largely precluded women's participation in mining activities in Zimbabwe.

However, as from the mid 1980s women have entered into formal mining operations by joining co-operatives engaged in chromite, tin and tantalite production. Previous studies (Chiwawa, 1989; Agren & Chiwawa, 1991) on mining co-operatives did not analyze the resultant power relations between men and women involved in mining co-operative activities. The purpose of this study, therefore, was to fill in this gap and determine whether this new development constitutes a real and sustainable change in attitudes and relations between men and women.

Conceptual framework

In determining changes and analyzing relationships in co-operative mining, the study has been greatly influenced by theoretical perspectives revolving around urbanization and gender relations (here considered to be the culturally defined power relations between men and women). In examining the legal structures and institutional framework under which co-operatives operate, the study made use of the supposed linkages between theories of development and women. According to Bell's (1991) literature review, the Women in Development (WID) approach emphasizes legal and administrative changes to ensure women's economic integration and thus transform the passive women into economic agents. The Women and Development (WAD) perspective focuses on the relationship between women and the processes of development, seeing women's condition primarily within the structure of international and class inequalities. The Gender and Development (GAD) approach sees women as agents of change and links the 'productive' (economic) and the 'reproductive' (domestic) parts of women's lives. The GAD approach leads to demand for structural change and power shifts within institutions.

In analyzing interpersonal relations at both the productive and reproductive levels, the study benefited from the concept of gender contracts as discussed by Larsson and Schlyter (in volume). The gender contracts are said to be invisible social contracts regulating the relations between men and women at all levels of the society. 'The concept gender contract allows us to analyze the space between men and women together with the ideas, rules and norms about places, tasks and qualities of men and women'. Taken together, the gender contracts are said to create a gender system.

Also at the productive and reproductive levels, the concept of household survival strategies from the same authors and from Bell's (1991) literature review proved useful in examining housing and survival strategies among co-operative miners.

In describing men's and women's living conditions on co-operative mines, the study has been inspired by the literature on human settlements and housing and on women, environment and urbanization (Bell, 1991).

Study objectives

Utilizing the above theoretical perspectives and concepts, the study specifically sought to:
+ Examine the legal and institutional framework under which mining co-operatives operate.
+ Determine and analyze the nature and level of men and women's participation in mining co-operative activities at both the 'production' and 'reproduction' levels and understand *why* women are peripheralized and subordinated.
+ Examine poverty levels and household survival strategies on co-operative mines.

Methodology and study outline

In meeting the above objectives, cognizance was taken of the observation that '... it has become clear ... that focusing on women alone is no more an accurate representation of social and economic phenomena than a focus on men alone.' (Imam, 1990, p. 243.) Consequently, an attempt was made to focus on both women and men and to provide as much gender-disaggregated data as possible. A mixture of both quantitative and qualitative research methods was employed. The main techniques used include:

The survey

To enable comparison of specific types of information, a survey was conducted using structured questionnaires at both the co-operative level and the membership level. Survey data was important for making comparisons between co-operatives, individuals in different co-operatives, and between women and men. While sampling of the co-operatives was not undertaken because of the perceived small size of the co-operative population in each mineral group, it was necessary to take a representative sample (20%) of co-operative members through systematic random sampling. To ensure a gendered analysis, an attempt was made to also interview the spouses of the sampled members.

The random sampling sought to capture both male and female co-operative members and their spouses in tin and tantalite mining, and only female co-operative members and the wives of members in chromite mining. This was because a similar survey of chromite mining co-operative members (97% of whom were male) based on a sample size of 358 members was conducted in 1990. (Agren & Chiwawa, 1991). In addition to the 1990 chromite survey findings and information obtained at the co-operative level, the study analyses have been based on a sample size of 236 respondents made up of 101 male and 33 female members, and 3 male and 16 female non-members in tin and tantalite mining; and 6 female members and 77 female non-members in chromite mining.

Observation

In the course of the field work, the researcher stayed at some of the urban centres where co-operators live. As a way of minimizing disruption of co-operative mining operations, most of the interviews of co-operative members were conducted at the mining sites. Observation was, therefore, an important data collection method since it was possible to see living conditions and to apply a gender perspective in interpreting what was going on at both the production and reproduction levels.

Relevant authority interviews, records and documents

Discussions and unstructured interviews were conducted of officials involved in the promotion of co-operative mining. These included co-operative Union leaders, government and Zimbabwe Mining Development Corporation co-operative advisers and other officials, Non-Governmental Organization representatives, etc. Other secondary and primary data were collected from published and unpublished official documents and records kindly made available by these authorities.

Group discussion

Given the scarcity of non-mining income-generating activities on co-operative mines, an in-depth study of the only 'women's project' was conducted through group discussion. The collective interview of key informants and women at the 'factory' allowed the subjects of the research to build on each other's ideas and to remind each other of past experiences, which proved to be an important source of information.

Study outline

In line with its stated objectives, the study firstly examines the legal structures and institutional framework under which co-operative mining is conducted and highlights the factors influencing men and women's participation in mining activities. It analyzes the resultant gender relations in co-operative mining at both the production and reproduction levels, and tries to show why and how women continue to be subordinated. The study also examines living conditions on co-operative mines and discusses how they affect men and women's everyday life. It then examines poverty levels among co-operative miners and how both men and women have responded to the deteriorating economic conditions.

Legal structures and institutional framework

The fact that women only got involved in formal mining as from the mid 1980s raises the question why women were finally recognized as 'economic agents' in this sector.

Responses to economic crises

In 1984/85 when ferrochrome prices declined following low demand by steel producers in developed countries, the two ferrochrome producers in the country, Zimbabwe Alloys Limited and Zimbabwe Mining and Smelting Company sought to reduce their chrome ore production costs. This was done by firstly laying off many workers on high-cost mines. These redundant workers (all male) were organized into mining co-operatives by the Zimbabwe Mining Development Corporation, a government-owned mining parastatal. The mining companies then subcontracted most of their high-cost, thin-seam chromite mining operations to co-operatives as part of cost reduction measures.

Co-operative miners have been producing, on contract, chrome ore from operations scattered on the Great Dyke – a geological feature where chromite deposits are found. As per tribute agreements or supply contracts, all the ore from co-operative workings, which is sold at negotiated prices, is for the companies' ferro-alloy smelters in the cities of Gweru and Kwekwe.

Following the collapse of the international tin market in 1985, Kamativi Tin Mines Limited, owned by the Zimbabwe Mining Development Corporation had no choice but to drastically reduce output, with lay-offs being inevitable. The redundant workers were also organized by the Zimbabwe Mining Development Corporation into co-operatives as from 1987 to produce tin and tantalite concentrates from mining claims around Kamativi. According to the supply contract, the concentrates are smelted and refined by Kamativi Tin Mines.

Subcontracting

Although mining co-operatives are registered in terms of the Co-operative Societies Act No. 6 of 1990, organizational autonomy has been greatly hampered by the established production and exchange relations. The production and marketing arrangements between mining co-operatives and mining companies were formalized through the signing of Tribute Agreements and Supply Contracts between co-operatives as 'tributors' and chromite mining companies as 'grantors' or claim-holders; and co-operatives as 'customers' and Kamativi Tin mines. This arrangement is provided for in terms of the Mines and Minerals Act (Chapter 165). In the vast majority of cases, co-operatives are tributing mining claims owned by the mining companies. In the few cases where co-operatives work their own or government mining claims, the co-operatives have also signed supply contracts with the smelting companies. In all cases, however, co-operatives do not have any land ownership rights.

Co-operatives in the chromite, tin and tantalite mining sub-sectors, therefore, emerged following supply-side adjustment and restructuring measures aimed at reducing costs after a glut in the traditional mineral export markets. Although co-operatives are really a new phenomenon in the post-independence period in the mining sector, they have had no impact on the economic structure since they have been subsumed by both private and state companies as a cost reduction measure. Further, the introduction of women miners was nothing of a planned measure towards gender equality in mining.

Co-operative mining as the least lucrative venture in the sector

While women have been only involved in formal mining operations by forming and joining co-operatives, this does not mean that co-operative mining is more 'gender-progressive' than non-co-operative mining. Without any organizational autonomy, land and mining claim ownership rights and any access to alternative markets, co-operative mining has proved to be the least lucrative and thus least preferred activity in the sector and co-operators have been at times likened to indentured labour. It has been mostly desperate people who found their way into co-operative mining.

The negative effects of the economic structural adjustment programme (ESAP), especially the retrenchment of mine workers, depressed world mineral markets, and the drought, all pushed not only men but also women into co-operative mining, from which they were not excluded as in the other mines. Thus, in the absence of any viable alternatives, both men and women, desperate for household cash income, have had to engage in chromite, tin and tantalite co-operative mining. However, asked about their preferred employment and career aspirations, women indicated preference for non-mining occupations such as domestic worker, crèche teacher, farm worker, dress-maker, policewoman, village health worker, etc. The majority of male co-operative members also indicated preference for employment in non-mining activities including general worker, driver, farm worker, domestic worker, etc. Of the few men who preferred mining because they once worked as miners and had some mining skills, the ambition was to be employed by the big mining houses. The main reasons given by both men and women for least preferring co-operative mining were that the pay was too low, the income was irregular as it depended on the output sold, and that there were long delays in payment for co-operative output by the buyers.

Conclusion

Two important observations follow from this discussion of the legal structure and institutional framework. Firstly, there has not been any deliberate strategy aimed at incorporating women into mining activities and challenging the biological approach. Instead, the co-operatives were created to serve as part of cost reduction measures by mining companies in reaction to economic crises in the mining sector. Secondly, there has been some tolerance of women's participation only in the least lucrative mining activities conducted under 'captive' production arrangements.

Key questions which should be raised at this stage concerning men and women's participation in co-operative mining include:
+ Why has the biological approach not been deliberately or consciously challenged?
+ Why has the number of women not increased relative to men under the same deteriorating economic conditions?
+ With more unmarried than married women, is it necessarily true that married women are not equally compelled by economic hardships to engage in co-operative mining?

A tentative answer to these questions might be given with reference to the concept of the dominant gender contract as observed by Larsson and Schlyter in some Southern African countries, including Zimbabwe. 'According to the dominant gender contract men are responsible for important decisions, especially those outside the household/family, and women's domain is restricted to the home and family. In public life, all women have been regarded as minors'. Thus, reference to the gender system becomes an important analytical tool in understanding why women have continued to be peripheralized and subordinated, despite their participation in mining co-operative activities at both the production and reproduction levels.

Gender system at the production level

Much as co-operative mining may be credited with more flexibility in allowing for female participation relative to the non-co-operative mining sub-sector, the level and nature of women's participation in co-operative mining activities have remained rather biased against them.

Gender-biased employment levels

There has been only one women's co-operative out of the sixty-eight co-operatives in chromite, tin and tantalite mining. The co-operative, called Equal Rights and engaged in tantalite mining, was formed at the initiative of an expatriate co-operative project manager (who has since left) at Kamativi in 1990. The fact that no other women's co-operatives were subsequently formed means that this initiative was not replicable in the sector. Thus gender biases against women could not be eliminated in the sub-sector; and the 'equal rights' in terms of men's and women's co-operatives were not achieved. Nor has female participation in terms of co-operative membership increased. Women make up an insignificant proportion (8%) of the total number of co-operative members in the sub-sector, and female participation has been on the decline, especially in chromite mining.

Gender-biased mining skills

In terms of mining skills, an examination of the background of co-operative members shows that, in tin and tantalite mining, virtually all the co-operators came from nowhere to become miners, and none of the female co-operative members have any previous mining experience. It would be fair to assert that, at this point in time, a vast majority of tin and tantalite mining co-operators, particularly women, will pass for unskilled mine labour. Thus, in the absence of any training programmes, beyond the provision of employment, the advantages of co-operative mining in terms of skills development are virtually non-existent in tin and tantalite mining.

In chromite mining, the picture is quite different. The majority of the joining co-operative members have previous mining experience. Mining skills and experience in chromite mining are relatively more advanced and longer than in tin and tantalite mining. Chromite miners can be said to be in the semi-skilled to skilled mining labour categories. The problem, however, is that this skills development has been grossly biased in favour of male co-operative miners only.

Mining skill levels and experience determine the role each individual member will play in a co-operative. The least skilled and least experienced, who include all the women, have been largely peripheralized at the production level.

The biological approach

In addition to this lop-sided skills development, it would appear the biological approach has greatly influenced the nature of women's and men's participation in co-operative mining operations. The mining method and the nature of the work involved have largely dictated the extent to which female labour has been employed. The majority (87%) of the total female co-operative members are engaged in tin and tantalite mining. While co-operative tin and tantalite mining involves surface operations only, chromite mining methods include both surface and underground mining operations.

In chromite mining, however, no women have been engaged in underground mining operations. In fact, the most frequently cited reason for there being few or no women co-operators was simply that 'women cannot go underground'. Even the women non-members gave the same reason for not joining chromite mining co-operatives. Similarly, although there are no underground co-operative tin and tantalite mining operations, no women ever worked underground before joining co-operatives. Consequently, underground mining has remained exclusively men's field, thus reinforcing the traditional biases against women in mining.

Further, the concept of 'heavy work for men and light work for women' has been widely adopted. In co-operative chromite mining, there are virtually no female members involved at the production level. At least a third of the female co-operative members are the 'village health workers' at mining compounds. Those engaged in actual production are confined to surface operations, where there is practically no specialization.

Specialization

It is, however, in tin and tantalite co-operative mining where an interesting specialization pattern has emerged. The division of labour at the production level has proved to be an extension of the traditional sexual division of labour. Taking operation of the 'sluice box' as an example, the digging and loading of the gravel using pick and shovel is undertaken by men; transportation by wheelbarrow is done by men; water pumping is done by men; screening and waste picking at the sluice box is carried out by women; panning is done by women; recording of production statistics is done by women; minding the children at the mining site is undertaken by women; and food preparation at the mine site is done by women.

In other operations, the drilling and blasting is undertaken by men; crushing is done by both men and women; process water is fetched by women; and panning is mostly done by women. These examples apply to co-operatives which have both male and female members. Even in the predominantly female group, Equal Rights, with ten women and two men, one of the men was recruited as a security guard and the other 'to provide the muscle and do the heavy work which we ourselves are not able to do'.

In all cases, prospecting for workings, also called 'sampling', is done by men, mainly because of their presumed mining skills and experience. A major problem cited by the co-operators is the trial and error siting of the workings caused by some of these 'samplers'. Again, in all cases, overnight security at workings is provided by men, who are popularly known as 'Guardnights'. What needs to be emphasized here is that the joining of co-operatives by both men and women has not changed sex roles even at the production level. The specialization pattern is still based on what is considered typically male and typically female.

Gender-biased technical skills development

Of course, it is undeniable that due to biological differences, in most cases men actually perform heavy manual work better than women.

However, this fact has been used as an excuse in subordinating women and extended to important tasks which require more skill than physique. E.g. there is nothing 'heavy work' about manning a water pump; 'sampling' or prospecting for mining claims; blasting and use of explosives; etc. Yet, as has been observed, these are skilled positions monopolized by men; and the concept of 'skilled work for men and unskilled work for women' has also been adopted. The overall result of linking specialization at the production level to traditional sexual division of labour has been the peripheralization of women at the technical level. In tin and tantalite mining, e.g. 25 percent of the management committee members are women. This implies that the women, who are 20 percent of the total membership, are rather over-represented and have greater say in co-operative policy issues. The same women are, however, grossly under-represented at the position of mine manager/'gang leader', where only 8 percent are women. This means that women have very little say at the production level, and production methods and decisions are dictated by men.

With this kind of specialization, therefore, it is highly unlikely that, at the end of the co-operative project, female co-operators will emerge as skilled miners. Nor can they take over from their male counterparts who have monopolized skilled positions. In short, in the absence of any gender focused skills development programme, or arrangements for women to understudy men in skilled positions, women will remain unskilled mine labour, specializing in an extension of their domestic chores at the production level.

Gender system at the reproduction level

Again, a closer examination of developments at the household level shows that conservative attitudes on gender have persisted in co-operative mining.

The male 'breadwinner' theory

The traditional view that the husband is the 'breadwinner' and the wife's place is in the home is still dominant in co-operative mining. The husband, being the head of the household, is seen as the provider of household cash income and the wife, seen as the helper, only provides supplementary income. Consequently, husbands as the dominant decision-makers, have sought to specialize in 'productive' labour and confine their spouses to 'reproductive' labour. Any efforts by wives to engage in productive labour have been widely resisted since such liberties have been often construed as threats to husbands' authority and decision-making powers.

According to the Kamativi Tin Mines General Manager there was a widespread sense of relief and jubilation among men when female waste pickers at the KTM Mill were retrenched in the restructuring process. In chromite mining, the near collapse of the chromite market resulted in outright discrimination against women. Male co-operative members were retrenched using various criteria including age, laziness, drunkenness, disobedience, chronology (i.e. last in first out), etc. When asked why such criteria were not applicable to female members, the quickest reply from the co-operative leaders was that 'women should look after the home'. When asked what would happen to those female members who were not married, the responses invariably included 'every woman should be married', 'a decent woman should be married', etc. Thus, women's (whether married or not) income was considered supplementary and as a luxury that could be dispensed with during difficult times. The worst affected were the female headed households whose 'breadwinners' were denied the chance to earn a living by being regarded as minors in public life according to the dominant gender contract.

Wives as home-makers

These attitudes are, therefore, largely responsible for the insignificant involvement of wives in co-operative mining. Married female co-operative members constitute an insignificant fraction (3%) of the total co-operative members. This contrasts sharply with the over-representation of husbands (77%) in co-operative mining. Nor have wives found formal employment in non-mining activities. While all the spouses of female co-operative members are formally employed mostly in mining by the co-operatives and mining companies, only a handful of co-operators' wives are formally employed mainly in the health sector as nurse aides, village health workers, etc.

The majority of the wives are housewives living with their husbands on co-operative mines and occasionally engaging in mining as 'casual' workers or looking after the home in the Communal Lands. Asked why they did not join mining co-operatives, married women gave such reasons as they were never invited, mining is men's work, husband refused, they were looking after the children, etc. Consequently, the majority (63%) of the female co-operative members are heads of households who are either widowed or divorced.

Unfounded male chauvinism

Yet the perceived threats from wives' engagement in productive labour have proved to be non-existent. The few husbands who allowed their wives to be formally employed told of democracy and joint household decision making, and there were no complaints of friction and disquiet in the home. Instead, there were widespread praises of the arrangement as being beneficial under conditions of drought and ESAP.

Nor is it true that only males are breadwinners. There is no evidence to suggest that male headed households perform better than female headed households. In tin and tantalite co-operative mining where there are both male and female headed households, the mean monthly income is Z$143 with women earning more (Z$158) than men (Z$138). Nor does it necessarily follow that a wife's income is supplementary (assuming supplementary means smaller). In tin and tantalite mining, female co-operative members earn more than their spouses employed mostly outside the co-operative sub-sector. The women earn an average Z$296 while their husbands earn an average Z$222. These women co-operators, therefore, contribute an average 57% to household income.

The 'roora' tradition and domestic chores

Initially based on the 'roora' (payment of bridewealth) custom, the man's authority and household headship is culturally determined and sealed. The man's area of specialization is 'productive' work aimed at generating cash income for the household. The woman, on the other hand, by having 'roora' paid (usually not in full) for her, is responsible for the 'reproductive' aspects, and her place is supposed to be in the home. The 'roora' tradition, therefore reinforces the dominant gender contract. With their full time jobs culturally confined to the home, it was no wonder that wives only attended to most of the domestic chores. Shopping, cleaning, cooking, laundry, water and wood fuel provision, gardening, child rearing, etc., are duties carried out almost exclusively by the female spouse. It is only in shopping and gardening that husbands occasionally assist. Husbands only attend to all other domestic chores if their wives are away (e.g. in communal lands) or ill. At Kamativi, husbands also bring home some firewood from their work places largely because of the relative ease with which it is obtained in the area. In the majority of cases, however, women are confronted with the arduous tasks of fetching water and collecting firewood.

The few couples where both spouses happened to be employed were asked why only women and not men, attended to most of the domestic chores. The women simply maintained that it was their duty since 'roora was paid'. The men simply laughed it off as being 'impossible' in the presence of the wife. On further probing, the men confessed that they could not 'interfere' in women's duties lest it implied inadequacy on the part of the wives; nor could they cook lest their wives and neighbours considered them greedy; nor undertake cleaning, laundry etc. lest the neighbours thought they had gobbled their wives' love potions. All these cultural considerations thus preclude male participation in reproductive labour and condemn women to virtual domestic slavery.

At the reproductive level, particularly where domestic chores are concerned, therefore, we see a reversal of the logic of heavy work for men and light work for women being legitimized by the 'roora' tradition. There is nothing 'light work' about travelling long distances and taking up to five hours to collect firewood; or about running the Communal Area home in the absence of the husband; or about undertaking domestic chores in addition to formal employment.

Reproductive labour under poor living conditions

While women attend to most of the domestic chores, their workload has been further increased by the poor living conditions under which they perform their reproductive labour.

Colonial era housing

In chromite co-operative mining, over half of the co-operative members live at isolated mining settlements planned and constructed along the lines of the archaic compound system. The balance live at former company mines. Housing at compounds is predominantly grass thatch pole and mud huts while that at former company mines consists of mainly old, two- to six-roomed houses, which were constructed in the 1930s and 1950s. While the huts are owned by individual co-operative members, the houses at former company mines are rented from the North Dyke Co-operative Union and Zimbabwe Alloys. This type of accommodation is proving to be inadequate with the families allocated up to two rooms being the worst affected. Consequently, shacks have been erected next to the houses to provide extra rooms.

In tin and tantalite co-operative mining, a vast majority of the members reside at Kamativi, and the rest live in the communal lands. At Kamativi, an agreement of lease was entered into between Kamativi Tin Mines and the union of tin and tantalite mining co-operatives, Chinamano Co-operative Union. The agreement is for the leasing of 167 housing units in the 'two roomed' housing area. The 'two rooms' are not only old but also do not have openable windows. The function of the sealed, three-pane 'windows' is only to provide light into the rooms during the day. Although there is a fireplace and chimney in one of the rooms, lighting a fire indoors is very inconvenient because of the poor ventilation. Consequently, firewood cooking is usually done outdoors and there is untold suffering in the rainy season.

Accommodation crisis and 'squatter' settlements

With three co-operative members per two-roomed house, there is a critical shortage of accommodation at Kamativi. The co-operators have been compelled to share the houses and even rooms (against the lease agreement), stay with relatives employed by Kamativi Tin Mines, or seek accommodation in nearby rural areas. About a fifth of the co-operative members have settled where they are regarded as 'squatters' by the Kamativi community. The history of the 'squatter' settlements was difficult to ascertain but the general opinion was that these were made up of people illegally and haphazardly settling on State land.

But most of the 'squatters' maintained that they had settled in a communal area with the permission of a local chief. The settlements are made up of scattered shacks which in times of rain or windy weather, cannot offer adequate shelter.

Because of the general shortage of accommodation, it has not been always possible for one to live with one's loved ones. As a result, there are very few female non-co-operative members at Kamativi. Further, female members who are heads of households have their children staying outside Kamativi, usually in the communal lands. The children are looked after by the co-operators' parents or grandparents.

Energy

In chromite mining, electricity has been historically supplied to almost all housing sections of former company mines. There is no electricity at the compounds. This means that more than half of the co-operative members have no access to electricity. However, having electricity supplied to the houses has not necessarily meant widespread use of electricity as a form of energy. Thus, even where electricity is available, poverty has limited its use in the home. In tin and tantalite mining, because no electricity has been nor will be supplied to the 'two rooms' section according to the lease agreement, a vast majority of co-operative members have no access to electricity.

Because of poverty, co-operators have resorted to cheapest energy sources. In general, firewood is the single most important source of energy in the co-operative mining sub-sector, accounting for more than ninety percent of household energy. This excessive reliance on wood as the source of energy has important environmental implications especially in terms of deforestation (Chiwawa, 1993).

Water and sanitation

In chromite mining, former company mines have piped water systems, while the bulk of the isolated compounds rely on unhygienic water sources. However, even where piped water and drainage systems exist, the majority of co-operators use the least convenient facilities. Drinking water is fetched from communal taps strategically placed in village sections. The bathroom, laundry and toilets are all communal. These communal facilities have proved to be insufficient and, in some cases, have had to be supplemented. The only facility to be supplemented, however, has been the toilet, and ventilated pit latrines can be seen at the outskirts of certain sections. The communal water system toilets are mostly of the trench type with an automatic flushing mechanism. The communal facilities are inconvenient particularly for women because of the time spent in the queue for laundry and bathing.

At the isolated compounds, the majority of the co-operatives have not invested in providing clean water to their members. Only one co-operative has managed to supply piped water to its compound in the form of a communal tap. The main water sources are borehole, well and river. Concern ought to be expressed about the rather large proportion (39%) of women who draw water from rivers in view of the possible outbreak of waterborne diseases such as cholera. At one co-operative, women have to enter a mine shaft to fetch water, and those who are afraid of mines draw water from the river. The toilets at co-operative compounds are predominantly pit latrines. Thus, sanitation in chromite mining is so bad as to receive press coverage. 'The main cause of the diarrhoeal epidemic in the affected areas was poor sanitary and unhygienic conditions which have resulted in the loss of life, especially in Mutorashanga' (Chabarika, 1992).

At Kamativi, co-operators have access to piped water although they also use the communal bath and toilet system. However, the 'squatters' have problems with water and sanitation since they travel a long distance to fetch water from Kamativi and resort to the bush due to lack of access to any type of toilet.

Poverty and survival strategies

Small scale co-operative mining is credited with the advantages of using 'appropriate' technology, employment generation, use of unskilled labour, small initial capital and infrastructural requirements, etc. but the trade-off has been low income levels and widespread poverty among the so-called self-employed workers.

Meagre incomes

The bulk of co-operators earn meagre incomes from mining activities. In chromite mining, co-operators have had a history of earning, on average, less than the minimum wage for the mining industry. Not only has the situation remained unaltered for a long time, but conditions deteriorated sharply from late 1992. The supply quotas had been drastically reduced for chromite mining co-operatives by the time of the field work. The mean monthly income in co-operative chromite mining is Z$211 per member implying that in real terms, the co-operative incomes have remained at their 1990 (Z$210) levels. It can be concluded that while membership figures dropped by an overall 25% over a three year period, average earnings remained at their 1990 levels in real terms. In real terms, the impact is up to the reader to imagine.

In tin and tantalite mining, the mean monthly income is Z$143, with women earning more than men, apparently because of the success of the Equal Rights Co-operative which is involved in tantalite production. Tantalite fetches much higher prices than tin, and the average monthly income in this predominantly female co-operative is Z$500. The co-operators' cash flow problems are compounded by delays of up to six months in payment for their concentrates by the buyer.

With a vast majority (95%) of co-operative miners earning less than Z$400 per month, sustained poverty in the co-operative mining sub-sector has generally precluded access to any type of social security scheme and acquisition of various types of assets such as bicycles, radios, furniture, stoves, cattle, land, etc.

Household survival strategies

Although men and women went into co-operative mining as a measure of last resort, efforts have been made to supplement the meagre incomes from mining in response to the deteriorating economic conditions. Survival strategies have been adopted at the initiative of both the co-operators and their spouses. In tin and tantalite mining, some of the female co-operative members have other sources of income which are mostly spouse's income, fruit sales and sewing; some of the male members have extra income from gardening, grocery shop, wood carving, carpentry, spouse's income, knitting, thatch grass sales, beer brewing, and meat, bun, fruit and cigarette sales. These activities are undertaken by the co-operators in their spare time or by their spouses.

In chromite mining, some co-operative members have extra income from spouse's employment, vegetable sales, hawking, knitting, sewing, contract mining, and poultry. A number of non-co-operative members, some of them women, have been employed by the co-operative members as 'casual' or 'contract' workers. In one area a number of women, some of them co-operators' wives, had just started working as contract labourers at a nearby commercial farm. The women were ferried by tractor from the compound around 6 a.m. and returned around 5 p.m. In fact, some of the sampled non-members could not be interviewed because they had gone to work on the farm.

Group non-mining activities – a case study

Non-mining group income-generating activities have been confined to retail ventures in the form of grocery shops and 'beerhalls' especially at the isolated compounds. Productive non-mining ventures have been a rare phenomenon. In the Ngezi area, however, Nehanda chromite mining co-operative benefited from the Domestic Development Service (DDS) programme operating under the United Nations Volunteers and funded by the United Nations Development Programme. In the context of community self-help, the DDS programme seeks to enable rural communities to start and sustain their own projects. In 1989, with the help of a DDS field worker, 28 women formed a sewing group called Kumboyedza Women's Club; and 40 men formed the Kubatana Poultry Group. While all the men are co-operative members, five of the women are members and the rest are non-members who also engage in mining as contract workers. Through the DDS revolving fund, the women's group got an interest-free loan and purchased three manual sewing machines, material and grocery stock. The men's group also got a loan to buy a refrigerator, fence, sieve and brick moulds.

By February 1993 each member of the women's group had earned Z$200 which was all paid out in December 1992. The three sewing machines proved insufficient and the members had to split into three groups, taking turns in using the machines. Productivity was said to have been increased as there is competition among the groups. None of the members is a qualified tailor or dressmaker, and neither was the DDS field worker. The group relies on someone from the nearby resettlement area for training in sewing. Consequently, the products have been limited to women's dresses and skirts, men's shirts and boys' shorts; although one would have expected such products as miners' overalls and school uniforms to be the priority. The group's main customers, the mining co-operative members and contract workers, are almost always in the red financially. The group therefore sells most of its products, including groceries, on credit terms. Unlike the Kamativi credit system where debts are settled on pay day by deducting the owed amount from a member's earnings, Nehanda co-operative has no centralized arrangements for members to repay their debts. As a result the defaulters are too many and the viability of the group's operations is adversely affected. Against the odds however, the women have managed to keep their group activities going. They also engage in chromite mining as co-operative members and contract workers and invest some of the income earned from mining operations into group activities. In December 1992 they afforded a repayment on the loan.

As for the men's group, there was nothing to discuss since the project had collapsed and all the members were back to full-time chromite mining. Poor debt recovery was cited as the main cause of the collapse.

Conclusion

It should be conceded that the undertaking of the study was not without its own hitches. The main methodological limitations were that the survey structured questionnaire precluded in-depth interviews and the learning of respondents' full stories, experiences, situations, etc.; the non-members were difficult to find; due to the language problem specially in tin and tantalite mining, confidential discussions and interviews were not possible since translators had to be present; because the researcher was male, and the translators were the co-operative leaders who were predominantly male, woman to woman discussions were missing and more sensitive information could not be captured. However, it was possible to meet the study objectives and the following conclusions can be drawn from the study findings.

The participation of women in co-operative mining has been a new phenomenon apparently contradicting the long-standing biological approach whose discrimination against women dates back to the colonial period in Zimbabwe. However, this new development was not a result of a deliberate strategy aimed at incorporating women and achieving gender equality in the mining sector. Instead, it was part of adjustment measures to reduce company mining costs after a glut in the mineral export markets. Co-operative mining has thus become the least lucrative venture in the sector and only desperate people, including female heads of households, have had to undertake it.

Since there was no deliberate gender planning and conscious challenging of the biological approach, a gender system based on the dominant gender contract has remained in operation at both the productive and reproductive levels. At the productive level, the biological approach and the cultural belief that men are responsible for important decisions outside the household/family and that in public life, women are regarded as minors, have resulted in the peripheralization and subordination of women. There has been only one women's co-operative and the proportion of female co-operative miners has remained insignificant.

Because of the biological approach, the general consensus has been that 'women cannot go underground', and the concept of 'heavy work for men and light work for women' has been widely adopted. The resultant specialization pattern has been an extension of the traditional sexual division of labour, with women being confined to unskilled tasks considered to be what they do best.

Although it is true that due to biological differences, men usually perform heavy manual work better than women, this fact has been extended to include important tasks which require skill rather than physique. Due to historical factors men have developed some mining skills and have had more mining experience than women. Men have, however, used this historical advantage to monopolize skilled positions and subordinate their female counterparts. Consequently, the notion of 'skilled work for men and unskilled work for women' has also been adopted.

While the over-representation of women in the management committee might imply their greater say in co-operative policy matters and appear to contradict the logic of the dominant gender contract, the issue of individual co-operative policy has not been important at all. Because of subcontracting arrangements and the consequent lack of land and mining claim ownership rights, there has been virtually no organizational autonomy among mining co-operatives.

At the reproductive level, the cultural belief that women's domain should be restricted to the home and family and the regarding of women as minors in public life have not only meant restriction of married women to the home but also resulted in outright discrimination against women and victimization of female headed households. The study has proved that these beliefs are unfounded since wives can also generate household cash income and it is not true that only males are 'breadwinners', thus clearly showing that if given the chance women can actually disprove the logic of the dominant gender contract.

Again, because of the cultural restriction of women to the home, married women on co-operative mines have been required to attend to most of the domestic chores, with the husbands undertaking these chores only if their wives are away or ill. Thus, at the reproductive level, there has been reversal of the concept of heavy work for men and light work for women being legitimized by the 'roora' tradition. Further, the women's workload has been increased by the squalid and poor living conditions under which they perform their reproductive labour.

Subcontracting and the companies' desire to reduce and minimize mining costs have meant meagre incomes and widespread poverty among co-operative miners. While both men and women have sought to supplement these meagre incomes by engaging in informal income-generating activities, economic conditions have continued to deteriorate. Thus poverty has generally precluded access to any type of social security scheme and acquisition of such assets as bicycles, radios, furniture, stoves, cattle, land, etc.

Although productive non-mining ventures have been a rare phenomenon, a case study of group income-generating activities has also clearly demonstrated that, if given the chance, women can be entrepreneurs just like men. This also serves to show that while its logic can be easily disproved, the dominant gender contract has been largely responsible for the denial of opportunities for women to meaningfully participate in the development process.

Chapter Eight

Gender Issues amongst Dombo Tombo Lodgers: A Case Study Approach

Sylvia Sithole-Fundire

Introduction

Urban housing inadequacy is a major problem in the developing world. This has forced some households into renting rooms from willing landlords as lodgers. Housing refers to a process of improving one's standard of living within any given shelter.

In this study, a lodger will be taken as anyone renting part of a house as their sole form of accommodation. The incidence of lodgers in Zimbabwe is as old as the provision of housing in the urban areas. The number of people lodging is always increasing due to the rapid urban population growth which outstrips the provision of housing (Patel, 1984). This study focuses on men and women lodging in Dombo Tombo, the oldest high density suburb in Marondera.

Patel quotes Van der Schyff as saying that lodging at that time reflected a potential need that was double the existing waiting list. By 1992 the lodgers' national occupancy rate in the high density areas varied from 9 to 30 people per 200 to 300 metre plots.

Justification

Very little has been published on lodgers in Zimbabwe (Schlyter, 1989) and, worse still, gender issues have been overlooked. Studies tend to reflect an assumption that whatever affects men equally affects women.

There is need to distinguish the housing needs of men and women, so as to avoid 'solutions' that never benefit the intended beneficiaries or solutions that merely benefit one section of the intended beneficiaries at the expense of the other equally deserving part.

The study hopes to show that both men and women are active agents in housing and that these men and women operate in the context of power relations which determine the position of one group relative to the other.

It is also hoped that this research will stimulate more action oriented gender sensitive research not only from women but from men too.

Objectives

The study aims at investigating:
- The reasons for lodging;
- Lodgers' usage of space and access to facilities;
- The impact that lodging has on social relationships;
- The lodgers's housing aspirations.

Data collection

Qualitative research was conducted in Dombo Tombo. This area was chosen on the basis of being the oldest suburb in the town and the accommodation is relatively cheap. Most of the houses belong to particular individuals through the home ownership scheme and therefore the suburb has very high rates of lodging by low income people.

Concentration on one suburb was due to limited financial resources. It also had the advantage of allowing an in-depth study and a comparison of male and female lodgers within the same suburb.

An extended case study approach was adopted. Since high levels of unregistered lodging were suspected, standard random sampling was not feasible hence snowballing was used. Five cases were studied in depth. (It should be noted that this research is merely a small part of a larger study.) Unstructured interviews and observation were used to collect data from lodgers. To cement the data on lodgers' background on the basis of gender, historical research was carried out and inferences were made on the position of men and women in urban housing from literature.

A household was taken as a group of people living and eating together (Schlyter, 1989, p. 15). Unstructured interviews were administered to heads of households, landlords/ladies and municipal officials.

The findings of this research can be used as examples to consolidate further research findings. When it comes to sensitive, personal or novel issues on which reliable data has not been documented, qualitative research yields fruitful results. It captures moments as they occur and thus gives a true portrait of issues. Qualitative methodologies can thus be used to capture truly reflective baseline data. It is on the realization of these strengths that this qualitative research was conducted amongst lodgers.

Access to housing in Zimbabwe

Urban housing research in Zimbabwe has mainly looked at the impact of colonialism on housing as if colonial discrimination on racial ground was gender neutral. The norm of the male experience as being generalizable to their female counterparts has been implied (Parpart, 1989). Some literature indicates that the colonial housing policy was heavily marred with gender discriminatory practices.

What then was the impact of colonialism on gender and access to urban housing in Zimbabwe? Male and female roles created in the industrial revolution were exported to the colonies. With the advent of the factory in the colonial towns the home ceased to be the place of production it used to be. This changed the relationship between men and women as women were relegated to housewifery whilst men's position and status of breadwinners was reinforced. However, the factory exposed some women to better horizons in that young women could leave their rural homes to seek employment in town. Working women were worse off than their male counterparts but were better off than non-formally employed women. This latter situation in itself acted as a strong incentive for more women to move into towns.

However, wage employment for women was more limited as compared to that of men mainly because women had and still have poorer skills-training than men. Men took up wage employment in towns, even domestic work, which was formerly perceived as feminine in the rural setting. Thus urbanization reconstructed gender roles for the colonized, mainly to the advantage of men.

Since residence in towns was a function of employment (Cutrufelli, 1983), male predominance in urban employment meant that whatever housing was provided was predominantly for men right from the servants quarters on the premises of their employers to single men's hostels and then rented municipal housing (Patel & Adam, 1981). This had gender implications on the post-Independence urban housing delivery systems particularly in the case of the home ownership scheme as it meant that beneficiaries of the scheme were the sitting tenants who were mostly men. Hence more men than women became home owners and landlords in the high density areas built before Independence.

Single women were not entitled to municipal housing as they were considered minors irrespective of their ages and they could not therefore enter into any contract of lease. The same applied to a deserted wife who only ceased to be a minor after divorce. It was only with production of proof that a woman was a widow or divorcee that she could apply for municipal accommodation on condition that she could pay the rent. Poorer education for women than for men and the role of women as rural-home managers meant that very few women relative to men were employed in town and, for the few who were, very few qualified for rented municipal housing.

Influx control measures such as the 1960 Vagrancy Act kept the unemployed, mainly women, out of the urban areas. However, in the late years of the liberation war, the Smith regime relaxed enforcement of influx control measures as concentration was mainly on the war (Patel, 1984). As a result, at Independence many more people had moved into towns (Patel, 1988).

With Independence all forms of sexual discrimination became legal offences thus implying that men and women could have equal access to housing. It is with this scenario that gender issues amongst lodgers are analyzed.

Who is a lodger ?

Research findings indicate that lodgers in high density suburbs come from all walks of life. Their reasons for lodging vary. However, what they have in common is that they have all taken up to lodging because they have problems securing their own houses. As illustrated in the cases that follow, there are various underlying reasons that lead people into renting rooms.

This can be initially due to the fact that one is new in the town, but has no relatives to stay with, and the only contacts one has in the town can only secure one accommodation in a particular residential area. This is common amongst people who came to Marondera on a job transfer.

Case 1

Chirwa moved to Marondera in 1986 from a small town east of Marondera to take up better paying employment. He was single then and had no relatives to stay with hence resorted to renting a room in Dombo Tombo. He was referred to the landlord by some Rusape church minister. The landlord was a church minister too. He initially rented one room and thought it would be some temporary accommodation whilst he sought his own house.

In 1985 he married and had a child. There was need for bigger accommodation. With the help of a friend, he managed to rent two rooms in the same suburb. It was then that he registered with the municipality for a housing stand and has since been on the waiting list.

Several other single lodgers had had a similar experience to Chirwa's – they took up lodging because they were new in the town and hoped it would be temporary before they secured their own house.

Not all immigrant lodgers proved to have come in on employment transfer, some had come in search of good opportunities associated with the urban way of life. Those concerned referred to urban areas as 'Kuchirungu', meaning 'where the whites are' and therefore where modernization, development and independence are. This view was mainly expressed by women in the informal sector. The case of Amai Bee illustrates this attitude.

Case 2

She came into Marondera in 1980 from some rural area close to the town. She was single and aged 17. Her education was poor – only four years of primary schooling. She had no hopes of getting formal employment but had come to Marondera because she believed that urban life was easier and more interesting than life in the rural areas.

On arrival in Marondera she initially stayed with a female relative who was also lodging in Dombo Tombo. A few weeks after her arrival, she found a boyfriend who offered to pay her rent if she became a lodger which she did. She had a child, then another. By 1992 she had five children by different men. She claims that all the men with whom she had relationships had at some point promised to help her get her own house even if they would not marry her, which they never did. However, these men, most of them married and residing in better residential areas, always helped Amai Bee with her rent in return for whatever extramarital services she offered them. She pointed out that in all her encounters with all these men it was initially because she needed money to pay rent and also because she had hoped some day one of her clients would buy a house or help her acquire a stand to build her own house. She quoted cases in which some 'big' married men had bought houses for their girlfriends.

Before she had children she did not mind being a lodger. Now that she shares one room with her five children, she desires her own house. She has not registered for a stand as she believes she would not be considered since she is not formally employed. She has registered with the municipality as a street-vendor and she mainly sells fruit and vegetables in the market.

Some rural immigrants in Dombo Tombo suburb had come into Marondera during the liberation war which had destabilized the rural areas and commercial farms. Others had come during times of drought. Many of these were women who came to seek refuge in the company of husbands and relatives who lived with them for some time and later returned to the rural areas or rented rooms once they got established.

Case 3

Mrs Musekiwa first became a lodger in Dombo Tombo in 1976 when she fled the liberation war in the rural areas to join her lodging husband. After the war she returned to the rural areas where she rebuilt their home with the husband's financial assistance. However, the 1991-92 drought forced her back into town and she then returned to the rural areas with the onset of the rains. When in town she illegally sells fruit and vegetables on the streets to supplement her husband's income.

The Musekiwas have six children, four of whom are doing their secondary education in two different towns. Of the four one is a boy and stays with his father in Dombo Tombo. Because of the nature of his accommodation, Mr Musekiwa cannot stay with his three teenage daughters: he has made arrangements for them to stay with relatives in Harare. They cannot stay with their mother in the rural areas as the parents feel the nearest secondary school is not good enough. The other two children stay with their mother. As a result of not having adequate urban accommodation, the Musekiwas live as a fragmented family.

The Musekiwas have not registered for a stand as they are contented with their rural home. Not all people who came into Marondera due to the war or drought managed to return to the rural areas. Some war victims no longer have any rural homes to fall back on. Not all lodgers in Dombo Tombo suburb are originally from outside Marondera.

Case 4

Bright is a 22 year old man who was born and grew up in the town and had been staying with his brother up to 1990. On securing employment as a till operator in one of the local shops, he felt the need for some individual freedom hence he decided to take up lodging in Dombo Tombo. For him, lodging was voluntary. He pointed out that should he encounter problems with his current accommodation he is still welcome at his brother's house.

He commented: 'Because I am a boy my brother does not mind me living alone as a lodger. My elder sister wanted to move out of my brother's house when she finished school and had found a job in 1988 but my brother would not allow her on the grounds that anything can happen to girls when they get the sort of freedom that I have as a lodger.'

In situations where lodging is out of choice, as illustrated by Bright's comment, it becomes a gender issue, that is, women should be protected whilst their male counterparts should be free. It seems more acceptable for a man rather than a woman to become a lodger thus implying that women take up lodging as a last resort whilst some of their male counterparts take up lodging out of choice. It is then not surprising that the few young single women who become lodgers are usually derogatively labelled prostitutes.

The research has also indicated that of the original (i.e. non immigrant) urban dwellers not all of them take up lodging out of choice, but other pressing issues may force them to. The most common problem being overcrowding as perceived by the occupants, in their original place of residence which might belong to parents or relatives.

Case 5

When the Rusikes got married in 1989 they lived with Mr Rusike's parents who own a house in Dombo Tombo. Mrs Rusike is a full time housewife and the husband is a till operator at some local shop. Realizing how difficult it would be for them to get their own house Mr and Mrs Rusike decided to save money and build a cottage on Mr Rusike's parents stand. The idea was for them to use the cottage whilst the rest of the family used the four-roomed house.

On completion of the construction of the cottage a misunderstanding arose between Mr Rusike and his brothers over his occupancy of the cottage. The young brothers felt that they had a right to use the cottage too. Mr and Mrs Rusike gave in to the demands of Mr Rusike's brothers and thus left to take up rented rooms in the same suburb. They had to move to allow for better sleeping arrangement for Mr Rusike's brothers and sisters.

Lodgers' economic situation

At the time of the study (1991–1993), the incomes of the cases studied ranged from $200 to $1 000 per month for men and below $100 to $600 per month for women. It should be noted that informal sector incomes are sometimes difficult to determine particularly in fruit and vegetable vending due to the uncertainties associated with the informal sector. At the time of this study, street vending was hard hit by a lot of problems, the major one being that of the cholera epidemic which forced the Ministry of Health to issue a directive over strict control of food vending. This meant that for those whose incomes were based on selling cooked food stuffs, fruit and vegetables, life became very uncertain as business was poor and that could mean the inability to pay rent and hence high chances of eviction. The majority of the lodgers affected were mainly women by virtue of being over-represented in food stuff vending.

At the time of the study, the lodgers had to pay a rent of not less than $60, food and other basic necessities such as the school fees also had to be paid for. Given the high cost of living, it is not surprising that hardly any savings were made. It should be noted that of the cases studied, most of the household only had two meals per day at the most. These were breakfast, that mainly comprised tea and bread, then supper which comprised sadza (maize-meal) and a relish (sauce) of either vegetables only and/or one or two small pieces of meat. Having lunch was a thing of the past. Even housewives and children who stayed at home all day did not have lunch. The idea was to cut down on expenditure as much as possible to ensure that at the end of each month there was some money for the rent.

Access to facilities and usage of space

Lodgers share the house from which they rent rooms and all that the house offers. Theoretically, all lodgers have equal access to these facilities. However, this study discovered that, in reality, equal access to facilities is not always the case particularly when it comes to the usage of the bathroom which is usually not separate from the toilet.

Where co-lodgers are of the same sex some degree of equal access to the bathroom tends to exists. However, it is those working in the formal sector who tend to be given first priority to the usage of the bathroom. In situations where the resident landlords/ladies share the bathroom with the lodgers, the landlord/lady's family are given first priority in the use of the bathroom and outdoor space. It is important to note that the sharing of the bathroom between landlords/ladies and their lodgers is very rare. Landlords/ladies tend to have a separate toilet/bathroom from that of their lodgers.

In cases where the co-lodgers are male and female, men use the bathroom first. Women and children have to bath only at times that will not inconvenience the men. Men are generally excused from cleaning the bathroom and the yard on grounds that house cleaning is a feminine chore. Women tend to bath last in the morning so that they can clean up the bathroom.

To separate the functions of the floor space, some lodgers have partitioned rented rooms into even smaller segments. The desire by lodging women to have a living room/kitchen separate from the main bedroom was expressed not only verbally but through the partitioning of the rented room into two or more sections.

This was normally done by use of a curtain or pieces of furniture which were arranged such that they formed a dividing wall between the segments of the rented room. Subdivisions are prevalent where there are female members of the household. Women therefore determine the usage of space within rented rooms.

Despite the fact that all women in lodging households expressed their desire to have a kitchen, a separate kitchen was not always a prerequisite in the face of limited indoor space. A corner in the living room can be used as the cooking area. Alternatively, food can be prepared outside in the open, on the veranda, passage or in an outdoor wooden room. The room or partition used as a living room is multipurpose: other than being used as a kitchen, it can also be used as a bedroom for some members of the household or visitors. In situations where two or three rooms are rented to allow for a bedroom, kitchen and dining room/living room, the kitchen and/or living room are converted into bedrooms at night. Girls slept in the kitchen whilst boys slept in the living room thus indicating that at household level the kitchen was always defined as a females' domain. However, if there was just a bedroom and living room/kitchen children under the ages of five could be allowed to sleep with their parent(s) in the main bedroom but for older children sleeping arrangements for the boys could be made with friends and relatives or with the landlord/lady whilst girls slept in the living room/kitchen which could be a second rented room or a partitioning. The general feeling was that girls should be guarded close to the home whilst boys, by virtue of being male, were believed to be in a better position to cope with their journeys to sleep. Girls were also kept at the house so that they could help with domestic chores such as cooking and cleaning up in the morning and evenings.

Outdoor usage of space was determined by landlords and co-lodgers. Whilst resident landlords rarely allowed their tenants gardening space, most absentee landlords left it up to their lodgers to decide on the usage of outdoor space. This was particularly true of absentee landlords with houses rented by not more than three households. In such instances lodgers apportioned each other gardening space. At the time of this study lodgers who had access to gardening space hardly grew any flowers but a few vegetable beds were observed. Gardening was generally discouraged at the time due to the 1991-92 drought and the subsequent municipal water rationing measures. Households with children and/or with females were more keen on gardening than male only households because children and females spent relatively more time on the stand than adult males. Also, households with children were relatively big hence the need to grow their own vegetables to save on the money spent on meat and vegetables for relish in the face of escalating prices of basic commodities at the time.

In situations where several (more than three) households rented rooms from an absentee landlord it became very difficult for lodgers to agree amongst themselves on how the yard could be subdivided. The desire for gardening space was always verbally expressed by female members of the lodging households and, at times, it was evidenced by the growing of vegetables under fruit trees within the yard. In cases of multiple lodging households (more than three) on the stand there was very little vacant space anyway, as the main house was usually extended and the backyard had a two- to three-roomed outbuilding. Women tended to use whatever little outdoor space for outdoor cooking in the event of a power cut or when there was no electricity connected to the house or in the event of lack of electrical, gas or paraffin cooking appliances.

For example, up to December 1991 the house from which Amai Bee rents a room had no electricity yet the stand housed 12 households in the main house and the outbuilding. So the lodgers had to either cook their food in the open space, outside using firewood which the women poached from the nearest Agro Forestry or indoors using paraffin stoves. Even after the house was electrified in January 1992, four of the 12 lodging households on that particular stand had no paraffin or electrical cooking appliances and still cooked in the open space available. There was hardly enough space for children to play.

Children were forced to play on the street. As late as 7.30 p.m. the children could be found playing on the street under a street-lamp. It is also not unusual to find women sitting relaxing and chatting with their friends by the street-side.

The street is very much a part of the lodging women and their children's outdoor space.

The impact of lodging on lodgers' social relationships

When asked about the impact of lodging on their jobs, the lodgers replied that there was no significant direct relationship between the two.

By contrast, lodging women, particularly those in the informal sector, complained that lodging did affect their income generation.

Case 6

Amai Chipo, a fruit and vegetable vendor, complained that she did not have enough space to store her fruit and vegetables ordered for sale or left over from the previous stock. She would love to grow her own vegetables but because she is a lodger she had no gardening space and she had to rely on fruit and vegetables ordered from the market. 'I can't even make a fire to cook green mealies to sell due to lack of free open space on the yard' she said.

The outcry from those in the informal sector – mainly women – was that lodging meant lack of space and freedom to embark on income generating projects. All lodgers, regardless of gender, strongly felt that lodging had a strong bearing on income expenditure. Rent ranged from $60 to $100 per month excluding water and electricity. Rent, water and electricity rates could rise any time at the will of the landlord/lady. This affected lodger-lodger and lodger-landlord relationships. Female lodgers usually get blamed for misuse of water and electricity such that husbands tend to blame their wives, male household members blame their female household members, adult male households or single households blame households with children for high water and electricity bills. It is interesting to note this case:

Case 7

Due to the 1991-92 drought, the Marondera Municipality imposed water rationing measures. Every high density stand was allowed $12m^3$ per month. A fine of $5 was levied for any extra cubic metre of water used. In May 1992 the water bill for the stand on which Amai Bee lived was $250 including fines. When the absentee landlord brought the bill to his 12 lodging households blame was put on all the female co-lodgers. One of Amai Bee's co-lodgers explained: 'When the bill came the man who lives in the cottage declared that all the single men were going to contribute $5 to the water bill and all the women with children had to then share the remaining expenses equally which meant that 10 families had to contribute $24 each. Six female co-lodgers who heard the declaration did not challenge this decision saying that the women couldn't argue with a man in case he should hit them. One of the women in the 10 families that had to pay $24 was beaten by her husband over the issue. The husband argued that the male co-lodger's decision was very right and he (husband) felt that his wife was wasteful as she always did the laundry and changed water from the basin each time she bathed their three children.'

In the lodging environment women can easily be harassed by their male counterparts. In the above quoted case, none of the lodgers questioned the rationality of the municipality water rationing procedure, preferring instead to blame the women. The socially defined role of women as being responsible for child rearing, laundry and cooking earns them the blame for high water and electricity bills: no-one stops to think of who is benefiting from all this work! In the quoted case the real cause of the problem, that of too many people scrambling for scarce water resource, is ignored and the women are used as a scapegoat. This problem is not only found amongst intra and inter-lodger households but is also prevalent in the lodger landlord/lady relationship as reflected in the landlords/ladies preferences when choosing their tenants.

The landlord/lady's choice

Whilst different landlords/ladies have different preferences, almost all those interviewed put female headed households at the bottom of their lists. Amongst the female headed households those living with children were the least preferred especially those with more than one child. Landlords/ladies strongly feel that women and children waste water, electricity and the children tend to mess up toilets and the yard. Women in female headed households are also blamed for bringing in boyfriends or seducing landlords yet single men are rarely blamed for bringing in their girlfriends. The impression created is that without some male in control, a household is disorganized. Landladies who head their household realized that the above outlined stereotype of lodging female heads of household was not always true.

Case 8

Amai Mukutsha, a widow and landlady, acknowledged that most home owners were not prepared to rent their rooms to female heads of households because they believed that such women were prostitutes. She hastened to add that this was not always true. She felt that one's personality rather than their sex determines how they interact with their landlords/ladies.

Given the general negative stereotype of female heads of households it is then not surprising that more female headed households are found in the worst housing structures than male headed household whilst male headed households are prevalent in cottages, or share the main house with the landlord/lady or one or two co-lodgers. Female headed households are over represented in the 'tangwenas' or share poorly maintained houses with several other co-lodgers in predominantly female headed households too.

Landlords/ladies have the greatest preference for male headed small households where the head of household is formally employed. This category of lodgers is believed to be more reliable in terms of paying their bills by virtue of their regular incomes.

Landlords/ladies prefer to take in lodgers who would have been referred by other people they know. It is then not surprising to find that co-lodgers usually have something in common as indicated by the following comments from some of the lodgers studied as regards their co-lodgers or landlord/lady.
- ✦ We come from the same home area.
- ✦ We go to the same church.
- ✦ We drink together.

The least preferred groups of lodgers are the most likely to have to endure bad housing conditions.

Case 9

Amai Bee has rented rooms in only two houses since she came to Marondera in 1980. She moved from her first rented lodging after she had her second child as her landlord said that he could not accommodate people with children. She then rented a room in her current residence in 1983.

Since then she has not moved. Factors that hinder her from moving to a new and better residence include:

- Her five children.
- Her marital status i.e. single parent.
- Informal sector employment.

In both male or female headed households the female members of these households are more disadvantaged than the male members. Due to their roles of cleaning up, ordering rooms, cooking, feeding the family, most of the women's time is spent at home. Even those who are formally employed or in the informal sector spend more time at home than their male counterparts, as such they feel the constraints of limited housing space and they interact more with co-lodgers and the landlord/lady.

Eviction

Even in the case of an absentee landlord/lady, in the event of arrears, it is mainly the women who face the rage of the house owner when he/she comes for his dues. Often it is the women who have the embarrassment of temporary eviction. They have to sit and guard their property that would have been moved out of the rented room(s) or they have to go around borrowing money from co-lodgers and neighbours to pay for the arrears. When all this happens usually the male members of the household are off the premises, perhaps at work, at the bar or otherwise occupied.

In the case of outright eviction it is always the women who face the embarrassment of packing their household goods into the hand-driven removal carts and walking alongside the removal boys to their new place of abode. The women have to clean up the new place of abode and start all over again.

The male head of household illusion

This is not to say male lodgers do not have their problems too. In male headed households, the head of the household is responsible for footing the accommodation bills and for making attempts to secure a full house for the household. However, despite the fact that the problems encountered by women lodgers are usually exclusive to women, those encountered by men are equally met by female heads of households. Even in male headed households some female members usually help solve the problems meant to be the responsibility of men.

Working wives (either in the formal or informal sector) often help shoulder traditionally male financial responsibilities and in some cases they totally take over. For example: Amai Bee's co-lodger, a soldier's wife, is a hairdresser. She described how her husband spends most of his money on beer and girlfriends. She, therefore, pays the rent, buys food and clothes for herself and her child.

Another example: Mr Musekiwa acknowledged the fact that his salary is too low to maintain his family. However, his wife who usually lives in the rural areas except in the case of war or drought, usually cultivates enough crops to feed the family and can even sell the surplus to educate the children. When in town she sells vegetables and uses the money to buy food and sometimes to pay the rent.

Such cases as quoted above, are indications that the supposedly male headed household norm needs questioning.

The responsibilities of women as home-makers is very prevalent amongst lodging working women. Given their limited income and housing space, it is very difficult for them to employ domestic workers if need be.

Lodger-landlord/lady inter-dependency

It is not always true that co-lodgers and their landlords clash. Whilst most male lodgers claimed to be indifferent about their co-lodgers some absentee landlords confessed that they relied on particular key lodgers for the collection of rent from the rest of their lodgers.

The majority of female lodgers maintained that they found social company from their co-lodgers and resident landladies.

One of the widowed landladies acknowledges that she derived a sense of security from the presence of her lodgers thus indicating that the relationship between lodgers and their landlords/ladies is not merely financial but can be cordial and two way. For example: Amai Murwisi has three lodging households, one in the main house two in the cottage. She says that the presence of her lodgers reduces any chances of her home being broken into. When she is away she informs her lodgers and they also do the same to her and to each other to ensure that they help to ensure that they guard each other's property. Therefore, she does not just generate income from her lodgers but derives some degree of security and companionship from them.

Lodgers' housing aspirations

All lodgers wished for a house of their own. Lodgers felt that lodging was not supposed to be a permanent type of residence especially for more than one person households. Therefore, lodging was only theoretically acceptable as accommodation for households in transition to home ownership. Indeed, all the cases studied pointed out that the first time they rented rooms they all expected it to be transitional whilst they sought their own houses.

House design

Men were not worried about the house design. As if to summarize all the male lodgers' views, Mr Musekiwa lamented: 'How the house looks is not important to me, all that I need at the moment is my own house.'

Instead, male lodgers wished for the local authority to control lodgers rent. There was a direct attack on the 1980 Lodgers Rent Restriction. It was argued that: 'There is need for government to enforce it otherwise lodgers would spend all their salaries on rent.'

Female lodgers gave detail on the design of houses they wished for. Common characteristics were:
+ Enough bedrooms for one's children.
+ A house with a big kitchen.
+ A house with a yard big enough for a vegetable garden and for the construction of an outer building that could be used as an extra kitchen in which firewood could be used for cooking and heating in order to cut down on the electricity cost.

Female lodgers emphasized the need for:
+ Independent outer doors to be used by each lodging household. This would ensure some degree of privacy as no lodgers would have to pass through any co-lodger's room(s).
+ More than one toilet/bathroom.
+ Outer buildings for lodging instead of the main house.
+ One garbage bin per household.

Male lodgers were worried about high rent whilst women complained of both high rent and poor living conditions, for example:
- Lack of privacy.
- Lack of gardening space and no room for children to play.
- Lack of kitchens for those renting one room.
- Too many people using one toilet hence clashes over cleaning or dissatisfaction with the maintenance of the toilet.

The general responses given by women as regards their desired houses, reflect preoccupation with their reproductive roles.

The lodger as a prospective landlord/lady

Cases studied in this research indicate that before house ownership, it is mainly male and female heads of household who want to take in lodgers whilst most married women dislike the idea on the grounds that lodgers do not maintain one's house as the owner would, Mrs Chirwa commented: 'If you want your house to deteriorate fast, rent it out to lodgers.'

Whether or not they desired to retire to the rural areas, lodging male heads of household indicated that they had a rural home or relatives in rural areas where they would be welcome in times of need. In contrast, lodging female heads of household, mostly those living with their children, felt that all they had were their rented rooms. Relatives, both in rural and urban areas, would not accept them in their homes if they were in trouble. There was a feeling that by heading their own household they had been labelled prostitutes. On the other hand, successful female heads of households are admired by the community at large: For example: Amai Tee, a landlady, is referred to by her lodgers and neighbours as 'Murume pachake' i.e. 'manly woman'. She inherited the house after the death of her husband then she took in lodgers and eventually built a cottage in which she took more lodgers.

Lodging female heads of household who had no intention of marrying (or remarrying) aspired to be manly women in the housing arena. Their desire was for the town-fathers to give them housing stands.

The lodgers' future

One's economic position directly affects one's chances of obtaining those things defined desirable in one's society. For those lodgers who can afford to pay the deposit for serviced stands or are able to prove financially that they can construct a house according to stipulated standards there is hope of acquiring an urban house of their own. These people can afford reasonable housing by virtue of being able to pay high rent. These are the educated, single or married with small households, and are normally employed in the formal sector earning above minimum wages. More men than women fall in this category.

Informants studied here lack economic power to ensure acquisition of their own houses. Those employed in the formal sector might manage to secure low cost housing and the majority of these are male. This can only be achieved on condition that these lodgers are formally registered and also registered on the housing waiting list.

Some of these respondents were unregistered, they felt that would mean payment of a lodgers fees which lodgers view as an extra financial costs. Some lodgers claimed to have registered for the housing stands as far back as 1987 but have since given up on renewing their registration and some have never registered at all. This is true for most female heads of household for whom lack of money is the major stumbling block to registration. For most married women, it is not just lack of finance that stops them registering but the mere belief that it is only the men's responsibility to register for a stand. For such people the housing future is very bleak, as they do not exist in the maps of the planners.

The only hope for registered lodgers who are also on the housing waiting list is the Ministry of Local Government, Rural and Urban Development's intention to cancel the requirement for applicants for housing stands to produce financial proof and thus allow people to construct their houses gradually (*Sunday Mail,* 23 January 1993). This would disadvantage the local authority in many respects but would go a long way in accommodating people in the informal sector in their acquisition of housing stands.

Conclusion

Lodging is one major way through which the housing problems in terms of having a roof over one's head can be contained. However, by virtue of being home-makers, women feel the impact of this limited space more than men. Continuities from the women's historical and socio-cultural background have affected women's chances of acquiring houses. They rent the worst rooms, in terms of maintenance and in terms of overcrowding of occupants per given room and per stand. Male lodgers have relatively greater choice than female lodgers in terms of the type of rooms to rent because they have better cultural and financial resources to fall back on.

Chapter Nine

Women in Micro-Enterprises: The Case of Mbare, Zimbabwe

Diana Nachudwa

Introduction

Small and micro-enterprises are a dynamic sector of the economy. They play a crucial role as an employer and a source of income for those who fail to make it in the larger sectors of the economy's private and public sectors. Despite the above, planners often impose regulations which impede the growth of this sector out of a desire to plan, control, and regularize the economic development of cities and towns so as to promote health and safety of the urban population. Those who suffer most from the planners' action are women and children, who constitute about two thirds of those involved in small and micro-enterprises.

As in most developing countries, planners in Zimbabwe are now moving towards enabling the small and micro-enterprises to grow, by providing land from which the enterprises can operate for a small fee. In the capital city, i.e. Harare, the council has set aside land for micro-enterprises in most high density areas. This paper will look at a small section of these micro-enterprises on such land in Mbare, a high density suburb.

Although Zimbabwean planners have moved towards enabling the sector to grow, they have carried little qualitative research to gain an understanding of the sector's needs in terms of space, service and land requirements, etc. Usually more quantitative than qualitative data has been used resulting in planners planning for the people and not with the people.

Objectives

The objectives of this paper are:
+ To assess the level of participation of the small entrepreneurs in Mbare in the preparation of the Mbare North Local Plan. Whether this was at the plan preparation stage or implementation stage.
+ To assess the impact of the Mbare North Local Plan proposals on the women, men and children who operate in Mbare.
+ To look at the problems faced by men, women and children in the micro and small scale economic sector at Mbare and assess how far their representations, if any, have been included in the Local Plan.

Definition of terms

The term micro-enterprises will be used to mean those small scale economic units operating around Mbare Musika (i.e. the market area). The paper will address only a small section of the numerous micro-enterprises operating in Mbare. It will focus on the fruit, vegetable and handicraft enterprises (both licensed and unlicensed).

Growers are the farmers who commute to Mbare from rural areas to sell their farm products at wholesale prices to traders and not to individual consumers.

Methodology

A qualitative research approach was adopted for the study. Simple random sampling was used to select the interviewees to get a general picture of how the enterprises are run at Mbare Musika. From the random sample, ten licensed traders were studied in-depth in the agricultural, retail, wholesale and handicraft sections of the market area. Of these ten cases, two were chosen in each of the agricultural, retail and handicraft sections whilst four were chosen from the wholesale section. More people were studied in the wholesale section because a subject plan for the area had proposed the redesigning of the wholesale market area so views of the traders on the redesign were sought.

The Mbare North Local Plan was also looked at to compare proposals in the plan and what the licensed traders felt should have been incorporated in the Local Plan. Informal interviews with the local authority were carried out to determine how the local authority collected information for the Local Plan and to determine whether the traders at Mbare Musika participated directly in formulating proposals for the Local Plan.

Constraints

The unlicensed vendors, especially children, could not be studied in-depth as they usually moved from one place to another in fear of the police. Some traders were not willing to participate because they felt they would not benefit from the study. This was so because many studies have been carried out before, especially by university students, but these studies have not been utilized to improve the traders conditions at Mbare Musika. However, this was not a serious problem because the researcher had a wide choice, considering the number of stalls at Mbare.

Location of the study area

The study area lies about 3 km south of the city centre, in Mbare high density suburb. It is the oldest high density suburb in Harare. The area is easily accessible by road from all parts of the city of Harare.

The largest long distance bus terminus in Harare is located here. Commuters to different parts of the country provide a market for the goods and services of the small enterprises which operate around the bus terminus.

Historical background

Before Independence, the economy of the then Rhodesia was a white dominated capitalist economy. The activities of blacks in this economy was limited to retail businesses and services most of which were concentrated in high density areas and rural areas. Manufacturing and commerce was little developed among blacks because competition with whites was limited through tight regulations such as zoning, licensing, financial constraints, etc.

The formal retail sector among blacks was dominated by men whilst women's activities were limited to vegetable vending and hawking because of the social relations in the black society. Men were supposed to be the breadwinners and women were to supplement what men brought home as well as to look after the home. Women thus found it easier to go into vending so that they could effectively accomplish both roles.

After Independence in 1980, the restrictive laws discouraging blacks from entering the formal sector were abolished. Blacks could now go into commerce, manufacturing and tertiary services. However, this opportunity was limited to men only since women could not own property according to the prevailing traditional customs. Women's participation in the formal sector was also limited by lack of education, so they were forced into small and micro activities such as sewing, knitting, vegetable vending and hawking. Most women ventured into vegetable vending and retailing. Today, about two thirds of the small enterprises are run by women. Most of these women are into retailing in the vegetables and fruit market, a typical female activity.

In most urban areas in Zimbabwe, the city fathers have realized the importance of small and micro-enterprises as a source of income for those who fail to get employment in the formal sector. The level of recognition varies from one local authority to another, as shown by the different levels of provision of facilities for use by these enterprises.

The planning process

In Mbare there was no comprehensive planning of the area and this resulted in haphazard development with a mixture of land uses. Therefore, at Mbare Musika, we find vegetable wholesaling, craft retailing, general retailing, etc.; all these activities are carried out by licensed and unlicensed entrepreneurs.

The Regional Town and Country Planning Act (hereafter called the Act) provides steps which should be followed when preparing Local Plans. These steps can be summarized as follows:

- Consultation:
  The Act simply says that at the preliminary stages the local planning authority should ensure that there is adequate consultation with government agencies and other local authorities (where necessary) but does not specify that individuals should be consulted about the intention to prepare a plan.
- Examination and analysis of the existing structure of the planning area i.e. population, social, economic and environmental characteristics as well as the sphere of influence of the planning area.
- Analysis of the information collected above.
- Preparation of the report.
- Public exhibition for comments and representations.
- Adoption and approval.

The collecting and analyzing of data stage ties in with the second step of the Act outlined above. The Act does not specify how the data and information should be collected. It is up to the local authority to decide how this should be done. In most cases data is collected by means of structured questionnaires. Little qualitative data is collected for planning purposes because more quantifiable data is needed to make projections into the future.

Views of the traders

The types of small enterprises around Mbare Musika are many but this paper will only look at the growers market, the retail and wholesale vegetable market and handicraft sections.

The growers market is used by rural farmers to sell their farm produce to traders from different parts of Harare as well as neighbouring small towns. The vegetable wholesale section markets vegetables in larger quantities both to consumers and micro-traders who buy in relatively smaller quantities than in growers market. The retail section sells directly to the consumers in very small quantities. It usually caters for people in Mbare who cannot afford to buy in bulk.

The growers market and part of the retail section do not have covered stalls. The wholesale section has covered stalls and the handicraft section is completely covered. Taps, toilets and bins are communal in all sections.

Growers

The inter-dependence between the Musika (Market) and the long distance bus terminus is that rural growers use the long distance buses to ferry their goods to Mbare. They find it convenient to sell at the nearby growers markets. The customers come from all over the city to buy wholesale vegetables for resale. Mbare is convenient and transport is not a problem because ZUPCO (the national bus company) has some parking bays next to the long distance bus terminus. Furthermore, 'emergency taxis' (local unmetered taxis services) operate from areas such as Mufakose, Highfield, Glen View to Mbare and so traders who come from other sections of Harare have little or no transport problems in getting to Mbare.

Rural growers come from different parts of the country to sell their fruit and vegetables at Mbare. Men dominate the growers market because both men and women feel that the growers market is tough for women to venture into, as one grower put it: 'I live in Devedzo (which is about 135 km east of Harare) and commute to Harare three times a week to sell sweet potatoes, tomatoes, beans, garlic, green mealies, etc. I am assisted by my twenty-year-old son. My wife stays at home to look after the home and plough the fields. I also feel that my wife is not strong enough to come to Mbare because this business is tough.'

This view was expressed by most of the farmers at the growers market. They felt that women have to do lighter jobs. It is more acceptable for men rather than women to do the tough work of selling farm produce to wholesalers because they are a stronger sex. Both men and women felt that women are too weak to fight off thieves who may pounce on them. (A farmer can earn as much as Z$2000 or more per day.) So it was not safe for women to carry large sums of money in Mbare.

As to services provided by the local authority, some of the farmers felt that they were adequate whilst others felt that they were not. The most needed service the growers require is a covered market to protect them from the rains and scorching sun. The growers also felt that the area around their market had to be paved because it was dusty and muddy during the dry and rainy season respectively.

Vegetable and fruit section

Traders in the vegetable and fruit section, both wholesale and retail, buy their vegetables and fruit from transporters who sell their goods at Mbare. The market was built in such a way that lorries can drive through the stalls to off-load their vegetables. More women than men were happy about this arrangement, as expressed by Mai Tee: 'This arrangement is convenient for me as a woman who not only earns money at the market but has a family of six to look after. I wouldn't be into wholesaling if I had to go to the rural areas myself to look for vegetables and fruit as this would be time consuming and too heavy for me. I would have little time to do all the household chores I handle at present, before and after work at the market.'

Mai Tee's view was expressed by most of the women interviewed because they are not only into trade but have the responsibility at home of carrying out the household chores and raising children. Thus, more women than men in the wholesale and retail sections felt that the Local Plan should maintain the status quo and not remove the driveways through the market as proposed by the Local Plan.

Traders in the retail section were not happy with the vegetable vendors who operate anywhere around the Musika bus terminus. They felt that they are losing customers to the vendors who are operating illegally but are not paying any license fees to council. The Local Plan, they felt, should address this problem by ensuring that there was a permanent police force to enforce the Vendors and Hawkers regulations. These sentiments were also expressed by women in the handicraft section who felt that they were being robbed of customers by young men operating illegally around the bus terminus area.

Services provided

The vegetable wholesalers and retailers were satisfied with the facilities provided and rental charges. They felt that the council was collecting sufficient money and should also upgrade the paving and deploy a permanent police force in the area. The need for a police force was expressed by both men and women in both trades and was put as the number one priority by almost everyone interviewed. Mukoma Sam's words express how strongly people need a police force around Mbare: 'Our customers are sometimes robbed of their money by the thieves who roam around this place pretending to buy vegetables. The area is usually congested on Saturdays and Sundays when we get customers from all over Harare who buy vegetables in bulk. Some customers buy over Z$100 worth of vegetables and these people are usually the target of thieves. If something is not done about these thieves we will lose customers to the shops or suburban markets. I strongly feel that our customers should be protected from these thieves. We also need protection because on weekends one can earn more than Z$1 000 per day and this usually attracts thieves. So the council should deploy more municipal police to this area for security reasons.'

Storage

Fruit and vegetables are stored on the stalls overnight as they are too bulky to carry home. The fruit and vegetable market is opened at 7 o'clock in the morning and locked at 6 o'clock in the evenings. The growers market is opened around 6 o' clock. There is no refrigeration so the vegetables tend to turn bad quickly especially in the hot season. There are several bins around the market area and there is a permanent refuse collection lorry based at Mbare Musika to empty the bins. Both men and women were satisfied with the frequency with which bins were emptied at Mbare.

Publicity in connection with the Local Plan

The city council informed traders at Mbare, through their chairman, of the intention to prepare the Local Development Plan and the dates when the survey would be carried out. This was done about a month in advance of the surveys. According to the city council this was done 'as a form of publicity and to ensure maximum response'. The question is, did the traders understand what a Local Development Plan (LDP) is?

Most of the traders interviewed did not know what an LDP is. Some thought that it was a plan to upgrade the hostels and squatter camp which lie to the north of the fruit and vegetable market whilst others thought that the plan was for the upgrading of the market area and bus terminus. This shows that the publicity in connection with the Local Plan was inadequate in informing traders at Mbare about the objectives of the plan.

There was consensus that the publicity was not good enough because traders did not know the intentions of the plan. The traders did not even know that there is an Act which guides development in urban areas and that the plan for Mbare was being prepared in accordance with that Act. The traders felt that the city council could have taken time to educate them about the procedures and requirements of the Act, so that they could have participated with a full understanding of what is required by the Act. This could have been done through the different committees.

Local Plan proposals in relation to peoples' needs

The Local Plan found that there is inadequate security at the Musika area for the goods sold as they are left in the open overnight. Council felt that there may be incidence of theft of goods among the traders so there was need for lockable stalls. Security was also needed to protect both the traders and the customers who come to Mbare from thieves. The council therefore proposed to deploy more municipal policemen to the area. It also proposed to set aside land within the existing shopping area for banks so that traders do not have to carry large sums of money to town. The banking proposal was welcomed by the traders especially by the women because they are the ones who usually fell prey to the thieves. The proposal to erect lockable stalls was, however, not welcomed by some traders because they felt that the cost of construction would be passed on to them in the form of increased license fees.

The city council also proposed to redesign the wholesale market area to remove driveways and create more stalls. A contractor was engaged to carry out the proposal soon after the plan was approved by council. This was, however, met with resistance from the traders so the activity had to be shelved to allow for negotiations between the council and the traders. The council had to pay the contractor for breach of contract. Traders at Mbare felt that the costly exercise could have been avoided had the council informed the traders of its intentions during plan preparation rather than wait for the traders to make representations at a later stage.

Every trader I talked to was bitter about the proposal to remove driveways as this would mean that they had to go and look for the vegetables and fruit rather than wait for the farmers to bring the fruit and vegetables to them. Women felt that removing the driveways would affect the smooth running of their micro-enterprises because some of their time would be spent looking for the fruit and vegetables. It would also impact negatively on their daily household chores as they would have to wake up early to go and buy fruit and vegetables for resale and this would reduce their time for motherhood duties.

The traders said they would agree to the proposal on condition the city council expanded the growers market to accommodate those farmers who used to drive through the stalls. However, the women felt that doing this would add an unnecessary burden to them because they would have to ferry the goods from the growers market to their stalls. They would be forced to hire help to ferry goods to their stalls which may prove to be very expensive.

Another proposal for the Musika (market) area was to discourage unlicensed vendors from operating everywhere around the market area as this was causing environmental decay. The vendors would be allocated stalls within the extended market area.

Conclusion

There is need for a review of the regulations relating to preparation of the Local Plans to incorporate public participation in planning. Public participation should be at the preliminary stages and formulation stages, and not at a later stage as proposed by the Act. If this is done, planners will have a better understanding of the people they are planning for and will have better proposals for their plans.

Planners should start education campaigns to inform people of the purposes of Local Plans before they prepare them, especially when the Local Plans relate to micro-enterprises. In micro-enterprises most of the entrepreneurs are women who have little or no education and therefore do not know their legal rights as far as town planning is concerned. Education campaigns will not only enlighten people of their legal rights but will enable people to contribute reasonably to the proposals. In turn, planners will get a better understanding of the people's social and economic needs which can then be incorporated into the Local Plans.

Chapter Ten

Ideologies on Everyday Life amongst Finalists at the University of Zimbabwe

Sibusisiwe Ncube

Introduction

This paper explores the attitudes and ideas about everyday life of final year students from the faculties of arts, engineering, social studies and medicine at the university of Zimbabwe. Everyday life was taken to mean the lifestyle these students anticipate to live after graduation. Emphasis here was placed on the similarity and differences between the male and the female perspective. This study gives insight into the ideologies held by this group which constitute the future leaders of society. It also gives insight into the formation of gender concepts especially from an ideological perspective.

Improved education makes people more critical of the prevailing conditions, be they political or socio-economic. It is therefore interesting to find out whether these students have a different understanding of the roles that men and women play, especially in marriage. Undoubtedly this would result in the questioning of culture and tradition because education and a change of environment results in a change of ideologies and values.

It must be pointed out that this study focused on ideas and beliefs and not actual practices. Educated people are generally looked up to and those who are less educated always aspire to be like the educated. It is therefore necessary to observe what society expects of a graduate and, in turn, what the graduate expects from society. Many of these students will be the decision makers or bureaucrats of tomorrow. Their perceptions on gender relations – on what is male and female – will undoubtedly influence how society will develop.

The researcher has noted that graduates generally aspire to own houses in the low density suburbs as well as to live a more western kind of life. The study therefore sought to discover how the finalists viewed the problem and what strategies they were going to employ to create a home and arrange household work. The study was conducted to find out the housing career (which was taken to mean the living arrangements these students were going to negotiate before actually settling down and buying their own property) these students were going to follow and, more importantly, the life they were going to lead in their households.

Here the key questions to be discussed were issues of the responsibilities that the husband and the wife have as regards the purchasing of property, the raising of children and the day-to-day running of the home. A major issue would be to find out whether the duties would be equally or equitably distributed, especially in relation to the career demands of both men and women which, in this case, would be more or less similar.

Another major aim of the study was to find out how female students anticipated coping with the demands of their careers and their households and to find out whether the assistance of their husbands would be solicited or assumed. If not, would they resort to the hiring of domestic help and, if so, what would her duties would be? How would they cope with the financial aspect – would the husband be called upon to contribute towards her salary or would that be the wife's responsibility?

Fundamentally, the study aimed at an understanding of the everyday life that the students anticipated to live and a comparison between the male and female perspective as well as to explore the difference between the male and female students and what they perceive as male/female in relation to housing and household duties.

Selection of respondents and methodology

The study chose to focus on a selection of 16 students with an equal number of males and females. The number was deliberately made this small so that in-depth interviews could be conducted using the case study approach. The students selected for the study were from rural and urban poor backgrounds thus allowing a comparison between their background and their anticipated way of life after graduating. This would also enable the researcher to measure the effect that education has on gender and everyday life issues.

The study comprised three main components. The first part required each student to write an essay about their childhood experiences vis-a-vis the day-to-day running of the home. Emphasis was placed on the chores that were performed by males and females as well as the issue of decision making, that is, what sort of decisions were made by the father and mother respectively.

Interviews were then carried out with each respondent. These were informal and the researcher sought to probe the aspirations of each respondent vis-a-vis:
+ The housing career they were going to follow;
+ Housing design, size and location;
+ Anticipated way of life;
+ Sharing of responsibility in the home;
+ The role of domestic help;
+ The relationship between gender roles and culture.

These sessions were tape recorded and the researcher was there merely as a facilitator. Respondents were given leeway to discuss what they thought, even though, at times, some of the issues had no direct correlation with the study. The discussion guide formulated was used by the researcher to ensure that the key issues were all covered. Interviews were carried out at a convenient time set by the respondents and in their own rooms to ensure that the atmosphere was as relaxed as possible. The researcher endeavoured to make the discussion as natural as possible and allowed the respondent to reflect about the issue being discussed if the need arose. These interviews revealed the most useful information for the study.

Generally each interview lasted about an hour although some did go well beyond that. One could not help but see that the respondents were keen on discussing these issues as one later said, 'I wish we could set up some form of club where we can regularly discuss these things'. Clearly, an in-depth type of investigation was the most suitable for obtaining the type of information that this study required.

Focus group discussions were then held so as to get an holistic understanding of some of the issues that the respondents had raised. Here, the main issue discuss was the problem of culture and relatives especially as regards men carrying out those chores that are traditionally regarded as female duties, namely cooking, cleaning and baby-sitting. Here the respondents raised the problems that could arise and also came up with suggestions on overcoming or handling these problems.

Background of respondents

As stated earlier, all 16 respondents came from rural or poor urban backgrounds. They told of how the family would have to share the two bedrooms available in the case of those from the urban areas, whilst those from the rural areas would have had to share the room with their siblings of the same sex. Three of the respondents from the urban areas said they at times had to give up this room to sleep in the lounge or kitchen when relatives visited. The average size of houses these respondents lived in was a four-roomed house although some had lived in the three-roomed houses typical of places like Makhokhoba (a low income residential area) in Bulawayo. A typical homestead in the rural area was made up of at most six huts three of which were used as bedrooms, one for the parents and the others for the boys and girls respectively.

When it comes to the household duties performed by these respondents as they were growing up, two patterns emerged. Three of the respondents, one female and two males, came from homes where there was no demarcation of duties for the children. The males had to do the duties that otherwise would have been done by females either because there were no girls in the family to do them or the sister/s were too young. Similarly, the female respondent had no brother and came from a single parent background where the mother, her sister and herself did all that had to be done around the house. The rest came from backgrounds where duties were clearly demarcated with the boys and the father doing only those that are traditionally seen as male. In all the cases, the father had absolute control in the home and took care of all the financial needs, the mother had very little power, if any at all. One male respondent stated: 'My father was really in control – all the assets in the house were in his name. My mother's only assets were her sewing machine and the kitchen utensils.'

Housing career

Given such a background, the second part of the study sought to find out the housing career these respondents were going to follow and the type of house they envisaged owning. The respondents envisaged following a particular pattern: they would start out renting or lodging and then later buy their own houses. Only two said they would start off living at home and then move out after about six months when they would have earned enough money to afford paying rent. One male arts student was definite that he would 'start out in the rural areas since I am most likely to be teaching there. I think I will move to town after accumulating enough money to cope with the urban environment.'

A preference for low density areas

There was little variation between male and female respondents, although the males seemed to want more elaborate houses both in terms of design and size. Invariably the majority aspired to own houses in the low density high income residential areas. This they believed was what graduates ought to do. Not only was living in the low density areas a sign of education, but also a status symbol – as one respondent stated: 'I would like to live in the low density suburbs, I think I owe it to myself especially after working so hard and, besides, it has to do with status as well because if you are a doctor, you tend to think you should live well.' Other factors were also highlighted, for example: 'In the low density suburbs the stands are bigger and are well serviced.'

A few respondents, however, had a different view. One male respondent did not want to live in a low density suburb because he found these areas to be 'rather too quiet'; he would much rather settle in the medium density areas. Another male wanted a house in 'a small town because it is more peaceful and you can get more land for a cheaper price than you would in Harare'. Perhaps the most striking response came from a respondent who wanted a house in the high density areas for two reasons. Firstly, he felt 'there are lots of people to interact with,' and 'it would be a way of generating income, I have seen people with an eight-roomed house using only three of those and letting out the rest. At the end of the day they don't pay a cent for rates and the maintenance of the house; the house pays for itself as it were'.

Lodging as a temporary measure

All the respondents realized, however, that owning a house would be a long-term achievement. The researcher therefore wanted to know where they would start out living and with whom. They were asked to say whether they would start out lodging, living at home or renting. Of interest also was from whom they would rent or lodge, would it be a relative, landlord or an estate agent.

Here, again, there was consensus that relatives were definitely out of the question, although one respondent was of the view that it could actually be advantageous to lodge with a relative 'so that, if for some reason I fail to raise the rent, we can negotiate'. Various reasons were given: 'relatives are unpredictable', 'they tend to want to control you', 'relatives are a problem, they become jealous when they see you prospering'. In the final analysis the respondents felt that 'when considering lodging, a relative is out of the question because naturally there would be some complications which could end up souring the relationship so it would be better neither to lodge nor rent from a relative.'

Estate agents were ultimately the best people to approach for those who saw renting as the most desirable thing for them. However, the long waiting lists that have now become synonymous with estate agents would ultimately lead to one resorting to renting from private landlords.

Evidently, the culture of living with relatives, especially in the urban areas, is dying amongst these respondents. Traditionally, young persons with nowhere to live would stay with their family or relatives until such a time as they were able to buy their own house. Ironically, some of the respondents aspired to own big houses so that they could accommodate their relatives whenever the need arose.

Becoming a house owner

Owning a house was seen as a status symbol. The house that one has conveys a lot of messages to the on-looker as well as to the owner. If one has a grand house, it could be a sign of wealth and a gratification to the owner that, 'yes' he has made it in life. The majority of respondents wanted to design their own houses so as to have one that was tailor-made to one's needs, again, this would give them something to talk about thus conveying more messages about their social standing. There was an expressed desire to have adequate room to accommodate relatives and friends when they visit. One respondent said: 'I want a big house so that when my friends come to visit they can still be comfortably accommodated without having to make the children sleep in the lounge.'

Although these respondents came from rural or poor urban backgrounds, whether they aspired to houses either in the low density or high density areas, they all wished for big houses. What this means is that the education they have acquired will now enable them to live in those areas, as some said, where they now belong. Education has been their key to upward class mobility and they will not be out of place in these areas because it is mainly the rich and/or educated who reside there. It therefore follows that their families will now be in a position to stay in these areas when they visit. Then their parents can truly say, as Zimbabwean parents do: 'It was well worth educating my son/daughter.'

In traditional Zimbabwean culture, women normally expected to marry into a house rather than buy one. The female respondents here interviewed, however, all aspired to own their own house even if this meant buying jointly with a husband.

The second main part of the study concerned itself with the kind of life that these respondents aspired to lead. Again, a discussion guide was formulated and the main issues discussed were:
✦ The character of the person they wished to marry;
✦ What his or her family was like;
✦ Their educational background and social status;
✦ What the husband's/wife's responsibility was regarding the purchasing of property, provision of shelter and the raising of children;

- Whether the husband would be in a position to assume some of the duties that are traditionally done by women such as cooking, laundry and baby-sitting if the wife was studying or working late and whether this help would be solicited or assumed by the wife;
- Would the man do this even in the presence of relatives, if so, what would the comments of the relatives would be and how would they respond to them;
- What the term 'head of household' means and who they felt should be the head of the house in a marriage relationship.

Visions of marriage

The female respondents looked to marrying an understanding, loving and caring person. One who had the same level of both education and income, if not higher. None was prepared to settle for anyone who earned less and had less education. Typical reasons given for this were: 'In our culture, the man has to earn more. Relatives talk a lot ... you couldn't suggest anything without them thinking you were trying to be bossy because you earn more. He has to be a graduate and have a reasonable job so that we don't quarrel in the end when I earn more than him'. They also wanted to safeguard against the man ending up feeling inferior because he is less educated. As far as background goes, a husband from a similar background was most desirable because they would understand each other. One respondent added: 'If I get someone from a higher background it would be an added advantage financially.' A prominent person, on the other hand, did not appeal to them because they feared he would live for the public and ultimately 'his attention would be taken away by other people and there would be little time left for me'.

Unlike their female counterparts, the male respondents described the type of person they wanted to marry more in terms of her role rather than her individuality. The general picture painted was that of a woman with 'acceptable morals, who can compromise and would be willing to accept me as I am'. A 'good, humble, down-to-earth woman'. Only three of the respondents were looking to marrying a degreed wife, the rest wanted an 'educated' woman, that is, one who had a full 'O' level certificate at least. One of the males wanted 'someone who is learned enough to be productive, who can be employed. I don't want to attach marriage to material things so I wouldn't mind even a non-graduate, it makes no difference, it all depends on her personality.'

All wished to marry someone from a similar background who would feel neither superior nor inferior to the husband, but would be able to 'understand my problems and be able to relate to my family'. Another respondent had this to say, 'I would prefer someone from a similar background because I think it would be embarrassing for us to visit her parents who have everything and when she visits my home she finds there are just three huts and nothing more. That would be very embarrassing for me.' Only two medical students were willing to marry a prominent person because they felt this would further enhance their status as medical doctors: 'She will not have a superiority complex because I am a doctor.'

Financial responsibilities

When it came to the financial responsibilities in the home, there were mixed views both among the male and female respondents. Whilst the females wanted to buy the house together and share the expenses of running the home, there was this underlying expectation that the husband should contribute more. There were, however, two who felt strongly that everything should be done fifty-fifty: 'I would really like to share in the buying of the house so that I am secure even when we later run into problems, he won't be able to chase me away because it would be his house not ours'. Others felt it would be best to divide the responsibilities: 'I wouldn't mind if the husband bought all the furniture, the house and pays the mortgage for it and I take care of the clothing, school fees and the daily expenses.' One respondent was of a totally different opinion: 'The husband should provide the money to run the home, be it for buying the food, maintaining the house, everything. I really wouldn't mind marrying someone who has a house already, I would simply move in'.

Only three males expected an equal contribution from their wives – one of them stated: 'If it is going to be 'our' home it has to be us doing everything even when buying a stove I should have a say since I will also be cooking. It will have to be a joint thing.' The rest believed that a wife could contribute but they were quite happy to shoulder the bulk of the responsibility. Even if she did contribute, there were certain things that her money should take care of: 'The wife should be in-charge of the food and the kitchen, otherwise the buying of property should be done by the man.'

Another male respondent was of the belief that the man should give the wife the money then she goes and chooses the property for the house. One female respondent was also in agreement with the idea of the woman being solely responsible for the kitchen: 'I would prefer us to share in the responsibilities of buying a house and maybe other furniture save that of the kitchen. That I would prefer to do on my own because it will be 'my' kitchen and every woman should be proud of her kitchen so I would want to furnish it myself.' Some did acknowledge, however, that they had not given it much thought, besides, it really was an issue that they believed had no clear-cut method of effectively handling. One male respondent stated: 'Finance is a bit of a complicated issue and I don't know how I will manage. I have a brother who is married and each has a separate account but they have what they call a 'kitchen' account – each one deposits a certain amount and they use that to buy groceries, pay the bills and other household expenses, but I think I would prefer a joint account but maybe my wife might not want that.'

Raising the children

Two differing opinions were given as regards the raising of children: there were those who thought 'the raising of children should be a mother's responsibility because she is closer to them than the father. His is an indirect responsibility through the financial contribution he would make but otherwise the mother is responsible for them'. Yet another thought 'the father should support her (the mother), and look after them when she is away.'

One male strongly believed that the duty of raising children lay with the mother: 'My character was moulded by my mother, I feared my father and I think this should be the case with my children.' Yet another agreed that this was largely a mother's responsibility: 'The father should take care of their financial needs and assist with disciplining them.'

It was interesting to note that the large majority of the males wanted to be involved in the raising of their children. As one said, 'Children need both parents, I won't let my wife do that on her own.'

They did not want the father to come in only when discipline was needed, as was the case when they were growing up. One of the female respondents was of the opinion that indeed father should be actively involved in the raising of children: 'In the first place, it's both who've made that baby so why should only one parent be responsible for raising it?'

Household chores

Generally, women would not mind their husbands doing some of the household chores but they were unlikely to allow this to happen especially in the presence of relatives, both the husband's and their own, because the relatives would not approve: 'They might go around saying I want to be the head of the home ... they could even stop coming to our house.' Another said: 'I wouldn't allow my husband to do that, I don't think the relatives would be pleased either. Women are expected to do these duties so it wouldn't be good if my husband is then seen doing them.' One female said she would love her husband to help but only if he was willing to ... I wouldn't demand it, I would want him to be happy and enjoy doing it so, if he is not, I wouldn't expect him to.' She was not worried about the comments that outsiders would make: 'I would tell them to leave us alone. Gone are the times when the extended family's views are considered when running a home.'

All but one male were willing to help their wives albeit in private. The exception said he would only help in certain situations: 'Well, here it depends. Say she finishes work at eight o'clock and I finish at four-thirty; in such a situation I would, but not when she is physically in the home, then I wouldn't, I am rather traditional.' Those who had been socialized into doing everything did not envisage running into problems even with relatives: 'I have never considered these as women's jobs because when I was growing up I cooked and did the laundry so I will continue even in marriage.' One acknowledged that he would not help in the presence of relatives for fear of the comments that they would make and the implications these would have, especially for the wife: 'They would probably think it is a daily phenomenon, so when they are there I wouldn't do it, they might even suspect I have been given some love portion.' Not all relatives were regarded as problematic: 'It depends on who the relative is; if it is someone who shares my outlook, that's alright, but if it is a sekuru (uncle/grandfather) from the rural areas it would be difficult because those are the hardliners. It could end up causing problems.'

The males were more willing to tell their relatives off or 'enlighten' them, but the females showed a genuine fear of the damage that relatives could cause.

Domestic help

The need for domestic help was another issue of contention even amongst respondents of the same sex. One female felt that it was not desirable to have a domestic helper: 'I feel we should be able to manage. I wouldn't really like to have a domestic helper unless it would just be for baby-sitting whilst I am at work.' A second female agreed that if it is just the husband and wife, there really would be no need for a domestic helper: 'We would only get one when we have children around, I don't think it would be necessary if there is just the two of us because I am sure we will manage.' One male did not want a domestic helper either: 'I would prefer things to be done by my wife.' The rest of the males generally thought it would be necessary to have a domestic helper although one added: 'I believe a domestic helper should just be a helper and not end up taking full responsibility of the house ... she would only perform certain duties just to relieve my wife.'

There were definite responses about the role of this domestic help. Emphasis was placed by females on the fact that her duties would be limited to looking after the children, cooking for them, cleaning and doing their laundry. Generally they preferred to cook, do the laundry for their husband and clean their bedroom, the main reason being' one of the duties of a wife is to look after her husband so I can't hire someone to look after my husband.'

Whilst the females did not want the helper to do anything for the husband, some males would rather the helper did not raise the children. Here a relative was seen as a better alternative: 'In the case of children I would rather look for a relative to look after them because I would not like to leave my children with a stranger whose background I am not familiar with – she could teach my children things I do not approve of. Another male gave this response, 'Theoretically I would prefer a wife whose job allows her to look after the family. I wouldn't want my children to spend most of their time with a domestic helper because they would imitate the characteristics of that person.' The females felt the hiring and dismissing of domestic helpers should be the wife's responsibility as she is the one likely to be able to tell whether or not the domestic was performing her duties as is expected. As they saw it, men would not really know what to look for.

Generally, male respondents were willing to assist in paying the helper although one said this: 'Since she will be helping my wife she should be responsible for that unless she can't manage.' One male would have liked to have a say about the domestic helper but he felt 'ladies seem to think that they are better at this than men so if my wife thinks that way too, I would leave her to do it on her own.' Indeed, one female respondent said this is the wife's territory 'because I feel women know more about domestic help than men do.' Another did not want her husband to be involved either although for a different reason: 'I wouldn't want him to be involved with issues concerning the domestic helper, you know how these men are!,' implying that the man could end up having a relationship with the domestic helper. It is interesting to note that all the respondents referred to the domestic helper as a she, none seemed to think there was any likelihood of the helper being male as is the case in some households.

Head of the household

Interesting responses were given about the head of household. All the females agreed that it referred to the person who had ultimate say about the goings-on of the particular household. One respondent stated the term is 'generally associated with the man who has the final say when it comes to major decisions but I think it now has a new meaning since decisions are now being made jointly'. There were those who felt that in a marriage relationship, both parties have equal say, whereas some varied slightly in that the wife should be there as an assistant not an equal. There was a strong feeling amongst three of these who felt 'the husband should be the head because that is how it is in our culture. My mother is very religious and she has brought me up to believe that the husband should be the head of the house and I feel I should respect him and let him be the head, he is the one who should have the upper hand. Another female agreed that the man should have the upper hand because 'it has always been like that, can we change it? Of course, we can share duties but he will still remain the head even the bible says that.'

Varied definitions were given by the male respondents for the head of the house or rather who it should be. One respondent defined it thus: 'According to the way I was brought up, the term refers to the man, but, in my ideal world, it's the individual with the stronger character. Perhaps the ladies don't want this; they think a man should be always be dominant even in marriage.' Another chose to look at it this way: 'The head of the house is the one who runs the house, personally, I don't want to be the head, my wife and I should be joint heads.' Yet another felt 'I would be the head in theory because I know what happens in these homes, the wife is the actual decision maker but she will make sure it appears as though the husband is the one who has made those decisions. Women dominate domestic affairs and men are used just to rubber-stamp.' The rest viewed themselves as 'traditionalists' and therefore believed a man should be the head: 'There can never be two heads in a home, the husband should have the upper hand.' One male, however, suggested that there was room for the separation of power: 'I can't be the head of everything, there are some things where the wife is the head, for example, in domestic work she has all the authority but there are some cases where the husband has ultimate authority.'

Looking after a husband

Two topical issues among professionals in Zimbabwe today arose from the discussions relating to the need as well as the role of domestic help. Respondents were wary of employing domestic help because of this belief that, in most cases, the helper ends up being the one who is more knowledgable about the goings-on of the home than the wife. There is this belief amongst some members of the society especially the older generation, that indeed this is the casein most modern homes today. What seems most deplorable to them is the very fact that, in some cases, wives hire these helpers to even 'look after their husbands' something which is next to taboo in traditional Zimbabwean culture. What the study reveals is that women do not do this intentionally. As the female respondents here stated that they would like to do the 'looking after of the husband' themselves, so, if in the end domestic helpers seem to take over, it is probably because of circumstances that the wife cannot help.

These respondents seemed to believe that, in a marriage relationship, the wife's primary responsibility is that of 'looking after the husband', the males expected it and the females thought it their duty. No mention was made even amongst the progressive respondents of men giving that attention back to their wives nor did the females seem to expect it save for the occasional times when the husband would assist with the various chores. The males saw themselves as the point of reference, they were willing to cook because they grew up doing it or enjoyed it, not because they wanted to relieve or 'treat' the wife. The females on the other hand were willing to forego their personal needs so as to maintain a healthy relationship. They would rather tire themselves out coping with professional and domestic work than give relatives reason to criticize them. It would appear as though the wife is there to please the husband and relatives without any claim to equal conjugal happiness.

There was also a persistent belief that a woman's domain in the home is the kitchen, this is where she has ultimate power: 'Every woman should be proud of "her" kitchen.'

The second issue was that of the domestic helper raising or looking after the children for most of the day. This study found that most males who did not look upon this favourably. Many believed that children's characters are moulded in the formative years by their environment and the people in that environment. This explains why the respondents disliked their children spending more time with the domestic helper than the parents.

Some young people in Zimbabwe today say that when they get to having children, the wife will take some time off work to raise the children until they reach nursery school going age. It was interesting to note that none of the respondents mentioned this as an alternative. Traditionally, children would be taken to the grandmother but, again, this was not mentioned although some respondents did say that they would rather a relative look after the children.

Conclusion

Three groups of people emerged from this study and I believe that they can be best classified under three headings: the traditionalists, the ambivalent ones and the progressive ones.

The traditionalists

This group comprises those who believe they are thus. These are the respondents in the study who continually referred to culture or tradition as their point of reference. They feel that they cannot depart from it neither do they have the capacity to change the way things are especially as regards issues such as the financial responsibilities in the home, the raising of children, the sharing and performing of household chores and the whole concept of power in a marriage relationship. There were, however, some inconsistencies in the responses given by these 'traditionalists' especially the females who aspired to buy houses: none of them mentioned the hindrance that could be caused by tradition but when it comes to issues like chores and the financial ability of their partners, then tradition is viewed as something one cannot depart from.

The ambivalent ones

Perhaps the majority of the respondents fall into this category. This is the group who really do not know where they stand. In their responses one could not see a consistent pattern of ideas or beliefs. They believed, for example, that everything in the home should be done jointly but when it came to the head of the house, they would then say it is the man who should be the head. To illustrate this I will quote one male who was willing to assist his wife even in the presence of relatives and had this to say: 'The relatives would be opposed to that but anyway it's a changing world ... I would try to explain that things are not as rigid as they used to be, it is all a question of mutual understanding.' When asked who he thought should be the head of the house he gave this answer: 'The husband, of course! Naturally the man should have the upper hand ... the wife should respect him ... actually, religiously, the man is the head.'

One could not help but conclude that these respondents do not have a clear understanding of what they really want or what they believe in. For instance, women wanted to have an equal share in buying property, marry someone who probably was a fellow student but when it comes to making decisions, they suddenly feel that this person who might even be less intelligent is by virtue of his being male, the one with the divine right to make decisions.

Perhaps the confusion here demonstrated is to a large degree true of the majority of young people in Zimbabwe. Yes, they want to be seen to be progressive and do that which educated people are expected to do such as buy or build a big house in the low density suburbs, have a presentable wife or husband who will not be a misfit in one's social circles and, to cap it all, have exemplary well-mannered and disciplined children. Here background or culture has little, if any, influence at all. The education that they have received has become their point of reference, as most of them said in the first part of the study, 'As an educated person I should have a big house or live in the low density areas'. None of them wanted to return to the rural areas or the high density areas they grew up in to live there. It is assumed that this is not what society now expects them to do. Even those who traditionally stood to inherit or were supposed to take charge of the homestead at the death of their parents, were not willing to go back to that life. To them that has become history, it is time for them to move on in life and yet when it comes to the lifestyle they will lead in these big houses, things are suddenly viewed differently.

Obviously this disparity was not apparent to them at all during the interviews and the group discussions. It is more subtle than that and yet it is, I believe a crucial parameter in assessing just how gender sensitive these respondents really are. Perhaps the majority Zimbabweans are caught in a similar dilemma. Besides, issues like buying a house are simple and clear cut whereas lifestyle issues are more complex. As one respondent said, 'I feel I shouldn't jump into this 'western' culture, there are some aspects of it which I feel I understand and at the same time there are some which I don't.'

Perhaps it is in cases where they don't fully understand these 'new' trends that the students would then want to revert back to that with which they are familiar than end up making 'mistakes'. Gender issues are still a fairly new phenomenon which many are only beginning to or have not yet fully understood. The responses here given are witness to this.

The progressive ones

There were, however, three male respondents who were sure that they wanted to lead lives where the man and the wife were equal in all aspects of the relationship. One of them said as far as he saw things 'marriage is an equal partnership, our society assumes that men always have the stronger character but this is not so, I think the one with the stronger character should be the head.' Whilst another viewed the issue of power relations thus: 'My wife and I should be joint heads.' There were two female respondents who could maybe also be classified as progressive although they had problems with the issue of the husband helping in the home.

Although I have classified the respondents in these three categories, it must be pointed out that there is really a continuum from the traditionalists to the progressive. In practise it would be virtually impossible to make such a clear distinction between the various groups, besides, as evidenced by the majority of the responses, people's attitudes and beliefs are constantly being modified as they reach a better understanding or with improved education and socio-economic status. Therefore, what some of these respondents expressed may not necessarily be what they will do when they eventually settle down, other factors may have influenced them to change their ideas and beliefs or may have influenced new changes in the prevailing cultural practices seeing as culture itself is forever changing.

Undoubtedly the issues here raised are by no means exhaustive. It is possible that the reader would be able to identify other patterns that the researcher overlooked. Moreover, much more research is needed into this topic and as the attitudes change and more understanding is reached, different patterns and results will emerge some of which will hopefully clarify some of the ambiguities highlighted in this study.

Chapter Eleven

Women's Access to Trading Space at Growth Points in Zimbabwe: A Case Study of Mataga

Agnes Zhou

Introduction

Throughout the third world, women are the major actors in primary production and basic commodity exchange especially in areas where agriculture and small scale enterprises form the base of the local economy. At agricultural resource based settlements, women are significant producers of crops for domestic consumption and local exchange. Apart from their contributions in agriculture, women's labour also sustains many family enterprises. Within most third world countries, up to 80% of buying and selling activities of basic commodities, especially in the informal sector, are done by women (Boserup, 1970). In Zimbabwe, many women work in small scale enterprises and in the informal sector. According to Jaravaza (1992), Zimbabwean women represent about two thirds of the informal sector and comprise 67% of Micro-small Scale Enterprises (MSE). In smaller settlements – 'growth points' or 'district service centres' (designated by the government according to population and economic criteria) –

women dominated activities of primary production/exchange and the provision of basic commodities are the first notable economic activities. However, despite their major role in production and exchange, women are under-represented in the ownership of productive resources, in particular land.

Mataga growth point is situated in the south east of Zimbabwe, in a district called Mberengwa. It has a resident population of about 2 000 and a hinterland population of seven thousand (CSO, 1992). The growth point lies in the midst of a densely populated rural area and was designated a district service centre because it was thought to have the potential to service the adjoining remote areas. It is still not developed enough to be called a town, but it is rapidly becoming a 'depot centre' due to the preponderance of commercial ventures.

Recently the Zimbabwean government made it possible for businesses at such growth points to acquire leasehold pending the survey and pegging of stands for full title. This development presents real opportunities for equitable allocation of land for trading activities because of availability of space and the fact that land is allocated to traders and producers at a concessionary rate subsidized by the government. The regulations for allocation of land at growth points are not discriminatory in nature, however, the register of leasehold at Mataga indicates that despite the high number of women participating in trading, fewer women are allocated trading space than men. This gender dichotomy in ownership of economic space at Mataga growth point raises questions such as:

i) What are the major constraints facing women entrepreneurs at Mataga growth point, and do these constraints account for their under-representation in the ownership of trading space?
ii) How can women be enabled to access trading space at growth points in Zimbabwe?

Using Mataga's case, this paper explores the implementation of space allocation policies at growth points to identify factors that inhibit women's access to trading space. Profiles of women traders at Mataga growth point are used to identify constraints in their operational environment.

An enabling framework

The conceptual framework of this study focuses on enabling women's economic initiatives. It emphasizes transfer of control and power over productive resources to women – a kind of empowerment (see Schlyter, Chapter Two). Defined from the developed world's perspective, the enabling framework makes a political statement by fusing the modernization idea of assistance and participation with the possibility of women's actual access to and control of resources (Zhou, 1993). With this approach, the level of productive engagement of Mataga women justifies their entry into the economic order. The concept also provides the basis for establishing a responsive and enabling environment for women either in the formal sector or in a stable informal sector. Creating production and exchange space for women can be seen as the enabling process for consolidating their economic activities at growth points.

Gender ideologies and the welfare concept

The concept of 'colonial welfarism' is important for understanding the observed gender contracts and gender ideologies in this study. Colonial welfarism saw women's position in the home as being paramount: a perspective in accordance with international norms of middle-class life. With the welfare approach, conjugal roles of husband and wife were brought to play on women's economic advancement hence the importance of family needs were emphasized over the individual needs of women. In policy implementation, the welfare of the principal wage earner (often seen as the male worker) was often played up thereby forcing women to chose their reproductive role over economic mobility. This legacy of the colonial state legislation still influences the system of things as seen in the attitudes of the administrators of space delivery at Mataga. It supports the system of patriarchy and men's protection of their privileges while compounding women's disadvantages within this gender contract. Communal land tenure laws of the colonial era which resulted from such gender ideologies were prejudiced against women. African women were made landless through legislation which emanated from the 'perceived' traditional gender power relations thereby alienating them from former sources of income. Gender contracts in the family relations referred to, were, firstly, rooted in the traditional place a man occupied and his power as a husband, secondly, the responsibility women felt for caring for the whole family and thirdly, cultural images of how women identified themselves as women (Schlyter, 1992). From these ideas, misconceived gender relations were enshrined in laws which still pose major barriers to women's advancement today. Although growth points should not follow such guidelines, decision makers and the women themselves are still influenced by them.

Gender issues in land allocation

Gender issues in land allocation hinge on equality of access between men and women. When access is defined in terms of actual process of getting the land, it becomes unclear to what extent women traders have access to trading space at growth points. In fact, if there is no conscious commitment to empower women, they may be denied economic opportunities by the patriarchal systems under which they live (Mies, 1989). Legal provisions for equal access to resources do not adequately situate women in mainstream economic development. They must be enabled and empowered to gain actual access to the space. As Batezat and Mwalo (1989) stated, the passing of legislation is a positive step for women but prevailing patriarchal attitudes and economic situation make enforcement weak. Although growth points still have much space for development, gender conflicts arise in the allocation of trading space because of entrenched attitudes within the system. The conflicts sometimes create situations where women are denied access to resources which have been legally provided for and they may not be equipped to fight this. Often there are no women in the decision making bodies of local authorities that distribute land in most areas hence women's interests are not represented. Consequently, women and men's initiatives are sometimes given differential weighting during planning due to traditional power positions that favour men. Also, the criteria for determination of project support and allocation of space could also lead to the relegation of those activities in which women are involved.

Qualitative research approach

Access to land has always been a difficult issue to discuss, more so with rural women. They view land-related discussions as political topics culminating in benefit for them or in recriminations. This was the case in the study of Mataga. In order to understand women's economic aspirations, constraints and frustrations it was necessary to use a combination of qualitative and quantitative research methods. A total of 58 women and 15 men were interviewed using structured questionnaires while 19 women attended three group discussions. Other interviews were conducted with Executive Officers of the local authority, consultants on project assistance to women and other organizations that assist women to set up their own business. The qualitative survey method of identifying processes and practice of resource allocation at Mataga was mostly adopted. Perceptions and testimonies of interviewees were paramount to the approach and questionnaires were merely used as confirmatory tools for group discussions and informal interviews. An extensive working session was held with two peer leaders during the pre-survey stage listing some of the discriminatory attitudes faced and other problems related to women's operations. Qualitative research methods proved to be more rewarding in this study as observed from the quality of information.

Background

Mataga growth point has two irrigation projects. The allocation of plots in the schemes is on the basis of households pooled from the surroundings of two small dams. Fresh produce is supplied by the scheme to the surrounding areas and most of the products are exchanged within the Mataga centre. Most of the exchange activities are by women, but in relation to total space at the growth point, women have only 26% of allocated space. Other activities of the growth point include hardware manufacturing and food processing and the trading/exchanging of manufactured goods and services to both the resident population and hinterland as well as to commuters who regularly pass through the area. Most of the trade is in consumer goods especially groceries and hardware but the building industry is developing too. Among these ventures are at least 10 women successfully trading in groceries, soft goods and hardware as general dealers. The only wholesale general dealer outfit is run exclusively by a woman.

The Department of Physical Planning developed a layout plan for plot subdivision and provision of title deeds at Mataga growth point. At the time of the study, the survey of the land was still in process and title deeds were not yet available for the transfer of plots to individuals. Most businesses were therefore operating under a 'lease with an option to buy' agreement with the state. From the local authority records, it was obvious that despite the non-discriminatory allocation policies at growth points and the laws of majority status to women on attaining the age of 18, women were still disadvantaged in allocation of trading space at Mataga. Very few women actually had leasehold or primary rights on commercial stands at Mataga, yet there were many women trading in and around the centre. The available records showed only 'accepted applications' (forms which had no recommendations were not accepted) and final allocation of space and could not indicate how many women had approached the council for stands. But interviews with the women confirmed that many more people had applied. From the record of land allocations, the trend of the imbalance in ownership of trading space shown in Table 1 below is similar to all other growth points in Zimbabwe. (The 1991 records examined at a central government department show that only about 29 percent of allocations at growth points were made to women.)

Table 1:
Allocation of trading space at Mataga growth point.
(Source: DPP Layout Plan/ MDC records, 1992)

Type of space	No. allocated to men	No. allocated to women	No. yet to be allocated
Commercial	58	12	40
Marketing/co-op. Agric.	86	23	0
Light industrial/service	60	0	27
Heavy industrial	5	0	100
Total (411 stands planned)	209	35	167

Access to trading space at Mataga

In order to obtain commercial or industrial space, applicants for stands were expected to apply in writing with an attached fee, to the council, after which they were issued with an application form. They had to obtain reference from the local councillor or headman after which the local authority recommended to central government where final approval of allocation is made. The local authority required building plans or architectural designs and proof of ability to develop in order to recommend the allocation of property in all cases. Applicants for trading space thus went through five stages involving the following steps:
+ The local traditional/political leadership;
+ Finance houses/banks (for proof of funds);
+ Private planning agencies (for architectural consultancy and plan drawing);
+ The local authority's finance and development committee;
+ The central government State Land Office.

The bureaucratic processes posed an obstacle for most women as they found themselves hard pressed to produce all the required documentation. They also had to go through many unsympathetic officials in the system. Most of the women did not understand this process and council had no systematic way of providing information to the women who may not always have access to their meetings and notice boards. These constraints resulted in the exclusion of many women from ownership of trading space as reflected by the profiles below.

Characteristics of the women traders

The 58 women traders interviewed at Mataga represented nearly all (94.1%) of the total number trading formally at the centre, excluding the agricultural sector. Three quarters of the women interviewed were under 45 years old while the remaining were 46 years and older but there were no women under the age of 25. Most of the women were previously engaged in other 'paid' employment or as assistants in family enterprises or had been housewives. Under a quarter (15%) of the women traders came to Mataga from other districts. Very few of the respondents had attained more than eleven years of schooling and even fewer had attempted 'Ordinary-level' examinations out of which none had the national minimum qualification needed to proceed with further education (i.e. five subject passes). The study showed that the low level of education among the women traders was a major deterrent to their business development and consolidation. Most of them were unable to follow through the paper work involved in property acquisition and development and the council did not have the capacity to give adequate guidance and support in this regard.

The case for economic space

Economic space is a prerequisite for business activity in small centres such as Mataga. As Todes and Walker (1991) commented, lack of access to land reduces the economic potential of women in Southern Africa. It is constraining for businesses at this level to operate without security of tenure. This is illustrated in the following cases which depict the different scenarios of constraint in obtaining space and some strategies used by the women traders. From group discussions, these profiles were developed to illustrate the case for trading space at growth points. The selection process for the profiles was based on individual contacts and introductions during group sessions.

Profile 1: The unsuccessful applicant for a business stand
The researcher engaged in a trial exercise to determine what actually transpires when an application for land is made from the growth point level, in this case – by a woman.

In agreement with a local woman who wanted to start a business, a project proposal was made and application filed for a commercial stand at Mataga. The council official who was to issue the forms did not readily accept the application because the woman applicant seemingly 'did not know what she wanted'. Due to the official's bias against women applying for such properties, he refused to discuss the application and insisted that the woman should bring a letter from the 'rightful owner of the proposal' who he expected to be a man. After three trips explaining the proposal to different council employees, the forms were finally obtained and filled out and the woman was required to obtain the stamp of approval of the local chief.

The local chief declined to do this requesting the applicant to file through her husband. Finally, the councillor was approached to recommend this applicant but again for unknown reasons this was not done. The case finally reached the attention of a central government staff who advised that the procedure followed and requests being made by local leaders were not right and advised that direct application be made to head office. It was, however, not possible to bypass the local council office and the applicant (a widow) then asked her son to make the application using the same project. The application was quickly accepted from her son despite the fact that he did not live in the area and had no prior business interest there. It was understood that the application went through because this woman's son had access to some council officials and was able to bypass the local leadership.

Profile 2: A successful business woman

Woman number two, is forty-two years old, single with three adult children one of whom worked with her. She owns the only wholesale general dealer venture at the growth point. Her enterprise provides inputs for most grocery, clothing and hardware businesses within the centre and hinterland. She had about twelve years of schooling. She also attended other non-certificate courses and seminars on business development which she admitted helped her in decision making and business improvement. Although she started her business when she was in a relationship with a man (the father of her children) she never really got married to him but continued to run her business single-handedly. Her first activity was moulding bricks for sale and she operated from her family home as she recalled: 'People thought I was strange when I first started. I had not even $2 to start my business so I decided to use the earth which will cost me nothing ... I started with things that don't cost money. I used to go down to the river to mould bricks for sale. My friends and some men used to laugh at me saying I had been rejected by men. They made fun of me and asked me to look for better work at home ... work for women. But it was the only thing I thought of. I noticed many businessmen were building and they needed bricks, so I sold a lot quickly.'

With the money she raised selling bricks and the help of her 'live-in friend', she soon managed to buy a shop at a near by village shopping centre. She retailed groceries, vegetables and any odd items of hardware she could source. As the growth point was being established, she joined the first group of formal ventures to open up at Mataga, where she established her general dealer store. She started expanding her inputs in the shop and soon was able to present a project proposal to financiers to develop a wholesale company which would also package indigenous vegetables and grain as well as retail hardware. She secured some primary capital for expansion and built up a sizeable warehouse floor to accommodate her stock. Her venture was a huge success and she was able to pay back her loan regularly. From own savings she was able to procure a residential property at the growth point and built a home for herself. She also developed a retail shop at a small local business centre, which her daughter administers. She has now made a proposal to the local council for larger factory space to establish a milling company. Having worked in the area for long she is more confident of picking up market trends and succeeding in the activities contained in her proposal.

This woman is an example of the successful woman trader at Mataga. She managed to move through the various stages of entrepreneurship and has now reached a level of accumulating enough capital to embark on further enterprises. Her assets were worth at least Z$250 000 but she required about 1 million dollars to complete the next phase of her expansion. This was revealed in her financial report and her project proposal to a commercial bank. The temptation to regard this as an exceptional case is great, but as her beginnings and current operations confirm, with the existing laws and given the relevant material support, women entrepreneurs are capable of consolidating their own initiatives if the operational environment is responsive.

Profile 3: The displaced vegetable trader

The woman in this profile is middle-aged and has very little education (seven years only). She is married with five children of school going age. Her husband is a migrant worker but spends the rainy seasons at home where he helps in the cultivation of food crops for subsistence. Together with 44 other women she started trading at Mataga from 1984 making her one of the earliest traders at the centre. Noticing the problems with mobile trading, they decided to squat along the commuter routes where they could hope to attract more customers. She supplied vegetables and fresh produce to the eating houses, bus operators, commuters, and the residents of Mataga. These inputs were usually obtained from the irrigation schemes near Mataga or far away eastern agricultural estates such as Chiredzi and Triangle. Her average 'take-home' income rate was Z$30 a day in a good season and was better when she could source other produce apart from vegetables. She recounts that when the reorganization of trading space started in Mataga, the women at the people's market were all displaced. The new layout indicated areas for agricultural co-operative marketing, but very little of the space was made available for them. Under the Public Sector Investment Programme, the council was allocated funds to construct a better market shelter which only accommodated less than 20 of the 45 market women. The council's response to this inadequacy of space was to terminate the activities of some women. At first they were asked to fill in forms for the allocation of stalls but after allocations, this woman was among those who were sent away. She recalls: 'We heard from others that we were to fill in forms for new places at the built-up market. Fours months later, a council official came around unannounced and gave out forms to only the women present. We had no prior information of this and all those who were absent did not get forms. When we tried to collect forms we were told they were finished and that we cannot operate from there again or from any other place otherwise we risk arrest. From that day we have been trying to get our own place to trade since it is our means of livelihood. Personally, I am lucky to be able to swop days trading at the same stall with my friend.'

She further explained that the council asked them to form co-operatives in order to get help to go into other activities. This was not acceptable to many of them and only four of the women joined some cooking co-operatives at the centre. Some of the women at the market were unable to meet the monthly rental cost for the stalls and opted to swop with friends. She cited the problems that they encountered at the market place as: lack of information about access to market stalls, lack of adequate storage to preserve their goods, high rental charges for the stalls, poor starting capital and consequent stagnation of trade and little family support.

Profile 4: The evicted butcher

Woman number four is 25 years old. She is married with three children of pre-school age and she has eleven years of schooling. On leaving school she joined the Ministry of Education as a temporary teacher in one of the local primary schools, a position she held until the massive retrenchment of temporary teachers in 1989. Her husband, a former council employee, is now unemployed. After her retrenchment, she started a supermarket which was to be completed with the help of her husband (at that time a council employee). Her husband leased the stand in his name and assured her that since he was employed by the council she could trade there on her own. Stands could be occupied on leasehold with the government, pending transfer to private owners, but leases can be bought over or transferred to other individuals who would then transfer the property to their names. To this woman's surprise the husband 'sold' the property without her knowledge and she was stranded. She then appealed to another council officer who had a building with butchery facilities. She was lucky to get this and thereafter changed her line of business to conform to the available space. She started a butchery within the rented premises and continued until the owner of the property was dismissed from council. Her landlord then decided to sell off this property and move away from Mataga, presumably in search of other work. He refused to negotiate the sale of the shop with her and she suspects that her husband's reluctance to assist her also influenced the landlord's refusal to transfer the shop to her.

During the first interviews and data collection exercise for this study, she was a butcher earning an average of Z$300 a day. But by the time of the final visit to Mataga two months later, she had been forced to close down her butchery and sell off all stock. In desperation she appealed to another shop owner to rent a part of an existing shop where she could open another line of trade, this time in soft goods and groceries. Her first venture lasted only two years, the second one three months and the third may not even last any longer than the first, judging from the conditions of rent. According to her estimates about one third of her meat stock was lost because the landlord did not even give her much notice of his intentions to evict her. It was also impossible for her to take any lawful action since she did not really have a contract with him. This constant movement made it difficult for her to consolidate her business and she did not receive any support to acquire her own place. She blamed her trading problems and inadequate income on lack of security of space.

Analysis of profiles

Production or trading activities could be seriously hampered by continuous movement of location as in profile 4, the evicted butcher. Even for seasonal enterprises such as the displaced vegetable trader (profile 3), continuous mobility was disruptive to their trade because they were unable to cultivate regular customers. In profile 3, all displaced women suffered loss of income and, though some of them managed to formulate strategies to acquire space for trading by sharing with their friends, the situation was constrained. Even this temporary solution was not possible for all women in similar positions and could lead to displacement creating more poverty for them. Looking at the problems encountered by traders who lacked medium to long term security of space in such small settlements, it is obvious that having their own property would contribute to their consolidation.

Attitudes of local authority staff

In the case of the unsuccessful applicant (profile 1), it was found that personal prejudices and stereotypical assessments could overshadow judgement on viable proposals. This was evident from the type of projects that received approval and allocations of space at Mataga. At least one third (30%) of the allocated stands were owned by absentee landlords who were gainfully employed elsewhere. Discussions held with council officials showed the gender bias of both councillors and council staff. Most of the officials did not see the need to study or improve economic initiatives of women at the centre. They commented that earning a better living would put ideas in the heads of the 'rural' women and make them revolt against their husbands. They did not acknowledge that already most of the shops at the centre, even those owned by men, were run by women. The local authority also required applicants to show proof of ability to develop such as readily available funds. Since most of the women did not own bank accounts, requiring proof of funds therefore created another level of problem because this could only be obtained from a bank or financial institution. The council used discretion to determine who showed adequate proof of ability to develop.

At committee meetings councillors were required to recommend or reject applications for property. They assessed applications from their constituencies without set criteria. According to a councillor, this posed problems for applicants who were not well known to their council representatives, particularly women. Councillors' recommendations of applicants were based on discretion. The process included a system of referees or guarantors and was open to abuse. Most senior people who could provide such guarantees refused to assist women. One of the women indicated that her attempts to get a guarantor led to accusations of infidelity to her husband while another woman was denied space on the grounds that she was single and thus unstable. The processes that entrepreneurs were expected to go through did not consider such gender specific problems which women experience. Hence, despite the law that made it possible for the women to obtain space for economic activities, the actual process covertly discriminated against them.

A question of bias

During the group meetings it was confirmed that in the application process women had to contend with attitudes of the headmen/councillors. Due to the traditional low esteem in which women's activities are held, individuals within responsible institutions were not supportive of the women. Some women were denied the chance to acquire a piece of property or even apply because the local leadership concluded that women were not capable of conducting viable business. Judgement of women's ability was mostly based on intuition of the decision maker and was not questioned. Records or history of previous trading of the applicants were not considered. For agricultural marketing and co-operatives, the displaced vegetable trader (profile 3), allocation of space also indicated bias. All respondents emphasized the displacement of former traders due to the size of the people's market. The planning process did not consider the women's need for trading space in allocating space therefore the inadequacy of marketing space excluded some women from their chosen trades. Responses of the women pointed to poor handling of the applications and allocation process by the council and the discrimination against the market because it was seen as women's trading activity. This is similar to local authority actions of banning vending and continuously arresting petty traders in all the cities of Zimbabwe. The bias was evident in most discussions as a local leader commented: 'Our women are rural, they are used to being subordinates and they want their men to dominate them. A woman cannot do tough business ... like the hardware business.'

Another council official reinforced the seeming collective prejudice against women when he said: 'Why worry about women when there are so many men out of jobs ... All that the women need to do is behave themselves and get married. They will be looked after by their husbands.'

The study also noted that the status of council officials/councillors and their relationships with the traders was central to the latter's access to trading space. This was illustrated in the unsuccessful applicant's case (profile 1), where the son was able to bypass some levels in the system. Because of the weaknesses in the system, there was evidence of nepotism in the recommendation and approval of applications. All of the 12 women found in formal trading managed to obtain space allocations due to affiliations or relationships with council employees and councillors, past or present.

Perspectives from the men

Male respondents concentrated mainly on how they view women in business. Most men were not happy with the idea of a woman doing large scale trading hence most of them referred to the successful business woman (profile 2) in derogatory terms. They could not view women in other ways except as wives and mothers and did not like the idea of this woman challenging existing gender contracts. This bias dominated the discussions and only in the case of differences in financial control between men and women, was there some consensus from both men and women. More than three quarters of the men interviewed admitted that women put their income to better use than men. They referred to a kind of stringent financial control which women are socialized into from the domestic scene. This was interpreted to be an admission of women's capacity to manage finances well. However, it could not be reconciled with the inability of women to get guarantors for their applications for loans or land.

The responses of the men would have indicated a level of confidence in women's ability to manage finances and thus made it easier to recommend and support women's access to land at Mataga. But this was not so. Being in positions of power, the men had imbibed and entrenched gender ideologies which stereotype women in society and this hindered the creation of the enabling framework for the local women traders.

Influences on choice of trade

The impression from group discussions was that decisions on resource distribution were based on culturally defined roles that put women in stereotype economic activities. Such unresponsive conditions were partly accountable for the replication of trading activities by the women. It was found that the choice of economic activity corresponded with the support that a woman got or hoped to get from both her family and the representatives of local institutions. This support was lacking so most women moved into sectors where start up capital was minimal. The successful businesswoman (profile 2) acquired the right level of confidence in her economic abilities to be able to access finance and resources on a higher scale. Her major thrust was developing her own business and getting a place of her own. Her first action was to save up enough money to purchase a shop as this was the type of activity she was exposed to through her 'live-in-friend' – a businessman. By owning the shop she was able to access more resources and enlist the confidence of even the institutions to support her proposals. She also had the added advantage of being single hence she could make decisions and sacrifices without negotiation or opposition from a husband figure. There were two major factors that enabled her success: her foresight and knowledge of the market and her ability to access commercial space. She showed foresight in her choice of business as she did in her decision to acquire her first shop and to expand. These qualities for success can be attained through training or material support in an enabling environment.

Effect of physical planning on women's trading

The trend at Mataga showed that the economic activities of women were not given adequate consideration in allocation of space in the physical planning of the centre. A major factor influencing this trend was observed within the institutional process which was biased against women's economic mobility. Patterns of women's participation in economic activities changed with the regulation and formalization of development space at Mataga. Women's participation, particularly in agricultural-produce trade, started to decrease during the period of reorganization of the centre as shown in Table 2.

Table 2:
Entry of women into trading activities at Mataga (1981-92)
(Source: MDC estimates, 1992)

Year	No. of women entrepreneurs	Net influx	Percentage increase
1981	38	0	0
1982	44	6	16
1983	57	13	30
1984	80	23	40
1985	85	5	6
1986	85	0	0
1987	85	0	0
1988	85	0	0
1989	100	15	18
1990	87	-13	-13
1991	70	-17	-20
1992	58	-12	-17

Resource distribution and control at Mataga confirmed the traditional gender ideologies of men's superior position in the home putting them at an economic and strategic advantage while women were constrained. This affected the role women played within Mataga's economy. In 1992, the number of women participating in own-account trading dropped by about one third (32%) to 58. Compared to the 1984-89 figures there was evidence of a decrease in the economic activities of women. From the responses of interviewed traders, issues of over-regulation of space, inadequate knowledge of allocation procedures, gender-prejudices in resource allocation and lack of funds have been major constraints on women's access to trading space.

At the irrigation schemes where women accounted for over half of the labour force, plots were allocated on the basis of households and only nine women (widows) were registered in both schemes. Women were not expected to be plot holders or to have shares in irrigation projects because household headship was traditionally male. According to the chairman of the local irrigation scheme, plot holders were expected to be members of the irrigation association that determined annual crop input levels and discussed matters pertaining to benefits from the scheme with the agricultural extension officers. The association's activities were guided by co-operative principles laid down by the Department for Co-operative Development. These absolute power of participation in decision making to a natural person, an individual member who is registered in terms of the constitution and not to a household or any other interests so represented. By definition the system did not recognize the female irrigation workers who contributed to household production and women were given plots only in cases where they prove that they have capable male dependants to work. The system undermined the agricultural production or exchange initiatives of its female members because they were not in a position to make any decisions. They were unable to make decisions on other extensions to agricultural marketing activities which may give more income. Further, the women were not expected to apply for commercial space at the centre because of their families' membership in the irrigation schemes.

Development of trading space

All the women indicated problems with accessing finance. Most of them were not clear on their business plans and aspirations. When the issue of financial constraint was pursued further they linked it to the possibility of developing a property according to council's development standards. In fact, some of them indicated that such standards should not be made to apply to them since their businesses were not on the scale anticipated by government when making the laws. About 26 women suggested a scheme of joint development of business premises where pool resources could alleviate the problems of high cash outlay for individuals. However, they still preferred to continue with sole trading.

Another group of women spoke of having 'lower' standard markets where basic sanitation facilities could be provided at a lower cost. This would enable more women to get stalls at the market. These options they would want to discuss with council. The women at the group discussions proposed more representation of women in the committees of council in view of the problems they encountered with council officials. They suggested an enhanced role of the local Women's League, a branch of the ruling political party safeguarding women's interests within the party, to include canvassing for women's projects and individual businesses. This was immediately recommended to the woman councillor who was present.

Options for raising capital

With regard to donors and assistance projects, it was pointed out that Mataga women did not want co-operative business ventures because of the insecurity they envisaged. They clearly outlined intra-personal conflicts that deter them from such group businesses. They acknowledged the need for clubs for social organization but rejected group income-generation projects as most of them clearly preferred to go it alone or with family members. In order to raise business capital for more substantial projects suggestions of joint ventures and partnerships were made by the researcher. All the women interviewed strongly opposed these except if it was with a spouse or child. In fact, they even opposed partnerships with other relatives. Most of the women cited cases that indicated their lack of information on formation of partnerships and genuine fear of losing businesses they have worked hard to build to a 'partner'.

Lessons learned

Often the argument of traditional gender roles is used to obscure major problems faced by women and their effect on the wider society. Contradictions were found between beliefs in preserving culture by continuing the traditional gender role divisions and rejecting women-in-development ideas, while enshrining a development pattern that discriminates against women thereby disinheriting them of stable productive roles and income/food security. The economic development of women has been shown to lag behind because of such traditional views. The socialization process sometimes ensures that women passively accept the existing gender contracts, discriminatory practises and prejudices against themselves. But local development must critically assess contributions of all sections of a population so as to support and create a democratic economic order where opportunities for progress can be optimised. In the case study, it was found that a lopsided development pattern was commencing, whereby sections of active economic population were being slowly frustrated out of the system. An imbalance difficult to redress was beginning to manifest itself. Testimonies from the group discussions and profile 3 proved that women's economic initiatives were being stifled by their inability to obtain trading space. Women entrepreneurs country-wide, as well as in Mataga's business sector, are an asset to the whole economy and should be encouraged to develop their initiatives alongside the men. The recurring theme of food security should be emphasized to create a basis for enabling women's initiatives in primary production and trade. In this respect, social support, particularly from immediate family, is critical.

Conclusion

The study concentrated on the themes of constraint to women's access to trading space. It was possible to identify some of the sensitive problems through the combination of research methods. Using participant observation, group discussions, personal informal interviews and formal interviews gave greater validity to the findings. However, the first three methods of enquiry did not allow for adequate objectivity due to the closeness of the researcher to all processes taking place as well as to the participants. In some cases the women gave information which was based on memory and this could not be verified except through personal contact with the subject. This may limit this approach to some extent but considering the situation and inaccuracy of records at council offices the research approach ultimately provided more insight into the questions. The research methods used were adequate for the objectives of the study because participants were able to convey concerns as well as make suggestions towards creating the enabling environment for their operation.

Constraints to trading

Women traders at growth points face many problems but this study highlights issues related to their access to trading space. There are, however, other constraints which are useful for reinforcing the role that access to space can play in the enabling framework for women traders. Regarding their participation in the local economy, the study identified the following constraints to women at Mataga:
i) Lack of adequate information on project ideas and options;
ii) Lack of information on procedures for obtaining or accessing productive resources and opportunities;
iii) Inadequate social support, particularly from their families, the officials of significant institutions and the wider business community;
iv) Inability to take advantage of training programmes on technological information due to poor levels of education;
v) Lack of access to more substantial start-up funds which is linked to inadequate collateral to access resources through formal borrowing;
vi) Isolation from the wider (national) economy due to their remoteness from larger commercial centre.

Gender specific constraints

While not all constraints are gender specific, the interventions required in order to confront and mitigate the situation must take cognisance of the gender conflicts. Socialization and its effects on how people access and utilize trading space and opportunity is a crucial issue in this regard. From the profiles some major gender specific constraints were identified, namely:
- Lack of support from the family which is very important since the concept of 'family' occupies a major place in most women's lives;
- Attitudes of men in authority such as council staff;
- Power of husbands to control women's trading;
- Constraints related to women's freedom to seek recommendation or guarantee for their development and sometimes sexual harassment.

The informal organizational relationships at the centre and

attitudes of the mostly male council members and workers, negatively affects women entrepreneurs and inhibits their access to productive resources. As Mies, (1989) wrote about patriarchy and accumulation, women were often particularly disadvantaged when discretionary powers were granted to gender insensitive authorities. In the study, most men believed in the stereotype of gender roles and 'a woman's place' in society. They neither recognized the contributions of women who worked for their family nor the female heads of household. This was the situation that led to prejudicial decisions on women's ownership of land at Mataga. Consequently, there was no support for women either in the informal sector or mainstream entrepreneurship development because council was not committed to seeking such support. Furthermore, the remoteness of Mataga deprives most women entrepreneurs of access to information and support of other organizations which provide services for small and medium scale entrepreneurs.

Creating space for women traders

In view of the economic structural adjustment programme and the role that women in small enterprises are expected to play in employment creation and economic development of local areas, non-governmental organizations, donors, government departments and financial agencies need to contribute to establish an enabling environment for the women to thrive. Women must be enabled to articulate and implement their economic aspirations. Relevant institutions and local authorities must provide appropriate back-up that is conducive to women's consolidation in local economies. The institutional regimes and policy implementation process should include women's contributions in macro-economic considerations. Women are capable and willing to explore economic opportunities at smaller centres such as Mataga and the proper enabling framework is to avail them of control over productive resources. Government efforts through legislation and activities to mainstream women traders may not have managed to reach the poorer and more remote areas because of the local-centre relationships but in the growth points such as Mataga, there is still scope for redefining planning criteria to accommodate development needs of women and link them to local economic goals.

Chapter Twelve

Social and Physical Living Conditions of Nannies in High Cost Residential Areas of Lusaka, Zambia

Mubiana Macwan'gi

Introduction

This study examines the living conditions of nannies in Lusaka. Both social and physical aspects of housing are covered. Physical aspects of housing refers to the 'hardware' of housing such as construction, structure, access to housing, building materials and type as well as quality of housing. Social aspects of housing refer to the 'software' – how people live within housing structures and/or quality of living within a household.

A large group of poor women are working as domestic workers, nannies, in high cost housing or in mansions they do not own. A nanny refers to an individual who is employ to be responsible for child care. The housing problems of women from low socio-economic groups residing in high cost areas are manyfold but invisible because it is erroneously assumed that their housing needs are met. This explains why no comprehensive research has been done on women in housing in high cost areas.

In order for research on gender and housing to be representative, it is imperative to recognize that there are a wide range of housing options in high, medium and low cost areas. Further, it is important to note that poor women are not restricted to low cost residential areas. Hence it is important to examine how women, especially those from low income groups, live in different types of housing in order to understand the problems they face. Such studies are presented in Zimbabwe (Schlyter, 1989) and in Botswana (Larsson, 1989) but not in Zambia, and only for women heads of households.

Few studies on gender and housing address the social aspects of housing and these concentrate on the division of labour, the decision making between men and women and on women headed households. Hudgen (1988) and Jiggins (1980) examined the relationship between housing and women headed households in rural Zambia.

Hansen (1989) in her study of domestic work in Zambia in a historic perspective presents one chapter on 'Lives Beyond the Workplace'. There is not much published on domestic work in the region outside South Africa.

Worth noting is that very few studies have examined how women from low socio-economic groups live in high cost areas.

Study rationale

This study is important because the proportion of women taking up paid jobs outside their homes is increasing (Government of Zambia, 1991). Coupled with lack of institutional child care, there will be a growing demand for nannies to take care of young children of working mothers while they are at work. Given the current socio-economic environment, nannies will continue to provide child care for the foreseeable future. Moreover, nannies play a very important role of caring and socializing children, the future generation. Therefore, their well being is important because it has an influence on the quality of child care they provide.

Study objectives

- ✦ to determine the socio-demographic characteristics of nannies in Lusaka.
- ✦ to determine the social and physical living conditions of nannies.

♦ to determine if nannies are aware of their employment rights such as minimum wages, social security benefits and leave benefits.
♦ to explore the social relationships between nannies and their employees as well as other household members.

Methodology

This study used three supplementary research methods to elicit both quantitative and qualitative data between November 1992 and October 1993.

First, four focus group discussions (FGDs) were held with a total of 25 females and one male. FGDs were used to generate and clarify question items for the survey, assist in the interpretation of the survey findings and to assist in understanding some sensitive issues such as those related to feelings and relationships between nannies and their employers. Second, a survey of 101 nannies selected randomly in Lusaka high density residential areas (Avondale, Chelstone, Long Acres and Roma) was conducted shortly after FGDs. Using a pre-tested questionnaire, information was collected in 'face to face' interviews. Survey data was used to describe the socio-demographic profile of nannies.

Finally, informal in-depth interviews with four nannies, purposefully selected, were conducted nine months after the survey. Informal interviews were prompted by the unexpected preliminary results of the FGDs and survey which showed that respondents did not experience or report physical or sexual harassment. In order to elicit information about harassment indirect and projective questions about other nannies and previous employment were used. This technique has been found to be useful when eliciting sensitive information (Kidder, 1985).

In this study, nannies are categorized into four broad types:
1. Day workers: those who report for work everyday and return to their homes after work.
2. Live-in nannies: those who live with their employers.
3. Relatives.
4. Non-relatives.

Study results

Female and male data from all the three research methods used in this study have been integrated in the presentation of the results. Description of the socio-demographic characteristics of the nannies is largely based on the survey data, while interpretation of results drew heavily from qualitative data. However, major points of departure between research methods and sexes are noted.

Types of nannies

As expected, females are more involved in child care than males. Culturally, child care is seen as a female's role. Out of a random sample of the 101, most (85%) of the respondents were females. However, this marks a shift from the pre-Independence period when, due to socio-cultural and ideological factors, men dominated the domestic service. This continued after Independence. However, the author observes that while men may dominate the domestic service, because white female bosses preferred to hire male helpers, in general, women take a lead in domestic work related to child care. Day workers are almost split into half, 44% and 56% respectively. This research expected to find many nannies who are related to their employers but, on the contrary, only 7% reported that they were related to their employers. In some cases one nanny was working for two single women sharing accommodation. No significant differences were observed between nannies of different types.

Socio-demographic characteristics of the sample

The majority of the nannies interviewed were young with about a third (34%) aged between 15 and 19 years, and a large proportion (78%) had received only primary education. On average males were older and better educated than females. The average age for males was 22 years and all males had attended formal school whereas 14 females never attended formal school. The fact that most nannies are young implies that, child care is a transitional job. This point is underscored by another study finding which indicates that very few respondents had stayed on the current job for more than a year. About half (48%) were single while about a quarter (21%) were divorced.

Only four males were not married. The study also revealed that half (50%) of the respondents had children, most (65%) had one or two children and the majority (78%) of those who had children were living with them. Most nannies have got children to support and care for, but to survive, they leave their children with very minimal care while they go and look after other people's children. A frequent comment was: 'I need money to survive.' And: 'A low salary is better than nothing'.

Employment

Over half (57%) of the nannies in the study had worked elsewhere before the current job. Males were more likely to have had previous work experience than females. A third reported that they got the current job through self initiatives, that is, going from house to house searching for a job until getting hired. Friends and relatives are equally important in providing information about employment. However, males were more likely to get a job through self initiative than females who relied more on friends and family members for assistance to get job.

Despite heavy workloads and long working hours, both female and male nannies get very low wages ranging between K1 300 (US$4) and K20 000 (US$67). However, more than half of the sample (66%) receive wages of less than K6 010 (US$20). The average wage being K6 167 (US$21). Some, especially relatives, are paid only in kind, exchanging their labour for food, accommodation, and personal items such as toiletries and used clothes which often do not fit properly because they are 'rejects'. However, this form of payment although practised is not popular among nannies. A majority (76%) described their salaries as inadequate to maintain even a minimum standard of living, especially because the monthly wage includes transport and housing allowance for day workers. Some were brave enough to ask for a raise but their requests were rejected on the grounds that they eat free meals at work. However, to compensate for this shortfall, over half of the respondents receive some support in kind from their employers.

Although there is a national scheme at National Provident Fund (NPF) with the aim of protecting the working interests of domestic workers, including nannies, over three quarters of the nannies in the study do not know of any public institution that could protect their employment interests and rights. A review of domestic servants' records at NPF for years 1991 and 1992 shows that only 222 domestic servants of all categories were enrolled and of these only 75 were women. This finding is echoed by the Zambian *Daily Mail* of 24 November 1993 which found that most of ununionized workers expressed ignorance about their unions existence.

Multiple roles

Although most respondents reported that they were hired for child care, almost all were doing multiple jobs combining child care with household and outdoor chores such as house cleaning, laundry, cooking, gardening and doing errands. However, the study noted that male nannies were more likely to walk children to school than female nannies. This may suggest that women are primarily employed as nannies, and as soon as they no longer need help with small child care they hire male servants. Because of multiple roles it is therefore not surprising that many described their workload as 'too much' and worked very long hours. About half of the nannies in the study (43) reported that they worked about ten hours while some (15) worked twelve or more hours per day without overtime. Live-in nannies are the most disadvantaged, they work much longer than others. As one nanny put it: 'For me, work never stops until bedtime. And I wake up early to prepare children for school'. One day worker reported that although her home is under two minutes walk from her work place, she is not allowed a short lunch break, because no one will stay with the children.

Housing

The study reveals that nannies do not have their own accommodation. About half (44%) of the sample live with their employers, 15% live with their parents or relatives, a quarter (26%) live in rented accommodation and only three live in own accommodation. It is important to note here that accommodation rent ranging between K700 ($2) and K1 000 ($3) is too high for most nannies: sometimes it exceeds the monthly income. Most could not even explain how they manage and are often heard to say: 'I survive by God's grace'.

Although live-ins do not pay any rent, their situation is equally difficult. The majority (79%) share a sleeping room with two or more people, often children, and sometimes they have to give up their shared space for visitors. Most complained about having to share a sleeping room with 'naughty' children. Although not expressed, there are likely to be problems of shared accommodation such as lack of privacy, undressing in the presence of children or other people who are not part of one's family. There is also difficulty in reaching consensus about when common facilities are to be used and who is responsible for putting off lights at night.

Relationships with other household members

To assess the quality of relationships between the nannies and their employers, questions related to freedom at home, use of free time, decision making related to what to eat, and preferences for personal items like clothing were asked. Information elicited by these questions indicate that nannies lead a subservient life. They are always under the control of their employers or relatives whom they live with as dependents. They lack control of their own lives and the freedom to even make basic choices in life is very minimal. In the case of live-ins, employers decide what food to eat, when to sleep, sometimes clothes for their nannies and how their free time should be used. This study revealed that nannies are not able to articulate their conditions of service and their concerns about living conditions. Many said: 'My salary is too low ... but I feel shy to ask for salary increment – it is up to my employer to decide, he/she knows I need a raise'. Most did not feel free at home: 'I do not stay in the living room with the rest of the family especially when the employers are around ... I feel shy ... and it is like I am intruding in their private discussions'. This finding is supported by Hansen (1989) when she described domestic servants and their employers as 'distant companions' and Cook (1989) when she observed that nannies are never fully integrated in the families of their employers.

Despite all these problems, a few respondents had good things to say about their employers or living conditions. Some of the good things cited are: 'My employer is good ... she does not talk too much; she gives me presents, food and clothing and sometimes helps me out when I'm sick'.

Problems encountered by nannies

The results of this study reveal various problems related to work and living conditions. Excessive work, low salaries and unpaid overtime are some of the common problems reported. Most complained about working long hours without getting off, getting few holidays or leave and getting no extra pay for extra work. Some work even when sick. One said: 'Last week I had a very bad tooth ache, but I had to work'. Mbilinyi *et al.* (1980) also make same observations for women in Tanzania.

Lack of respect by employers and their children is also a major problem. Nannies are treated like children or 'servants' and do not have input in their conditions of work. They rarely discuss their working and living conditions with their employers. A common remark was: 'They do not listen to us'. Employers' children are described as 'spoiled' or 'unruly' – 'If you try to discipline the children, parents get angry and start shouting at you for the children's mistakes – children dirty the house and play with water ... I cannot advise them to stop ... I just clean the house again and again because I live in their house'. The way children interact with or treat nannies reflects society's attitudes towards the nannies or domestic workers in general.

Abusive or threatening language especially by female employers, is also a common problem perhaps because nannies interact more with female than male employers. One respondent reported that her female employer beats her sometimes. Further, indirect and projective questions revealed that physical and sexual harassment do exist. One female nanny, aged 28, narrated a story of another female nanny who used to work in the same neighbourhood: 'She was beaten by a jealous wife who suspected her of flirting with her husband ... I do not know the truth about the suspected love affair ... but sometimes men misbehave when their wives are not around'. One nanny, aged 40, had a personal history of sexual harassment: 'One morning my male employer tried to force me to bed ... he tore my clothes ... with God's power, I managed to get away ... That day I did not stay at work, I went back home. The following day I came back just to ask for my money – I got it all. I told his wife that I had decided to quit my job for personal reasons. She was surprised and tried to persuade me to stay ... I could not stay, I knew it was going to happen again – I did not tell the wife the truth because I did not want to cause trouble for their marriage.'

One female nanny who had no history of personal harassment, knew of another female nanny who was beaten. This nanny was assaulted by her employers because her husband, who also worked for her employers, stole from them: 'She did not report this to the police or lay assault charges because her husband had made a mistake ... She knew her husband was wrong'. The findings of this study suggests that male nannies do not suffer any sexual or physical harassment, but this is not necessarily correct as data relates to a small number of males who participated in the study.

Discussion

This study explored the social and physical living conditions of nannies in Lusaka and found that nannies, in general, lack accommodation. They live as dependents with employers or family members in high cost areas. As dependents, nannies' freedom to relax at home and to make personal decisions or choices is minimal. Though the study did not directly assess the health status of the respondents, the conditions under which nannies live are detrimental to health, especially their social and psychological wellbeing. A sense of insecurity fostered by a lack of accommodation undermines self confidence and can lead to a sense of helplessness. Larsson (1989) points out that for most women, 'a house of their own offers both short term and long-term security. It provided a place where a woman can run her own life and take care of and enjoy her children'.

Despite government guidelines for minimum wages and ages, nannies start their career early in life, sometimes as children looking after other children. They work long hours and carry out multiple responsibilities beyond their terms of reference and earn very low salaries. Of serious concern is that, in general, nannies are not aware of their employment and human rights. When not satisfied, the easiest solution is to quit the job. As a result, this group of workers, mostly women, are perpetual job seekers, searching for better working and living conditions. As a result, they never earn the rewards or security of long service. They are always at the mercy of their employer and can be fired any time without terminal benefits or any form of compensation.

This study brought to light some methodological issues. It observed that sensitive questions related to salary, relationships with employers and personal harassment of any form are best studied by qualitative research methods using indirect and projective questions. And it raises more questions which need to be investigated. Given salaries which are lower than monthly housing rent, how do nannies manage? What strategies do they use to supplement their low incomes? Do nannies have other options to child care? What proportion of men work as nannies, and are working conditions for female and male nannies the same?

Conclusions

From this study it is clear that more comprehensive studies to examine the living conditions of both female and male domestic workers should be undertaken. Such studies of domestic workers should include the employer's perspective in order to fully understand the situation.

For a better understanding of the question of housing it would be useful to define housing and living conditions in a much broader way so as to include their social aspects.

There is need for the responsible authorities, in Zambia it is the Ministry of Labour and Social Services, to look into conditions of services for domestic workers. Universal standards of workers, minimum wages and hours of work should be put in place.

The study also reveals that it is not enough to create schemes to protect the workers interests. In Zambia, neither the employers nor the employees know that the Zambia National Provident Fund has a Domestic Servant Scheme.

Domestic workers need to be educated on their rights, how such schemes work, and how they can benefit from them.

Domestic workers, not only nannies, need to get organized and fight for better wages and living conditions.

Chapter Thirteen

Choice of Law: Theoretical Perspectives on Urbanization and Women's Rights to Property

Mulela Margaret Munalula

Introduction

Women's rights to property in Zambia have, to a large extent, been affected by their lack of equality with men. In this paper this unbalanced relationship is examined in the light of Zambian women's rights to real property. Under Zambian law, all land belongs to the state so property rights are limited to leaseholds which maybe purchased or subleased. Thus, rights are used here to include ownership of the leasehold, renting from the state, councils, housing companies, employers and individuals, and control between the members of the a family or household. Therefore, the issue of women's equal access to ownership of their homes has legal implications, in that it questions the role of the law and the legal system in bringing about equality, but more importantly, it raises issues of competing interests within the household unit and family structure. The fact that property rights are not static but a result of constant renegotiation determined by a variety of socio-economic factors, magnifies the complexity of the situation.

One such factor is the urbanization process which has led to profound changes in law and Zambian society. This dynamic process, currently enacted in the face of a severe economic recession, has resulted in a multiplicity of rules regulating property rights in society. Most people believe that these rights are regulated by either custom or statutory law. Regarding customary law, the Zambian constitution allows for the application of customary and personal laws in matters to do with private property. Thus different customs will apply to different ethnic groups depending upon membership of a particular group. The actual customs are defined by the courts. With respect to statutory law, these are the family and property law statutes which are generally based on English law and are applicable in Zambia. People also assume that patriarchal elements which deny women equal access to property can be eliminated through the enactment of gender neutral legislation. Hence the women's movement in Zambia has sought to determine women's options by consolidating what they consider to be the most secure and equitable source of rights i.e. the general or statutory law.

The thrust of this paper is that this is an overly simplistic view, in that lived reality portrays more than a clearly defined dual legal system and, in many instances, women 'choose' to solve their everyday property disputes by relying on multiple and highly flexible, officially unrecognized norms in society which maybe aptly called the 'living law' (Friedman, 1964).

This paper, which is analytical in substance, seeks to develop a theoretical framework for a more realistic and in-depth understanding of the prevailing situation in urban Zambia. The framework for analysis is Hirdman's theory of a gender system in which chronic conflict results in the continuous creation of new gender contracts (1991). As such the analysis includes a historical element which shows the developments in gender concepts and conflict resolution, as Hirdman's theory is linked to Ehrlich's theory of the 'living law'. Having set out a summary of the research methodology and the empirical findings, the paper moves into an analytical review of the urbanization process following the advent of colonialism. The process of law reform is outlined to show the limitations of action based on preconceived and narrow notions of solutions which are not grounded in sound locally specific theoretical conceptions. The main body of the paper is devoted to a discussion of the 'living rules' operating in the current gender system to determine women's 'choice' of 'law'.

Background, methodological considerations and findings

The paper is based on the findings drawn from research conducted in the Lusaka urban district in the latter half of 1992. As a socio-legal study with a gender perspective, the major objectives of this study were to bridge the gap between law and society by articulating and theorizing the options available to different classes of women, rather than men, for the resolution of their property disputes and to make policy recommendations advocating more pertinent research objectives and procedure.

Achieving these objectives necessitated the ascertainment of personal laws and practices relating to property in the context of competition between men and women, particularly following the dissolution of marriage. The basic research instrument being the gender contract depicting a systematic gender order operational at various levels in society. Consequently, the study relied on qualitative data made up of in-depth interviews conducted in five different socio-economic areas of Lusaka, several case studies sourced from the Women's Rights Clinic of the Law Association of Zambia, legal provisions and court cases, and a review of literature on the subject.

Once the research sites had been selected, a section of each area was made at random and ten interviews obtained at alternate houses. Due to the fact that the interviews were conducted during office hours, most men were away from home so that, in line with the research objectives, more women than men were actually interviewed. The similarity of the responses to open ended questionnaires meant that ten interviews in each locality were adequate to elicit the requisite data on cultural aspects. The deliberate sampling from different socio-economic areas was intended to elicit data on the effects of class distinctions on the options open to women. Though useful in this regard, this method was not able to elicit information on the existence of intra-household property disputes.

Sourcing court cases was achieved through a physical search of the law reports and the records at the high court and subordinate court registries. Gendered property disputes within the courts were very few, and in the case of the high court, it was necessary to include all reported cases in the sample. With regard to the unreported cases the search covered the records for the periods January to June 1983 and July to December 1988. Subordinate court cases were obtained from the Chikwa and Boma court registries and the search covered the records for the period 1989 to 1991. The property disputes dealt with here were appeals from the local courts and totalled sixteen out of which only eight files were available for scrutiny. These were, without exception, incomplete, having been abandoned for undisclosed reasons.

Several case studies were followed up from the legal clinic run by the Women's Rights Committee of the Law Association of Zambia. Because of long term involvement with many of the respondents, it was possible to obtain very intimate information relating to progressive developments in the resolution of their personal disputes. This was a rich source of data on the living elements of social regulation.

The findings from the research which are discussed in greater detail in the analytical section of the paper indicated, first and foremost, that women were experiencing problems relating to property, but that these problems were revealed only in cases where serious conflict had developed and the matter had been taken to outside parties for resolution, such as where marriages had been dissolved whether by death, separation or divorce. Secondly, that although these problems were extensive, few of them were actually resolved by the courts using either the general or the customary law, indicating the existence of more popular informal dispute settlement mechanisms. (During the period 1989 to 1991 there were only 16 property disputes in the Lusaka subordinate courts between men and women despite its population of close to one million.) Thirdly, that dissatisfaction with existing gender contracts was evident in activities outside the court room and often surfaced in the argumentation used in the lower court cases.

Gender and the urbanization process in Zambia

With the advent of colonialism, came profound changes in African society which irrevocably altered the old way of living in groups on the basis of matrilineal or patrilineal kinship. Urbanization, which commenced under a gender biased policy which encouraged temporary male migration but prohibited female movement to the urban centres, was intended to retain a rural base which could subsidize the male wage and reabsorb the male labour force when it was no longer required (Cutrufelli, 1983). Thus, while the supervision of the village home was mostly left to women, urban housing was an employment benefit reserved for men. When women were finally allowed into towns, they moved there as dependants of male kin (Heisler, 1974). This Victorian ideology of the male breadwinner supporting a dependent spouse is still an ideal propagated by the state despite the obvious contribution of women to the household income and their increasing role as heads of single parent households (Schlyter, 1988). Opposing ideologies are inevitable in the face of western ideals imposed at the same time as the promotion of a dual legal and socio-economic system in which native issues were to be administered under the customary law. The mixing of white and black cultures, and the inter tribal relations required a new system to regulate the increasingly blurred rights and duties. If customary law was to apply effectively then it had to be redefined.

The official policy was to treat customary law as a 'given', requiring only to be ascertained but Chanock (1982) argues that what took place was actually the creation of a customary law centred on the control of women. The process of proving customary law in the courts using male assessors and the establishment of rules through a series of inquiries, achieved little more than a legitimation of male claims of control over women. The effects of these developments were that African family disputes were resolved in the bottom rungs of the formal court structures by English adjudicators using newly created customary law which was not necessarily a reflection of what was taking place in practice. Once rules were sanctioned by the courts as customary law what happened outside the courts was considered to be extra legal and irrelevant. But women's position with regard to property rights and other family law issues could not be ascertained from the law in the courts alone because, as social science researchers find, many disputes were resolved outside the confines of the formal legal system (Hay & Wright, 1982).

Independence brought an end to the restriction to customary law in the sense that Africans were now free to opt for their relations to be governed by either the general state law or custom. The general laws of property were apparently gender neutral in relation to the state but this situation was dramatically altered by marriage. By simply marrying under the relevant law property rights could be created or erased conclusively. A marriage under the general law was defined as a union for life between one woman and one man. It implied monogamy, joint interests and permanence. Property was jointly owned and divisible in the event of divorce, with each party being legally entitled to inherit from the other and to maintenance including housing both during and after marriage. (WLSA Research Report, 1992). Marriage under customary law, on the other hand, validated by the payment of 'lobola', meant the separation of income, no maintenance or sharing of matrimonial property after divorce and no right for a woman to inherit from her husband (Himonga, 1990). This rule was settled by the court in the infamous **Mwiya vs Mwiya** (1977) Z.R. 113, when it stated that under Lozi customary law, a man is not obliged to either maintain his former spouse nor to share the household property with her.

The lifting of barriers to accessing the general law which is presumably more equitable has made little difference to the majority of the Zambian people; they have not embraced the system (Fortman and Mihyo, 1991). Thus, in practice, customary rules apply even to people who have contracted marriages under the Act (Schuster, 1979 and Munachonga, 1988). At the same time, however, the deteriorating economic situation has meant greater competition for resources both within and outside the home (Munachonga, 1989). Intra household and extended family conflicts over property have led to a great furore over women's entitlement, as is evident from the process of law reform.

Women and family property law reform

The legacy of Zambia's socio-legal history is a pluralist system of law in which general law is regarded as superior. It is the law which is taught in the law schools, printed in legal materials and generally applied in the courts of record. Customary law is only applicable when it does not contradict the general law or offend 'English' sensibilities and morals. But, in addition to this, there is the 'living law' which is not formally recognized by the state institutions. The assumed omnipotence of the general law has been a major contributory factor to the worldwide women's movement's strategy of pursuing gender equitable social change through the law (Smart, 1989). In Zambia this strategy is manifest in the overwhelming passion for a consolidated and uniform law of marriage in the long term and a restatement of the law of succession immediately.

According to Longwe and Clarke (1990), the calls for a change in the laws of inheritance were prompted by the one common practice referred to as the 'property grabbing' syndrome. By the 1960s, it had become common practice for a widow whether married under the general or customary law, to be stripped of all the family property by her deceased husband's relatives as soon as he was buried. Justification for the 'custom' of property grabbing was the traditional and broadly accepted notion of separation of property rights within the African context. Because a wife is never considered to be a part of her husband's kinship group, she has no rights to inherit from the husband (Munachonga 1989). The assumption that all the family property belonged to the husband being itself a result of the 'dependence' created by women's migration into towns as dependants of their male kin. And yet research indicates that property grabbing is a distortion of custom which leaves out widow inheritance and/or support by the heir (Law Development Commission Report, 1976).

The new law of succession was enacted in 1989, in the form of two Acts, to cover both intestacy and testate succession. It provides for a spouse to, *inter alia*, inherit a life tenancy in the matrimonial home. This supposedly progressive statute employs gender neutral terminology which serves to dilute the gender bias of the problem it seeks to solve because it denies the underlying cause of the problem in the first place i.e. the assumption that the house belongs to the man and can be 'grabbed' by his relatives. Also, it fails to give women full rights in that they are only tenants till death or remarriage, whichever is the earlier – a situation which applies less frequently in the case of men since property is more often registered in the name of a husband than a wife. On the more positive side, however, is the local court requirement that the appointment of an administrator of the estate must be endorsed by the widow, a clause which creates the potential for her protection.

Concerned with the lack of comprehensive property rights for women during marriage and after divorce, activists, including the Women and Law in Southern Africa Research Project (WLSA), are researching into how the law can be used to rectify the situation. Beginning with research into maintenance after dissolution of marriage, WLSA for instance, have sought consolidated law reform to ensure that the English-based family laws of property apply to all women instead of the small minority married under the Act (WLSA MIZ Report, 1992). Curiously enough, the recommendation for more law is made despite the fact that research indicates that the women who have the rights to matrimonial property do not avail themselves of these rights. Further research is currently looking for ways in which to make the inheritance laws more effective.

In the face of the furore created by the enactment of the inheritance legislation, the value of law in creating a framework for change cannot be denied, but the level at which it can achieve prescribed changes is debatable. Furthermore, the focus on law means that other regulatory factors in society receive inadequate attention. The superiority of the general law in a legal system in which multiple factors actually regulate property rights, mean that only the official law is accountable to the requirements for gender equity. The other factors are not subjected to scrutiny or rationalization. And yet unless the law is actually resorted to, its equity or otherwise are of no real use to women. Several researchers have already found that due to factors operating at three different levels – ideological, institutional and interpersonal, many women do not resort to law to solve their problems; and when they do, they very often find justice remains elusive (WLSA, 1992 and Himonga, 1990).

Property rights in a 'living' system

The gender system based on the logic of the separation of the sexes and the propagation of the male norm, is an arena of struggle in which gender contracts are reconstituted (Hirdman, 1991). This dynamic process is operational at various levels in society. Although they maybe separated for purposes of analysis, these levels are interconnected, feeding into each other and affecting each other in such a way that changes at one level must inevitably have some effect on the others. At the abstract cultural level, images of the ideal male-female behaviour in which women are subordinate, are concretized at the institutional level such as the legal system. Besides the courts, employment institutions were of particular interest because a large proportion of housing in Zambia is still obtained through employment. The institutional level is the easiest to alter, but the least effective, in bringing about profound change. The third level is the inter-personal one at which the gender contracts are enacted on a day to day basis. For ease of clarity these levels form the theoretical base for the interpretation of the research findings while at the same time, the gender system is illustrated by the latter.

Ideological level

The interviews carried out in all the socio-economic areas and the court decisions brought about strong indications of the male norm, manifested as a belief by both male and female respondents in a male head of the household. This was the case even in the homes in which home purchase was largely contributed to by the woman, which was more prevalent in the lower socio-economic areas of Kalingalinga and N'gombe. There were some claims to shared decision making but there were few households in which final authority was not reserved for the man. This applied regardless of socio-economic class and the type of marriage contracted. Women generally assumed the position of head in single households.

In the higher class areas i.e. Northmead and Kabulonga, most of the houses were owned by virtue of employment and this was heavily biased in favour of the men. But it was only in two cases where the husband was not only the head of the household but vested with absolute decision making powers. However, it was only in the Kabwata area where housing is rented from the local council and where women were not only in paid employment but were also the registered owners of their homes, that there was a concretization of aspirations expressed by women from other socio-economic areas. The women here claimed single ownership and headed their households even where they were married as was the case with the majority of respondents. Thus the combination of home ownership, employment and education were clearly emancipatory factors.

Besides the issue of the head of the household, other interesting side issues were raised. These included views on the role of law and custom. Customary law was well known and there was clearly a rudimentary knowledge of the state law, but, with it, also fear of its power and its effect on established but non-legal rights. These fears were specially visible during the process of enacting the new law of inheritance. One of the male respondents in Kalingalinga objected very strongly to the statutory law of inheritance which he felt prevented relatives from benefiting from their kin and was a form of 'interference', indicating the confusion arising out of opposing but concurrently applicable ideologies.

The value of legal title in protecting property rights was reiterated by nearly all female respondents although they lacked knowledge of the legal niceties. For instance, while all respondents felt that women could own a house in the village under customary law, the women preferred to have title deeds to urban property because the documents of title meant more security.

Although not referred to directly by the respondents there was a refusal to admit to property disputes within a subsisting marriage which could only be hypothesized as a manifestation of the strength of the sanctity of marriage and the shame of publicizing difficulties. Values such as these are powerful in keeping women in their place.

Institutional Levels

Property rights in the courts

Although marriage under the Act entitles women to a share of the matrimonial property, the court's interpretation of this is that it is a form of charity directed at the women rather than a justified right. Cultural constraints clearly affect the court's stance. The court cases revealed a tendency to compensate women for their contribution to the acquisition of the home on the basis that they had merely assisted in the purchase. This is apparent even in High Court decisions where the law is applicable and is not confined to the courts applying customary law. The following cases which include **Mwiya vs Mwiya** in which the court failed to exercise its power to disregard a custom which is blatantly repugnant to justice, equity and good conscience, are testimony to this.

In the case of **FMB vs the Estate of the Late JWB** (unreported) the plaintiff whose husband died intestate, sought a court order to enable her to assume legal authority over various properties left by the deceased which were falling into disrepair. The letters of administration granted to the Administrator-General had been revoked earlier upon her application claiming gross mismanagement by his office. The court refused her application on the grounds that there were life interests involved and the properties could only be administered by the administrator. Considering that the life interests involved were hers and those of her children, the court failed to recognize this and accord it appropriate consideration, raising implications of women's minor status.

In **AB and Anor vs CAS AS** (unreported) the petitioner, who never married the deceased, sold her own house in order to help meet the mortgage payments on a house in his name, but which they occupied together for eighteen years before his death. It was not until then that she discovered that he had left a will leaving the house to his estranged wife in Portugal. The High Court ruled that she had no rights since her contributions were a gift to him. However, on appeal, it was held that, since the house was constructed for and used as home during the duration of a stable relationship which could be equated to marriage, and since she had made a substantial contribution to its acquisition, she was entitled to one third of its sale value.

The decision in this case sets the tone for the type of awards generally granted by the courts in situations where they apply the statutory law. They award no more than one third of the value of the property, further confirming that women are being 'given' something which was not theirs of right.

Employers, state bureaucracy and housing rights

The institution of gender at the bureaucratic and policy level reflects many cultural expectations; in particular, it reflects western patriarchal ideology of the nuclear family and the dependent wife and mother. The struggle by the Zambian women's movement to secure maintenance and inheritance rights for women is a logical result of this belief. However, it also reflects indigenous cultural and customary law expectations.

Much of the available housing is acquired through employment or the state institutions such as the local council or housing authority. Therefore, whether directly or indirectly, they are major players in the determination of property rights. They can make it easier or harder for women to acquire or secure housing rights. Ideological conceptions are applicable here too; but since these institutions are often meticulous about following the law and regulations to the letter, it is here that the value of equitable laws is most valid as the following cases illustrate.

In **SC vs LHC**, the deceased's brother was appointed administrator by the local court, without the widows consent, and in violation of the Local Courts Act; so, when he wished to administer the estate, the deceased's former employer wrote to him to regularize his appointment. This he failed to do since the widow did not trust him and had filed a complaint at the legal clinic to have his appointment revoked. She then also appealed to her own employers, to take over the mortgage so she could acquire control over the house. Due to the force exerted by the two institutions and the legal clinic, the administrator finally handed over control of the estate including the house to her. Her employers took over the mortgage and the property was transferred to her name. All these parties were able to exert force because they had the backing of the new inheritance laws with which they were able to make the court do the right thing. Interestingly enough, this serves as a check on the court which is not above manipulation due to ideological considerations. For instance, the disappearance of files in property disputes, which is a common occurrence at the courts, may not always be solely attributable to bribery and corruption but reflect negative attitudes on the part of court personnel. Also, interviews of court personnel during the WLSA group study into inheritance, indicated that they not only misunderstood the provisions but were often hostile to the new law.

Involvement of institutions and bureaucracy have not been as positive in other cases. In **MM vs TM**, the widow whose husband, an army officer, died in November 1991 was under threat of eviction by the administrator who is the deceased's brother. She was living in the family house in Kabanana compound and he wanted it sold. When she complained to the legal clinic, the lawyers immediately filed a caveat to prevent a sale of the property. They also wrote to the army to offer her some protection – but the army adjutant wrote back to say it was none of their business and they could not interfere.

Even the local council, in its zeal to apply its regulations, has often acted in an inhumane manner. This was the case when **M.C.** approached the clinic for help because her estranged husband was threatening her with violence and eviction from the family home which was leased from the council in his name. The council would not consider her application without a letter authorizing them to do so from the husband indicating reliance on cultural beliefs in the sanctity of marriage. The clinic's pleas to both the council and her husband proved fruitless and she was eventually advised to obtain a divorce through the local court as the only alternative open to her.

The inter-personal level

At the interpersonal level the competing interests took on a dynamism rendering specific rights and their attainment very elusive. This was demonstrated by the cases resolved under the auspices of the legal clinic.

In **RM vs BM**, after the husband's death in January 1991 leaving two houses in Chawama, his brother was appointed administrator. Upon the instigation of the deceased's aunt, the widow was told to vacate the family house so that it could be rented out since the deceased's relatives were in occupation of the other. She then went to the legal clinic to complain. She stated that all she wanted was to keep her home and that the deceased's aunt should be stopped from continuing to threaten her children since two had already died. The administrator and his aunt were called to the legal clinic for a meeting and in the presence of the widow claimed that they only asked her to find a room to rent so that when the house was leased out, she would have some income. After protracted discussions it was finally agreed that the administrator would ensure that she remained in her house while the other one was rented out and rentals would go to her and the children.

A key observation from the cases at the clinic is the large number of disputes between women. This prompts views in many quarters that women are the worst property grabbers and indicates that competing interests and ideologies are all at play even among women themselves, so that at any given time different women may have different interests.

'Living law' and the courts

Very interesting at the interpersonal level was the maximization of options exercised by women which maybe viewed as survival strategies as women fight for their rights. For instance, even where a legal right exists, women may not exercise the right if the emotional cost is too high. This innovative characteristic is most useful where it has enabled women to demand a re-interpretation of established rules; and they have maintained their stance all the way to the lower courts.

The local court cases were not directly examined because the local court is administratively excluded from making adjudications on issues of real property. However, the study revealed that they do deal with the issues by the way, because they in fact, make awards of compensation which are based on contributions to the construction of the house. This is evidenced by the cases which came up on appeal in the subordinate court. The rate at which the cases were abandoned before they could be resolved by the subordinate court implies negative gains for the women who make the effort to go that far; but the response of the local courts in granting their claims reflected a felt need to create more equitable gender contracts even though that need was unsupported by law or custom. The courts still assumed male ownership, but were more than ready to award compensation for recognized contributions even if those contributions were only in kind. Despite occasional references to customary law, men, and women in particular, employed argumentation reflecting practical considerations.

In **LP vs ZS 1990/ssp/lca55**, after granting the divorce, the local court ordered the defendant husband to pay his former wife a sum of K10 thousand as compensation for labour and cash which she had contributed towards the construction of the family house. He denied she had made any contributions, substantiating his claim by producing receipts to show that all payments were made in his name. The court was not swayed, and insisted that even if she had made no financial contribution, she had contributed labour, and, in any case, while the husband's income was going towards the construction of the house, the family must have been dependant on the wife's income for living expenses. The husband appealed, but as the subordinate court was interested only in assessing the value of the house to determine whether the sum awarded to the wife was correct, he abandoned the matter. Most of the other cases covered in the study followed similar lines.

A further interesting feature is the mixture of ideological concerns which are evident in the arguments raised. Often these are contradictory or rely upon unexpected principles of justice, equity, custom and law. To illustrate: in the case of **GM vs MB** lca/34/89, the husband appealed against an order attendant upon the grant of a divorce, to pay his former wife K4 000 as compensation since he would retain the matrimonial house. He claimed the adjudicating court was biased since his former wife had no legal rights to his house and had contributed nothing to its construction. Furthermore, he claimed she had left the matrimonial home of her own volition and, in any case, they were not legally married. He testified that he had searched for a plot and constructed two rooms. A further two rooms were added with the help of his new wife. The former wife acknowledged that no dowry had been paid but insisted she had contributed to the construction of the house to its four-room level.

Since all the cases examined were abandoned before they were finalized by the subordinate court, the present study relied on earlier studies to analyze the response of the subordinate court. Himonga's study of family property dispute settlement, was particularly useful in bringing to light some incredible developments within the legal structure which had very little to do with channelled law reform. These developments which are confined to the lower courts appear to be a direct response to socio-economic developments (Himonga, 1987). In her study which examined extra legal dispute settlement mechanisms as well as the general law, she found that the customary law, as applied in the court, is based on an economic structure in which, purportedly, women did not have the opportunity to earn an income independent of their husbands. But today it is generally recognized that women work outside the home, earning wages or engaging in all sorts of income-generating activities. Their independent incomes are used to maintain their families and it is unrealistic to argue that the husband as head of the household owns the family property to the exclusion of his wife. The mantle of dependency thrust on them by pre-colonial minor status, colonial and post-colonial 'wife' status has served more to hide their productivity than to shelter them from the strife of economic pursuits.

Himonga states that the local courts seem to have recognized the hardships of customary law and made some attempts to ameliorate the position of women through three types of orders against the husband upon divorce. Thus, the husband maybe ordered to pay compensation to the wife and share family property with her regardless of whether she can prove direct cash contribution to its acquirement or not. According to Himonga, compensation is paid by the husband to the estranged wife in order to meet her immediate financial and rehabilitation needs as well as to compensate her for loss of marriage. Where women could prove direct contribution to family property, they were able to secure cash compensation for their contribution to the construction or purchase of a house, which generally remained the property of the man. Himonga supports this claim by referring to several cases in which this was done.

Although the cases in the present study were all abandoned and therefore inconclusive with regard to the subordinate court's stance regarding property settlement, Himonga's cases indicate that the subordinate court was not sympathetic to women's claims. She found that the subordinate courts were quick to undermine the local court awards by regularly overturning them on the grounds that they are contrary to custom and are not sanctioned by law. Not only do the subordinate courts not examine custom critically under the repugnancy clause, but they appear to be guided by ideological considerations which take precedence over equity and the principles of justice intended to guide legal decisions. From Himonga's sample of cases, all those which went to the subordinate court on appeal, because the husband was disputing the order to compensate his wife, resulted in orders quashing the original decision.

Conclusion

Women's need to secure property rights is a facet of the deep-seated and gendered power relations within society, arising from the logic of separating between men and women. Socio-economic changes, both in terms of women's increasing ability to contribute to the acquisition of matrimonial property and the deepening levels of poverty, has made women more vocal and insistent about their rights to property. At the same time, they still believe in the rule of the father. This means, firstly, the conjugal unit and, secondly, the social structure as a whole, are turned into arenas for struggle and renegotiation of the male norm.

The type of gender contract in which women are not regarded as owners of property in their own right is no longer satisfactory in today's situation. Inevitably new terms are being drawn up in the framework of a living law. To do justice, courts must acknowledge the redefinition of gender rights and look to bridging the gap between law and society, otherwise women look elsewhere in order to secure their rights to matrimonial property.

Many gender sensitive women who have recognized the difficulties women face in securing property rights are leading the struggle for new gender contracts. In this regard they have directed much energy towards law reform. This, of course, has certain consequences which are not wholly effective within the Zambian context. For instance, one aspect of revering law, has been the corresponding disregard of custom. For feminist reformists, customary law became the source of oppression and the barrier to equal protection of the law, with traditionalist arguments being greatly feared. But, should we fear custom in its own right or simply in its present manifestation as a static patriarchal set of rules?

An obvious limitation of regarding law as right and custom as wrong is the simplification of a reality which has a lot of 'grey matter' in such a way that the latter remains untackled. Since it is in this grey matter that I perceive the factors which govern family relations in reality, I consider it an unfortunate development of the legal centralist approach, that there has been a failure to come to terms with and theorise it. By treating anything other than black letter law as either non-existent, oppressive or temporary, the process of law reform has paid inadequate attention to the role these factors play in social regulation particularly as they are the lived embodiment of patriarchy.

Researchers need to revise their theories to take into account local specificities and indigenous values in order to make effective policy recommendations. Changing the law to ensure that women have equal access to and power over property is empowering only in that it provides the framework within which rights can be enforced and claimed but it does not guarantee that those rights will be achieved in practice.

Chapter Fourteen

Changing Gender Contracts and Housing Conflicts

Anita Larsson and Ann Schlyter

Introduction

Most governments in Southern Africa support a policy of home ownership and many people have found that a house of one's own is an important means for survival in town. This study focuses on the urban house as property and, more precisely, on the relation between gender and housing, that is, how men and women respectively relate to housing.

In previous studies (Larsson 1989, Schlyter 1988 & 1989) we found that single women as house owners were more successful than married couples with similar incomes in improving and enlarging their houses. We became interested in understanding what prevents married couples from putting as much effort as single women into the improvement of their urban house. Why do married women not try to improve the houses they live in to the same extent as unmarried women?

Further studies (Schlyter, 1991) revealed differences in household survival strategies. Married couples could rely on several strategies. By contrast, the investment in an urban house was one of the few alternatives for single women largely excluded from the formal labour market and having difficulties in obtaining land in rural areas.

Different household strategies thus offer one type of explanation, but, to understand married women's actions, their own individual strategies, as elaborated within the constraints set by cultural and legal structures, have to be taken into account.

This paper explores the relationship between gender and housing by using a theoretical framework elaborated around the concept gender contract. It summarizes findings of three country studies. In order to understand married women's housing strategies the analysis focused on their actions in case of housing conflicts. We envisaged that a study of women's legal right to housing would be a way to find empirical material and identify their space of action.

In the analysis presented in this paper, a dominant gender contract, placing married women in a subordinate position, is identified. State actions after independence, aiming at improving women's situation through legislation, are then analyzed by presenting some new laws as well as today's legal praxis. With this background, some examples of women's strategies are given.

Conceptual framework

The central concept in our previous studies on women and housing was that of strategies. We identified the housing strategies of women heads of households as well as those of the state. The concept proved to be helpful in the analysis of individual women's actions, and, for that reason, we will continue to use it.

In order to reveal the impact of power structures on individual actions within the marriage, a broader theoretical framework was needed; a theoretical framework which could be applied not only to actions between individuals but also to customs of marriage and property, to legislation and to state policy.

Changing gender contracts

A model of changes in gender contracts and the gender system has been developed by Hirdman (1991). The concept gender contract allows us to analyze the space between men and women together with the ideas, rules and norms about places, tasks and qualities of men and women. The gender contracts are invisible social contracts regulating the relations between men and women at all levels of the society. Taken together they create a gender system.

We first felt hesitant to adopt a concept with associations to contract theories. We felt that such an approach might lead to a blindness for other types of explanation than that of the 'economic man's rational choice'. Contract theories have also been criticized for assuming equally strong parties. Hirdman stresses that this is not her assumption. On the contrary, she points out that the contract is drawn up by the party who defines the other. This is due to two characteristic patterns – or logics – that history demonstrates. They are the logic of separation between the sexes and the logic of male norm, that is, higher value is automatically given masculine things. This does not mean that women are passive; there is a space of action for women. Pateman (1988), who uses the term sexual contract synonymously with gender contract, shows convincingly how such contracts are formulated around the dichotomy of protection and subordination.

The concept gender contract allows us to consider changeability and historicity. In focus is the fact that this gender shaping relationship plays a fundamental social, economic and political role. Thereby studies of gender are not just to visualize women, but to show that gender dynamics are driving forces in history and important in the creation of a local urban culture decisive for the content of urbanization.

Change is a dialectic process not necessarily in a straight direction from oppression to emancipation; it may also result in an ideological reinforcement of abstract meanings of what is male and what is female.

Particular gender contracts are specific in time and setting. These specific gender contracts provide the point of departure for actions by women and men. Variations in gender contracts can be found between different ethnic groups and between urban and rural populations. In times of rapid change, such as urbanization, there are more evident changes in the contracts.

Levels of analysis

Hirdman discusses the contracts in relation to three levels in society: the abstract level of cultural images, the institutional level, and the interpersonal level. On the second and third level class structure, family relations and age operate and shape the gender contracts. Changes in contracts on one level have an impact on contracts on other levels.

An important actor at the institutional level is the state. Its legislative power allows it to take an active part in ongoing gender negotiations. It can be sensitive to demands for changes from certain groups, or it can actively preserve existing laws whereby existing contracts are confirmed and perhaps even reinforced.

Gender contracts at the individual level are developed in relation to the existing contracts at other levels. There might be points open for negotiation while other points are seen by one of the parties as completely unnegotiable. Within this context, the strategy concept is useful. Women elaborate their strategies within the space of action given by the gender system or they try to extend the space through negotiations.

Research design and methodology

Three parallel studies in Zambia, Zimbabwe and Lesotho were conducted with the aim of revealing some kind of general patterns in gender contracts within the context of family and property. Gender relations related to such sectors of society as the labour market and politics are thus not discussed here. We are primarily concerned with urban low income people. Due to the explorative character of the research, to local conditions, and to individual interests, the studies have been allowed to develop in slightly different directions.

The following concrete research questions were formulated for the field studies in each respective country:
✦ What are women's rights to housing?
✦ How is the law implemented in actual judgements?
✦ What are the arguments used by men and women in court?
✦ What strategies were elaborated by women (and men)?
✦ What views do women and men hold regarding housing rights?

The concrete answers to these questions are presented in separate papers (Larsson & Schlyter, 1993). In this paper we will compare and analyze these findings in terms of gender contracts at three levels of analysis.

The interpersonal level

At this level we will analyze our findings about the strategies elaborated by women, and to some degree by men, as we identified them in interviews carried out in different types of low income housing areas in the capitals of the three countries. Men's and women's views are also made explicit and clear in their argumentation in courts. Court records have been an important source of information.

The institutional level

At this level we have studied family law. The written law is here regarded as a tool for state intervention in gender relations. The state is an important actor in the creation of new gender contracts by legal instruments. We have studied literature analyzing the legal situation rather than studied the original law texts.

For women's housing rights, access to court and legal praxis is more interesting than the law itself. We therefore carried out interviews in housing areas as well as studies of court cases. The dual legal systems in these countries with one general (common, English and statutory) law and one customary (local, community) law make the study of legal praxis even more important as the customary law is flexible and largely unwritten. In this paper the term general law is used for statutes and laws applied in the Magistrate's Courts and the High Courts although these laws, originating from European laws may be differently named in the three countries. The term customary law is used for laws derived from local traditions. The courts in which customary law is applied are, in the presentation, called by their local names. Nevertheless, the application of customary law can, in the last instance, be seen as state action.

The level of cultural images and ideologies

This is an abstract level of analysis for which empirical material is used from both the interpersonal level and the institutional level. In interviews with women and men explanation to behaviour was often of the kind: 'This is our tradition' or 'this is how we do it now-a-days'. Such explanations reflect cultural images and ideologies. These are also reflected in laws, but not in a simple and direct way. Old law might have lost its relevance in reality.

In the colonial situation, imported laws might never have had support in the views of the populations of what is right and what is wrong. New laws might be introduced that reflect only the ideologies of certain groups of the population. The flexible customary laws have a much more direct connection to cultural images and ideologies. These laws are mostly unwritten and exist only in their praxis. One might say that the legal praxis in courts of customary law is directly guided by cultural images and ideologies, which they in turn confirm or transform.

A dominant gender contract

According to Hirdman's model, gender contracts can be identified on all levels of society. These contracts are not likely to be consistent, especially not in societies undergoing rapid change. They may even be contradictory. Nonetheless, limiting our analysis to the context of family and property, a dominant gender contract can be identified in the three studied countries, despite some differences in organization of traditional societies, colonial history and contemporary policies.

According to the dominant gender contract, men are responsible for important decisions, especially those outside the household/family, and women's domain is restricted to the home and the family. In an old but challenged contract, all women were regarded as minors. Married women were under the guardianship of their husbands, unmarried women under their fathers or other male relatives. In case of divorce or the husband's death the woman would either return to her own family or remain under the custody of the in-laws.

One can assume that this gender contract came out strongly in the Southern African countries as there was a basic concordance in customs and laws between those of the colonizers and those of the colonized.

The gender contract of a married couple permeates all levels of society including family laws, whether customary or general. The husband is the head of the household and the wife is subordinate to him. Although a wife may have a say in some family matters, in public she is represented by her husband. The husband is also, as a rule, the manager of the matrimonial property, whether it is considered to be jointly owned ('in community') or not. An urban house is viewed as belonging to the husband.

In theory, a means to get away from this gender contract (in Lesotho and Zambia) is to marry 'out of community' of property. To ask for such a property regime is indeed for a woman to challenge the man as it has to be agreed upon before the marriage. Furthermore, the option does not take into account a wife's unpaid work as a contribution to the household wealth. 'Out of community of property' has meaning only for women who have enough income or capital to allow them to live economically independently of their husbands.

At the personal level, the dominant contract is enforced by identifying the husband as the main income earner and by referring to him as the breadwinner. Nonetheless, the wife is supposed to be responsible not only for general household chores but also for feeding the family. Traditionally, the task to feed the family meant that women's input in agriculture was extensive. Today it means that when the wife has some own earnings, these are primarily used for food and other daily necessities. The husband's income can be spent on implements such as a radio, tools, a bicycle or on house investments. If a marriage comes to an end the property derived from the husband's income can easily be identified.

Unmarried women no longer have to live in the custody of men, and in that sense the gender contract has been modified. Still, unmarried women are often indirectly controlled by men. Concerning adult unmarried women, today's gender contract can be interpreted as follows: they have not only the right to run their own lives, but also the duty to support themselves and, as the case may be, their children as well. Today, many urban widows and divorcees live their own lives, although their access to the matrimonial property is only to a limited extent recognized by the laws and by courts.

The dominant contract does not stand unchallenged. It has been challenged by state action and by the individual women's actions. The state can change laws and supervise its implementation.

New laws to change the dominant gender contract

At the level of ideologies and cultural overlays, some important modifications of the dominant gender contract were introduced at the time of independence. After almost a century of colonial oppression, and, in the case of Zimbabwe, a liberation war as well, independence was gained and each country formulated its own constitution in line with modern democratic notions.

Constitutional rights

Every citizen was accorded equal protection and enjoyment of rights. Adult men and women are recognized as majors and they are entitled to vote. These constitutional rights were, in Zimbabwe, confirmed in legislation through the Legal Age of Majority Act of 1982. The gender contract assumed in the constitutions seems to be a contract of equity. However, the ideology of the constitutions has not had much impact on the dominant gender contract. Further reading reveals that the constitutions (of Zimbabwe and Zambia) do not include sex as a ground for unlawful discrimination. Such a writing in the constitution would have required radical changes of most existing family laws. If the constitution is interpreted as not only giving women voting capacity but equal opportunities in all sectors of society, deep contradictions occur between the gender contract assumed in the constitutions and legal reality. It can be concluded that the constitutions rather assume a gender contract of domination and subordination, covered by an ideology of harmony in spite of different rights. According to this ideology, men and women hold equal value in spite of different roles and different rights.

Contradictory land laws

Contradictions also exist between different laws regarding the rights of women within a country. In both Lesotho and Zimbabwe all citizens have the right to own land according to recent legal reforms, but the Deeds Registry Acts lags behind in the reforms. In Lesotho married women are still not allowed to register as owners of land without the consent of the husband.

Marriage laws

With the exception of the Zimbabwean Legal Age of Majority Act, there have been no legal reforms aimed at strengthening of a married woman's position. A number of new laws strengthened women's positions at the dissolution of a marriage. These might indirectly strengthen women's position within marriage.

Widows' rights to a share of the matrimonial property has recently been strengthened through legal amendments in all three countries. In Lesotho a widow's right to rural land that formed part of the joint estate has been legally confirmed through an amendment to the Land Act in 1992.

In Zimbabwe and Zambia widows may be made destitute by their late husband's relatives. A law was therefore introduced in Zimbabwe in 1987 to protect the widow. According to the Deceased Persons Family Act a court can decide to distribute the estate in the interest of dependents. But a widow has to go to court to claim her share of the property and the outcome depends on the court's decision.

In Zambia a similar law was delayed by the Parliament for years. Only after a lengthy struggle involving and strengthening women's groups was the law finally approved in 1989. A widow today can inherit a fifth of the property value, and also be given the right to stay in the house until children are grown up.

The general law in Lesotho allows for the property to be split between the spouses in case of divorce, while in Zimbabwe divorcees have only recently got a legal right to a share of the matrimonial property. The Matrimonial Causes Act from 1985 empowers courts to transfer some of the matrimonial property to the wife after divorce. It is not regulated how large a share of the property value a divorcee should get, but the courts are required to consider 'all circumstances'.

Implementation of constitutional and legal rights

Although adult women in the three countries are constitutionally recognized as majors, they often experience difficulties when approaching a court. In Local Courts in Zambia women may represent themselves today, but only after having explained why their guardian is not present. In 1992 there was a case of clear violation of the constitutional right of a woman to exercise her constitutional right as a citizen to choose her place of residence.

In Lusaka a battered woman had moved from her husband's house to that of her to her mother. Her husband charged his mother-in-law claiming custody of his wife. The judgement said, 'In accordance with Ngoni customs, the Defendant is supposed to return the Plaintiff's wife immediately when she arrived at her home.

Defendant is ordered to return wife.' This woman is clearly seen as a minor or even as property belonging to the husband.

The constitution of Zambia is not supported by legal assessments to change an antiquated gender contract. There is no law overruling this interpretation of customary law.

In Zimbabwe it has proved difficult to get the Community Courts and the governmental departments to fully adapt procedures to the new conditions spelled out by the Legal Age of Majority Act, although the law in principle overrules customary law. Women continue to be asked for affidavits of separation or a consent from the husband in order to be put on the waiting list for a plot, or sign a house contract.

The flexibility of law

An important characteristic of customary law is its flexibility. By contrast, general law tries to be exact and to objectify its rules. Nonetheless, some new general laws include elements of flexibility. If the flexibility is used to adapt to new socio-economic conditions, it can result in a more egalitarian treatment of women and men. It can, however, also result in an enforcement of traditional values to the detriment for women.

Division of property at divorce

The Matrimonial Causes Act in Zimbabwe is very flexible and leaves a lot to the discretion of the court. A study of all divorce cases during 1991 in the High Court and in the Community Courts of Harare and Chitungwiza which involved conflicts over urban houses was conducted in order to see how the law was implemented. (Larrson & Schlyter, 1993)

By reading the judgements, one can easily identify the paragraph of the dominating gender contract saying that the husband is the sole owner of property. Judges hold a strong view of matrimonial property as belonging to the husband alone. The judges see themselves as having the power to take from the husband's property and give to the wife so that she and the children can have a decent life. Only in ten of twenty-six cases the women got a share of the value of the matrimonial house.

There were also great differences in the sizes of the share. Seldom was the property properly valued. As the wife was not entitled to a specific share this was not necessary. A rough estimate of the property value in the studied cases reveals that one wife got less than one per cent while another got forty per cent of the total assets. Consequently, it is not easy for a woman to know if she will gain or lose by taking her case to court. It is like gambling.

The law also becomes flexible by the fact that the concept of matrimonial property is not properly defined. It is not unusual that the husband claims that the property is matrimonial with his other wife.

According to the law many circumstances should be considered by the court, among them, the direct or indirect contribution made to the household economy. Usually, a direct contribution of cash to the household economy is a heavy argument for giving the woman a share of the property.

The new and progressive issue with the Matrimonial Causes Act was that indirect contributions, the home-making work of a woman, should also be considered. Lack of indirect contributions was, however, in a few cases in Community Court, held against wives who had been working as domestic workers and spent little time in their own houses. The unpaid domestic chores were instead done by some relative. Applied in this way the Act gets the character of 'damn you if you do, damn you if you do not', and women are the guaranteed losers.

Now, the situation is not that bad, although it can generally be assumed that by divorcing in court a woman will not be able to stay on in the matrimonial house. She has a chance to get a share of the value of the property, especially if she is educated herself, has contributed with cash to the building of the house, and belongs to the high income group. In conclusion, a less flexible law would probably be of benefit to women, at least until a new and better praxis has developed.

Houses registered to widows

The position of urban widows in Lesotho today illustrates how the flexibility of customary law can operate in favour of women. According to tradition, a widow was not entitled to inherit the matrimonial property. Instead, it was inherited by a son who administered the estate to the benefit of all other members of the family, including the widow.

Due to labour migration and more recent urbanization the traditional settlement patterns and related kinship responsibilities no longer work. When married women become widows, they often live a life independent of the husbands' relatives. This is a fact that customary law, as applied by local chiefs in the peri-urban areas of Maseru, recognizes and supports. In such areas traditions and customary law govern the everyday life of the inhabitants. Land is under the control of local chiefs and most elderly people are married according to custom.

Interviews with a large number of widows, both plot holders and tenants, in the peri-urban areas, revealed that plots registered in the name of the deceased husband had been transferred to the widow (Larsson & Schlyter, 1993). As a rule, the plot was transferred shortly after the husband's death and without any problems. No widow had been forced to leave the matrimonial home. The majority of interviewed women had become widows a long time ago. One woman had become a widow as early as 1939 and the plot was transferred to her without any problems shortly after the husband's death.

Only a few widows had experienced some conflicts over the plot but, in the end, the widows received the plots. Claims were only occasionally raised by a male relative who, according to tradition, could be regarded as the proper heir to the house or plot. The cases had been taken to the chief, sometimes even further up in the court hierarchy. The interviewed women felt that they were protected by the law and got the necessary support from the chiefs.

Also, widows who had migrated to Maseru after the husbands' death, because of lack of means to support themselves in rural areas, had been allocated plots in peri-urban areas. This happened despite the fact that traditionally women were not entitled to own land.

No share – but compensation

In Zambia where there has been no legal reform to protect a wife in case of divorce, the Local Courts have fully adapted the gender contract saying that an urban house and all other property except kitchen utensils belong to the husband. In customary law in Zambia the fruits of the wife's labour are regarded as belonging to the husband. This can be seen as a distortion of traditional law. In the rural society a woman had a high degree of control over the fruits of her work, and income from special skills, such as pottery or midwifery, were regarded as their own. Flexible customary law has been able to adapt to colonial rule and to the demands made by men.

As everything is regarded as belonging to the husband and his relatives, there is usually no discussion on sharing of property, not even if the wife built the house and paid for the building materials. The Local Courts, nonetheless, have shown an openness to change custom in order to avoid leaving a divorcee destitute. A divorcee may be awarded a lump sum in so-called compensation for the maintenance she was entitled to as a married woman. The courts have been flexible enough to introduce the compensation which has no base whatsoever in traditions. This praxis of compensation underlines the common notion of the man as the breadwinner.

Access to courts

Although women's legal opportunities to claim their rights in court have improved to some degree after independence, the result of legal modifications is rather discouraging when looking at court cases. A major finding is that only a very limited number of conflicts over a house are brought to court, and only a small proportion of these cases is actually finalized. The court cases studied demonstrate a common way of courts to act, which, to some extent, provides an explanation for the few court cases. In the case of High Courts, economic barriers and unwilling husbands as well are severe obstacles for women.

Expensive lawyers

The most important finding in all the countries was that very few cases of conflicts over an urban house are taken to court. People married according to general law have to divorce in High Court. To do so you have to consult a lawyer which is beyond most people's means. There are possibilities of getting legal aid, but in practice the hindrances are many.

In Zimbabwe (Larsson & Schlyter, 1993) one woman tried for more than eleven years to get a divorce. She was once left in the street with five children while her husband let their home to tenants. From that he got a good income, but he never contributed to the upbringing of the children. She paid lawyers and she waited. She could not pay enough for the lawyer to continue when the husband put up obstacles. With the help of the researcher she finally, after nine years, got legal aid. The economic barriers are, however, not the only ones. It seems as if the legal system can do nothing if the husband really wants to delay the case.

In eight of nine Harare High Court cases on division of urban houses at divorce, the wives were the plaintiffs. This might be interpreted as if both women and men anticipated that the court was going to support the woman.

Access to Community Courts is easier. The distribution of men and women plaintiffs in Zimbabwean Community Courts is not as uneven as in the High Court. The study of cases in these courts confirm that women cannot be sure of getting any support. That might be why they do not frequently approach the courts.

Reluctance by courts to consider conflicts within marriages

In Zimbabwe a woman was scolded by the judge in High Court for bringing her domestic problems to court. The judge did not want to get involved in them. She was a married woman who was long separated from her husband and lived in their matrimonial house. Now the husband, who lived with a second wife, wanted to sell the house, and she wanted the court to prevent him from doing that, without asking for a divorce.

In other cases married but deserted women wanted the court to guarantee occupancy rights to the matrimonial home. The courts were very reluctant and, in the few cases they approved the claim, it was only for the period until a divorce case could be brought. It seems as if most courts do not want to violate the dominating gender contract defining the husband as the head of household.

Similarly, in four cases reported by Mamashela (1991) the High Court in Lesotho judged in favour of the husbands sued by their wives for maladministration of the marital property. Mamashela's conclusion is that the cases 'all paint a very sorry and sad picture of the wife's disadvantaged position in this regard. They also illustrate the nigh impossible burden placed on the wife to show that the husband's administration/dealing with the joint estate is fraudulent, unreasonable and to her detriment (p. 220).'

Judges in Lesotho often ask divorcing couples to reach an agreement themselves. This agreement is then confirmed by the High Court in a judgement. If no agreement is reached, the case is not brought up for decision in court. Through such behaviour by courts, marriage conflicts are referred down to the personal level to be solved between a husband and a wife in conflict. The message is that conflicts should not be solved in courts at the institutional level. Consequently, few women look upon courts as a resource to be relied on in order to get support.

This legal praxis can be interpreted as being in line with traditional notions, that is, conflicts are to be settled by agreement rather than finding a guilty party who is to be punished. It can also be interpreted as a reluctance by the state to intervene in order to change the gender contract. Traditionally in a village the division between institutional and interpersonal levels was not clear. A marriage was not a personal affair, but an agreement between two large families. Conflicts were settled within the family hierarchy.

In an urban context people often live far away from relatives who may not be involved in arranging a marriage, still less in settling a divorce. To ask a husband and wife today to settle a marriage conflict through discussions at home is often to put the woman in a very vulnerable situation. Being at the same time a minor in relation to the husband, in conflict with him and without the support of relatives, the wife is indeed at the mercy of her husband.

Women's strategies

Women's strategies to maintain access to their houses seldom include taking their cases to court. Their limited access to courts is not enough to explain the small number of cases. Another explanation could be that women do not know that they can get legal support. But according to our interviews, urban women know their rights fairly well, and about their lack of rights. They also know that it can be hazardous to take their cases to court. Therefore women devise other strategies.

In order to settle conflicts over matrimonial property in their favour, women develop strategies within the space of manoeuvre that existing legal rights and legal praxis provide at an informal and interpersonal level. Women may turn to informal conflict-solving among relatives or institutions within their residential area.

In Lusaka a variety of conflict solving institutions on community level were found. During the one-party system the local party chairman served as a conflict-solving institution. With the disappearance of the local party structure elderly men held similar positions entirely in their own capacities as respected men. These institutions cannot be seen as part of the state's implementation of laws, but it is still a way to take the conflict out from the family and individual husband-wife relation. Many women felt this level of informal or living law as a support in conflicts which they did not dare to take to a formal court.

Postponing of conflicts

A major strategy seems to be one of postponing open conflict. This is illustrated by cases from Maseru. In a governmental low income housing project women, who had been deserted by their husbands and had remained in the joint house, were interviewed. The interviews did not reveal a situation of open conflict over housing. Instead, the women developed strategies aimed at giving them full control over the house step by step and which avoided an open confrontation. Women's responsibility for the household's well-being was the force behind achieving control over the home/house. Ownership as such was not their prime goal. Thus, the position of the husband and his responsibilities as head of the household were as a rule not challenged. Women's subordinate position in marriage was, in principle, accepted.

According to the rules of the housing project and the laws of the country, plots were registered in the name of the husband. A first strategy was, despite no changes in the registration, for the women to recognize themselves as plot holders. Women claimed they were the plot holders or even lawful owners. A major reason for women's claims was that they paid the monthly charges and had remained in the house.

To legally gain the house through asking for a divorce was, however, not regarded a viable strategy by most women, or at least not a quick way. Some women were afraid of the outcome, like this woman who said about the possibility of divorce:

'I don't know whether, when we divide, he will be given the plot and I will be given the children or the children might get the plot ... I have never been to court to hear what they say. That's why I am afraid

... So that's my problem, I really don't know what the law says about this. So till I know, I think I can carry on'.

The answer by another woman illustrates reluctance to take a conflict to court in order to secure access to a house. She realized she needed a divorce to be recognized as the lawful plot holder. As she did not know the husband's intentions, she felt she might be busy paying while he had his own plans for the house. She had asked herself if it would be fair of the court to give him the house, when she remained in it.

She had approached a lawyer to start the divorce, but still it should be settled as a family matter. They had decided to call her in-laws so the two parties could discuss the case. It was to be determined by both families. The purpose of the gathering was to find out if both wanted to go on with the divorce and who would take the case to court. Although the families were involved, she feared that she might not be able to defend herself when the case appeared in court. Because of lack of money, she regarded her chances to be very slim.

An educated woman had developed the divorce strategy in a more straight forward way. She aimed at getting a divorce, but to make sure she would win, time had to work for her: 'In fact I wanted the case to be simple so that they should see me separated for a long time and then it shouldn't take me long time to be told to go on separation and all that, that is why I give him enough time. So I think it will be over this year.'

She had taken care of the children since he left her nine years ago. He had not paid maintenance and he had no objections to the children staying with her. Her lawyer had assured her that 'whoever stays with the kids will have to be in a home.' So she was very confident about the outcome of the divorce concerning custody of children and the house. This woman had no hesitation in having the house registered in her name.

Indirect control

Many women in the Maseru project area did not aim at having the house registered in their names. Their strategy was instead to gain indirect control over the house by having it transferred to and registered in the name of the eldest son or, in some cases, a nephew. Through such measures, the women felt that the husband could not interfere if the woman died. Many women regarded the child who was most helpful to be the one who deserved the house. Some childless women looked upon their nephews the same way. There were also other advantages with appointing a younger relative as the owner of the house, the women could expect support in the future when needed.

Widows in Lusaka have also applied a strategy of indirect control, by arguing for sons as heirs. An urban house was viewed as belonging to the husband, and according to traditions it was his relatives, not his wife/wives and children who inherited. Consequently, widows often become destitutes, but custom has been under change for a long time. Women have argued primarily for their children in conflicts over urban houses. The new inheritance law, which finally was approved in 1989, made the children the main heirs but also gave the widow life-long occupancy rights to the house.

Conclusions

The concept gender contract has helped us to see common patterns in the relationship between men and women in the context of housing. It has enabled us to identify a dominant gender contract. To discuss contracts on three analytic levels has helped us to be aware of and to understand the existence of seeming contradictions concerning women's legal right and matters of equality in today's society.

At the different analytic levels there are various actors, who aim in different directions and have different power to influence. Thus changes in contracts should be understood as ongoing negotiations, perhaps even the result of a struggle, rather than a simple one-way evolution from worse to better. Time alone cannot be assumed to solve the existing problems.

The state as an actor

We have stressed that the state through legislation can be an important actor in the creation of new gender contracts at the institutional level. The state in the three countries studied has not, however, imposed any major changes regarding a woman's legal position within marriage. Instead it has so far favoured men over women by supporting the dominant gender contract and only allowing legal reforms to apply when a marriage comes to an end. The notion of equality manifested in the constitutions has not been allowed to penetrate marriage laws.

New laws of importance for women are limited to situations when the marriage is dissolved, either through divorce or the husband's death. The divorcee or the widow is then given some opportunity to be awarded part of the matrimonial property through a court's decision. How much, however, is left to the court's discretion. It falls upon the woman to take the case to divide the property to court, it does not follow automatically upon a granted divorce or reported death of husband.

The need for information and policy changes are often called upon when the purpose is to promote equal opportunities and equal rights for women. Women should be informed about such things as existing laws and how to approach the court. The application of Hirdman's model to the context of urban housing clearly shows that information and gender aware policies are not enough. The dominant sex makes use of many different means, often very subtle ones, to control the other sex. Negotiations and actions must take place simultaneously in many different arenas located at different levels in order to effect considerable changes.

Perhaps the most subtle means to hamper women's action for improvements is to refer conflicts, which could have been solved in the court room, to be settled between individuals. In this way women are not only denied the legal rights they may have according to the law, they are also denied the chance to have their cases visualized in the public sphere. There will be no or few records available for the public, no comments in media for people to watch or read, to discuss and learn from, and only limited incitements for actions by women groups. What could have been of public interest in the society becomes highly individualized.

A challenged gender contract

The first step in negotiating a new gender contract is to question the existing one. This contract determines what strategies women elaborate to secure access to a house. The first strategy at hand is, therefore, to find and please a husband and to try to manipulate him to consume less and invest more in the house. This is a strategy of adaption to the existing contract; it does not mean that women would not like to see it changed. On the contrary, most women seem to question the dominant gender contract. Interviews in a poor urban area in Lusaka show a clear cut difference between the views of women and those of men on three central paragraphs in the dominant gender contract:

- Women certainly regard themselves as major persons, while men want to see married women as dependents in their custody.
- Women claim joint ownership, while men see themselves as sole owners of matrimonial property.
- Women want pooled incomes and joint control, while men claim control and ownership over not only their own but also their wives' incomes.

Furthermore, women regard the present state of affairs concerning their housing rights as unfair, especially in case of divorce. Women use militant terms urging other women to fight against the injustice, while they often find excuses to submit to male power themselves. They have, in their survival strategies, to avoid conflicts with relatives which might put them in a worse material position.

Many individual women expect the state to take actions. A Mosotho woman comments on the fact that men are legally recognized as house owners:

'I think women should be the house owners, because they know all the difficult things, ... So I think if there can be something like a law to help the women to upgrade them, ... We still want to change everything, because it was a custom, it is still our custom, but I can say this was a custom of past days. But now it is up to us to jump to the conclusions because we feel we are the ones that are hurt, so I think that it is better that the laws protect us, and help us, to have something.'

It is obvious that women in all three countries would like to see a new dominant gender contract governing the relationship between men and women. Even if many women find it difficult to negotiate in the present situation, they question prevailing ideologies in different ways. There are women, often those with some education, who feel that they have the strength:

'We Basotho women ... find that women are stronger than men. Men don't care whether an account had been paid, or something is done with the homes. We find that we are almost equal to, or even better than, men. We no longer consider that the man is the head of the household.'

REFERENCES

Agren, A. & Chiwara, H. 1991. *Chromite Mining Co-operatives in Zimbabwe.* Sweden: Uppsala University.

Batezat, Elinor & Mwalo, Margaret. 1989. *Women in Zimbabwe.* Harare: SAPES Trust.

Bell, J.K. 1991. 'Women, Environment and Urbanisation: A Guide to the Literature'. In: *Environment and Urbanization* Vol. 3 (2) pp. 92-103. London: Russell Press.

Boserup, E. 1970. *Woman's Role in Economic Development.* London: George Allen and Unwin.

Bruce, J. 1989. 'Homes Divided'. In: *World Development* Vol.17(7).

Brydon, Lynne and Chant, Sylvia *1989 Women in the Third World. Gender issues in rural and urban areas.* London: Edward Elgar Publishing.

Central Statistical Office. *Census 1992 – Zimbabwe Preliminary Report.* Harare.

Chabarika, S. 1992. 'Health Officials Cry Foul Over Diarrhoea Epidemic'. In: *The Daily Gazette,* 19 November 1992.

Chanock, M. 1982. *Custom and Social Order.* Cambridge. Cambridge University Press.

Chant, S. 1985 'Single-Parent Families: Choices or Constraints? The Formation of Female Headed Households in Mexican Shanty Towns'. *Development and Change* (Vol.16), pp. 635-656.

Chant, S. 1991. *Women and Survival in Mexican Cities.* Manchester: Manchester University Press.

Chiwawa, H. 1989. *Co-operative and Contract Mining in the Zimbabwe Chrome Industry.* Harare: Zimbabwe Institute of Development Studies.

Chiwawa, H. 1993. *The Environmental Impact of Co-operative Mining in Zimbabwe.* Paper presented at the 4th OSSREA Congress, 9–12 August, 1993. Debre-Zeit. Ethiopia.

Clarke, D.G. 1974. *Contract Workers and Under Development in Rhodesia.* Gweru: Mambo Press

Clarke, J. 1987. 'The Lusaka Human Settlements Programme: The Case of Florence'. UN/NGO Workshop Paper, Oxfam, Oxford.

Cook, Jacklyn. 1985. *Maids and Madams: Domestic Workers Under Apartheid.* London: Women's Press.

Cutrufelli, M.R. 1983. *Women of Africa: Roots of Oppression.* London: Zed Books.

Durban Municipal Transport Authority Board. 1990. *Inanda Release Area 33 and Newtown: Socio-economic Travel Survey* Vol.2.

Fapohunda, E. 1988. 'The Non-Pooling Household: A Challenge to Theory'. In: Dwyer, D. & Bruce, J. (eds.) *Home Divided: Women and Income in the Third World.* Stanford: Stanford University Press.

Fortman, B.D.G. & Mihyo. P. 1991. 'A False Start: Law and Development in the Context of a Colonial Legacy'. ISS Working paper No.112. The Hague.

Friedman, W. 1964. *Law in a Changing Society.* Middlesex: Penguin Books.

Giddens, Anthony. 1986. *The Constitution of Society.* Oxford: Basil Blackwell.

Guyer, J. 1986. 'Intra-household Processes and Farming Systems Research: Perspectives from Anthropology'. In: Moock, J. (ed.) *Understanding Africa's Rural Households and Farming Systems,* pp. 92-104. London: Westview Press.

Guyer, J. 1988. 'Dynamic Approaches to Domestic Budgeting: Cases and Methods from Africa'. In: Dwyer, D. & Bruce, J. (eds.) *A Home Divided: Women and Income In the Third World,* pp. 155-172. Stanford: Stanford University Press.

Gwagwa, N. (unpublished) *Low Income Household Resource Allocation: The Case of Inanda Newtown, Durban – Preliminary Results.* Paper presented at GRUPHEL Project Seminar, Maseru, 1993.

Hansen, K.T. 1989. *Distant Companion: Servants and Employers in Zambia, 1900-1985.* New York: Cornell University.

Hartmann, Heidi *et al.* (eds.). 1981. 'The Unhappy Marriage between Marxism and Feminism: Towards a More Progressive Union'. In: Sargent (ed.) *Women and Revolution*. Boston: South End Press.

Hay, M.J. & Wright, M., (eds.). 1982. *African Women and the Law: Historical Perspectives*. Boston: Boston University African Studies Centre.

Heisler, H. 1974. *Urbanisation and the Government of Migration*. London. C. Hurst.

Himonga, C. N. 1987. 'Property Disputes in Law and Practice: Dissolution of Marriage in Zambia'. In: Armstrong, A. (ed.) *Woman and Law in Southern Africa*. Harare: Zimbabwe Publishing House.

Himonga, C. N., Turner K.A. & Beyani C.S. 1990. 'An Outline of the Legal Status of Women in Zambia'. In: Stewart, Julie & Armstrong, Alice (eds.). *Legal Situation of Women in Southern Africa*. Harare: University of Zimbabwe Publications.

Hirdman, Yvonne. 1991. 'The Gender System'. In: Andreasen, Tayo *et al.* (eds.) *Moving On: New Perspectives on the Women's Movement*. Aarhus: Aarhus University Press.

Hudgen, R. E. 1988. 'A Diagnostic Survey of Female Headed Households in the Central Province of Zambia'. In: Poats, S. *et al. Gender Issues in Farming Systems Research and Extension* pp 373-387. Boulder: West View Press.

Imam, A.M. 1990. 'Gender Analysis and African Social Sciences in the 1990s'. *Africa Development* 3(4).

Jaravaza, B. 1992. *Women Entrepreneurship in Zimbabwe*. Paper presented at MCCD workshop for women in small scale enterprises. Harare.

Jiggens, J. 1980. *Female Headed Households: Moika Sample, Northern Province, UNZA*. RSDB Occasional Seminar Paper, No. 5.

Jonasdottir, Anna. 1984. *Kvinnoteori – några perspektiv och problem inom kvinnoforskningens teoribildning*. Orebro: Hogskolan i Orebro.

Kidder, H., Louise and Judd, M. Charles with Smith R. Eliot. 1985. *Research Methods In Social Relations*. New York: Holt, Rinehart and Winston.

Larsson, Anita. 1989. *Women Householders and Housing Strategies. The Case of Gaborone, Botswana*. Gävle: The National Swedish Institute for Building Research.

Larsson, Anita. 1991. 'Governmental Housing Strategies Versus Women's Housing Strategies in Urban Southern Africa'. In: Stolen, Kristi Anne (ed.) *Gender, Culture and Power In Developing Countries*. Oslo: Centre for Development and the Environment (SUM), University of Oslo.

Larsson, A. & Schlyter, A. 1993. *Gender Contracts and Housing Conflicts in Southern Africa*. Gävle: The National Swedish Institute for Building Research.

Law Development Commission. 1976. *Working Paper On The Customary Law of Succession*. Lusaka: Government printers.

Longwe, S. & Clarke, R. 1990. 'Perspectives on Research Methodology'. In: *Women and Law in Southern Africa*, W.P.I. Harare.

Mamashela, M. 1991. *Family Law. Through Cases in Lesotho*. Roma: The National University of Lesotho, Roma.

Mascarenhas, Ophelia & Mbilinyi, Marjorie. 1980. *Women in Tanzania: An Analytical Bibliography*. Motala Grafiska: Motala.

McFadden, Patricia. 1993. 'Epistemological Issues in Conceptualising Gender in Africa'. In: *Southern Africa Political and Economic Monthly* Vol.7(2).

Meena, Ruth. 1992. *Gender in Southern Africa. Conceptual and Theoretical Issues*. Harare: SAPES publications.

Mencher, J. 1988. 'Women's Work and Poverty: Women's Contribution to Household Maintenance in South India'. In: Dwyer, D. & Bruce, J.A. (eds.) *A Home Divided: Women and Income in the Third World*. Stanford: Stanford University Press.

Mies, M. 1989. Extract from 'Patriarchy and Accumulation on World Scale'. ZWRCN Discussion papers. 1991.

Moock, J. 1986. *Understanding Africa's Rural Households and Farming Systems*. London: Westview Press.

Moser, Caroline, 1989. 'Gender Planning in the Third World: Meeting Practical and Strategic Gender Needs'. *World Development* 17(19).

Moser, Caroline. 1993. *Gender Planning and Development: Theory, Practice and Training*. London: Routledge Press.

Moser, C., & Chant, S. 1985. *The Role of Women in the Execution of Low Income Housing Projects Training Module*. DPU Gender & Planning Working Paper No.6, London.

Munachonga, M. 1988. 'Income Allocation and Marriage Options in Urban Zambia'. In: Dwyer, D. & Bruce, J. A. (eds.) *Home Divided: Women and Income in the Third World*. Stanford: Stanford University Press.

Munachonga, M. 1989. 'Women and the State: Zambia's Development Policies and Their Impact on Women'. In: Parpart, J.L. & Staudt, K.A. (eds.) *Women and the State in Africa*. Boulder and London: Lynne Rienner Publishers.

Nimpuno-Parente, P. 1987. 'The Struggle for Shelter: Women in a Site and Service Project in Nairobi, Kenya'. In: Moser, C., & Peake, L. *Women Human Settlements and Housing*. London: Tavistock Publications.

Parpart, J. L. 1989. *Women and Development In Africa*. University Press.

Patel, D. 1984. 'Housing the Urban Poor'. In: Schatzberg, M. G. (ed.) *The Political Economy of Zimbabwe*. Praeger Publishers.

Patel, D. 1988. 'Some Issues of Urbanisation and Development in Zimbabwe'. In: *Journal on Social development Africa* Vol.3, No.2, 1988.

Patel, D & Adams, R. J. 1981. *Chirambahuyo: A Case Study in Low Income Housing*. Gweru: Mambo Press.

Pateman, Carole. 1988. *The Sexual Contract*. Stanford: Stanford University Press.

Sayers, J. 1982. *Biological Politics – Feminist and Anti-Feminist Perspectives*. London: Tavistock Publications.

Schlyter, Ann. 1988. *Women Householders and Housing Strategies: The Case of George, Zambia*. Gävle: The National Swedish Institute for Building Research.

Schlyter, Ann. 1989. *Women Householders and Housing Strategies. The Case of Harare, Zimbabwe*. Gävle: The National Swedish Institute for Building Research.

Schlyter, Ann. 1991. 'Gender Dynamics and Progress in Home Ownership. A pilot study in Zimbabwe'. In: Saglamer & Özüekren (eds.) *Housing for the Urban Poor.* Istanbul.

Schuster, G.M.I. 1979. *New Women of Lusaka.* USA: Mayfield Publishing.

Smart, C. 1989. *Feminism and the Power of the Law.* Routledge, London and New York

Sorock, M., et al. 1984. *Women and Shelter.* Washington D.C.: Office of Housing and Urban Programs.

Thorbek, Susanne. 1993. *Slumculture and Gender. A Study of Women's Lives in Colombo and Bangkok.* London and New Jersey: ZED Press.

Todes, A. & Walker, N. 1991. 'Women and Housing Policy: Analyzing the Past, Debating the Future'. Policy paper presented to GRUPHEL in Harare.

UNCHS 'Habitat' Report. 1988. In: *Environment and Urbanization* Vol.3(2), 1991.

Urban Foundation. 1985. 'Subsidisation of Inanda Newtown' unpublished Internal Report.

Wilson, G. 1987. 'Money: Patterns of Responsibility and Irresponsibility in Marriage'. In: Brannen, J., & Wilson, G., *Give and Take in Families: Studies in Resource Distribution.* London: Allen & Unwin.

WLSA, Women and Law in Southern Africa Research Project. 1992a. *Inheritance Law in Southern Africa.*

WLSA, Women and Law in Southern Africa Research Project. 1992b. *Maintenance in Zambia.*

Women In Development Research Unit (Handbook April 1979) *Women's Guide To Law Through Life.*

Zambia *Daily Mail.* 'Classified Employees Surviving by God's Grace'. 24 November 1993.

Zambia, Government of. 1991. *Women and Men in Zambia. Facts and Figures.* Central Statistical Office.

Zambia National Provident Fund. *How to Claim Your Benefits*. Lusaka: The Public Relations Unit, Provident House.

Zhou, A. O. 1993. 'Enabling Economic Initiatives of Women Entrepreneurs at Growth Points in Zimbabwe: A Case Study of Mataga'. M.Sc. Dissertation, Department of Rural and Urban Planning, University of Zimbabwe: Harare.

Zimbabwe, Government of. 1991. *Zimbabwe: A Framework for Economic Reform (1991-95)*. Harare.

CONTRIBUTORS

Henry Chiwawa is a full-time researcher at the Institute of Development Studies, University of Zimbabwe. He holds a B.Sc. (Econ) degree from the same university and his research interests include development problems of mineral exporting countries, science and technology, and gender issues.

Nolulamo (Lulu) N. Gwagwa is a lecturer in the Department of Town and Regional Planning at the University of Natal, Durban. Her work on gender issues includes local government, 'the family', and development planning. She is currently working on her Ph.D.

Anita Larsson has a Ph.D. in Architecture, Lund University, Sweden. She is a senior lecturer at the School of Architecture, Lund University. Her research on housing in Botswana has focused on the transition from traditional to modern housing and its consequences for low income people, especially for women. Today low-cost housing, urbanization, changes in everyday life and governmental housing policies are studied with a gender perspective.

Mubiana Macwan'gi holds a Ph.D. and is presently a research fellow/co-ordinator at the University of Zambia, Institute for African Studies. Her field of research comprises women's health, population, family planning, support systems for under-privileged women and the elderly, more recently also on community capacities to cope with HIV/AIDS. She has worked for the World Bank, WHO and the Population Council.

Tiitsetso Matete-Lieb has a Bachelor of Commerce degree, a Master's of Urban Affairs and a post-graduate diploma in Housing, Planning and Building. She has worked for the Lesotho Government Department of Housing. She has undertaken housing research, participated in national gatherings on women, urbanization, etc., and represented Lesotho at several international fora.

Mulela Margaret Munalula is a lecturer in the School of Law, University of Zambia. She is involved in the Women and Law in Southern Africa project and a member of the Women's Right Committee of Zambia dealing with issues of gender equity. Her research is in the field of legal anthropology/sociology and she has had several works published.

Diane Nachudwa works at the Physical Planning Department in Harare, Zimbabwe.

Sibusisiwe Ncube holds a B.A. and a post-graduate certificate in Education from University of Zimbabwe. Apart from the GRUPHEL programme, she has also worked on a few other research projects in Zimbabwe.

Symphorosa Rembe is a lecturer at the University of Fort Hare in South Africa. She has a B.A. in Public Administration and Sociology and a M.A. in Public Administration. She was a researcher at the Institute of Extra Mural Studies, National University of Lesotho for six years. Her research has comprised women and youth, evaluation of non-formal education, and public administration.

Ann Schlyter is an associate professor at the School of Architecture, Lund University, presently working as a research co-ordinator at the Nordic Africa Institute in Uppsala. Since the early sixties she has been engaged in research on housing and urban development. Starting with a study on women headed households and housing strategies in Zambia and Zimbabwe, her research interest has been concentrated on gender issues.

Sylvia Sithole-Fundire holds a B.Sc (Hon) Sociology and a post-graduate diploma in Rural and Urban Planning from the University of Zimbabwe. She has taught at the University of Zimbabwe and has worked for the Zimbabwe Women's Resource Centre and Network as a gender trainer. She has also been actively involved in a survey that investigated the cultural practises that militate against a fuller participation of women in development in Zimbabwe. She is currently working on her M.Phil.

Agnes Zhou holds an M.Sc in Rural and Urban Planning from the University of Zimbabwe. She also has a background in Education. She has worked for the Ministry of Local Government in Zimbabwe. She is actively involved in the women's movement in Zimbabwe.

Distributed in Europe by:
Nordiska Afrikainstitutet
P.O. Box 1703
S-751 47
Uppsala
Sweden

In Southern Africa, women are faced with many socio-economic problems which can be attributed to unbalanced gender relations in their societies. Many issues arising from these constraints do not receive priority in research agendas for development planning. This publication is an attempt to meet that challenge.

Gender Research on Urbanization, Planning, Housing and Everyday Life presents papers that are based on research that was conducted during the first phase (1992-1993) of a programme called Gender Research on Urbanization, Planning, Housing and Everyday Life (GRUPHEL ONE).

ZWRCN
Zimbabwe Women's Resource Centre and Network